The Collected Works of Edith Stein

IX

The Collected Works of EDITH STEIN

Sister Teresa Benedicta of the Cross
Discalced Carmelite
1891–1942

Edited by
Dr. L. Gelber
and
Romaeus Leuven, O.C.D.

Volume Nine

ICS Publications
Institute of Carmelite Studies
Washington, D.C.
2002

EDITH STEIN

Sister Teresa Benedicta of the Cross
Discalced Carmelite

FINITE AND ETERNAL BEING
An Attempt at an Ascent To the Meaning of Being

Translated by Kurt F. Reinhardt

ICS Publications
Institute of Carmelite Studies
Washington, D.C.
2002

The original of this work was published in German by the
Archivum Carmelitanum Edith Stein under the title
Endliches und Ewiges Sein: Versuch eines Aufstiegs zum Sinn des Seins
Band II of *Edith Steins Werke*
Translation authorized.

ICS Publications
2131 Lincoln Road, NE
Washington, DC 20002-1199
800–832-8489
www.icspublications.org

Cover design by Rosemary Moak

Library of Congress Cataloging-in-Publication Data

Stein, Edith, 1891–1942
[Endliches und Ewiges Sein. English]
Finite and eternal being: an attempt at an ascent to the meaning of being / Edith Stein (Sister Teresa Benedicta of the Cross); translated by Kurt F. Reinhardt.
p. cm. — (The collected works of Edith Stein ; v. 9)
Includes index.
ISBN 0-935216-32-4 (pbk.)
1. Ontology. I. Title
BD331 .S74513 2002
111—dc21

2002007643

Table of Contents

V. Existents as Such (The Transcendentals)

VI. The Meaning of Being

Foreword to the ICS Publications Edition

Finite and Eternal Being is Edith Stein's master work, the culmination of her lifelong search for truth in all its philosophical, psychological, and spiritual dimensions. ICS Publications is honored to make this text available in English for the first time, as part of our ongoing series of Edith Stein's *Collected Works.*

A. Biographical Sketch

Born into a practicing Jewish family in Breslau in 1891, Edith Stein abandoned her faith as a teenager but continued her restless intellectual searching. She later became a student and assistant of Edmund Husserl, writing her doctoral dissertation for him *On the Problem of Empathy.* Known as a brilliant philosopher in her own right, she was one of the most important contributors to the early stages of phenomenology, the influential philosophical movement that Husserl inaugurated.[1]

Yet despite her remarkable accomplishments, she found that attaining a university professorship was not easy for women in prewar Germany, no matter how brilliant the candidate. Moreover, with her Jewish ancestry, Edith Stein's academic prospects further dimmed as the Nazis rose to power.

In the meantime, however, she had undergone a profound conversion experience in 1921 upon reading the *Life* of St. Teresa of Avila, and the following year she was baptised and confirmed in the Catholic church. She became a leader in the Catholic women's movement in German-speaking Europe, lecturing widely on the education and vocation of women. She continued her research and writing, taking what teaching positions were still available.

Then in October 1933, with academic doors closing to her, she found herself free to pursue a calling she had already felt for many years, and entered the community of the Discalced Carmelite nuns in Cologne, Germany. But the darkening political situation outside the convent walls did not leave her untouched. On 31 December 1938, for safety reasons, she was transferred out of Germany to the nearby Carmel of Echt in the Netherlands, where she was joined by her sister, Rosa. But the imagined safety of this new assignment proved illusory when the Germans invaded and occupied Holland. In 1942, in retaliation for a letter of the Dutch bishops denouncing their anti-Semitic policies, the Nazi authorities rounded up Catholics in Holland of Jewish descent, including Edith and her sister. The prisoners were eventually taken to Auschwitz-Birkenau, where Edith and Rosa died on 9 August 1942, two among the millions of victims of Hitler's "final solution."

B. Background of the Text

In 1931, as part of the process of applying for a professorship at the University of Freiburg, Edith Stein had begun writing her *Habilitationsschrift,* in effect a further doctoral dissertation required by the German academic system. This work, entitled *Potenz und Akt* (Potency and Act), was published posthumously in 1998 and is currently being translated by ICS Publications. It is a study of the founding principles of the philosophy of St. Thomas Aquinas from a phenomenological perspective, and thus an "attempt," as Edith explains, "to come from scholasticism to phenomenology, and vice versa."[2] In this way she hoped to bring together the phenomenological method in which she had been trained and the modern Thomism of the Catholic church she had embraced.

Though her application for a university position was rejected, Stein's efforts were not wasted. After entering the Carmel of Cologne she was encouraged by her religious superiors to take up the work again, revising and expanding it. The resulting text was more than twice as long as the original, with ample new material on divine being and other topics. At the same time, she confessed that she often felt unequal to the task, given the limited time and few scholarly resources available in the monastery as well as her own belated introduction to Thomistic philosophy.

The work was essentially completed by the beginning of 1937 and submitted to the publishers, but by then the German anti-Aryan laws prevented its release. *Endliches und Ewiges Sein* remained unpublished until 1950, when it finally appeared as the second volume in the series, *Edith Steins Werke,* from Verlag Herder and E. Nauwelaerts.

C. An American Connection

Less well known is the fact that even after her disappointment with German publishers and her transfer to Echt, Edith Stein still hoped to find a publisher for her book overseas. By 1940, some of her companions in the "Göttingen Circle" and other phenomenologists had emigrated to North America. Already Professor Marvin Farber at the University of Buffalo was in frequent contact with Edith's longtime friend, Professor Fritz Kaufmann, then at Northwestern University, about the establishment of a new International Phenomenological Society and its journal, *Philosophy and Phenomenological Research.* In fact, presumably at Kaufmann's suggestion, Farber had written to Stein inviting her participation. In a letter dated 4 April 1940, Stein replied that while she was grateful for the invitation, her new life as a nun would make it impossible for her to pay the membership fees or attend meetings.[3] She continued:

> May I now, despite your finding this reply hardly satisfactory, in turn ask for your advice, and if at all possible, even for your help? During my novitiate time I wrote, despite the unfavorable circumstances for this kind of undertaking, a very large 2 volume book "Finite and Eternal Being: An Attempt at an Ascent to the Meaning of Being." It treats of the fundamental ontological questions in the comparison [*auseinandersetzung*] between scholasticism and phenomenology. Being a "non-Aryan," I never, even from the very beginning, thought of a publisher in the German Reich. But then, since my former publisher Otto Borgmeyer volunteered his services, after some hesitation I gave him the manuscript. With long pauses, it was set in type. But when that was completed, the work went no further since the publisher no longer had the courage to publish it under my name. He has now used 3,000 lbs. of lead [type] for the work. While he was at this job, the Order paid him 3,000 R.M. [Reich's Marks] as an allowance toward the printing. He claims these were used up for the job. I would consider it as the best solution if a foreign publishing firm could take over the project. We looked in vain in

> Holland and Belgium for someone. Do you believe there is a possibility in America? Mrs. Husserl advised me to make an excerpt to appear in your periodical. But that would not be any substitute for the book and would only have meaning as an indication of the book if that were to appear. I think shipping 3,000 lbs. of lead would prove difficult. It would be more practical if a publisher were to be ready to have the book printed by Borgmeyer with the American firm's name on the title page—and give him [Borgmeyer] part of the edition as compensation. Were it possible for you to do anything in this affair you might be able to consult with my friends and relatives over there, inasmuch as they are capable: Gerhart Husserl and Fritz Kaufmann are close [friends] from the time of my student days.... I would like to mention also that the publisher has repeatedly suggested an alternative proposal: that [the book] be brought out under another's name, preferably the name of the prioress of the Carmelite Monastery in Cologne (to which I formerly belonged); she it is who signed the contract for the publication. I decidedly turned down that suggestion, not only for reasons of truthfulness, but as well for fear of putting the convent or the order in jeopardy.... Were you able to do anything in this matter, I would thank you with all my heart.[4]

Farber consulted Fritz Kaufmann about these matters, and Kaufmann responded on May 7 that Stein should be allowed to join the new society despite her inability to pay the dues because of her "most valuable and authentic contribution" to the early development of phenomenology. He continues:

> The problem of her book is a very difficult one indeed. I do suppose that this book is identical with a work she spoke [to] me of years ago. Then it had the title "Potency and Act"...: a problem, by the way, whose central importance just in the present situation of philosophy (and phenomenology in particular) I realize more and more. As Miss Stein was a productive phenomenologist and has, e.g., as the translator of Thomas' *Quaestiones Disputate* [*de Veritate*], a first-hand and first-rate knowledge of scholasticism I would heartily welcome the being inserted of her work [sic] in our publications-series—though, perhaps, under two conditions. First, I think, it should be translated into English. (If she cannot do it herself, her order will certainly have the necessary relations to English-writing people.) Second it should refrain from every

> Catholic propaganda apart from that which the exhibition and defense of the scholastic position necessarily implies....[5]

After receiving Kaufmann's comments, Farber wrote to Stein on May 9 informing her of her acceptance into the society, and adding:

> It is my hope that we shall be able to do something about the problem [of the book] which you described. The matter has been referred to a Catholic professor for his advice. That is one of the possible sources of help for the publication of your book. I wrote to Fritz Kaufmann about your problem, and he too has hope that something may be done by means of Catholic scholars. Should that fail we shall make further inquiries. You may be sure of our interest in your work.[6]

Stein replied on November 4, enclosing a copy of the original contract with Borgmeyer:

> I received your kind letter of the 9th of May at the end of September. Only today do I find time to answer it. I thank you sincerely for making me a member of your Phenomenological Society and for all your kind endeavors to publish the unfortunate opus. I can well imagine that in the last months you have hardly been able to do anything about it. In any case, I wanted to send you a copy of the contract with the publisher so that you and any other gentlemen who show an interest in the matter can become familiar with all the business details. In case of any possibility there, it would probably be best to deal from there directly with the publishing firm Franke (Owner: Otto Borgmeyer, Breslau...) and with the Rev. Mother Prioress of the Carmel in Cologne (Rev. Mother Prioress Teresia Renata de Spiritu Sancto, O.C.D., Köln-Lindenthal...). As you see from the enclosure, I did not finalize the contract; the convent did so....[7]

Six months later, on 9 May 1941, Farber wrote again to Edith Stein, indicating that: "Several efforts were made to get people interested in your book. We tried to interest some Catholic publishers, but it seems that only an English translation of your book would meet with a response. Right now a last effort is being made to interest a prominent Catholic philosopher...."[8] To this Stein responded on 12 September 1941, in her final note to Farber: "For all the trouble taken regarding the big book I am most grateful, even though it was without success," and she adds in the margin: "Would you know a translator? It would of course be a giant undertaking."[9]

On October 25 Farber again wrote to Edith Stein, thanking her for having submitted her article on Pseudo-Dionysius ("Ways to Know God") but lamenting again that "unfortunately, we have not succeeded in interesting a publisher in your large book because it is not in English. Several persons tried to do something about it."[10] There matters remained until Edith Stein's death less than 10 months later. But it is interesting to note that, had a translator been found, the first edition of Stein's masterpiece might have appeared in English during her lifetime, published in the United States.

D. History of the Present Translation

In the end, *Endliches und Ewiges Sein* remained unpublished until 1950, when it finally appeared as the second volume in the series, *Edith Steins Werke,* from Verlag Herder and E. Nauwelaerts. The background to this first German edition, and the details of how it was compiled out of existing manuscripts, can be found in the "Editors' Appendix to the First German Edition," found at the end of this volume. Subsequently, Hilda Graef included a very brief two-page excerpt from this work in her anthology, *Writings of Edith Stein* (Westminster, MD: Newman Press, 1956).

Meanwhile Kurt F. Reinhardt became interested in the project. He was a professor of Germanic languages at Stanford University who had been born in Munich and studied at the Universities of Munich, Heidelberg, and Freiburg. Author of numerous works, including *Fundamentals of Mysticism* and *The Existentialist Revolt,* he is perhaps best known to contemporary Catholic readers for his essay on St. John of the Cross in Clare Booth Luce's anthology, *Saints for Now.* Apparently in the 1960s he had begun a translation of *Endliches und Ewiges Sein* for the Frederick Ungar Publishing Company of New York, which had produced his abridged translation of John of the Cross's *The Dark Night of the Soul* in 1957. His friend Sr. Fleurette Sweeney, S.C.H., currently on the faculty of education at the University of British Columbia, picks up the story from there:

In 1969 I moved to Portola Valley, California, where I took up the position of Assistant Director of an educational research institute, The Richards Institute of Music Education and Research. Mary Helen Richards and her husband, Professor Cedric of Stanford University, had recently converted to the Catholic faith and the three of us attended the five o'clock daily Mass at St. Anne's, the Newman Center for Stanford University. It was there that I met Dr. Kurt Reinhardt, Professor Emeritus of Stanford. The four of us became fast friends; Kurt lovingly referred to us as his "four-leaf clover."

In one of our after-Mass chats, Kurt mentioned that he had received his manuscript back from Ungar Publishers. My understanding was that in the interim between their having commissioned Kurt to translate *Finite and Infinite Being* there had been a change in policy of their editorial staff and this highly scholarly text of more than 900 [manuscript] pages was seen as having too limited a readership to warrant their continuing on with the publication. I sensed Kurt's personal disappointment at this turn of events and asked, "How do you feel about this after so much work—having it end this way?" His reply astounded me then, as it does still today: "It was a work of love."

At the time Edith Stein was someone I had never heard of before. Kurt shared the manuscript, complete with all the editorial notes from the publisher, and that was the first of many conversations about her and about phenomenology. As a student of Husserl at Freiburg University, Kurt was a contemporary of Edith Stein and Heidegger. He knew her as a phenomenologist and as "Husserl's favorite student." I do not think that there was a personal connection between Kurt and Edith Stein themselves, although Kurt, also a convert, retreated to the Benedictine Abbey of [Beuron] for Holy Week and other principal feasts of the liturgical year. He recalled seeing Edith Stein there deep in prayer in the front of the chapel.

When Kurt died in 1983 he willed his entire library to the Richards. I moved to Vancouver, British Columbia in 1986. Shortly after, one of the sisters who knew of my deep interest in Edith Stein, shared an article by Father Jan [Nota, S.J.], the last scholar to visit Edith Stein in the Carmelite Monastery in Holland prior to her death.

In connection with the article, I read of the intent to have the complete works of Edith Stein published in English. I was intrigued; so I placed a telephone call to MacMaster University

> where Father Jan was located only to find that he was not there. I followed that with a call to Father John Sullivan [of ICS Publications] in Washington who was also referenced in the article. I just wanted to inquire if someone had already translated *Finite and Infinite Being.*
>
> I can still remember the amazement in Father John's voice when, after telling me that no one had tackled it yet, I said that I had a copy of the complete, edited manuscript in English. He made some quick checks, just to see if I was "for real"! Then he said, "I'll call you back." It did not take long for him to make that return call. Father John asked if I would send some pages of the manuscript so that scholars could check Kurt's interpretation of Edith Stein's phenomenology. Of course, I could not do that because the manuscript belonged to Mary Helen and Professor Richards; and besides, I did not know Father John and I was reluctant to have anything happen to Kurt's "work of love." Shortly afterwards I received a call from California telling me that Father John had visited Portola Valley and had returned to Washington, manuscript in hand. Now, some fourteen years later, I am happily responding to his request to "tell the story" once again![11]

As the last sentence of Sr. Sweeney's letter suggests, even after its delivery into our hands, Reinhardt's translation has taken a slow and circuitous route to publication. The late Father Jan Nota in fact reviewed the entire text and suggested changes. Dr. Waltraut Stein, Edith's grand-niece and the translator of earlier volumes in this series, painstakingly typed the manuscript onto computer, developed an index, and in places adapted the language to be more "inclusive." The De Rance foundation provided a grant to help subsidize the publication. Unicorn Press typeset the work but then went out of business, which meant that the entire set of original galleys had to be rescanned by Darden Brock of Trinity Communications and proofread again. A series of qualified scholars were engaged to assist with the proofreading, but each in turn withdrew from the project after some months (and in one case, over a year). In the meantime, Fr. John Sullivan, who had begun the project, had been elected to serve in the general administration of the Discalced Carmelite friars in Rome, for a six-year term. The history of Edith Stein's fruitless efforts to publish her *magnum opus* seemed to be repeating itself all over again!

Finally, Mr. Volker Schachenmayr (now Br. Alkuin, O.Cist.), a young German-American with a background in editing, was able to review carefully the entire text. Prof. Walter Redmond of the University of Texas at Austin also made valuable suggestions. Stephen Tiano undertook the page layout. At long last, the translation is ready, and we are very grateful to all of those mentioned here as well as countless others who contributed in their own way.

E. Matters of Style

As the "Editors' Appendix to the First German Edition" indicates, *Finite and Eternal Being* originally included a number of appendices (e.g., on St. Teresa's *Interior Castle* and on Heidegger), which the German editor, Dr. Lucy Gelber, decided to move to a different volume of the *Werke* for reasons of space; nevertheless, Gelber indicates that she included a few relevant extracts from these appendices as footnotes in the main text. This confusing situation should be rectified with the eventual publication of a two-volume critical edition of *Endliches and Ewiges Sein* in the new German series, *Edith Stein Gesamtausgabe* from Verlag Herder.

In the meantime, we have tried to follow the existing German edition and Kurt Reinhardt's translation. For the sake of ease in typesetting, we have moved all footnotes to Stein's text to the end.The numbering of the footnotes, however, does not precisely follow that of the German edition, since Reinhardt in certain cases inserted shorter footnotes directly into the text, or shifted long parenthetical remarks to the footnotes.

In general, we have tried to preserve the italics and quotation marks of the German edition, insofar as these do not violate American typographical conventions. Because of the amount of Greek in the text, Waltraut Stein opted in certain cases to substitute Latin lettering for more frequently occurring Greek words (e.g., *ousia* for οὐσία). For greater clarity, Edith Stein's original German terms have sometimes been included in the text in brackets. And though not all her sources are clearly identified in the original German edition, we have made some effort to add what information we could find about the texts cited.

German philosophical tomes are notoriously difficult to translate, especially since the expressions used and distinctions made often have no exact English language equivalent. In standard English, for example, according to context the single term "being," so crucial to this study, can mean the *act* of existing or being as such, or *that which* exists, meanings for which distinct terms are available in philosophical German. The translator obviously invested great effort in attempting to render Stein's subtle distinctions clearly. But the reader untrained in scholasticism and phenomenology should not be surprised if some sections of this work seem dense and hard to follow. The effort required to follow Stein's argument is regularly repaid by passages of great clarity and beauty, such as the one which contains her famous remark "What did not lie in my plan lay in God's plan" (p. 113) which turns out to be part of a longer meditation on divine providence. Edith Stein invites us all, scholars and ordinary readers alike, to follow in her footsteps as she attempts "an ascent to the meaning of being."

STEVEN PAYNE, OCD
ICS Publications

Editors' Preface

The work entitled *Finite and Eternal Being* is one of the great philosophic studies of Edith Stein. This fruit of her intellectual labors was ripening at the time she withdrew from her secular career to devote herself to her spiritual vocation. A pupil and, later on, an assistant of Edmund Husserl, the founder of phenomenology, she made important contributions to her master's *Jahrbuch für Philosophie und phänomenologische Forschung* (Yearbook for Philosophy and Phenomenological Research). She then turned to teaching and subsequently held a lectureship at the German Institute for Scientific Pedagogy at Münster in Westphalia. Finally, she laid down her intellectual and literary gifts as well as her solid philosophic and pedagogic knowledge before the altar of the convent at Cologne-Lindenthal to take in deep humility the veil of a Carmelite nun.

Within the span of the few years that she was privileged to live as a religious in the convent, she ascended in internal and external crucifixion to the peak of Mount Carmel. She was not to see the publication of the present volume and was unable to complete the study entitled *Kreuzeswissenschaft* (The Science of the Cross), her last work and the one in which she actually reached the pinnacle of the mountain. She was called to depart from this earthly life, to suffer martyrdom at the hands of the National Socialists in the course of the wave of antisemitic persecutions.

If in the light of this inward and outward crucifixion we look upon Sister Benedicta's attempt to arrive at an understanding of being, the guiding idea in her dual way to this goal becomes evident: As finite being unfolds, an original and boundless ground is revealed which leads to Eternal Being. As far as Sister Benedicta's own way of life is concerned, this idea springs from the joyful certitude of her faith. "What did not lie in *my* plans," she writes, "lay in

God's plan.... [The] more lively becomes in me the conviction of my faith that—from God's point of view—nothing is *accidental,* that my entire life, even in the most minute details, was pre-designed in the plans of divine providence and is thus for the all-seeing eye of God a perfect coherence of meaning. Once I begin to realize this, my heart rejoices in anticipation of the light of glory in whose sheen this coherence of meaning will be fully unveiled to me" (p. 113).

As to the other way—the ascent to the meaning of being—the breakthrough from finite to eternal being is not merely divined or mystically experienced but philosophically and methodically sought and achieved. Starting out from the experience of her own personal being, Edith Stein analyzes the ontological conditions of this unified experience. Step by step she then ascends on solid, scientifically tested ground.

What does this mean for readers of this book? They, too, must studiously grope their way to the height. They, too, must engage in lengthy and difficult analyses. The context and interrelation of the ideas they encounter on the way will not be revealed to them until they have reached the peak of the mountain. Then only will they appreciate their truth and therewith also their beauty. At that point the various analyses will be joined together and permit a deep insight into the nature of things as they unfold in time. And in the end they will be led toward the primordial ground of all being, the ground which is illumined by the radiance of the eternal. This does not mean, of course, that we will then be capable of penetrating the ultimate depths of being. To do that we would have to know the *summum analogon,* that is, the Eternal as such. It does mean that from this height we are able to recognize the natural beginnings of those lines which lead to the mysterious depths of being. And the sight of the image of God in all nature, a valid likeness of the eternal Logos, will fill us with reverent awe. Moreover, a glance backward toward those who did not reach the peak or who preferred to remain in the valley may then distinctly impress upon us the loftiness of our newly gained insight and vision.

It is quite possible that at several junctures in the course of the ascent questions and doubts may arise. At one point a direction which would allow us to remain closer to St. Thomas may seem preferable. At another point we may feel inclined to insert some time-honored conceptual distinction with which the author appears to be unfamiliar. Another path to the pinnacle of the mountain may suggest itself. Let us admit then that wherever human beings are on the upward climb to the heights of being, many possible ways are open to them. In Edith Stein's own words, "The knowledge and science of reality remains forever fragmentary."

May this work reach all those who in their unredeemed being are striving for redemption, including those who do not understand as yet the language of Christian philosophy. For in Edith Stein they meet a guide whose authentic leadership bears the stamp of approval of the master of phenomenology himself. By way of analysis she proposes to advance—insofar as this is humanly possible—to an intuition of essences [*Wesensschau*].

THE EDITORS

Preface of the Author

This book was written by a beginner for beginners. At an age when others may confidently call themselves teachers the author was compelled to start all over again. She had been intellectually formed in the school of Edmund Husserl and had been using the phenomenological method in several philosophic treatises published in Husserl's *Jahrbuch*. Her name had thus become known at a time when she had ceased working in the field of philosophy, at a time when nothing was further from her mind than the thought of any public activity. She had found the way to Christ and his church and was preoccupied with the task of drawing the practical consequences out of this newly gained position. As a teacher at the Pedagogic Institute of the Dominican nuns at Speyer she was privileged to acclimatize herself to the actual Catholic world. She naturally felt an increasing desire to familiarize herself with the intellectual foundations of this world. Almost as a matter of course she first seized upon the writings of St. Thomas Aquinas. Her translation of *Quaestiones disputatae de veritate* paved the way for her return to philosophy.

St. Thomas found a reverent and willing pupil. Her mind, however, was no longer a *tabula rasa:* It has already received the firm impress of her philosophical training, which could not be ignored. Her reason had become the meeting place of two philosophic worlds which demanded a dialectic elucidation. The first philosophic expression of this demand was an essay written as a contribution to the *Husserl-Festschrift* entitled "Husserl's Phenomenology and the Philosophy of St. Thomas Aquinas."[1] It was composed while the author was still working on the "Investigations of Truth."[2] When the translation was completed and in the press, the attempt at a philosophic clarification of the basic concepts of Husserl and St. Thomas was resumed, this time on a broader scale. A comprehensive outline was drafted in 1931. It centered on a discussion of the concepts of *act* and *potency* which were also to provide the title of the entire work. A thorough revision of the manuscript was even then deemed unavoidable, but vocational work of a different kind made it necessary to defer such a plan.

After the author had been received into the order of the Discalced Carmelites and had completed the year of her novitiate, she was ordered by her superiors to prepare the original outline of her work for the printer. Actually, an entirely new version has thus come into being; only a few pages of the original draft (the beginning of Part 1) have been taken over unchanged. Although the Thomistic doctrine of act and potency was retained as a starting point, the discussion is now centered on the *inquiry into the meaning of being.* And the attempted comparative elucidation of Thomistic and phenomenological thought proceeds on the basis of an objective exploration of this problem.

Both the search for the meaning of being and the attempt to arrive at a synthesis of medieval thinking and vital present-day philosophy are not only the personal interest of the author but dominate the philosophic scene. And since many feel the inner need to find an answer to this question, the author believes that her attempt, inadequate as it is, may yet help others.

As to the inadequacy of this undertaking, there can be no doubt. The author is a novice in the field of scholastic philosophy, and as such she can only seek to acquire little by little the knowledge she lacks. For this reason she had to refrain from giving an historical account of the questions under discussion. Whenever she bases an argument on historically established solutions, she simply uses them as a starting point for an objective investigation. This procedure, it would seem, may not only lead to a factual clarification of the issues involved—and there is no human system of thought that can dispense with this kind of analysis—but also to the establishment of vital contact with the great minds of the past. We may then begin to realize that above and beyond the limitations of historical epochs and peoples there is something in which all those share who honestly search for truth. If this attempt contributes in some degree to encouraging such vital thinking in philosophy and theology, it may not be entirely futile.

The question may be asked in some quarters how this book is related to Fr. Erich Przywara, S.J.'s *Analogia Entis.*[3] The problem discussed in both works is actually the same, and Fr. Przywara has pointed out in his preface that this author's endeavor to confront and compare the philosophies of Thomas and Husserl proved significant for his own study. Although the first version of her book and the final version of the *Analogia Entis* were written at about the same time, the author was privileged to look over the earlier drafts of the *Analogia Entis.* Moreover, the lively exchange of ideas between the author and Fr. Przywara in the years from 1925–1931 has in all probability decisively influenced both his and her approach to the identical issue. To the author this exchange of ideas was an additional powerful stimulus when she resumed her philosophic research.

The first volume [the only one published—Trans.] of the *Analogia Entis* presents a methodical and critical preliminary consideration of the questions which are the subject matter of this book and which Fr. Przywara reserved for his second volume (consciousness—being—world).[4] There is nevertheless a certain amount of overlapping, since on the one hand analogy is shown to be the fundamental law that rules over all existents and that must therefore also determine the method of investigation, which, on the other hand, the factual analysis of existents with respect to the meaning of being leads to the discovery of the same fundamental law.

The investigations of this book do not encompass the entire breadth of the problem as it has been presented in the first volume of the *Analogia Entis.* Consciousness is discussed as a way and means to gain access to the world of existents as a particular genus of being. The investigation, however, is not based in its entirety on the mutual relationship existing between consciousness and the data of the objective world, and no inquiry is made into the specific forms of consciousness which correspond to the structure of the objective world.[5] The pure concepts of the intellect, furthermore, were only adduced as the genera of "that which is" [*Seiende*], and the mutual relations existing between that which is [*Seiende*] and its conceptual formulation were only occasionally considered but not comprehensively discussed as a central theme of the investigation. This was done in conscious self-restraint; for this attempt aims at an ontology [a doctrine of being], not at the elaboration of a philosophic system. The very fact, on the other hand, that the ontological problem *was* taken up separately presupposes a point of view regarding its relation to the doctrine of the constitutive forms of consciousness and to logic which could only be convincingly substantiated in a complete system of knowledge and science.

A comparison of the procedure followed in this book with the one demanded in the first volume of *Analogia Entis* will show that in the former the thinking in the categories of "historical immanence" [*innergeschichtliche Denken*] gives way in large measure to the striving for "supra-historical truth."[6] A justification of the way chosen by the author may be found, however, in Fr. Przywara's references to what he calls "creaturely thinking."[7] A different mentality often necessitates a different methodological approach. The contributions which different minds are capable of making on the basis of their one-sided intellectual endowments supplement each other, so that in this way a progressive approximation to "supra-historical truth" may be obtained. *Some* thinkers may have to gain access to the realm of "objects" [*"Sachen"*] by means of concepts which other minds have formulated and handed down to them. The strength of such a thinker lies then in "understanding" [*"Verstehen"*] and in the faculty of gaining profound insight into historical constellations. *Other* thinkers, owing to a specific mentality, may feel compelled to devote their efforts to a direct investigation of the actually given world of things. These thinkers will then arrive at an understanding of other minds and of the products of their intellectual labor only with the aid of what they have been able to ascertain by the exertion of their own intellect. The former—whether they be great masters or only modest apprentices—make intelligible the original historical pattern [*Urgeschichte*], that is, those events with which the history of ideas is concerned. The latter kind of mentality, on the other hand, is the characteristic mark of all born phenomenologists.

It is thus to be expected that the second volume of *Analogia Entis* when eventually it is published, will—in virtue of its comprehensive "intro-historical perspectives" [*Innergeschichtlichkeit*]—represent an essential complement to this book. In regard to certain questions even the first volume offers such a complement.

Agreement in principle prevails on the views concerning the relationship of creature to Creator and also concerning the relationship of philosophy to theology. Regarding the latter, however, some qualifying remarks will have to be made later on.[8] In respect to Aristotle and Plato, the two works take a position which does not rest on any either/or but rather attempts a solution that does justice to both thinkers. And the same may be said in regard to St. Augustine and St. Thomas.

The question may perhaps be asked why the author has followed the lead of Plato, Augustine, and Duns Scotus rather than that of Aristotle and Thomas. The obvious answer is that she did indeed start out from Thomas and Aristotle. The fact that the actual discussion led in the end to certain goals which might have been reached faster and with greater ease if a different point of departure had been chosen, constitutes no sufficient reason to disavow the way which has been followed. The very difficulties and handicaps which had to be overcome on this way may prove of advantage to others.

Finally, a word should be said about the relationship this book bears to the most significant efforts that have been made in our time to arrive at a foundation for metaphysics, namely, Martin Heidegger's *philosophy of existence* and its counterpart, the *ontology* [*Seinslehre*] embodied in the writings of Hedwig Conrad-Martius. At the time when the author was Husserl's assistant at the University of Freiburg, Heidegger's thinking was moving in the direction of phenomenology. This common interest in the philosophy of Edmund Husserl led to the author's personal acquaintance with Heidegger and to a first contact with his thought. The author's subsequent course in life and a change of environment caused the interruption of this contact. She read, however, Heidegger's *Sein und Zeit* (Being and Time) shortly after its publication and was deeply impressed with it, but without being able at that time to evaluate it objectively.

Though the first acquaintance with Heidegger's great work dates back many years, certain reminiscences may have found their way into this present study. The desire, however, to confront these two decidedly different approaches to the meaning of being was not felt until after the conclusion of the work. This explains why the section dealing with Heidegger's philosophy of existence has been appended.[9]

The writings of Hedwig Conrad-Martius, with whom the author was closely associated during an earlier period of her life, which was decisive for both of them, have influenced her own thinking in several ways, and the reader will find repeated evidence of this influence.

I wish to thank all those who have contributed to bringing this work to a successful conclusion.

Cologne-Lindenthal, 1 September 1936

THE AUTHOR

FINITE AND ETERNAL BEING
An Attempt at an Ascent To the Meaning of Being

I.

Introduction: The Inquiry Into Being

§1. Preliminary Discussion of St. Thomas Aquinas's Doctrine of Act and Potency

A preliminary exposition of the doctrine of *act* and *potency* of St. Thomas Aquinas is to serve as an avenue of approach. It is no doubt a rather bold undertaking to single out in the structure of a philosophic system an isolated pair of concepts with a view to arriving at an understanding of their meaning. For the *organon* of philosophic reasoning is an *undivided whole*, and the individual concepts which one may be able to disengage from it are interlinked in such a way, that they illuminate each other, and none of them can be exhaustively understood apart from the context. There is indeed only *one* Truth but it unfolds itself to our human perspective in a manifold of individual truths which must be conquered step by step. If we succeed in penetrating to a certain depth in one particular direction, a larger horizon will be opened up, and with this enlarged vista a new depth will reveal itself at the point of departure.

The distinction between potency (possibility, faculty, power) and act (actuality, actualization, efficacy) is related to the ultimate problems of being. And the discussion of these concepts leads immediately into the very heart of Thomistic philosophy.[1]

The first question which Thomas asks in the *Quaestiones disputatae de potentia* reads as follows: *Can God be said to possess any potency?*[2] His answer reveals a dual meaning of potency and act. The entire system of basic concepts is cut in two by a radical dividing line which splits every one of them—starting with Being—so that each of them presents a different aspect depending on whether it is seen from the point of view of infinite or finite being. In other words, *nothing can be said of God and creatures in the same sense.* If nevertheless the identical terms are legitimately used to describe both types of being, the reason for it lies in the fact that these terms are used neither *univocally* nor *equivocally* but *analogically*. Thus the dividing line itself might

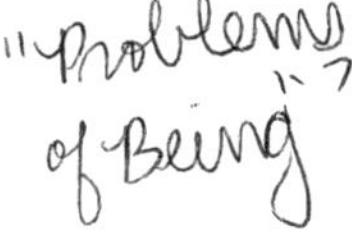

be designated as *analogia entis,* a designation which would then indicate the relationship existing between God and creature.

Potency of a sort must be attributed also to God, but this kind of potency is not opposed to act. We must distinguish between active and passive potency, and the potency attributed to God we call active potency. As to God's "act," this term does not apply to him in the same sense as it does to the creature. A creaturely act—in any of the several but intrinsically interdependent meanings of the term—indicates an efficacy or activity which has a beginning and an end and which presupposes a passive potency as its ontological foundation. God's efficacy or activity, on the other hand, has no beginning and no end: It is from eternity unto eternity; it is his immutable being. There is nothing in him that is not act; he is *actus purus,* and for this kind of act no potency is presupposed as a ground or foundation of his being, least of all a passive potency moved or activated from without. Even that active potency that is attributed to God does not exist aside from or outside his act: His potency, his power expresses itself in his act. And if externally—in the created universe, its preservation and its direction—he does not effect everything that he could possibly effect according to his power, and if in this respect there seems to open a gap between potential and actualized power, there is nonetheless to God no surplus of potency vis-à-vis his act, no unactivated potency. For the self-limitation of his power as regards its external efficacy is itself act and effect of his power. God's potency is one, as his act is one, and in this one act his potency is completely actualized.

§2. The Problem of Being in History

The reader who is unfamiliar with scholastic thought may gain the impression that when we speak of *creator* and *creature* we have thereby entered into a theological discussion. Later on, however, it will be shown that these terms are used here in a strictly philosophic sense, notwithstanding the fact that their philosophic meaning has disclosed itself only to those thinkers who had already learned by revelation to know God as the creator. With his doctrine of act and potency St. Thomas stands firmly on the ground of Aristotelian philosophy.

When Aristotle arrived at this distinction, he thereby made an epochal contribution toward the solution of a problem which had occupied Greek thought from its very beginnings: He suggested an answer to the question as to the nature of the *first* and *true* being. Καὶ δὴ καὶ τὸ πάλαι τε χαὶ νῦν καὶ αἰεὶ ζητούμενον καὶ αἰεὶ ἀπορούμενον, τί τὸ ὄν, τοῦτό ἐστι, τίς ἡ οὐσία. (The question asked at all times and still unanswered, "What is that which is?" is identical with the question, "What is meant by οὐσία [*ousia*]?"[3]) Let us at this time simply quote this sentence without making any attempt to interpret its meaning. It may be regarded as the *leitmotif* of Aristotle's *Metaphysics,* that strange book in which we find the compact expression of the as yet unsolved problem with which the Greek mind wrestled for centuries.

It is not the purpose of this book nor the task I have set for myself to show how the philosophic system of Aristotle as a whole has developed. I consider it quite possible, however, that it may have grown out of this question as from a living seed. The ardent desire of the masters of philosophy in later centuries[4] to give a consistent explanation of Aristotle's thinking is quite understandable if one considers that it was centered in a question which in his opinion was destined to remain the perennial "embarrassment" (the real *aporia* [ἀπορία]) of philosophy.

St. Thomas took up the inquiry into the nature of being at the point where Aristotle had left it. He could afford to do this because he regarded philosophy as a discipline which proceeds strictly on the basis of natural reason. On the other hand, in the course of the Christian centuries, philosophy—owing to the close association of philosophy and theology—found itself confronted with facts and tasks of which it had been unaware in its pre-Christian phase: Aristotle knew nothing of a *creation;* nothing of a God-Man, *in whose one person two natures were united;* nothing of triune Godhead or of *one nature in three persons.* His ontology, as far as he had developed it, was insufficient to do justice to these truths of faith.

St. Thomas first found a certain continuity of thought, suggesting a further development of the Aristotelian doctrine of being, in Boethius and then in larger measure in Avicenna (for whom the idea of creation had at least significance as a first motivating force and impulse). Fearlessly, yet carefully, Thomas followed in the footsteps of both the Arabic and Greek thinker, and he safely passed by the errors of Avicenna as well as those of Averroes; in both instances he examined everything and retained the best.

The opusculum *De ente et essentia* was written by Thomas, the young bachelor of arts of the University of Paris, upon the request of his brothers and companions.[5] It follows closely the *Metaphysics* of Aristotle. Even the title[6] calls to mind the sentence which I designated as the *Leitmotif* of the Metaphysics: The *ens* is the Greek ὄν and *essentia* stands for *ousia.* The short treatise presents a concise outline of the saint's *doctrine of being* [*Seinslehre*], to which he subsequently adhered in all essentials, even though he indefatigably further elaborated the main ideas until the time when, a few months before his death, he ceased working on his *Summa Theologiae,* because God had revealed to him certain truths in comparison with which everything he had previously written appeared to him as little more than chaff.

Already in this early treatise, Thomas had taken his most decisive step beyond Aristotle: He had within the realm of that which is [*Seiende*] distinguished between being [*esse*] and essence [*essentia*]. The equation of ὄν and *ousia,* from which Aristotle had started out, remains valid only for the First Existent [*Seiende*]. With this distinction, being as such—as distinct from that which is [*Seiende*]—was understood for the first time as comprising both finite and infinite being and as simultaneously encompassing the abyss which separates the former from the latter. From this vantage point, a way to seize upon the entire *manifoldness of all that which is* [*Seiende*] could be envisaged.

The inquiry into the meaning of being may be regarded as the dominating theme in both Greek and medieval thought. There is, however, this difference: While the Greeks were led to this inquiry in view of the natural givenness of the created world, for the Christian thinkers (and to a certain degree also for the Jewish and Moslem scholars) the problem assumed larger dimensions in view of the revealed truths of the supernatural world.

Modern thought, on the other hand, dissociating itself from tradition, no longer centers its efforts on the problem of being but on the problem of knowledge, and has thus severed again its linkage with faith and theology. It could perhaps be shown that modern philosophy, too, was at bottom concerned with the truth of being and that by seizing upon certain ideas which likewise have their roots in the early stages of Greek thought (and which mark necessary trends in epistemological speculation), has rendered valuable services to the question of being.

Much more serious is the complete separation of modern philosophy from revealed truth. It no longer sees in revealed truth a standard of measurement with which to test its own findings. Nor is it willing to have theology assign to it certain tasks for the solution of which philosophy would then have to use its own specific ways and means. It not only considers it a duty to confine itself to the natural light of reason but it is determined never to reach out beyond the world of natural experience. It wants to be an autonomous discipline in every respect. This ambition has caused modern philosophy to become to a large extent a godless discipline. And it has led, moreover, to the division of philosophy into two separate camps in which two different languages are spoken and in which no attempt is made to arrive at a mutual understanding.

On the one side we have modern philosophy and on the other Catholic-scholastic philosophy. The latter claims to be the *philosophia perennis,* but outsiders look upon it as a private affair of theological faculties, seminaries, and colleges of religious orders. To these outsiders the philosophia perennis appears as a rigid system of abstract and lifeless ideas and concepts which are handed down from generation to generation while the stream of life is flowing on in its own self-created river bed.

There is no doubt, however, that this situation has gradually changed during the past few decades and that this change has come about as the result of sincere efforts on both sides. As far as the Catholic position is concerned, it is well to remember that *Catholic philosophy* (and *Catholic scholarship* generally) was never quite the same as the philosophy of Catholics. Catholic intellectual life had in a large measure become dependent on *modern* intellectual life and had lost contact with its own great past. In this respect the second half of the nineteenth century witnessed a real renaissance, a rebirth brought about by Catholic scholars delving again into the primary sources of their own intellectual heritage. Is it not truly astonishing that the decrees of Leo XIII and Pius XI were needed to revive the study of St. Thomas and that it had become necessary first of all to prepare adequate editions of the texts that were to be used in Catholic institutions of higher learning? A great many hitherto unpublished and entirely unknown manuscripts were lying in European libraries and had to be rediscovered. And only the last few years have witnessed a concerted effort on the part of translators.

This multifarious scholarly research has yielded some admirable results, but the work is far from completed. Nonetheless, what has been excavated to date reveals a whole forgotten world—a rich and dynamic world—which holds much promise for the future. The newly aroused interest in the history of ideas [*Geisteswissenschaft*]—itself a fruit of the late nineteenth and early twentieth century—has in large measure contributed to these successes. We know today that Thomism did not spring from the mind of St. Thomas as a ready-made system of philosophic concepts. We have learned to see it as a living intellectual structure which we can observe in the successive stages of its organic growth. It is a way and method of thought which must be personally appropriated in order to gain new life within us. We are also aware that the great thinkers of the Christian Middle Ages wrestled with the same problems which concern us today and that they have therefore much to tell us that may prove of great help in our present situation.

It should not be forgotten, after all, that there is also another side to this question. At about the same time when *Christian philosophy*[7] awakened from its sleeping beauty sleep, *modern philosophy* made the discovery that the way it had pursued for about the past three centuries led it into a blind alley. Mired in materialism, it sought at first to regain its freedom of inquiry by a return to Kant. But that was not enough. The several brands of Neo-Kantianism gave way gradually to those trends of thought which turned once more to being and reality [*Seiende*], thus vindicating the long despised term *ontology*, the science of being. Ontology reappeared first as *Wesensphilosophie* (philosophy of essences) in the phenomenology of Edmund Husserl and Max Scheler. This development was seconded by Heidegger's *Existenzphilosophie* (philosophy of existence) and its opposite pole, the ontology of Hedwig Conrad-Martius.

The question then arises whether the reborn philosophy of the Middle Ages and the newly created philosophy of the twentieth century can possibly find a common meeting ground in the one broad river be of the *philosophia perennis.* They still speak different languages, and the task immediately at hand is therefore to find an idiom which may serve as a means of communication and mutual understanding.

§3. Linguistic Difficulties

A real cross for contemporary philosophy is the language barrier. We are living in the midst of a veritable Babylonian confusion of tongues. Today it is hardly possible to use any expression without having to fear that the reader or listener may completely misunderstand its intended meaning. Most of our technical terms are imbued with several historically conditioned connotations.

In the preceding preliminary discussion I have advisedly let St. Thomas speak in his own tongue without attempting to translate the terms *potency* and *act.* It is, however, not my intention to let the matter rest here. In Germany we have for some years witnessed serious endeavors to create an indigenous philosophic language. The writings of the great German mystics of the middle high German period provide a valid basis for such an undertaking. A bold pioneering effort in this direction is the German edition of St. Thomas' *Summa Theologiae* by Joseph Bernhart.[8] The translation of the *Summa* published under the auspices of the *Katholische Akademikerverband* [9] has the same end in view but uses much more caution and moderation in pursuing it.

These attempts, however, clearly reveal also the dangers inherent in translations of this kind. People who have themselves tried their hand at translating from foreign languages know how much there is that is simply untranslatable. On the other hand, it should be emphasized that the possibilities for making the concepts of a foreign tongue intelligible by way of translation are certainly much greater than the usual complacency in this matter would let us surmise. And anybody who has given some thought to the nature of language as well as to the nature of languages knows that it cannot be otherwise.

Languages grow out of the spirit of different peoples and are thus a fruit and formal expression of their lives; their languages mirror both their individuality and their diversity. The Greeks, a philosophical people, created for themselves a philosophical language. But where and how could the Romans find a philosophical language? The answer is, of course, that they took their philosophy from the Greek universities, from their visiting Greek friends, or from their slaves. They probably fared best as long as they did their reading and writing in the Greek language. As soon, however, as they became engrossed in creating a Roman literature they had to struggle laboriously to wrest from their own language something which it actually lacked.

A letter written by Seneca to the Roman satirist Lucilius[10] contains the following illuminating passage: "Your criticism of Roman narrow-mindedness," the Roman philosopher writes, "will be even more severe when I tell you that there is one short syllable [in Greek] which I find myself unable to translate. You naturally will want to know which one it is. Well, it is the syllable ὄν (*das Seiende* [that which is]). I may appear to you inept. The translation *quod est* immediately suggests itself. Nevertheless, I find a considerable difference of meaning in the two expressions: I have to use a Latin phrase to render a single Greek word (*verbum pro vocabulo*). If, however, it cannot be avoided, I shall use *quod est.*" Evidently, the form *ens* [*Seiendes*][11] never occurred to Seneca. (It is used occasionally by Boethius, although he too in most instances writes *quod est*). Seneca probably would have regarded *ens* as too barbaric a word formation. He thought that even the term *essentia*[12] was more than a man of good taste could be expected to tolerate. Beginning his letter with an impressive lament on the poverty of the Latin tongue, he goes on as follows: " 'What,' you may well ask, 'is the purpose of this long introduction? What is it trying to accomplish? ' I am not going to leave you in the dark: I want you to listen, if possible with favor, to the sound of the word *essentia;* if you find that impossible, I shall have to pronounce it in spite of your disapproval. ... How shall we translate the word *ousia*—that necessary thing, that nature which contains in itself the foundation of everything? I therefore ask you to permit me to employ this word [*essentia*]. In return I shall make every effort to use the privilege granted me most sparingly: I may even be satisfied with the mere permission to use it."

Are these linguistic difficulties not the very same with which this present attempt has to contend? To be sure, there is no reason to lament the poverty of the German language! In this respect our position with regard to Greek is far more favorable than was that of the Romans.[12a] Our difficulty in relation to Latin is rather the opposite one: It appears impossible from the outset to render the several shades and meanings of Latin terms by *one* particular German word. The attempt to do this will of necessity illumine only one aspect of the Latin expression and will thus in diverse contexts entail serious semantic distortions.

What, then, must be done to overcome this difficulty? In order to do justice to the multiple shades of meaning, we must utilize the natural richness of our language and employ, to the extent this is necessary and possible, different terms in different contexts.[13] And yet this procedure is not without its dangers. In the first place, the translator who adopts it must not only have a sure command of both languages—his own mother tongue and the foreign idiom—but he or she must also feel at home in the intellectual world of the foreign work and its author, and must moreover live in immediate contact with the problems which are under discussion. What translator, however, will confidently claim to have the confidence of fulfilling all these requisites?

In order not to succumb to the danger of offering personal opinions in place of the ideas of an author, the translator must in many instances have recourse to the Latin terms.[14] This is also occasionally necessary because, in spite of the greater richness of the German language, *some* Latin concepts simply have no corresponding equivalent in German. But the most cogent reason which seems to make it impossible to dispense entirely with the technical Latin terminology is another one: The relative poverty of the Latin language is its weakness as well as its strength. While Greek with its freedom and ease of expression is a *language of vital intellectual mobility,* Latin with its strictly disciplined orderliness and its almost austere stringency is especially suited for forming *boldly cast expressions of summary conclusions.* The great number of meanings embodied in a Latin word is not arbitrary but orderly and semantically consistent. By simply discarding the Latin terminology we relinquish our hold on many significant semantic units which cast abundant light on the order of that which is [*das Seiende*]. We thereby deprive ourselves of the mature fruits of centuries of intellectual endeavor and of the spirit of a people which—as is the case with every *Volksgeist*—was preordained to fulfill a special task in the history of humankind. Who would be presumptuous enough to brush aside lightly such a heritage or bold enough to offer a substitute for it?[15]

Let us try then to do one thing and yet not leave the other thing undone. Let us attempt to find the most adequate expression for everything that can be convincingly stated in German. But let us retain and make visible the firm scaffolding of the traditional scholastic language. Let us cling to it as our guide and have recourse to it whenever the danger of one-sidedness or a distortion of meaning threatens.

With these objectives in mind, we might well be satisfied if it were only a question of the relationship existing between German and Latin. We know, however, that the Latin terminology follows the Greek model, and we are aware of the difficulties which had to be overcome in the attempt at assimilation. We will therefore most likely succeed in arriving at a correct understanding of the Latin terms and in rendering their meaning faithfully if we turn back to the Greek original. Medieval scholasticism has not invalidated Greek philosophy, and neither has Latin made the Greek language obsolete.[16]

What has been said is strikingly illustrated by the terms *potency* and *act* with which we started our discussion. The word *act* is comprised of the meaning of the Greek terms ἐνέργεια, ἔργον, ἐντελέχεια. Others might be added to these, but for our present purpose an exhaustive enumeration is neither necessary nor appropriate.

'Ενέργεια (energy) designates actual being in contrast to possible being (δύναμις). While the figure of Hermes, for example, is potentially in the wood out of which it can be carved, it is actually found only in the finished statue. Scientific thinking is a possibility for a person endowed with the capacity to think, even at a time when that person is not actually engaged in thinking: It is actual in the exercise of the faculty of thought, and ἐνέργεια thus means an efficacious operation [*Wirksamkeit*]. The possibility or capacity (δύναμις, potency) has as its end (τέλος) actuality: The end of the capacity to think is actual thought. If this actualization of the possibility results in some *work*, it is called ἔργον. This latter term is used regardless of whether the being of this work abides in the one who operates—as thought abides in the thinker—or whether it extends to certain effects of the operation which acquire an existence [*Dasein*] of their own—as, for example, the house which owes its origin to the activity of the architect. The former case makes it quite clear that ἐνέργεια and ἔργον (efficacious operation of the work) are identical. And since possible being reaches its fulfillment or end in actual being, the latter is also designated as ἐντελέχεια (entelechy), a term which might properly be translated as perfection of being [*Seinsvollendung*].[17]

This is not yet the proper place for a thorough discussion of all these concepts. It was merely to be shown how the citation of Greek texts may prove helpful in finding valuable clues for the deciphering of the multiple meaning of a Latin expression and for its correct translation. Actuality, efficacious operation, work, activity, perfection of being—there is certainly no lack of shades of meaning. But the above example also illustrates how perilous it would be to use one and the same term indiscriminately to reproduce the meaning of the Latin word *actus*. For example, a person well versed in the terminology of modern philosophy and accustomed to associating with the term *act* the meaning "freely operating activity," will of necessity completely misinterpret certain scholastic texts if that person uniformly applies to them this specific preconceived meaning.

The following investigations will attempt to proceed in accordance with the principles outlined above. Wherever basic ideas of scholastic thought form the point of departure, they will first be presented in scholastic terminology. To assure ourselves, however, that we have understood their true meaning and are not using verbal clichés, we shall try to find in our own language expressions which correspond as closely as possible to the particular Latin phrasing. In this endeavor the search for the origins of the scholastic concepts must come to our aid: We shall look for the *historical* origins and more eagerly still for those *factual* [*sachlichen*] origins which are only revealed to us when we inquire once again into the repeatedly posed and never resolved problem relating to the nature of that which is [*das Seiende*], and to the nature of *ousia* itself.

We shall earnestly strive to join our thinking to that of the ancient masters, and yet not only to these but also to those others who in our time have in their own manner and method resumed the identical inquiry. This latter procedure appears fully justified in view of the fact that these modern thinkers have out of an inner necessity—not under the influence of any traditional intellectual ties—penetrated anew to the depths of the problem of being. They are living in closest proximity to its reality and can therefore help us to understand the original intentions and motives of the old masters.

This procedure seems especially appropriate in the case of the author of this book: Her philosophic home is the school of Edmund Husserl, and her philosophic mother tongue is the language of the phenomenological thinkers. She therefore uses phenomenology as a starting point to find her way into the majestic temple of scholastic thought. She believes that her awareness of this ultimate goal suffices to permit her to choose it as her guide.

§4. Is There a Christian Philosophy?

Any attempt to arrive at a mutual understanding between modern and medieval philosophy has to overcome an even greater obstacle than the language barrier: The two differ radically in their attitude regarding the interrelation of knowledge and faith or philosophy and theology.

We have already pointed out that Catholic philosophers and theologians are not even agreed among themselves as to whether it is permissible to speak of a *Christian philosophy.*[18] But no matter whether one regards philosophy as a purely natural science—that is, a discipline resting exclusively on reason and natural experience as its sources of knowledge—or whether one grants to it the right to draw additional light from revelation, there can be no doubt that the philosophy of the great medieval doctors of the church grew to its maturity in the shadow of Christian doctrine. In revealed truth it saw the measure of all truth, and it made every effort to resolve those problems which were posed by Christian dogmatics. It put its trust in the power of faith to impart to human reason greater certitude about its own natural operations.

In this matter *modern* philosophy has cut itself off completely from the medieval tradition. The question therefore arises whether there is still common ground for constructive intellectual effort between such heterogeneous ways of thinking. St. Thomas Aquinas himself answers this question strongly in the affirmative. His own relationship to Aristotelian and Arabian philosophy presents sufficient evidence that he believed in the possibility of a philosophy founded on pure natural reason, unaided by revealed truth. He clearly demonstrates this conviction in his *Summa contra gentiles,* commonly known as his *philosophical Summa.* Here he points out that in discussions with pagans and Moslems, the Christian thinker cannot refer to a common faith based on the Scriptures (a common ground which in the case of the Jews is provided by the Old Testament and in the case of heretics by the New Testament). It therefore becomes necessary, he says, "to have recourse to that natural reason to which all must assent."[19] There are, according to St. Thomas, two ways of truth,[20] and though natural reason cannot attain to the highest and ultimate truth, it can nevertheless ascend to a stage of knowledge which enables it to reject certain errors of judgment and to recognize the accord between the naturally demonstrable truths of reason and the truths of faith.

But if, on the one hand, St. Thomas is convinced that there is a common way and a common field of research for all seekers of truth, it must, on the other hand, be emphasized that for him natural knowledge and supernatural faith (philosophy and theology) are not so radically separated as to be entirely unrelated to each other. After all, in writing the *philosophical Summa,* it was precisely his intention to *demonstrate the truth of the Catholic faith* and to refute the errors of the gentiles. And almost every page of his works testifies to the fact that for him the truth of faith is the measure of all truth. The simple phrase, *Sed haec sunt contra fidem* [but these opinions are contrary to faith] appears to him as a perfectly convincing refutation of even the most respected philosophic authority.

In his presentation of the Thomistic solution of the problem of reason versus faith, Jacques Maritain[21] points out that to obtain a satisfactory answer to the questions, "Is there a Christian philosophy and, if so, what is its meaning?," one must distinguish between the *nature* and the *actual situation* or condition of philosophy. As far as the nature of philosophy is concerned, he says, it is entirely independent of faith and theology. But this nature is actualized within a specific frame of changing historical conditions, and with respect to this actualization one may justifiably speak of a *Christian situation or condition of philosophy.*

In order to clarify further what he means by the nature of philosophy—that is, what philosophy is in itself or as such[22]—Maritain explains that "according to St. Thomas substances are absolutely and autonomously determined in their specific and particular essence, whereas the possibilities of their operation are determined by those acts which essentially correspond to the substances, and these acts in turn are determined by their apportioned objects. Now when there comes into being that specific formation of the mind which we call philosophy, it is essentially related—as is every form of knowledge, inquiry, and judgment—to some objective reality. In assimilating reason to this objective sphere, philosophy receives from it its specific character, and its particular form is thus entirely determined by its object. Its nature depends exclusively on the objects to which it turns in conformity with its essence, and by no manner of means does it depend on the subject in whom it resides."[23]

Let us now carry this work of clarification a little farther.[24] Philosophy is described by Maritain as "a structure and … formation of the mind," as a form of "knowledge, inquiry, and judgment"; it is said to be related to some objective reality and characterized in its nature by nothing but this objective reality. It is a formal structure of the mind: This is to say that the philosophically formed mind adheres to a definite direction, that it is firmly set within a frame of definite possibilities of action (the potency acquires the form of a habit [*habitus*]). In speaking, however, of knowledge, inquiry, and judgment, one thinks not so much of an enduring mental habit but rather of the corresponding *act,* that is, of a vital activity. Let us conclude therefore that philosophy may imply both, namely, vital intellectual activity and an enduring intellectual habit. (The philosopher remains a philosopher even in those moments when he or she is not actively engaged in philosophic thought.)

A third consideration must be added, and I feel even tempted to say that this third meaning of philosophy should have been mentioned first: *Philosophy is a science* [*Wissenschaft*]. Both the Latin word *scientia* and the German word *Wissenschaft* denote knowledge [*Wissen*] (as a habit and as act) as well as science. And, as a matter of fact, theological usage associates with the term *science* the meaning of knowledge (e.g., when it calls sc*ientia* a gift of the Holy Spirit). Modern logic and the modern theory of knowledge and science [*Wissenschaftslehre*], on the other hand, mean by *Wissenschaft* a mental construct and attribute to give it an existence independent of individual thinking minds. It is regarded as a structure of concepts, judgments, and demonstrations, all interrelated and joined together according to definite laws. What establishes one specific scientific discipline as an intrinsically unified and coherent whole, setting it off from all the others, is its relation to a circumscribed sphere of objects. It is conditioned in its structure by this objective sphere and receives from it its rules and methods.

If *Wissenschaft* is then understood as a structural whole that is not tied to or dependent upon an individual thinking mind, it nevertheless presupposes the existence of an objective reality and of knowing intellects—even of intellects of the specific kind that acquire their knowledge step by step by means of discursive reasoning. And if *Wissenschaft* is defined in this way, there still remains attached to it that dual meaning corresponding to the difference between its *nature* and its *actual situation or condition.* Using for the moment the latter meaning as our frame of reference, we may then try to interpret it on the basis of its historically conditioned and thus variable factual content. We use this kind of interpretation, for example, when we describe the concrete situation of contemporary mathematics. Viewing the matter in this perspective, Husserl correctly states that "*Wissenschaft* exists as an objective entity only in its literature: Only in the form of its written documents can it be said to have an objective reality, notwithstanding its manifold relations to man and his intellectual activities.[25] In this form *Wissenschaft* perpetuates itself through the ages and outlasts individuals, generations, and nations. It thus represents a sum total of external designs and projects which, having sprung from the actual knowledge of individuals, may ultimately also terminate again in the actions of countless individuals. ..."[26]

In an earlier passage of Husserl's work we read, "*Wissenschaft,* as the name implies, tends toward knowledge [*Wissen*]." And a little further on, "In knowledge, however, we possess truth." *Wissenschaft,* we conclude, in every one of its historical situations, represents the total precipitate of the efforts of the human mind in its pursuit of truth. It manifests itself in forms and structures which have dissociated themselves from the searching mind and have thus acquired an existence of their own. To the extent that these forms reveal themselves to *sensory perception,* they carry a *meaning* which calls for interpretation and understanding. *Wissenschaft* in its historical situation is always fragmentary; aside from intuitions of truth, it also embodies all the errors, pitfalls, and distortions of truth to which the searching mind has succumbed.

From this meaning of science and knowledge must be distinguished *Wissenschaft* as it subsists according to its *nature* or, better, *Wissenschaft as an idea.* We might theoretically assume that some special field of science was completely explored (although we know well that the human mind in its earthly striving will never achieve this kind of perfection). We might further imagine that everything that can be predicated of this special scientific sphere has been set down in the form of true statements and that all of these were causally and logically correlated or—what amounts to the same thing—that all have been integrated into a conclusive scientific theory. This would then represent a *Wissenschaft* in ideal perfection, without a flaw or wrinkle. But such an ideal science will never enter into the field of our actual experience: It remains rather the guiding paradigm which we try to approximate in all our search and endeavor.

Let us then ask the question: To what extent is such a paradigm meaningful? Is there any field that could ever be exhaustively explored by a particular science? To make this latter query more intelligible, we must briefly consider (again anticipating some of our future discussions) what we mean when we speak of the *truth* which we possess in our knowledge. I know, for example, that right now the cherries in our garden are in bloom. This sentence, then, "The cherries are blossoming," is true. The cherries blossom "in truth." As a linguistic structure this sentence expresses a meaning which I embrace and comprehend with my knowledge; it comprises a series of intelligible terms. The fact that I embrace this meaning knowingly (and not merely hold an opinion about it) indicates that this sentence is not only intelligible but "true, "or that something corresponds to it "in truth." The term "true" in these two phrasings does not carry a strictly identical meaning, but the two shades of meaning are nevertheless intrinsically related to one another.

If one speaks—as is customary—of *truths,* one has in mind such true sentences or propositions. But this is an imprecise way of expressing oneself. The sentence is not a truth [*veritas*] but a true thing [*verum*]. Its *truth* in the strict sense consists in its being in *adequate correspondence with something which is* [*mit einem Seienden* (with an existent)] or in the fact that something corresponds to it which has an independent existence. The truth of the sentence, in short, is founded upon a *true being* (that is, a being which has its foundation in itself and which provides a foundation for the sentence).

Every *Wissenschaft* aims at true being. Being antecedes every *Wissenschaft:* Not only every human knowledge and science understood as an arrangement for the elaboration of true propositions and for the description of the tangible total residue of all the endeavors leading up to true propositions, but even *Wissenschaft* conceived as an idea. The propositional sentence [*Satz*] *is* concerned with a *subject* (or *object*) of which it makes some predication and which we therefore call the subject of the sentence [*Satz-Gegenstand*). But what the sentence "aims" at intentionally in positing a proposition is not this subject or object (in our example: the cherries), nor what is predicated of the subject (blossoming), but rather the entire existing state-of-affairs [*Sachverhalte*] (that the cherries are blossoming).

Sentences express existing states-of-affairs *and have their ontological* foundation in them. These states-of-affairs in turn are not founded in themselves but have their ontological foundation in *objects* (in a specific sense of this term). To each object belongs a sphere of states-of-affairs which reveal the object's inner structure and the relative position which it occupies with respect to the total texture of existents. Again, to each state-of-affairs belongs a sphere of propositional sentences in which these conditions may manifest themselves. (There are many possibilities of expression for a particular state-of-affairs because of the semantic richness of the component parts of these individual states-of-affairs [*einzelnen Sachverhaltsglieder*]).

In their structural organization these different states-of-affairs are already related to the potential cognition of minds which acquire their knowledge step by step in discursive reasoning. This latter statement should not, however, be construed as if these states-of-affairs were "produced" by the mind: They rather prescribe for the mind the rules of its procedure.

Propositional sentences with their manifold possibilities of expression have their foundation in the states-of-affairs [*Sachverhalte*], and in this sense it may be said that these propositions are or "exist" prior to their being conceived by a human mind and prior to their being formulated in the *material* medium of a human language, that is, in the media of sounds and letters.

Wissenschaft as an idea—that enduring substrate of every concrete human knowledge and science—is then to be understood as the "pure" (quasi, as yet bodiless or disincarnate) expression of all those states-of-affairs in which that which is [*das Seiende*] unfolds itself according to its own inner necessity.

But now the question arises whether all those states-of-affairs which correspond to that which is [*Seiendes*], or even that particular state-of-affairs which corresponds to a single object, can be conceived as a definitive totality that exhausts all the possibilities of its object. As far as the objects of the exact sciences are concerned, the question may here be left undecided. In regard to the real world in its plentitude, however, the answer must be emphatically in the negative: It proves itself inexhaustible for any analytical or discursive cognitive reasoning. And if this is the case, then any *Wirklichkeitswissenschaft* (that is, any knowledge and science of reality as a whole) is in its very idea a project that remains forever unrealizable.

That there exists a diversity of disciplines of knowledge and sciences [*Wissenschaften*] is due to the multiple division of that which is [*das Seiende*] into series of spheres of objects [*Gegenstandsgebiete*] which are integrated in themselves and set off from one another according to their genera and species. As to what constitutes the domain of objects in the case of philosophy, Jacques Maritain writes: "Whatever idea one may form of philosophy, one negates rather than defines it unless one attributes to it that domain of objects which is accessible to the natural powers of the human mind."[27] This statement indicates the clear dividing line which St. Thomas draws at the beginning of the *Summa Theologiae*, where he says that "the philosophic disciplines ... confine themselves to the sphere of human reason," whereas theology "is based on divine revelation."[28] Evidently, the saint means here by philosophy every type of natural knowledge and science [*Wissenschaft*]. This definition, however, is no longer admissible in contemporary research which has to take into account a number of completely separate *disciplines*—differing from one another according to both their objects and their methods—and which must thus attribute to philosophy a unique position with respect to all the individual branches of knowledge and science [*Einzelwissenschaften*]. While mathematics and history, for example, need not (and actually do not) take cognizance of one another's efforts, philosophy finds itself compelled to interest itself in both mathematics and history. But though the average mathematician and historian pursue the beaten path of their particular disciplines without paying attention to philosophy, there will always arise situations in which a particular discipline stands in need of considering its own philosophic foundations if it wants to define clearly its own specific tasks.

No discipline can afford to proceed arbitrarily: The rules for its method of procedure are determined by the nature of its specific sphere of objects [*Sachgebietes*]. This is why in the initial stages of the evolution of the individual disciplines we usually find some creative minds earnestly concerned with the clarification of the basic concepts of their particular field of endeavor (such as Galileo and Newton in the natural and exact sciences or Friedrich Schiller and Leopold von Ranke in the field of historiography). But once the procedure or *method* has been determined, it becomes possible to employ and exercise it in accordance with the established rules.

It cannot be denied, on the other hand, that there are some disciplines which embark on their exploits as upon an adventurous voyage of discovery, treading unknown paths and advancing into unknown regions, without any previous clarification of fundamental principles. Sooner or later the scholars who follow this kind of procedure will be overcome by a feeling of helplessness, finding themselves at their wits' end. For such a situation there is only one remedy: They must re-examine their own foundations and then evaluate their methods and their findings in the light of the basic principles of their particular discipline. The crisis, for example, in which psychology has found itself since the turn of the century is merely an inescapable consequence of the amazing feat which the psychology of the nineteenth century performed when it simply discarded the concept of the soul.[29]

It is one of the functions of philosophy to elucidate the fundamental principles of all the sciences [*Wissenschaften*].[30] What the individual disciplines accept and adopt without questioning from pre-scientific thinking must be subjected to philosophic investigation.

And whenever the research worker carries on such an investigation in her or his particular field—as is done, for example, by the mathematician who speculates on the nature of numbers or by the historian who meditates on the meaning of history—this research worker acts as a philosopher. We can thus well understand why St. Thomas designates philosophy (or wisdom in the sense of being naturally preliminary to the supernatural, spiritual gift) as *perfectum opus rationis* (a perfect work of reason).[31]

But philosophy is not satisfied with a preliminary clarification: It aims at ultimate clarity. It wants to give an account (λόγον διδόναι) of the ultimate attainable causes. The world of experience, with everything that it presents to the senses and to the intellect, stimulates the natural desire for knowledge and provides proper perspectives for human research in several directions. It thus points toward the ultimate sphere of intelligibility, that is, toward *being as such* and toward the *structure of the totality of that which is* [*das Seiende als solches*] with its *essential divisions according to genera and species.* In this direction toward being as such, experience gains access to pertinent problems and adequate methods of research.[32]

The inquiry into the meaning of being and of existents as such [*des Seins und des Seienden als solchen*] is, according to Aristotle's statement in his *Metaphysics,* the task of *first philosophy.* Later on, this first philosophy was termed *metaphysics.*[33]

The different principal species of existents are studied by those particular branches of philosophy which provide the foundation for the individual disciplines of knowledge and science [*Einzelwissenschaften*]. They thereby link philosophy with these individual disciplines. If at any time the work of philosophy were completed and the individual disciplines firmly established on a philosophic foundation, then they would all have been transformed into truly philosophic sciences and we would have arrived at one unified *Wissenschaft* in perfect accord with the unity of the sum total of existents. Here again, however, we are speaking of an ideal which can only be approximated but never actually attained.

As long as we are *in via,* philosophy and the individual sciences will have to carry on their research separately. The two types of knowledge are nevertheless destined constantly to set new tasks for each other and mutually to strengthen, deepen, and generally benefit each other. Once we are *in patria,* the glimpses[34] of earthly wisdom and knowledge will give way to the plenitude of divine wisdom, which will then permit us to envision with one single glance what human reason has been trying to compile during the millennia of its laborious efforts.

Having clarified the meaning of philosophic speculation, we may now further inquire into the meaning of the specifically Christian situation or condition of philosophy. Maritain mentions several characteristics relevant to this matter. Grace purifies and strengthens the human intellect, making it less vulnerable to error (though by no means safe from erring) than it was in its fallen state.[35] This observation bears on philosophy if we consider it as an attitude [*habitus*] and an activity [*actus*] of the intellect. But Christian doctrine also enriches philosophy with certain concepts (such as that of creation) which actually remained foreign to it as long as it did not draw from this source (though it was never intrinsically impossible for it to discover them.)

The latter observation applies to philosophy considered as a science [*Wissenschaft*]. What has been handed down to us as the philosophy of the Christian centuries contains essential ingredients deriving from Christian ways of thinking. Moreover, the world itself had assumed a new meaning once it was seen with the eyes of faith: "From then on the world was manifestly given to us as the work of the *Word,* the Second Person of the Trinity, and everything in it—addressing itself to those *finite* spiritual beings who know themselves as spiritual beings—henceforth proclaims the *infinite* spirit."[36]

At this Christian stage philosophy gained a new insight into its own nature: It could envisage what both Maritain and Gabriel Marcel call a "scandal" to human reason—the "fact, namely, that the validity of the contents of revelation lies beyond any experience based on purely human foundations...."[37] If philosophers then want to remain faithful to their goal, if they want to understand that which is [*das Seiende*] in the light of its ultimate causes, they will be compelled by their faith to extend their reflection beyond that which is naturally accessible to them. There are existents which are beyond the reach of natural experience and natural reason but which have been made known to us by revelation; and they confront the receptive human mind with entirely new tasks.

"In those things," writes Maritain, "which concern the data of sense, philosophy turns for information to the natural sciences. Why should it not turn to faith and theology to gain information concerning the divine? In the words of Malebranche, 'The facts of religion or the definitions of dogmatic theology are among my experiences ... '; after they have been recognized by me as valid I use my mind with respect to them in the same way as do those who study physics with respect to scientific data."[38]

Faith and theology enlighten natural reason as to the true nature of the *first existent* whom it had previously reached by its own efforts, and they also throw light on the relationship which obtains between all that which is and the first existent. This illumination natural reason could never have gained unaided. Reason would turn into unreason if it would stubbornly content itself with what it is able to discover with its own light, barring out everything which is made visible to it by a brighter and more sublime light. For it ought to be emphasized that what is communicated to us by revelation is not something simply unintelligible but rather something with an intelligible meaning—a meaning, to be sure, which cannot be comprehended and demonstrated in the way natural facts are understood and demonstrated. What is communicated to us by revelation cannot be comprehended at all (that is, it cannot be exhaustively described by means of concepts) because it is in itself immeasurable and inexhaustible and at any time reveals only so much of its mystery as it wants us to understand. In themselves, however, the contents of revealed truth are supremely intelligible, and they become intelligible for us in the measure in which we receive light and with it the medium of a new understanding of natural facts, of which we now learn for the first time that they are *only* natural.

As regards human action, Maritain has pointed out that it must be considered in the light of the revealed truths of original sin and redemption and that therefore no system of ethics can be complete if it rests exclusively on a *purely* philosophical basis. It can be completed only if, acknowledging its dependence on the supernatural (i.e., on theology), it supplements its own basic truths with the truths of revelation. This statement, it seems to me, applies—with some modifications and additions—to all finite existence and also to the whole of philosophy. In the light which the fundamental truths of the Christian faith—the truths of creation, original sin, redemption, and supernatural perfection—throw upon the totality of existence, it appears impossible for a pure philosophy (i.e., a philosophy based exclusively on natural reason) to perfect itself or to perform a *perfectum opus rationis.* It needs for its completion the aid of theology without, however, becoming itself theology.

While it is the task of theology to establish the facts of revelation as such and to elaborate their specific meaning and interrelation, it is the task of philosophy to harmonize those propositions at which it has arrived by using its own devices together with the truths of faith and theology. Only thus can reality be made intelligible in its ultimate reasons and causes.

To harmonize—this means, negatively speaking, that for Christian philosophers revealed truth is the standard of measurement to which they have to subordinate their own judgment. They will, for example, have to sacrifice a philosophic insight as soon as they themselves recognize or are told by the magisterial authority of the church that their supposed discovery is incompatible with Christian doctrine. Although philosophers must strive for clear evidence as a final criterion within the sphere of their own rational argumentation, they must nevertheless—in view of the undeniable fallibility of all purely human knowledge—accept in the interest of truth the infallible judgment of a supernaturally enlightened supreme authority. They can, of course, submit to this authority only if they have received the gift of faith. But even unbelievers will understand that the believers must bow to this authority not only as believing Christians but also as philosophers.

Furthermore, philosophers, in taking account of revealed truth, may discover for themselves certain tasks which they would never have envisaged without this additional theological knowledge. In his address at Juvisy Fr. A.R. Motte, O.P., pointed out that the doctrine of God and of divine creation taught philosophy to distinguish between essence and existence [*Wesen* and *Dasein*]; that the doctrines of the Holy Trinity and of the Incarnation informed as to the distinction between nature and person, and the doctrine of the Holy Eucharist forced it to elaborate clearly and distinctly the meaning of substance and accident.[39]

When philosophy thus finally encountered a type of existence which it had hitherto not known, it discovered entirely new aspects of existence and being. Revelation speaks in a language accessible to natural human reason and offers subject matter for the formation of purely philosophic concepts. The latter may—as happened in the case of the concepts of *person* and *substance*—later on become the common property of philosophy and may then be used independently of those facts of revelation from which they originally derive.

The aforementioned two modes of paying heed to the truths of faith bring to light a distinct temporal phase of the historical structure of philosophy—a structure which depends on faith and theology as the external conditions of its full realization. We may then call such a philosophy Christian in the same sense in which *Thomism* may be called a *Christian philosophy,*[40] but certainly not in the sense that it embodies in its own structure revealed truth as such. If, on the

other hand, philosophy in its exploration of that which is meets with questions which it cannot answer by making use of its own devices (as, for example, the question concerning the origin of the human soul) and if, in order to arrive at a more comprehensive knowledge of things that are, it appropriates for itself the answers given by Christian theology, then we have a Christian philosophy which uses faith as a source of knowledge. In this latter case we can no longer speak of a *pure* and *autonomous* philosophy. Are we justified in calling it theology? I do not think so.

Let us assume, for example, that in a historical work dealing with the intellectual life of the twentieth century the changes in modern physics under the influence of Einstein's theory of relativity are being discussed: In this case the historian has to supplement his knowledge with certain findings of the natural scientist. But does his work thereby become a textbook of natural science? By no means. What is decisive is the guiding intention of the author.

Now the relationship existing between philosophy and theology does not offer an exact parallel to the above example. The historian is not concerned with the problem of whether Einstein's theory is true or false but rather with its historical significance. The philosopher who borrows from theological doctrine, on the other hand, is concerned with revealed truth qua *truth.* The common element in both instances lies in the fact that another discipline has to be consulted to make it possible for scholars to progress in their own field, so that with the aid of this second science they may be able to go on with their own research.

One thing is certain: Philosophy cannot claim for those propositions at which it arrives with the aid of Christian doctrine the same degree of intelligibility that characterizes its own independent and strictly philosophical conclusions. Whatever derives from the synthesis of theological and philosophic truth bears the imprint of this dual source of knowledge, and faith, as we are told, is a "dark light." Faith helps us to understand something, but only in order to point to something that remains for us incomprehensible. Since the ultimate ground of all existence [*alles Seienden*] is unfathomable, everything which is seen in this ultimate perspective moves into that "dark light" of faith, and everything intelligible is placed in a setting with an incomprehensible background. This is what Erich Przywara means when he speaks of a *reductio ad mysterium.*

As has become clear from our last remarks, we hold with Przywara that philosophy reaches its perfection with the aid of theology, not by being itself transformed into theology ["*durch* Theologie, nicht *als* Theologie"].[41] On the other hand, I was not able to understand clearly from what aspect Przywara envisages the union "of theology and philosophy within the frame of a metaphysics."[42] To be sure, the *formal primacy* of theology[43] must be acknowledged in the sense that the final judgment on the truth of both theological and philosophic propositions is left to theology, taken in the sense of its supreme significance as God's word through the medium of the *magisterium* of the church. But precisely because philosophy (not theology) must have its contents augmented, it faces the task of elaborating a unified and comprehensive doctrine. It is therefore our conviction that the term *Christian philosophy* designates not only the mental attitude of the Christian philosopher, nor merely the actual doctrinal system of Christian thinkers but, above and beyond these, the idea of a *perfectum opus rationis.* A Christian philosophy in this sense must aspire to a unity and synthesis of all the knowledge which we have gained by the exercise of our natural reason and by revelation.

The striving for this goal is reflected in the *Summae* of the Middle Ages.[44] These monumental and comprehensive presentations reveal even in their external form a type of research that aims at total knowledge. But the realization of this ideal—in the sense of a total comprehension of reality in its unity and plenitude—transcends the capacity of any and all human *Wissenschaft*. Even finite reality can never be exhaustively understood by means of conceptual knowledge, and much less the infinite reality of God. Thus pure philosophy as a *Wissenschaft* of beings and of being, in the light of the ultimate reasons and causes (and staying within the confines of natural reason), remains even in its greatest conceivable perfection essentially fragmentary. But it is candid in respect to theology and may thus be complemented by it. Nevertheless, even theology is not a closed nor an absolutely conclusive structural whole. It evolves historically in a progressive appropriation and penetration of the original contents of revealed truth.

Furthermore, it must be emphasized that the contents of revelation do not comprise the infinite plenitude of divine truth. God reveals himself to the human mind in a measure and manner commensurate with his wisdom. His sovereign will may see fit to enlarge this measure and to reveal the divine mysteries in a way commensurate with the modes of human thinking: with discursive reasoning, conceptual knowledge, and critical judgment. Or he may raise human beings above their natural ways of thinking to a totally different level of knowledge, making them partakers of that divine vision which embraces everything with one single and simple glance.[45]

The perfect fulfillment of everything at which philosophy—as a striving toward wisdom—aims, is the divine wisdom itself, the simple *visio* with which God embraces himself and all his creation. The highest perfection to which a created spirit may attain—but, to be sure, not without divine aid—is the *beatific vision.* This is the divine gift of union with God by which the created spirit partakes of divine knowledge in sharing divine life. The *mystical vision* or mystical union represents the closest approximation to this highest goal that is attainable in this earthly life. A preliminary stage, however, for which this highest favor is not required, is a true and living *faith.*

According to the teaching of the church, "faith is a supernatural virtue by which, with the inspiration and aid of divine grace, we hold true what God has revealed and what the church teaches, not on account of its intrinsic and objective truth which we are able to know with the light of natural reason, but on the authority of the revealing God himself, who can neither deceive nor be deceived."[46]

Theological terminology designates as faith not only the virtue (*fides, qua creditur*) but also the contents of faith, namely, the revealed truth (*fides, quae creditur*) and, moreover, the vital actualization of the virtue of faith (*credere,* actual faith) or the *act of faith.* And it is this living or actual faith with which we are here concerned.

Several elements are implicit in the act of faith: By accepting the truths of faith on the authority of God, we *hold them to be true* and we thereby *give credence to God* (*credere Deo*). But we cannot give credence to God unless we believe in God *(credere Deum)*, that is unless we believe that God *is* and that he is *God:* We use the name *God* to designate the supreme and absolutely truthful being.

To accept the truths of faith means thus to accept God, for God is the real object of faith, and to him all the truths of faith are related. But to accept God also means to turn to him in our faith or to believe in God as the end of our faith (*credere in Deum),* that is, to strive toward God.[47] Faith is thus a taking hold of God. This kind of seizure, however, presupposes a being seized. In other words, we cannot believe without divine grace. And grace means participation in divine life. Once we open ourselves to grace and accept the gift of faith, we have "within us the beginning of eternal life."[48]

We accept faith on the testimony of God himself and thereby gain a certain knowledge without, however, obtaining a thorough comprehension. In other words, we cannot accept the truths of faith as evident in themselves as we do in the case of the necessary truths of reason or of the data of sense perception; nor can we deduce them logically from certain self-evident truths. This is one reason why faith is called a "dark light." Moreover, faith as a *credere Deum* and a *credere in Deum* always aspires beyond all revealed truth, that is, beyond all truth which God has confined in concepts and judgments, in words and sentences, in order to make it commensurate with the human mode of cognition. Faith asks of God more than individually separated truths: It desires God himself, all of him, who *is* truth, and it seizes him in darkness and blindness ("although it is night").[49]

This night denotes the profound darkness of faith as compared with the eternal light to which it aspires. And our holy father, St. John of the Cross, refers to this dual darkness of faith when he writes, "In the course of the progress of the understanding, faith becomes stronger, and thus this progress brings on increasing darkness, since faith is darkness for the human reason."[50] But it is an advancing, nevertheless, a going beyond all conceptually intelligible particularized knowledge unto the simple comprehension of the one truth. Faith therefore is closer to divine wisdom than any philosophical or even theological knowledge and science [*Wissenschaft*]. But because it is difficult to go forward in the dark, every ray of light that pierces our night gives us a glimpse of the future brightness and is therefore an invaluable aid in keeping us from going astray. And thus even the feeble light of natural reason may render good service.

A *Christian philosophy* will regard it as its noblest task to prepare the way for supernatural faith. This is the precise reason why St. Thomas was so deeply concerned with the problem of how to build a pure philosophy on the basis of natural reason. He knew well that this was the only way of finding some common ground with unbelieving thinkers. If the latter are willing to join us at least part of the way, they may perhaps subsequently allow themselves to be guided farther than they originally intended to go. From the point of view of *Christian philosophy,* there should then be no misgivings about a common effort. Adhering to the principle, "Examine everything, and retain the best," Christian philosophy is willing to learn from the Greeks and from the moderns and to appropriate for itself whatever can meet the test of its own standards of measurement. On the other hand, it can well afford to display generously what it itself has to offer and then leave to others the task of examination and selection.

Unbelievers have no good reason to distrust the findings of Christian philosophy on the grounds that it uses as a standard of measurement not only the ultimate truths of reason but also the truths of faith. No one prevents them from applying the criterion of reason in full stringency and from rejecting everything that does not measure up to it. They may also freely decide whether they want to go further and take account of those findings which have been gained with the aid of revelation. In this case they will accept the truths of faith not as "theses" (as do believers) but only as "hypotheses." But as to whether or not the conclusions at which both arrive are in accord with the truths of reason, there prevails again a standard of measurement which both sides have in common. Unbelieving thinkers may then calmly consider whether or not they find themselves able to make their own the synthesis which results for Christian philosophers from the two sources of reason and revelation. And unbelievers must judge for themselves whether by accepting this additional knowledge they may perhaps gain a deeper and more comprehensive understanding of that which is. They will at any rate not shrink back from such an attempt if they are really as unbiased as, according to their own conviction, genuine philosophers ought to be.

II.

Act and Potency as Modes of Being

§1. Presentation of the Problem According to St. Thomas's *De ente et essentia*

The *doctrine of act and potency* is like the portal of a huge building which appeared to us in its commanding height from afar. Even this first glance made us realize in a preliminary fashion that this pair of concepts may well encompass the entire amplitude of that which is. On the other hand, our brief linguistic investigation has shown that the terms *act* and *potency* are not semantically univocal but comprised of manifold meanings. It will therefore be our next task to analyze and inquire into these several shades of meaning.

Our introductory discussion of the doctrine of act and potency followed closely the exposition given by St. Thomas in the *Quaestiones disputatae de potentia,* the work which deals with these questions in the most detailed and comprehensive manner. Representing one of the mature works of the great master, this treatise was, according to the findings of Martin Grabmann,[1] composed between 1265 and 1267, at about the time the saint was writing on the first part of the *Summa Theologiae* (which contains the questions concerning the existence and nature of God).

Certain problems which could be treated only cursorily in the *Summa* (which was intended as a compendium covering the entire field of theology) could be discussed more thoroughly and at greater length in the *Quaestiones.* This is the reason why in this latter work the *theological* point of view prevails, although—as everyone familiar with the works of St. Thomas knows—a great deal of information concerning purely philosophical matters may be gained by its perusal. But it is not always easy to disengage what is philosophically significant from the theological context. And especially readers who are not clear in their own minds as to the ways in which theological and philosophical questions are interlinked, will be apprehensive lest, as philosophers, they tread on forbidden ground.

In the interests of an objective analysis it therefore seems advisable to turn from the *Quaestiones* to the aforementioned opusculum *De ente et essentia,*[2] that early treatise of St. Thomas in which he shows himself a faithful disciple of "the Philosopher" [Aristotle]. To be sure, the discussion in *De ente et essentia* is not much more than a first approach to the problem. If we compare this early attempt with the fully developed doctrine, it resembles a seed that later on grows into a mighty tree. But precisely for this reason a careful analysis of the earlier work may prove helpful in our endeavor to arrive at a clear understanding of the original meaning.

Even in this first brief outline of an ontology [*Seinslehre*], Thomas regards the totality of that which is as a hierarchically ordered realm composed of three major gradations:

1. *Material or composite substances* (composed of *matter* and *form*); these comprise the material world, both *inorganic* [lifeless] and organic beings, including humanity.
2. *Intelligent* [spiritual] or *simple* substances. While Aristotle, in using these terms, had in mind those intelligences which in his opinion caused the movements of the celestial bodies, the medieval thinkers used the same terms in relation to the angels. Thomas called these intelligences "simple," because he wanted to emphasize that they were *pure forms.* The question whether the structure of *pure intelligences* includes some matter was hotly disputed in the Middle Ages.
3. The *first existent,* that is, God. All the medieval writers were agreed that the first existent, the cause of all the other existents, was absolutely simple and pure being. Those, therefore, who denied with St. Thomas that the created intelligences [the angels] were composed of *matter* and *form* had to look for some other characteristic to distinguish them from the first existent. In this endeavor Thomas arrived at positing separately the *form* and the *being* [i.e., the act of existing] of created intelligences. Their *form* is identical with their *essence* [*essentia*]: "An intelligence [*intelligentia*] is form and being, and it has its act of existing from the first existent, who is pure being, and this is the first cause, which is God. But every being which

receives something from another is *in potency* with respect to what it receives, and what it receives is its *act.* And thus potency and act are found in the intelligences, but not form and matter. ... And because the quiddity [*quidditas*] of the intelligence is the intelligence itself, its quiddity or essence is identical with itself, and *its being* (act of existing) which it has received from God *is that whereby it exists independently in the world of things (quo subsistit in rerum natura)*. ... "[3] "And since in the intelligences both potency and act must be admitted, it is not difficult to account for their multiplicity. If, on the other hand, there were no potency in them, there could not be a multiplicity of them, either. ... The intelligences thus differ from one another in accordance with their respective *degrees of potency and act,* so that a higher intelligence, being closer to the first existent, has *more actuality* and *less potency,* and the same is proportionately true of the others."[4]

This brief quotation shows how closely in the ontology of St. Thomas the concepts of *act* and *potency* are linked with a number of other basic concepts of Aristotelian philosophy, such as form, matter, substance (what sub-sists), etc. It will therefore become necessary later on to devote our attention to these also. To lean on them for support at this time would merely amount to an attempt to explain one unknown quantity by another. We shall therefore confine ourselves to taking from the above passage whatever can be gleaned from it without making necessary a discussion of those other Aristotelian concepts.

St. Thomas, as has been shown, distinguished in pure intelligences *what* they are (their quiddity) from the fact that they *are.* Their being he designated as their *act* of existing. This is in conformity with his idea of the *first existent,* whom he defined with Aristotle as *pure being* and as *pure act.*

On the other hand, it was stated that whatever receives being is in potency with respect to this very being which it receives. If we now adhere to the verbal meaning of *potentia* (or δύναμις), which denotes a *possibility* or a *being able to,* then *esse in potentia* means possible being, having the possibility of being, or being able to be [*im Vermogen sein;*

in der Moglichkeit sein; Sein-konnen]. That which can be, however, does not—as has been explained—by itself have the *power* of giving to itself its being or its act of existence.

On the other hand, being able to be means more than the mere assertion that something is not barred from receiving the act of existence. Having the possibility of *being,* rather, implies already being in a dual sense: first of all, a being ordained or being oriented toward that being which we have designated as *act,* and, second, a certain *mode of being.* For "being possible" does not simply mean "*not*-being." Unless even possible being were already a mode of being, it would be meaningless to speak of *degrees* of *potentiality.* If we were to assume that the meaning of *being* were always and everywhere one and the *same,* and if act and being were absolutely identical and convertible, it would also be impossible to say that something is more or less in act and thus closer to or farther removed from the first being.

We are justified, then, in distinguishing between *gradations of being* and in calling act and potency *modes of being.* The transition from potency to act or—as we may now express it—from *potential* to *actual being* is not only a transition from one mode of being to another but from an inferior mode of being to a higher one.

There are, however, gradations even within the spheres of possible and real being. This is why it makes sense to speak of a *pure act* and why this pure act designates the *highest being.* Our former remarks should have made it clear that these considerations by no means exhaust the meaning of the terms *act* and *potency.* For the time being, however, we shall rest satisfied with the results so far achieved.

What we have gained up to this point is, in the main, some understanding of the *terms.* We have learned to associate with them a definite meaning. But have we simultaneously acquired a sufficient *understanding* of the content as such? When a blind person is told about the colors red, blue, and green, that person knows that these words are not meaningless but signify different colors; but the blind person has no *experiential knowledge* of these colors. And do we at this juncture know more about act and potency than our blind person knows about the different colors? Yes, I think we do know a little more! We have become aware of the differences between possibility and actuality. But as soon as we try to picture the finer nuances, new difficulties arise. And all in all, we are still far removed from a real understanding of what is meant by act and potency as degrees or modes of being. Is there a way, then to bring us closer to such an understanding?

§2. The Starting Point of the Inquiry: The Fact of Our Own Being

People unfamiliar with medieval thought may find the subjects discussed by St. Thomas in his investigation of the nature of being quite beyond their reach. What, after all, do we know about God and the angels, and whence could such knowledge come to us? "Cherubim and seraphim: ... we believe in them as in beings that are far removed from our experience; we can rely only on what we are told about the existence of certain heavenly powers."[5]

There is, however, something which is not only very close to us but even inescapably near. Whenever the human mind in its quest for truth has sought an indubitably certain point of departure, it always encountered the inescapable *fact of its own being or existence:* "Of all the things we know, how much do we know with the same certitude as we know that we exist? In this knowledge we have no fear at all of being deceived by a mere appearance of truth, since it is indubitably certain that even the one who is being deceived exists." Here then we are well beyond the delusions of the senses, "for here we do not see with the eyes of flesh. The knowledge of our own existence is a most intimate kind of knowing, and no skeptic can tell us: Maybe you are asleep without realizing it. ... People who have the certitude of their own existence do not say, 'I know that I am awake,' but rather, 'I know that I live,' and no matter whether they be asleep or awake, one thing is certain: They exist."[6]

When Descartes in his *Meditationes de prima philosophia* [*Meditations on the First Philosophy,* i.e., metaphysics] made the attempt to reconstruct philosophy as a trustworthy science on the foundation of indubitable certitude, he started out methodologically with his familiar effort of a *universal doubt.* He eliminated everything which—owing to possible deception or illusion—could be subject to doubt. What remained as an irreducible datum was the *fact of doubt* itself and, generally speaking, the fact of thought itself and of the *being* implicit in the thinking: *Cogito, sum.*

In a similar manner, Edmund Husserl, in his endeavor to lay the foundations for a phenomenological method, demanded a suspension of judgment [*Urteilsenthaltung*] (ἐποκή) in regard to everything that we simply and naively accept in our natural attitude as human beings living in the world of our experience. He demanded such an abstention of judgment in regard to the total existence of the *natural world* as well as in regard to the validity of the actual contents of our *knowledge and science* [*bestehende Wissenschaft*].[7] What remains after this phenomenological reduction as the field of investigation is the area of *consciousness* understood as the *life of the ego* [*Ichleben*]. While there may be some questions of whether or not the *object* which I perceive with my senses exists in reality, there can be do doubt of the reality of my *perception.* I may doubt whether the conclusions which I draw from certain premises are correct, but my syllogistic reasoning as such is an indubitable fact. And the same applies to all my desires and volitions, my dreams and hopes, my joys and griefs—to everything, in short, in which *I live and am,* to everything that manifests itself as part of the being of the self-conscious ego. For in all of this—in the "I live" of St. Augustine as much as in the "I think" of Descartes, and in Husserl's "being conscious of" or "experiencing"—there is implied the same *I am.* And this I am is not a conclusion, as seems to be suggested by saying, *Cogito, ergo sum,* but it is implicitly given: I *am,* whether I be thinking, or willing, or in whatever other way I may be intellectually active: and I am conscious of my being.

This certitude of my own existence is in a sense the most *primordial knowledge* I have. It is *not* my first knowledge in any *temporal* sense, for a person's natural attitude tends above all else to the external world, and it takes a long time to learn to find oneself. Nor is this knowledge first in the manner of a *first principle* from which all other truths may be deduced or by which they may be measured. The certitude of my existence is rather most primordial in the sense that it is the most intimate or immediate knowledge I have: It is a knowledge of that which is inseparable from me, and it is therefore a primordial starting point.

The certitude of my own existence is thus an "unreflected" knowledge, i.e., it precedes all reflective or "retrospective" thinking.

In self-knowledge, the intellect relinquishes its natural attitude of being concerned with external objects in order to turn upon itself. If, in turning upon itself, the intellect contemplates the simple fact of its own being, it reads in this fact a threefold question: (1) What is that being of which I am conscious? (2) What is that self which is conscious of itself? (3) What is that intellectual movement in which I am and in which I am conscious of both myself and the movement itself?

When I turn toward being as it is in itself, it reveals to me a dual aspect: that of being and that of not-being.[8] The "I am" is unable to endure this dual perspective: that in which I am[9] is subject to change and since being and the intellectual movement ("in which" I am) are not separated, this being is likewise subject to change. The "former" state of being is past and has given way to the "present" state of being. This means that the being of which I am conscious as mine is inseparable from temporality. As actual being—that is, as actually present being—it is without a temporal dimension [*punktuell*]: It is a "now" in between a "no longer" and a "not yet." But by its breaking apart in its flux into being and not-being, the *idea of pure being* is revealed to us. In pure being there is no longer any admixture of not-being, nor any "no longer" and "not yet." In short, pure being is not temporal but *eternal*.

And thus eternal and temporal, immutable and mutable being (and also not-being) are ideas which the intellect encounters within itself; they are not borrowed from anything outside itself. This means that we have now found a legitimate point of departure for a philosophy based on natural reason and natural knowledge.[10]

What is meant by *analogia entis* (as indicative of the relationship existing between temporal and eternal being) also becomes faintly visible at this point. *Actual being* at the moment at which it is reveals something of the nature of being as such, i.e., of the fullness of being which knows of no temporal change. But precisely because this actual being is only for the moment, it is not at this moment the fullness of being: The very reason for its caducity [*Hinfälligkeit*] lies in its being momentary, and it is thus only an *analogon* of that eternal being which is immutable and therefore plentitude of being at every moment. Momentary or temporal being, on the other hand, is merely a remote image or likeness [*Abbild*], related to the primordial prototype of its similitude but yet infinitely far removed from it by its dissimilitude.[11]

§3. Our Own Existence Viewed as Actual and Potential Being; Temporality

We need not discuss here the question whether in the similitude or analogy that exists between temporal and eternal being there is also implied a causative relationship, as might be concluded from the use of the terms *creator* and *creature*.[12] Before we turn to that problem, we must first further examine the position from which we started.

Simultaneously with the idea of being and not-being, that of *actuality* has become clearer. That being which became manifest to us we termed *actually present*. We might just as well call it *fully alive* (because the being under consideration is that of the living self). But its actual state is thereby not yet completely described.

That which once was but no longer is and that which will be but is not yet is not simply not-being. This means not only that past and future have an epistemological existence in memory and expectation, an *esse in intellectu (sive in memoria)* but that the actually present being of the moment is not *conceivable* as existing by itself in isolation. As a point does not exist apart from a line, so the moment does not exist apart from some temporal extension or duration. If then our consciousness takes hold of the actually present, this latter *reveals* itself to us as something which, rising out of darkness, passes through a ray of light only to sink back again into darkness. Or we may picture the actually present as the crest of a wave which itself is part of a mighty stream. These metaphors are evidently employed to describe a kind of being which endures but which is not actual throughout the entire extension of its duration.

How are we to understand this last statement? There is something in what I am now which I am not actually but which I shall be actually at some future time. And what I am now actually I was at some time in the past, but not actually. In other words, my present being contains in itself the *possibility or potentiality* [*Möglichkeit*] of future actual being and presupposes a possibility or potentiality in my former being. My present being is simultaneously actual and

potential being; and insofar as it is actual, it is the concrete realization of a possibility which antecedes my present actuality. This means then that actuality and potentiality as modes of being are implicit in the simple fact of being [*Seinstatsache*] and can be deduced from it.

The potentiality which can change into actuality, and the very meaning of which it is to become an actuality, is thus not not-being. The joy, for example, which filled my heart a moment ago but which is now "fading away" can no longer be called fully alive, but neither is it entirely extinguished and forgotten as if it had never been real. It is still there, but—as compared with its full vitality—it is in a weakened state of being. This is, in varying degrees, true of all that exists in the present but is not fully alive; it is true of everything which at one time was but no longer is fully alive, inasmuch as it can pass over again from its present mode of being into a state of full vitality; and it is true of everything that will be fully alive in the future, provided it once possessed that seminal mode of being in a preceding span of time.

We do well to remember that the two different modes of being in which I "still" am what I once was, and in which I am "already" what I shall be in the future are both parts of my present existence. In other words, my past and future existence *as such* are completely void [*nichtig*]: I *am now,* not at any other time past or future. Only by having—in memory and expectation, and within a not too well-defined range—a certain intellectual grip on my past and future, can I *picture* for myself these temporal dimensions as filled with the *existential breadth* of enduring being. In the meantime, however, I know full well that my existence is, as it were, suspended over a sword's edge.

Hedwig Conrad-Martius has strikingly depicted the contrast between the phenomenal breadth of existence and its non-dimensional [*punktuell*] actuality.[13] There is (in time!) no dimension in which existents could disappear in such a way that they are, "as it were ... still preserved in it"; nor is there "a dimension which could release something previously contained in it, so that it might pass over into existence. Past and future do not actually contain what, in the phenomenal view, they seem and promise to be."[14] Here, then we get a glimpse of the enigmatic nature of *time* and of *temporal existence.* Although the present moment could not be without past and future, these latter two dimensions of time are not static: They are not containers in which something could be preserved or from which something could emerge; no enduring being can be concealed in them.

The peculiar nature of enduring being cannot be understood from the point of view of time, but rather, conversely, time must be understood from the point of view of non-dimensional actuality. The "ontic birth of time" takes place "in the fully actualized present," in that "actual existence ... which establishes a contact with being...at only one point,"[15] as something which is given and which in its "givenness is simultaneously something privative": a "being-suspended between not-being and being."[16]

What appears to us as enduring being is merely a *continual passing* over the point of contact. This is what may be called the original *existential movement,* a movement which creates time and creates it as its "space." Time *is* in the point of "existential contact," and it is experienced as "present."[17] "Time is this *absolute* present which continually passes over the point of existential contact." Past and future are not presuppositions of the present but are constituted "with and in the present"; they are vacuous formal dimensions [*Leerdimensionen*],[18] owing to that original movement which makes them rise out of nothingness and allows them to sink back into nothingness. This original movement is either a movement into being toward nothingness or it is a movement out of nothingness toward the temporal dimensions themselves (i.e., toward whatever is being posited).

"Being," understood in *this* sense, "is and always remains a becoming; it can never be static [*ruhend*]. "This being stands in need of time. The "position" which has to be gained and regained again and again posits of necessity a formal dimension as its habitat; it posits actuality or the present in the strict sense, as the place or space in which the act of positing can be performed.[19] "Wherever this primordial ontic act occurs, 'there' is the present. But this place can only be a 'point,' never a breadth. ... The present continually breaks in upon nothingness ... , and actuality, according to the way it is constituted, advances one step farther. This *means,* however, *that* a new position has been reached and that the former one is no longer valid. The dimension of time, after all, is *nothing but* this progress of actuality."[20] The firm anchorage of time lies in the *passing present.* Time cannot furnish any concrete existential hold nor any breadth dimension of the present, "because all temporal positing is the existential form [*Existenzform*] of an existent that is, not essentially but only factually; and, furthermore, because this merely factually existing being cannot *in and by itself* arrive at a definitive positing of being, that is, at a true possession of existence [*Existenzbesitz*]."[21]

The preceding considerations go far beyond the scope of our present preoccupation with the contrast between actuality and potentiality in our personal existence. We have now learned to understand this personal life in its temporality, i.e., as a nondimensional actuality continually illuminated by flashes of light. But this temporal existence is not pure actuality: In my nondimensional present there is simultaneously actual and potential being. I am not in the same manner and degree everything that I presently am. In order to clarify the meaning of "pure actuality," it is necessary to confront an existent in which potentiality and actuality are united in the manner described with an existent in which these opposites are sublated [*aufgehoben*]. Here again we are compelled to anticipate some of the results of our future investigations.[22]

Whatever human beings *do* is a realization of what they are *capable* of doing; and what they are capable of doing is a manifestation of what they *are*. In the realization of their capabilities, their *essence or nature* reaches its highest *ontological development* [*Seinsentfaltung*]. What is separated in human nature is united in God. As all his capability is realized in action, his entire essence [*Wesen*] is eternal and immutable in the fullest and highest actualization of his being. His *existence is* his *essence.* He is *who is:* This is the name which he himself used to describe his being (Exodus 3:14). And, according to St. Augustine, this name best expresses what God is.[23]

In contrast to the unity of the divine being, the being of the creature is broken and divided. But notwithstanding the abyss which separates the creature from the creator, there is something which is common to both, so that it is possible to speak of *being* in either case. Everything that is (or has being), insofar as it is, bears some semblance of the divine being. But all being, aside from the divine being, also bears some admixture of not-being. And the consequences of this are manifest in everything that pertains to *creaturely* being.

God is a*ctus purus*. Unlimited being is purely actual being. And the greater a creature's share in being [*Seinsanteil*], the stronger is its actuality. As long as the creature exists, some part of its being is actual—but never all of it. A creature can actually be more or less of what it is, and its actual being can be more or less actual. There are thus differences in the extent and degree of actuality.

Whatever is, without being actual, is in potency; and potentiality, too, differs with respect to extent and degree. This is the character mark of all creaturely *potentiality*. Both actuality and potentiality, as they have here been defined, are *modes of being* [S*einsweisen*]: The divine being is pure actuality, while the creaturely modes of being are differently graduated mixtures of actuality and potentiality (or of being and not-being). Pure potentiality is ascribed to that mode of being which is attributed to pure matter and, like the latter, does not actually occur. Potentiality, in the sense in which this term is here used, is not found in God. While the two modes of being of finite existents are *in potentia esse—in actu esse* (potential and actual being), God cannot be otherwise than in *actu esse*.

We have been using the terms *actual* and *potential being* (actually-present and possible being; fully alive and debilitated being); we have also spoken of *actuality* and *potentiality*. St. Thomas, too, speaks of *in actu esse, in potentia esse* as well as of *actualitas* and *potentialitas*. Are these terms equivalent among themselves and also with respect to *act* and *potency*? According to Thomas, what receives being is in potency with regard to the being which it receives. Being itself, however (in the sense of realized or perfected being), he designates as *act*. Potency, on the other hand, is for him, strictly speaking, no "possible being" but a "being in possibility" [*Möglichkeit zu sein*] or a being ordained to real existence. Whatever is or can become is either *in actu* (actually) or *in potentia* (potentially). Actual and potential being signify thus the modes of being of something which may enter into them. Act and potency are designations applied to these two modes of being as such, that is, independent of what may enter into them. We may then translate these terms by saying: being in a

state of perfection (or *actual being*)[24] and a *rudimentary stage* [*Vorstufe*] *of being*. Potentiality and actuality denote modes of being in general, i.e., modes which are not attributed to any particular existent.

The differences in the several *modes of being* may now in some measure have become evident. But further clarification is needed if we want to understand what exactly is meant by mode of being [*Seinsweise*]. To this end we must consider the nature of what may enter into different modes of being.

§4. Units of Experience and Their Mode of Being; Becoming and Being

Actually present within me is right now the process of *my thinking,* my meditation on the problem of being. But this reflection does not date from this present moment: It has been going on for quite a while and probably will go on for some considerable time until it gives way to some other intellectual activity or until it is cut off by a sudden impression coming from extra-mental reality. But while it lasts, this thinking process forms a whole that possesses a temporal structure.

Modern psychology and phenomenology call this structural whole an intellectual *act* [*Denk-Akt*], and scholastic philosophy too occasionally used the term "act" in this sense. But since the meaning associated with act in these instances differs from the one which we are trying to clarify, we shall substitute another name. The term "intellectual movement" which we employed in an earlier passage in connection with the thinking process is not a very happy one, since "movement" ordinarily signifies something involuntary rather than a free action. We have therefore chosen the name *experiential unit* [*Erlebnis-einheit*],[25] and by this we mean, generally speaking, a structural whole which during a certain period of time grows up organically in the conscious life of the individual self and thereby "fills" this temporal span. It is quite irrelevant in this connection whether it is a question of free action or some involuntary happening or any other kind of experiential content.

The mode of thinking in which I exist at this moment differs as *Erlebniseinheit* from my meditation on the same subject a few hours ago. While the "present unit" began only a few minutes ago, the "past unit" has been disconnected, and in the meantime a whole series of other experiential units has forced its way in between my present and my past thinking.

As against the "past unit," the "present" one has the distinction of being *actual.* But upon closer view we recognize that this so-called *actual* unit is not actual in its entirety. Strictly speaking, only what takes place in the immediate now is "fully alive." We know, however, that this now is an indivisible moment, and whatever fills it "sinks" in the next moment "back into the past." And every new now is filled with new life.

But here we meet with a great difficulty: If temporal being always immediately passes over into not-being, and if thus nothing that is past can "stand firm and remain," is it then not meaningless to speak of enduring units? How can we arrive at a unit that extends beyond the fleeting moment? The life of the ego thus appears to be nothing but a continuous living-from-the-past-into-the-future whereby the potential is constantly actualized and the actual constantly sinks back into potentiality. Or, to express it differently: That which is not fully alive reaches the height of its vitality, and that which is now fully alive becomes a moment later "life that has been lived" [*gelebtes Leben*].

The "fully alive" is the "present"; what "has been lived" is "past"; and what is not yet alive is in the "future." Let us ask then whether it is possible to speak of an enduring unit, reaching (as an *existent*) from the past through the present moment into the future and thus filling a span of time [*Zeitstrecke*]? This seems impossible if we keep in mind what has been said with respect to the nature of temporal being.

To be sure, we constantly take it for granted that there are such enduring units. And, moreover, by "present" we mean not only the fulfillment of the present moment, nor do we mean by "past" and "future" only what precedes and follows this moment within the circumference of an enduring experiential unit, but we also call present, past, and future such individual enduring units as are experienced in acts of deliberation, of fear, or of joy. We then designate as past an experiential unit which in its entirety has "moved into the past" and is thus no longer organically and structurally active; we designate as future an experiential unit which has not yet reached the height of the present [*Gegenwartshöhe*]; and we call present an experiential unit which, though not fully alive in its entire extension, is engaged in a vital process of becoming and is at every moment in vital contact with the fullness of life.

We are, however, aware by now that neither in the past nor in the future can anything really "be." There is no actual "being" in these two temporal dimensions: There *are* only lacunae [*Leerstellen*], indicating the stretches of time which either have been or will be traversed. All real *fullness* or *fulfillment* is in the present moment.

The aforementioned misleading ways of speaking rest, nevertheless, on some factual basis. After all, we really *do* experience joy, fear, and so on, and, moreover, we experience these as units which are construed in a time-consuming movement. This movement is my life or my living being. Whatever structures "arise" within this movement, I encompass (each individually) from the vantage point of this present moment in which I am alive. Nothing of all this "stands" in the past. Whatever of all that I have been is still alive, is within me, and with me in the present moment.

But where, if not in time, do these units of experience have their stand? And how, if at all, can we form a concept or an adequate idea of them? These questions we shall soon have to consider. For the time being, however, let us insist on the following: My existence is a continuous movement, a fleeting and, in the strictest sense, a *transitory* kind of being and thus the extreme opposite of *eternal* and *immutable being*.

We can easily understand why this tremendous contrast was so profoundly experienced by the ancient Greek thinkers that it occupied all their speculative powers and that they could not persuade themselves to call these opposites by the same name. While Heraclitus saw the *true being* of existents in their constant flux and regarded as real only a perpetual *becoming*, for Parmenides true *being* was the eternally immutable, and the world of *becoming* was an illusory world of mere appearances.

Becoming and being: If once we acknowledge this contrast, does this not mean that for us, too, the unity of that which is breaks asunder? And yet we must not allow our vision of the all-embracing totality of being to be dimmed by our discovery of this yawning abyss. We have already recognized a common property in being and becoming, and we have designated their common denominator as *analogia entis* (i.e., a comparative similitude of being in all existents, but a similitude outweighed by an even greater dissimilitude).

Becoming cannot be divorced from being, i.e., not from actual and *true being* or from being in the true sense of the term. Becoming cannot be actual and true being because it is, as has been shown, a *passing over into being* and can therefore be determined only by being itself. If one were to deny the possibility of being as distinct from becoming, then the possibility of becoming would also have to be denied, and we would arrive at nothingness. And thus that continual becoming and passing away, as we experience it within our own selves, points constantly beyond itself. It strives toward being (this is, of course, merely a metaphorical manner of speaking), but it touches it only fleetingly from moment to moment.

Our own *being* then—which is this continual becoming and passing away and as such always only on the way to true being—reveals to us the *idea of true being*, i.e., of the perfect and eternally immutable being of the *pure act*. It is not yet time to ask whether on this way we simultaneously touch upon being as a *reality* and thus become aware of the mode and manner in which we ourselves are related to it.

§5. The Structure and the Ontological Conditions of Experiential Units [*Erlebniseinheiten*]

First of all, we shall have to consider further those enduring units which are customarily designated as *present*, i.e., those units which are engaged in a vital process of becoming. Owing to the fact that one or another part of such a unit steadily—though only for a brief moment—reaches the height of being, the whole unit receives a share in being and reveals itself as actually present, i.e., as something actual. We must, however, distinguish between *what* bears this character mark of the actually present and loses it as soon as it moves as a closed structural "whole" "into the past" (i.e., what can be kept in sight as something which once *was* but no longer is), and that specific character or mode of being as such. The former we call the *experiential content* [*Erlebnisgehalt*].

The experiential content is essential for the unity of the structure. Such a unity or unit, for example, is the joy which one experiences upon the arrival of good news. This joy presupposes my appreciative listening to the news and my knowing comprehension of its gratifying nature. Nevertheless, these presuppositions are not part of the joy unit [*Einheit der Freude*] as such. It may well be that I have known of this news for some time prior to my experiencing joy over its content. I may either not have fully grasped its significance right in the beginning, or, having understood the gratifying nature of the news, I may not have been able to experience joy over it owing to my preoccupation with other matters.

We may say then that the experience of the content "joy" is conditioned in a twofold way: by the *object* and by the *ego* [*Ich*]. The object—in our example, the content of the news[26]—is not itself a *part* of joy as experiential content, whereas the tending toward [*Richtung*] that object is indeed a part of the experiential content. (Phenomenology uses the term *intention* to designate this tending toward.) The characteristic which makes this experience joy with respect to this particular object is a constitutive part of joy, and the same is true of the intentional object (i.e., the object "toward which joy tends"). The entire *Erlebniseinheit,* "this particular joy," is closed or completed at the moment when I no longer experience this joy or at the moment when I may "again experience" joy but not with respect to the same object.

And the *ego* too shares in several ways in the experiential unit. When I say, for example, "I realize that this is a joyful message, but at the moment I am unable to experience joy," it is evident that the ego cannot be eliminated from both my experienced "realization" and my experienced "not-being-able-to." I can experience nothing without the "I" [*Ich*] experientially involved.

But what kind of a *self* or *ego* is it that we have in mind here? When I try to give an account of the reason why I am not able to experience joy, I may discover that I am so engrossed by some profound grief that there is no room left for joy. Or I may simply find that I cannot experience joy without being able to name any specific reason. But I am convinced, nonetheless, that the reason for not being able to experience joy "lies in me" even if I find it impossible to track it down. I must conclude therefore that there are things hidden "within me"—all kinds of things—which are unknown to me. And in this sense it may be said that the ego is not part of the experiential content: The ego transcends my experience, as does the object in a similar and yet not identical manner. This is why Husserl applies the term *transcendent* to both the object and the "psychological ego" [*"das psychische Ich"*].[27]

§6. The "Pure Ego" [*"Reine Ich"*] and Its Modes of Being

To emphasize the contrast to this hidden ego that lies behind immediate conscious experience, Husserl calls that self which is immediately given in conscious experience the *pure ego.* We shall speak of this latter ego exclusively as long as our discussion is confined to the realm of immediate consciousness, i.e., to what is nearest to and inseparable from us.[28]

Husserl says of the pure ego that It has no content and cannot be described as it is in itself. "It is pure ego, and that is all."[29] This means, then, that the pure ego is alive in every such statement as "*I* perceive," "*I* think," "*I* draw conclusions," "*I* experience joy," "*I* desire," etc. and, furthermore, that the pure ego in one way or another tends toward what is perceived, thought, desired, etc. We need not decide here the question whether the *purity* of the pure ego must be so interpreted that, as far as its content is concerned, it is completely unspecified and therefore differs from other selves only numerically. Right now the important thing is to make it clear that the pure ego is alive in every experience and cannot be eliminated from it. It is inseparable from the experiential content but nonetheless not actually a *part* of this content. Rather the converse is true: Every experience is part of the pure ego; the pure ego is alive in every experience; *its life* is that very flux in which ever new structures of experiential units arise.

This last statement, however, means not only that all experiential *contents* are part of the pure ego. This ego is *alive,* and its life is its *being.* It lives perhaps right now in the experience of joy, a little while later in longing, and again a little later in thoughtful reflection, but most of the time in several such experiential units simultaneously. But while joy fades away, longing dies, and reflection ceases, the ego does not fade or pass away: It is alive in every now. This does not mean, however, that it possesses *eternal* life.[30] We need not ask at this time whether it always has been and always will be. We are merely trying to show that this pure ego does not come into being and die away like the experiential units but that it is a *living* ego whose life is filled with changing contents. And this latter assertion again does not mean that its life is comparable to a ready-made vessel that is gradually being filled with varying contents: It is rather a life that wells up anew at every moment; *in every moment its being is actually present.*

The fact that the experiential contents attain to real being, although they touch it only punctually [*punktuell*] at any given moment, may now appear a little less enigmatic. The real being they touch is in fact not *their* being, since in and by themselves they are incapable of real being. The experiential contents receive a share in real being only by virtue of the ego into whose life they enter. With respect to what owes its being to the ego and rises to the level of being only by virtue of and within the ego, the latter thus exists in a preeminent sense. The ego is not, to be sure, *existentially superior* in the sense that it could be said to embody the *height of being* (as compared with *rudimentary degrees of being*) but rather in a sense that indicates a relationship existing between a *carrier* and the *thing carried* [*das Tragende* and *das Getragene*].

But before we look further into this significant distinction between a carrier and the thing carried, we must first clarify the way in which the ego is related to the height of being and the rudimentary stages of being (act and potency). According to what has been established up to this point, it would seem that the ego must always be in act and can never be in potency. It will be remembered that by potentiality we did not mean the mere logical possibility of passing over from not-being to being, but rather a rudimentary phase of being which itself, however, is already a mode of being.

For the ego, too, it is possible to step into existence [*Dasein*] out of nothingness.[31] But to be without being alive—in the sense in which a past joy is said to have a "lifeless being"—that seems to be an impossibility. If the self is not alive, it neither *is* nor is it an ego: It is nothing. It is empty in itself, and all its fullness derives from the experiential contents; and these in turn receive their life from it. But it nevertheless seems possible and even necessary to speak, with respect to the ego, of different degrees of vitality [*Lebendigkeit*]. In order to understand this clearly, we must scrutinize still further the specific life of the ego.

We have observed that whatever life there is in the experiential contents derives from the ego and is present in all of the ego's experiences. It is therefore obvious that the experiential units—although they are compact in themselves and separated from each other—

are not juxtaposed like the links of a chain. Husserl is thus justified in speaking of a *stream of experiences.* The ego, always alive, proceeds from one content to the next, from one experience to another, so that its life is *one* constant flux. From the point of view of the ego, on the other hand, it is also clear why "what is no longer alive" or "is past" does not simply sink into nothingness but continues to subsist in a modified form and why what is "not yet alive" or "will be in the future" is already in a certain manner before it is actually alive. The ego does not release immediately what it has experienced, but for a while retains its grip on it[32] and, similarly, it stretches forward and reaches out for what is to arrive. And even what the ego does not presently have in its grip remains in some way within its reach.

The question whether something can really be so completely forgotten that it can never "rise again" and "be called back to memory" need not be discussed here. It is certain, however, that things which lie far back and of which I have not been thinking at all for a long time can be "made present" by way of recollection (as, for example, the joy which we children felt when our mother returned from a trip). This making present can happen in several ways: I may simply *know* as a *matter of fact* that and how deeply I felt this joy at that particular time. In this case I presently live in this knowledge, and the object of my knowledge is the fact that at that particular time in the past I experienced joy. The joy of which I merely know is neither really alive nor "actually present": The ego does not live in it.

There is, secondly, the possibility that I allow myself to be "carried back" in my memory to that particular time so that I live, as it were, "once again" in the expectation of that *Wiedersehen* with my mother and thus re-experience step by step this joyful event. How, then, does the description "really alive" or "actually present" fit this situation? What was at that time an *original* occurrence I now *repeat* in retrospect. The situation is similar to the one in which I may co-experience by way of empathy what a *companion* of mine presently experiences. As long as the joy of this other person or my own past joy is only *re*-experienced in recollection, my present life is nothing but this *retrospective* experience. But this kind of joy is not fully alive: It is merely an experience of a "past" joy or, in our second example, the experience of the other person's joy in the mode of a making present. In both instances the experience of joy lags behind the being-fully-alive of my present joy.

Now what does all this mean with respect to the ego? At what time am I really alive? When my memory carries me back to the past? In the present now? Or in the moment that has just passed? Is my present ego really alive in my past joy? Or is it another—a past ego—that lives in the past joy and that is therefore not actual?

As far as time is concerned, it seems that my ego lives now and at that past time simultaneously. It lives "now"—for my memory carries me back from the present moment into the past moment, and yet I do not relinquish my hold on the present moment. And my ego lives "at that time"—for my memory carries me into the past moment, and hence I live in it. What does all this mean, however, if we remember what has been stated above, namely, that nothing can really be or be real in the past? I really *am* only now, and I cannot actually return *to* the place at which I really was in the past. Intellectually, however, I have in my grip this place in the past as well as everything which was real "then and there," including its approximate distance from my present now, and I can freely recall what was real at that time to the extent, at any rate, that it is still within me in *potency*.

In sober truth, then, it must be stated that it is not possible to live now and at that past time simultaneously: What has passed remains past, and I can merely recall *what* was real at that time and, in doing so, I must remain conscious of the fact that I merely repeat or recollect the past intellectually. But the past—i.e., the former now—does not thereby become the present now. The two remain separated in my consciousness by my experience of "carrying myself back," i.e., by the experienced contrast between my total situation now and then and by the span of time which stretches from the then to the now, a span of time "filled" with my past life.[33]

I do not live in my past joy as I live in my present joy, inasmuch as I merely *re*live the past. It may happen then that I (my present ego) occupy the place of my past ego and relive its life. But though I am conscious of the fact that "at that time" my joyful experience differed from my present reliving of that experience, there are not two egos, but only one. It may also happen, however, that in the making present my past self appears to me as a stranger and that I co-experience its joy as if it were that of a strange ego. In this case I (the presently living ego) stands at the side of that past ego which is not now alive. All I know is that this past ego—or rather I myself—was alive at that time. Does this mean then that in this case we are dealing with a potential ego and that we must thus speak of two egos, one actual and one potential? Such an assumption would not correspond to the situation. The "past ego" is nothing but an image of myself, an image of the manner in which I was once alive, and no mere "image" of the self can properly be called an ego.

There is finally the possibility that the past joy is reborn in me and thus becomes a real joy; and the same may happen with respect to my sympathetic co-experience of another person's joy: It may result in a genuine personal experience of joy, The past is said to be within me *potentially* in the strict sense precisely because the *making present* implies the possibility of a passing over into the actually present. The being of the past is thus truly a preliminary phase of that reborn actually present being into which it may pass over again and again.

The ego is then, we conclude, always actual, always actually living present. On the other hand, there appertains to it an entire stream of experiences, comprising everything that lies "behind it" and "ahead of it," that is, everything in which it was once alive in the past and everything in which it will be alive again in the future. It is this very totality which we designate as the "life of the ego." But this totality is not actual as a whole. Only that part of it which is alive "now" is a present reality. In other words, the vitality of the ego does not embrace everything which appertains to it: The ego is always alive as long as it is, but its *vitality* is *not that* of the all-embracing being of the *pure act* but rather the *temporal* vitality advancing from one moment to the next.

And let us not forget this qualifying condition: *as long as the ego is*. We have seen that the ego can, as it were, "go backward," surveying the stream of its past life and calling back into life one or another part of it. What is thus recalled or resumed is then always the ego's own former life. But in doing this the ego's freedom is not unlimited: It always encounters some lacunae which it cannot fill. In these empty temporal spans the ego finds nothing that could be made present, nor does it discover in them its own self. Occasionally this failure may be due to *blanks in the ego's memory*. In this case other persons may possibly aid in filling these gaps and in calling back to the ego's memory some of these forgotten things.

But there are also other reasons for such blanks. Let us take, for example, a dreamless sleep or a fainting spell: *Was* the ego alive in these temporal intervals or did its being suffer a real break? And, furthermore, the stream of experience is for the experiencing ego neither definitely limited nor altogether unlimited. Viewing its past and going back farther and farther, the ego is in the end unable to distinguish anything definite: Everything begins to "blur." Is there an outer limit to this kind of "haziness"? The ego itself, it seems, does not arrive at any beginning. True enough, others may testify to the beginning of its bodily existence, but what about the ego as a whole? Has its being also had a beginning? The ego's immediate experience answers neither the question relating to its actual beginning nor the question relating to its possible end. And thus there gapes a vacuity at several points.

Has the ego risen from nothingness? Does it move toward nothingness? Is it suspended above the abyss of nothingness at every moment? The being of the ego, of which we stated only a little while ago that it is being in a preeminent degree (cf. p. 49 above) appears suddenly as very frail indeed. And yet, it is being in a preeminent degree, even in a dual sense: It is *always alive* in comparison with what is no longer or not yet alive, and as a *carrier* in relation to what is carried (the latter owing to the ego the ontological height of its life).

Although this double preeminence of the being of the ego is unshakable, it reveals at the same time the peculiar weakness and fragility of this *preeminent being*. The ego, as we have pointed out, is always alive, but it is nevertheless unable to keep enduringly alive those experiential contents which it needs to sustain its own life. Without these contents, the ego is an empty nothing. The ego imparts life to those contents, but only momentarily at any given time, whereupon they fade away again. They remain *being* of a sort, not as possessing any sovereign ruling power, but merely in that weakened mode which pertains to things that are no longer truly alive.

Furthermore, whence does the ego acquire those contents without which it is nothing? When, for example, a noise "breaks in upon me" from *without,* this noise obviously does not originate in the ego but only "falls upon" the ego, and the ego "lends an ear" to it. If, on the other hand, joy arises "within me," then this experience evidently originates *within,* though as a rule it responds to some external stimulus. What, however, is the meaning of this *within?* Does the joy originate in the *pure* ego? If by pure ego we understand with Husserl only that self which is alive in every "*I* think," "*I* know," "*I* desire," etc. and which is conscious of itself as a thinking, knowing, desiring ego, then we must conclude that this joy originates in a transcendent [*jenseitige*] depth which discloses itself in the conscious experience of joy, without, however, becoming transparent. The conscious life of the ego depends thus by virtue of its contents on a twofold *beyond* [*transcendence* in Husserl's sense of the term], an *external* and an *internal* world both of which manifest themselves in the conscious life of the ego, i.e., in that ontological realm which is inseparable from the ego [*immanence* in Husserl's sense of the term].

But what about that life itself which, as has been stated, the ego imparts to the experiential contents? Is the ego then a source of life? Since life is the *being* of the ego, this would mean that the ego *imparts to itself* or *posits its own being.* This, however, does not accord with the previously established peculiar characteristics of the ego's being: The mystery of its whence and whither, the lacunae of its past which cannot be filled, its powerlessness to call into being and sustain in being the experiential contents. Above all, it does not accord with the manner in which the ego itself is and experiences its own being.

The ego knows itself as a living, actually present existent and simultaneously as one that emerges from a past and lives into a future; *itself and its being are inescapably there: It is a being thrown into existence* [*ins Dasein geworfen*].[34] This, however, marks this being as the extreme opposite of an autonomous and intrinsically necessary being *a se* (by itself).

The being of the ego is alive only from moment to moment. It cannot be quiescent because it is restlessly in flight. It thus never attains true self-possession. And we are therefore forced to conclude that the being of the ego, as a constantly changing living present, is not autonomous but *received* being. it has been *placed into existence* and is sustained in existence from moment to moment. This, however, implies the possibility that this being may have a beginning and an end and that it may suffer a break.

§7. The Being of the Ego and Eternal Being

It is time now to ask: Whence comes this received being? According to what has been said concerning the life of the ego, there seem to be several possibilities of answering this question. Either the ego receives its life as well as the contents of its experiences from those "transcendent worlds"—external or internal or both—which manifest themselves in these experiences, or the ego owes its being directly to that pure being which is by itself and in itself [*a se* and *per se*], eternally immutable, autonomous, and necessary. This second possibility would not absolutely exclude the first one. If it were admitted that the ego is placed into and sustained in existence by a direct act of pure being, then there might well be assumed an additional dependence of its life on either the external or the internal world, or on both, A received being, on the other hand, that is independent of eternal being is inconceivable because, aside from eternal being, nothing exists that is truly in full possession of being.

Everything finite is placed into and sustained in existence and therefore by itself incapable of positing and sustaining being or existence. We cannot, however, predicate anything concerning the manner in which the ego is related to those transcendent (external and internal) worlds unless and until we cease to confine our investigation to that realm of being [*Seinsbereich*] which is directly and inseparably linked with our own existence. We may legitimately ask nevertheless whether it is possible to make some valid predications concerning our relationship to pure being within the limitations of this finite realm of being.

My own being, as I know it and as I know myself in it, is null and void [*nichtig*]; I am not by myself (not a being *a se* and *per se*), and by myself I am nothing; at every moment I find myself face to face with nothingness, and from moment to moment I must be endowed and re-endowed with being. And yet this empty existence that I am is *being*, and at every moment I am in touch with the fullness of being.

As was stated above (p. 37f.), the becoming and passing away which we discover in ourselves reveals to us the *idea* of true and eternally immutable being. Those experiential units which are in the modes of becoming and passing away stand in need of the ego in order to attain to being. But the being they receive through the medium of the ego is not eternally immutable but is merely this very becoming and passing away, with an added crest of being at the moment of transition from the phase of becoming to the phase of passing away. The ego itself seems to be closer to pure being because it attains not only to the crest of being for one single moment, but is sustained in it at *every* moment (though not, to be sure, as immutable being, but as being that constantly changes in its existential content).

The ego is capable of arriving at the idea of eternal being not only by way of envisaging the becoming and fading away of its experiences, but also on the basis of the experienced specific nature of its own being, which is confined to an existence from moment to moment. The ego shrinks back from nothingness and desires not only an endless continuation of its own being but a full possession of being as such: It desires a being capable of embracing the totality of the ego's contents in one changeless present instead of its having to witness the continually repeated disappearance of all these contents almost at the very moment they have ascended onto the stage of life. The ego thus arrives at the *idea of plenitude* [*Idee der Fülle*] by crossing out from its own being what it has come to know as privation.

The ego, moreover, experiences in its own self *various degrees of approximation to the fullness of being.* Its *present* (what fills it now) does not always exhibit the same circumference. This may be explained by the fact that the ego may be comprised of more or less content at different moments. But there is also the further fact that the ego itself has at different moments a larger or smaller *amplitude.* And a similar observation may be made regarding the manner in which the ego is related to what it—still or already—firmly holds in its grip of the contents of past and future.

To these differences in amplitude must be added those in the degrees of *vitality in the ego's present existence,* i.e., its greater or lesser *intensity of being.* Proceeding intellectually beyond all the stages within its own reach to the outer limit of what can be conceived by the human mind, the ego is capable of arriving at the idea of *all-embracing* being in its *highest degree of intensity.* This procedure confirms our previous contention (pp. 49–50 above) that the continuous actuality of the ego admits of varying degrees. In comparison with the perfect being of the *pure act,* the *actual* being of the ego appears as an infinitely far removed and feeble image, but even in this remoteness from the primordial prototype there are found different *gradations* of being. And as against those rudimentary modes of being which we designated as *potentiality,* the actual being of the ego appears so clearly marked off that it would be highly inappropriate to include it in the category of potentiality, notwithstanding its gradations and the possibility of its passing over from lower to higher degrees. At most one might be entitled to speak of a combination of actuality and potentiality.[35] This "combination," however, is different from the one we referred to in our discussion of experiential units (pp. 43–44f. above).

If we now designate *real being* as *act,* then we have on one side the *pure act* (i.e., perfect, eternally immutable being, super-eminently alive in its plenitude), and on the other side the *finite acts* (that is, infinitely feeble images in varying degrees of imperfection). To these finite acts, in turn correspond different potencies as rudimentary stages of these acts. The finite act as such is, however, in our present frame of reference first and foremost the *being of the ego,* and it is only by virtue of the ego that the experiential units share in the finite act.

For the ego that has once grasped the idea of the pure act or of eternal being, this idea becomes the *measure* of its own being. But how does the ego learn to see in eternal being also the *source* or the *genuine cause* of its own being? The nullity and transiency of its own being becomes clearly manifest to the ego once its *thinking* seizes upon its own being and seeks to lay bare its deepest roots. But the ego also touches upon these depths of its own being prior to all reflective and retrospective existential analysis in the experience of anxiety [*Angst*]. Existential anxiety accompanies the unredeemed human being throughout life and in many disguises—as fear of this or that particular thing or being. In the last analysis, however, this anxiety or dread is the fear of being no more, and it is thus the experience of anxiety which "brings people face to face with nothingness."[36]

Anxiety, to be sure, is under ordinary circumstances not the dominant mood of human life. It overshadows everything else only under pathological conditions, while normally we go through life almost as securely as if we had a really firm grip on our existence. This may in part be explained by the fact that we feel tempted to pause at any superficial view of life which simulates an appearance of "lasting" existence within a "static temporal continuum" and which under the veil of our multiple "cares" [*Sorgen*] hides from us the sight of life's nullity. Generally speaking, however, this feeling of security in human existence cannot be called a mere result of such an illusion and self-deception. Any circumspect reflective analysis of the being of people shows clearly how little reason for such a feeling of security there is just in actual human existence, and to what extent the being of people is indeed exposed to nothingness.

Does this mean then that the feeling of existential security has been proven objectively groundless and "irrational" and that therefore "a passionate … consciously resolute and anxiety-stricken *freedom toward death*"[37] represents the rational human attitude? By no means. The undeniable fact that my being is limited in its transience from moment to moment and thus exposed to the possibility of nothingness is counterbalanced by the equally undeniable fact that despite this transience, I *am*, that from moment to moment I am *sustained in my being*, and that in my fleeting being I share in enduring being. In the knowledge that being holds me, I rest securely. This security, however, is not the self-assurance of one who under her own power stands on firm ground, but rather the sweet and blissful security of a child that is lifted up and carried by a strong arm. And, objectively speaking, this kind of security is not less rational. For if a child were living in the constant fear that its mother might let it fall, we should hardly call this a "rational" attitude.

In my own being, then, I encounter another kind of being that is not mine but that is the support and ground of my own unsupported and groundless being. And there are two ways in which I may come to recognize *eternal being* as the ground of my own being. One is the *way of faith* when God reveals himself as *he who is*, as the *creator* and *sustainer*, and when our redeemer says, "He who believes in the Son possesses eternal life" (John 3:36). Then I have in these pronouncements clear answers to the riddle of my own being. And when he tells me through the mouth of the prophet that he stands more faithfully at my side than my father and my mother, yea that he is love itself, then I begin to understand how "rational" is my trust in the arm that carries me and how foolish is all my fear of falling prey to nothingness—unless I tear myself loose from this sheltering hold.

The way of faith, however, is not the way of philosophic knowledge. It is rather the answer of another world to a question which philosophy poses. But philosophy has also its own specific way: It is the way of discursive reasoning, the way or ways in which the *existence of God is rationally demonstrated.*

The ground and support of my being—as of all finite being—can ultimately be only one being which is not some received being (as is all human being). It must be a *necessary being,* i.e., it must differ from everything that has a beginning in that it alone cannot not be.[38] Because the being of this existent is not received being, there cannot be any separation between *what* it is (and what could or could not be) and its actual existence: It must be its very act of existing.[39]

This necessary being *a se,* which is without a beginning and itself the cause of all beginning, must be *one;* for if there were several such beings, a distinction would have to be made between those characteristics in which they differ and which make one of them that *particular being,* and those qualities which the one shares with the others. But the first existent does not admit of such a distinction .[40]

It may be that my fleeting being has a "hold" on something finite and yet, being finite, this something could not possibly be the ultimate hold and ground. Everything temporal is *as such* fleeting and therefore needs an eternal hold or support.[41] If my own being is tied to some other finite being, we are *together* sustained in being. The security which I experience in my fleeting existence indicates that I am immediately anchored in an *ultimate* hold and ground (notwithstanding the fact that there may also be some mediate supports of my being). But this experience is a rather dim and indefinite feeling that can hardly be called *knowledge.*

St. Augustine, who groped his way to God preeminently from the experience of his inner being and who emphasized in ever new verbal expressions the fact that our being points beyond itself to true being, is always equally emphatic in affirming our incapability of comprehending him who is incomprehensible. "Those who ... believe," he writes, "that it could occur to someone, while in this mortal life, to attain to the radiant brightness of the light of immutable truth and to adhere to it steadily and unswervingly with the mind totally detached from the habits of this life—these people have not understood the nature of what they seek nor the nature of those who seek. ... "[42] And again, "When you begin to step nearer, conscious of some similitude with him, and when you then try to probe the being of God—in a measure proportionate to your growing love (for your love also is of God)—then you experience something you expressed in words and something you did not and could not express in words. ... For prior to your search you thought you had enunciated something pertaining to God, but once your search has begun, you feel how impossible it is to make articulate the object of your search. ... "[43]

This groping search in darkness reveals to us the incomprehensible one as inescapably near, as the one in whom "we live, move, and are" (Acts 17:28), but who remains incomprehensible, nevertheless. Our discursive reasoning is certainly capable of coining clear concepts, but far from grasping the incomprehensible one, these concepts rather move him still farther away into that peculiar distance in which all conceptual knowledge is shrouded.

The way of faith gives us more than the way of philosophic knowledge. Faith reveals to us the God of personal nearness, the loving and merciful God, and therewith we are given a certitude which no natural knowledge can impart. But the way of faith, too, is a dark way. God himself attunes his language to the measure of human understanding, so as to make the incomprehensible intelligible to some extent. "When he commissioned his servant Moses and told him, 'I am who am' and 'Tell the sons of Israel: He who is has sent me to you'—for this true being is hard to grasp by the human mind, and Moses was sent as a human being to human beings (though not by a human being)—he immediately added, 'Tell the sons of Israel that the God of Abraham, the God of Isaac, and the God of Jacob has sent me to you. This is my name in all eternity. ... What I told you—I am who am—is true, but you cannot comprehend it. But when I said that I am the God of Abraham and the God of Isaac and the God of Jacob—this is true and comprehensible as well. ... For this, *I am who am*—that pertains to me. But this, *the God of Abraham and the God of Jacob,* pertains to your understanding.' "[44]

III.

Essential and Actual Being

§1. Temporality—Finitude—Infinity—Eternity

Simultaneously with the contrast between actual and potential being—understood as height of being and the rudimentary stage with respect to that height—other distinctive qualities of being have become manifest. Whatever is at the same time actual and potential in the described sense requires time to pass from one stage to the other. Actual-potential being is thus *temporal* being. As such it expresses an existential movement: It is an ever repeated flashing up of actuality. Whatever exists in the mode of temporality does not *possess* its being but receives it ever anew as a *gift*. Here we are confronted with the possibility of beginning and ending in time.

One of the meanings of *finitude* is therewith described. We may accordingly call finite what does not possess its being but needs time in order to attain to being. Even if it were endlessly sustained in being, it would not on that account be infinite in the true sense. What is truly infinite is essentially and intrinsically incapable of ending. The genuinely infinite does not receive being as a gift but is in *possession of being;* it is the master of being, yea, it is *being itself.* We call it *eternal being.* It does not stand in need of time; it is the master of time, too.

Temporal being is finite. Eternal being is infinite. Finitude, however, means more than merely temporality, and eternity means more than merely the impossibility of coming to an end in time. Whatever is finite needs time to become what it is. And whatever it is, is always something that is *objectively limited:* Whatever is placed into being is placed there as *some thing,* i.e., as something that is *not nothing,* but neither is it *everything.* And here we have the second meaning of finitude: To be something and not to be everything. Eternity (understood as the full self-possession of being) correspondingly means being of such a kind that there is *nothing that it is not:* It *is everything.*

If temporality as such is tied to finitude as its objective limitation, it does not follow that everything that is objectively limited is necessarily temporal. In order to clarify the interrelationship of temporality and finitude, it is important to take into consideration not only being but also that which is—and to do this first of all within that realm to which we have confined our preliminary investigation. We return thus to a problem which we have already approached but for which we have as yet not found an adequate solution. The *experiential units* appeared to us as structures which arise in the fluctuating, temporal being of the ego and which are retained in their *wholeness,* notwithstanding the fact that they lack the capacity of standing and remaining in the flux of time. These noteworthy relationships require further clarification.

§2. Essence [*Wesenheit*] (*Eidos*) and Essential Being [*wesenhaftes Sein*]

In the simple fact of being [*Seinstatsache*] from which we started out, we first distinguished the intellectual movement in which I become aware of my own being, the ego, and being itself. Upon closer examination we had to add the further distinction between the being of the ego and the being of the ego's intellectual movement or the experiential unit: The actually-alive being of the ego (revitalized from moment to moment from hidden sources), on the one hand, and, on the other, the being of the experiential unit arising and growing in the life of the ego. This being of the experiential unit is, as we have learned, a becoming and passing away, a rising to the height of living actuality followed immediately by a descending movement.

We now find, however, that our description of the experiential unit is still incomplete. It is necessary to make a distinction between the becoming and passing away and *what* becomes and passes away and which, after it has become, still is in a certain manner despite its being *past.* We have pointed out that the unity of an experience and its demarcation from other experiences is (not exclusively, but essentially) determined by its *content:* The joy, for example, which I derive from some successful work is something different from the working process itself. The two may follow each other temporally, but even when I work and enjoy my success simultaneously, the two are distinct from one another.

My joy—the joy which I experience right now—comes into being and passes away. Joy *as such,* on the other hand, neither comes into being nor does it pass away. And in order to elucidate what we mean, some further distinctions are necessary.

I may consider my joy precisely as I experience it, i.e., as the full and unabridged *what* of my experience. This implies that my joy derives from success in my work, that it is a heartfelt and grateful joy, and so on. Or I may consider *joy as such.* In this latter case it is irrelevant from what *source* joy derives, what *sort* of joy it is, whether it lasts a long or a short time, and whether it is *my* joy or the joy of some other person.

Here we encounter one of those forms [*Gebilde*] which Plato had in mind when he discussed the nature of *ideas* (ἰδέα, *eidos*). Thus he speaks of the beautiful as such in virtue of which all beautiful things are beautiful or of the just as such in virtue of which all just actions are just, and so on. Although Aristotle categorically denied the independent existence of *ideas* and unremittingly tried to demonstrate its impossibility, he nevertheless showed his indebtedness to Plato's doctrine. The Platonic ideas reappear in Aristotle's philosophy under the names of *eidos* [*Urbild*] or μορφή [*form*], but he presents a different interpretation of their mode of being and of their relationship to things.[1] Rather than applying to these forms the much disputed and ambiguous term *ideas*, we prefer to use the phenomenological expression *Wesenheiten* [ideal essences].[2]

There are many different experiences of joy, differing according to the experiencing ego, according to the object of the joy, according to the temporal determination and duration of the joy, etc. *The essence of joy, however, is one.* It is not mine or yours, not now or later, not of shorter or longer duration. It has no being in space and time. But wherever and whenever joy is experienced, the essence of joy is *actualized.* The essence of joy thus determines all individual experiences of joy with respect to what they are, and they all owe their name to the essence.

What does it mean when we say that the essence of joy is *actualized?* If joy is not experienced anywhere in the world, is there still an essence of joy? "There is," but this essence is not in the same way in which experienced joys are. There could, however, be no experience of joy if there were not an essence of joy prior to the experience. It is the essence which makes possible any and all experienced joy. This "prior," of course, does not mean that the essence precedes the experience temporally. The essence is not in time at all. For this reason it is not potential in the sense in which the not yet fully alive joy is said to be potential. The being of the essence is not an inferior rudimentary phase of actual being. "I am referring," says Hering, "to something that is ... in itself without any relation to objects, something that is what it is regardless of whether there are real and ideal worlds of objects or not. We can think essences without any reference to the world. They ... need no objective *support* [*Träger*] but ... abide *independently in themselves.*"[3] But though the essence belongs to a sphere entirely different from that of objects, it nevertheless enters into a relationship with them. We thus say that there are objects which *partake* of the essence, and also (though not quite correctly) that the converse is true: that the essence can be realized in objects."[4] "If there were no essences," Hering continues, "neither would there be objects. The essences are the ultimate reasons of both themselves and of the possibility of the being of objects. ... The essence or *eidos* ... does not exist (as does the object) by participation [μέθεξις] in something extraneous that could impart to it its essential nature (as the essence imparts objectivity to the object), but it gives to itself, as it were, its essential nature. The *conditions of its possibility* lie not outside itself but fully and wholly within itself. Only the essence is thus truly πρώοτη οὐσια [*ousia*]."[5]

Some of Hering's statements, especially the last sentence quoted, evidently overshoot the mark. In writing this sentence, Hering was probably concerned only with describing the relationship that exists between essences and *finite* objects. In my opinion it was not his intention to confront the essence with the *first existent*, this latter term understood in the sense in which we have been using it and in which it is used by Aristotle and the medieval schoolmen. To clarify this relationship was, as we know, the aim of the Christian Platonists, who were faced with the task of harmonizing the idea of God (as they knew it from their Christian faith) with the Platonic doctrine of ideas. And the relation in which the *ideas* stand to the existing *world* can ultimately be clarified only within the larger frame of reference of the relationship that exists between the *creator* and the *ideas.* But this is not yet the place to enter into a discussion of this problem.[6]

Our own procedure demands that we first of all clarify the nature of being to the extent that this is possible within the circumference of the life of the ego, i.e., within that sector of being that is in our immediate proximity and indeed inseparable from us. In that region we have met with a type of existent that is removed from the flux of the life of the ego and that itself conditions this flux: We mean the experienced essences [*Erlebnis-Wesenheiten*]. In comparison with the experiential units which become and pass away, these experienced essences are in fact a kind of *first existent.* Unless essences were realized in the life of the ego, this latter would be a chaotic maze in which no formal structure whatever could be distinguished. It is the essences which impart to the life of the ego unity and multiplicity, organic articulate structure and order, meaning and intelligibility.

Meaning and intelligibility: Actually we are face to face here with the primordial source of all meaning and intelligibility. For what is *meaning* [λόγος]? What does this word signify? We are unable to define or explain it because it is itself the ultimate ground [*Grund*] or reason of all definitions and explications. All human speech rests on the certainty that words have a meaning, and every explanation and argument rests on the conviction that all our questioning and reasoning arrives in the end at an ultimate intelligible reason or ground. This ultimate ground is the meaning [*Sinn*], intelligible in itself and through itself. *Meaning and understanding belong together.* Meaning is what can be understood, and understanding is the grasping of meaning [*Sinnerfassen*]. To understand what is *understandable* (*intelligible*) is the precise nature or being of the intellect which for this reason is also called the *understanding* (German: *Verstand;* Latin: *intellectus*). In its *logical* or *rational* procedure, the understanding inquires into *semantic associations and contexts* [*Sinnzusammenhänge*]. *Ratio*[7] (i.e., logical procedure) signifies the derivation of one meaning from another or the reduction of one meaning to another. This *ratio* comes to rest in some ultimate which can itself no longer either be derived from anything else nor reduced to anything else.

According to Hering, true essences are the only "entities which carry within themselves the possibility of *becoming wholly* [*restlos*] *intelligible*," and "it is only our knowledge of essences that makes us capable not only of verifying but also of understanding everything that is."[8]

Essences are manifold. There are derived essences which are related to simpler ones and which can he made intelligible by referring them back to the latter (e.g., the essence "bittersweet"). The ultimate simple essences, however, can no longer be derived from one another. Within the sphere of consciousness such simple essences are designated by the names of different experiential contents, such as mourning, joy, grief, lust, but also by the names of the essences of consciousness, experience, or ego. These essences must, of course, not be mistaken for the realities which derive their names from them. Thus the essence ego is not a living ego, and the essence joy is not an experienced joy.

The danger of mistaking the essence of a *concept* is even greater.[9] This would indeed be a serious misunderstanding. We *form* concepts by bringing into relief certain characteristic *marks* of an object. We thus have a certain amount of freedom in the formation of concepts. Essences, on the other hand, are not formed by us but rather *found or discovered.* Here we have no freedom whatsoever. We are free, of course, to seek but the finding, i.e., the found essence, does not depend on us. And because the ultimate essences are simple, there is nothing in them that could be brought into relief. For the same reason essences cannot be *defined* in the manner we can define concepts. The words we are using to find our way to them have, as Max Scheler used to say, only the significance of a pointer. They tell us: Look for yourself, then you will understand what I mean. I myself, life, joy—who can understand the meaning of those words unless they have experienced this meaning within their own selves? But once they have experienced the meaning of these words, they then know not only *their* self, *their* life, and *their* joy, they also know the meaning of self, life, joy *as such.* And only because they now understand this essential meaning are they able to know and understand *their* ego, *their* life, *their* joy as *ego, life,* and *joy.* At this point many new questions arise.[10] But we must defer an answer and pursue further our present line of argument.

What we have called experienced essences are, strictly speaking, not experiences: They are rather the preconditions of experiential units. What kind of *being* must we attribute to them? Their being is not like that of experiences—a becoming and passing away. Nor is it, like the being of the ego, a vitality that is ever received anew from moment to moment. Theirs is a *changeless* and *timeless* being. Do they then possess the *eternal being* of the first existent? Plato's description of the being of the *ideas* actually makes use of the identical terms that were later on employed by Christian philosophers to describe divine being. And Aristotle, too, did not arrive at a clear distinction between divine being and the being of the unchangeable essences (by the latter, to be sure, he did not mean ideas but intelligences). It is only the Christian thinkers who made an endeavor to separate the two types of being and to determine their mutual relationship.

There is really a great difference between the first being in whom we recognize the author of all other being and the being of ideal essences. The first being is being in absolute *perfection:* It is not only changeless being that never becomes or passes away, but it is infinite being, comprising in itself all *plenitude* and *vitality.* The being of ideal essences, on the other hand, is not perfect in this sense. Its preeminence in comparison with the actual experiential units lies in the fact that, raised above the flux of time, it changelessly rests and abides on its ontological summit. But if the individual semantic unit of the ideal essence is taken by itself in its delimited subsistence, it is not living being but appears rigid and dead.

This is precisely the point which even in antiquity gave rise to the main objection against the Platonic doctrine of ideas. How are the ideas *realized?* How does any *participation* in the ideas come about? What sets the ideas in motion? The fact that a real joy arises within me cannot be attributed to the ideal essence of joy, nor can the fact that *I* live be attributed to the ideal essence of my self. We are touching here on the relationship that exists between *actuality* and *efficacious activity,* a relationship which upon closer examination will presently reveal to us a new meaning of the term *act.*

The being of the limited and separate essences is *inefficacious* and therefore also *non-actual being.* The first existent, on the other hand, is absolutely primary in both efficacy and actuality. The being of the essence is nevertheless *not potential being* in the sense of a preliminary phase of actual being. Although it is not perfect being in any *absolute* sense (since it does not comprise the total plenitude of being), it is nonetheless perfect *in its own right* because it cannot experience any accretion beyond itself nor suffer any diminution of itself. It is thus the condition of the possibility of real being and of the latter's actual and potential preliminary stages.

The *realization* of the essence does not mean that the essence as such becomes real but that *something* that corresponds to it becomes real. The possibility of real being has its ground in the being of the essence. For this reason its unreal being cannot be called not-being. Anything which is the condition of another's being must itself possess being. The very fact that it is something indicates that it *is*. Only what is *nothing* is *not*.

Now what kind of being is this something of the essence? In contradistinction to real being, we shall call it *essential* being, and for the present phase of our investigation this terminological distinction may suffice. But in order to determine the peculiar character of this essential being, it seems advisable to mark off the essences from some other aspects of being which, though related to them, are by no means equivalent to them.

§3. Essence [*Wesenheit*], Concept [*Begriff*], and Nature [*Wesen*]

It was stated above that essences cannot be defined. No one can make me understand what joy is unless I myself have experienced joy. But once I have experienced joy, then I also understand what "joy as such" is. Is it nevertheless not true, however, that we find various definitions of joy in psychology textbooks? And does not St. Thomas offer us a carefully elaborated *theory of the emotions* and passions with precise definitions, with divisions and subdivisions?[11] Joy, for example, he defines as a *passion of the appetitive faculty*.[12] It is by its *object* that "joy (which is related to some good) differs from grief (which is related to some evil)." Joy, furthermore, corresponds to a definite phase in the *progress of the appetitive movement:* "The enjoyment ... enters first into a certain conjunction with the appetite, inasmuch as the enjoyment is considered as equal to or commensurate with the appetite; and from this conjunction results the passion of love (*amor*), which is nothing but the appetite's being formed by its object. This is why love is called a union of the one who loves with the object of that love. But what is thus conjoined in a certain way is still desire ..., so that the union may be completed *realiter* and the one who loves may enjoy the object of that love; and this is the way the passion of desire originates. But once the object of desire has actually been attained, it generates joy. The first phase, then, in the appetitive movement is love, the second phase is desire, and the third and final phase is joy..."[13]

Joy in a more restricted sense of the term (*laetitia*) is set off by St. Thomas from a number of closely related affective states: "Some of these indicate a high degree of joy, and this great intensity is found to exist either with respect to the inner disposition (*dispositio*) where joy signifies an inward expansion of the heart so that *laetitia* then almost has the meaning of *latitia* [widening]. Or this great intensity of joy relates to a glad inward exuberance (*gaudium*) expressing itself in outward signs. This state of joy we call exultation (German: *Frohlocken;* Latin: *exultatio*). The inward joy of exultation leaps out, as it were (*exterius exilit*), and this leaping out manifests itself in a change of facial expression which, owing to the intimate relationship that exists between facial expression and imagination, is indicative of the state of mind which we call hilarity (German: *Heiterkeit;* Latin: *hilaritas);* and insofar as such a highly intensified joyfulness tends to express itself in words and deeds ... it turns into cheerful gaiety (German: *Aufgeräumtheit;* Latin: *iucunditas*)."[14]

All these observations are certainly correct and highly illuminating. They assign to joy its proper place in the inner life of the soul; they teach us how to distinguish joy from other affective states which are either related or opposed to it; they point out the conditions from which it derives its origin as well as certain concomitant and consequent phenomena; and with all this they establish a solid foundation for a correct evaluation and practical analysis. But do these observations of St. Thomas predicate anything concerning the *essence* of joy? Certainly not. The essence of joy is not a state of the soul; it has no degrees of intensity; it does not manifest itself in the phenomena of bodily expression, and it does not impel to words and deeds.

We might ask then whether it is not true nevertheless that the essence of joy is related to the good and, generally speaking, tends toward an object. Yet even this contention must be denied. While it is true of *every* joy, it is not true of the essence of joy. None of these characterizations constitutes the essence of joy. We are therefore forced to the conclusion that the definition of joy which results from the descriptive analysis of St. Thomas is not a definition of the essence of joy. It cannot be the definition of the essence because an understanding of all his detailed observations presupposes that we already know what joy is.

Let us ask then what it is that is determined by the concept of joy? It is neither the essence of joy nor a particular experienced joy (one joy alone, at any rate). *Every* joy is related to some good; every joy has a definite emotional pitch [*Höhe*], and every joy tends to express itself. But *one* joy is related to this particular good, while another joy is related to that particular good; one has a higher and another a lower degree of intensity. The concept comprises the common elements of *all* joy (insofar as the intention in forming the concept has been to include everything that pertains to joy; a concept need not have this kind of generality; it may even relate to only one particular thing). For some purposes it may suffice to select but a few characteristic marks which will then make it possible to demarcate everything that pertains to joy from everything else. If, however, we want to answer the question, *What is joy?* and if we want to give not only some correct answer (as, for example, "Joy is an experience," or "Joy is an emotion") but a truly exhaustive answer (amounting to a definition of the nature of joy), then the concept must comprise everything that belongs to the nature of joy. And by nature [*Wesen*] we mean to denote something which coincides neither with the essence nor with the concept.

Hering has formulated the following principle of nature [*Hauptsatz vom Wesen*][15]: "*Every object* (whatever its mode of being) *has one and only one nature which as such constitutes it in the fullness of its particular individuality.* Conversely, ... *every nature is (in accordance with its nature) nature of something and, more precisely, nature of this particular and of no other something.*" The nature is thus "what constitutes the particular *individuality* of the object,"[16] "its sum total of essential predicables."[17] Hering also uses the term *thisness* (German: *Sosein;* Greek: ποῖον εἶναι)[18] to designate the nature. The fact that the *nature is nature of something,* i.e., the particular individuality of *an object,* denotes its being *dependent.* The nature, in short, is *that which determines the "quid" or "what" of the object* (τὸ τί ἦν εἶναι). A "nature-less" [*wesenlos*] object is therefore inconceivable; without a nature it would no longer be a real object but only the empty form of an object.

Within the frame of the realm of the ego—the realm which has been the object of this preliminary investigation—we were able up to this point to avoid speaking of *objects.* But now that we have advanced beyond that frame, this is no longer possible. Although in the realm of the ego, too, we have encountered *natures* and *essences,* we have already sufficient evidence that both are not only found in this particular realm but in all that which is [*Seiende*].

The term *object* [*Gegenstand*][19] has several connotations: It may be understood as what stands *counter* or *opposite* the knowing intellect. Object in this sense is equivalent with *something* or anything at all: Everything which is *not nothing,* which therefore can be *known* and of which something can be *predicated* [*subiectum logicum*], is thus an object. There are independent and dependent objects in this sense. Thus understood, "experience," "joy," "natures," and "essences" may be called objects. It is possible, however, to think in connection with a "Gegen*stand*" primarily of its *standing* aside or standing apart from other things, of *Selbständikeit* and *Eigen-ständigkeit* (standing in itself and the standing on its own). In this sense not every something is an object but only what sub-sists or in-sists in itself [*ein Sein in sich*].[20] "Things" and "persons" and in some way also numbers and concepts are objects in the latter sense (though numbers and concepts are not objects in the strict sense of a *substantia subsistens* or a *hypostasis*). On the other hand, neither qualities nor experiences nor natures are objects.

When Hering's "principle of the nature" stated that every object has a nature, he had in mind not only objects in the narrower sense of the word. Qualities and experiences also have a nature, and even the nature itself has a nature. Everything has *its* nature. If it is a question of an individual person or thing [*individuum*]—for example this particular man or woman, or this particular joy (*my joy*)—then the nature of this person or thing too is an *individuum.* "Two (individual) objects which are absolutely alike have two absolutely alike natures but not one and the same nature, each of two like flowers, each of two congruent triangles has *its* own nature."[21] It pertains to the nature of *this particular* person that he is easily aroused to anger and just as easily pacified; that he is fond of music and that he likes to mix with people. It does not pertain to his nature that at this moment he is crossing the street and is caught in a storm.

But we can and must also speak of the nature *of* man [*Menschen*]. It pertains to the nature of man that he has a body and a soul, that he is endowed with reason and free will. It does not pertain to the nature of man that his skin is white or that his eyes are blue, that he was born in a big city, that he goes to war or dies of a contagious disease. The nature thus does not comprise everything that can be predicated of an object. We must distinguish between *essential* and *non-essential* qualities; and to the determination of what and how the object is must be added what happens to it: its *fate,* i.e., its *actio* and *passio* (ποιεῖν χαὶ πάσχειν),[22] its relation to other objects, its spatial and temporal determinations.[23]

Only what provides an answer to the question, "*What* is the object?" and "How is the object?" pertains to the nature (and only part of it, not all of it). On the other hand, not everything that does not pertain to the nature is *fortuitous;* some of it has its *foundation in the nature.* Thus, it did not pertain to the nature of Napoleon that he embarked on the Russian campaign, but it had its ground or foundation in his nature.[24] And among those things which are founded on the nature, there are some which follow *necessarily* from the nature. The Russian campaign of Napoleon appears delineated in his nature as a *possibility.* We can *understand* this undertaking as proceeding from his nature, but we cannot say that it followed necessarily from his nature. It is conceivable that he might have decided upon a different course of action.[25] On the other hand, it *follows* from the nature of the square that its area is larger than that of an equilateral triangle with an identical length of its sides. It is impossible that it could be otherwise; it *follows* from the nature of the square but does not *pertain* to this nature, because no relationship to any other object pertains to the nature of a square. But it does pertain to its nature that it has four sides of equal length.

The foregoing observations concerning the nature are merely indicatory and incomplete, but they suffice to make us recognize the difference between nature, concept, and essence. The *concept* is *formed* in order to make possible the determination of the object. The *nature* is *found or discovered* in or on the object. It is safely withdrawn from our arbitrary will. While the nature thus belongs to the object, the concept is a formation that is separate from the object but intentionally "related" to it.[26] *The formation of concepts* [*Begriffsbildung*] *presupposes the seizure of the nature* [*Wesenserfassung*] and is nurtured by it.

The nature is also distinct from the essence in that the nature belongs to the object, while the essence is independent [*selbständig*] with respect to the object. Thus we speak of the essence "joy," but of the nature *of* joy. The nature shows a *structure of essential features* which can be traced in it and expressed conceptually. The nature, in short, is that *which* can be conceptually seized and that *by which* the object itself can be seized and determined.

§4. The Nature [*Wesen*] and Its Object [*Gegenstand*]; Nature, "Full Quid [*volles Was*] and Nature-Quid [*Wesenswas*]"; Change and Transmutation of the Nature

In order to be able to predicate something concerning the nature's *mode of being,* we must examine still more closely the relationship existing between the nature and the object which has this particular nature. We may speak of the nature of *this (my)* joy, but we may also speak of the nature *of* joy Here we have different objects and different natures. "This (my) joy" denotes my present experience, i.e., something that is unique, temporally fixed and delimited, something that belongs to me exclusively and to no other human being. When this joy is past and when I try to "make it present" again in recollection, this making present is not identical with my present experience: It is a new experience, but an experience with a content which both experiences have in common. And this common content is the *full quid* [*volles Was*] of this (my) joy, while the "being present" and the "being past" are its modes of being.[27] It pertains to this *full quid* of my joy that it is joy over the message which I have just received, that the joy is lively, and that it endures for some length of time. It does not pertain to this full *quid* that simultaneously I hear noises coming from the street, nor does it pertain to it (it rather follows from) this full quid that now, "filled with joy," I can no longer concentrate on my work as I did before. But, above all, it pertains of course to this full quid that my experience is *joy*, i.e., a realization of the essence of joy.

Let us ask then whether the *full quid* of my joy coincides with the nature of this (my) joy. The answer must be in the negative. We must rather add here a further twofold distinction:

1. If we understand nature [*Wesen*] as ποῖον εἶναι or τί εἶναι, then this nature denotes not the what of joy but rather the whatness [*Wassein; Sosein*] or the quidditive determination [*Wasbestimmtheit*] of joy.[28]
2. To the *full* whatness of joy (in which we now include every ποῖον εἶναι) belongs also the *quantitative magnitude* of my joy.

This joy can grow in intensity: It can become stronger, richer, and deeper, and yet is still "this (my) joy," the same as before—it is *different*, but it is not *a different joy*. The *full* whatness has changed, but the nature of my joy has not changed. To the nature of the object, in other words, belongs all (and only) what must be preserved, so that "the object" will remain the same.

This (my) joy is of course no longer extant if I no longer experience *joy*. If, for example, I convey the message I have received to some other person and if this person is thereupon filled with a *like* joy, her joy is surely not my joy. We therefore say that the determination of *whose* joy it is also belongs to the nature of this joy. And, as has been pointed out, the joy does not remain the same if it is no longer referred to the same *object*.

The difference between the full whatness and the nature exists only where an object whose being "extends over some duration," i.e., an object which needs time to attain continuously to being, undergoes some changes in the course of this duration. This applies to all objects whose being is a "becoming and passing away." Included in this class are, as we have also pointed out, all experiential units, but added thereto must be the entire world of perceptible and perceived objects of sense [*sinnenfällige Dinge*] or all that we mean when we speak of *nature* [*Natur*]. The difference between the full whatness and the nature of objects does not exist in the case of numbers, of pure geometrical forms and figures, of pure colors and sounds—in all those instances, in short, where we deal not with *real* but with *ideal* objects. In ideal objects, whatness and nature coincide. In the world of becoming and passing away, on the other hand, we distinguish in the *what* which an object is at any given time some elements that are constant and others that are changing.

The constant elements constitute what may be designated as the quid of the nature [*Wesenswas*]. This does not mean, however, that owing to these elements of constancy the nature is free from all change. In the case of a human being we regard a person's *character* as that constant which serves as a basis for our judgment and which provides the key for the understanding of the person's changing appearance and behavior. But it sometimes happens that this key, after having served us well for an extended period of time, suddenly falls. This particular human being appears then "like a changed person." We need not necessarily have misjudged up to now. The person may actually have undergone a "transformation," and as soon as we discover the new key, we regain the proper orientation. He or she is still the same human being, but we ask ourselves whether the person's nature has merely "changed" or whether it has actually been "transformed" into a different nature. Both possibilities seem plausible to me.

It seems proper to speak of a *change* of the nature if certain individual characteristics of the nature pattern [*Wesensbild*] undergo a mutation so that gradually a changed picture of the character emerges, as happens, for example, in the process of evolution from childhood to adolescence and adulthood. But in this changed pattern there remains nevertheless a certain basic element of continuity with the former state. The same phenomenon may be observed in the case of sudden *conversions* such as "Saul being transformed into Paul." The passionate champion of the Mosaic law can be clearly recognized in the "prisoner of Christ" (Ephesians 3:1) who utterly spends himself in the service of the Gospel, even though the unbending severity of the fighter has given way to a generous self-consuming benevolence, and in place of legalistic rigidity we find a flexible sensitivity to the gentle breath of the Holy Spirit.

There are, however, other instances where the change is so complete that no element of constancy remains and where it is therefore appropriate to speak not merely of a "changed" nature but of a "new or different" nature. If the human being in question can nonetheless still be called the "same," it is because the *bearer* of the nature must be distinguished from the nature the person bears and because the same bearer may be said to possess first one and then a different nature-quid [*Wesenswas*].[29] In those instances where the nature is not merely changed but has become another, we shall then not speak of "change" but of a complete "transmutation" (i.e., a change of the nature that amounts to a change of the object).

Both change and transmutation of the nature occur, of course, only in mutable objects. The nature of numbers, of pure colors, and of pure sounds is always immutably the same.

§5. Individual and Universal Nature

These differences between the quid and the nature suggest that the corresponding modes of being are likewise without uniformity. But before we examine this question, we may profitably complement our inquiry into the nature of individual things with an examination of that *universal* element that is actualized in them.

It was pointed out above that the nature of "this (my) joy" differs from the nature *of* joy. It pertains to the nature of joy that it *is* joy (i.e., it is an embodiment or incarnation of the essence *of* joy); that it is joy experienced *in or in view of an object* (without any specific reference to this or that particular object); that it is the experience of a soul-nature (but not my experience nor the experience of any other particular being).[30]

We might refer here once more to St. Thomas's previously discussed analysis of joy. The nature *of* joy is actualized in "this (my) joy" as well as in every particular experience of joy (and *only* in such individual experiences). For what is meant by the expression "joy"? There is certainly no such thing as a "joy in general" which, apart from the individual experiences of joy, would have its place in the real world in the manner of some particular thing (in our example, in the experiential context of a specific soul nature).[31] There are nevertheless certain predications possible with respect to "joy" which are not related to any particular experience of joy. We say, for example, that "joy strengthens vitality" or that "joy can be profound or superficial." Now a particular joy is *either* profound *or* superficial:

I may be in doubt whether it has one quality or the other, but in itself it is objectively determined. *Joy,* on the other hand, is ”profound or superficial”: It cannot be decided whether it is the one or the other. Linguistically, it is even possible to say that “joy can be profound and superficial.” Such a saying would obviously be absurd if we were to refer it to a particular experience of joy.

There exist, however, certain relations between statements concerning “joy in general” and statements concerning this particular joy. Because *joy* can be “profound and superficial,” a particular joy can be *either* profound *or* superficial. If *joy* as such were profound, then no particular joy could be anything but profound. As often, therefore, as some statement is made concerning *joy,* something is simultaneously predicated that relates to every particular joy.

Is it then perhaps necessary to say that the term “joy” comprises “everything that joy is”? As a matter of fact, in some contexts the two expressions are interchangeable. We may say, for example that “everything that is of the nature of joy strengthens vitality.” In the case of our second sentence—“joy is either profound or superficial”—the interchange is not quite so simple. We may perhaps change the phrasing, so that the sentence reads: “Everything that is of the nature of joy is in part superficial and in part profound.” In other words, the linguistic structures and the possibilities of their mutations point to certain contextual relations in the realm of those existents which are their intentional objects.

Joy, at any rate, is a *name* which designates everything that is of the nature of joy, i.e., every actual and potential experience of joy. In different contexts it designates at one time the particular experience of joy. When I say, for example, that “joy has restored my health,” I have in mind not “joy in general” but a very definite joy. *In* this definite joy, however, I refer especially to the fact that it is *joy.* At another time the name joy designates in summary fashion all possible and actual experiences of joy. The name “joy” may also refer to something which is more comprehensive than any particular experiential unit but not so comprehensive as to include everything that is of the nature of joy. Thus I may say, for example, “In that person’s life joy outweighed grief.” In this case I refer to the sum total of joy in the totality of a human life.

If we now say that only the individual or the particular is real and that the universal or general is a "mere name," this by no means disposes of the issue. The question immediately arises: What is a name? It is not the mere wording [*Wortlaut*] but the wording (or *sign*) plus its specific *meaning* or *significance*. The word which *means* an object always definitely restricts this meaning with respect to what it signifies. Thus the same may be meant but with different aspects of signification. When I refer to "Bonaparte," to "the Emperor of the French," to "the victor at Jena," and to "the prisoner of St. Helena," the meant or intentional object is the same, but the significance differs in each case. And even if the wording remains the same, the significance and correspondingly also the objects may differ. When I hear, for example, the Latin work *ora*, I may take it as either signifying "face" or "coast," or the imperative form of "to pray." What meaning the word carries in each particular instance I can learn only from the context.

The name "joy" also had different meanings in the several sentences in which we have used it, and it referred to different objects. This was, however, not simply a question of an ambiguity of meaning or of an equivocation, but there was in these several meanings of the same word a common stock of signification. In one instance the identical name may designate a distinct particular joy. In another it may signify everything that is of the nature of joy, simply because in both instances reference is made to "joy," and because what is recognized is "the same" in both instances. The objects, as we have seen, are not identical, and we can take cognizance of their difference by using more adequate expressions, i.e., by speaking in the one instance of "this (my) joy" and in the other of "everything that is of the nature of joy." It is probable that there are languages which can express such differences by mere modifications of the word *form*, possibly by varying endings. But what remains as the common element of the different wordings is then the expression of a common stock of semantic significance which as such is indicative of some common element in the objects themselves.

What then is the common element which underlies everything that we designate by the name of "joy"? Could it possibly be the *essence* [*Wesenheit*] of joy? It will be recalled that we previously stated with respect to essences that they represent the ultimate meaning and are the truly intelligible. If this is the case, then it must be the essences from which the meaning of words ultimately derives. As a matter of fact, that which is the ultimate ground of all intelligibility also makes possible all linguistic understanding and all linguistic communication. We therefore now conclude *that all names are actually and ultimately expressions of essences.*

If this, however, were all we could express linguistically, then our language would consist only of names for *individual or particular things* [*Eigennamen*]. But in ordinary life we very rarely speak of essences. What we do speak of and what we are concerned about in our daily lives are objects, and especially things that are tangible. It remains for the meditating thinker to discover that there are essences, and such a thinker makes this discovery while pursuing paths that are far removed from the highways of everyday life; and, after having made the discovery, this thinker has a hard time trying to explain to others what he or she means by essences. And yet, if there were no essences, even the purely practical person could not speak of the things with which that person is occupied in everyday life. One blames fellow human beings for "selfishness" [*Selbstsucht*], and one probably thinks that such people are overly concerned for themselves. The interesting thing is that *Sucht* actually means "disease," but who thinks about the kind of vice expressed in this German word for egotism? In a similar way one wonders how many people who talk about the feast of Corpus Christi realize that this means the body of Christ.

Our language—and this is true of every human language—abounds with expressions which denote something definite, expressions which have some universally intelligible meaning, but this meaning is neither the *original* one nor the one *actually expressed* by the word used. Only the linguist who is familiar with the history of language knows the original and real meaning. "Original" and "actually expressed," however, do not signify one and the same thing: The fact that words no longer have their original meaning must be attributed to the historical process of semantic change in its various forms. But even if we take the words in their original meaning, they usually signify more than they actually express. Thus we apply, for example, *universal names* to *individual* things, and we use *one* name to designate *many* things. No language is so rich that it could afford an *individual proper name* for each and every particular thing. And even when we use an individual proper name to designate a particular thing, this name is *poor* in content and meaning compared to the richness of its intentional object, a richness which the name in vain tries to express.

The Goths named their king *Dietrich* [*thiuda-reiks*] and thereby designated him as a *ruler of and by the people* [*Volksherrscher*]. When we hear or read of this name, we may think of the first of their rulers to whom it was applied, and we may further assume that the name was then still understood in its original meaning and used only to designate this one particular individual. But when the Goths chose this name, they meant to designate with it the *entire* man, not only his position of rulership or a particular trait of character by virtue of which he had received his exalted calling, but his entire being or nature [*Wesen*].

The aim of our brief linguistic excursus was this: *The words we ordinarily use are not generic names* [*Wesensnamen*] and much less expressions of the full quid. By means of either one or a few particular characteristic marks, occasionally also by some essential (yet more frequently by non-essential) marks, they describe a totality which includes a multitude of essential and non-essential *features.* The name represents for us the whole, and most of the time we are no longer aware of what it really stands for. In short, the reason for the imperfection of our language is the imperfection of our knowledge of the nature of things [*Wesenserkenntnis*].[32]

The simple names we are using can only express simple things. However, only the *ultimate* essences are *truly simple.* We know of them without recognizing them *as* essences, and we make use of them as often as we recognize and name things. Both our cognition and our naming would be impossible without essences.

We have already learned that the being of essences differs from the kind of being we encounter in the realm of becoming and passing away. Essences are not *actual,* but if they were not, there would be neither actuality nor potentiality. The *actual has a share in the essence by virtue of the fact that the actual has a nature* [*Wesen*]. *Every quid of the nature* [*Wesenswas*]—aside from the borderline case [*Grenzfall*] of the absolutely simple nature, which can only be one, and in which the quid and the essence [*Was und Wesenheit*] coincide—*shows a structure of essential features* [*Wesenszüge*]. *These essential features, however, bear the imprint of the essences; they copy the essences.*

But it would be misleading to say that the essential features are essences, for there is only *one* essence in each particular class, while there are many essential features copying the essence. Thus the essence redness is copied in the red color of each and every red object."[33] But the color red as an objective quality occurs with a frequency proportionate to the occurrence of red objects. In some things—not in all—the being red is part of the nature of the thing (e.g., in the case of a "red rose"). It is, of course, not a question of stating the self-evident truth that a red rose is red but rather of asserting that the being red pertains to the red rose in a different manner than it pertains to some other red objects (e.g., a red apron, which has been dipped into a bucket filled with red paint to use up some paint that was left over). The being red does not pertain to a rose as such: It pertains to a specific *type* of rose. (The question of what is meant by a *type* may be left undecided for the moment.) The being red cannot be dissociated from the specific nature image [*Wesenbild*] of the rose, whereas the being blue of those blue roses that were "fashionable" some years ago represented a strange and unnatural element in the structure whole [*Gesamtbild*] of the rose.

In concluding this section, we must try to determine more clearly the difference between the *universal* and the *particular nature* [*allgemeines und Einzelwesen*]. "This my joy" is "a joy," and it is *an experience.* Implied in these expressions are different degrees of universality and particularity: There is the nature of this my joy, there is the nature of joy, and there is the nature of the experience as such. Both the quid and nature of this my joy are unique. They are *actual* in this particular joy. They are the "essential" elements in it. The essential elements of joy are actualized wherever joy is experienced, i.e., "in" each and every individual joy. They lie hidden in every particular joy, and this is why we call them *universal.* The essential or universal elements thus stand in contrast with the *individual* elements, if by "individual" we mean that cannot be communicated to others.[34] For what can be communicated to others is precisely the universal nature which can become actual in a multitude of individual things. If therefore the nature of the individual thing must be said to be *lacking in autonomy* because it can be actualized only in another (viz., its own proper object), the universal nature is doubly lacking in autonomy, for in order to become actual it needs the individual natures and their objects. But though the universal nature "occurs" in several individual natures (and their objects), it is *one.* It is one and the *same* universal nature which is actual or may become actual here and there and in all the individual natures that pertain to it, whereas the individual nature is actual and potential only in one (in *its*) object. There may be other natures "like unto" it, but it cannot "occur several times."

§6. Actual and Essential Being [*Wesenhaftes Sein*]

When we speak of the "*possibility* of becoming actual" or of actual and possible individual things, we are immediately carried back to the problem of *actual* and *potential being*. We have now learned to know several meanings of that *which* is: It may signify the object with its full quid (what), with both its essential and nonessential thisness [*Sosein*]; it may further denote the full quid taken by itself, and it may also mean what the object is according to its individual or universal nature. In addition, we can distinguish different degrees or stages of universality: The nature of joy, the nature of emotion, the nature of experience as such.

Let us now put aside the problem of the *object* as such and concentrate our attention exclusively on the different possible significations of its *quid* in relation to being. If we start out from the experience of "this (my) joy," we must, in order to grasp its full quid, take into account the entire duration of its ascent to being. In this duration this quid is not rigid and solid but in constant flux and change. It becomes and passes away, and its being is neither absolutely actual nor absolutely potential: It is both actual and potential at every moment, and at every moment some part or element in it attains to the height of being [*Seinshöhe*].[35] *The nature and the nature quid* [*Wesenswas*] *of this (my) joy is actual as a whole at every moment of the joy's duration.*[36] This holds true without any restriction if the nature remains unchanged for the entire extent of the duration (in our example, as long as the joy remains the "same").

In the particular case under discussion, the question of what kind of being pertains to the nature prior to the beginning of joy and after the passing of joy must be asked. There is no doubt that the nature of this (my) joy is *actual* only as long as the joy itself is actual.[37] Prior to the actuality, the nature of my joy has no being in the "real world," i.e., in our example, in the experiential actuality of an ego. Nevertheless, it cannot be said that the nature of my joy is not prior to this actuality. Since we are able to grasp the quid of the nature independent of its actualization in its object, the quid of my joy must possess some sort of being in accordance with our assertion that everything which *is something* must also *be*. But it does not possess the same kind of being that it has in the actualized quid of its object. And because—by virtue of this mode of being (which precedes the being of the object) and by virtue of the not yet actualized nature [*Was-Sein*] of the object—actual being becomes *possible*, we may say with St. Thomas that both the quid and the nature are *potential* being.

To say this, however, means more than merely to point to the logical possibility of the nature of becoming actual in an object; and it denotes more than that rudimentary and preliminary stage of actual being which we designated as potency. We are speaking of the *potentiality of the nature* [*Wesensmöglichkeit*], but what we really mean is that possibility of the nature's actualization which has its reason or ground in that same nature.[38] The nature, in other words, has a being of its *own*, an essential [*wesenhaft*] being which is more than merely a phase on its way to actuality (its ultimate goal). This being of the nature is a preliminary stage, nevertheless, because (1) only by starting out from the being of the nature can actual being be attained; (2) the nature lacks autonomy and stands in need of supplementation; and (3) to the nature pertains the possibility of entering into the actuality of the object. But the being of the nature is not an *inferior* preliminary stage because the object, in a certain sense, becomes actual by virtue of the nature, not vice versa.[39] The nature is in the actual which is *fundamentally* actual. This consideration may help us to understand why the term *act* (which originally denoted actual being) was applied to *that whereby* something actual attains its *actuality*.[40]

We have previously employed the term *essential being* to designate the being of *essences*. If at this juncture this same term suggests itself for the designation of the being that is comprised in the nature, it seems necessary to examine whether it is used in both instances in an identical sense. I am indeed convinced that it is characteristic of the peculiar relationship which exists between natures and essences that their respective modes of being belong closely together.

According to what we have learned so far about essences, it appears certain that their essential being is the only kind of being they possess. On the other hand, as far as the natures are concerned, they may possess an additional actuality in their respective objects, and a relationship to those objects whose quid they determine is already implied in their pre-actual being, This duality in the being of the natures corresponds to the mediating function which they exercise with respect to the essences, on the one hand, and the "real world," on the other.

The world of essential being[41] must be conceived as a hierarchically ordered realm in which the *essences* represent the simple *prototypes* of the highest stage. *Fashioned* in the image and likeness of the essences are the essential features of those composite structures which we have designated as the nature quid. To the latter we may perhaps profitably apply the term whatness [*Washeit*] or *quiddity,* because we cannot form a plural of *quid* [Was]. The term "what*ness*" is, however, not quite adequate because the English suffix "-ness" (and the German suffix *-heit*) implies a *to be* (*esse*; *Wassein*). We are using it merely for lack of a better one.[42]

The natures and whatnesses [*Washeiten*] show a gradation according to their greater or lesser universality. We may feel inclined to regard the individual whatnesses as representing the lowest grade of universality. We must, however, include in this same sphere the *full quid* of things, inasmuch as to it, too, a duality of being must be attributed, namely, the previously described being-in-the-objects, which is a becoming and passing away, and, secondly—distinctly apart from the being-in-the-objects—being as a pure quid which as such is free from this kind of change.[43] The structures of different grades are separated from one another as far as their essential being is concerned, and they are related to each other only in the manner of subordination and coordination. But as far as their actual being is concerned, the natures and whatnesses of a higher grade are present with their full quid *in* the subordinated less universal ones and ultimately in the individual natures and their corresponding objects.

We have encountered a separation of essential and actual being in those individual natures which persist without change during the entire length of the process of their actualization. It now remains for us to examine the situation as it prevails in the case of changeable natures. Some person, for example, whom we knew in the stage of adolescence, has now grown into adulthood. We find her nature changed. How can this fact be reconciled with the statement that the nature and the nature quid [*Wesenswas*]—in contrast to the full quid—is actual during the entire length of the process of its actualization? The simplest solution to the problem seems to be to speak of two natures which are actualized in this particular individual, *one after the other.* As far as the essential being is concerned, we shall, as a matter of fact have to distinguish as an other what was *prior* to the change and what *follows* the change. In addition, however, we have to assume a third element which comprises and provides the foundation for the two others as well as for the transition from the one to the other, for this transition is founded on the *possibility of the nature* [*Wesensmöglichkeit*]. Of this enveloping and founding nature[44] we shall have to say that it is actual at every moment during the entire length of the life span, whereas the partial natures [*Teilwesen*] are actual only for the length of the respective periods of their duration.

§7. The Nature and Its Core [*Wesenskern*]; Essence and Essential Form [*Washaftigkeit*] (μορφή)

If we want to gain a more thorough understanding of natures and whatnesses [*Washeiten*], we must proceed to an examination of their internal structure. We have been able to distinguish between the *founding nature* and the *foundation which it establishes.* We have stated, moreover, that both are composed of *essential features* [*Wesenszügen*]. But we desire to know not only these individual features; we are looking for that *inner relation* between them which will make the nature *intelligible.* Unless we gain this knowledge we remain without "the key which will disclose to us the fullness of the nature as an integrated structure."[45] "It is a question ... of making understandable why precisely these particular features may appear in this specific combination and why, once a certain number of them are present, they have to manifest themselves jointly in their totality in accordance with a strictly regulated inner homogeneity." We are looking for "a more or less simple core of essential features ..., the presence of which will make intelligible the presence of the remaining strands of the nature in accordance with either clearly intuited or perhaps only instinctively discerned a priori laws." "It cannot be maintained, however, that each and every nature possesses such a core or even an integrated structure that can be understood as the expression of an intrinsic necessity."[46]

In the case of the particular nature of a human being, the presence of a *core of nature* is very conspicuous. Here more than in any other nature we look for some basic constituent element by virtue of which all the other elements become intelligible. And it is very similar in the case of other intellectual and historical formal structures [*Gebilde*]. In trying, for example, to understand the political actions of Frederick the Great or to interpret a work of poetry, we are looking for a "key" that will disclose the structure of that particular nature. There are, on the other hand, a large number of objects where such a search for a core would be useless and meaningless. Only a fully developed theory of the nature of the different spheres and classes of objects[47] could tell us in what instances we may expect to find a *nature with a core* and in what instances such a search will be futile. For our present purpose it will suffice to gain an understanding of the nature structure [*Wesensaufbau*] as such.

Hering designates the nature as ποῖον εἶναι (thisness [*Sosein*]) But he understands the ποῖον (the *this* or *So*) so broadly that it includes also the τί, i.e., the *what* of the object.[48] Thus, to the nature of a particular object belongs not only its being red, its being soft, its being fragrant, but also its being a rose or its being a bud, which provides the answer to the question of what it is. It appears even that the τί εἶναι reveals the nature more directly than the individual essential features because the τί εἶναι comprises the nature in its totality. The individual essential features are nevertheless indispensable for our knowledge of the nature. The τί and the ποῖον, the τί εἶναι, and the ποῖον εἶναι, are interrelated, and with the discovery of this interrelation we gain access to the nature structure as such.

It pertains to the rose as a physical object to have form, size, color, and a number of other qualities. This *particular* rose has its particular form, size, color, etc. We say, "The rose is red," and "red" thus belongs to the ποῖον of the rose. We may also say, "The color of the rose is red" (or some *shade* of red, for red is not an ultimate determination). In speaking of color, red does not designate the ποῖον (the *this* or *So*) of the rose but rather relates to its τί (the *what*). Red is a color, and color is an objective quality. Color may be considered in its specific character as distinguished from form, size, etc., and it may also be considered in its distinct qualification as red, blue, etc. What makes this particular color a *color* is that element in it which corresponds to the essence "color." And thus what makes this particular color red corresponds to the essence "redness." Both "color" and "redness" are simple essences. But "red" is already a composite: It is not only red but is simultaneously "a color." It thus partakes of the two essences, "redness" and "color."

It was stated a moment ago that what makes the red color red *corresponds* to the essence "redness." What makes the red color red *is* not the effect redness, but it is something *in* the red, and something different in this red and in that red. This something Hering calls the *essential form* or μορφή [*Washaftigkeit*] "which 'imparts' to the object the form of its being."[49] "What we have said of the nature," Hering continues, "also holds true of the μορφή: It is, *according to its meaning,* μορφή of or on something (and, to be sure, of or on a very definite something). It is the μορφή *of* this definite something."

The color of the rose bears within itself a μορφή which makes it red, and it thereby partakes of the essence redness. The μορφή of the color is not directly the μορφή of the rose, but *indirectly* or *mediately* it has a share in the structure of the rose. Hering therefore calls this μορφή the *immediate* μορφή of the color and the *mediate* μορφή of the rose, and he correspondingly designates the rose as the *mediate* and its color as the *immediate carrier* of the μορφή. The rose as a whole possesses its own particular μορφή.

It is *not* possible to formulate a law stating that "the morphes of a part are parts of the morphes of the whole."[50] The morphe "equilateralness," for example, is not a part of the morphe "triangularity."

But there is such a thing as a fusion of individual morphes in one total or universal morphe as, for example, the fusion of the redness and "color"[51] in the "color of the rose, which is red." The "being horse" of this particular horse, on the other hand, and this horse's "being a domestic animal" (which both determine this horse's τί εἶναι) do not fuse.

Generally speaking, "it may be said that every μ [= μορφή or morphe] stands in need of being complemented by its carrier. Now if this need for a complementary integration of different μ's (μ_1, μ_2, μ_3, ...) is satisfied by the same object A, then these several μ's *together with A* form a whole. The individual μ's, though mediately linked by A, can be relatively independent in regard to each other. In other words, such a linkage establishes no actual unity among the several μ's."[52]

"Accordingly, certain special relationships must obtain between μ_1 and μ_2 if their combination in a firmly established unity is to result." Of such a nature is, for example, the combination of μ_1 (color) and μ_2 (redness) in a definite color. "It is no mere accident that μ_2 cannot appear in a carrier without μ_1; the reason lies in the nature of μ_1 and μ_2. It seems certain, moreover, that this foundation in μ_2 is not mediate: The two morphes are not linked, as it were, by the carrier acting as an intermediary and under a mandate of μ_2 that would compel it to provide an abode simultaneously for μ_1. The latter is in fact also true, but only because μ_1 has to enter into a direct relation with μ_2, such a relation being the only way in which μ_2 can appear in an object."[53]

"This fusion of the two morphes, however, is of such an intimate nature that it results not in a mere *linkage of two essential forms* [*Washaftigkeiten*]—namely, "coloration" and "redness"—but in *one* (new) *Washaftigkeit,* namely, "Rothaftigkeit" or, more correctly, "Rotfarb-Haftigkeit" (red-coloredness). To be sure, this new essential form *has not the character of a simple essence but of an essence in which different component parts* (which account for its complexity) can be discerned. This need for a complementary integration of μ_2 by μ_1 we call a direct or *immediate* need.[54]

The need for the complementary integration and fusion of different morphes points to the important distinction (1) between *derivative* or *composite* and *simple* or *primordial essences* [*Ur-Wesenheiten*]; and

(2) the corresponding distinction between *derivative* and *primordial morphes* [*Ur-Morphen*].

Now—aside from the fusion of morphes which stand in need of mutual complementary integration to form a new composite morphe—a combination of such morphes as stand in no such need is also possible. Thus, in contemplating "the essential form [*Washaftigkeit*] which makes the horse what it is in the zoological sense," we find "that all those multiple individual characteristics which are listed by the zoologist form merely a more or less tightly knit bundle of different elements, but not a *novum* endowed with a specific quality of its own. We are evidently dealing here with a *conglomerate or complex of morphes* and not with an individual composite or (much less) a simple morphe. In this particular instance we can therefore not speak of a *genuine* morphe."[55]

We now understand the difference between a *nature with a core and a nature without a core.* "The essential forms" writes Hering, "which appear in the object, determine its thisness [*Sosein*] or its nature. In those instances where the sum total of the morphes, as they appear in their carrier, fuse to form a new and genuine total morphe—a morphe which *as such* cannot suffer any accretion or diminution of its sum total—the nature of the object, too acquires the character of a definitive unity. The comprehension of this unity constitutes a new act of cognition and is as such distinct from the act which comprehends the multiplicity of the individual features of the nature viewed as a grouping."[56]

There are two further ways in which the term *core of the nature* may be understood.

1. "If the this [*So*] of an object is a complex and genuine essential form [*Washaftigkeit*], the individual characteristics of the thisness (which have been established without considering, for the time being, their interrelation) form an orderly organic structure as soon as we have succeeded in intuiting that particular morphe and the total thisness which is conditioned by it. The thisness and its function are in this case comparable to the function of a core or nucleus [*Kern*]." Hering here evidently designates as nucleus the totality of the nature.

2. "The metaphor of the core or nucleus seems more appropriate in instances where it is a question of fundamental interrelations among parts of the object and where an understanding of the presence of the remaining parts as embodiments of the underlying μορφαί and εἴδοη (essences) becomes possible on the basis of an awareness of the one or several essential forms and essences (which animate them) and their need for complementary integration by others. Here that part of the nature [*Wesensteil*] which corresponds to the parts of the object fulfills the function of the nature core [*Wesenskern*]."[57]

§8. Act and Potency—Essential Being

The liberal use of Platonic and Aristotelian terms in the quoted passages of Hering's work calls for a confrontation of this attempt at the elaboration of a fundamental theory of the nature [*Wesenslehre*] with the earlier endeavors of *the philosophia perennis*. But before we venture such a comparison it will be necessary to throw some light on the ways in which what we have now established as *essential being* is related to *act* and *potency* in the sense in which we have previously described these two concepts.

Following the terminological usage of St. Thomas, we have up to now discovered a twofold meaning of act: that of *perfect being* (which is totally actualized only in *pure* being), and that of *actual* being (which admits of gradations, in accordance with its relative nearness to or remoteness from perfect being). By *potency* we meant—if we disregard the initially mentioned divine potency, i.e., the sway of divine *power* with respect to being—a *preliminary stage of actual being* (which itself shows again several gradations). Potency is thus not conceived as mere possible being divorced from actual being. It will be remembered that in the case of finite being we found that it is at every moment simultaneously actual and potential. And thus even in the case of actual being we must speak of an element of potentiality, because all actual being includes as a possibility an ever renewed ascent from potentiality to actuality and a rise to a higher perfection of being. We found the opposite to be true in the realm of *becoming* and *passing away,* which is as such to be understood as a constant transition from *potential* to actual being and from actual to potential being—a movement which itself has its basis or ground in a transition from not-being to being (which presupposes potentiality in a different sense).

But now we have discovered in *essential being*—in the being of essences and in the being of natures and whatnesses when they are considered apart from their actualization—a type of being that is not a *becoming* and *passing away* and that stands *in opposition to actual being.* Does *actuality* have the same meaning here that it had when we understood real being as actual in contrast with possible (potential) being?

In the realm of the life of the ego (from which we started out), *actual* being signified *presently alive being,* while *potential* being signified being that is *not yet* or *no longer alive.* The reason for this signification was said to lie in the peculiar character of the sphere of the ego. If, however, actuality or reality is not to remain confined to this particular sphere of the ego—and in everyday language the term "actual or real world" bears a closer affinity to the "external" (understood as objective) than to the "internal" world—the term actuality must needs have yet another meaning than that of vitality [*Lebendigkeit*]. Whether (and what kind of) an inner relationship exists between the former and the latter will be examined later.

As a matter of fact, we have already encountered such a different meaning of actuality: In our introductory remarks (cf. p. 1 above) we designated *efficacy* as the primary meaning of *act* and thus understood actuality as *efficacious activity* [*Wirksamkeit*]. An interrelation between this latter meaning and that of the fully alive becomes immediately apparent: The joy which is not yet alive neither impels me to act nor does it express itself externally in audible jubilation. And the same observation applies to other spheres: The not yet lit lamp gives no light, and the not yet vibrating string emits no sound. Such instances show that efficacious activity is, strictly speaking, not identical with actuality. Although efficacious activity seems to pertain to actuality, it arises effectually from a deeper ground. And it is this deeper ground which we designated as *perfect being.*

We were led to conclude that only pure, eternal being is absolutely perfect. But even in the case of finite being it makes sense to speak of perfection, since finite being is that *maximal measure* [*Hochstmass*] of being that is commensurate with a particular existent [*Seiende*]. Once this height has been attained, being burst forth, as it were, in efficacious activity, and this bursting forth or breaking out is simultaneously its unveiling or revelation. Before this summit has been reached, the corresponding *rudimentary stage of being* (i.e., *potency*) possesses only that *possibility* of *efficacious activity* [*Wirken*] which is called *capability* [*Fahigkeit*].

The present vitality represents the ontological summit of the experiential unit. What is actual and actually alive in this vitality is the ego. Objective conditions or processes (e.g., the possible or actual sounds of the string of a musical instrument)[58] are what correspond in the objective world to the experiential units. As soon as a sound "becomes audible," it reaches that height of being which corresponds to the present vitality of an experience, such as joy or grief. But what becomes actually "audible" *in the sound,* thereby revealing one summit of its being, is the string or—more precisely—the violin (for the string is a part of the violin). We say advisedly *one* summit, for the sounding of the being-sound neither represents nor exhausts the total being of the string. It can therefore, as a sounding string, be potentially and in other respects "on the summit" and can thus be called actual.

If we then understand *actuality* as *reality* and reality as *perfection of being,* "working itself out" [*sich auswirkend*] and revealing itself in *efficacious activity,* we shall have to ask further whether real being and its rudimentary stages (actual and potential being) comprise all the being there is, or whether we can and must speak of being in yet another sense. In addition, we must ask what constitutes the common denominator of being as such in either case.

In "essential being" we believe we have discovered a kind of being which is *not a rudimentary phase* of actual being and which, on the other hand, is *not efficaciously* active being [*wirksames Sein*]. There is no preliminary stage from which the essence could ascend to being. And the essence is not efficaciously active: The essence "joy" does not vivify, the essence "light" does not illuminate, the essence "sound" does not emit any sound. If this is the case, what then remains of the meaning of being? It seems to me that in essential being—the "being-on-its-summit" in the "being-perfect" in its nature—the meaning of the almost untranslatable Greek phrase τὸ τί ἦν εἶναι (to be that which was) is purely and fully realized.[59]

Whatever is essentially *is* immutably what it *was*. More exactly, in essential being the difference between present, past, and future is suspended. Whatever is essentially, does not step into existence: It is. And it is not as something which from moment to moment is wrested from nothingness; it is not in any temporal sense. But precisely because it is independent of time, it *is* also in every instant. *The being of essence and whatness reposes in itself.* This condition is most poignantly described by the German verb *wesen,* because this verb expresses even more emphatically than the Latin *esse* [*essentiae*] the intimate connection between being and nature.

Becoming and passing away, on the one hand, and *wesen,* on the other, are arrayed against one another as being in motion and being in repose. Both are being. If one of the two may be said to precede the other in point of fact, it is *wesen.* For just as all motion aims at repose, so all becoming aims at some enduring *wesen.* Both *Wesen* (nature) and *wesen* (enduring being) are required if something is to be and if something is to be.

The intimate connection between nature and being accounts for the fact that the problem of distinguishing that which is [*das Seiende*] from being [*das Sein*] presented such formidable difficulties that it was solved only relatively late in the history of philosophy. A similar difficulty was encountered in the task of distinguishing nature from being within the sphere of that which is (if this *Seiende* is nothing real). For the same reason it becomes understandable why—with seeming inconsistency—now being as such and then again the nature was designated as *act.*

St. Thomas, guided by the desire to set off with all possible clarity and stringency the first existent (God) from all other existents, separated in the case of *pure* forms their *essentia* from their *esse.* He designated being as act and stated that the nature or quid is in potency with respect to the being it receives. The question then arises of how we are to understand this being that is added to the nature quid. Our description of *wesen* as a reposing of the essence or whatness in itself (in contrast to becoming and passing away) seems to exclude a transition of the essence or whatness from notbeing to being, as appears to be implied in the phrase *to receive being.* We may legitimately speak of a reception of being when we have in mind the *actualization of the nature,* but essential being does not seem to admit of a beginning, and the nature quid does not seem to permit a separation from its essential being.

Does St. Thomas contradict this statement when he says, "We call the whatness created, for prior to possessing being it is only in the mind of the creator, and it is nothing outside the divine mind; and it is in the mind of the creator not as a creature but rather as a creative essence."[60] *(Quidditas creari dicitur: quia antequam esse habeat, nihil ist nisi forte in intellectu creantis, ubi non est creatura, sed creatrix essentia.*[61]) If we try to clarify the meaning of this sentence and keep in mind the sense in which St. Thomas used the term *whatness,* we may find in it a confirmation of our own thesis. The *whatness* [*quidditas*] is that *into which* a thing is formed; it denotes *what* the thing is, namely, "a part of the composite whole."[62] The whatness is also called the *form* of the thing. And from this form St. Thomas distinguishes the *idea* in the sense of what in the passage just quoted he terms "creative essence." "For this term *idea* seems to denote a form which is separated from the thing whose form it is." "The idea is that *in accordance with which* the thing is formed. It is thus the exemplary form in the image and likeness of which something is formed."

These exemplary forms have their being—according to the Augustinian interpretation of Plato's doctrine of ideas, which Thomas follows here—in the divine mind. Distinct from them are those *created forms* which have their being in things. And these created forms we must evidently understand as the *actualized* natures in things. The being they receive is the *actual* being which they have in things. And the "being created" is a further interpretative qualification of what is meant by *reception of being.* If this expression, "reception of being," is not to be void of meaning, *that* which receives being must possess some kind of being prior to its receiving actual being. This Thomas could admit only in the same sense in which he attributes being to the archetypal ideas, namely as a being in the divine mind. In this sense he would indeed have to admit it. For even if we assume that the image or copy lags behind the ideal archetype and that the quid of the thing is not congruent in its content with the creative idea, it is inconceivable that the creator had no foreknowledge of the image, such as it is (i.e., with its lagging behind the ideal archetype).

It is thus clear, at any rate, that essential being is distinct from and independent of the actual being of things. The further questions which must be asked concern the interrelation between essential being and the actual being of things and the nature of the relationship that exists between essential being and the eternal being of the first existent (God). To answer these questions we shall have to examine what is meant by "being in the divine mind" and whether this kind of being *describes* and *exhausts* the meaning of essential being.

§9. The Essential and Actual Being of Things

If we want to examine the interrelation between essential and objective actual being, it is necessary to remember that the kind of existence which is characterized as essential being is manifold: It comprises essences and whatnesses as well as some other modes of being which we have only touched upon in passing without actually discussing them. If we consider the noun *Wesen* (nature) and the verb *wesen* (an enduring to be) in their intimate connection, and claim for *Wesen* all that which is in the manner of essential being, we understand *Wesen* not in the restricted sense (as nature) in which we marked it off from *Wesenheit* (essence) and *Washeit* (whatness), but in a broader sense.

To gain clear insight, however, into the interrelationship that exists between essential and actual being, we must make an additional distinction. Nature quid [*Wesenswas*] such as the "joy of a child" was in its essential being prior to all time, prior to the "existence" of the world, prior to the existence of children in the world, and prior to the existence of the joy of children. But at the moment a child in the world experienced joy for the first time, at that same moment the *Wesen* (nature) and *Was* (quid), "joy of a child," was also *actual* for the first time. When this child jubilantly "leaped with joy," it was joy which *by virtue of its Wesen* revealed itself efficaciously.

Joy, then, is actual and efficacious *by virtue of its Wesen:* The *Wesen* is actual and efficacious *in joy,* in the joy *of this child,* and it is actual in a *unique and unrepeatable way.* Considered from the point of view of its essential being, the nature quid [*Wesenswas*], "joy of a child," is *one* regardless of how many times it may be actualized. There are as many correlative actual natures and whatnesses as there are joyful children. And the relationship which obtains between the *one essential quid* and the *many actual natures* and whatnesses is adequately expressed in the statement: *The same quid is actual here and there and at any place and time* where the joy of children [*Kinderfreude*] is alive. Only those who cannot rid themselves of the idea that all that which is rigidly fixed in and attached to space and time will find it difficult to understand that something can be simultaneously at different times and in different places. They mistake existence in space and time for existence as such. Just as I can transpose myself "mentally" to another place and can thus in my mind be here and there simultaneously (though with my real body I am only in this particular place), so the identical *essential quid* [*wesenhafte Was*] can be actualized here and there simultaneously. What is required thereto is, to be sure, that a *something* be here and *another something* be there in which the essential quid can be actualized.[63]

If it is correct to say the quid and the nature become actual and efficacious in individual things and that quid and nature are *that whereby* individual things are actual and efficacious, is it then necessary to ascribe to quid and nature also the *process of actualization in individual things,* i.e., the becoming actual or the transition from essential to actual being? If this were the case, essential being could be said to possess an efficacious activity which would qualify it as actual being in the full sense. For we understood actual being as a "perfection of being which works itself out and reveals itself in efficacious activity" (cf. p. 92 above). We attributed perfection of being to essences and whatnesses in the sense of a reposing in themselves. If we were now to discover that the whatness spontaneously passes over into the being of individual things, then it could be said that essential being had acquired the full meaning of *actual being.* The actuality of the whatnesses would then even be superior to that of individual things on account of the fact that the former precede the latter as their true *primordial causes* [*Ur-Sachen*] which engender the actuality of individual things. In their relation to individual things, the whatnesses would not only be πρῶται οὐσίαι, but truly *creatrices essentiae* (creative essences).

If, however, we consider the whatnesses as we have described them—as the pure *quid* of the actual nature—we are unable to discern in them such a superior actuality and such a spontaneous efficacious activity. As compared with actual things and their actual natures, the whatnesses appear rather as peculiarly pale and feeble formal structures [*Gebilde*], so that we feel more inclined to designate them as *non*-actual than as *supra*-actual entities.

§10. Universals

What we have called *whatness, nature quid,* or *essential quid* is comprised in the scholastic *universale.* According to the original meaning of the word, the *universale* denotes *unum versus alia seu unum respiciens alia* (the one as against others, or the one with respect to others).[64] And since the one can be related to another in different ways—either designating, representing, or causing it, or related to it in its being—we distinguished a *fourfold meaning* of the *universal:* universal *words,* universal *concepts,* a universal *cause* (God), and universal *natures.*

The controversies concerning the correct interpretation of universals are almost as old as philosophy itself. From the days of the Pre-Socratics there have always been *nominalists* who were willing to admit only to *universality by names* and who related the meaning of these universal names exclusively to individual things. There have always been *conceptualists* who conceded that there was a *universality of concepts* but who regarded these concepts as constructs of the mind with no corresponding reality. And there have always been *realists* who were convinced that there actually existed a *nature* which corresponded to the universal name and concept.

Realism is itself again divided into different branches. The Thomistic school brands the idea that the universal exists as such either aside from or within things as *exaggerated* or *extreme realism.* To this category of thought belongs Platonism (according to the interpretation it has received at the hands of the scholastics, who based their verdict on Aristotle), which attributes to the universal an existence apart from the mind and apart from individual things. Duns Scotus, on the other hand, taught that the universal exists in individual things. The Thomists—leaning above all on the authority of such thinkers as Aristotle, Boethius, St. Anselm, and St. Thomas—call their own point of view *moderate realism.* They make a distinction between the *matter* (or the quidditive content) of the universal concept (i.e., the nature) and the universal *form:* To the matter they ascribe a being in the individual thing, while to the form they attribute a being only in the mind.[65]

Let us ask then whether in any one of these points of view we can find an explanation of what we have called the *essential quid* [*wesenhaftes Sein*] and its essential being. It is obvious, of course, that what we had in mind was not a mere name but something objective [*etwas Sachliches*]. One might feel tempted to designate the *essential quid* as a *concept* (in contradistinction with the actual quid).[66] The concept (as a *mental structure*) is, after all, something *unreal,* although in a certain sense it is "realized" or "actualized" here and there, inasmuch as to *one and the same concept* may correspond an entire series of individual things. The concept, finally, possesses a certain amount of independence with respect to the thinking in which it is conceived: The same concept can be conceived by a large number of human beings. As compared with actual being, the concept shows the same paleness and lifelessness which we associated with essential being. If we try to grasp it apart from the word which expresses it and apart from the object which is comprehended by means of it, the concept easily vanishes from sight.[67]

It is nevertheless impossible to regard as concepts the nonactualized quid and nature (or the quid and nature apart from their actualization). Concepts are *formed:* They are "products of thought" and as such they leave a certain room for choice. Natures and whatnesses, on the other hand—as was previously stated with respect to essences—are *found* and are thus removed from our arbitrary choice.

According to Pfänder, the *content* of the concept of an object constituted by the intentional character of the concept, i.e., the concept tends toward a particular *object.* "Therefore, *neither* the intended objects themselves nor anything on or in these objects form the content of the concept."[68] By *nature* and *quid,* however, we mean to designate something which we find in objects, even if we disavow their actual being in them. We shall soon have to point out why we are nevertheless unable to accept without qualification Pfänder's description of the content of the concept.

Let us insist on the following: The essential *quid* is neither a mere name nor a mere concept. It is something *objective* (*aliquid a parte rei*). Does it fit then the point of view of *moderate realism?* We answer that we can go along with moderate realism when it distinguishes between *matter* and *form.*[69] *Matter* is the *quid* [*das Was*] of the nature, regardless of whether this quid possesses actual or essential being. We further agree with moderate realism in its contention that the quid has some being in individual things. But what about the *form* of universality to which only a *being-in-the-mind* is attributed? To answer this question we must first inquire what exactly is meant by this being-in-the-mind.

Let us listen to what St. Thomas has to say regarding this problem. "The *universale,*" he writes, "may be understood in a twofold way: It may be referred to the nature itself to which reason ascribes the meaning of universality (*intentionem universalitatis*) … ; or we may conceive of the *universale qua universale,* inasmuch as the nature itself carries the meaning of universality, i.e., inasmuch as the "animate nature" [*das Lebewesen*] or the "human being" is regarded as one in many. In this sense the Platonists asserted that the "animate nature" and the "human being" in their universality are substances. Aristotle, in the chapter under discussion, endeavors to refute this contention: He shows that the "animate being in general" or the "human in general" (*animal commune, homo communis*)[70] are not substances in the real world (*in rerum natura*). This kind of universality (*communitas*) has rather the form of the animate being or the human being, inasmuch as it is in the mind; and the mind receives into itself a form that is common to many objects by detaching it from everything that conditions individuation (*ab omnibus individuantibus*). …"[71]

"Reason," St. Thomas continues, "knows things to the extent that it is assimilated to them with respect to the *species intelligibilis* … ,[72] but the species need not be in the mind in the same manner as in the known object; for everything that is in an object is in it in the manner of that in which it is. It thus follows necessarily from the nature of reason—which differs from the nature of the known object—that the mode of cognition according to which reason acquires knowledge differs from the mode of being according to which the thing exists. *What reason knows in the thing must be the same, but reason does not know it in the same manner.*"[73]

The last sentence in our quotation is of special significance for our problem. St. Thomas speaks of *the same* that is in the thing and that is "known" by reason. The "being known" is for him identical with the "being-in-the-mind" (i.e., *in intellectu*). What the thing is, is an intelligible, i.e., something which can enter into the intellect, and once it is known, it becomes *actu intelligibile* (the *actual* object of knowledge).[74] *The same,* accordingly, has the capacity of receiving a twofold *additional* mode of being[75]: the being in the thing (i.e., *actual* being if the thing is actual) and the being in the mind. And it seems to me that this same which can have several modes of being and which can be grasped apart from these modes, is precisely what we have called the *essential quid.* If we say that it is "in the mind" or "in actual knowledge," this does not mean that it is a constitutive part of the knowing mind or of actual knowledge understood as experiential unit. In this respect the frequently enunciated principle of St. Thomas that the thing known is in the knower according to the mode and manner of the knower is open to misinterpretation.

The knowing mind is an individual actuality; the thing known, on the other hand, can as such by its being known never become such an individual actuality. It merely becomes something that is encompassed by the mind, something pertaining to the mind. The mind encompasses it and possesses it as transcendent [*ein im Jenseitiges*].[76] The thing known is not "mine" in the same sense as is the knowing. *My* knowledge is mine exclusively: It cannot simultaneously be the knowledge of another human being. But what I know—and this means not only the object of knowledge but also the known according to the manner in which it is known (e.g., in a specific conceptual formulation)—can also be known by others. My knowing it does not withdraw it from any other person's knowledge.

The "being-in-the-mind" or the "being encompassed by the mind" is added to what is comprehended in knowledge in the same way in which the being actual is added to what is actualized. "Being actual" and "being known" are different modes of being of the name nature quid [*Wesenswas*] which, actualized in *rerum natura* (in the real world), becomes an *actu intelligible in intellectu* (an actual object of knowledge in the intellect).[77]

What the mind encompasses is, as a matter of fact, identical with what it encountered in the actual nature as the nature's quid. This identical element preserves a peculiar intactness and integrity with respect to both its *actualization* and its *intellectualization*. It is what it is, regardless of whether it is actualized or not and regardless of whether it is known or not. And it is precisely this being indifferent with respect to *actualization* and *intellectualization* which we call its *own essential being.*

It is well to emphasize here that *intellectualization* implies something else in addition to "encompassing with the mind": Thought "tends toward" [*meint*] an object, and it does so through the medium of a concept with which it seeks to grasp the object. The ideally perfect concept would be congruent with the nature quid without, however, being identical with it. And the concept which is formed by an individual human being aims at this ideal concept (provided that what is aimed at is really the concept of the nature [*Wesensbegriff*] and not merely some "universal determination"), but the formed concept lags more or less behind this ideal goal, either owing to its incompleteness or owing to its inadequacy. Every human being possesses his or her own "conceptual world" which may coincide more or less not only with the *real world* but also with the *world of ideal concepts* and with the conceptual worlds of other human beings.

Because the known nature quid is the *identical* element that we find in a multiplicity of individuations, we are able to attribute to it the *meaning of universality.* For the same reason it is possible to pay *no heed* to the conditions of its individuation; this paying no heed [*das Absehen*] is implicit in the meaning of universality and is called *abstraction.*

The known nature quid is as such neither *universal* nor *individual.* It cannot be duplicated in the realm of essential being—and this it has in common with the individual. But it is *communicable* and admits of individualizations—and this distinguishes it from the individual in the full sense of the term and makes it possible to ascribe universality to it.

These last observations show clearly that our own answer to the problem of universals goes somewhat beyond the position of *moderate realism* without, however, going as far as *Platonic realism* (in the traditional interpretation).[78] We do not ascribe to the *essential quid* any being in the manner of real things. It would seem that our own point of view is closest to that of Duns Scotus.

In the realm of what we have tried to determine as *essential being*—in contradistinction to actual being, on the one hand, and to "being-in-the-mind" (in its several possible forms of being known, being thought, etc.) on the other—the *essences* [*Wesenheiten*] are the constitutive *elements* of the *composite structures* of the *whatnesses* [*Washeiten*]. These latter in turn enter into the *full quid* of things as their substantial core [*Kernbestand*]. Only through the media of the whatnesses [*Washeiten*] and natures [*Wesen*] do the essences [*Wesenheiten*] enter into a relation with the real world. The whatnesses and natures acquire reality in things as their solid substance [*Bestand*], while the full quid is actualized in things as their fluctuating substance.

If we approach this entire question from the point of view of the *natural human attitude* (which tends toward the world of real things), we gain a hold on the quid of things or on their positive meaning [*sachlichen Sinn*]. If, on the other hand, we start out retrospectively from what the mind encompasses in the processes of apperception, thought, cognition, and comprehension, the same sphere is seen as constituting the content of our *objectively oriented consciousness,* i.e., as a sphere of *intellectual meaningfulness* [*geistiger Sinn;* Husserl's *noëmatischer Sinn*]. And if we start out from an analysis of linguistic terms, the identical sphere reveals to us its *linguistic meaning* [*sprachlicher Sinn*].[79]

§11. Rejection of Some Misconceptions of Essential Being

In view of certain persistent misinterpretations which the phenomenological doctrine of essences [*Wesenslehre*] has experienced in many quarters—and also at the hands of some scholastics—it seems desirable to determine with all possible accuracy the real meaning of this doctrine, at least to the extent that we have tried to expound it up to this point, and also determine what it does *not* mean.

It was stated in the preceding pages that nothing temporal, i.e., nothing whose being is becoming and passing away from moment to moment, can exist without a supra-temporal ground. Nothing temporal can exist without a timeless *formal structure* [*Gestalt*] which regulates the particular course of the temporal sequence of events [*das Geschehen*] and is thereby actualized in time. In developing this thesis, we proceeded from that temporal sequence of events which we encounter in our own being, and we understood the timeless formal structures as the meaningful contents [*Sinngehalt*] of our experience. It was therefore implied in our statements—though we have no intention of further pursuing this line of thought—that no temporal *cognition* and no cognition of a temporally real nature [*Zeitlich-Wirklich*] is possible that is not simultaneously the recognition of a timeless meaning. It is only the recognition of such a timeless meaning that makes knowledge in the strict sense possible.

We did *not* state, on the other hand, that as human beings we are capable of acquiring knowledge of a timeless meaning independently of the temporal actualization of this meaning and independently of any sense data. To discuss this latter question, we first of all have to ask what is meant by sense data [*sinnliche Gegebenheit*] and what might be meant by sense data in instances where it is not a question of the perception of external things but of the contents of that consciousness which pertains to our very being. However, we have not discussed this question at all in our previous considerations, and have made no prejudgments about it.

When we lay claim to a *knowledge of essences* [*Wesenserkenntnis*]—understood as the grasp of a timeless meaning—as a condition of the possibility of all knowledge, we do not wish to assert that such a knowledge of essences—independent of the knowledge of temporal things—is possible for such creatures as we are (our knowledge, after all, is part of our temporal being), whose knowledge is confined to the dimension of time. It should be clear, therefore, that we do not attribute to human beings a quasi-divine knowledge.

Nor do we maintain that human beings are naturally capable of having a direct or immediate knowledge (i.e., a knowledge without the aid of our experience of the temporally real) of purely spiritual natures (such as God or the angels). This much only may be inferred from what we have pointed out: If and when we speak of "God" or of "angels" and if we connect some meaning with these names, then this meaning signifies something timeless. We do *mean* something by these names; they *signify* something; and different names mean different things. If the things which are meant are "genuine" units of meaning [*Sinneinheiten*] and not merely arbitrary products of fanciful "thinking,"[80] they must be something which we have found or discovered, some gift we have received, something which prescribes rules and laws for the formation of our concepts and for our name-giving [*Namengebung*]. Still further questions concern the where and how of what we have thus "found." But there can be no doubt that it is something that is neither temporally real nor "merely thought." And this something we call "essentially existent" [*wesenhaft Seiendes*].

Although so far we have discussed the temporal flux of life and the underlying formative units of meaning only within the sphere of our personal being, the description applies to all temporal being, i.e., to the entire world of our internal and external experience. When we speak of "things," we thereby mean something that comes into being and passes away but which in its becoming and passing embodies a timeless meaning. Accordingly, even though we distinguish in the world of our experience a fluctuating "quid" and an "essential structure" [*Wesensbau*] which rules over this flux, and even though we recognize our "experience" as "conditioned and animated" by a knowledge of essences, we do not mean to assert that we know things as they are "in themselves" [*an sich*], independent of our experience; nor do we claim that we are capable of seeing the "ultimate ground of things." But even if we should have to acknowledge that we can get hold of things only by means of "appearances"—appearances which as such are not determined by the things in themselves but by the laws of our knowing mind—the *givenness of appearances* [*Erscheinungsgegebenheit*] and the fact that the knowing mind is proportioned to the known world (i.e., the "subject-object relationship") is something which is subject to essential laws and cannot be comprehended in any other way.

The very possibility that something can "appear" to creatures who possess our intellectual constitution can be understood only from the "nature" of things and from the nature of our mind. Everything that can be said concerning this question rests on the presupposition that there is a knowledge of essences in the manner described. This by no means repudiates the contention that we have no direct or immediate access to the nature [*Wesen*] of God, of angels, and of things (maybe even to our own nature) and that our knowledge of essences is never exhaustive but always "fragmentary."[81]

But all these questions concerning the manner and extent of our knowledge and its natural objects are really not what interest us at this moment. We have inquired into the meaning of *being* and have hit upon the contraries of temporally real and essential being. At this point, however, we run into a difficulty.

§12. Essential and Eternal Being

Let us cast a backward glance upon the road we have travelled. We started out from the ineradicable fact of our own being. It revealed itself as fleeting, narrowly limited from moment to moment, and therefore inconceivable without another kind of being which, resting firmly in itself, is supremely creative and—as Lord of all being—is being itself.

We encountered something else, something which arises with in our fleeting and fluctuating being and which, after it has arisen and grown, can be seized and firmly held by us as a definite structural whole. Though risen in the flux of time, it appears now raised above this flux and timeless. The temporal flux, the experience in which the structural unit arises *within me* and *for me,* is subject to laws which determine its course and which are themselves not fluctuating and fleeting but firm and abiding. What confronts us here is a multiplicity of units of meaningful existence differing in content and marked off from one another. The realm of meaning is the foundation of the "real world" with its manifold becoming and passing structures, the world of fluctuating (simultaneously actual and potential) being. This real world has the ground of its possibility[82] in the realm of meaning.

The units of meaningful existence are *finite* inasmuch as they are "something, yet not everything." But they lack the possibility of beginning and ending in time. Does this mean that they are neither temporal nor eternal (in the sense of all-encompassing being)? Did Hedwig Conrad-Martius pronounce a premature "either/or" when she summarized the main result of her investigation on time in the following words: "Either a being exists in essential commensurability with the nought—in this case that being is *eo ipso* an eternal universal person [*Allperson*]. Or it exists in factual opposition to the nought—in this case that being (taken in its ontic isolation) is *eo ipso* in the grip of that constitutive tension which obtains between being and not-being and is thereby (in its contact with being) confined to a mere punctual [*punktuelle*] existence: It is a finite being in the specific sense of the term"?[83]

"Commensurability with the nought" means that every "possible abyss of nothingness" is "*eo ipso* ... filled" by eternal being. "This, however, denotes a direct ontological sovereignty over every possible not-being. Creation [*das Schaffen*] is the self-evident manifestation of this sovereignty in its factual efficacy."[84]

"Fleeting" being is not in possession of an existence whose very nature it *is* to be fleeting: It must receive this existence ever anew as a gift. But only he who truly possesses being and who is thus the Lord of being can present such a gift. And only a *person* can be Lord. This person, however, would not be Lord of being if anything were exempt from his ontological might [*Seinsmacht*], if without him or independent of him there could be either being or not-being. And thus also the being of the units of meaningful existence cannot subsist independently of God.

Is the being of these units of meaning then abandoned to or immersed in the flux of time? This is not possible, either, because their *meaning* proved to be the law which, reposing in itself, rules over this flux. But do these units of meaning really repose in themselves? Is the being we ascribe to them really *their* being?

If some experiential unit is actualized within me, then it is *I* who receive the gift of being, and the experiential unit is actualized by means of this gift. I do not receive this gift by virtue of the meaning informing the experiential unit, but this meaning and my subsequent formation in accordance with it are given to me simultaneously with the gift of being.

He who gives me being and simultaneously fills this being with meaning must not only be the Lord of being but also the Lord of meaning: All plenitude of meaning [*Sinnesfülle*] is contained in eternal being, and eternal being can draw the meaning with which every being is filled that is *called into existence* from no other source but from itself. Consequently, the being of essences and whatnesses cannot be conceived as independent in relation to eternal being. Within itself, eternal being molds (in a non-temporal process) those eternal forms in whose image and likeness it creates the world in time and with time. This statement sounds enigmatic and yet familiar.

"Ἐν ἀρχῇ ὁ Λόγος"—thus eternal wisdom answers the puzzling query of the philosopher. "In the beginning was the *Word,*" translate the theologians and mean thereby the eternal Word, the second person in the triune deity. But we do no violence to the words of St. John when, in line with our previous argument, we translate with Goethe's Faust: "In the beginning was *meaningful existence* [*der*

Sinn]." It is customary, after all, to understand the eternal Word in analogy to the inner word of human speech and to compare the incarnate Word with the eternal, spoken word.[85] To this we may add what eternal wisdom speaks through the mouth of the apostle Paul (Colossians 1:17): "αὐτός ἐστιν πρὸ πάντων, χαὶ τὰ πάντα ἐν αὐτῷ συνέστηχεν." ("He precedes all things, and all things subsist and cohere in him").[86]

These two texts from Scripture carry us far beyond what our searching reason has disclosed. But the philosophic meaning of the logos to which our own inquiry has advanced may perhaps help us understand the theological meaning of the Word [*Logos*] *and, conversely*, revealed truth may aid us with our philosophic difficulties.[87]

Let us try then first of all to elucidate the meaning of the two scriptural passages. The Gospel of St. John understands by *meaning* or *meaningful existence* [*Sinn*] a *divine person,* i.e., not something *unreal* but, on the contrary, *supreme reality.* And St. John adds immediately: "πάντα δἰ αὐτοῦ ἐγένετο—through him all things came into existence."[88] The same idea is reaffirmed by St. Paul, who says that "in the Logos" all things "subsist and cohere." It is thus clear that the divine Λόγος is to be understood as a *real nature* [*wirkliches Wesen*] and, according to the doctrine of the holy Trinity, as the *divine* nature. That this nature is called *meaningful existence* [*Sinn*] is explained by the fact that what is meant is the divine nature *as comprehensively known by God* [*als verstandenses*], i.e., as *content of divine knowledge* or as the "intellectually conceived meaning" [*geistiger Sinn*] of divine knowledge.

This divine knowledge may also be called *word* because it comprises the Word of God, i.e., the content of revelation, and thus carries *linguistic meaning.* Or—in a yet more fundamental sense—because it is the Father who speaks the word and who generates the word by his speaking. This meaning, however, is actual, and its essential being cannot be separated from its actual being, because the eternal being is essentially actual and because as the *first* being it is the author of all being.

The reason why the essential being of the divine nature cannot have had a beginning lies in the existential meaning of the essential being as such. But this reason can also be understood from the nature of the divine *intellect:* The actual being of the intellect is *life* and *vital intellection* [*lebendiges Verstehen*]. God, as "pure act," is immutable vitality. Intellectual life or intellection, however, is not possible without a content, without an "intellectual meaning" *[Sinn]*. And this meaning must be as eternal and immutable as the divine intellect itself.

Is it possible at all—even in a purely *intellectual* manner [*gedanklich*]—to separate the essential being of the Λόγος from its actual being, as it is possible in the case of finite natures? The doctrine of the Trinity seems to suggest such a possibility. In the Athanasian Creed, the Son is designated as *co-eternal* with the Father, but as *generated* by the Father, which means that the Son *receives* his eternal being from the Father. Now the *divine being* is *one* and can therefore not be designated as generated. What is *generated* is the *second person,* and the being which the Son receives can thus not be the essential being of the divine nature but must be its *actual being* in the second person. And because the person of the Son and his actual being is a *novum* [*etwas Neues*] with respect to the person of the Father, the second person may be said to receive the nature [*Wesen*] of the Father. This nature, however, does not receive the Father's essential being. Even the ἐν ἀρχῇ ὁ Λόγος admits of such an interpretation if we recall the meaning of ἀρχῇ in Greek philosophy. For what is meant is not a "beginning" in the sense of "the beginning of time" but rather the "first or primordial existent" [*das Ur-Seiende*]. And thus this mysterious saying acquires the following meaning: In the first existent was the *Logos* (i.e., the *primordial meaning* of the *divine nature*); in the Father was the Son; the primordial meaning was encompassed by the primordial actuality.[89] *Generation* means a positing of the nature of the new personal actuality of the Son, a positing which, to be sure, denotes not a position outside or aside from the primordial actuality [*Ur-Wirklichkeit*] of the Father.[90]

The metaphors which are used to illustrate the interrelation between the divine persons might suggest that not only an intellectual but a real separability of essential and actual being would have to be assumed. (This, however, cannot be the case, since in both instances it is a question of eternal being.) On the other hand, if the first existent is understood as existence as such—as an existent whose *nature* is *being*—not even an intellectual separation seems admissible. In this inseparability of the nature from the actual being, St. Thomas sees the distinguishing mark of the first existent by which it is set apart from every other existent. Everything finite *receives* its being (i.e., its *actual* being, according to our interpretation) as something that is added to its nature. And this is a declaration of a *real* separability of nature and actual being.

It appeared to us that essential being was intellectually (but not really) separable from the nature quid. However, if it is true that being is the nature of the first existent, then it is impossible even to conceive of the first existent without being. If being were thought absent, nothing would remain—no quid that could be conceived as a non-existent [*das Nicht-Seiende*]. It is impossible here to distinguish among quid, nature, and being. If this could be understood with all possible lucidity, such an understanding could provide a valid foundation for an "ontological proof of the existence of God," a foundation which would be more substantial and more luminous than the idea of the *ens quo nihil maius cogitari possit* (the being greater than which none can be conceived), i.e., the idea of the most perfect *ens* conceivable, which is the starting point of St. Anselm's argument.[91]

Strictly speaking, our own argument cannot be called a *proof.* When we say that God's being is his nature, that God is not conceivable without being, that God *is* necessarily—there is no question of a real *inference* but merely of a transmutation of the original idea. St. Thomas, who, as is well known, rejects the proof of St. Anselm,[92] does not deny the validity of this transmutation. He admits that the truth of the statement, "God exists" [*"Es gibt einen Gott"*] is immediately *self-evident,* because God *is* his being. "But because we do not know what God is, the statement, 'God exists,' is not immediately self-evident [*per se notum*] *for us;* God's existence must therefore be demonstrated from his effects which, in the order of nature, are later than the cause and thus less *self*-evident, but which are given to our knowledge prior to the cause and therefore more easily accessible."[93]

Undoubtedly it is not self-evident for us to think of God as "He who is" [*den Seienden*] and even less as "he whose nature is being." In the five ways of his proofs of God's existence, Thomas starting out from God's effects, leads up to that idea, and once we have grasped the idea, the necessity of the divine being follows inevitably.[94]

But the question is: Can we really *comprehend* this idea, he who is? *Si comprehendis, non est Deus* ("If you comprehend it, it is not God"), says St. Augustine. And he asks, "With what power of insight could human beings possibly comprehend God, since they do not even comprehend that power of insight with which they intend to comprehend him?"[95]

If we say that God's being is his nature, we may well associate a certain meaning with this statement, but we attain to no "exhaustive intuition" [*erfüllende Anschauung*] of what we really mean.[96] We cannot comprehend a nature which is nothing but being. We barely touch upon its meaning, and this only owing to the fact that our intellect aims beyond everything finite—and is induced by the finite itself to aim beyond it. Our intellect aims at something which comprises in itself everything finite without exhausting itself in it; no finite thing can ever saturate the human intellect, and not even the sum total of all finite things can do that. But that which could fully saturate the intellect, that the intellect cannot grasp. It withdraws itself from the intellect's view. Faith, however, promises us that we shall see it in the light of glory. But whenever we try to seize it here *in via,* we grasp only a finite likeness—a finite in which quid, nature, and actual being fall asunder.

This paradox of the human intellect—its being distended between finitude and infinity—seems to account for the peculiar fate of the ontological proof of God's existence: Its defenders and its adversaries return again and again in the history of Christian theology and philosophy.[97] Anyone who has penetrated to the idea of divine being—the first, eternal infinite, the *pure act*—cannot remain unaware of the necessity of being which is comprised in this idea. But if that person seeks to seize it in the manner in which one seizes something in the process of cognition, it recedes and no longer appears as a sufficiently strong foundation upon which to erect the edifice of a proof.

To believers who in their faith are certain of their God it seems so impossible to think of God as non-existent that they confidently undertake to convince even the *insipiens.*[98] The thinker who applies the rules of natural knowledge shrinks back again and again from the leap over the abyss. But do the *a posteriori* proofs—the inferences from created effects to an uncreated cause—fare much better? How many unbelievers, after all, have become believers on the strength of the Thomistic proofs of the existence of God? These proofs too demand a leap over an abyss: The believer leaps across lightly, the unbeliever stops this side of the precipice.

But to return to our original queries: There is no doubt that the equation of the divine being and the divine nature affirms the intellectual *inseparability of both and therewith also the inseparability in God of essential and actual being. God's essential being is actual being, and it is actual being in the highest degree,* the *pure act* [*das allerwirklichste Sein*]. But because God is for us incomprehensible either as being or as nature[99] and because we can never approach him in any other way than with the aid of finite images and *likenesses* (in which being and nature are separate), our approach will have to proceed at one time from the aspect of the nature, at another time from the aspect of being. This is why we speak of that which is in itself inseparable as if it were something that could be separated.

How is it possible, however, to reconcile this inseparability with the kind of separability that is suggested by Trinitarian theology? Can the persons and their distinct personal being be separated from the divine nature if nature and being are inseparable? As far as I can see, the only solution to this problem is to regard *the being in the three persons* as *essential being.* But in this case even the separability of nature and being and of essential and actual being in the Logos becomes a mere figure of speech. And this is hardly surprising, for how could we ever expect to speak of the greatest of all mysteries of faith otherwise than by figures of speech?

These figures of speech may not lead us to an understanding of the way in which the divine Logos is related to the *meaning* [*Sinn*] of finite natures. We found that the reason for applying the name *Logos* to the second divine Person lies in the fact that this name expresses the divine nature as known or encompassed by the divine intellect. Here we are again using figures of speech deriving from human knowledge and from the naming of finite things. We attribute to the Logos a place in the deity which corresponds to the *meaning* understood as the positive content of things and, simultaneously, as the content of our knowledge and our language in the realm of the comprehensible. This is what is meant by *analogia,* i.e., the similitude-dissimilitude relationship that exists between *Logos* and *logos,* between the eternal Word and the human word.

However, the scriptural passages to which we have referred affirm not only a relationship of similitude which makes it possible for us to "catch sight of the invisible nature of God ... as it is known through his creatures" (Romans 1:20), but they state that these creatures were *created* and *are sustained* in their existence *by the Logos*. The meaning of these passages is further explained in a specific version of John 1:3–4, which was quite common in the Middle Ages. Whereas today we read, *Sine ipso factum est nihil, quod factum est* ("without him [the Logos] nothing was made that was made"), the medieval version stated, *Quod factum est, in ipso vita erat* ("what was made was life in him"). This seems equivalent to saying that all created things have their being, their actual being, in the divine Logos. And this latter interpretation of the scriptural passage is evidently closely related to the Augustinian conception of the ideas as "creative essences of the divine intellect."

One of the doctrinal decisions of the church states how the being of things in the divine Logos must *not* be interpreted[100]: Created things are not in God as the parts are in the whole, and the actual being of things is not the divine being but their own being and as such distinct from the divine being. If this is the case, what does it mean when we say that they "subsist and stand together" in the Logos?

Let us first try to understand this standing together (*con-stare*) in the Logos. The verb evidently denotes the unity of all that which is [*alles Seienden*]. Our experience shows us things as self-contained units, separated from one another but nevertheless depending on each other in such a way that we are led to surmise a universal causal connection between all real things. But this causal connection appears to us as something external. We try to explore the structure of the object world, we discover that it is the nature of things which determines in what causal relations they enter. The causal relations, on the other hand, reveal to us something of the nature of things.[101] In both instances we recognize that the nature is something which is deeper and which underlies the causal relations. The *universal causal interrelations*, therefore, do *not* yet signify a *universal correlation of meaning* [*Sinnzusammenhang*]. Moreover, the sum total of all real things does not yet encompass the totality of all finite existents. To this totality belong also many "unreal" [*unwirklich*] things, such as numbers, geometrical forms and figures, concepts, and so on. All of these are encompassed by the unity of the Logos. The interconnection in which "everything" subsists in the Logos must be conceived as the *unity of a totality of meaningful existence* [*Sinn-Ganzes*].

The coherence of our own life is perhaps best suited to illustrate what we mean. In ordinary speech we distinguish what is "planned" or "well-designed"—and this appears simultaneously as "meaningful" and "intelligible"—from what is merely "accidental" and which seems by itself meaningless and unintelligible. For example, I intend to pursue certain studies and to this end select a university which promises to provide some special incentive in my chosen field. Here we have a meaningful and intelligible coherence of motives and circumstances. But the fact that in that particular university town I make the acquaintance of a person who is "accidentally" matriculated at the same institution and that one day I "accidentally" become engaged in talking on questions regarding an outlook on life—this seems at first glance hardly a thoroughly intelligible coherence of events. And yet when, many years later, I reflect upon my life, it becomes clear to me that this particular conversation turned out to be of decisive significance for my life, that it was perhaps more "essential" than all my studies so that now I am inclined to think that this encounter may have been "precisely the reason" why I "had to go" to that town. In other words, what did not lie in *my* plan lay in *God's* plan. And the more often such things happen to me the more lively becomes in me the conviction of my faith that—from God's point of view—nothing is *accidental,* that my entire life, even in the most minute details, was pre-designed in the plans of divine providence and is thus for the all-seeing eye of God a perfect coherence of meaning [*Sinnzusammenhang*]. Once I begin to realize this, my heart rejoices in anticipation of the light of glory in whose sheen this coherence of meaning will be fully unveiled to me.

What has been said applies, however, not only to the individual human life but to the life of the entire human race and beyond that to all existents. Their *standing together* in the Logos is a totality of meaning [*Sinn-Ganzes*]. It may be compared to a perfect work of art in which every single feature in its *particular* place and in pure and strict proportionality fits the total pattern and contributes to the harmony of the whole. What we grasp of the "meaning of things," what "enters into our understanding," is in relation to that totality of meaning like some forlorn sounds of a symphony which are carried a long distance by the wind until they finally reach our ear.

In theological language the coherence of meaning of all existents in the Logos is called the *divine plan of creation* [*Schöpfungsplan*] (*ars divina*).[102] Its actualization is the history of the universe from its very beginnings. But *behind* this plan, *behind* the "artistic design" of creation, stands (without being separated from it ontologically) the eternal plenitude of divine being and divine life.

The foregoing already contains the answer to this further question: "How is the *con-stare* of things, their *subsisting* or *being alive* in the Logos, to be understood? It has been pointed out that it cannot be understood as their actual being. Otherwise it would be meaningless to speak of a "plan" and its "actualization." The name *Logos* seems to indicate that what is meant might be the *essential being* of things, that the meaning of things (which we previously characterized as "not-become" [*ungeworden*]) might have its habitat in the divine Logos. That which from eternity subsists as a component part [*Glied*] of the divine plan of creation is "imparted" [*mitgeteilt*] to things as their meaning and is actualized in them. It pertains, we have seen, to essential being that it can "impart" that which subsists in this manner so that it may be actualized in a multitude of individual things.

However, it seems that the essential being as we have encountered it in things does not exhaustively describe the being of things in the Logos. If it did, this being would hardly merit being called *life,* nor would it make sense to speak of *creative essences.* Moreover, we recall that in God essential and actual being are inseparable and the Gospel of St. John says of the Logos that *through* him everything was made. What is actual in things is not pre-designed in the Logos as something "non-actual," but it is actual and efficacious in him, and the actualization in things is the effect of this efficacious activity. It is in this way that we must understand the designation of the *ideas* as creative archetypes in the divine intellect.

But this answer does not solve all the riddles which confront us. According to our earlier description of essential being, we seem to be forced to conclude that what was from eternity in God in "archetypal actuality" and what becomes actual in things in time is "the same." However, in things it is possible to separate the quid and the nature from their actualization. In things it is possible to separate their essential from their actual being. On the other hand, in God such a separation is impossible.

Closely connected with this difficulty is another one to which we have also previously referred concerning the unity of the divine being and the multiplicity of the *ideas.* We compared the coherence [*Zusammenhang*] of all existents in the Logos with a perfectly composed and proportioned work of art, with an organically integrated manifold that is perfectly unified and coherent. Is this compatible with the simplicity of the divine nature (which is identical with the divine being)?

St. Thomas attempts to resolve this difficulty by saying that the one and simple divine nature is the cause of all things and that multiplicity is introduced by its being related to the manifold of things: "The divine intellect, which causes all things, generates everything in the image of its nature. Its nature, therefore, is the idea of things. ... However, created things are not a perfect likeness of the divine nature. The divine intellect therefore does not conceive the nature as the idea of things in an absolute sense but relative to the particular thing that is to be created in the image of the divine nature, i.e., relative to the greater or lesser proximity of the copy to the archetypal divine nature. However, different things copy the divine nature in different ways—each of them in its own way—for it is an inherent characteristic of each of them to differ from the others. If then the different relations that exist between the divine nature and individual things are intellectually compounded in the divine nature, the latter is the idea of each individual thing. And since there is a multitude of relations, there must necessarily be a multitude of ideas. From the point of view of the divine nature, there is only one nature for all things, but there is multiplicity on the part of the differing relations of the creatures to the divine nature."[103]

The unity and multiplicity of the divine nature is not curtailed by the fact that the divine intellect encompasses the manifold of all existents *qua* manifold, for this encompassing is done *uno intuitu,* i.e., with one single glance from eternity—immutably. This glance encompasses everything "that was, is, and will be."[104] It encompasses *quid* and *nature* as actualized in things, but also every possible that never becomes actual and—enclosing both—everything potential and actual, irrespective of their potential or actual being, the pure quid or the *meaning,* understood as an all-embracing manifold of meaningful existents [*Sinn-Mannigfaltigkeit*]. In this manifold of meaningful existents every individual existent has its place—finite things as self-contained and delimited meaningful units and real things as "pre-conceived divine thoughts."

We thus arrive at a twofold meaning of the being of the finite in the eternal:

1. all *meaningful existents* are encompassed by the divine intellect; and
2. all existents have their archetypal-causal ground in the divine nature.[105]

This consideration also suggests a possibility of resolving a difficulty to which we have alluded on several occasions. It appears possible now to regard objects as *created* which are neither actual nor do they become but which nevertheless are not mere concepts. We have spoken several times of *ideal objects* and have included them in the sphere of *essential being*. Geometrical forms and figures—point, line, triangle, circle, and their *individual parts*, such as a section of a straight line with a definite length or a triangle with definite sides and angles[106]—are not *actual*. Their "actualizations," their corners, edges, and the surfaces of actual bodies, are really not actualizations but "imperfect likenesses" of or approximations to the pure geometrical forms. It is not possible to designate them as "merely mentally conceived" [*bloss gedacht*] if by mentally conceived we mean arbitrarily constructed in the mind. I am able to fashion mentally the concept of a "triangular circle," but such a concept is self-contradictory: It cannot be perceptually realized. Nevertheless, such a concept has a "being in the mind" [*gedankliches Sein*]. But I cannot "perceptually think" a triangular circle (i.e., I cannot visualize it with my mind's eye), because "there is no such thing." This not only means that it does not occur in reality but that it is impossible in itself, because it lacks that being which is the property of geometrical forms as such. Nor is this being-in-the-mind the *being* of a nature in the previously determined sense of nature of *something*. The nature requires an object in which it can be: Its being is dependent being [*unselbständiges Sein*]. The individual triangle, on the other hand, is itself an object: It needs no other for its particular being. And each triangle has its nature which, though not "actualized" in it, has "attained geometrical existence" in it. This "attainment," however, denotes no temporal process of becoming.

Geometrical existence has no temporal beginning. When we "construe" a triangle, this does not mean that we "produce" or "create" it. Rather, we search for that form or structure in which are found conjoined those parts and elements which are known to us *analytically*. The *construction* is a faithful *copying* [*Nachbilden*] in some real material or a *construing* of the form in space. In this mentally guided procedure we are indeed "free," because the geometrical form can assume different positions. Its position at a definite place is thus something which (with respect to the particular form) can have a beginning and end. We are able "to move it about in space," to change its position. As seen from the perspective of the geometrical form, this is something which can happen to it, something to which it submits. Nonetheless, this is not *real* movement nor a *real* happening: What we do with the triangle is a mental activity.

This suggests the idea that the specific position does not pertain to the geometrical form at all but is merely our own "mental addendum." We have already pointed out that the position pertains to the geometrical form in a different way than do structure and size. But since two equal triangles are distinguished only by their respective positions, the further question arises of whether perhaps even the individual being [*das Einzelsein*] of geometrical forms is merely such a "mental addendum." In this case the ultimately determined object of which geometrical existence is predicated would be the triangle of definite length of sides and definite size of angles; its individual being in one or another position or in several positions simultaneously would then be something "merely mentally conceived." However, this evidently is not true. The six equal faces which confine a cube are *six* in number: Each of them has its own geometrical existence, and we cannot say that it is merely a question of *one* mentally multiplied by six. It is quite legitimate, on the other hand, to state that "the same" face (according to its essential being) occurs six times on the cube. To be sure, the question is whether this "occurrence" can be called individual existence [*Einzeldasein*] in the true sense. As a matter of fact, the cube with its six equilateral faces can in its turn be "conceived" multiplied in space.

In the structure of a geometrical body a definite position pertains to its lateral planes, and in the structure of geometrical planes the same is true of the confining lines. But to bodies—and also to their structures if they are independently conceived and not conceived as structural parts of bodies—pertains no definite but just "some" position in space. To a body pertains the *possibility* of being in a certain definite position. If this position is merely a "mental addendum" to it, its individual being is likewise "merely mentally conceived." On the other hand, if there is a natural object in space in which the geometrical form is "actualized," we speak of a genuine (not "merely mentally conceived") individualization. However, in addition, we must distinguish between the individual being of the geometrical form and the actual being of the object in which the individuality stands out in relief. Geometrical objects are, after all, only imperfect actualizations of geometrical forms, and the *pure forms* must be extracted [*herausgeholt*] from the objects by means of a special kind of intuitive perception.

There is no need to pursue the individual being of geometrical forms any further. The important thing in our context is to gain some understanding of the specific being of *ideal objects*—as examples of which we used geometrical forms—in contradistinction to actual being, on the one hand, and to merely mentally conceived being [*Gedachtsein*], on the other. These ideal structures can be "actualized" or "mentally conceived" in time but, aside from that, they have an independent, timeless being: As structures that are definitely determined in themselves, they do not *become*. Does it then still mean anything when we call them "created" or designate them as "actualizations of the creative ideas of God"?

To answer this latter question, we must keep in mind the twofold meaning that attaches to the being of *ideas of God*. In one sense these ideas are the quid of all that which is, as it is encompassed by the divine intellect in the organically conjoined manifold of meaningful existence [*Sinn-Mannigfaltigkeit*]. In this manifold the ideas too have their definite place. Their own being is not, with respect to that being *in the Logos*, some later derivative. Rather, they are encompassed in their own being by the Logos; and their own being—in contradistinction to the beginning and fluctuating real being of things—is timeless and changeless being. The ideas as *primordial cause* [*Ursache*] of all finite existents[107] are the one, simple divine nature to which everything finite is related as its image and likeness [*Abbildverhältnis*]. This image and likeness relationship must be assumed for all finite existents, the timeless as well as the temporal. Inasmuch as the "archetype" [*Urbild*] is the first and the "images" are derivatives which received the meaning of their existence from their image and likeness relationship, all finite existents must be regarded as having been placed into their particularized being *by* that simple, archetypal first, and in this sense we call them *created.*[108]

From here some light is thrown on the intimate connection between Logos and creation. The Logos occupies a peculiar intermediate position. It shows, as it were, a double countenance, the one mirroring the one and simple divine nature, the other mirroring the manifold of finite existents. The Logos is the divine nature (as object of divine knowledge), and it is the manifold of meaningful existence of created things as encompassed by the divine intellect and as reflecting the divine nature in images and likenesses.

We now can see a way which may lead us to an understanding of the twofold visible revelation of the *Logos: In the incarnate Word* (the God-Man) and *in the created universe.* And one further step allows us to grasp the idea of the inseparable oneness of the Logos become flesh and the Logos "become world" in the unity of head and body—*one* Christ, as we encounter it in the theology of St. Paul and in Duns Scotus's doctrine of Christ's kingship.[109] These problems, however, are of a purely theological nature and thus fall outside the frame of our discussion.

The truths of faith to which we have referred—the dogma of the Trinity and the doctrine of the creation of all finite existents by the divine Logos[110]—were to enlighten us concerning the difficulties into which the purely philosophic inquiry into the problem of being have led us. On the one hand—starting out from finite existents and their being—we have encountered a first existent who has to be one and simple: quid, nature and being in one. On the other—starting out from the *quid* of finite existents—we have arrived at a manifold of ultimate elements of the nature. It is impossible to arrive at an understanding of the first existent by a purely philosophic investigation, because no fully comprehensive view of the *first existent* is within reach of natural reason. While theological considerations cannot lead us to a purely philosophical solution of our philosophic difficulties (i.e., they cannot lead us to an inescapably compelling "insight"), they nevertheless point to a possibility of a solution beyond the frontiers of philosophy (but not beyond the proximate sphere of philosophic understanding). And, conversely, the philosophic exploration of being will aid us in disclosing the meaning of the truths of faith.

IV.

Essentia (*Ousia, Wesen*)—Substance—Form and Matter

§1. *Essentia* [*Wesen*], Being [*Sein*], and Existents [*Seiendes*] According to *De ente et essentia*. Different Concepts of Being [*Sein*] and Object [*Gegenstand*] (States-of-Affairs [*Sachverhalte*], Privations and Negations, "Objects" in the Narrower Sense of the Term)

The domain of essential being which we have tried to approach and interpret from the phenomenological point of view presents a large area for intensive investigations. The insight we have gained so far amounts to little more than what is revealed at first glance. But even this limited view, and the distinctions which it taught us to make, necessitates (for the sake of further illumination) a confrontation with the *doctrine of being* and *essence* [*Seins- und Wesenslehre*] of traditional *metaphysics.*

We recall our previous discussion of St. Thomas's *opusculum, De ente es essentia,* which made us recognize potency and act as modes of being (cf. pp. 32ff. above.) We stated on that occasion that the Latin *essentia* [*Wesen*] is a translation of the Aristotelian *ousia,* it is our next immediate task to compare the meaning of the German *Wesen* (as we have defined it) with the meaning of St. Thomas's *essentia* and Aristotle's *ousia.*

The first chapter of *De ente et essentia* is dedicated to the clarification of the meaning of *ens* and *essentia.* Aristotle uses the term ὄν (= *ens* = *Seiendes,* that which is) in a dual sense.[1] St. Thomas adopts this usage for his point of departure.

> "In one sense," he writes, "the ὄν designates what is divided into the ten categories. In another sense it denotes the truth of propositions. The difference between the two meanings is this: If ὄν is used in the second sense, it may designate everything of which an affirmative predication can be made, even if thereby nothing is posited that subsists by itself [*nihil in re*].[2] In this sense even privations and negations are said to be existing [*seiend*]. For we say

> that an affirmation is opposed to its negation [*negatio*], and that blindness [*a privatio*] is (i.e., exists) in the eye. If on the other hand, ὄν is used in the first sense, it can designate only an existent that is posited as subsisting by itself [*in re*]. In this first sense, then, blindness and the like are not existing beings [*sind nichts Seiendes*]."[3]

In the foregoing passage St. Thomas discusses *that which is* [*das Seiende*] with a view to determining *essentia* as that which is. But there still attaches a dual meaning to the term "existing" [*seiend*]: It denotes, first, that being which is predicated in the *copula,* i.e., in the "is" of the judgment. This is what is meant (in our text) by the "truth of propositions." "The rose is red" and "This rose is not yellow" are two true propositions. Both express an objectively known factual relationship, and the "is" is the linguistic form in which the affirmation of this state-of-affairs [*Sachverhalt*] is clothed.[4]

The state-of-affairs [*Sachverhalt*] which is affirmed in the "is" of the judgment represents again a specific kind of being—that kind of being, namely, which pertains to states-of-affairs. These latter are forms of a specific organic structure: They are founded on *objects* in that more narrowly restricted sense of the term to which we have referred previously. Such *Sachverhalte* are what is *known* (in a definitely limited sense of the word *to know*), what is *affirmed* in judgment, and what is (by the judgment) *expressed* in a proposition.[5] What is enclosed in compound form in the objects is unfolded in the structural organization of the *Sachverhalte:* essence and being (the act of existing) become manifest in their separateness and their intimate connection simultaneously, the essence. The essence unfolds itself in its essential characteristics. It reveals that which can be inferred from it, and so on.

Although the *Sachverhalte* have their counterpoise in a mind whose knowledge proceeds intermittently step by step, they are certainly not formed by the mind. What is "formed" by the mind is the judgment. It is "con-formed" to the *Sachverhalt.*[6] The judgment—like all thinking—is "free": I am free to judge or not to judge, but if I want to judge "correctly," I must not proceed arbitrarily.

The organization of the *Sachverhalte* and the step-by-step process of thinking follow the exactions of the structure of the objective world. The being of the *Sachverhalte is* thus no "mere being thought": It has *a fundamentum in re* (a foundation in reality). But because it needs such a "foundation," it is "derived being." The existence of the *Sachverhalte,* therefore, is not of a kind that would permit an immediate access to the *essentia.*

There is, however, still another meaning of *being* which St. Thomas wants to have excluded from the determination of *essentia:* that being, namely, which is attributed even to *privations* and *negations.* In the judgment, "The person is blind," the word "blind" expresses something which this person *lacks.* Instead of denoting the capacity to see, the word denotes here the absence of this capacity. It is thus at any rate that the matter appears to St. Thomas. Strictly speaking, there might be some doubt whether "blindness" really means nothing more than the absence of the capacity to see. (We may, for example, remind ourselves that a "blind person" represents a particular type of human being.) But let us disregard this question for the moment. What really matters here is the adequate understanding of the specific mode of the being of *privation* [*Mangel*], and it is certainly possible to interpret "blindness" as a "lack" of the "capacity to see."

The capacity to see is something which pertains to seeing human beings: It inheres in them; it has its foundation in their nature; it is something that is *real* in them and part of their real being. (But it is a preliminary stage [*Vorstufe*] of actual being—mere *potency*—whenever and as long as they do not actually see, i.e., exercise the faculty.) The lack of the capacity, on the other hand, is nothing real in the blind person despite the fact that, owing to this lack, the person is specifically determined in his or her individuality.

One kind of being undoubtedly pertains to "blindness": The word as such has a very definite meaning, and inherent in this meaning is the same kind of being that is associated with each and every meaning. But is the blindness of this particular human being not something more?

If in my imagination I picture a blind person, this person's blindness (as well as the entire person) is "merely intellectually conceived" [*bloss gedacht*]. If I picture a seeing person as blind, the blindness is merely "conceptually added" [*zugedacht*] to the seeing person, and it is, moreover, at variance with that person's "real" manner of being [*Beschaffenheit*]. In contradistinction to both these instances, it makes sense to speak of real blindness. Blindness, to be sure, is not as "real" as is the faculty of seeing: It cannot efficiently operate in a corresponding action (i.e., in seeing) and in this way achieve its ontic perfection [*Seinsvollendung*]. It is not a *potency* that can be *actualized.* But blindness nevertheless has a *fundamentum in re,* namely, the actual manner of being of the "blind person" as distinct from the manner of being of the "person with normal visual perception" [*der Normalsinnige*].

Privations are found only in the realm of real being [*wirkliches Sein*], i.e., in the realm of becoming and passing away, and only the supreme reality is without any privations. Only where there are faculties which can efficiently operate in real action is a corresponding lack or "lapse" [*Ausfall*] possible. What is perfect and immutable can suffer no *privation. Negations,* on the other hand, are possible also in the case of *ideal objects.* In the sentence, "This triangle is not equilateral," the expression "not equilateral" has a definite restricted meaning. However, beyond this it has its *fundamentum in re* in the factual determinations of a triangle, and these determinations exclude what has been "conceptually added" [*zugedacht*].

The being of the *Sachverhalte,* the being of privations, and the being of negations differ among themselves, and these three kinds of being in turn differ from mere being thought as well as from the being of meaning as such. But what the three modes of being (*Sachverhalte,* privations, and negations) have in common is the *fundamentum in re,* i.e., the real foundation of their being [*Seinsgrundlage*]. And St. Thomas has in mind this *fundamentum in re* when he speaks of being (ὄν) in the first sense and marks it off from other modes of being. Following Averroës, he says, "Being in the first sense of the term is what signifies the essence of a thing."[7] In the second sense, however, "we attribute being to some things which do not have an essence, as is manifest in the case of privations."

The foregoing two sentences strongly suggest what is meant by *that which is* [*das Seiende*] and by essence or *nature.* Can we reconcile these sentences with the previously mentioned *principle of the nature* which stated that every object has its specific nature or essence (cf. p. 70 above)? Or should we not rather have to say that, according to this principle, privations and negations too have their specific essences? To be able to answer this question, we must remind ourselves that privations and negations are objects only in that widest sense in which anything may be called an object of which something can be predicated. They are not objects in that narrower sense in which we call an object something which itself presupposes other objects.

Furthermore, it should be kept in mind that the term *essence* too is used with different semantic connotations. If, for example, we were to assert that it pertains to the nature or essence of privation to have no reality [*nichts Wirkliches*] in things, then *nature* [*Wesen*] would be merely another expression for *meaning* [*Sinn*]. And the implication would be that the "nature of privation" can certainly not be a real nature.

Finally, it should be observed that the meaning *of* privation is a property of privation *as such,* while the *individual* or *particular* privation is determined in its meaning, its *quiddity* (or essence) by that which in this particular case "is" lacking, i.e., by that being [*Seiende*] which is the opposite of privation and which is something that has its own real nature.

Let us turn then with St. Thomas to *that* kind of being [*Seiende*] which—in its meaning—has an *essence* or *nature,* so that we may understand what he means by *Wesen* (*essentia*). "And because ... being in this sense is divided into the ten categories, the essence must be something that is common to all those natures by which the manifold of existents is placed [*collocatur*] in different genera and species. Thus, for example, being human is the essence of the nature of humanity, and so it is with other things."[8]

With the foregoing sentence, however, we have become entangled in the meshes of Aristotelian concepts, and our understanding cannot progress until we have gained sufficient clarity concerning these concepts. The *categories, natures* [*Naturen*], *genera,* and *species* are to elucidate for us the meaning of *Wesen* [*essentia*]. This they can only do if and when their meaning has become clear and familiar to us.

§2. An Attempt to Clarify the Concept of *Ousia*

1. Categories as Modes of Being and Genera of Beings [Seiende]*;* Substance *and* Accident

That which is [*das Seiende*], we have learned, is divided into the ten *categories.* "All that," says Aristotle, "which is signified by the forms of predication is said to exist by itself. The several ways of

predication are indicative of the several modes of being."[9] This means that to the different forms of predication correspond different modes of being and different *genera* of beings. And in the *Metaphysics* the *categories* primarily denote modes of being and genera of beings. They are listed by Aristotle immediately following the passage quoted as follows:

- τί ἐστι (*what* something is)
- ποιόν (being constituted in such and such a manner or having such and such a *quality*)
- ποσόν (being of such and such size or number, i.e., *quantity*)
- πρός τι (being related to something, i.e., *relation*)
- ποιεῖν ἢ πάσχειν (doing and suffering, i.e., *action* and *passion*)
- ποῦ (where, i.e., spatial determination whereby place and relative situation must be distinguished)
- πότε (when, i.e., temporal determination)

Although these are all the categories mentioned in this particular passage, the category e1xein (to behave in such and such a way, i.e., attitudinal condition)—which is discussed later—must be included.

Everything that is signified by these terms is designated by Aristotle as *being* [*Seiendes*]. However, it is no accident that he names first the τί ἐστι. It occupies a preeminent position with respect to every other mode of being, and it is thus a presupposition for the other categories. The τί ἐστι denotes *what* the thing *is,* and this category therefore designates the thing in a more authentic sense than the statements that it has such and such a quality, that it is such and such size or number, that it is related to another, and that it is active or passive. For this reason the being of all the other categories is designated as *accidens* (i.e., as something that is *superadded attributively*). What "underlies" the accidents [*das Zugrundeliegende*], on the other hand, is called in Latin *substantia*[10] (from *sub-stare* and *subsistere*), while Aristotle uses the term *ousia.* The latter is linguistically derived from the stem ὄν and signifies *that which is or exists in a preeminent sense* [*Seiendes in vorzüglichem Sinn*]. And, as previously mentioned, it is this word, *ousia,* which St. Thomas translates by *essentia.*

Does this mean then that we arrive at the equation: *ousia* = substance = *essentia* = *Wesen?* This would no doubt be too hasty a conclusion. St. Thomas claims that the being to which an essence pertains is that particular kind which is divided into the ten categories. He thus has in mind not only substances but all the different kinds of accidents. All of these (not substances alone) have an essence.

2. πρώτη *and* δευτέρα Ousia

Moreover, if we confine ourselves for the time being to the simpler and narrower explanations of Aristotle's *doctrine of the categories,*[11] the meanings of both τί and *ousia* are ambiguous. What ultimately underlies the accidents may in one sense be understood as that of which something is predicated but which itself is predicated of no other thing. However, it also signifies that which is not in another but in which others are. *Ousia* in the first sense is *that* which *is* and which is determined as *what* it is, i.e., the individual thing of which is predicated *what* it is, *how* it is, and so on, but which itself is no longer predicated of anything else. *Ousia* thus understood is τόδε τι (a "this-something-there" or "this-there," which can be pointed out and identified in its individuality). This Aristotle calls πρώτη *ousia* (that which is first in being: *erstes Seiendes*).

If, on the other hand, the categories are understood as forms or figures of predication, then the πρώτη *ousia* (since it is not predicated) can have no place among them. In this case the τι denotes that which responds to the question *what* the thing is, i.e., the determination of the thing according to its genus or species. It is then not τόδε τι, but ποιόν τι (a what of such and such a quality or constitution). And this Aristotle calls δευτέρα *ousia* (that which is second in being: *zweites Seiendes).* He terms it "second" because it is predicated of something else, namely, of the πρώτη *ousia.* And yet, says Aristotle, it is *ousia,* i.e., being in a preeminent sense, because it underlies all other predications and because it is not in another ("humanity" is not in "this particular person").[12]

Aristotle points out some additional distinctive marks which the δευτέρα *ousia* has in common with the πρώτη *ousia* and by virtue of which it holds a privileged position in comparison with the other categories: It is without an opposite, it admits of accretion or diminution (something can be more of less *ousia*—as a species is more *ousia* than a genus—but it is impossible to be more or less "human being" or more or less "animal"); and the δευτέρα *ousia* has the further peculiar characteristic of being capable of receiving into itself opposite qualities. (It can, for example, be or become white and black, large and small.)

On the basis of the above explanation, it appears no longer possible indiscriminately to translate *ousia* by *essentia,* because if we mean by *essentia* the "nature [*Wesen*] of a thing," it certainly does not signify the thing itself (i.e., the πρώτη *ousia*). Nor does it seem appropriate to render *ousia* universally by *substance* and to speak of *first* and *second substances* (as is customary in German [and English] translations of Aristotle). If these terms are used, the meaning (still to be specified) which we associate with *substance* is lost and the highly significant close interconnection between *ousia* and ὄν is obscured. For this reason we shall avoid for the time being the term *substance* and shall—as long as we have not sufficiently clarified the issue to permit the employment of an unequivocal terminology—continue to speak of *ousia* or use a paraphrase that fits the respective context.

3. A Discussion of Ousia *on the Basis of Aristotle's* Metaphysics

The traditional terminology and the simple distinction between first and second substances find their explanation in the close adherence to the texts in which the doctrine of categories is elaborated and in which the conception of *ousia* as the ultimate *underlying* principle [*das letzte Zugrundeliegende*] is almost exclusively emphasized. But for the structure of a genuine ontology [*Seinslehre*] it is essential that we do not lose sight of the close connection that exists between *ousia* and ὄν. It is this connection in which Aristotle is especially interested in the discussions of the *Metaphysics.* As we stated earlier [cf. p. 3 above], the well-known sentence, "The question asked at all times and still unanswered, namely, 'What is that which is?', is identical with the question, 'What is *ousia*?'"[13] appears to us as a kind of *leitmotif* of the entire work. And the explanations which Aristotle offers in the discussion of the doctrine of the categories do not suffice to clarify this complex problem.

Aristotle himself made ever repeated attempts to set forth conclusively what *ousia* really means. In most of the respective passages he distinguishes several meanings of the word. Some of them he uses in an exclusive sense, while others he employs side by side or alternatingly.

He speaks of *ousia* in the case of simple bodies, such as earth, fire, water, and the like, as well as in a general sense with reference to bodies and the things composed of them, such as animals, physico-spiritual beings,[14] and their parts. The name *ousia* is applied to all of these because they are not predicated of some underlying principle ὑποκείμενον, subject) but are rather themselves the subjects of every predication.

In a different sense Aristotle speaks of *ousia* with reference to that which in the mode of a cause is immanent in things of this kind (i.e., things which are not predicated of some substrate), as the soul, for example, causally inheres in the animal nature. The name *ousia* is applied furthermore to the immanent parts of things of this kind—parts which delimit them and mark them out as this thing-there or these things-there (i.e., as individuals). The destruction of the parts entails the destruction of the whole. Thus, as some say, a solid is destroyed by the destruction of its confining planes, and the plane is destroyed by the destruction of its confining lines. To others, number appears to be of this nature. For, they say, as soon as number is destroyed, nothing remains, and thus all things are delimited in their existence by number. And, finally, "to be that which was and still is" [τὸ τί ἦν εἶναι]—the conceptual formula of which is the definition—is also called the *ousia* of each particular thing.

Thus we now see clearly that the word *ousia* is used in a twofold sense: (1) it signifies the ultimate substrate [*das letzte Zugrundeliegende*] which is no longer predicated of anything else; (2) it signifies a separate, individual this-there *[Diesda;* τόδε τι ὂν καὶ χωριστόν]; and this latter is the form [μορφή] of each thing or its idea [*eidos*].[15]

It is rather surprising that in the final summary statements of the *Metaphysics* only a twofold meaning of *ousia* is mentioned, while in the earlier passages many more shades of meaning were listed. It was presumably Aristotle's intention to arrive at the relatively simple distinctions of the *doctrine of the categories*. He obviously includes in the concept of the "ultimate substrate" or "subject" [ὑποκείμενον] everything that a *sensorially perceived individual thing* [*sinnenfälliges Einzelding*] is or everything which pertains to it as an independently separate part (i.e., simple and composite bodies, animals, *demons* [*Dämonen*] as well as the parts into which such beings may be split by physical division). To all this he opposes the *Platonic idea,* which is conceived in this context as the idea of the individual thing, an idea endowed with a quality of independent being that separates it from the thing whose idea this quality is. The fact that no more mention is made of the "immanent causes inherent in things" may perhaps be explained by assuming that Aristotle considers these causes as the real *ousiai* in individual things. And if there is no longer any reference to the previously enumerated geometrical forms and to numbers, the reason for this omission may be that Aristotle includes these among the "ideas."[16]

It is no less surprising to find in the summary conclusions a similar omission of what is grasped in the definition of a thing. Are we to assume that what Aristotle designates as τὸ τί ἦν εἶναι is likewise included among the ideas? We gather from many passages that the philosopher regarded only the *universal* as conceptually comprehensible and definable. In the passage under discussion, on the other hand, the idea is explicitly designated as a "this-there." The explanation therefore suggests itself that the idea—even if many individual things pertain to it—must itself be regarded as a "this-there."[17] If everything that is not an individual thing and is nonetheless named *ousia* is to be classed as πρώτη *ousia,* it is obvious that much will have to be included that must also be *ousia,* but in a different sense. We propose to seek and hope to find further enlightenment on this question in the pages of the *Metaphysics.*

Immediately following the above quoted sentence (p. 128), which referred to the problem of that which is and which stated that this question was identical with the one concerning *ousia,* Aristotle resumes his inquiry and continues as follows:

> It seems that *ousia* is most manifestly revealed in bodies. This is why we speak of *ousia* not only in the case of animals and plants and their parts but also when we deal with (inanimate) natural bodies [φυσικὰ σώματα], such as fire, water, earth, and the like, and in the case of all things that are either parts or composites of these (either of some of their number or of all of them), such as

> the firmament and its parts: stars, the moon, and the sun. Whether these are the only *ousiai* or whether there are others, or whether none of these are *ousiai* and we must therefore look for others: All this must be carefully considered.
>
> Some hold that the limits of bodies or solids—surface, line, point, and unit—are *ousiai*, and more so than bodies or solids. Some, furthermore, believe that there is nothing of the nature of *ousia* aside from sensible things, while others think that there are eternal existents which are real in a higher degree. Thus Plato designates the ideas (*eidos*) and the objects of mathematics as two different kinds of *ousiai*, and he distinguishes from them sensible bodies as a third kind. And Speusippos adds still more *ousiai*: He starts with the one and assumes primordial principles [*Urgrunde;* ἀρχαί] for all *ousiai*, a different one for each of them: one for numbers, another for spatial quanta, and yet another for the soul. ... Again, some say that ideas and numbers have the same nature [φύσις], and that other things are attached to them in a temporal sequence: lines and planes, and finally the *ousiai* of the heavens and of sensible bodies.
>
> It is necessary then to inquire which of these several statements are correct and which are false, and what *ousiai* there are, and whether or not there are any besides the sensible ones, and in what manner the latter exist, and whether there is an *ousia* that exists separately[18] (and, if so, when and how) or whether there are no *ousiai* aside from sensible ones, All these problems must be thoroughly explored, but first of all the nature of *ousia* must be determined.[19]

So far Aristotle has merely set down the different doctrinal tenets. He has enumerated everything to which the name *ousia* has been applied, and in doing this he has given a more detailed account than in the previously cited passage. He is now ready to begin the actual investigation: "The word *ousia* is used in at least a fourfold sense, for the *ousia* of each thing seems to be (1) a 'to be that which was and still is' [τὸ τί ἦν εἶναι], (2) the universal [τὸ καθόλου], (3) the genus [γένος], and (4) the substratum [ὑποκείμενον]."

Regarding this fourth meaning the previous statement is once more repeated, namely, that it is not predicated of anything else, while everything else is predicated of it. To determine the nature of this fourth meaning is thus the first object of the inquiry:

For that which primarily underlies a thing seems to be *ousia* in a preeminent sense. And in one sense matter [ὕλη] is called such a primary substratum, in another sense form [μορφή] and in a third sense the compound of matter and form. As matter I designate, for instance, the bronze; as form I designate the pattern of the image (to be embodied in the bronze [σχῆμα τῆς ἰδέας]); and by the compound (of matter and form) I mean the completed statue. If therefore the formative principle [*eidos*] is prior to the matter, and if it is (or has being) in a higher degree than matter, it will for the same reason be prior also to the compound of matter and form.[20]

Aristotle himself finds the definition of *ousia* as the ultimate substratum inadequate:

For one thing, this definition itself is not clear, and, moreover, in this view matter becomes *ousia.* For if matter is not *ousia,* I confess that I am unable to say what else it could be. When everything else is taken away, nothing but matter seems to remain. For all the other properties of bodies—what they suffer, what they do, what they are capable of producing [πάτη, ποιήματα, δυνάμεις = passions, actions, potencies); their length, breadth, and depth—are determinations of extension [ποσότης = quantity] and not *ousias.* (That which is of such and such a size or such and such in number is not an *ousia.*) That rather is *ousia* to which these properties pertain as to their primary substratum. If therefore length and breadth and depth are taken away, we see that there is nothing left unless it be something that receives its determination from that material substratum. And so it is evident that to those who view the problem in this manner matter must appear as the one and only *ousia.*

I call matter that which in itself is neither identified with a particular quid [*Was*], nor with a certain size or quantity, nor with any of the other categories by which that which is [*das Seiende*] is determined. For there is something of which each of these are predicated and whose being differs from all those forms of categorization [καταγορίαι]. While all these others are predicated of *ousiai, ousia* is predicated of matter. The ultimate substratum is thus neither a particular quid nor a particular quantity nor anything else that is positively determined. On the other hand, it is equally impossible to say that the ultimate

substratum is the negation of all these determinations, for negations too belong to it only in the manner of adherent consequence [κατὰ συμβεβηκός].[21]

If this point of view were adopted, it would of necessity follow that matter is *ousia*. But this is impossible, for it seems to pertain essentially to the nature of *ousia* to subsist independently [χωριστόν = separately] and to be a this-there [τόδε τι]. Therefore, the formative principle [*eidos*] and the compound of matter and form—rather than matter—would seem to be *ousia*. Now that kind of *ousia* which is a compound of matter and form we need not consider here, for it comes into being later, and its nature is obvious. And the nature of matter, too, is manifest in some measure. It is thus the third kind of *ousia* which presents the most formidable difficulties and which for this reason we must now make the object of our inquiry. And since it is generally admitted that *ousias* are found among the objects of sense, it is with these that we must begin our investigations.[22]

4. *The Basic Meaning of* Ousia. *The Sense Object as* πρώτη Ousia; *Its Composition of Form and Matter*

The section of Aristotle's *Metaphysics* from which we have just quoted is, it seems, very enlightening if we want to understand the ultimate aim of Aristotle's inquiry. He calls *ousia* an *existent to which being pertains in a preeminent sense.* That *natural objects* [*Naturdinge*], as we know them from sense experience, possess such a preeminence of being appears to Aristotle as something that is generally admitted and therefore hardly needs to be discussed. (Some remarks concerning the nature of this preeminence are found in the *doctrine of the categories,* and some further discussion of this problem will follow.[23]) Things and objects are, however, not of simple but of complex structure, and if they are *ousiai* they must owe it—so it would seem—to that of which they are composed. What is predicated of a thing in judgments is always something that accrues to it "additively" [*etwas ihm "Zukommendes"*] (this need not always be something "accidental" or "fortuitous").[24] There must be something else, on the other hand, to which the accrument accrues [*dem das Zukommende zukommt*], and there must finally be an *ultimate fundamentum* or *substratum* [*letzte Grundlage*] which no longer pertains to anything else and which can therefore no longer be predicated of anything else. This ultimate substratum is ὕλη (*materia,* matter).

Thus it would seem that we have at last arrived at that in the thing which is *ousia* in the true sense. But then—quite abruptly—comes the surprising turn: "This is impossible!" Pure matter, we learn, is something completely undetermined; we cannot tell at all *what* it is, and therefore it *is* not at all if we conceive of it without any determinations. And yet *ousia* is said to exist in a preeminent sense. And now we also learn wherein its preeminence consists: It is a χωριστόν (something separate) and a τόδε τι (a this-there); it exists *by itself, in separation* from all other existents, and as a *this-there* it is an *individuum,* i.e., a single, undivided being that possesses something of its own which it shares with no other existent.

The sense object as a whole has this preeminent distinction: As a *self-contained unit* and as something that is distinct from everything else it stands out from the context of nature in which our sense perception and sense experience encounter it. It is therefore unquestionably *ousia* and can—if we proceed from that which is first in our experience—be designated as πρώτη *ousia,* i.e., as the first *independently* or *autonomously* existing being [*das selbst-eigene Seiende*].

However, since the sense object as a whole is not a simple and primordial existent but is composed of different structural parts, it seems that these parts—one of them, or several, or all of them—must impart to it this ontological preeminence.

This preeminence cannot lie in that which merely *accrues* or *falls to* the thing (i.e., what is predicated of it in the form of the accidental categories); nor can it lie in the *matter* which is determined by certain qualities, but which is *nothing* and is not without some such determination.

What then is left when both matter and the "determinations" of matter are taken away? It seemed to us at first that in this case nothing at all remains; there must, however, be something else that has a share in the structural whole of the thing, and this *third* principle must be the one which imparts to the thing hold and ground and makes it the kind of being that it is.

Aristotle calls this third principle μορφή (form) or *eidos* (formal archetype, *Urbild*). Up to this point he had used both terms as if they signified the same. Actually, however, linked intimately with these two terms is the major problem to which the philosopher returns again and again in his *Metaphysics* and which is generally regarded as the main issue of the controversy between Plato and his most illustrious disciple.

Eidos is the name applied to the Platonic *idea,*[25] and—according to the exposition given in the *Metaphysics*—the Platonists saw in the *ideas* the πρώτη *ousia,* i.e., the first independently or autonomously [selbst-eigene] existing beings. But it is precisely here where Aristotle encounters indissoluble difficulties. A thing must certainly have a *form,* i.e., something which is distinct from matter and from everything that accrues to it from the outside, something that determines its being. But can this be something that is separate from the thing? Must it not rather be something in the thing itself—its *inner form,* its πρώτη?

The investigation has thus shown that the inquiry into the nature of that which is inevitably demands an analysis of the doctrine of ideas. Aristotle had set out using the objects of sense as the subject matter of his investigation because they were generally recognized as *ousiai* and because they are what is best known to us.[26] What immediately follows in the text is, however, not an interpretive analysis of the object of sense. Aristotle rather reverts to the fourfold meaning of *ousia* from which he had originally started out (cf. p. 131 above). Of these four meanings, only that of the substratum has so far been discussed. The latter was recognized as *ousia* in the sense of being the entire compound of form and matter, while matter by itself was excluded. Form was made the principal object of the investigation. But now the analysis turns to that meaning of *ousia* which was listed as the first among the four, namely, the τὸ τί ἦν εἶναι (to be that which was and still is). Evidently, this is done in order to come closer to an understanding of the nature of form.

5. τὸ τί ἦν εἶναι *and the Nature or Essence* [Wesen]

Logically considered, "the τὸ τί ἦν εἶναι of each thing is what it is said to be in itself; for being-yourself [*Du-sein*] is not your being-liberally-educated [*Gebildet-sein*], since it is not part of your very nature that you are liberally educated."[27] One's *being formed by education* [μουσικός] is something that "accrues" to one or "is added" to one [*etwas Hinzukommendes*], but before one was so "formed" [*gebildet*] one was already something that did not "accrue" to one—something *that* one will *always be* as long as one remains "oneself." We are therefore induced to regard as the nature or essence [*Wesen*] of a thing that *which* makes it what it is—that which a thing is *enduringly in itself.*[28]

This latter consideration makes it understandable why *ousia* has been rendered in Latin by *essentia.* But it becomes immediately manifest that this rendition denotes a meaning entirely different from that of *substance.* Every something—not only the thing itself, but its qualities and everything else that can be predicated of it—has a nature or essence in the sense of an enduring determination of its quid [*Was*]. This nature or essence *of a thing* must, however, be distinct from "everything that additively accrues to it," because the peculiar ontological preeminence of the thing must have its foundation in its nature or essence. That therefore which distinguishes the thing as such from every nothing—its being thing or thingness [*das Dingsein*]—must be found in each and every thing as its ineradicable property [*unaufhebbar eigenes*]. And because this is something that is found *in each and every thing,* it can be *universalized conceptually* and enters into the *definition* of the thing. This is why Aristotle regards the τὸ τί ἦν εἶναι as what is expressed in the thing's definition.[29]

To each thing there must belong, on the other hand, *its own* prior being a thing or thingness because otherwise it could not become, by virtue of its *Dingsein,* an *ousia* in the sense of an independent and authentic existent. Its being a thing, moreover, cannot constitute its entire nature, for the nature of a thing must be determined not only by what it has in common with others but also by what is specifically *its own.* The being-a-thing is therefore *only one*—albeit fundamental—*characteristic of the thing's nature or essence* [*Wesenszug*]. And thus we once again encounter that peculiar structure of the nature as we have learned to know it previously: a *composite structural whole* in which a number of essential features are integrally joined together. And if this nature "has a core or nucleus" [*"mit Kern" ist*], the entire structure obeys a definite morphological law. It *can be grasped as a universal* [*allgemeines Wesen;* universal nature] and is nonetheless the nature of *this* particular thing and as such a *this-there* (an individual nature). Finally, its nature is the nature *of this thing* and as such dependent on others [*unselbständig*].

If the τὸ τί ἦν εἶναι were to signify *only* what can be grasped as a universal (such as the being *human* [*das* Mensch*sein*] of Socrates, but not his being Socrates [*das* Sokrates*sein*]),[30] it would evidently not coincide with the individual nature. This distinction might possibly indicate the difference between τὸ τί ἦν εἶναι and μορφή (cf. n. 34 on p. 569 below). It is not our intention, however, to explore at this time the question of how these two concepts are related to each other. Rather, we would like to call attention to another substantial difficulty.

We are searching for that in the thing to which it owes its ontological preeminence as *ousia*, and this ontological preeminence was thought to lie in the fact that it is an independent and authentic existent. The question then arises whether this ontological preeminence may possibly be traced back to something which itself possesses no such prerogative. Can the being-*ousia* of a thing be grounded in something which is not *ousia* in the same sense? With this question, however, the entire object of our inquiry seems to have become problematical.

6. Matter, Form, and the Individual Thing [ὕλη, μορφή, *and* τόδε τί]

We turn once more to the passage where Aristotle distinguishes among the several meanings of *ousia* (cf. p. 131 above.) After having previously enumerated the different meanings traditionally associated with *ousia*, the philosopher inquires here into the actual semantic implications of the term. The fourth meaning on which he comments—the ὑποκείμενον—is manifestly opposed to the three others. The word ὑποκείμενον itself carries a threefold meaning: It signifies ὕλη (matter), μορφή (form), and the compound of matter and form, i.e., the τόδε τί (the individual thing). Evidently, matter, form, and the individual thing (as a whole) have something in common which is related to the meaning of *ousia* considered as an independent and authentic existent. Neither matter nor form, however, is independent (χωριστόν), but only the thing (the compound) as a whole is independent. On the other hand, both matter and form are τόδε τί (a this-there) and as such unique (neither matter as such nor form as such is unique, but the matter and form of this particular thing are unique). And for this reason one might be tempted to associate with these constituent parts of the thing (matter and form) that ontological preeminence to which it owes the name *ousia.*

In contradistinction to the ὑπολείμενον, the other three meanings of *ousia* are evidently held to be truly different. In other words, although they too signify an existent that possesses an ontological preeminence, this prerogative can by no means consist in their being χωριστόν and τόδε τί. It will thus perhaps be possible to understand πρώτη and δευτέρα *ousia* as two species of existents, each of them distinguished by a different kind of ontological preeminence.

7. Nature (Essence), Universal, and Genus [τὸ τί ἦν εἶναι, καθόλου, γένος]

We are now facing the task of trying to gain an understanding of the meaning of τὸ τί ἦν εἶναι, καθόλου, and γένος, so that we can ascertain whether each of these means something different and whether these terms are perhaps interrelated in a similar way as are ὕλη, μορφή, and τόδε τί.

It appeared to us that the τὸ τί ἦν εἶναι signified the nature or essence of the thing—not the individual, but the universal nature or essence (as, for example, the being human [*das Menschsein*] of this human being).[31] The much disputed linguistic meaning of the strange word formation τὸ τί ἦν εἶναι may also prove illuminating. Aristotle used the expression τὸ ἀγαθῷ εἶναι to designate goodness [*Güte*] in contradistinction to the good [*das Gute*] or what is good.[32] Goodness is what makes every good thing good. Using Platonic terminology, we might feel inclined to say that goodness is the idea of the good. This phrasing, however, is not permissible, since, as we know, what makes a good thing good is for Aristotle not separated from the thing, but in the thing itself. The term "goodness"—if we mean by it the "essence"[33]—is therefore not quite appropriate.

It seems to me that the word εἶναι indicates that what is meant is the *being-good* [*Gutsein*] which is a property of every good thing: and the being-*itself* [Eigen*sein*] of the thing is expressed in the dative form ἀγαθῷ. If we conceive of ἀγαθόν as signifying some definite action, ἀγαθόν εἶναι denotes neither the being of this action as such nor the being of goodness as such, but the being good of the action or its essential goodness. Although the ἀγαθόν εἶναι does not express the essence in its entirety, it does express one essential characteristic.

In the expression τὸ τί ἦν εἶναι the general term τί ἦν corresponds to ἀγαθῷ. In the case of each individual thing, the answer to the question τί ἐστι? (What is it?) must be inserted in place of τί ἦν. Accordingly, τὸ τί ἦν εἶναι would have to be understood as what makes a thing what it is, its *whatness* [*Wassein*] or its *essence* [*Wesen*], but only inasmuch as this essence is universally comprehensible and is found in all individual things of the same species.[34]

Some difficulties have also been encountered in the attempt to determine why we read in the text τί ἦν (that which was) and not τί ἐστι (that which is). And again different interpretations have been offered. Personally, I give preference to an interpretation which is in essential agreement with our own distinction between the *full quid* [*volles Was*] and the *nature quid* or the *quid of the essence* [*Wesenswas*] (cf. Chapt. III, §3).

Among the determinations of *what* a thing is there are some which belong to it only temporarily and accidentally and which are therefore subject to change. The nature or essence of a thing, on the other hand, is its *enduring* whatness [*Wassein*]. It is that which belongs to the thing inwardly—independent of external influences—and which endures in every change that is brought about by external influences. And ἦν expresses this enduring Wassein.[35] The thing "is" what it "was" because its nature or essence is lifted out of the stream of time.

Our brief linguistic consideration seems to have confirmed that τὸ τί ἦν εἶναι must be understood as the universal *nature* or *essence*, and we shall use this basic meaning in the following discussion. From here we may perhaps find access to an understanding of the interrelation that exists between τὸ τί ἦν εἶναι and καθόλου.

Aristotle writes:

> Ὅλον (a whole) means (1) something which lacks none of those parts on account of which it is said to be naturally a whole, and

> (2) something which comprises the things which it contains in such a way that they form a unity. But this happens in a twofold manner: Either each individual (of the things comprised) is a unified one, or all the individual things (which are comprised) form a unified one. For what is predicated καθόλου (universally; of the whole) ... is καθόλου (universal) because it comprises many things by being predicated of each of them, and because each of them is one single thing by itself. In this way, for example, person, horse, and, god are comprised in one class, because all of these are living beings.[36]

καθόλου, therefore, is the *concept* which comprises what belongs to its "extension" [*Umfang*]. It is, furthermore, the objective content which is grasped by the "universal" concept. In the example cited by Aristotle something is named which in turn comprises universal unities and an extension of individual things only by virtue of these universal unities. But no matter whether we consider the more comprehensive or the less comprehensive *universal,* the difference between this καθόλου and the τὸ τί ἦν εἶναι is obvious. "Human being" and "living thing" are not the same as "*to be* a human being" and "*to be* a living thing." Only the latter ("to be" a human being and "to be" a living thing) belong to this particular human being and aid in the formation of the τόδε τί. The concept "human being" is no part of this particular human being.

Our next and final question concerns the γένος (genus). Aristotle distinguishes a threefold meaning of this term.[37] It denotes:

1. The continued *generation* of living beings of the same species (γένεσις; *generatio*);
2. The entire *progeny* that descends from one generator or procreator [*Erzeuger*];
3. It is used in the sense in which the plane is called the genus of plane figures and a solid is called the genus of solids. For every spatial form is either a such and such determined plane or a such and such determined solid, but plane and solid are what underlie these determinations (τὸ ὑποκεί μενον ταῖς διαφοραῖς).

Finally, the term is also used in the sense in which we call γένος that which is the first constituent element in concepts—that which is defined as the quid of something (ὃ λέγεται ἐν τῷ τί ἐστι)—and in the sense in which the qualities (ποιόται) are said to be the differentiae (διαφορά) of concepts.[38] In this latter sense the genus is also called *matter* (ὕλη). "For that to which pertains the differentia or quality is the substratum (ὑποκείμενον) which we call *matter*."[39]

It is evident that only the last two meanings of γένος can be related to καθόλου and τὸ τί ἦν εἶναι, namely, (1) the *universal* concept which is differentiated by special *characteristics* and (2) the existent as such [*das Seiende*] which is intellectually grasped in universal concepts and their differentiae. What is subsequently said concerning generic differences must likewise be referred to genus in this twofold sense.

Aristotle continues:

> Those things are called differing in genus whose primary substratum is different, so that the one cannot be reduced to the other nor can both be reduced to the same (i.e., to an underlying third thing). Thus, form (*eidos*) and matter (ὕλη) are different in genus, and the same is true of all things which are said to belong to different categorical forms (σχῆμα κατηγορίας)[40] of that which is [*des Seienden*]. For some of the things which are said to be signify a "what" (τί ἐστι), while other things signify a "thus" (ποιόν τι) in accordance with the distinctions we have previously noted. These categorical forms cannot be reduced one to another, nor can they be reduced to some common substratum.[41]

If we meet here again with the term *matter* (which we encountered earlier in the course of our discussion of the objects of sense), its meaning is obviously different: It is used in an analogical sense. Concepts and the *universal* that is grasped in them consist not of matter as is the case with physical bodies.[42] The only common element in both instances is an indetermination (which needs and can be determined). In the case of genera, however, there is no question of a complete indetermination: Being distinctly marked off from each other, they are also determined to a certain extent, but their being determined leaves room for further determination.

The *categories* are designated in this context as genera of that which is [*des Seienden*], but they are only mentioned to serve as examples and are thus not to be regarded as the only genera of that which is. Generally speaking, we may consider the *genera as the basic formal structures of that which is* [*Grundgestaltungen des Seienden*] which as such can neither be reduced to each other nor derived from each other nor traced back to some common (third) substratum. This formulation suggests the conclusion that there are other formal structures of that which is which admit of such a reduction or derivation. They are the *species* (εἴδη) or what Aristotle calls *parts of the genus.*[43] Conversely, "the genus is also called part of the species,"[44] because the concept of the genus is contained in the concept of the species. "Those things are said to differ in species which belong to the same genus and are not subordinated one to the other; further, those which differ within the same genus; and those which have a contrary in the *ousia.* And the contraries (ἐναντία), too, differ in species. ..."[45]

Different in species are also those things which belong to the ultimate underlying species [*infima species*] of a genus and which differ in their concepts: Thus man and horse are undivided in genus, but their conceptual definitions are different; and finally those things which—though belonging to the same *ousia*—have a difference.[46]

Human being [*Mensch*] and animal [*Tier*] offer an example of things which within the same genus—living being—are not subordinated one to the other and show a difference (rational—irrational). *Ousia* may here be rendered by *thing.* In a thing, different colors are contraries which the thing cannot have simultaneously. For example, color and shape [*Gestalt*] are different but not mutually exclusive. Human being and horse are said to be conceptually differing *ultimate* species. This suggests—as does the possibility of super-ordination and sub-ordination [*Über- und Unterordung*]—several stages of universality within a genus.

Genera are "divided" into species. Every basic formation of existents is divided into separate subordinate formations: the thing into its different species, the qualities of the thing into different species of qualities. This division proceeds until the ultimate species are reached which no longer have any subordinated species. But even these ultimate species have something "below themselves" or "encompass" something, namely, the *individual existent* of the species, the individual thing or the individual thingly quality—*this* person, for example, or the brown color of this person's hair.

Our analysis has now advanced far enough to make us understand the way in which καθόλου and γένος are related to one another. Both signify a universal, in the dual sense of the conceptually universal and of the existent that is conceptually grasped. But καθόλου is more universal than γένος: It signifies *everything* that is "encompassed" [*umfasst*] by something, including the species of every degree as well as the differentiae of the species, whereas γένος signifies only the highest and most general basic formations.

The way is now open to determine also the relationship which exists between these two species of universality and the τὸ τί ἦν εἶναι. Aristotle understood this relationship as what is expressed in the definition. Not every concept is a definition, but only "what is related to something primary; and the primary is what is not predicated in the way one thing is predicated of another. τὸ τί ἦν εἶναι, then, is found nowhere except in the different *species of the genera,* i.e., in species exclusively; for these latter are not predicated in the sense of participation and received determination (πάθος) or in the sense of accident (συμβεβηκός) … ."[47] All this is expressed in a meaningful concept, but there is no question of either a definition or a τὸ τί ἦν εἶναι.

> But perhaps definition—like "what a thing is" (τὸ τί ἐστι)—has several meanings; for "what a thing is" signifies in one sense the *ousia* and the τόδε τί and in another sense it signifies all the forms of that which is (i.e., the categories), such as quantity, quality, and the like. For just as "it is" pertains to all things, yet not in the same way, but to some in a primary and to others in a secondary, derivative sense, so also what a thing is pertains absolutely only to the *ousia,* but in a certain sense to the other categories as well: Even in the case of a "qualitative determination" (ποιόν) we may ask what it is, so that quality too is a quid (what the thing is), but not in an absolute sense. …[48]

The τὸ τί ἦν εἶναι is attributed only to the *ousia* in an absolute and primary sense and to the other categories merely derivatively and with certain modifications. There can be no question, moreover, of a mere ambiguity of terms: The different meanings bear rather a definite inner relation to each other.[49]

From the statement that the τὸ τί ἦν εἶναι is that which is apprehended in the definition, we concluded that it must be a *universal* and that it is not the concept but rather that which is "seized" in the concept [*das "begriffene"*]. We may now add that the term comprises less than καθόλου, which denotes every kind of universal. It is limited to the *species*—not to all the species of that which is, but exclusively to the several species of the genus *thing* (i.e., *ousia* in the previously indicated sense of an independent and authentic existent or a *substance*). The τὸ τί ἦν εἶναι is not the thing itself and thus not πρώτη *ousia;* rather, it is *what determines the species of the thing.* Likewise, the mutually non-derivable genera of things indicate what the thing is. τὸ τί ἦν εἶναι denotes then the lowest kind of specific determination, a determination which is no longer divisible into species but is merely further individuated or "particularized" [*vereinzelt*]. It is the ultimate [*das Letzte*] that can be conceptually apprehended and by which the individual thing can be grasped.

The τὸ τί ἦν εἶναι—by which the thing is determined as what it is and by which it can be conceptually determined—is not πρώτη *ousia.* It is distinguished from the thing by its universality and by its lack of independence [*Unselbständigkeit*]. *By* virtue of these two characteristics, it ranges alongside with καθόλου and γένος. If the name *ousia* is applied to all concepts, it must—as previously indicated—be used in a sense differing from that in which the individual thing is called *ousia.* This is why—in order to distinguish it from the πρώτη *ousia*—it must be termed δευτέρα *ousia.* And the *specific* ontological preeminence of the δευτέρα *ousia* must be sought precisely in this difference from the πρώτη *ousia,* i.e., in the fact that the δευτέρα *ousia* is a *universal* and as such something that can be *communicated to others* [*ein Mitteilbares*] and can *encompass others* [*ein Umfassendes*]. Thus the genus can be communicated to those species which "partake" of the genus; and by way of the species it can be "communicated" to those individual things which partake of the species. The communicable [*das Mitteilbare*] comprises everything into which it enters by way of participation [*als ihm Mitgeteiltes*]. It is, on the other hand—in a different sense—"encompassed" by that into which it enters, by virtue of the fact that the communicable really enters into species and individual things and partakes of their structures.[50]

8. Different Meanings of Ousia *and Their Common Semantic Basis (Existence, Thingly Reality, Quidditive Determination, Essential Being as Different* Ontological Perfections*)*

The time has come to apply to πρώτη *ousia* and δευτέρα *ousia* what was previously said concerning equivocal signification and semantic inter-relation (cf. pp. 143f. above). It would seem that πρώτη and δευτέρα *ousia* must have something in common that provides an explanation for the fact that both are termed *ousia.* We attempted to express this common semantic basis [*Sinnbestand*] by saying that *ousia* in the sense in which it encompasses the meaning of both terms is an existent which possesses an ontological preeminence [*Seinsvorzug*]. We must ask now whether this preeminence is not that common element which distinguishes both from something which is in turn distinct from them.

Several other factors must be taken into consideration. When we distinguished the concept from *that which is* [*das Seiende*], which is seized by means of the concept, we thereby already attributed to that which is a certain preeminence, since some sort of *is* or *being* also pertains to concepts. However, the being of concepts is not being in a primordial sense but rather is a derivative, "second-hand" being.

Concepts are formed: They are patterned after something which is and whose being is independent of the concept. The being of concepts is tied to what stands over against them [*das Gegenüber*], i.e., the objective world and those knowing intellects which take hold of the world of objects step by step in the process of discursive reasoning. The being of concepts is thus a twice conditioned and twice dependent being. Compared with this conditioned and dependent being of the concepts, that which is (after which the concepts are "patterned" [*"nachgebildet"*] or to which they are "con-formed" [*"angemessen"*]) possesses the ontological prerogative of *primordiality* [*Ursprünglichkeit*] and *independence* [*Unabhängigkeit*].

We might be tempted to say that concepts are *unreal,* whereas the existents which are seized by concepts *are real.* However, according to what we have previously stated concerning *essential* and *real* being, the term *real* being must be reserved for a special sphere of primary and independent being, i.e., for that world in which there is real and efficient activity [*Wirken und Wirksamkeit*]. Numbers, pure shapes and figures, pure colors, and pure sounds are not concepts. Rather, they are the primary substrate upon which the concepts of number, shape, etc. are formed. They are not "real" in the same way as is the world of those things which move and change, which come into being and pass away and are themselves causes of such changes. Nor do I propose to have the term *Dasein* (being-there = existence) applied to this *primordial [ursprünglich]* being. The term *Dasein,* as is well known, has been used with very different connotations in some recent philosophic discussions. While for Martin Heidegger *Dasein* signifies exclusively the being of the human self [*das ichafte Sein*],[51] Hedwig Conrad-Martius means by it real being (which includes the being of the human self.)[52] And it can easily be seen why existence [Da*sein*] may be attributed to the real world (and in a very special way to the human self) with greater justification than to those other structures which do not inevitably arrest our attention but must be sought out and drawn forth from a certain concealment.

But even the terms *primordial* [*ursprünglich*] and *self-dependent* [*selbständig*], which seemed to fit the particular kind of being that we call existence, are unsatisfactory as definitive designations. For, while this kind of being is *ursprünglich* and *selbständig* in relation to concepts, it is—as will presently be shown—not *ursprünglich* and *selbständig* in any absolute sense. The term *existence,* therefore seems to be more fitting than any of the others as a designation for this kind of being because, on the one hand, it is common in everyday language to call "non-existent" what is "merely intellectually conceived" [*bloss gedacht*] and on the other, to attribute existence not only to real things but, for example, also to speak of *mathematical existence.*

We thus call existence that mode of being which is distinguished as more primordial over against what is only being thought [*Gedachtsein*]. And in *what exists* [*das Existierende*] we get hold of the meaning of *ousia,* a meaning which we recognize as the common semantic foundation [*Sinnbestand*] in both the πρώτη and δευτέρα *ousia.* The existent [*das Existierende*] is that to which the concepts are con-formed [*angemessen*] and in which they have their formal "measure" [*Mass*].

But within the realm of what exists there are again found differences of being and corresponding differences of existence. The dual meaning of the *categories*—their being simultaneously forms of predication and forms of being—corresponds to the distinction between (logical) being and existence. As *logical forms*, the categories divide conceptual structures into different classes. As *ontological forms*, they divide what exists into classes. The strictest dividing line in each of these spheres is the one which separates what *accrues* to an existent (what is predicated of an "object") from that existent to which the accruement accrues [*dem das Zukommende zukommt*] or from that existent which "underlies" the "object" of which something is "predicated."

What accrues [*zukommt*] to an existent is dependent in relation to the substrate, while the substrate itself is primordial and independent in a novel sense. What accrues [*das Zukommende*] (the shape, color, size, etc. of the thing), *exists*. However, it exists *not in itself*, but *in another*, viz., in the "substratum." What accrues owes its being to the substrate. It "partakes" of the substrate. And this is why, according to Aristotle, the ποιόν, ποσόν, etc. are "in some way" but not "absolutely" [*schlechthin*]. These accidents, too, possess their quids ("what they are"), but not in the same manner and degree as the substrate. The substrate, in turn, which exists in itself in a truly authentic sense and which authentically possesses its *what*, was said to be τόδε τί, i.e., the individual thing.

The individual thing was also called πρώτη *ousia*. The term τί ἐστι, in contradistinction to τόδε τί, was used to designate "*what* a thing is," i.e., not the thing itself, but its what. This what, however, may again have several significations: It may denote genus or species, down to that ultimate universally conceivable particularization which determines the τὸ τί ἦν εἶναι. Thus understood, the τί no longer denotes the πρώτη *ousia*, but the δευτέρα *ousia*. It must be asked, however, whether *everything* that may be understood as *quidditive determination* [*Wasbestimmtheit*] can be said to be δευτέρα *ousia* and as such endowed with some ontological preeminence in the realm of existents and over against "what accrues to them" [*gegenüber dem Zukommenden*].

The πρώτη *ousia* was characterized as an ultimate substrate on account of the fact that it is the subject of predications, while it cannot itself be predicated of anything else. Now, *what* a thing is is no ultimate substrate in this sense.[53] Thus it can be predicated of Socrates that he is "a human being" [*ein Mensch*] and that he is "a living being" [*ein Lebewesen*]. We can also say [in German] that he is [a] "human being" [*Mensch*] or "living being" [*Lebewesen*]. Although these two predications differ in meaning, they both predicate of an individual thing its determination according to genus and species. Is there a difference then between this kind of predication and one which refers to some "accruing element," such as the statement that Socrates was "great" or wise or that he lived in Athens?

When we say that Socrates was "a human being," we include him in the totality of those who make up the *species* "human being." The *species* in this instance is conceived as a *whole,* the *parts* of which are those individuals who belong to the species. In the same way the genus living being can be conceived as the whole that is composed of all the species of living beings and therewith of all individual living beings. Thus understood, species and genus are "all-encompassing" or "universal" [*umfassend-allgemein*]. But Socrates—and each and every human being—is "a human being" because he is "human," i.e., because "human being" is precisely what he is. However, in the being-human is included his living-beingness [*das Lebewesensein*]; the latter is *part* of what he is.

We do not intend at this point to raise the question whether the being human [*das Menschsein*]—wherein Aristotle sees the τὸ τί ἦν εἶναι of the individual human being—exhaustively describes what every individual human being is or whether the ultimate essential determination [*Wesensbestimmung*] does not rather lie in the being Socrates [*Sokratessein*]. We must first elaborate more distinctly the difference between "being human" [*Menschsein*] and "being a human being" [*ein Mensch sein*].

An individual person is "a human being" [*ein Mensch*] because the being-human *belongs* to that person's nature or essence [*Wesen*].[54] That the person is "a human being" (i.e., this particular human being) does not belong to that person's nature or essence but rather has its foundation in his or her nature or essence or follows from it. And that there exists the *genus human being* [*die Gattung*

Mensch]—understood as the *whole* whose *parts* are individual human beings—follows from the fact that "human being" is a *universal* in the sense of "what can be imparted" [*im Sinne des Mitteilbaren*]. And from the impartibility [*Mitteilbarkeit*] of what is denoted by the term "human being" follows the possibility of a plurality or multiplicity of individual beings all of whom "are *Mensch*," and therewith the possibility of a totality of "all that which is *Mensch*."

We have previously designated such structures as "human being," "living being," and the like as *essential quids* or as *units of meaningful existence* [*Sinneinheiten*] and their being as *essential being* [*wesenhaftes Sein*].[55] This kind of being is in fact *not yet universal*. It is rather *what makes possible both universal and individual being* and at the same time what *makes possible* both *intellectually conceived being and existence* (including *real being*).

We have thus encountered something that is not only more primordial than any intellectually conceived being but also more primordial than existence and existents.[56] We believe that this is precisely the meaning of Plato's *eidos,* and we can now understand why the Platonists attributed an ontological preeminence to the πρώτη *ousia* rather than to real things. If, on the other hand, we understand the ideas in Aristotle's sense, they can neither be designated as πρώτη *ousia* nor as δευτέρα *ousia.* In the Aristotelian view the ideas signify a third principle (as the philosopher himself emphasized when he attempted to lead the Platonic concept of ideas *ad absurdum*). But this third is, as we have seen, the foundation of the "first" and "second." At this juncture, however, the "second" (the δευτέρα *ousia*) stands in need of further clarification.

9. Genus, Species, and the Determinateness of the Essence [Wesensbestimmtheit]

The preceding considerations have shown us divers meanings of the terms *genus* and *species.* We call those *concepts of genus* and *species* to which there does not pertain the ontological prerogative of *existence* merely exclusive [*ausschliessend*]. Adjoining these we find the genera and species as *wholes* whose *parts* are the individual things pertaining to them. To these latter types of genera and species, existence or even real *Dasein* must be attributed, depending on whether their individual *specimens* [*Exemplare*] are real or not. For their extension [*Umfang*] must be enlarged to embrace "all real and possible specimens" with which such a distinction (between real and possible) has meaning. (It only has meaning in the realm of becoming and passing away, i.e., in the realm of temporal-real being. In the field of mathematics, for example, this distinction is not valid, because here everything that is possible exists.)

Furthermore, we must consider what makes individual things into *specimens* of a genus or species. We have pointed out that the fact that each individual *Mensch* is "a human being" has its ground or foundation in the "being-human" [*das Menschsein*] of every *Mensch*. What makes the individual being a specimen of a species or genus we may designate as the *determinateness* [*Bestimmtheit*] of its *genus* or *species*. It pertains to the thing as such.[57] Being the *ultimate* determination of the species, the determinateness is the thing's τὸ τί ἦν εἶναι, and the "more universal" determinations are contained in it as structural elements.

Strictly speaking it is not quite correct to call the specific properties of the thing *universal*. The *meaning* [*Sinn*] which is *the same* in all the specimens of a species or genus must be "inferred" [*entnommen*] from the determinations of the genera and species of things. This meaning is "what can be imparted" [*das Mitteilbare*] or communicated, what can "occur" [*vorkommen*] in the multiplicity of the different specimens. But *what has been imparted* or *communicated* and has been received into the individual thing is no longer *universal*. It now belongs to the individual nature of the thing, and, though it may have a "likeness" in other things, it cannot be strictly *the same* here and there.

We must next ask how the determinateness of genus and species is related to the individual nature or essence. But before this question is answered, we must first discuss the still unsolved problem of how the determinateness of genus and species (which answers the query concerning the whatness [*Wassein*]) is related to those determinations which are called *accidental categories*. We are, after all, primarily interested in finding out whether an ontological preeminence can be attributed to the τί (εἶναι) over against the ποιὸν (εἶναι), ποσόν (εἶναι), etc. For the time being, we shall confine our inquiry to an investigation of the interrelation of τί εἶναι and ποιόν εἶναι.[58]

10. τί εἶναι *and* ποιὸν εἶναι *(Determinateness of the What and of the This)*

"This thing is a rose." "It is red." Here we have two predications referring to the same individual thing. The first predication establishes a fact relating to this thing's τί εἶναι, while the second predication establishes a fact relating to its ποιὸν εἶναι. We now recall that Hering[59] designated the nature or essence of the thing as τὸ τί ἦν εἶναι, τί εἶναι, and ποιὸν εἶναι. Although these different expressions are used to designate the same thing, they are not identical in meaning, and this difference in meaning may enable us to gain an understanding of the structure of what is designated by them.

There is undoubtedly an interdependence between *what* a thing is and *how* it is. To being-a-rose there pertains the being-red (or being-yellow or being-white), being-of-such-and-such-a-shape, being-fragrant, etc. (whereby the such-and-such signifies different—but definite and limited—possibilities). If we take away all the ποιόν, there is no τί left. But the τί is more than a "sum total of qualities," and this is why the τί εἶναι tells us more about the nature or essence of a thing than the ποιὸν εἶναι.

The being-red is an individual essential characteristic [*Wesenszug*] of the rose. The being-rose is a structure in which the individual characteristics are conjoined in accordance with definite structural laws. τί εἶναι and ποιὸν εἶναι coincide, if we mean by ποιὸν εἶναι the sum total of essential characteristics, in the order which is imposed upon them by the τί.

Among the qualities of a thing are some which do not belong to its nature or essence, if we mean by *nature* or *essence* [*Wesen*] the firm and enduring constitution [*Bestand*] of its whatness and thusness (e.g., the bedewed-ness [*Betautsein*] of the rose). But such qualities contribute to the *full quid,* which we understood as the totality of both the enduring and changing elements in the constitution of the things.[60] Both the enduring and changing qualities are of the nature of "being-in-something" [*In-etwas-Sein*], which is a mode of being peculiar to all *accidents.* The determinateness of genus and species too is "something which accrues to the thing"; and the *whatness* [*das Wassein*] also is "in" the thing and is not the thing itself. This being-in [*in-sein*], however, differs from the being-in of accidents. It is a fundamental being-in: The *thisness* (or thusness: *Sosein*) is received into the *whatness* [*Wassein*]: every individual "this" or "thus" and every thisness or thusness finds its predesigned place in the "what" or quid. The τί εἶναι thus possesses an ontological prerogative over the ποιὸν εἶναι, not only in the sense of an ultimate determination of the species but of every kind of determinateness of genus and species. This ontological prerogative seems to justify us in applying the term δευτέρα *ousia* to this entire complex of being, even though it applies to the τὸ τί ἦν εἶναι in a preeminent sense.

11. Tabular Classification of the Different Meanings of Ousia *and* ὄν

According to what has been established so far, the forms of being and of beings [*des Seienden*] show a greater manifoldness than is suggested by the simple distinction between πρώτη and δευτέρα *ousia.* The following is an attempt to present a preliminary tabular classification:

῎Ον = beings, "that which is" [Seiendes]

I. *Ousia* = existents, what exists [*Existierendes*]

1. πρώτη *ousia* = τόδε τί (the individual thing)

2. δευτέρα *ousia* = determinateness of the essence [*Wesensbestimmtheit*] understood as determinateness of the what [*Wasbestimmtheit*]. This includes the determinations of genera and species down to their ultimate determination = τί εἶναι.[61]

2a. δευτέρα *ousia* (πῶς) = the determinateness of the essence understood as determinateness of the this or thus = poio\n ei]nai [*Wesensbestimmtheit als Sobestimmtheit*]

II. Λόγος νοητός = beings (existents) which are intellectually conceived [*Gedanklich Seiendes*]

III. Ὄντως ὄν = *eidos* (that which is essentially [*Wesenhaftes Seiendes*], understood as the ground of being and essence [*Seinsgrund und Wesensgrund*] of I and II).

1. Essences [*Wesenheiten*] = elements of being [*Seinselemente*]

2. Whatnesses (essential quid [*Wesenswas*]) = composite structures of meaningful existence [*zusammengesetzte Sinngebilde*]
Πρῶτον ὄν = Πρώτη *ousia* = Λόγος
first being [*erstes Seiendes*] = being of essences
[*Wesen – Sein*] = meaningful existence [*Sinn*]

Some parts of this preliminary outline stand in need of still further explication.

§3. Form and Matter

1. τί *and* ποιὸν τί εἶναι *and* ποιὸν εἶναι

Although we have now gained some understanding of the way τί is related to ποιόν, we may still find it difficult to distinguish τί εἶναι and ποιὸν εἶναι (whatness [*Was-sein*] and thusness [*So-sein*]) from τί and ποιόν (what and thus [*Was und So*]). According to Hering, the τί εἶναι (and the ποιὸν εἶναι, in the sense in which it coincides with the τί εἶναι) is the nature or essence [*Wesen*] of a thing (e.g., the *being*-a-rose). Strictly speaking, this implies a deeply rooted interconnection of essence [*Wesen*) and being [*Sein*] in the thing. It was our own understanding that the τί "[a] rose" is: 1) the *essential quid* [*das wesenhafte Was*] or the meaning [*Sinn*], that which is neither an individual rose nor the nature (essence) of an individual rose, but which is actualized in every individual rose; and 2) the *whatness* [*das Was*-sein] of the individual rose, its inherent specific determinateness which, though it is not yet the ultimate determinateness of the essence [*letzte Wesensbestimmtheit*], nevertheless pertains to the latter. Only the what of *this particular* rose is such an ultimate determinateness, for it is this what or quid which distinguishes this rose from every other rose (at any rate from all roses which are not "entirely like unto it," granted the possibility that there might exist roses which are entirely like unto it).

The question then arises whether in this ultimate determinateness of the essence there is still a distinction between the what and the whatness. And *if* there is such a distinction, is the individual nature or essence the what or the whatness? Hering distinguishes very strictly between the ποιόν of the thing or its "qualitative constitution in the widest sense" and the ποιὸν εἶναι: "To the ποιόν of this horse, for example, belongs the brown color of its hair of which I am able to say that it is a lighter brown than the brown color of the riding habit worn by the horseman. The *being*-brown [*Braun*sein] of the horse, however, cannot be of a lighter shade than the *being*-brown of the riding habit."[62]

For Hering only the *being*-brown is a mark of the essence. But if this holds true of one mark of the essence, it must be equally true of the essence as a whole.

Now it is fairly obvious that the *being*-brown (rather than the brown) pertains to the nature or essence of this particular horse. And the *being*-horse [*Pferd*sein] likewise belongs to the essence of this horse as its specific determinateness. However, since the ultimate determinateness is more manifestly evident in people than in animals, we shall use a different example to illustrate the meaning of this expression on the human level.[63] In other words, is the being-Socrates [*Sokrates-sein*] rather than "Socrates" the essence of this particular person? And if the answer is in the affirmative, is there still a difference between "Socrates" and this particular person, and a difference between the being-Socrates and the *Dasein,* i.e., the actual being of this particular person? If there is no difference, then we have to say that in the individual person *Dasein* and essence coincide in the "actual essence" [*wirkliches Wesen]* of the πρώτη *ousia.* In this case it would be entirely appropriate to designate the individual formal structure as a "living essence" [*Lebewesen*] or an "animate (souled) essence" [*seeliches Wesen*]. To say this, however, would invalidate everything that we have so far established concerning nature (essence) and being. The *principle of the nature* [*Grundsatz vom Wesen*]—the principle which states that every object *has* its nature and that every nature is the nature *of an object*—would collapse if nature (essence) and object were one and the same thing. And it would no longer be possible to understand with St. Thomas the nature as potency and being as act. As far as the individual thing is concerned, the possibility of its not being would become inconceivable, and the distinction between finite and eternal being would disappear. This shows that our assumed premises cannot be correct. In other words, "Socrates," as a designation of the ultimate determinateness of the essence, signifies something that is distinctly different from this person Socrates, and the being-Socrates of this particular person must signify something that differs from this person's *Dasein.*

2. Pure Form and Essential Form (Eidos *and* μορφή*); The Individual Essence; Essence, Potency, and Act;* πρώτη Ousia *as Primordial Cause* [Ur-Sache]

"Socrates" signifies *what* Socrates is, and this what—as is likewise the case with "human being" [*Mensch*] and "living being" [*Lebewesen*]—can be disengaged from the quidditive determinateness [*Wasbestimmtheit*] of this particular person and can be seized in its purity as an *essential quid* [*wesenhaftes Was*].[64] "Being-Socrates" means to possess the what of "Socrates" or to be "in this particular form."

What is implied in the phrase, "in this particular form"? It is customary to use the word "form" to render in German [and in English] the Aristotelian μορφή. Aristotle often uses this term interchangeably with *eidos*, but we have previously pointed out that this can be done only if *eidos* is not understood in the sense of the Platonic idea; for μορφή denotes not something that is separate from the thing, but something which belongs to it. This form is today sometimes called the essential form [*Wesensform*], because in modern philosophy the meaning of "form" has vastly changed (cf. pp. 205ff. below).

Μορφή by no means signifies something like an empty receptacle into which some *content* is poured. Aristotle places the concept of μορφή opposite to that of ὕλη (matter) as an apparently necessary complement to form. We have referred to the example which the philosopher uses to explain what he means. He calls matter the bronze, he calls form the pattern of the image (to be embodied in the bronze), and he calls the complete statue the compound of matter and form (cf. p.132 above).

This form-matter relationship, as described by Aristotle, became decisive for the understanding of the created universe and determined the entire thinking of the Middle Ages. We have already mentioned in passing the lively disputes which arose over the question of whether *pure spirits* must also be conceived as being composed of matter and form. Of necessity, this question had to be answered affirmatively if form and matter were understood exclusively as correlative and complementary concepts. We know, on the other hand, that St. Thomas always insisted on the "purity" of *pure spirits* and that he therefore designated them as *formae separatae*, i.e., as "forms which were free from all matter." Now, if such a view is at all possible, then the meaning of form can neither be exhausted nor exclusively determined by its contrast and complement-relationship with *matter*. And thus being-formed or being-in-a-form must have some other meaning besides that of being shaped in the manner of a work of the "plastic arts."

"Being-Socrates" means that all the what and all the how of this particular person, including all his doing and suffering, and, in short, everything that belongs to his being, grows out of one single root.[65] The simile of organic evolution and growth—which is used just as frequently as that of artistic formation to illustrate the nature of the μορφή—seems to fit the real situation much better. It is even more than a simile because it vividly and directly describes the thing itself: As it unfolds from the seed, the plant follows an invariable formative law. Root and stalk, leaves and blossoms, position and movement, and even the particular manner of growth, of ripening and withering, are in perfect accord as a diversified "manifestation" of the one *nature* or *essence*.

Socrates walks and Socrates talks. He converses with an artisan or refutes a famous sophist. Again, all these activities are "manifestations of his nature or essence." Walking, talking, conversation—they carry a universal meaning, a meaning which is realized wherever and whenever a human being engages in such activities. But no other human being walks, talks, and converses *precisely* in the way Socrates does. All of his actions conform to the way he *is* "himself" and may therefore be described as manifestations of his *thisness* (or *thusness* [*seines Soseins*]). But the *particular* thisness of Socrates signifies something else than either an individual essential characteristic [*Wesenszug*] or the sum total of his essential characteristics. It is a simple and

invariable phenomenon which recurs in every essential trait and which makes his entire nature as well as every essential trait of this nature something unique. Thus, the friendliness and kindliness of Socrates differs from the friendliness and kindliness of every other human being, notwithstanding the fact that the *same* essence is actualized here and there. A totality—which is *this* and *thus*—unfolds itself in the individual traits and in the entire life of this *particular human being,* constituting his individual essence.

But let us now ask in what sense this individual essence is the *being* [*das Sein*] of this particular person. As soon as we inquire whether Plato or Xenophon gave a more accurate description of the way Socrates existed "in reality," the difference between real and essential being, between *Dasein* and *Was-sein* (or *So-sein*) comes into relief. It is possible that the "real Socrates" differed from the picture drawn by Plato, but this "picture," nevertheless, shows us a human being of a very definite "formation of character" [*Gepräge*]. We have before us an *individual essence*, but this Platonic Socrates (supposing the real Socrates was actually different from the Platonic Socrates) is not the "real Socrates": His individual essence is not the "real essence" of Socrates. In this case the "Platonic Socrates" would have to be regarded as a "poetic figure." This reflection, however, gives rise to two further lines of inquiry: 1) Is the poetic character with its individual essence something "merely intellectually conceived" [*bloss gedacht*]? 2) How is the essence of the "real Socrates" (*qua* real) distinguished from the essence of the poetic character?

We begin with a consideration of the first question. There are characters of poetic fiction of whom we say that they are true to life, and there are others whom we call "untrue," "distorted," or "impossible." "True to life" in this case does not mean that the characters must be exact copies of real life models. The true poet is endowed with the gift of "creating" characters that are true to life. This kind of creativity, to be sure, is of a peculiar nature. It is not "free" in the sense of being completely arbitrary. The more genuine and the greater the art of the poet, the more his creation will resemble a conception and birth and the less will it show the marks of a mechanical construct. The "artistic structure" [*Gebilde*] has its immanent organic law to which the "master" must submit if his or her creation is to be a work of art rather than a mere "artifact" [*Machwerk*]. The formal structures which artists mold have their own nature, a nature which "unfolds" before their very eyes. They "watch" them, observing how they "behave" in this or that particular situation; they have no dictatorial power over them.

Thus for artists there exist *archetypal forms* or *images* [*Urbilder*] which they must seize and the being of which is independent and a precondition of their workmanship. Here we are dealing with *pure forms*, and they may make it possible for us to grasp the meaning of *a form* that is unrelated to a particular matter.

It follows from the nature or essence of Homer's Achilles that he cruelly avenges the death of his beloved friend; that he mourns and laments the death of Patroclus as a loving maiden bemoans the loss of her lover; that Achilles treats Priam, the aged father of Hector—the enemy whom he has slain—with the tender reverence of a son, and that he faces his own destiny with calm composure.[66] This is the way then in which the quid [*Was*] and the nature [*Wesen*] of Achilles unfold. And a special significance attaches to this "unfolding": The nature is a structure which unfolds itself in individual essential traits that are enclosed in it, and the nature discloses itself fully and becomes actual in doing and suffering.[67]

It is the peculiar character of "structural form" [*Gestalt*] to be a unified manifold [*ein Manigfaltig-Einheitliches*], i.e., to be whole and to be at the same time unfolded in the manifoldness of individual traits. And this is precisely the meaning of *pure form* and the way it can be seized without being related to some matter which has been formed or which is to be formed by it. The unfolding of what is enclosed—an unfolding which does not dissolve the unity—and the being-enclosed of what unfolds itself constitute that being which pertains to the essential quid [*Wesenswas*].

In a spatial structure [*Raumgestalt*] the unfolding of the essence is actualized in spatial expansion. And in a *temporal structure* [*Zeitgestalt*]—as, for example, in a musical tune or in an experiential unit—the unfolding of the essence [*Wesensentfaltung*] is actualized in a temporal sequence. Space and time thus pertain to these particular modes of being.

But to return to our original query: *Genuine* poetic characters are essential structures and not something merely intellectually conceived. They obey the law of a form the unfolding of which they copy: They unfold in accordance with this formative law. Such poetic characters *are*, however, not *pure forms* because their structure includes some *material elements* by means of which they take hold of the form and make it intelligible to others. In the case of poetry the chief (though not the only) material element is language. If the works in question are not accomplished masterpieces, they are bound to deviate more or less from the archetypal form [*Urbild*].

It is thus possible for us to distinguish not only in the real Socrates but even in the Platonic Socrates his being-Socrates from his being-himself (always assuming that the Platonic Socrates is not the real Socrates, but a poetic character). Being-Socrates means—as we have pointed out—to be in the form of "Socrates." This seems now equivalent to saying that being-Socrates means an unfolding in accordance with the form of "Socrates." In the case of a pure form, quid, essence, and being are inseparably joined together. They are the self-unfolding of the quid. Their essence and their being consist in this self-unfolding quid. In *essential being* [*wesenhaftes Sein*], *essence* and *being* coincide, and the essence can in this case no longer be distinguished from its object. The Platonic Socrates, on the other hand, "has" an essence: Essence and object do not coincide. The essence of Socrates determines how he has to unfold in accordance with the pure form. And in this case it is still possible to distinguish the quid from the essence: The essence is the whatness [*das Wassein*] of the object. The self-unfolding pertains to the quid as the latter's being, and the self-unfolding determines the corresponding unfolding of the object.

Our second question reads as follows: "How is the essence of the 'real Socrates' (*qua* real) distinguished from the essence of the poetic character?" To be able to answer this question, we must first somewhat enlarge upon what has been said. We understood the concept of *pure form* or *structure* so broadly that it included spatial and temporal structures as well as the structures of things and persons (and possibly some others), but we recognized that to different structures correspond different modes of unfolding. The unfolding of a triangle, for example, differs from the way a melody unfolds itself. But these several modes of unfolding have something in common if we compare them with that entirely different unfolding which pertains to the forms of *real objects*. In the case of a triangle of definite length of sides and definite size of angles the manner of its unfolding is determined. There is only the *one* circumstance of relative position or situation for which different possibilities are left open.

But this does not entail any change in the triangle as such. Although it pertains to the nature of the triangle that it must unfold itself at a definite place or in a definite situation, this external fixation adds nothing to what the triangle is in itself. And it is similar with the unfolding of a melody as a definite sequence of sounds. Such structures unfold themselves, as it were, only in one plane or dimension: They comprise no opposites of surface and depth, of foreground and background.[68] *Real* objects, on the other hand, have a much more complex and deeply grounded [*tiefgründig*] structure, and their essences correspondingly unfold themselves in a very different manner.

We said of this particular man, Socrates, that his nature or essence "unfolds itself" in the essential traits of his character and that it "fully discloses itself" in his actions. We thereby evidently indicated different modes of self-unfolding. The loyalty of Achilles as a friend and his cruelty as an enemy, his gentleness and kindliness—these are obviously different traits of his character. But when he chases the fleeing Hector around the walls of Troy and later on even mutilates and desecrates the corpse of the slain enemy, there seems to be no trace left of any gentleness and kindliness. And when Achilles is seated with his mother by the shore of the sea pouring out his sorrow and allowing himself to be soothed by her consoling words, we might again not believe him capable of any inhuman cruelty. Thus we see how in his behavior now one and then the other essential trait of character prevails. What does not "express" itself in vital action remains hidden, not only veiled to our knowledge, but ontically [*seinsmässig*] undisclosed like the inner life of a closed bud.[69]

Once again we meet here with the contraries of act and potency. We call an act the vital activity of the human being In doing and suffering [*Tun und Lassen*].[70] And by *potency* we mean the *inner power* [*Vermögen*] for a corresponding vital activity. In relation to this activity, the potency represents a preliminary stage, a *possibility* of being [*ein Sein*können], while on the other hand it is the basis of the activity and as such distinguished by a greater constancy[71] as compared with the fleeting nature of changing activities. The potency is thus something which lies beneath the "surface."

The *faculties* [*Vermögen*] or *capabilities* [*Fähigkeiten*] are the essential traits into which the essence unfolds itself. The essence discloses itself when an *ability* [*ein Können*] passes over into the corresponding *doing* [*das Tun*]. The essence thus represents the deepest stratum in the entire structure: It is its "ground." However, it is not a ground which lies immobilized in the depths, separated, as it were, from the "surface" of vital activity by the faculties as by an "intermediate layer" [*Zwischenschicht*], but a ground which reaches from the deepest stratum to the surface, a root which grows into a tree and spreads out into the finest ramifications. And thus the vital activity is not "merely surface," but deeply rooted in the essence.

At this point, however, new doubts arise. Did we not previously state that the contraries of act and potency are confined to the realm of real being, the world of becoming and passing away? Assuming that this is the case, we can easily understand that for "real human beings," the unfolding of the essence consists in passing over from potential to actual modes of behavior. But what about those poetic characters who are not real? And what about *pure forms?* Do the contraries of act and potency apply to them, too? A consideration of these queries will lead of necessity to an answer to the question concerning the way in which the *real essence* is related to the essence of the poetic character.

It is noteworthy that in our present inquiry we have encountered the contraries of act and potency precisely in considering a poetic character. There was a distinct difference between the cruelty of Achilles as an enduring essential trait of his character and the "activation" [*Betätigung*] of this trait in his attitude toward Hector. But if Achilles as such was never alive, if he is altogether unreal, does it make any sense to speak of a contrast between his potential and actual conduct?

The peculiar nature of what we call a "poetic world"—or more generally speaking, a "world of poetic imagination"—plays an important part in the consideration of our question. However, since both real and poetic characters have their archetype [*Urbild*] in the *pure form* and unfold in accordance with its injunctions, we do well to ask ourselves once more in what sense one may speak of an unfolding of pure forms.

Assuming that Homer's Achilles was designed in every particular trait as a faithful copy of the pure form of the *Urbild*, we may conclude that in this *Urbild* were enclosed all individual traits of his character and all *possible* modes of his actions. We may further state that the form unfolds itself in the individual traits pertaining to it and in its possible modes of action (whereby the *unfolding* must not be understood as a temporal process). The form is really not an "unfolding" but an "unfolded" structure: It knows of no mutation and change and therefore of no passage from potentiality to actuality. This is why we have placed emphasis on the expression *possible modes of action.* The pure form "Achilles" has no mode of action at all: It does not "behave" in one way or another, but in it are predesigned all the possible modes of action of the particular human being who has it "as his form." There is no human life in which all the possibilities of human nature of the essence "human being" are actualized. And even a work of poetry must select among the many possibilities of the essence [*Wesensmöglichkeiten*] and cannot hope to exhaust them. Poetic characters are "true" or "real" to the extent that they are kept within the confines of the possibilities of the essence.

In actual human life the unfolding of the essence is a temporal process. We are not at this time interested in the question of the extent to which this also holds true in the case of the "unfolding" of essential traits. To determine this would require a more thorough knowledge of the structure of the human soul than we have at our command right now. It may suffice therefore to demonstrate the process of "unfolding" with respect to that self-disclosure which takes place in vital activity.

We first observed the contraries of potential and actual being (not yet alive and presently alive being) in *experiential units,* and we recognized the passage from one state to the other as the peculiar mode of the being of the "life of the ego" [*Ichleben*]: We stated that this mode of being is a constant becoming and passing away (cf. Chapt. II, Sections 2 and 3). From the structures of experiential units, we were led to the interrelation which exists between essential and real being, and the investigation of this relationship made it necessary for us to go beyond our original field of vision, partly for reason of an intrinsic nature (i.e., on account of the very far-reaching significance of the potency-act contrast), and partly because we were leaning on Aristotle, for whom the reality of nature [*Naturwirklichkeit*] was the "most immediate reality" [*das Nächstliegende*] from which he started out.

From the "reality of the nature" of human beings we were then led back to the experiential units. But these latter now appeared in a different light. What we had previously designated as the "life of the ego" we now recognized as the "vital activity" [*lebendiges Verhalten*] of human beings. While the life of the ego appeared as a mere interconnection of experiential units passing over into one another, the human being's vital activity we saw rise "from the depths" of human existence. Later on we shall have to inquire into the relations which exist between the "pure ego" and the "human ego" [*Ich-Mensch*] and between "pure experiences" and "human modes of action" (cf. chap. VII, §3). Certain points of departure were already suggested in the considerations of Chapter II. A discussion of these questions at this time, however, would break the continuity of our presentation. We must therefore assume, for the time being, that the structure of the experiential units as such remains unchanged when it is viewed under the aspect of modes of human action. We are thus able to make use of what we have previously learned concerning these experiential units.

The emotional strain which Bismarck showed during the peace negotiations with Austria at Nikolsburg (1866) represents an experiential unit of a definite duration. The events are familiar to us from Bismarck's own description in his *Reflections and Reminiscences.*[72] The old Kaiser Wilhelm (at that time only King of Prussia), who at other times willingly submitted to being guided by the counsels of his great chancellor, was on this occasion in no mood to listen to the mild peace terms which Bismarck proposed. All the endeavors of Bismarck to persuade his sovereign of the weight and validity of his arguments were to no avail. At last the chancellor gave up the seemingly hopeless struggle and withdrew to an adjoining room. There his extreme nervous tension found release in a convulsive crying fit. After another fruitless attempt on the following day, Bismarck was in such a state of mind that he "pondered the idea of whether it might not be better to throw himself out of the window of the four-storied building."[73] At this moment someone taps him on the shoulder. It is the crown prince, the future Kaiser Friedrich, who at other times had often opposed Bismarck's policies. However, this time he offers his services to plead Bismarck's cause with the king. When he does so, he has better luck than Bismarck and the king's resistance is broken.

Does not this emotional crisis of Bismarck reveal a hidden depth? In the simple and succinct narrative of the chancellor, we sense the sequence of inner experiences: the violent straining of an iron will bent on the right objective, the unrelenting efforts of a penetrating intellect to set forth convincing rational arguments, the bearing up against a stubbornly hostile will, the yielding in view of the apparent futility of the struggle, and finally the momentary failing of strength following the excessive strain. All of this emanates from the depths of a "nature" revealing itself in these manifest "expressions." Here is a man who is willing to live and die in the fulfillment of his task, who is passionately giving his all for a cause which he can inwardly not abandon, even though he finds himself forced to forsake it externally.

Thus the essence discloses itself. It becomes manifest in those individual traits which are enclosed in it. In "vital action" it attains to that height of being that is within its reach. And our example illustrates at the same time the way in which *act* as *being* and *act* as *doing* are factually interrelated and perfect themselves mutually.[74] Here the "actual" [*das Wirkliche*] manifests itself simultaneously as the "efficacious" [*das Wirksame*]: The essence receives impressions and, stirred by this impress, it produces out of its depths certain modes of action which "manifest" themselves externally. This then is what we mean by an *unfolding of the essence* in the form of *actual events* [*wirkliches Geschehen*]. Here the difference from the unfolded being [*Entfaltetsein*] of a pure form is evident.

But now the question arises once more: Can all this happen also in the realm of poetry where no real events are involved? The rancor of Achilles, too, is an experiential unit of a definite duration: It persists almost throughout the entire span of time in which the events take place that are recorded in the *Iliad*. In the initial verses this rancor of Achilles is explicitly designated as the main theme of the epic. We witness the arrogance of King Agamemnon which gives rise to the rancor in Achilles.[75] We observe how this mood is obstinately maintained[76] in the face of all the attempts to assuage the temper of the hero, and how in the end the rancor dissolves under the impact of an even more severe grief and through the interventions of higher powers .[77]

In the Homeric epic, too, then, the action arises from the depths of a nature and reveals the essence. And the efficacy [*Wirksamkeit*] extends far beyond the life of this particular human being, since the fate of two nations is determined by it. But what can be the meaning of the "efficacy" of "something unreal"? In the "world of Homer" things happen in precisely the same way as they do in the real world. Homer's characters behave and are "construed" like real human beings: They have a nature or essence, and this nature or essence unfolds in their lives. And yet this entire Homeric world is not real: It is a "poetic world of appearances" [*Scheinwelt*] and as such a product of *poetic imagination*. In other words, the human mind is capable of creating something which resembles the real world because it copies the archetypal images [*Urbilder*] of real existents [*des Wirklichen*], but this something is nevertheless only *apparently* [*scheinbar*] real. The rancor of Achilles is no real rancor: It does not really arise out of the depths of the essence, and that which unfolds itself is no real essence. In short, Achilles is no πρώτη *ousia*, no independently and authentically existing being [*Existierendes*]. Achilles, and with him the entire "world" into which he has been placed, are sustained by the spirit of the poet (or of the empathetic reader). Achilles does not "possess" his nature or essence: It has been "given" or "loaned" to him. And to this loaned essence correspond the modes of action which are either actually attributed or may possibly be "attributed" to him in the poem.

The contrast between the real world and the world of appearance may now aid us in our understanding of reality and real existence [*Seiendes*] and in answering all those questions which have arisen in the course of this inquiry. *That which is real possesses its nature or essence and allows it to unfold in a temporal sequence of events.* The real [*das Wirkliche*] is the *primordial cause* [*Ur-Sache*] of these events, and these events are in turn—by virtue of the primordial cause—actual and efficacious, i.e., they engender other events. The *nature* or *essence* is in this case an *individual, real essence*—pertaining to this object and to no other—and the *actualization of a pure form*, i.e., the "being-in-this-form" of the object. All the whatness [*Wassein*] and thisness [*Sosein*] of the object—all the generic and specific determinations—are thus enclosed in the essence but, in addition, there is predesigned in it all the object's qualitative being, all its doing and suffering, all its relational conditions [*In-Beziehung-stehen*], which pertain to it or "accrue to it" [*zukommen*] either necessarily or potentially. If all these "determinations" are taken away, there remains neither an essence nor an object. And it is thus understandable that without these determinations there can be no πρώτη *ousia*, notwithstanding the fact that these determinations themselves do not have the nature of a πρώτη *ousia.*

If we then decide to designate the essence as τὸ τί ἦν εἶναι, we must be aware that in contradistinction to Aristotle, we understand the essence as an individual rather than as a specific determinateness. We have tried to illustrate this by the example of this man, Socrates, whose being-Socrates differs from and yet includes his being-a-human-being [*Menschsein*]. In this example the person Socrates is πρώτη *ousia,* i.e., primordial cause [*Ur-Sache*]. On the other hand, we are in agreement with Aristotle inasmuch as he too regards the being-human (which for him is the τὸ τί ἦν εἶναι of this particular human being) as pertaining to this particular human being, despite the fact that it can be grasped as a universalized concept [*allgemeinbegrifflich fassbar*]. It must be left to our future special investigation of the nature of the human and thingly essence to ascertain to what extent the distinction between the individual essence and the ultimate determinateness of the species [*letzte Artbestimmtheit*] can be maintained when we deal with infra-human things and beings. The concept of a *thing* can be taken so broadly that it includes all primordial causes: human beings, infra-human animate natures, and dead objects. Customarily, however, we are using the term *thing* in a restricted sense: We apply it either to *dead* objects, in contrast to living beings, or to the impersonal, in contrast to *persons.*

Individual objects which are not real—as, for example, an individual triangle of definite length of sides, size of angles, and position—are of the nature of a this-there *(Diesda:* τόδε τί), not of the nature of an primordial cause (*Ur-Sache;* πρώτη *ousia*). Their unfolding is not a temporal, real, and efficacious event, not a rising out of an essential ground [*Wesensgrund*], and they can therefore not be said to be truly in possession of their essence [*Wesensbesitz*].

3. The Aristotelian Concept of Form (First Schematic Outline)

We must now endeavor to gain a clear understanding of the way in which what Aristotle calls *form* (μορφή) is related to the *essence* (τὸ τί ἦν εἶναι) as the ultimate determinateness of a thing and to the *pure form* (*eidos* = *archetypal* image [*Urbild*] of the thing). To this end, however, it is first necessary to determine more precisely what Aristotle means by μορφή. Aristotle looks for form in the realm of *becoming*. He writes:

> Everything which comes to be, comes into being by the agency of something; it comes from something and comes to be something; and this something I understand in the sense of any of the forms of being or categories. For it comes to be either a this or a thing of such and such a size or of such and such a quality or in such and such a position. That out of which a thing comes to be we call matter, and that by which it comes to be is something which exists naturally (τῶν φύσει τί ὄντων); and that which it comes to be is either a human being or a plant or some other existent of the kind which in a preeminent sense we call *ousia.* Now all things which come to be either by the agency of nature or by artistic creation have matter, for each of these (i.e., things which come to be) can either be or not be, and it is the matter in each of them which accounts for this capacity of being or not being. And, generally speaking, both that from which the thing is produced and the type or image in whose likeness it is produced are nature. For what comes to be (e.g., a plant or an animal) has a nature. And the same is true of that by which the thing is produced: The specifically same nature, which is called the archetypal image (*eidos;* [*Urbild*]), although it comes to be in another individual. For a human being begets another human being.[78]

"What comes into being through art is something of which the archetypal image *(eidos)* is in the soul (of the artist). *Eidos,* however, I call the essence of each thing τὸ τί ἦν εἶναι) and the πρώτη *ousia.*"[79] In this passage, *eidos* evidently has a double meaning. It signifies: 1) the essence of the become (that which has come to be), and understood in this sense, *eidos* is equated to the immanent form (μορφή); and 2) the *archetypal image* [*Urbild*] which is anterior to both the becoming and the become and which is the starting point of the movement by which that which is in the process of becoming comes to be.

This movement is at first intellectual mobility [*Denkbewegung*], but then passes over into external operational creative activity. But even the archetypal image is not a pure form: It has its being in a "this there" [*Diesda*], and while in the case of creative artistic activity the *Urbild* is in the mind of the artist,[80] in the processes of natural becoming (e.g., in the generation of animate beings) it is the essence (i.e., the specific determinateness) of the progenitor. With respect to this double meaning of *eidos,* it may thus be said "that health comes from health, and house from house, and that what has matter comes from what has no matter. For the medical art and the art of construction are the archetypal images of health and house. Thus, when I speak of being without matter (*ousia* a!neu u#lhj), I mean the essence (to_ ti/ h}n ei]nai).[81]

> It is therefore ... impossible that anything should come to be if there were no being prior to it. It is clear then that some part of the being produced must of necessity pre-exist. For the matter is a part which is in the process of becoming that which is to be, and matter itself thus becomes something. But now we assert that even of that which we call the conceptual (τῶν ἐν τῷ λόγῳ) something must already pre-exist. For we describe, for example, in a twofold way what rings of bronze are made of: We describe the matter by designating it as bronze, and we describe the form by saying that the rings have such and such a shape. And this shape is the proximate genus in which the form is placed. The concept of the ring of bronze, then includes some matter.[82]

However, the statue which is made of stone we do not designate as "stone," but we say that it is "of stone" [*steinern*]. For "upon closer examination we find that we cannot even state without qualification that a statue is produced from stone, because that out of which something comes to be is characterized by change, not by permanence."[83]

That which truly comes to be [*wird*] is neither the matter nor the form but that which contains both: not the bronze, nor the bowl, but the bronze bowl.

> Obviously, then, neither the shape (*eidos*)—or by whatever name we call the form (μορφή) which is present in the object of sense[84]—comes to be, nor can the becoming be attributed to the essence (τὸ τί ἦν εἶναι). For these (form and essence) are what come into being in something else, whether it be by artistic creation, by nature, or by some power (faculty). What we make or bring into being is the bronze bowl. For it is made of bronze and of the bowl,

> and when we bring the form into the bronze, the bronze bowl comes into being. However, if there were such a thing as a becoming of the being-bowl, then something would have to be made of something else. For that which is in the process of becoming must always be divisible, and one of its parts must be this and another that—the one must be matter and the other form (*eidos*).[85]
>
> ... It is evident then from what has been said that what is called *eidos* or *ousia* does not come into being: What comes to be is the unified concrete thing (σύνοδος), whose name derives from *eidos* or *ousia*. It is clear, moreover, that in everything that comes to be, matter is present and that what has become is partly matter and partly form.[86]

Aristotle subsequently emphasizes once more that the *eidos* must not be regarded as an archetypal image that exists separated from individual things and that no such separate *Urbild* is needed for the explanation of becoming, for the philosopher argues that in the things of nature the progenitor and the progeny are of the same kind, "not indeed in number, but in species...; for a human being begets a human being...."[87]

> Obviously, therefore, it is by no means necessary to set up an idea (*eidos*) as a paradigm (παράδειγμα). For such ideal paradigm should have to be postulated in any things of nature, because they are *ousiai* in a preeminent sense. However, we find that in this case the progenitor is fully adequate for the production of the progeny and for causing the presence of form (*eidos*) in matter. However, the whole (i.e., such and such a form in this particular flesh and in these particular bones) is what we call Kallias and Socrates. And the whole differs according to its matter (which is a different one in Kallias and in Socrates), but it is the same according to its *eidos* (species; form). For the *eidos* is indivisible.[88]

When Aristotle says that the form (*eidos*) does not come to be, he is probably thinking primarily of what the thing is. But he emphasizes specifically that this statement holds true not only of the what of the thing but also of all the other forms of being (categories): "For the quality (ποιόν) does not come to be, but rather the wood or the living being of such and such a size. However, it is the peculiar nature of *ousia*[89] ... that another real *ousia*,[90] which produces it, must pre-exist, whereas it is not necessary that there should pre-exist a quality or quantity otherwise than potentially."[91]

Though it must have become clear by now that our own views concerning *form* and *essence* differ in some important points from those of Aristotle, we shall try to set forth our dissenting opinion with all possible precision. Before we do so, however, we would like to point out some of the difficulties which result from the standpoint of Aristotle.

The philosopher states that to all *becoming* belongs something *out of which* that which is in the process of becoming comes to be. He know of no becoming that entails a *being-called-forth from nothingness,* i.e., the *idea of creation* is foreign to him. Only the composite of form and matter *comes to be. Matter and form must thus be assumed to be eternal.*[92] Are matter and form then to be conceived as united from eternity or as originally separated? Are we to assume a pure matter or a pure form?

4. The Aristotelian Concept of Matter (First Schematic Outline)

It is impossible to gain an understanding of *form* without first elucidating the nature of *matter.* The examples given for matter in the previously quoted passages—wood, bronze, stone—do not signify pure matter, but a matter that is already "formed" in the sense of a specific determination, and this matter "occurs" in individualized "pieces," each of which is a "this-there" of a definite spatial structure, a real thing, a πρώτη *ousia.* When Aristotle says, "I call matter that which is a this-there, not actually (ἐνεργείᾳ), but potentially (δυνάμει),"[93] this statement might at first glance appear to refer to matter conceived as a whole, irrespective of its formation in definite individual pieces or bodies (e.g., all the wood that exists anywhere in the world). However, this cannot be the meaning of the quoted passage, for a little later the philosopher states that for matter there can be neither generation nor corruption. What he means is, rather, the substratum that underlies the becoming and passing away of things.

Aristotle counts the becoming and passing away among the *metamorphoses* [*Veränderungen*] (μεταβολαί) and gives this further explanation: just as there pertains to every change something that changes—to a change of place something that is now here and then there, to a change of quantity something that is now larger and then smaller, and to a change of quality something which (to name only one example) is now healthy and then diseased—so it is also in the case of a *change in the ousia (substantial change)*. There must be something involved "which is now generated and then destroyed, something which now underlies this process as a this-there and then as a wholly indefinite substratum (κατὰ στέρησιν, in the manner of *privation*)."[94] This kind of becoming and passing away takes place, for example when different elements enter into a chemical compound: The elements pass away and the compound comes to be.

Now Aristotle holds that this becoming and passing away has a substratum which itself does not become and pass away, and this underlying principle remains self-identical in the process of change from one state into the other. This substratum is matter, which is only potentially (not actually) a this-there and for which there is no longer any generation or corruption. Aristotle emphasizes that each and every thing has its own particular matter, even though all material elements might possibly be reduced to a single (or perhaps a plurality of) prime matter [*Urstoff*].[95]

If Aristotle appears undecided whether or not to accept matter as πρώτη *ousia,* this may perhaps be explained by the fact that at one time he means by matter the materials (such as wood or iron) which are known from experience and have the form of real objects, while at another time he has in mind the indefinite substratum. His indecision may, however, also be due to the fact that there is in matter this indefinite element, so that it is quite properly called a potential (but not an actual) *ousia.*

From the passage last quoted we gather that there are *degrees of indefiniteness*. The particular matter of the individual thing is indefinite in relation to the thing which is determined in its objective form. If, however, these "particular materials" (οἰκείαι ὕλαι) can be traced back to a single (or a plurality of) prime matter, then this *Urstoff* must be something even more indefinite, something that is particularized in the specific materials by a graduated scale of determinations (genus, species, down to the ultimate determinateness).

Though it seems to me that Aristotle's concept of the *particular matter* (or material) is not entirely clear, it may help us to understand why and how in his opinion the determinateness of the species is particularized in individual existents by the *specific material* in which it is embodied (i.e., why and how matter becomes the "principle of individuation"): Several individuals of the same species are possible because "the divisible matter receives the same form into its different parts."[96] Here also, it appears, lies the starting point for the formation of the concept of the *materia designata* or *determinata* (of spatially confined and determined matter), to which both Avicenna and St. Thomas Aquinas refer as the principle of individuation.[97] "I call *designated matter* [*materia signata*]," writes St. Thomas, "matter which is determined in its dimensions."[98] This problem we shall have to discuss later.

Although each thing has its matter, it is possible that different things are made of the same material. Thus, wood may be used for making a box or a bed. It is the *moving cause* [*bewegende Ursache*] which accounts for the difference. This moving cause, however, is not unlimited in the choice of what can be made out of a given material. Thus, "a saw, for example, cannot be made of wood."[99] Furthermore, the same things can be made out of different materials: For example, a statue of Hermes can be made of wood or of stone. In this case "the labor of the artist (τέχνη) as the moving ontic principle [*Seinsgrund*] (ἀρχὴ κινοῦσα) must be the same. For if both the matter and the moving cause were different, the product would show the corresponding difference."[100]

With this last thought Aristotle proceeds from the consideration of matter to the discussion of form: He wants to demonstrate that matter by itself does not suffice to explain becoming. However, we had hoped that Aristotle's views on matter might throw some additional light on the concept of the *specific material.* But here we have to contend with the difficulty that all his examples are taken from the field of creative human workmanship and not from the realm *of* natural becoming. All human work, however, starts out from an already firmly determined matter, from some real thing. For example, if a bed is fashioned out of a piece of wood, this does not mean that one natural material is changed into another but that the same material is given a different spatial structure. And this latter is not a new substantial form [*Dingform*], but merely a new accidental form or a new quality. There is no question of a thingly becoming [*dingliches Werden*] but only of a change or a *transformation* in the narrower sense of the term.

As a matter of fact, the "product" of human creative workmanship is for Aristotle not a πρώτη *ousia*.[101] Human works do not rest in themselves as do things of nature: They rest on the human mind which imparts to them that meaning or purposive determinateness in which their particular being has its root and ground. These human works are sustained both by the in mind of the human being who determines their purpose and fashions them accordingly and the minds of those who understand their purpose and "deal" with them accordingly.

The question is whether in view of such a far-reaching difference in structure human "works" can be of any help in an attempt to understand the "things of nature," their matter and their form. The human "work," if it is a sensible object, has matter which itself is already a thing of nature. To conceive of things of nature in the manner we conceive of human works is possible only if we regard them as structures which have been formed by some "artist" or "master craftsman" out of some given material.[102] But such a world would not be a "creation" in the Christian sense.

We mentioned before that Aristotle was unfamiliar with the idea of creation out of nothing. Nor is it his opinion that the world was formed out of a prime matter which anteceded it in time. For Plato such a theory of the origin of the world was possible because he posited *pure* forms separated from matter. If, on the other hand, one regards with Aristotle the objects of sense as πρώτη *ousia* (i.e., as the primary reality), one can at no time conceive of matter as existing separate from things. If therefore prime matter was conceived as not become, it could be understood only as formed: The "world" or "nature" would then have to be posited as "eternal." "The world," writes Aristotle, "is non-become and noncorruptible. Whoever doubts this and holds that such mighty visible divinities as sun and moon and all the heavens with their planets and fixed stars—which indeed comprise a true pantheon—are in no way distinguished from those thing which are fashioned by human hands, that person is guilty of a horrible impiety."[103]

This passage is followed by another significant statement which seems to have been handed down by oral tradition: "Aristotle, as we are told, used to say scornfully that while hitherto he had only feared for his house (lest it might be destroyed some day by violent storms, by decay, or because of it flimsy construction), he felt now that a much greater threat was contained in the teachings of those who by their doctrines endangered the very structure of the universe."

When we read such statements in some of Aristotle's early writings, we get a glimpse of the philosopher's original personal attitude toward the world, and in comparison with these utterances, his later philosophic arguments seem like a subsequent rational elaboration and confirmation of his earlier views. The world appears to him so firmly constituted and of such overpowering beauty that nothing can impair it. "The world has not come to be, because a work of such splendor cannot have had a beginning consequent upon some new resolve, and it is so perfect in every one of its aspects that there is no power which could cause such tremendous commotions and changes nor any imaginable age in the extension of time which could ever bring about the decay and destruction of this cosmic structure."[104] All matter is formed in the totality of the universe, and all formative power is enclosed in this totality, so that there is nothing external to it whereby it might be destroyed. "Nor can the world be decomposed by some inherent principle, since in this case the part would have to be greater and mightier than the whole, which is absurd. For with unrelenting force the world sets in motion all of its parts without being itself moved by any of them."[105] There is hardly a greater contrast conceivable than this trusting and joyous world affirmation of Aristotle and the negative attitude regarding the world of Plato, for whom the world of sense was only a feeble, transitory image or copy of the ideas.[106]

The mildly pantheistic tinge of Aristotle's praise of the world is absent from his later theological views. While he remains unfamiliar with the idea of a creator of the world, he acknowledges that there must be an eternal, purely spiritual *world mover.* The world itself leads him to that conclusion: While he regards the *whole* of the world as not become and eternal, he observes an incessant movement, a continual becoming and passing away *in* the world. And since each individual movement refers back to one that causes it, and since the series of these movements cannot be infinite, there must be a first mover himself unmoved.[107]

We do not intend to pursue this line of thought any further until we have gained an even clearer insight into the nature of "matter." We have learned now that in Aristotle's view matter can never have been or can ever be real or actual as "pure matter." To matter as such pertains only *potential being,* and it is *actual* only as formed matter.

5. Matter and Form—Potency and Act

We are confronted at this point with the question of how the *form-matter problem is linked with the act-potency problem.*[108] And we must make an attempt to illuminate the one by means of the other. If, as we have done, we try to understand act and potency as *real and possible being,* it is evident that the inquiry into the nature of *ousia* cannot bypass this distinction. *Ousia*—so we stated—signifies a kind of *existence* [*Seiendes*] *which possesses an ontological preeminence* over against another kind of existence. This is why we designated *ousia*—in a broad sense—as *that which exists* [*das Existierende*] in contradistinction to that which is merely intellectually conceived [*bloss gedacht*]. And among that which exists the *autonomous existent* [*das Selbständige*] in turn possesses a preeminence over against the dependent existent [*das Unselbständige*]. The latter partakes of the being of the former only by virtue of its sharing in the generic and specific determinateness and in the qualities of autonomous objects.

The highest ontological preeminence was ascribed by Aristotle to *real things:* To them the term *ousia* applies in a preeminent sense, and the real thing is therefore called a πρώτη *ousia.*

We have thus established a relation between *ousia* as a preeminent existent and ἐνέργεια (reality, act). *Reality is the highest ontological preeminence, and the real is what is an existent in the truest sense.* *Possibility* (δύναμις, potency), on the other hand, is a *preliminary stage* of reality. The possible is not yet an existent in the full sense. But wherever there is a preliminary stage there must also be an ascent to a higher stage, and the passing from possibility to reality is *becoming* or, more precisely, this passing from one stage to the other pertains to becoming. For we have previously seen that becoming is truly a being lifted out of nothingness into existence [*Herausgehobenwerden aus dem Nichts ins Dasein*]. The being, however, into which becoming is lifted is always simultaneously "actual" and "potential" being (cf. Chapt. II, Sections 3 and 4). Thus the contraries of actuality and potentiality have their place in the realm of becoming. They permeate all existents of this realm, not only those which exist most authentically, i.e., things as such, but also everything which "actually" accrues to them and everything which "can" possibly accrue to them. In short, every kind of *movement* or *change* is a *passing from potentiality to actuality* or vice versa.

However, because the actual which comes to be is—according to Aristotle—a composite of form and matter, the "component parts" of the actual must likewise be somehow involved in the contraries of actuality and potentiality. To *unformed matter*—so we heard it stated—pertains only *potential being*. The meaning of this statement, however, still lacks precision, because "potentiality" and "actuality" have several semantic connotations.

Logical possibility is mentioned by Aristotle only in an exclusory sense [*ausschliessend*]. To state that something is possible in this sense would merely mean that its opposite is not necessary.[109] This kind of possibility does not yet constitute a preliminary stage of actual being. What is implied here is δύναμις (potency) as a *power* [*Vermögen*], i.e., an "ontological ground or primordial source [*Seinsgrund*] ἀρχή, principium)[110] of the change or movement in another thing (*qua* other) or the source of a thing's being moved by another thing (*qua* other)."[111] Thus being cured takes place in the patient who is getting well. However, medical art as the power of healing which produces that "movement" has its being not in the patient, but in the physician (except perhaps in that particular case where the patient is and acts as a physician). But the art of medicine does not by itself suffice to bring about the cure: In addition there must be in the patient the power or capability of getting well or of being cured. While the former is a *power of doing or acting* [*actio*], the latter is a *power of suffering* [*passio*] or of being acted upon (active and passive potency).

A thing is said to have a power [*vermögend*] or c*apability* [*fähig*] in a preeminent sense when it is capable of doing something *well*. (*Incapability*, conversely does not signify a complete lack of power, but only the inability to produce some good or to do something well.)

And, correspondingly, an extraordinary power of suffering or of being acted upon entails a capability of undergoing a change toward the good. And we speak of a preeminent capability when a thing has the *power* to resist all external influences and to endure completely unchanged, i.e., when it is not subject to any suffering (*passio, Leiden*). The basic meaning of "power" [*Vermögen*], however, remains for Aristotle that of being the ontological ground or primordial source of change in another thing qua other.[112]

The powers of acting and of being acted upon are interconnected in several ways. First, both are united in the same thing, which simultaneously has the capability of suffering and of causing suffering in other things. Second, to all suffering [*passio*] belongs a doing or an activity [*actio*], although, to be sure, that which acts [*das Wirkende*] and that which is acted upon are different things. But as the cause of suffering Aristotle mentions not only the capability of being acted upon of the one who suffers, but he adds that "matter, too, is an ontological ground (ἀρχή). ... Thus, what is greasy can be burnt, and what yields in a particular way can be broken...."[113]

If matter is regarded as the ontological ground or primordial source of particular powers, it cannot be conceived as wholly indefinite, nor can it coincide with those powers which have their ground in it. If *prime matter* itself is said to be a *potency,* it can either not be an ontological ground or it cannot be wholly indefinite. G. Manser[114] decides in favor of the second alternative. Though *prime matter* is "according to its inner being not some definite substance, it is nevertheless something substantial in relation to the *compositum*" and "can therefore not be *nothing.*" In this way we arrive at the peculiar notion of an "indefinite—yet not wholly indefinite—something."[115]

To this difficulty is added another one. This indefinite something cannot be a potency in the sense of a power or capability (e.g., the power of being inflammable or of being luminous). By "power," however, we mean the capability *for something,* i.e., the capability for some definite acting or being acted upon. Now it is not any easier to conceive of an "indefinite capability" than to conceive of an "indefinite something." Manser seems to think that he has found the solution of the difficulty in the supposition that: "there is an intermediate principle between *nothingness* and *actuality,* namely, potential being (κατὰ δύναμιν). And this intermediate principle in all physical substantial becoming is precisely prime matter, which is the substratum of all becoming and passing away: What this moment was actualized in prime matter is effaced owing to the loss of form, and the *novum* comes into being owing, to the acquisition of another form."

It seems to me, however, that Manser's proposed solution does not remove the difficulty, for he evidently pays no heed to the distinction between *being* [*Sein*] and *existents* [*Seiende*]. Of potency—in the sense of power or capability—we can say only that it is an immanent possibility of an existent. *Prime matter,* accordingly, would have to be designated as this existent rather than as potential being. It would have to be "something" to which being "accrues" (as least according to the view of St. Thomas, if not according to the view of Aristotle. The former regards the *materia prima* as *created,* and he has being and existence coincide only in the case of the uncreated first existent). It may be left undecided, for the time being, what may be meant by this strange something.[116]

In the passages quoted from Aristotle's *Metaphysics* the difficulty is perhaps circumvented owing to the fact that what the philosopher describes as *matter* is not to be conceived as *prime matter.* When he designates the "greasy" as the ontological ground or primordial source of what is fit for burning [*Brennbarkeit*], he means by "grease" the matter and by "fit for burning" the capability, and these two do not coincide. The *capability* (power) is rooted in *matter.* However, *matter* in this case is not indefinite, unformed, and

thus not yet actualized, but definite and actual. What can happen to the thing or what may become of it is predesigned in it as a possibility. The actualization of such possibilities, however, is tied to the working capacities [*Wirkfähigkeiten*] of other things. Becoming warm is tied to the warmth of what emits warmth [*des Erwärmenden*] and the becoming-joined-together of building stones of a house is tied to the art of the builder. But what "forms a natural unity cannot itself suffer being acted upon by itself [*durch sich selbst leiden*]."[117]

This last remark touches upon the passing from potential to actual being. And this passing proceeds—as will be shown—differently in natural becoming and in creative work [*Werkschaffen*], depending on whether the *power* is an irrational or a rational one.[118]

It is important for our purpose to analyze these distinctions because—as we have seen—the examples taken from the sphere of creative work obscure rather than clarify the interrelation of form and matter in the reality *of nature* [*Naturwirklichkeit*].[119]

6. Nature, Matter, and Form

Nature (φύσις) denotes in one sense the genesis of what grows (a meaning which is suggested by a lengthening of the υ in φύσις). In another sense we call nature that out of which the growing thing grows as from its first immanent principle. We also designate as nature that from which the first movement in each and every existent takes its start, insofar as this movement is present in the existent as in an object of such and such a specific constitution.[120] Of growth (φύεσθαι), however, we speak in all instances where things derive an increase from something else, by direct contact, by organic unity, or by organic adhesion, as in the case of embryos. And organic unity differs from mere contact. For in the latter case there need not be anything besides the contact, whereas if two things form a unity of organic growth, there is something identical in both which makes them not merely touch each other but grow together and be one with respect to continuity (συνεχές) and quantity(ποσόν), though not with respect to quality.

Moreover, *nature* is said to be that of which those things consist and are made which are not things of nature,[121] i.e., something which is not formed and which cannot change itself by its own power, as we call bronze the nature of a bronze statue or of bronze utensils, and wood the nature of wooden things ... ; for each thing is made up of such natures, and *prime matter* (πρώτη ὕλη) is preserved in them. It is in this sense that one also calls the elements the nature of the things of nature. Some say that this nature is fire, others earth or air or water or something else of this sort. Some mention a few elements, and others all of them.

In yet another sense, *ousia* is called the nature of the things of nature. Thus it is said by some that nature is the primary mode of the composite, and Empedocles asserts that no thing has a nature, that the word "nature" is nothing but a name used to designate mixture and separation, and that these latter are the really real. Hence we also say of those things which are or come to be

> in the order of nature (φύσει)—even though that from which their becoming and being naturally derive is already present—that they do not have their nature unless and until they have their structure (*eidos*) and form (μορφή). Only what consists of these two (of the not yet formed and of the form)—for example, living beings and their parts—is said to exist in the order of nature. And nature is on the one hand prime matter (πρώτη ὕλη) in a twofold sense[122]: either as the primordial principle relative to a particular thing or as the primordial principle as such. Thus, bronze is the primordial principle relative to works made of bronze, while water is perhaps the primordial principle as such (assuming that everything that can be melted is water).[123] On the other hand, nature is form (μορφή) and *ousia*, the latter being the end of the process of becoming. In a broad and more general sense we have thus come to call *ousia* a nature, because the nature of a thing too is an *ousia*.
>
> According to what has been said, then, nature in the primary and real sense is the *ousia* of things which have in themselves as such the ontological ground or primordial source of movement. For matter is called nature because it is capable of receiving *ousia*, and becoming and growth are called nature because they are movements proceeding from *ousia*. And this ontological ground or primordial source of movement in the things of nature is present in them in different ways, either potentially or in full actuality (δυνάμει ἢ ἐνεργείᾳ).[124]

When Aristotle in this summary statement designates the *ousia* of things as nature in the true and full sense, he evidently does not have in mind the thing as such but what he had previously called τὸ εἶδος χαὶ ἡ οὐσία or what in scholastic terminology is known as substantial form or *Wesensform*. To nature in the broader sense would then correspond *ousia* in the general meaning of that which exists as such [*des Existierenden überhaupt*].

7. *Becoming in the Order of Nature* [Naturhaftes Werden]

Of special importance for our inquiry are Aristotle's statements concerning the matter of the things of nature. This matter must presumably be what is given prior to the thing's having attained its *form* or *nature,* i.e., the "unformed substratum"[125] from which the natural becoming derives. Since this unformed substratum is what underlies becoming, i.e., the principle from which passing over into actual being takes its start, it bears within itself the *power* of becoming the corresponding *actual thing,* or it *is* this thing *potentially* (δυνάμει). It is not a non-existent but rather located at that peculiar stage of being which ties in between not being and actual being (ἐνεργείᾳ) and which we designated as a preliminary phase of actual being.

According to Aristotle, the unformed substratum "receives into itself" the form or nature, and this expression is pregnant with significance for an understanding of natural being and becoming. This phrase, nevertheless, presents a formidable difficulty: It seems evident that bronze "receives into itself" the "form" of a shield and that the bronze is given prior to its becoming a shield. But what is it that "receives into itself" the "form" of the rose bush? What is there or given before the rose bush "comes to be"? How are we to conceive of this "receiving" and this "becoming"?

Once again we turn to Aristotle for illumination:

> The production of another of their species is the most natural act for all living beings which are fully developed, not mutilated in one way or another, and not spontaneously generated. Thus, an animal generates an animal and a plant produces a plant in order that, as far as this is possible, they may partake of the eternal and divine. For this is the end toward which all beings strive, and all their natural activities are directed toward that goal. But because they can have no immediate contact with the eternal and divine (since none of the transitory individual creatures can endure forever), they partake of it in the measure which their nature permits, the one in a greater, the other in a lesser degree. And in this way they endure, not indeed as self-identical individuals but rather in something that is like themselves, and thus they remain self-identical or one in their species.[126]

The capability of living beings to produce others of their species is regarded by Aristotle as a power [*Vermögen*] of the soul, since the soul is the essential form (*ousia*) of animate bodies and as such the cause of their being. "For in all things it is the substance which is the cause of their being, and in living beings their being is their life."[127] The soul is also the immanent ontological ground or primordial source of movement, of growth and decay, for:

> ... growth and decay can only take place if they are sustained by nutrition, and nutrition can only take place in a being which has a share in life. ... Since nothing, then, takes in nutriment that has no share in life, it is the besouled [*beseelt*] body as such which takes in nutriment, and nutriment thus pertains essentially (and not merely accidentally) to besouled beings. There is, however, a difference between nutrition and growth. Inasmuch as the besouled being has a quantitative determination, it is capable of a quantitative increase, and inasmuch as it is this definite thing and a substance,[128] it is capable of taking in nutriment. For nutrition sustains the substance, which is maintained as long as it is nourished. Nutrition, moreover, effects *generation*, not indeed the generation of the being which is nourished, but the production of another being of the same species. For the substance of the being which is nourished is already in existence, and beings do not generate themselves. They only maintain themselves.
>
> This principle of the soul, therefore, of which we are speaking, is the power of maintaining the being which bears this power within itself, such as it is, and nutriment imparts actuality to the power. This is why, when deprived of nutriment, the being cannot exist.
>
> Since this process of nutrition involves three factors—that which is nourished, that wherewith something is nourished, and that which does the nourishing— the soul on its first or basic level is what nourishes a thing, the body in which the soul is immanent is what is nourished, and the nutriment is that wherewith a thing is nourished. But since it is reasonable to name things with a view to their goals and since it is the goal of this kind of soul to generate a being of the same species, the soul on this first level should be defined as the power to produce a being of the same species.[129]

The processes of nutrition and generation, which in the above quotations are seen in their close interconnection, must now be considered separately. In this way we may be able to see more clearly how form and matter are related to one another in things of nature. Later on we shall have to ask whether part of what has been shown to be valid for living beings applies equally to "dead things," insofar as they are "purely natural," i. e., not fashioned or shaped by human hands.

8. Nutrition Considered as an Example of the "Formation" of "Material Elements"

We distinguished three elements in the process of nutrition: the soul which does the nourishing, the body which receives the nourishment, and the food or nutriment wherewith the nourishing is done. In this process the soul functions as the *form*, the body (i.e., the besouled body) as the matter which is being formed, and the nutriment as a matter which is to receive form but is as yet unformed. This "being-as-yet-unformed," however, is not to be understood in an absolute sense, for the nutritive material elements are "unformed" only inasmuch as the body is as yet not informed by them and inasmuch as they bear in themselves the *potentiality* of such an information (*passive potency*). Thus, the nutritive material elements are not *prime matter* in an absolute sense, but only with respect to the body, for they are, after all, definite and real objects. In order to encounter genuine prime matter, i.e., something which is absolutely unformed (if such a thing could be encountered "at all"), we should have to go back even further. The important thing is, for the time being, that in the phenomenon of nutrition we have evidently found a natural process to which the term "formation" can be meaningfully applied.

Two additional distinctions must be made and should be kept in mind: 1) the chemical transformation of the nutritive material elements that are absorbed by the body into material elements with which the body can be "informed"; and 2) the building up [*Aufbau*] of the body from the thus prepared material elements.[130] In the process of "preparation" the body extracts from the nutritive material elements whatever it finds useful and eliminates what is useless. Prior to this work of digestion, the received material elements are foreign matter, and whatever cannot be used remains foreign matter and must be eliminated. What is useful, on the other hand, undergoes the process of "information": It is conjoined with the spatially formed and organized body, and once it is "besouled," it becomes part of the besouled body and therewith a *tool* or *organ* of the soul and its activities.

The use of nutritive material elements in the building up of a body of definite structure reminds one of the way a work of art is formed. The essential formation, however, consists in the besouling information [*Beseelung*]. The latter is basic for the organization of the spatial structure [*Raumgestalt*] which in the case of nutrition does not come about—as it does in a human work (e.g., the building of a house)—by means of a workmanlike external operation, but *naturally* inside the natural whole in which the nutritive substances are incorporated owing to the activity of that vital center which we call the *soul* (in the broad sense in which Aristotle and the scholastics use this term). And the work of art is not a *nature* or *substance* (*ousia*) precisely because it does not possess the unity of an internally cohering whole.[131]

Viewed from the perspective of the living being which maintains itself in existence and grows by means of nutrition, the nutritive process implies that the living being animates the lifeless material elements by "appropriating" them and by thus making them part of its own being. The *power* to do this belongs to the essence or nature of the living being: The latter is so constituted that it is capable of appropriating foreign matter, and the realization of this power (the act of this *potency*) is a mode of its being, which is life. This realization is thus a *vital activity* [*Lebenstätigkeit*]. And this process presupposes the living being as actually alive. It does not "come into being" [*es wird nicht erst*] by taking in nourishment. It does not thereby receive its *form.* Rather, it displays its activity by virtue of its form. The absorbed material elements in turn undergo a genuine new formation in the process of nutrition: They become something which they were not prior to this transformation.

9. Elements and Prime Matter: The Ambiguity in the Aristotelian Concept of Matter

When hydrogen and oxygen combine to form water, we have a new substance in place of the original elements. In Aristotle's view, there had to exist a substratum which subsequently assumes a new *nature* or *form* by losing the one it previously had. And if this underlying principle is the *ultimate* substratum, it must be the looked-for *prime matter* in the true sense of the word: an indefinite and—taken by itself—unreal element.

As a matter of fact, Aristotle sees in nature a graduated structure of forms and material elements: The experientially known physical bodies are composed of the elements (the heavenly bodies are composed of ether, earthly bodies of fire, water, air, and earth), and it is the elements which represent the lowest stage of *formed matter*. What has been formed in them is *prime matter*. This prime matter, however, has never existed by itself without form, and there has never taken place a formation as a temporal process whereby prime matter could have received the form of the elements.

If this is the case, what need is there for assuming such a strange substratum (viz., prime matter) and for making a distinction between form and matter in things of nature? The need for such an assumption evidently lies in the possibility of a passage from one state into the other. Aristotle believes in the possibility of the transmutation of one element into another, and he can explain such a transmutation only by assuming a constituent part common to both being potentially one or the other. The *meaning of prime matter* is thus a *general receptivity* [*Empfangsbereitschaft*] for the forms of all things or the *possibility of becoming everything*. This meaning has its outer limit in the fact that prime matter is a *preliminary stage of actuality* [*Vorstufe des Wirklichen*] (δύναμις, potency). It thus seems that *potency* and *matter* coincide.

We have encountered this latter idea before on pp. 177f. above, and we have seen what difficulties it entails. All being is the being of some existent [*Sein eines Seienden*].[132] A "potential being," without a "something" whose being it is, cannot be posited. We have clearly seen that every finite actuality is simultaneously actual and potential and that some elements of its nature are actualized while others are still waiting for their actualization. The actual is here the basis of the potential. Is any potentiality conceivable without such a foundation of actuality?

Aristotle's concept of matter has both of these connotations: It denotes material elements which, though formed, bear within themselves the possibility of further formation, and it denotes what is totally unformed, totally non-actual, and merely possible.

We have encountered this double meaning again and again. Aristotle believed he could get hold of a unified principle by calling—in order to explain the process of becoming—the underlying ὕλη an existent [*Seiendes*] "that is, relatively speaking, a non-existent, or a non-existent that is, relatively speaking, an existent."[133] In point of fact, however, the first and the second half of this definition signify different things. What Aristotle called the relatively non-existing existent is the actual which is opened toward further determinations, and what he calls the relatively existing non-existent is what is as yet non-actualized and therefore merely possible. While the former concept is familiar to us from our visual experience of the actuality of nature [*Naturwirklichkeit*], the latter concept presents such difficulties that it is understandable why Bäumker wanted to see it eliminated altogether.[134] He tried to circumvent the difficulty by characterizing the Aristotelian concept of matter as a "too extreme form of realism" and by attributing a specific kind of reality to that possibility of a new state which has its foundation in an actual nature.[135] However, the question is whether *prime matter* can be disposed of so easily. Does this difficult concept not perhaps point to something which can be brought into our field of vision?

10. The Aristotelian and Platonic Concepts of Matter

It is rather surprising that Aristotle and Plato, using entirely different approaches, should have arrived at what Aristotle calls ὕλη (the term as such is not used by Plato). For Aristotle, ὕλη is the *raison d'être* of the undeniable experiential phenomena of *becoming*. Plato, proceeding from the consideration of the *distance* or *gap* that exists between the *ideas* and their *images* or *copies* (i.e., worldly objects and beings), arrives at the conclusion that there must be a third principle which may serve to explain this gap—a "nurse" or a "recipient" of all becoming: "an invisible, formless, all-receiving being, partaking of the intelligible in a way that is difficult to explain and more difficult to understand...."

With great ingenuity Bäumker endeavored to show that for Plato this *primary matter* signified nothing but empty space,[136] that *wherein* bodies exist, not that *of which* they consist. Plato, he points out, did not distinguish between mathematical and physical bodies and consequently not between space and what fills space. When Plato in his *Timaeus* speaks of *primary* and *secondary* matter, of "a matter which precedes the formation of the world, a matter which is independent of God and therefore eternal, visible, and corporeal"—an orderless, irregularly moving mass upon which God impresses order and rule—both Bäumker and Eduard Zeller comment that this does not actually express Plato's point of view, but that the Greek thinker "only temporarily lent an ear to the ancient idea of the chaos that was in the beginning."

We might object that what Plato presents in mythical form should be taken a little more seriously and that he presumably introduced a second matter in addition to the first (which he himself designates as space) because the first matter appeared to him insufficient to accomplish what he regarded as the function of the "third" principle, namely, explain the gap between the ideas and the things and beings of the world. But it is not our intention here to weigh the pros and cons of different possible interpretations of Plato's philosophy. What intrigues us is the fact that two thinkers of such widely differing philosophic outlook as Plato and Aristotle should meet in their demand for a principle which appears to them absolutely essential for the understanding of visible nature (plus the additional fact that Aristotle, despite his different view of the world as a whole, firmly adhered to Plato's suggestion). We gather from such a meeting of minds in this complex question that both thinkers envisaged—albeit dimly and from afar—something of objective validity and significance. It will be our task to bring this something into clearer focus.

11. Attempt at an Objective Clarification of the Problem: The Material Element [Stoff], *Matter, Pure Mass*

If we mean by "Platonic ideas" what we have previously designated as *essences* [*Wesenheiten*] or *whatnesses* [*Washeiten*] or *pure forms* and if we then confront these with the world of sensible objects, the contrast is immediately evident. On the one side we find what is withdrawn from all becoming and change, what rests in its own fulfillment untouched by the events of this world and accessible only to the intellect. On the other side we find a world of things which "enter into existence" [*Dasein*], which develop by working upon others and by in turn being subject to various influences, which "maintain" themselves in the struggle with others and yet, after a variety of "fateful encounters," perish in the end; a world, moreover, which peremptorily "strikes the senses."

Everything that we have just stated concerning the nature of Platonic ideas applies equally to structures in the constitution of which the intelligible or spiritual element has a preponderance over the spatial material elements.[137] In the present context, however, where we endeavor to explore the nature of the material as such, we are confining ourselves to *external nature.*[138] "External nature" does not refer here to what is outside myself but to what is essentially "externally formed" [*ins Äussere hineingestaltet*],[139] i.e., to everything material [*stofflich*].[140] To be externally formed, however, does not yet mean to be a material thing. A real image, for example, that has been produced by means of mirrors is likewise externally formed: It is "real," not merely "apparent." But if at first we believed it to be the real thing and then found out its illusory nature, the situation has "changed completely": What we had accepted as filled and weighted with reality turns out to be empty and fragile. "It rests not in itself but depends ... on a different source of reality." It is *not in itself* [*in sich*], *but only outside itself* [*nach aussen*] and "therefore ... not outside *by virtue of itself....*"[141] What is material, on the other hand, stands and rests in its own fullness and thereby transcends itself [*tritt nach aussen*]. It reveals itself in its sensible nature which as such is both the manifest and the self-manifesting phenomenon.

Mere apparent units [*Erscheinungseinheiten*] have no "place of their own" [*eigene Stätte*]. They are produced by something which is external to them, and they disappear as soon as these external conditions of their existence are suspended. A material thing, on the other hand, cannot simply vanish from existence. It is safely rooted in itself, but it has at the same time a certain *ontological immobility* and *rigidity*. It is thus not only distinguished from the fleeting and weightless being of the mere apparent unit but also from beings which in a similar manner only fleetingly manifest themselves in the external world and which do so not by virtue of external conditions, but by virtue of their own strength—beings which are "capable of ... clothing themselves with their corporeal existence."[142] The natural constitution of material things excludes the possibility on their part "of incorporating themselves in existence out of their own substantial power or of placing themselves outside this existence." The material body is not an authentic expression of a free substantiating power.[143]

If we now try to understand the nature of materiality as such, we must certainly attribute to it *dependence on space* [*Raumgebundenheit*], but a dependence of a *special kind.* The apparent unit, too, is a spatial structure, but one which does not *fill* space and which does not arise from the *depth* of space. Everything material, on the other hand, has a hidden depth which manifests itself in the form of an external surface. By means of sectional cuts, ever new elements come to the surface, but even an infinite number of sectional cuts could not reveal the entire depth, because "none of these can really touch the ultimate depth."[144] Because matter "fills space in its continuity not merely superficially, but *totally* and thus in actual reality, and because to do this is the specific character of its ontological constitution, matter is, as it were, irrevocably tied to space and always transcends any merely superficial or punctual (i.e., two-dimensional or one-dimensional) condition."[145]

Space is an "abyss," an "absolute and quasi-universal, bottomless depth. It is that which in its emptiness is beyond all measure," but in this very boundlessness it is "the basis of everything that is measurable of every structure that is constituted in external, measurable proportions."[146] Matter is essentially spatial. "Where there is matter or anything material, there is space. No previously given space is needed."[147] Yet there is a difference between space as a dimension of material being and space as such. Where space is filled with material being it appears as a suitable receptacle, while space as such is emptied of everything, even of itself. *Matter* [*das Materielle*] *as such totally fills the abyss,* thereby not only annulling it, but entering into it. Whereas everything that is real is in full possession of its effectually manifest content and is thus self-contained and self-enclosed, it is "the peculiar character of material units that they are compelled to posit their self-enclosed nature ... in the form of absolute transcendence, flight from self, and emptiness."[148]

Matter [*das Materielle*] is "what is *materialiter* commensurate with the abyss and thus commensurate with the immeasurable as such, and which has become a material (self-immanent) unit—a unit which at no point rests *in itself,* but is wholly outside itself and which, *despite* this formal being-outside-itself, *is* yet unified." The content acquires its fullness by filling the abyss. "Prior to this filling, the content possesses no fullness. ... Material fulfillment (matter) and a thoroughly spatially determined substantiality originate in the consummate union of the content and the abyss."[149] This process marks the origin of *real space.* "The abyss plus the substantially effectual content yield space plus matter."[150]

While matter "rests" upon the ground of the abyss, the merely apparent unit is "held in suspense" [*schwebt*] by a fixed transcendent point. But from these two types of spatial being we previously distinguished a third one: a type of existent which lifts itself to a certain height and maintains itself at that level without sinking into the abyss. It is possible to conceive of a *spatially effectuated* [*raumhaft ausgewirkt*] *body* which is *born up from within,* but in such a way that it is held totally "in suspense" [*in der Schwebe*]. Such a body is thoroughly grounded in *energy* [*Kraft*]. Its ontological propensity [*Seinsrichtung*] is from the inside out. It cannot be weighted down internally and thus become a burden unto itself; and it represents "a genuine material entity, i.e., an entity of spatially extended fullness," but "an immaterial materiality [*immaterielle Stofflichkeit*] ... which at no point relapses into itself and can thus not fall prey to the bottomless depth of space."[151] Its quiescence is the *calm of strength,* while the quiescence of matter is the *calm of impotence.*

Matter is "a pure stuffing [*Füllung*] ..., an infinitude and boundlessness of pure accumulation, corresponding to ... the empty and boundless infinitude of the abyss that is to be filled."[152] In this case the *ontological propensity* is from the *outside in,* and in place of a supporting bearing up [*das Tragen*] we have a heavy bearing down [*das Lasten*]. On the other hand, where an existent is its own carrier [*Träger seiner selbst*], i.e., where "the existent's own being effectuates a representative manifestation," we have a *vital positing of reality* [*Lebendige Realtitätssetzung*]. "Vital" in this context does not denote restriction to a definite sphere of reality (of "living beings"), but indicates precisely the peculiar nature of this self-forming from the inside out. Material living beings possess no such vitality in any primordial sense. Matter [*das Materielle*] as such is a "carrier" only formally, not materially. It "rises not to itself ... but ... lies *buried* under the fullness of its being which is simply commensurate with it. ... The ontic task which must be fulfilled and is actually fulfilled by any simple material positing consists in being (in substantial fullness and upon the ground of absolute emptiness and boundlessness) something which carries and unifies itself without a substantiating carrier that could impart unity, measure, and uniformity from within."[153]

That which is substantially immanent forms itself into space without falling prey to the abyss. Any substantialization into the abyss [*Substantialisierung in den Abgrund hinein*], on the other hand, leads to an "immanence of absolute transcendence" and therewith to an "unconditional positing of the external," i.e., to "external nature" in the narrower sense.[154]

The above quotations give no unequivocal answer to the question concerning that objectively demonstrable principle at which the Aristotelian ὕλη seemed to aim. We have encountered several concepts which may have some bearing on our problem. *Stoff* and matter were used [by H. Conrad-Martius] with different significations. While *Stoff* was described as "substantial fullness with spatial breadth,"[155] *matter* appeared as a darkened fullness, heavy with and stifled by its own weight, a fullness in which every "internal and external freedom of qualification is obliterated."[156]

There are *material whatnesses* [*Stoff-Washeiten*] which require actualization in spatial fullness, but not every kind of content is capable of such actualization. The forming-into-space, however, can take place in a twofold manner: 1) as a formation from the inside out, born up by an indigenous energy which dominates space without falling prey to it; and 2) in the peculiar manner of things material which are "swallowed up" by space and which would be struck in their innermost being if they were deprived of their position in space.

Material substances [*Stoffe*] differ "according to their structural relations which in varying ways cause their substantial fullness to unfold itself into space and to give the appearance of its filling that space. These structural relations express the manner in which the material substances are internally united among themselves."[157] But now a peculiar difficulty arises. Specifically differing material structures (i.e., structures which differ according to their *materiality*) embody different material whatnesses [*Stoffwasheiten*]. However, what causes the *materiality* of these structures, what causes their fullness to possess that peculiar weight and darkness—what "boundlessly fills the abyss," the *pure mass*—is as such incapable of assuming different formations. "Being wholly commensurate with the abyss, the mass simply is what it is: thoroughly wedded to space and thus in its own ontological sphere factually excluding everything else."[158]

Whatever "is absolutely outside itself cannot be joined to itself, either closely or remotely, either firmly or loosely. ... " Nor can it—in the so-called secondary qualities—appear on the surface. Pure mass is dark through and through, dead and dumb. It is "what is essentially unqualifiable ... , a dead, dumb, and obtuse something which is distinguished from nothing only by the fact that it is mass and thus in its very massiveness *eo ipso* set apart from nothingness."[159] On the one hand, then, a material substance is only possible when a qualitatively determined content is wedded to the abyss. On the other hand, the pure mass resists such a wedding. Is there a way out of this difficulty?

12. The Atomistic and Dynamistic Theory of the Constitution of Matter

Hedwig Conrad-Martius sees a possible solution of the problem in *atomism.* The mass is divided into *particles* "which, despite the fact that as mass-particles they are again divisible *ad infinitum,* actually represent the ultimate building foundation of concrete matter." This is only possible if certain *forces* "work upon the mass particles and tie them together." These forces "are ... potencies for an efficacious activity of a definite kind, and they are not in the possession of the mass itself, but accrue to it *externally* and are thus taking possession of it." In this way mass becomes *externally* capable of a qualification which it cannot assume internally, and therewith:

> ... the qualitatively determining content (i.e., the material whatness [*Stoffwasheit*] which as such is to be substantialized) becomes in turn subject to the material form of substantialization.... Corporeal fullness is here impossible, since the qualitatively determining

> element can be vitally qualifying only in a kind of fullness which remains *overt,* transparent, and in suspense with respect to all potencies and all possibilities of formation. ... Only *fixed* potencies can take possession of the mass. ... A qualification which is posited once and for all from without then takes the place of a vital and actually continuous qualification from within.[160]

On the basis of such an external fixation "the entire wealth of possible qualification can then become manifest," but only "shadowlike and by way of intimation."[161]

Atomism is thus mentioned as *one* possible solution of the problem. It may explain how, notwithstanding the demonstrated peculiar nature of pure mass, a material world of varied structures can arise. But, as previously indicated, an entirely different world of material fullness [*stoffliche Fülle*] is conceivable: a world without any massive weight, totally born up and permeated by vital forces. This world "*is* only what it is (i.e., a substantial fullness which nevertheless is no mass) *as* a world born up and permeated in this manner."[162] This alternative solution, based on dynamism, does not mean that pure force would allow us to dispense with the material element [*Stoff*] as such. For both solutions the material element as a spatially extended fullness [*raumgebreitete Fülle*] is indispensable. *Fixed potencies* (the physical forces) are tied to mass.

"*Free* forces, on the other hand ... are only what they are in and with the fullness in which they become effective [*sich auswirken*]. ... A separation is here no longer possible. The material element *is* the continuous actual efficacy of the potencies as such, and the potencies *are* the inner being of the material element, a being which is posited by force. The material element and the force [*Stoff und Kraft*] coincide." The material element, resting as it does on a free inner dynamism, "corresponds to the genuine being and essence of what nature and what is posited by nature are and ought to be," and this being and essence are what they are "in a more genuine sense than the matter which has its foundation in pure mass and its externally posited potencies."[163]

This latter description, however, hardly corresponds to the world of our experience in its present state. We are confronted here with two entirely different views of the basic constitution of *external nature*. A passing from the one to the other is inconceivable in the way of natural evolution. It is possible only by means of a "leap," i.e., by a complete reversal [*Umkehrung*].

In the case of dynamic constitution a manifold of specifically differing material elements without a common foundation is conceivable. In the case of atomistic structure, on the other hand, "external nature has as its necessary substrate an ubiquitous dead element."[164] Thus it seems that in the case of *pure mass* we are dealing with something which corresponds to the Aristotelian ὕλη insofar as this term refers to that substratum of all external nature which we designated as *prime matter*. There are nonetheless considerable differences in particular details. While Aristotle's prime matter must *as such* be capable of becoming everything, pure mass has as such no potentialities of formal becoming [*Ausgestaltungsmöglichkeiten*]. And while for Aristotle the ὕλη Is the indispensable foundation of all becoming, a possible relationship of the pure mass to the process of becoming must be envisioned in an entirely different way.

Massive weight [*Massenbeschwertheit*] does not at all represent the primordial state of external nature. This primordial state, i.e., the truly "natural" in external nature, is the inner unity of force and material elements, the free, efficacious realization [*das Sichauswirken*] of force in space-filling material formations [*Stoffgestaltungen*]. The breaking apart of *Kraft* and *Stoff*, the "breaking away" [*Herausfallen*] of the material elements from this unity, which turns them into pure mass, is a reversal of the primordial ontological state.

Pure mass, therefore, cannot be conceived as an eternal, not-become prime matter. Nor can it be conceived as non-transitory. For even if external nature in its actual present state is massively weighted [*massenbeschwert*] this state is by no means immutable. External nature can be "redeemed," i.e., it can be raised to its original state. "Pure mass as such is unredeemable, but matter can be redeemed from its bondage to pure mass. The latter would cease to *be* wherever and whenever the free dynamic constitution could gain ground."[165]

Stoff is never without *Kraft*. In the case of dynamic constitution, material elements are effectuated by force and *inwardly* ruled. In the case of atomistic constitution, mass is subjected to aggressive forces that work from the outside, and it cannot be conceived apart from these forces. Mass can therefore neither be equivalent to *chaos* nor to Plato's *secondary matter.* No initial state of the world is conceivable in which *pure mass,* entirely unformed, could have filled space. In order to be, pure mass needs a hold which it cannot give to itself. It is "held" by those forces which rule it and form it. It *is* a constructive constitutive part of external nature which as such is characterized precisely by this constitutive part as a nature that has "fallen" from its original state. Does it make sense to call mass a pure "possibility"? By itself it is neither real nor possible. It is real within the total structure of external nature, upon the actual being of which the pure mass confers the peculiar characteristics of massively heavy, "darkened," and "fallen" being.

13. Matter in the Structure of the External World: The Graduated Scale of Material Elements [Stoffe] *and Formations*

In our inquiry into the possible meanings of *Stoff,* several things were anticipated which stand in need of further clarification. Thus, we shall have to devote special attention to an investigation of what is meant by *force* [*Kraft*], *substance,* and the *carrying principle* [*Trägerschaft*]. But before we approach this task, we must first determine the role which the material elements play in the structure of external nature. In this connection we shall have to take into consideration the different meanings of *Stoff* which we have so far encountered: 1) the basic meaning of space-filling as such and as the substrate of all formation; and 2) the distinctive characteristics of *Stoff* according to the manner of space-filling and according to the graduated scale of formations. Pure mass we have learned to know as the boundless stuffing [*das masslos Füllende*] and the totally unformed which, taken by itself, is never actual. Pure mass shares this non-actuality and the incapability of existing by itself with Aristotelian prime matter. All actual material elements are formed, and the specific manner of their formation and of their space-filling are interdependent.

Material stuff-structures [*Stoffgebilde*], i.e., structures of massive weight, are not only *filling* space but also *tied* to space, and their formation proceeds from the external toward the internal. Pure apparent-units (which have light as their material element) are produced in space by something external to them without filling space or maintaining themselves in space in their own right.

Vital stuff-structures are placed into space by some internal force. It seems that Aristotle confined himself in this respect to the consideration of material nature. Within the latter he distinguishes between *dead* and *living* beings, while he is not cognizant of the above described two possible basic constitutions of material being.

In material nature the lowest stage of actual existents is represented by the simple material elements [*Stoffe*]. They are *formed* inasmuch as each of them has its definite and distinct character which sets it off from the others. They are *Stoff* in the dual sense of that which fills space and that in which other things (mixed bodies, e.g., minerals) may originate.[166] These latter are on a higher level of *formation* inasmuch as their particular nature presupposes the nature of the elements and is yet a distinct *novum.* But these mixed bodies, too, are *Stoff* in view of and with respect to a twofold formation. They are: 1) what serves to build up the bodies of *living being,* and 2) what provides the foundation upon which human *works* can arise. In both instances the "structure" which comes into being has a self-enclosed *spatial form* [*Raumgestalt*] which is organized according to definite laws and is thereby distinguished from the lower material elements (insofar as they are fixed elements). The latter, to be sure, exist likewise in "pieces" and have as such a definite spatial limit, but one which is externally conditioned, i.e., one which derives not exclusively from their own structural law.[167]

While on the lower levels the particular nature of the material element was designated as *form,* on this higher level the particular spatial structure belongs so essentially to the *form* that it is customary to apply the name "form" to the spatial structure as such. Because of the strongly pronounced Greek "sense of form" [*Formgefühl*] and because of the high esteem in which the Greeks held everything that was formed, firmly bounded, and duly ordered as against what is formless and without boundary or measure—perfection was for the Greeks equivalent to what is thoroughly formed and ordered, while imperfection was equivalent to the unformed and boundless. The former was called *cosmos,* the latter *chaos.* This common characteristic alone made them draw a strict dividing line between the structures of nature and art, on the one hand, and the lower levels of material elements, on the other. Thus the structures of nature and art were for them in close proximity. The lower stages exist for the sake of the higher ones and are ordained to them as their "end."

And in view of the thoroughgoing teleological determinateness of the Aristotelian cosmos, this "for the sake of" applies in all strictness also to works of art.

The human mind is ordained to the forming of works and so there must be some material element [*Stoff*] destined to be formed by the human mind and by human hands. In and by creative work the human mind and simultaneously the human work are fully actualized (cf. pp. 222f. below). Inanimate elements in turn are destined to serve as building material for living bodies, and—in the view of Aristotle—they undergo this "formation" at the moment living beings originate and from then on progressively in the growth, evolution, and reproduction of these beings by means of nutrition and procreation.

This "formation" is the actualization of the dual potentiality of the "pliability" [*Bildsamkeit*] of material elements [*Stoff*] and the "formative power" [*Bildungskraft*] of living beings. The process of "formation" as such evidently cannot be observed by us either at the moment living beings originate or at the time the material substrate originates. What is visible is the already "formed being" [*Geformtsein*] in its specific determinateness. The progress of a human work, on the other hand, and the development of a living being are processes of a formation which can be perceived. It is thus understandable that examples taken from these spheres present themselves to our mind whenever it is a question of explaining the way in which form is related to matter.

There is, of course, no doubt in the mind of Aristotle that natural becoming and artistic creation are distinctly different processes. In natural becoming that *out of which* the becoming thing comes to be (i.e., the material element [*Stoff*]) is an actuality of nature [*ein Naturwirkliches*] (*ousia,* substance), and the same is true of that *which* comes to be (i.e., the new living being). In artistic creation, on the other hand, that *whereby* the work of art comes to be is not an actuality of nature, but the "project" or "design" "in the soul" of the artist, and likewise that which comes into being (i.e., the "work") is not *nature* in the same sense as is a living being: It is not *ousia* in the sense of an independent actuality.[168]

To say that that *whereby* the work comes to be lies not in the work itself means at the same time that the material *elements* [*Stoff*] do not have in themselves the ontological ground of that movement which leads toward their end, as is the case in the development of a living being. These are certainly far-reaching differences. It is nevertheless understandable that Aristotle could regard natural formation and artistic formation as being very closely related to one another. For that *out of which* the becoming thing comes to be is in both instances an actuality of nature, albeit not a full actuality [*Vollwirkliches*], inasmuch as it bears within itself the potentialities of further formation. There are certain material elements which can and must serve the building up of living beings, and there are certain material elements which have the aptitude and the "calling" [*Berufung*] of being formed into works of art. And in Aristotle's opinion both sets of material elements bear within themselves these "possible" structures as inner possibilities.

In fully developed living beings and in perfected works of art the process of formation seems to have reached a certain consummation. This does not mean that these structures cannot furnish any *material elements* for further formations and for the latter's in-formation in structures of a higher rank. But such a development would even go farther beyond the frame of *external nature* than is the case in works of art. And our main concern, for the time being, is, after all, to arrive at a more adequate understanding of spatial-material nature as such. We have learned to know the material elements [*die Stoffe*] as filling space and as having an aptitude for being molded into structures of a closed spatial form [*Raumgestalt*]. With respect to both these aspects certain complemental determinations appear to be necessary if we are to understand the way in which these two essential characteristics are intrinsically interconnected.

14. The Basic Modes of Filled Space [Raumerfüllung]

Material elements differ among themselves by virtue of the particular mode in which they fill space. Of essential significance for the total structure of the material world are the *three basic modes of filling space* which in natural science are known as *states of aggregation:* the *solid,* the *liquid,* and the *gaseous* state. A structure of comprehensively closed spatial form and persistent external limitation—the *corporeal structure*—is possible only in the case of solid material elements. At the extreme opposite end are the gaseous elements. With them there seems to be no longer any massive weight. Nothing seems to remain that could be called completely self-enclosed, fixed in itself, and demarcated as a whole. Everything is absolutely volatile and without a hold in itself. But this apparent "nothing" is nevertheless a something that lightly and imperceptibly penetrates everything, partaking of everything in an almost playful manner, and enveloping everything.

The opposite of the constitution of the body is the constitution of the *sphere.* "While the 'body' is self-centered [*in sich gesammelt*] and fixed ... the sphere in its volatility is without a hold in itself, giving itself in freedom, and "self-lessness" to everything else. ... While in the former the self is securely maintained ... the latter is a free 'un-selfish' outpouring."[169] If volatility appears, on the one hand, as a privation, it makes possible, on the other hand, that lightness, freedom, and overtness which solid bodies lack. Material elements of massive weight cannot possess both of these qualities in unison, whereas in material structures which have no such massive weight and which are formed from within, corporeal fullness in unison with volatile freedom is possible.

That which is in the liquid state "partakes neither of the force of self-maintaining fixation nor of self-transcending volatility. Liquid has a hold in itself without, however, being firmly centered in itself or even capable of such a firm self-concentration."[170] While liquid cannot be formed, it does not resist (as does the gaseous) confinement but "is rather destined to being enclosed in a receptacle." It needs "such a confinement ... in order not to glide unrestrainedly away *from itself* into an infinite depth." In falling it does not maintain itself (as does the solid), but is dominated (not only as a whole, but *throughout*) by the attracting force of the depth. ... "[171] It not only falls, but it *glides away from itself* [*entfällt sich selber*]. Being essentially "that which falls" [*das Fallende*] it is as such incapable of being formed [*nicht formbar*]. But this *flux* of a "continuous self-defection" [*Selbstabfall*] nevertheless presupposes a fullness which continuously maintains itself. Owing to this fullness and its unstable incapability of offering resistance, liquid becomes "the suitable material for the positing of fluid structures"[172] and therewith the bearer of life.

We designated the three, states of aggregation as the basic modes of space-filling, and we stated that the material elements differ among themselves by virtue of these basic modes. While each *Stoff* may under suitable conditions pass over from any one of the three states into another, one particular state of aggregation is the *natural* state of each particular *Stoff,* so that such a passing over is a more or less artificial process. Water is the purest embodiment of liquid as such—"fluidity as such."

The three modes of space filling we have described denote essentially different basic structures of material being.[173] Mass as such cannot assume the form of any of them. Although on an atomistic basis an external copying of pure essences is possible, they all must needs suffer a deformation and distortion. The "self-lessness" of gaseous elements is achieved at the expense of volatility. The vitality of liquid elements turns into a dead and feeble instability, and the self-containment of solid elements becomes an impenetrable rigidity.

To the three basic structures of material being correspond three different atomistic constitutional states: the *communistic* state (its principle: *everyone for anyone*), the *anarchial* state (*all stand against all*), and the *atomistic* state in the narrower sense (*everyone stands for himself or herself*). On an *atomistic basis* a solid body can come into being only:

> ... if the atomistic members are juxtaposed in a fixed association of communistic attachment. The phenomenon of gaseous modification and thus of material self-detachment, in turn, can come into being only if the atomistic members oppose themselves in principle and in universal mutual repulsion to any kind of union and association. And, finally, in the liquid state we witness the realization of the absolute indifference of specifically atomistic structures, owing to the fact that in this state the ever present possibility of the continuous defection of members from one another may—upon the slightest external influence—bring about atomistically and externally what was shown to be the pure essence of fluidity (i.e., self-defection).[174]

Every material element [*Stoff*] *possesses* one of these three basic structures, either one which is naturally its own, or one into which it has been placed by suitable conditions and circumstances. Each *element* as such is characterized and set off from other elements by the fact that one or the other basic structure—and, in addition, one of this structure's possible particularizations, such as brittleness or softness, refractoriness or fluidity, etc.—is specifically its own.

15. Elements and Combinations [Verbindungen]

Elements represent a manifold of material formation. When they enter into *mixtures* [*Mischungen*] and *combinations* [*Verbindungen*], there result further particular material formations. Now the question must be asked whether it is essential for the understanding of the material element [*das Stoffliche*] as such that a union of the originally existing elements in new ones is possible. The fact of the transformation of material elements into one another has, as we know, been cited as the reason for assuming a *materia prima* [*Urstoff*].[175] We found it impossible, however, to accept the notion of prime matter in the strictly Aristotelian sense.

In *pure mass* we indeed discovered something which in some respects is closely related to Aristotelian prime matter, but we also found that massively weighted, atomistically arranged material elements are not the only ones possible. We must ask then whether and how on the basis of either atomism or dynamism a mixture and combination of material elements is conceivable.

We speak of mixture when different material elements enter into a composition without surrendering their particular materiality [*stoffliche Eigenart*]. Parts of several material elements enter into a spatial whole, the external appearance and efficacious activity [*Wirkung*] of which are determined by the particular nature of the *mixture* and by the being and working together (based on the mixture) of the building materials. While this presents no particular difficulty, it is different with *combinations* which arise from elements as complete *nova*. Water, for example, differs completely from both hydrogen and oxygen. We would not even suspect that these "constituent parts" were contained in water if we could not actually observe that water originates from these elements and that it can again be "resolved" into them. The "constituent parts" are in this case not spatially differentiated and delimited material parts (as they are in mixed material elements, such as minerals and chemical solutions).

Water is not partly hydrogen and partly oxygen, but wholly water. And as long as water exists it behaves in accordance with its particular nature and not in accordance with the nature of "constituent parts." For this reason it seems not quite appropriate to speak of constituent parts. For as long as the composite lasts, the elements are non-existent [*nicht vorhanden*], even though they were present before and may "present themselves" again [*wieder auftreten*].

In all such instances "something" becomes "something else," and this becoming we call *transformation* (*substantial change*), in contrast to *alteration* (*accidental change*), in which only the quality of the thing changes, while the thing itself persists. What then compels us to assume something "persistent" also in this kind of transformation, something which receives into itself first one and then another "form"?

Transformation proceeds not irregularly but in accordance with definite laws. This means that it is not possible for something to become anything whatsoever, but definite elements enter under certain conditions into definite combinations or compositions. Elements entertain among each other more or less close or more or less distant "family relations" and accordingly disengage themselves from certain combinations in order to form new ones. Finally, elements must fulfill definite requisites of proportional relations to enter into combinations, and these proportional relations find their mathematical expression in chemical formulas. The natural sciences regard these formulas as structural laws which determine the proportional relations of the parts which make up the whole.

The atomistic theory considers all material elements as parts of the one space-filling mass. These parts are divided and held together in different ways, but exclusively by their immanent forces, and they accordingly fill space and react to external aggression in various ways. It is thus conceivable that the ultimate structural parts of some material elements become disengaged from one another and that others of a different kind combine so that the former may join with the latter in the building up of a new material whole [*Stoffganze*]. It appears that in this interpretation the process of "combination" moves into close proximity to that of a mixture. The structure of a molecule is composed of atoms in analogy to the way in which the structure of a mixed material element is composed of sensorily perceptible quantities of simple material elements. The difference is that the building up of a molecule proceeds more strictly in accordance with definite physical laws. The question which remains unanswered concerns the nature of the ordering "forces."

The dynamistic theory assumes an original manifold of material elements without a common substratum. Each material element is formed, as it were, out of its own root principle. Is something in the nature of a "combination" conceivable on the basis of this supposition? It seems to me that precisely the dynamistic explanation makes it possible to speak of combinations in a "vital" and "inward" [*innerlich*] sense. Vital transformation and a free cooperation of differentiated forces for the sake of forming a new material whole is possible only where something forms itself into space out of its own inner strength and where the material fullness into which and by virtue of which it forms itself is not rigidly fixed and determined. But here again the question concerning the meaning of these forces imperatively asserts itself.

Both the atomistic and dynamistic theories are trying to justify what we believe we perceive in our natural experience, namely, that a combination actually arises "out" of the material elements. When, in place of the elements, the combination "appears," the elements have not been "reduced to nothing," nor has the new *Stoff* arisen from nothing, but what has happened is that a *transformation* has taken place. What is it then that has undergone this transformation? What of that which existed prior to the transformation has passed over into that which exists now? According to St. Thomas, the *forms* of the elements are in the combination not in their fully actuality [*actu*] and essentiality [*secundum essentiam*], nor have they wholly disappeared. They are maintained virtually [*virtute*] "inasmuch as the properties [*accidentia propria*] of the elements, in which their *force* [*virtus*] rests, are preserved in a certain way."[176] What then is the meaning here of *form* and of *force* [*Kraft*], and what can the knowledge of this meaning contribute to an understanding of material being?

16. *Formation Considered as a Specific Determination of the Material Element* [Stoff] *and as the Forming of a "Structure"* ["Gebilde"]

We have repeatedly emphasized that all actual material elements are formed, but this *formation* carried different connotations.

It signified (1) the particular nature of the internal structure by which one element is distinguished from another, and (2) the formation of the material element into a unified, self-contained structure. Is there an inner connection between these two meanings? Does the one directly lead to the other, and is the *form* which "performs" the same in both instances?

The different basic structures of material elements as such seemed to indicate that not all elements are (by virtue of their particular nature) suitable for the building up of self-contained structures. Solid elements are naturally adapted to combine in delimited spatial structures, while liquid and gaseous elements can acquire such an aptitude only by being bounded externally or by submitting to the rule of a superior force. They too can be so compressed as to form solid bodies, and when this happens their circumscribed bounds will bear the stamp of their particular materiality. It may thus be said that all material elements bear within themselves the aptitude for being formed into specifically delimited spatial structures, but it is not "natural" for all of them to attain to this state. Generally speaking, we may affirm that every "structure" [*Gebilde*] results from different "forces," working partly from within and partly from without, and the immanently working particular material nature has a varying share in the final result. This statement implies that there must be a diversity of form if we mean by "form" that principle which imparts to the *material element* (*Stoff* understood as spatial fullness) its particular nature [*Eigenart*] and structure.

17. The Formal Structure of the Thing (Form *Understood in the Sense of* Formal Ontology)

What Aristotle called πρώτη *ousia* and what we ordinarily designate as a *thing* are the *formed material elements* [*geformter Stoff*], understood as a space-filling structure of a definite and particular intrinsic nature and of a distinct external shape. We made an attempt to clarify the meaning of *Stoff,* and we are about to proceed to a further elucidation of the meaning of form. But before we do so, we wish first to draw the outline of a general frame into which everything that bears the name *thing* can be fitted. In referring here to the

"formal" structure of a thing, we are using the term *form* in a sense which differs completely from the one we have hitherto associated with it.

We have previously pointed out that in every finite existent *that* which is must be distinguished from both *what* it is and from its *being.*[177] Of *that* which is we predicate *what* it is as well as the fact that it *is.* We call it an object [*Gegenstand*], using this term in both a broader and narrower sense. In the broader sense, "object" means *something* or *anything* at all, i.e., everything that can be known of which something can be predicated—anything which is [*Seiendes überhaupt*], regardless of whether it is actual or nonactual, independent or dependent. Even the "nought" is still an *object* in the sense that it is something that can be conceived and of which certain predications can be made. In the narrowest sense, on the other hand, an object is that which stands by itself, that which is *self-sustaining* and *self-dependent* [*selbständig und eigenständig*].

An object can be called a *form* regardless of whether we speak of *object* in the broader or in the narrower sense. But the meaning of *form* here differs from the meaning of the Aristotelian μορφή (essential form, [*Wesensform*]). This meaning differs even more from that of form understood as spatial structure, of which we stated that in the case of material "formed" structures (in the linguistically familiar sense) it is intimately related to the essential form.

Every spatial structure has its definite particular nature, its particular constitution, and understood in this sense, it is something filled with content [*inhaltlich erfüllt*], of the nature of matter rather than merely of the nature of material elements [*materiell* = *stofflich*].

The essential forms too are, of course, filled with content or rather they are "fullness" as such, since it is owing to these forms that objects attain to their definite, particular, and inwardly filled nature. Those forms, on the other hand, which are not under discussion are completely empty and stand in need of being filled with some content. To avoid any confusion, we shall therefore refer to them as *empty forms* [*Leerformen*].

This latter usage of the terms *form* and *formal* is familiar to us from the discipline of *formal logic,* and it is moreover *the* concept of form that is quite common in modern philosophy. In formal logic we deal almost exclusively with such empty forms (i.e., the forms of mental structures). Their lack of content is made evident by the fact that they can be expressed in universal symbols.

"This rose is red" is a judgment, and the symbolic expression, "A is B," is the corresponding form of this judgment. *Concept, judgment,* and *conclusion* are the most general logical forms. Although the object (in the broadest sense of the term) of that of which something can be predicated is usually called the *logical object,* this object belongs, strictly speaking, not to the sphere of logic. Rather, it is the presupposition of all *logical objects* (i.e., of all those mental structures with which we deal in logic). It is, after all, a special mark of the being of mental structures that they are "second-hand existents" [*Seiendes aus zweiter Hand*] which must be referred to that more primordial type of existents that are precisely the presupposed objects of logic.

Concepts [*Begriff*] serve to "apprehend" [*begreifen*] objects. *Judgments* serve to affirm known *states-of-affairs* [*Sachverhalte*] or—which amounts to the same thing—to establish certain facts with respect to the apprehended object. By means of *conclusions* one judgment can be derived from another, i.e., some state-of-affairs can be affirmed on the basis of another, so that thereby an *interconnection of states-of-affairs* may be established. Thus we see that objects, states-of-affairs, and interconnections of states-of-affairs are those more "primordial existents" to which mental structures—concepts, judgments, and conclusions—are related and upon the pattern of which they are "formed."[178] The fact that these mental structures are patterned after those more primordial existents indicates that the latter must correspond in their structures to the former. In these more primordial existents, too, it must be possible to distinguish the empty forms from the contents. To the forms of mental structures (i.e., logical forms) must correspond *forms of being* (i.e., ontological forms).[179]

Objects, states-of-affairs, and *interconnections of states-of-affairs* are thus ontological forms, and they are *objects* in both the broader and narrower sense of the term. Object in the broadest sense is "everything that is in any way" [*Seiendes überhaupt*]. "Object" denotes here the most universal form of this particular sphere, the form by which the frame of an *ontology* (understood as a doctrine of being and existence [*Seiende*]) is circumscribed. In this most general sense states-of-affairs and their interconnections must also be called objects. *Object* in the narrower sense, however, is a form of existence which is distinguished from and superior to *states-of-affairs* and *their interconnections.* Objects in this narrower sense provide the foundation for all other forms of that which is [*Seiende*].

What an object is, *how* it is, *that* it is, in what relations it stands to other objects, or into what relations it can enter—all this becomes manifest in states-of-affairs. These latter are particular organic structures, and their "existential constitution" [*Bestehen*], which is their particular mode of being, presupposes the structurally differing being of objects.[180]

Object in the broader sense may be something perfectly simple (as, for example, the simple essence "redness"), whereas object in the narrower sense is an existent of organic structure, comparable perhaps to the scaffolding of a house or the skeleton of an animal (if we are looking for an illustration by means of sensible images of something which cannot be immediately grasped in sense perception). In such an object, *what* it is (in the graduated scale of genera and species) is distinguished from *how* it is, and these "determinations" are firmly fitted into the orderly organic structure of the whole.

The Aristotelian categories in their twofold signification as modes of predication and modes of being illustrate quite well the interrelatedness of logical and ontological forms. As ontological forms the categories describe the structure of the object (in the narrower sense), although they reach out beyond this frame and simultaneously represent the forms of the object's organic insertion in the "universe" of objects. The name *ousia* (i.e., the existent in a preeminent sense) applies to the object (in the narrower sense). Preeminence pertains to the object inasmuch as its determinations are exclusively within and inasmuch as *in* their being they "share" in the object's being, and also because the structures on a higher level (such as the *states-of-affairs*) must be referred back to the object as their ontological foundation.

18. *The Thing as Foundation* (ὑποχείμενον, *Substratum) and Carrier* (ὑπόστασις). *Form and Content. Universality and Particularity (Genus and Species)*

It is now time to ask whether the object with respect to its "determinations" has the nature of a *foundation* [*Zugrundeliegendes*] (ὑποχείμενον, *substratum, subjectum*) or *carrier* [*Träger*] (ὑπόστασις, substance). According to Aristotle, the ὑποχείμενον is that of which everything else is predicated, while it is itself not predicated of anything else.[181] This definition applies to the object insofar as it is a presupposition for logical structures, and it applies more specifically to the object in the narrower sense. For there are many things which are objects in the broader sense (i.e., something can be predicated of them, while they in turn can be predicated of other things and are thus not objects in the narrower sense).

If we stay within the confines of that which is as yet not logically defined, there is more than one meaning for the Aristotelian ὑποχείμενον: It is the *individual thing* (e.g., a living being) which "underlies" this thing's properties and qualities, and it is the *material element* [*Stoff*] which underlies this thing's ontologically perfected form (ἐντελέχεια).[182] Of the individual thing we may say forthwith that it corresponds to the concept of the *object.* While the former was always recognized as *ousia,* we have now found the *object* to be *ousia* also. But what do we mean when we say that the thing underlies or is the substratum of its own properties?

A thing can "assume" and "lose" properties and qualities. When a green leaf "changes to red," it loses the green color and assumes the color red. The thing changes and yet remains the same. The color, however, does not merely change: It becomes another. Green does not become red, but the thing itself changes *from* green to red: It changes its color. It remains a colored thing, but it was first green-colored and is then red-colored. To have color pertains irrevocably to colored things (what is sometimes designated as "colorlessness" is likewise a particular kind of color). Color as such is thus an enduring *quality.*[183] However, color must always be definitely determined, and this determination can change.

To distinguish the changing color determination from the enduring quality [*Eigenschaft*] we shall call the former the *qualitative condition* [*Beschaffenheit*]. The thing structure thus shows a peculiar stratification. While the enduring qualities belong to its "scaffolding," i.e., to its irrevocably firm structure, the changing qualitative conditions do not belong to the thing's *firm* constitution. Whatever belongs to this firm constitution of the thing can be regarded as the "foundation" or "carrier" of the changing qualitative conditions which are inserted in the thing at some preordained place.

It pertains to those natural corporeal objects (which we generally have in mind when we speak of *thing*) to have a definite shape, size, weight, and that specific material individuality which is the foundation of these qualities. The thing's size and shape may change, but it must always have some definite size, shape, and so on. And the same may be said of the colored thing: It must always be a thing of some definite color. This color is determined as blue or red, and owing to this determinateness the thing is a thing of some definite color. The thing, moreover, can be a colored thing only when it has a definite color. Only *qua* determined can color be a definite color. Although according to its meaning color is something definite, there is in it a lacuna [*Leerstelle*] which needs to be filled. And this filling or fulfillment cannot be of any kind whatever. The being of "color" as such determines what can impart content to the lacuna. It can be filled only by the different color nuances (down to the ultimate determinateness), and by nothing else.

We call a *genus* something which, though determined in its content, shows a lacuna and can therefore attain to the full determinateness required for actual being once the lacuna has been filled, and that which is capable of filling the lacuna we call the corresponding *specific difference*. The specific differences determine the several species of the genus. While the contents of the different species of a genus have something in common—the generic determinateness—the contents of genera have nothing in common.[184] But different genera may nevertheless have a common form (i.e., an *empty form* [*Leerform*]). Thus, "color" and "shape" are different fillings of the *Leerform* "thingly quality." The categories, which we previously designated as *forms of that which is* [*Formen des Seienden*], are such only in the sense of *empty form*. When Aristotle also applies the term genera to them, this is, strictly speaking not quite correct: They are merely the empty forms of genera.

To describe the way in which genus and specific difference are related to one another, neither the terms *substratum* [*Grundlage*] and *accrument* [*Hinzukommendes*] nor the terms "carrier" [*Träger*] and "that which is carried" [*Getragenes*] are quite adequate. But "form" and "content" will not suffice, either. The content fills only the *lacuna* in the genus. The relation of genus to species is equivalent to that which exists between the *universal* and the *particular*, and it is the specific difference that particularizes the species [*das Besondernde*].

This relationship cannot be reduced to that of form and content, because it crosses [*sich kreuzen*] the latter. There are empty forms as well as contents of greater or less universality, and in each stage of universality form and content can be distinguished from one another. Genera are the most universal objects (in the broader sense of the term) which may be said to have a content. But because they have a lacuna, they are not objects which are fully determined in their content. There is in them some element of empty form. The species, on the other hand, are less universal and less "formal" (in the sense of empty form). We may thus call the thing which is fully determined in its content the *foundation* or *substratum* of the changes which this same thing undergoes as well as of the qualitative conditions [*Beschaffenheiten*] which newly "accrue" to it. Substratum and accrument (i.e., the thing and its "accidental" qualitative conditions) then occupy the same state as far as particularization and being filled with content [*inhaltliche Erfüllung*] are concerned.

There is however, another sense in which we may speak of *foundation* or *substratum,* and one which is of special significance to our context. We pointed out that the material enduring quality [*Eigenart*] lays the foundation [*ist grundlegend*] for the shape, size, and weight of the thing. It likewise lays the foundation for the so-called *secondary qualities,* i.e., for that which presents and makes manifest externally the particular nature [*Eigenart*] of the thing. *As* a material thing of such and such a species, it must collect and confine itself externally. It must behave in this particular way with respect to other things, and it must "strike the senses" in its particular individuality. In this case, then, the foundation of the accruing elements [*Hinzukommendes*] is not the thing as a whole, but some element of what the thing is or how the thing is—and, indeed, what the thing is as *material element* [*Stoff*]—lays the foundation for everything else this thing may be. And this may explain why Aristotle calls the material element a ὑποχείμενον. To understand this designation we must keep in mind that the material element assumes this function of laying the foundation in its particular character of determinateness. If, however, the material element has the character of massive weight, then it is the *pure mass* which—though it does not "lay the foundation" [*begrundet*] for the determinations—lays the foundation for what "underlies" and "lies in the ground" of the determinations [*auf ihrem Grunde liegt*].

With these latter reflections we have advanced from the consideration of the form to the consideration of the content. What we stated above may, however, be expressed in a purely formal way. Among the immanent structural elements of the thing, there is something which lays the foundation for everything else that pertains to the thing's structure. If the form of the thing can find its fulfillment in any other element but that of its material being, then something else—in place of the spatial material individuality of the thing—will have to fill the empty form of the *foundation.*

There exist—as was made evident in the relationship of genus and species—definite relations between the empty form and what can fill it. This becomes quite clear when we now ask how material element and thing are related to one another. By *material element* [*Stoff*] we mean a spatial fullness of a particular kind, and by *thing* we mean a πρώτη *ousia* in the Aristotelian sense, i.e., an independent actuality.

What is independently actual depends or stands only on itself [*ist auf sich selbst gestellt*] and operates from its own nature. It is evident that pure mass cannot be a thing, because as such it neither "stands" nor "operates," nor has it a "nature."

To every definite material element pertains a particular kind of operation [*Wirken*] but, obviously, not every material element has the aptitude of building a self-sustaining structure by itself. Self-sustaining independence [*Selbständigkeit*] requires a tightly fit and unified structure firmly bounded and confined. Liquids and gases are by themselves incapable of forming such structures. They stand in need of a firm "receptacle" or of a controlling force in order to attain to a definite shape and outline. Only solid material elements can thus by themselves build up structures which correspond to the thingly form. But while liquid and gaseous elements cannot by themselves form a thing, they may well contribute to the formation of things, if by "thing" we understand a whole in which the diversity of the structural material elements is controlled by a single formative law. Such a thing is then not merely a liquid or gaseous quantity, externally held together by a receptacle, but an organism.

We have stated in what sense the thing can be called a "foundation" or a "substratum." Is the word *carrier* [*Träger*] merely a synonymous term or does it have a new and different meaning? When we say that the thing is the *carrier* of its color, we mean that thingly color—and the same is true of all thingly qualities—is something not self-sustaining which must be carried by something which is self-sustaining. This, however, is not equivalent to saying that the carrier is self-sustaining without that which it "carries." In other words, the essential qualities are not merely externally "added" to an already "finished" thing, but it is these very qualities which build the thing up. Nor can it be said that the color is in the thing as the content is in its form. *Thing* denotes a form in relation to this particular thing, and "color" denotes the determinateness of the content of something which pertains to the structure of the thingly form. "Color" denotes the filling of that empty form which we termed enduring *quality* [*Eigenschaft*].

Color, by virtue of its specific determinateness, fulfills or complements itself as this particular color, and the entire thingly form fulfills and determines itself as this particular thing by virtue of that determination of its what and how which is pre-designed in its own structure. The particular qualities are related to the particular thing—and likewise the qualitative forms to the thingly form—as the part is related to the whole (i.e., as one structural characteristic is related to the essential whole [*Wesensganzes*], which includes several characteristic traits). This is to say that the particular qualities are not related to the particular thing in the way cut-off or cut-out "fragments" (such as spatial, temporal, or corporeal "parts") are related to a homogeneous and continuous whole. Because no thing can be without these structural parts, we shall refrain from calling the thing the *foundation* of these parts. The thing is, however, the foundation of those changes which it can undergo—as it is also the foundation of non-essential qualities—of everything that can happen to it and of every "happening which it can cause." If we exempt local change, every other kind of change in a thing is simultaneously a change either in the constitution of its enduring qualities or a change in its qualitative conditions.

On the basis of these different relationships, we may now try to define our terms. We call *foundation* [*Grundlage*] (ὑποχείμενον, *subiectum)* the fully determined individual thing as related to the qualitative conditions which it can "assume" and "lose," and as related to all the contingencies in which it can share (among which are the "assumption" and "loss" of qualitative conditions). Included in the

contingencies of the thingly world are also the combination and separation of *elements* and the transformation of *material elements* into higher structures. A material element in this sense we may thus designate as a ὑποχείμενον, and we recognize, moreover, in the material nature the foundation of the structure of a thing and the standard of measurement of its enduring qualities.

Carrier [Träger] (ὑπόστασις, subsisting substance) we call the self-sustaining whole as related to its structural parts. Strictly speaking, the carrier is once again the individual thing (not something which remains if the entire "what" and "how" of the thing are conceptually eliminated). The term "carrier," however, may also be applied also to the *empty form* of the self-sustaining whole as such, considered in its relation to the partial forms. Owing to the fact that the content belongs to the structural parts (without which the whole could not be), the whole that is filled with content is the *carrier* of the *content* (i.e., the entire "what" and "how"). The form of the whole is the carrier of the "form of the content," and no matter how strange it may sound it pertains to the formal structure of a thing to have a content.[185] The individual thing is thus simultaneously *foundation* and *carrier,* but with respect to different aspects of the thing.

Form, finally, we call the "scaffolding" [*Gerüst*] of the entire thing (as well as the parts of the scaffold), considered in relation to what imparts to it content and determines it as *this* individual thing. The form "thing" corresponds to the form *object* (in the narrower sense). But nevertheless we must ask whether these two coincide completely or whether the *thing* is not already one particularization among possible others. This question is significant for the elaboration of an ontology [*Seinslehre*]. But other matters are of even greater importance for the solution of the difficulties with which we are faced at this juncture.

19. *Material Element* [Stoff], *Essential Form, and Accruing (Accidental) Forms*

What enters into the thingly form as its content is formed matter, i.e., something which fills space in a particular way by being structurally conjoined to form a unified whole, and manifesting itself externally in sensible appearance. What makes this formed matter a thing of such and such specific qualities we call its *essential form* [*Wesensform*]. The Wesensform is—in contradistinction to the *empty form* [*Leerform*]—precisely what imparts content—a content, to be sure, for which it is essential to become enclosed in this empty form. There is then an inner connection between these two forms, and the process of filling must not be conceived in the manner in which a receptacle may be filled with any kind of content.

With respect to those material elements which were already transformed into thingly being, we stated that they could either serve as the *foundation* of changes or as the *Stoff* underlying transformations and re-formations. Reference was made in this connection to the second meaning which Aristotle associates with *Stoff* (the material element). It bears within itself the possibility of receiving new formal determinations. These latter may be accruing or accidental forms, in which case we observe a change in the qualitative conditions [*Beschaffenheiten*]. The thing becomes *different* from what it was before. One of its properties "undergoes a transformation" [*formt sich um*], and the corresponding empty form is filled with a different determinateness of content. A potentiality which was actualized becomes once again mere potency, while a hitherto not yet actualized potentiality is actualized. This happens, for example, when a green leaf assumes the color red or when a rock changes its shape under the influence of atmospheric conditions. In these instances the thing which undergoes these changes remains the same (accidental change).

The *transformation* can, however, be so far-reaching that the thing itself becomes "another." When natural material elements are transformed into works of art, we may be in doubt whether what is taking place is a *change* or a *transformation.* The wax out of which the plastic image of a deity has been formed is—as a mere thing of nature—the same that it was before the modelling: It has merely changed its shape. On the other hand, if we consider the work of art as such, i.e., the spiritual significance of the thing—as an image of the deity—then we must say that a *novum* has come into being. The lump of wax has been transformed into an image of the deity.

An even more radical transformation takes place when a new organism grows out of a seed. In this case there occurs not only a change of individual properties and qualities, but another essential form appears to be present from the moment the *evolution* and with it new vital activities begin. A living being has grown from something which prior to this evolution was not a living being but merely bore within itself the "possibility" of such an evolution. Is it still possible in this instance (where apparently the essence or nature has changed) to speak of something which remains "the same," to speak of "the same object" which has first this and then another essence [*Wesen*]?

In the case of the lump of wax which has been changed into the image of a deity, we may be inclined to speak of a "sameness" before and after the process of formation, because the *material element,* after all, remains the same. For this very reason, however, we hesitate to call such a change a genuine *transformation.* In the case of organic evolution and growth, on the other hand, not even the material element remains the same. The grain of wheat must "die" so that a new fruit-bearing stalk may sprout forth. The material element must be transformed in order to be revitalized. "Out" of something, something else has to come to be. That which was there prior to the transformation is there no longer as the same that it was before. Nor has it been reduced to nothing. It has acquired a new being—a being "in a new form"—in the thing into which it has been transformed.

In this connection the same expressions which we used in the case of combinations of elements to form new material elements [*Stoffe*] suggest themselves. Evidently here we are witnessing a similar process on a higher plane. The grain of seed is not reduced to nothing, and the plant does not grow from nothing. Rather, it develops out of the grain of seed and grows with the aid of those nutritive elements which it absorbs. The plant grows by degrees, and this gradual process of growth can—at least in its major phases—be observed. And the particular nature and qualitative conditions of both the grain of seed and the nutritive elements determine the particular nature and the qualitative conditions of the plant. The essential form of the plant, on the other hand, differs from the essential form of the seed.[186]

The following conclusions may be drawn from the above statements: 1) We may say that the same thing which was previously a grain of seed is now a plant; and 2) It seems that there is a material foundation which remains when the new form is assumed. Is this "remainder" the *Stoff,* then, that element which is first one and then another?

Even though decomposition and transformation of material elements are taking place in the processes of growth and nutrition, the material elements of which organisms are constituted in their structures are absorbed from inanimate nature. Not all material elements, but only certain definite ones, are fit to "become animate." To plant organisms is assigned the task of transforming *inorganic* into *organic* elements, i.e., into elements which can serve the building up of living bodies. This kind of transformation must be distinguished from the process of "vitalization" [*Belebung*]. This latter does not add "life" to that essential form which pertained to the inanimate material elements, but the "living form" (i.e., the form of an organism of definite individuality) replaces the form that was present prior to the "vitalization."[187]

The new organic being is what it is owing to *its* essential form, even though it shows a certain kinship with those material elements which were necessary for its coming into being. Despite this "kinship," the animate *material* elements differ from those inanimate ones out of which the former were formed.

In considering these relationships, we must distinguish between the nutritive elements, which are absorbed and with which the growing organism is being "in-formed," and the seed which initiates this absorption and in-formation. To the seed, too, pertains—as soon as growth sets in and independently of the material elements which are absorbed—a material element out of which it is formed, an element of a definite material individuality. Its form, however, is more than mere material individuality, for the structure which the seed assumes with the aid of the absorbed material elements—as soon as life beings to stir—depends on the form of the seed. And this consideration leads us to the question: Does the form, which is "dormant" [*schlummernd*] in the seed, become "alive," or is the "dead" form replaced by a "living" form?

An answer to this question cannot be given before the concept of form has been further elucidated. There is no doubt, at any rate, that a transformation of the essence or nature has occurred. The *what* of this object is no longer the same that it was before.[188] But *that* (i.e., the *object*) of which the essence has undergone a transformation has remained the same. That which was first a seed and which is now a plant is the same. And while its *being* persists without a break, its mode of being has changed. *Life* is a particular mode of being, distinct from the modes of being of either lifeless material elements or of material elements which are potentially alive [*lebensfähig*].

If the being of the thing were to cease and a new being were to begin, the object too would no longer be the same.[189] What remains as the same is the empty form of the object—not indeed the universal form of the object, but the form of the individual object (i.e., the *individuum*). Since, however, the empty form cannot be without a content and since the content is not something that is "poured in" from the outside, such a continuity is possible only if some element of the content is likewise continuous. Either an enduring essential form must underlie the changing constitution of the essence, or some element of the former constitution of the content must be preserved in the domain of the new essential form (cf. pp. 254ff. below).

20. *Material Element* [Stoff] *and Thing, Material Element* [Stoff] *and Spirit* [Geist]

We summarize once more what we have learned from the preceding considerations concerning the relationship that exists between *thing* and *material element* (cf. pp.204ff. below). The *thing* is a self-enclosed, independent actuality, a πρώτη *ousia* in the Aristotelian sense. It is an *object* in the narrowest sense of the term, i.e., a "something" which bears its essence within itself and which with the essence stands upon itself—a "subsisting substance."

The thing as such must not necessarily be spatial material. There also exist "spiritual" substances. Though it is true that in his attempt to elucidate the meaning of *ousia* Aristotle referred primarily to the realm of material things, it was for him and is for us indubitable that all finite things point toward one first existent—one πρώτη *ousia*—which is pure spirit. Aside from this first existent, Aristotle knows of finite spirits (the movers of the heavenly bodies and of human souls) which he regards as *ousiai.*

In contrast to material elements, the spiritual is non-spatial, invisible, and intangible. While the material thing fills space in such a way that every part of the space completely coincides with a part of the thing—the thing is not wholly at any particular point, but is spread out with its total being and is as such sensorily manifest—*spiritual being* is a *being-in-itself.* The spiritual has "inwardness" in a sense entirely foreign to spatial material elements. And when the spiritual steps forth and communicates itself [*aus sich herausgehen*]—and this it does in diverse ways either by turning toward *objects* (in what Husserl calls the *intentionality* of spiritual life) or by a purely spiritual self-disclosure to other spirits and by a sympathetic entering into them or by forming itself into space (by means of informing the body and by a formative molding of foreign material elements)—it remains nonetheless in itself. From its own vital center it forms itself, unifying everything that it is and everything that it appropriates. And this kind of appropriation is once more an exclusive potentiality of the spiritual.

A further detailed investigation will have to determine the meaning of "formation" and "confinement" in a context where there can no longer be any question of spatial fullness, structure, and boundary in the usual sense. At this point we can give no more than a preliminary indication in order to articulate more distinctly the peculiar nature of the spiritual over against the material.

The *material element* thus is a *genus* within the realm of the thingly actual. We have described it as the *space-filling* element as such, and we have pointed out that not every material element is by itself fit to enter into the form of a thing. Only solid elements have the peculiar aptitude to enclose and delimit themselves in a firmly circumscribed external form. Liquid and gaseous elements are incapable by themselves of attaining to such a self-enclosure, and even solid material elements by no means exclusively obey their own inner law in their thingly formation.

There no doubt exists an interrelation between the particular nature of the material element (i.e., the particular manner of space-filling) and the "external" behavior of the material thing, i.e., the more or less of its mobility in space, the manner of its movement, and its spatial structure. After all, it is the confining spatial structure which imparts unity and self-enclosed particularity to the brute material thing. However, matter is in most instances not a "structure" that has been formed purely from within, but merely a "chunk of matter" which can "easily" be divided into two or more pieces (crushed, torn, or cut up in diverse ways depending on the particular nature of the material element). This material thing, moreover, does not impart to itself its external spatial structure, but the latter is determined to a large extent by the external "fate" [*Schicksal*] of the thing. To be sure, it cannot assume just any kind of structural form. Its particular material nature is determined by the qualitative conditions of its surface. Different material elements have different planes of fracture, section, and so on.[190] But the face of "inanimate" nature is determined by a reciprocal working upon each other of different material elements. The unbounded volume of water turns into forms—brooks, rivers, lakes—which are clearly confined by enclosing shores. The river bed and its brinks are in turn formed by the pressure of the rushing currents. Wind and weather carve out the outlines of the rocks. Each and every form, however, works and is worked upon in accordance with what it is in its own nature. Nature as a whole is thus the product of formative forces or of potent plastic forms. And thus we find verified what became more and more evident in the course of our inquiry. We are unable to gain an adequate understanding of the nature of material structures unless we first succeed in clarifying the meaning of *form* and *force*. This is why we must now once more inquire into the nature of *formed matter*, but this time we must undertake the investigation from the aspect of form.

§4. A Summary Discussion of the Concept of Form

In the course of our investigations we have repeatedly—in different contexts and with varying connotations—spoken of the concept of form.[191] We must attempt now to present a summary clarification of the way we understand and interpret this concept and how our own interpretation is related to that of Aristotle.

1. Once More the Aristotelian Concept of Form

For the time being, the concept of the *empty form* [*Leerform*] need not be considered. Whenever Aristotle speaks of the contrast between form and matter, he has in mind essential form [*Wesensform*]. We already know from which two fields Aristotle ordinarily chooses his examples: from human creative work (*Werkschaffen*], which imparts a form to some given matter, and from organic structures [*Naturgebilde*] which are in the process of becoming or changing. However, since natural organic structures and human works [*Menschenwerk*] are not *ousia* (i.e., independently or autonomously existing being) in the same sense, the form, too, which makes the being what it is, cannot have quite the same meaning in both cases. It is impossible, therefore, to achieve clarity in both these categories at one and the same time, and we thus deem it advisable to concentrate our attention on the forms of nature [*Naturformen*].

A natural organic structure bears its form within itself. It is determined from within as that which it is. Some further distinctions, however, are in order. As was shown earlier,[192] Aristotle looks for form in the realm of becoming. In the realm of the *become* [*geworden*] he equates the form to the *nature* or *essence* [*Wesen*] (τὸ τί ἦν εἶναι). Accordingly, the being human [*das Menschsein*] of this particular human being is its in-dwelling form, which is alternately designated as μορφή and *eidos*. However, in the case of that which is *in the process of becoming,* the form *by virtue of which* it comes to be is, in Aristotle's view, not the one that abides *in it* but rather the form of the progenitor. It will be remembered that we found the reason for this distinction made by Aristotle between τὸ τί ἦν εἶναι and μορφή in the fact that what is designated in the one instance is being human as such—i.e., as universally conceivable—while in the other instance it is the being human of this or that particular human being, a being which is different in each case (cf. pp. 136f. and165f. above). In these structures, moreover, which are composites of form and matter, the nature or essence too shows this composition (cf. pp. 250ff. below).

In the generation of living beings, one of these forms is obviously regarded as being produced by the other. Aristotle points out that the form of the generating living being produces the seed or sperm out of surplus materials but that the seed contains within itself the form of the new living being.[193] In another context, however, he states that what comes to be is neither the matter nor the form, but the composite of both.[194] If what the philosopher had in mind here was human workmanship—that neither brass nor the sphere comes to be, but the brazen sphere—then the same reasoning would seem to apply to the case under consideration. What comes to be is a new human being to whom being human pertains. In a sense, it is correct to say that *being human* does not come to be, and yet every human being has *his or her* specific being human which differs from that of every other human being and which is not prior to the existence of this particular human being. Should we want to speak of *form* in both instances, and the two statements are not in contradiction, the meaning of *form* must obviously be different in each case.

The seed is not *potentially* the living being, because only in the fully developed living being is realized what it was to become. Prior to its coming to be what it is, this "is" was an unattained end [*Ziel*], and to this end Aristotle applies the term *form.*[195] According to the principle that actual being precedes potential being[196] (act = ἐνέργεια of potency = δύναμις), we might be justified in assuming the priority of that which is fully developed. However, since Aristotle uses the terms "prior" and "posterior" with different connotations, we shall have to listen more closely to what he has to say concerning this question.

Potentiality or capability [*Vermögen*] (δύναμις) denotes for Aristotle:

> ... not only the ontological principle [*Seinsgrund*] of change in another thing qua other, but in general every ontological principle of movement or change. Nature (φύσις), too, belongs to this genus of potential being. For nature is an ontological principle of movement—not indeed in another thing, but in the thing itself *qua* self. Now actuality (ἐνέργεια, act) is prior to all potentiality of this kind, both conceptually and in the order of being καὶ λόγῳ καὶ τῇ *ousia*). In the temporal order, actuality is prior in one sense, but not in another sense.[197]

It can easily be shown that the actual is prior conceptually. The faculty of seeing can be defined and determined only by actual vision, i.e., that activity in which the faculty is actualized. In the temporal order, however, the actual is prior in this sense: In the individual being that is in the process of evolution, potentiality precedes actuality (as the seed is prior to the fully developed plant), but this potentiality is in turn preceded by something actual (in our example, by a plant of the same species, a plant from which the seed derives). Prior to every movement there is something which causes the motion [*ein Bewegendes*], and this cause or principle of the motion is an actuality.

Now what do we mean when we say that in terms of *ousia* the actual is prior to the potential? In the individual being that which is temporally prior is the seed, and that which is temporally posterior is the developed plant. However, the seed is that which is to become this plant, and the plant is related to the seed as the more perfect to the less perfect. And this is why we render τῇ οὐσίᾳ by "in the graduated order of being" [*in der Rangordnung des Seienden*] keeping in mind the general meaning of *ousia* (an existent which has an ontological preeminence). Moreover, the fully developed with respect to the seed has the meaning of an *end.* For "all becoming strives toward an end. That for the sake of which a thing is, is its ontological *Seinsgrund* (ἀρχή, principle), and the becoming is for the sake of the end. Now the end is being in full actuality (ἐνέργεια, act), and it is for the sake of the end that the potency (δύναμις) has been given."[198] We have been given the faculty of seeing so that we may have actual vision, and we have been given the faculty of thinking so that we may exercise it in actual thought. *Matter,* too, is in potency (δυνάμει) inasmuch as it can attain to form (ἔλθοι ἂν εἰς τὸ εἶδος), but once matter is fully actualized (ἐνεργείᾳ), it is then in the form (ἐν τῷ εἴδει ἐστι[199]).[200]

"The operation (ἔργον) is thus the end, and the efficacious activity [*Wirksamkeit*] (ἐνέργεια) is the operation. And this is why we call the *operation* an *actuality,* a term which points to a perfection of being [Seinsvollendung] (ἐντελέχεια)."[201] The meaning of this significant passage becomes clear from what immediately follows. In the case of some faculties the ultimate end is "the use that is made of it, or its exercise (e.g., the ultimate end of the faculty of sight is vision, and no other operation besides vision results from the faculty of sight). From some faculties, however, some additional results follow (e.g., from the art of building results not only the act of building but also the house). And the act is by no means the end of the faculty to a higher degree in the one case than in the other."[202]

The meaning here implied is evidently that even where the ultimate end is an activity which remains confined in the active principle itself and where this activity produces no separate operation (i.e., no "objective accomplishment"), the faculty or capability

is fully actualized and therewith reaches its ontological perfection [*Seinsvollendung*]. For the truly actual is the operation [*das Wirken*], not the result or product of the operation [*das Gewirktsein*]. The *opus* is actual only by virtue of the operation, and the latter bears the *opus* within itself as the ground or cause of its being actual [*Wirklichsein*].

> For the act of building is in the house that is being built, and this act of building comes to be, and is, simultaneously with the house. Where, then, that which comes to be is something apart from the exercise of the faculty, the actuality (or the being active [ἐνέργεια, *das Wirken*]) is in the thing that is being made, as, for example, the act of building is in the thing that is being built, and the act of weaving is in the thing that is being woven ... and in general the movement is in the thing that is being moved. But that which produces no result apart from being active has its actuality in itself. Thus, actual vision is in the one who sees, and actual thinking is in the one who thinks, and actual life is in the soul (and therefore also natural beatitude, which is a qualitatively determined kind of life). It is clear, then, that both *that which exists in a preeminent sense and form are actualities* (ὅτι ἡ οὐσία χαὶ τὸ εἶδος ἐνέργειά ἐστιν).[203]

We have had previous occasion to point out that the manifoldness of meaning which is comprised in the word *act* is unfolded in the terms ἔργον, ἐνέργια, ἐντελέχεια (*opus*, operation, efficacious activity or actuality, perfection of being) [*Werk, Wirken, Wirksamkeit oder Wirklichkeit, Seinsvollendung*].[204] In operating [*Wirken*] the faculty or capability attains its end and therewith its perfection of being. Being active or being operative is that highest degree of the being of that which is [*das höchste Sein des Seienden*] to which the faculties or capabilities of existents are ordained. In those instances, however, where the actualization of the potency is a process of *evolution*, the end is neither a separate *opus* nor a particular activity, but the ontological perfection of the totality of that which is [*Seiende*], which in the process of evolution strives toward its perfection. In this stage of perfection, that which is, is called *ousia*. 
Ousia is thus not a particular operation (i.e., the "particular operative act" [*Tätigkeitsakt*]), but that which operates [*das Wirkende*] in

its operation [*das Wirken*]. That which is "independently or autonomously" is substance in its operation, and this operation is the highest degree of the being of substance.

The particular *accomplishment* [*Leistung*] is called ἔργον in that broader sense of the term *opus* [*Werk*] according to which it may denote both deeds (i.e., the good or evil works of people) and such independent structures as have their being apart from the human creative mind. If we refer opus to human deeds, it is immediately evident that *opus* and *operation* (ἔργον and ἐνέργια, *Werk* and *Wirken*) coincide.

The problem is more complex in the case of independent structures. Precisely these latter, however, are important in our context, for here it is evidently a question of material structures. And again Aristotle's examples are taken from the realm of human artistic and technical still. He refers to a house or a woven fabric, and he states that the operating is in the thing which is being produced by the operation [*im gewirkten*]. Thus, the act of building has its place in the thing that is being built. In this case, then, operation and *opus* (*Wirken* and *Werk*) do not actually coincide. The *opus* is formed matter, while the operation is the forming [*Formung*] which is performed in and upon the matter. And because the *opus* owes its actuality to this kind of operation, the operation itself may be called the act (ἐνέργια) of the *opus*.

In the operation a twofold capability is actualized: the "skill" [*das Können*] of the artist (*active potency*) and the "plastic pliability" [*Bildsamkeit*] of matter (*passive potency*). In the course of the operation both potencies attain to the perfection of their being. The *opus* is an existent in the state of ontological perfection, and this is why in it ἐνέργια and ἐντελέχεια coincide.

However, the operation is also designated as *form* (*eidos*). In the completed work matter "has attained its form." It appears that Aristotle calls *ousia* (i.e., "the existent in the state of its perfection") the entire work as well as the form to which it attains. The question then arises whether the form to which the matter attains must not antecede the matter and the forming of the matter. And this same difficulty presents itself when we look at the problem from a different aspect. *Ousia* was determined as an existent in the perfection of it being (ἐντελέχεια) as the end toward which evolution is oriented. But as long as the end has not been attained, the perfection does not appear to be an actuality. Here, then, ἐντελεχεια and ἐνέργια—the perfection of being and actuality—seem to fall apart. It even appears as if the less perfect and the more perfect were changing places. Whereas up to this point the less perfect was designated as potency (δύναμις) which became actual only in the more perfect, it now seems that the more perfect is that which is not yet actualized and therefore only a "potential" end, while the living being in its factually attained stage of evolution appears as the "actual." And we are equally bewildered when we ask which, after all, is the "real" *ousia*—the not yet perfected actuality or the not actualized perfection? A proper balance is found only in the end, once it has been attained. Here *ousia* is both the fully unfolded and the fully actual. And here (i.e., in the end) it also becomes evident that only that which has reached its perfection is also fully actual, since the not yet attained end lacks that actuality which could impart to it the perfection of being, and the not yet fully developed lacks that perfection which could make it fully actual.

One other matter, however, must be considered. The *end* is, according to Aristotle, a *cause* (αἰτία) of movement. But that which is moved does not only strive toward the end, but is set in motion or, as it were, attracted by the end. Only something which is in act can thus set in motion or cause movement. That "existent in the perfection of its being" at which the evolutionary process aims must therefore—strange as it sounds—be actual prior to its actualization in order to be able to start the evolutionary process and to keep it going. A resolution of this seeming contradiction appears possible only if "actuality" has more than one meaning. In fact, in order to explain this difficulty, a threefold meaning of actuality must be assumed. Actuality denotes: 1) the imperfectly actual (i.e., the actual in the process of evolution); 2) the not yet attained end; and 3) the attained end.

2. *The Distinction Between Pure Form and Essential Form* (εἶδος *and* μορφή)

The difficulties referred to above force us first of all not to equate *eidos* [εἶδος] and μορφή, but to set them apart as *pure form* and *essential form.* The pure form or the *meaning* [*Sinn*] that is signified by the word "human" does not come to be and does not pass away. This pure form is above and beyond the realm of becoming. Its being stands above the contraries of actuality and potentiality and is eternally "perfected" [*vollendet*]. And this form prescribes both the end and the way to the end for the thing in which this form is "actualized." That which in the process of becoming [*Werden*] "attains this form" and which as a become [*Gewordenes*] "is in the form"—i.e., the individual human being—has as its *nature* or *essence* precisely this "being-in-this-form" and this "attaining-to-this-form." Therein is constituted the *being human* [*Menschsein*] of the human being [*Mensch*] and Aristotle designates it as τὸ τί ἦν εἶναι and *eidos.* However, we find it necessary to make some distinctions here.

It is possible, to be sure, to derive a universal *meaning* from being human, a meaning which is realized in all three concepts of Aristotle, and a meaning which neither comes to be nor passes away. But the being human of this particular human being is actual and actuating [*wirksam*] in this person. This person shares it with no other human being. It is not, prior to the person's own being, but steps into existence [*tritt ins Dasein*] together with the person. It determines *what* this particular human being is at any particular time, and this changing what expresses a more or less extensive approximation to the end, i.e., to the *pure form.*

The individual human being lags more or less behind that which is prescribed for the person as the end by the pure form "human being," and the person does so in more than one sense. The person is either "not yet truly the end" (e.g., the being imperfect of the child), or the person is the end in a *defective* manner (e.g., the being imperfect of a deformed person or in the moral order of a "bad" person). And even where the individual human being has reached perfection (i.e., in the state of glory, since there is no real perfection for us humans prior to that state), not *everything* that is predesigned in the pure form "human being" has been actualized, but only that which determines this individual nature or essence (e.g., the pure form "Socrates"). Here, as was pointed out earlier, we again deviate from Aristotle, for whom form coincides with specific determinateness [*Artbestimmtheit*]. The term *eidos* is a also used to designate the *species* [*Art*]).[205]

This consideration leads us to the question of individuality understood as the specific particularity of the individual, and this problem is in turn linked with the function which is attributed to matter in the building up of the individual thing. Aristotle cannot discuss this question, however, before having inquired into the nature of the *causality* [*Ursächlichkeit*] of the pure form.

3. Pure Form and Essential Form Considered as Causes

Aristotle distinguished *four* causes of actual things[206]: matter, the generator of motion, form, and the end. In the case of a human being, these four causes would be constituted by the material elements of which the body is formed, the semen (or progenitor), being human, and the perfection of the human being. It is evident that in all four instances there is a common element of meaning [*Sinnbestand*] which permits us to speak of *cause*. All four causes represent an ontological *ground of actuality* [*Seinsgrund des Wirklichen*] to which the actual owes its existence. But each of the four is cause in a *different manner*, and what is caused by them also differs, so that an additional element of meaning accrues in each case to the common *Sinnbestand*.

When matter is called a cause, the implicit meaning is that the thing as a whole could not be without matter and that matter codetermines *what* the thing is. But it is not matter that gives the first impulse to the process of becoming. Unless some other principle were added, no new thing could ever originate from matter. This fact is expressed by stating that to matter is attributed only a passive potency, not an active one, i.e., only the potency of suffering [*pati*] or receiving, not the potency of doing or effecting anything by itself.

To operate efficaciously [*wirken*] or to give a first impulse to some operation or action is, however, precisely the function of cause in the second sense. The causal principle here causes some becoming, movement, or change (in the narrower sense of the latter two terms: They neither coincide with each other nor do they include the element of becoming). An efficacious operation is the activity of something that is in act, an activity in which the being of this actual thing attains to its perfection in a certain respect. Nothing that is not actual can actualize (cf. pp.221ff. above).

The actual thing which gives the first impulse to the becoming of a new living being is—if we exclude *primary* origination—a living being of the same species. The efficacious operation by which the actual gives the impulse is, however, not its enduring being, but something transitory. The actual has its ontological ground in some enduring faculty or power (the generative act has its ground in the generative *potency*), and the power in turn has its ground in the nature or essence, i.e., in the living being-ness [*Lebewesensein*] of this particular living being (i.e., in what Aristotle calls the form of the living being). What is an *efficient cause* for the newly becoming nature or essence (or, more precisely, the foundation of the efficient cause, if we regard as the cause of the becoming the generative *act* rather than the progenitor or the progenitor's specific determinateness) is a *formal cause* for generating nature or essence, i.e., the ontological ground of what it is, of what it is capable of doing, and of what it actually is *doing*.

As soon as the new living being has become actual, it can itself operate efficaciously. It bears within itself its own formal cause or ground of its operation and of its operative power. As a cause of efficacious operation, the form itself must be called actual (in its capacity as an actual essence—if we do not regard the generic and specific determinateness as the full determinateness of the essence).

The new living being is now *actual,* but *not yet actually perfected.* Its perfection lies ahead as an *end* and as such effects the evolution which leads this new being toward its proper end. Thus, the end or final cause operates not in the manner of moving [*bewegend*] or efficient cause. Evolution is not kept going by an operation that has as its basis an actuality of the same species as the thing which evolves. At the moment evolution begins, that which evolves is an independent entity, cut loose [*abgelöst*] from its progenitor, an entity which bears within itself the formal cause of its operation.

A child moves, expresses its needs, receives it first impressions, etc. in accordance with its nature or essence [*Wesen*]. But the process of evolution—which again and again carries the child beyond the status it has attained at any given time, and which again and again gives rise to a new ontological ground for new operations or activities—receives its impulse and direction from something which the child is not yet, but which the child is destined to become. If thus the end effects the evolution, and if only something actual can actuate, the end obviously must have actuality prior to the time the movement of the evolving thing or being reaches this end and is thereby "actualized."

Is this efficaciously operating end then the pure form, the essential form, or possibly a third principle? Since we previously stated that the being of the pure form is above and beyond the contraries of act and potency, it would seem difficult to attribute actuality to this kind of being. It was shown, moreover, that not only the actuality of nature [*das Naturwirkliche*] but also the "creations" of art are fashioned after an archetypal pure form. And it seems that the pure form remains indifferent to whether or not something is a real or only an "apparent actuality." The actual happening [*Geschehen*] occurs on the part of that which moves toward the end—whether it be by means of natural evolution or through the medium of the artist's creative activity. But even if by one or another kind of "actualization" nothing is changed as far as the pure form as such is concerned, the latter evidently remains not unaffected by the one or other mode of happenings.

In the mind of the artist the *idea* flashes, attracts the artist, leaves the artist no rest, urges the artist on to create. And in a similar manner an "attraction" seems to issue from that which stands above the living being as its end and perfection, an attraction which directs and guides the development of the living being. This attractive force may be felt not only in the mature human being, but from the time of the first awakening of reason. And the image of what the individual is to become may be grasped more or less distinctly, and the individual's free acts may—in the striving for perfection and self-education—be informed accordingly. All infra-human development, however, as well as the early development of the human being (and also to a large extent the human being's later development), do not proceed in the manner of a conscious and rational striving for the attainment of a known end, but rather—seen from the point of view of the living being—in accordance with a non-voluntary and hidden finality. And even where it is a question of a conscious striving for a known end, this striving comes to serve a purposive finality [*Zielstrebigkeit*] which has not been posited by this known end but which—being the immanent force of that which is freely active—existed independently of this known end and has only now been drawn from its concealment and brought to light.

It is *immanent to the nature* of the artist to create, and this immanent principle also determines what kind of designs the artist can appropriate and make his or her own [*sich zu eigen machen*]. This is why there are certain *ideas* which are "attractive" and which the artist is able to actualize. If and when the artist does actualize them, not only do the corresponding works become actual, but the artist's own nature or essence is being actualized: The artist himself attains to a higher stage of ontic perfection [*Seinsvollendung*]. If on the other hand, the artist's striving reaches out for something which according to its nature is denied to him or her, then not only is the work a failure, but the artist also makes a parody of his own self.

And the dual meaning of "self" that is evidenced here cannot be exhaustively characterized by speaking of *pure form* and *essential form*. The "self" in one sense refers to the person as that person really is, a human being with a nature or essence that is actualized in this person, while the second "self" may be understood in the sense of *pure form* to which the person as that person really is does not correspond.

But this is not all. The human being who attains to his or her end does not thereby become a *pure form* but rather a perfect image or copy of the pure form. And whether the person attains to the end or not, the person bears within the self the "seed" of the end. The person's ἐντελεχεια—understood now as the end *structure* [*Zielgestalt*] rather than as perfection of *being*[207]—is actuating within that person from the very beginning of that person's existence, but this ἐντελεχεια is not the only actuating force, and for this reason it may happen that its formative power cannot fully actualize itself [*sich auswirken*].We must therefore distinguish from the pure form—which stands *above* the evolution as a guiding archetype—that vital law which actuates *in* the process of evolution itself and determines this evolution with respect to and in the direction of the end.

It should be remembered in this connection that, according to our previous findings, in the case of an existent whose being is a process of evolution, the nature or essence itself is subject to change.[208]

And what we have just now called the *actualized essence* [*das ausgewirkte Wesen*] is not the same before and after such a change. However, that which is before and after is grounded in something deeper which determines the entire process of evolution and leads it toward the end. And this something we have called the *essential form* [*Wesensform*]. In the essential form is alive that purposively directed power to which the *actualized essence* owes its existence if and whenever it corresponds to the end.

Does this mean, then, that pure forms must be regarded as incapable of causative impulses, as non-real and non-actuating? So it would seem if these pure forms are understood as pure units of meaning [*Sinneinheiten*], as self-enclosed, free-floating essences or whatnesses. This standpoint, however, becomes untenable as soon as we inquire into the manner in which pure forms are related to real thing and their essential forms. If these things are regarded as *images* or *copies* [*Abbilder*] of the pure forms and if these latter are regarded as primordial *archetypes* [*Urbilder*] to the actualization of which the essential forms tend, then it is hardly possible to imagine a merely "accidental" conformity of two worlds which as such are entirely separate. Both worlds, rather, in accordance with their origin, point to that same primordial reality that also accounts for and makes intelligible their interrelation. Comprised and incorporated in the unity of the divine *logos,* the pure forms are primordial prototypes of all things in the divine mind,[209] which places them into existence and which has inscribed in them their end-structure [*Zielgestalt*]. In this sense we may then speak of the being of things in God, and St. Thomas calls this being in God a truer being than the one which things have in themselves.[210]

The causality of the eternal primordial archetypes is simply the creative, sustaining, and ordering efficacious action [*Wirksamkeit*] of God, and the actuality of these archetypes is the divine actuality or rather super-actuality.[211]

When Aristotle concludes from the movement in the world that there must be a prime author of this movement and when he attributes to this prime mover a purely spiritual being, the kind of causality here implied must be considered as finalistic [*Zielursächlichkeit*]. Through it everything that is in the process of becoming is directed toward the one and only supreme end. By virtue of the archetypal forms, we should then have to regard the divine essence not merely as the mover of the universe as a whole, but as linked in a specific manner with every created thing and being. This point of view makes it necessary that there be a peculiarly strong and close interrelation between the archetypal and essential forms. Plato's and Aristotle's doctrines of form suffer, it seems to me, from the defect of Plato's laying undue stress on the archetypal form and of Aristotle's placing too much emphasis on the essential form. And the reason for this deficiency in both instances I see in the fact that to both philosophers the idea of creation and its sequel, the divine sustenance and directive governance of the created universe, remained unknown.

4. Form and Matter in Aristotle's World View and in Ours

We shall now attempt in a brief summary to confront the world view of Aristotle with the one at which we have arrived on the basis of a philosophic inquiry into the nature of finite existents and on the basis of the Christian doctrine of creation. The world is for Aristotle a well-ordered whole consisting of a manifold of formed structures and kept in motion from all eternity and into all eternity by that first cause of motion which is itself unmoved. Thus, human thought is set in motion by its object, and appetition and will are set in motion by their respective ends. Now whatever is a cause must be in act. Whatever moves the will must be a good, but that which moves everything must be the ultimate end and the highest good. And this unmoved mover endures in eternally immutable being—a mind or spirit whose being is the thinking of its own self in a state of eternal bliss. To it must be attributed the order of the universe, that order by virtue of which all things entertain definite relationships among themselves and owing to which every individual thing is guided toward its predestined end.[212]

To the unmoved mover is due also the union of form and matter in things.[213] Matter is from eternity and thus uncreated, but, being unformed, it is in a state of mere potency. Its actual being is owing to the form and ultimately to the first cause which causes everything that *comes to be,* as it leads everything from potentiality to actuality.

Now it seems to me that the reproach which Aristotle levels at his precursors[214]—that they failed to show how matter and form can combine—applies equally to his own doctrine. One particular passage, the interpretation of which has proved very difficult and is by no means uniform today, has perhaps some bearing on this problem. "The final cause," Aristotle writes, "is both *for the good* of something and *for the end* of something. And of these two the former is already given, while the latter is not yet given."[215] Lasson interprets this passage as follows: "That *for which* the end is a cause is something changeable, e.g., a sick person. And that *of which* the end is a cause is some enduring state, e.g., health."[216] This obviously means that the sick person comes to be healthy again, but he does not come to be health. Applied to the origination of human life, the meaning of Lasson's statement is that a human being—but not being human—comes to be. It was previously pointed out that the "unmoved entity" is neither this particular human being nor the being human of this human being but rather that which is expressed by the term "human being" [*Mensch*]. If the *pure form* or the *divine idea* of people is viewed as the measure and end, it makes perfectly good sense to say that this particular person is more or less a "human being" than that other one, or this person comes to be more and more a "human being."

The assumption of a non-become and non-corruptible prime matter is based on the premise that nothing can come from nothing and that something that is cannot become nothing. Both of these propositions, however, are invalid once we acknowledge an infinite existent who has the power of calling something into existence out of nothing or of annihilating that which exists,. The difficulty of explaining how matter can attain to form and how formed matter can acquire actual existence is resolved if there is no matter that could have existed—not even in potency—prior to and independently of the divine creative *Fiat!* And the question of how something that is merely "in potency" can become actual is satisfactorily answered if form and matter as well as existence [*Dasein*] itself are created by this *Fiat!*

Those structures which we designate as "formed matter "whereby matter must be understood as that which fills space [*das Raumfüllende*] as such—do not represent the sum total of all created things, but only *external nature.* The question of whether there are created beings who might be designated as *pure forms* in a novel sense—not in the sense of archetypal essences or whatnesses, but of actual essences which can attain to perfection without any space-filling matter—we have not yet taken into explicit consideration. For the time being, there remains for us the task of clarifying the mutual relationship of matter and form within the narrowly circumscribed field of spatial-material entities.

5. The Mutual Relationship of Form and Matter in the "Original" and "Fallen" State

Whatever is placed into existence [*Dasein*] is a *something* the *being* of which is the molding of some matter so as to form an integrated [*geschlossen*] structure. *Whatever* this something may be, there is always involved some matter that is being formed and some form that is molding matter [*stoffgestaltende Form*]. The one is never without the other. Is it then possible to designate one of these two principles as more primordial than the other? Considered from the temporal point of view, there is certainly no such possibility on the lowest level of material being.[217] Ontologically [*seinsmässig*] speaking, however, priority must be attributed to the form.

This entire question must be considered separately in regard to the two possible modes of the forming of matter [*Stoffgestaltung*]—internally free and externally massively heavy formation. Wherever a form molds itself freely into space, the material fullness results not from the forming of something that is already given, but this fullness derives from the interiority of the form itself. Just as the thinking mind forms the word—no vital movement of the thinking mind would even be possible without such a formative process[218]—so the form actualizes itself in the material fullness as in its co-created and thoroughly pliant and proportionate medium. We may thus say with St. Thomas that matter is for the sake of form. However, since matter is co-created, we shall have to admit with Duns Scotus[219] that matter has a being of its own: not an independent being, to be sure, nor one that is fully actual, but that peculiar kind of being that has a real share in the building up of independent being.

Paradoxically enough, the determinateness of matter lies in its determinability. Essential forms that form matter are thus inconceivable without a material fullness which is molded by them. Such forms are *alive,* i.e., their being is a movement that is automotive [*aus sich selbst heraus*]. And these forms are endowed with *power,* i.e., they are capable of acting or operating in a definite manner. This makes us understand the interconnection between *form* and some qualified creative *power: Essential forms are as such endowed with formative power* [*gestaltungskräftig*]. And now we see also why the form may be called an existent in the most genuine sense: Matter owes whatever being it has to form, so that we may even feel inclined to ask ourselves whether form by itself (and not the composite only) deserves to be called *ousia* or substance.

The decision to designate as *ousia* not the form by itself, but the composite of form and matter, takes into account the fact that it is of the essence of form to form matter and that form is thus never encountered without matter. Form and matter are placed into *Dasein* in a very real sense, and their being is the self-actualization of the form in spatial fullness, the being formed of matter—a self-formation which terminates in a formed whole. In the matter the form is the *carrying principle* [*das Tragende*] in a peculiarly fulfilled and radical [*wurzelhaft*] sense of the term. Where we previously designated the whole as the carrying principle in relation to everything that belongs to its essential constitution, we may now designate the form as that principle which carries or bears up the whole from within. And where we said before that the particularity of matter was basic [*grundlegend*] in the structure of the whole with respect to everything in which this particularity manifests and actively asserts itself, we must now say that what is ultimately basic is the form which forms matter [*stoffgestaltende Form*]. For is it not precisely this form which establishes and *constitutes* the wholeness of the whole, which makes of the "structure" of the whole a demarcated unity and thereby inserts it in the empty form [*Leerform*] of the thing?

According to what was said in previous passages concerning the different basic kinds of space filling, it would seem that not all forms possess this power of self-enclosure [*Selbstabschliessung*].[220] It will therefore be necessary to examine the different forms with respect to the specific manner in which they form matter. Before we do this, however, we must first inquire how this forming is to be conceived when it is a question of massively heavy [*massenbeschwert*] matter. We are already familiar with the atomistic point of view, according to which pure mass is divided up into ultimate indivisible units, while these units in turn are thought to be grouped together in various ways. We stated that such a division and regrouping is conceivable only as resulting from *forces* which are not properties of mass as such. If this is so, whose properties are they? For "free forces," i.e., forces without something to which they pertain as properties, are inconceivable.

It should be pointed out in this connection that pure mass is not to be conceived as something primordial but rather as something resulting from the disintegration of an original unity. Matter which is brought forth from and molded by living forms becomes pure mass as soon as it is taken out of that essential unity which binds it to the molding forms, so that it falls prey to space. The question of how such a "fall" is possible need not concern us here.[221] But if this fall had been radical and definitive—i.e., if the union of form and matter had been totally dissolved, if the form had been forever deprived of its power of forming matter, and if matter had been reduced to a no longer formable mass—then *nature* or the spatial-objective world of things would no longer be possible. However, we know that this is factually not the case. Mass remains subject to formation, and forms have retained some of their power of forming matter, but this forming has become an external subjugation of a matter which has "slid away" [*entgleiten*] from the form and which is no longer quite proportionate to the form. This does not mean, however, that at one time pure mass as such—i.e., completely formless mass—was just there [*vorhanden*] and that it was subsequently subjected to formation by a superimposed form. Rather, what we know by actual experience is formed matter—even on the lowest stage. But forms are no longer capable of dominating and molding freely and without impediment an essentially proportionate commensurate matter, because forms are now tied to spatially captive [*raum-verhaftet*] mass and thus have merely the power of ordering mass in a manner corresponding to its material particularity. From this situation derives the possibility of a manifold of material elements which fill space in varying ways and which manifest themselves sensorially [*sinnenfällig*] in accordance with their material particularity.

6. *Forms of Diverse Formative Power. First Stage: Matter-Shaping Forms* [Stoffgestaltende Formen]

We encounter matter [*Stoffe*]—as elements, mixtures, and combinations—in "pieces" or "quantities," such as, for example pieces of gold or quantities of water. The differences among them are due to the previously discussed particular natures of the basic modes of space-filling. Thus it pertains only to solids to form delimited closed units in an objective, thingly sense, while liquids and gases stand in need of a "receptacle" or some superior, dominating force—a force not internally their own—to attain to such a delimited enclosure. And "pieces," too, in most instances do not exclusively owe their actual structural bounds to the formative power of that form which determines material particularity. The size and structure of external spatial limits are, to be sure, co-determined by material particularity, but they are primarily conditioned by those external influences to which material elements are exposed in their natural contextual environment [*Naturzusammenhang*]. Size and structure therefore appear as something "accidental," i.e., something that has its ground not in the essence, and the essence or nature of things of this kind seems to be equivalent to the thing's ultimate specific determinateness.

Are we then permitted to say that on this level the forms which mold matter lack the power for the formation of autonomous structures that are delimited in accordance with their essence? This can hardly be maintained—not at any rate as a general law—since there are material structures, such as *crystals,* which are formed autonomously from within. Structures of this kind seem to be located on the borderline between the spheres of "dead matter" and "living beings." We regard it as pertaining to the particular nature of living beings that they *form* themselves from within according to a law of their own, that they *grow* with the aid of nutrition until they reach the full stature of their natural measure,[222] that they *maintain* themselves in their developed structure, sustained by changing material elements, that they *reproduce* themselves by generating other living units of the same species, and that they *die* in the end. Now very similar phenomena may be observed in a crystal. It "grows" in accordance with an intrinsic formative law, and if something interferes with this structural growth, the crystal breaks into two parts of identical structure and seems thus to "reproduce" itself by division or fission like an amoeba. In the case of the crystal there is, of course, no question of genuine growth, for the crystal merely accumulates already present particles of the same matter, whereas in any vital growth, foreign material elements are transformed and molded in accordance with an internal formative law. Nor can there be a question of true generative reproduction, since crystals do not only—and not as a rule—originate by fission, but in most instances derive from uncrystallized solutions, whereas living beings always descend from living beings and never from dead matter.[223] There can therefore be no doubt as to which class of formal structures crystals belong.

Shall we then have to restrict the power for such a terminative formation from within to certain material elements? H. Conrad-Martius calls the "crystalline nature" [*Kristallität*] the "natural condition of matter."[224] The meaning implied in this statement is that there are contained in each and every material element those directive forces which may lead to crystalline formation. But just as it is not in the "nature" of every material element to pass over into the solid state—although such a passing over may be brought about by special conditioning—so it also pertains only to certain material elements to form themselves "naturally" as crystalline structures, and it is of essential importance for the formation of the *cosmos* as a whole that not all material elements attain to that end.

We must insist, on the other hand, that, as far as the formative power of the forms of this class is concerned, they are in themselves sufficiently powerful to form things of an autonomous and integrated structural unity. The total structure of external nature, however, results from the cooperation of manifold matter-shaping formative forces, and this total structure presupposes diverse stages of formation on the part of the participating material elements. The crystal represents the highest stage attainable. It is a supremely autonomous structure and can therefore lay claim to the title of *ousia* in a very authentic sense. The crystal exemplifies a principle frequently enunciated in the writings of St. Thomas Aquinas, namely, that each sphere of being in its highest stage touches on the next higher one.[225] We can thus recognize in the crystalline structure the outer limit of the formative power of those forms whose function it is to actualize pure material whatnesses [*Stoffwasheiten*]. Not all the forms of this class actualize themselves to the extent that they reach the outer limit of their formative capacity. Some form no *structures* that are bounded from within, but merely *material elements* [*Stoffe*] as such. And these latter become structures or contribute to the formation of unified structures only by virtue of external influences (e.g., water, which becomes a lake by virtue of the enclosing shores). Material elements are *matter* in a dual sense: as that which fills space and as that which permits further formation, either by the forces and events of nature or by human workmanship.

7. The Pure Form and the Essential Form of Material Structures. Their Symbolic Character. Essence or Nature as "Mystery"

Every structure and every material substance [*Stoff*] is the embodiment of some whatness, i.e., of a *pure form.* Its actualization is brought about by the essential form [*Wesensform*]. A pure form (e.g., the pure form of a landscape) may require for its actualization a diversity of material substances and therewith also of essential forms. Even in the case of simple material substances the distinction between the pure form and the essential form remains valid.

The gold that is found in the universe was created as a specific material substance. It has had a diversified "fate" in the course of the millennia. In part it rests still undiscovered and is thus exposed to no other influence but that of the forces and events of nature. In part it has been discovered and molded by people and has been made to serve any number of purposes. But what the name "gold" signifies and what is actualized in all the "pieces of gold" or "things made of gold" was not created—not at any rate in the same sense as "real" gold—nor has it had any fate. It was before the world came to be, and it will continue to be even after the world with all the gold it contains will have perished. This real gold we call the *essence* or the *pure form of gold.* And all the gold that we know is "gold" only because and insofar as it corresponds to this pure form. The pure form, however, we know only through the medium of the gold we encounter in our experience. And on the basis of our experience we can then reach out beyond it and attain to something which becomes the standard by which we measure the things of experience.

"Real" gold is "pure" gold to a greater or lesser degree. This means, first of all, that it may be mixed with other material substances and that it therefore cannot unfold its own essence or nature without impediment. But even unmixed or unalloyed gold need not have the radiance of pure gold. We shall even have to say that no earthly gold fully actualizes the pure essence. We can conceive of gold that is much more radiant, much "more golden" than all the gold we know from experience, but we can conceive of none that could surpass in splendor of perfection the *pure form* in which is enclosed the highest perfection. The pure form is thus the *ideal,* i.e., the "limit" which all real gold, as well as our own idea of gold, seeks to approximate.

The thing and its actualized essence thus lag behind the corresponding *pure form* to which they owe their entire being. Here we are face to face with the enigma of the "participation of things in the ideas." Aristotle tried to circumvent the difficulty involved in this problem by completely eliminating the ideas (understood as *pure forms*). However, we have seen that this does not solve the riddle, since new difficulties immediately arise.

Things are what they are owing to the essential form actuating from within. Is matter to blame for the fact that things lag behind the pure form? In the world as it was originally created, matter was to serve the pure actualization of form. In that original state matter was molded purely by and in accordance with the essential form. Only in the "fallen" state can matter—cut off from the original unity—impede pure formation [*Ausgestaltung*].

From a strictly philosophic point of view, the "fallen" state can be understood only in terms of a possible metamorphosis of nature. The theological doctrine of original sin, on the other hand, offers us a firm basis which permits us to relate the actual state of the

world to people's rebellion against God and to discover a link between the perversion of the original order of human nature and the fallen state of the world as a whole.

It was pointed out earlier that everything created has its archetypal reality [*Urbild*] in the divine *Logos*.[226] All finite existents must be regarded as images or copies of the divine essence, reflecting as in a mirror the majestic splendor of God. Out of his own being God has placed these finite existents into their own and has endowed them with their own essence and independent [*selbständig*] existence (*ousia* = substance). The essences or natures of these finite existents are determined throughout by the divine essence, but they must necessarily lag behind the divine essence in several respects. In their finitude they cannot comprise in themselves the infinite plenitude of the divine essence, and they can neither in amplitude nor in degree attain to the divine perfection. While they have been given a limited measure of their share in being (essence and existence), the divine being is without limit or measure (also as archetypal reality of a finite being).

And finite existents lag behind the highest degree of being which they could potentially attain in still another respect. This *second* lagging behind is due to the *status naturae lapsae* (the state of fallen nature), i.e., the general corruption of all things in the fallen state. Thus, even the splendor of "gold has been dimmed."[227] There is henceforth a split or crack [*Bruch*] even in the determinateness of the essences of things. They are still a mirror of divine perfection, but the mirror is broken. There is a discrepancy between what things essentially ought to be and what they actually are. And there is, moreover, a disproportion between what things could essentially come to be and the state to which they can actually attain.

This latter observation no longer refers only to particular material substances in their specific determinateness, but to the entire context of natural phenomena and to material substances in their capacity of serving as *material* for human works. As we have previously seen, material substances bear within themselves potentialities which can be actualized only by external influences. Their external constitution is determined by whatever happens to them.

Now we may assume that in the original order of being all natural forces and events were to aid things in the full unfolding of their essences and therewith in becoming pure mirrors of the archetypal reality. And we may further assume that the forces and powers which were implanted in things were commensurate with and subject to the perfect formation of each individual thing as well as to the entire *cosmos,* so that these forces could not act "crudely," senselessly, or destructively. And thus also the "creative work" of people was destined to reveal ever more luminously the God-likeness of nature. Every human *work* was meant to be not only *useful* (i.e., to serve human ends) but also *beautiful* (i.e., to be a mirror of the eternal). Owing to the curse, however, that was pronounced over the created world, its elements were not only "corrupted," but they are in rebellion against each other, so that the forces and events of nature may actually impede the unfolding of essences and thus exert a "destructive" influence. And if people "are to eat their bread by the sweat of their brow," the fault lies not only with the earth, which bears thistles and thorns and yields good fruit only after hard travail, but with the resistance that is offered by each and every *material element* on which people lay their laboring hands.

Original sin and the fallen state of creation thus provide a clue for the understanding of the difference between the actualized essence and the pure form. It is necessary, however, to consider yet a littler further the way in which both were interrelated in the original order of things. This investigation will in turn be conducive to a better understanding of the meaning of *essence* or *nature.*

It was stated above that the essences of things are determined throughout by the divine essence. And the endeavor was made to understand *pure form* as the *archetypal reality* [*Urbild*] of things in God. However, the divine essence is inaccessible to us in this earthly life. Not only on account of its infinitude is it impossible for us to "comprehend" (i.e., to embrace as a whole) this divine essence. We cannot see it face to face at all. We can have no insight into it, and we are therefore unable to "discern" in it the archetypal reality of things.  This is the reason why the *phenomenological intuition of essences* [*Wesenserkenntnis*] has again and again been opposed by representatives of the *Thomistic-scholastic* tradition. They see in such a doctrine the presumptuous claim to a share in the *visio beatifica* already in this life. The discussions of this chapter, as well as in the preceding one, have perhaps made it clear that there can be no question of such a claim on the part of phenomenologists. What has been said up to this point, however, stands in need of some further implementation if we do not wish the truths of faith and philosophic knowledge to remain in unconnected and unbalanced juxtaposition.

We arrive at the essence or nature, understood as the firm and enduring quidditive determinateness [*Wesensbestimmtheit*] of things—an inner determinateness which is independent of external influences—exclusively by the contemplation of those finite existents which we encounter in the world of our natural experience without having recourse to the truths of faith and most certainly without any special supernatural illumination. And we can even go further than that. The actual quidditive determinateness of things points beyond itself to *what* they should be, i.e., to that archetypal reality which is their measure and model. However, the riddles which are posed by the being and intelligibility of these archetypes, pure forms, or essences—we seize them without really holding them, we merely draw close to them; and yet we cannot do without them, because it is only with their aid that we grasp whatever we seize of things—make us seek that answer which a philosophy of purely natural reasoning cannot give, in an entirely different realm, namely in the truths of faith and in traditional theological doctrine.

The divine Logos, by whom and in whose image everything was created, is for us the archetypal existent who comprises in himself all finite archetypes. These latter do not thereby become more intelligible for us, but we begin to see the reason for their non-intelligibility. They are enveloped in the very same veil of mystery which hides from us and simultaneously reveals to us in certain general contours everything that is divine. And now this veil covers even that inner determinateness of the essences of things which first appeared to us as something quite clear and mater-of-fact and which are actually for us the "conceivable" or that which we try to seize by means of concepts.

Gold is scientifically determined according to its color, its firmness, its specific weight, its reaction to other material elements, etc. When we attempt to grasp its essence, we regard color, luster, malleability, the capacity of assuming various shapes, and some other qualities as "essential" or as "having their foundation in the essence." Nevertheless, the essence can neither be reduced to nor construed of any number of such individual characteristics. The essence is a unified whole and always more than the sum total of all individual characteristics which we may be able to discover, and in its unity and wholeness it can ultimately only be designated by some name.

Moreover, there is something contained in the essence which cannot be conceived as "material quality" at all.

It will be remembered that *matter* (in one specific sense of the term) must be regarded as denoting generically that which fills space, expands in space, presents itself and is actualized in space.[228] But the essence or nature of material things is not exhausted in their spatial being. Why is it that crowns and ornaments are made of gold? Certainly not only because gold is rare and therefore precious, but because gold is "fit" to be used in this way, i.e., because in its luster there is something of the nature of royal splendor. And why is it that we say of a human being that he or she is "true as gold"? One reason is that gold is durable and not easily corroded by external influences. But such a saying refers not only to a mere external analogy. Linguistic metaphors often express an inner relationship that exists between different genera of existents as well as a relationship between finite existents and the divine archetypal reality. For it is of the essence of every finite thing to be a *symbol* [*Sinnbild*], and it is of the essence of everything material and spatial to be a *symbol* [*Gleichnis*] of something immaterial or spiritual. This is its mysterious meaning and its hidden inwardness.[229] Precisely what makes the material and spatial a symbol of the spiritual makes it likewise a symbol of the eternal. For God is spirit, and finite spirituality is a more proximate symbol of the infinite spirit than the material and spatial.

And so we see that in its essence each and every thing bears within itself its own mystery and thereby points beyond itself. And just as the fleetingness and debility of finite being discloses to us the necessity *of* eternal being, so the imperfection of all finite *essences* or *natures* makes manifest the necessity of an infinitely perfect essence or nature.

How can there be eternal being?

8. Second Stage: The Living Being.
Body — Soul — Spirit as the Basic Forms of Actual Being

Let us now deal with *living beings* [*Lebewesen*]. They constitute another special class of material being. Their particular nature—as distinguished from the inferior realm of *dead* things as well as from the nature of crystals—has already been characterized. Living beings are capable of transforming and "incorporating" in themselves foreign material elements and of bringing forth new structures of their own species. The formal principle which commands such a superior formative power is called the *soul* by Aristotle and the scholastic thinkers, while the material structure that is molded by this form is designated as the *body.*

The terms *soul* and *body* imply a different content in the several classes of "the living" [*des Lebendigen*]. Beyond this, however, these terms denote different *basic forms of actual being,* and to these must be added *spirit* as a third basic form. According to H. Conrad-Martius:

> Corporeal being is essentially a kind of being in which an entity possesses itself in a quasi-fully-born-out [*ausgeboren*] form, i.e., in a form which is actually unfolded and thus self-enclosed and self-delimited. Such a formal structure, resting in itself, represents and makes manifest what it is. ... The being of the soul is the hidden "life" or the hidden source which empowers such an entity to attain to corporeality. ... On the level of spiritual being, however, a thus substantiated corporeal entity is in turn capable of transcending itself in a selfless and non-fixed [*unfixiert*] manner and—purified and freed from the mass of the limited self—to "give itself freely" to others in vital participation.[230]

These three basic forms [soul, body, and spirit] demarcate three different *realms* of actual being, albeit not in an exclusive manner [*ausschliessend*], but in such a way that "the individual formations *within* these realms are in their turn subject to the dominating formative power of these three classes," determined and modified in each instance by the principle class or category.

> The realm of corporeality is the realm of "nature" or ... the "earthly" realm in the strict sense. ... While the realm of the spirit is the sphere of the supra-earthly [*Überirdisch*], the realm of the soul is the sphere of the infra-earthly [*Unterirdisch*] and as such the dimension of an as yet non-revealed [*unoffenbar*] life ... which tends toward its unfolding in corporeal being. The supra-earthly, however, is the realm of fully unfolded being—a being which is actual through and through and thus abiding in the splendor of perfect selflessness (conjoined with the highest possible plenitude of essential reality!), lightness, and brightness.[231]

There are two reasons why it is not possible to speak of genuine corporeality on the level of *dead* things: 1) The structure of these things is not a pure actualization of their own essential form, but is conditioned to a large extent by external influences and thus "accidental"; and 2) in "fallen" nature, material fullness is not found in vital union with the essential form, but material fullness is subject to the domination of the form only in an external sense. This is precisely why it makes sense to speak of *dead* nature. What is it, on the other hand, that entitles us to speak of *body, life,* and *soul* in the case of *living beings,* since, after all, these latter receive into themselves, together with the matter which they embody in their structures, also the *dead nature* of this matter? The answer is that we are justified in speaking of a *body* because the self-enclosed structure is molded by the essential form (which thereby expresses its own self), even though the structure of the living being is formed out of a matter which has the capacity of positing an obstacle to this formation, the capacity of dimming the purity of the "expression" and of thus contributing to a possible disintegration of the structure. And the essential form as such may be called a *soul* because it is something that is "hidden" and that tends toward formation and revelation in corporeal fullness. Such a forming from the inside out, however, is properly called *life,* although it is the kind of life that is subject to death.

9. The Soul of the Plant

In a limited sense even the plant may be said to have a soul and a body. H. Conrad-Martius calls the plant soul a "forming soul."[232] The latter is distinguished from the animal and human soul by the fact that its being exhausts itself in the process of "forming" and that all the activities of the plant serve this one purpose, while in the case of the souls of other living beings, the task of forming is but one among others.

If by *soul* we mean the innate essential form of a living being, then it must be said that each and every soul bears within itself the power of forming matter in a particular way, i.e., in a way that is superior to the formative power of purely material structures and that makes it possible for the soul to transform foreign material elements. It is the particular mode of being of living beings that they build and form themselves *progressively from within* with the aid of the received and absorbed material elements. And this particular mode of being we call *life.* It is not, however, a true and full life because it is not radically and unrestrictedly a formation from within, i.e., from the innate formal principle. The form is truly "alive" inasmuch as it has the power of forming, but this form is tied to a matter in which it cannot freely and completely actualize itself. The vitality of this form is stronger and freer than the vitality of *dead things,* only because the matter over which it holds sway from the outset is already molded into a whole from within, but also because the vitality of this form is not confined to this particular matter. The form is capable of appropriating material elements from "without"—from a region which lies beyond the limits of this whole and thus beyond its original realm of formation [*Gestaltungsbereich*]—and it is capable of incorporating these extraneous elements into the whole and of further molding the whole with their aid. But this dominion over matter is not unlimited. To what extent the formed whole is an actualization of the form depends on the degree of autonomy possessed by these "foreign" material elements.

10. The Evolution of Living Beings

Actualization comes about *progressively,* and it pertains to the nature of living beings nor to step into existence "ready-made" [*fertig*]. This holds true in a sense for all earthly things. Every earthly reality, the entire visible creation, is in the realm of *becoming.* Every formed thing bears within itself possibilities of future actualization. This applies even to those material elements which have as yet not received a thingly enclosure [*dinglich geschlossen*].

We do not know how to picture that *chaos* which, we are told, was the initial stage of the created world. However, we may imagine that it was a kind of total "disorder" [*ein Durcheinander*], a fortuitous medley of all the elements that made it impossible for any of them to unfold in accordance with their particular natures. Some "kinetic impulse" was needed to arrive at that orderly play of forces which we call causal relations and which rests on the principle of causality. The creation of material elements and the kinetic impulse, however, must not be conceived as two temporally separate events. Nor should one conceive a stretch lying betwen two points in time as a period of "Tohu wabohu" [formless waste, a Hebrew expression used in Genesis 1:2]. Material elements can, after all, step into existence only formally actuated, i.e., engaged in a process of formation and manifesting themselves actually in their external appearance in accordance with their internal form. And thus there pertains to the existence of material elements also the movement by which they are separated or united and by which they attain in any particular instance to either separation or orderly junction of a kind that enables them to unfold as *structures.* Solids unfold as self-enclosed and firmly delimited spatial structure while liquids and gases are either delimited by solids or move freely about [*umspielen*] solids.

It may be assumed, moreover, that according to the original order of creation, the movements and interactions of material elements were to aid them in forming and unfolding themselves, so that they might manifest in their entire external appearance their anchorage in the eternal. This form-language of material elements cannot be expressed in words, nor can its meaning be conceptually grasped, but it is still unmistakably visible and audible in the towering mountains, in the waves of the sea, and in the raging storm no less than in the gentle breeze. The fact that the forces and events of nature often cause grave disturbances, mishaps, and the destruction of natural structures, has its reason and cause in the fallen state of nature. And yet a glimmer of the original order is still discernible. Even now the world is a cosmos rather than a mere chaos.

There is, then, becoming and passing away, change and transformation, even in the realm of *dead* nature. Nevertheless, the *becoming* of that which is alive is quite distinct from the kind of becoming that we associate with dead nature. A mere material structure—rigid in its massive weight—would persist as it is, unchanged, unless it were exposed to some external influence. This is precisely the reason why we call it "dead." That which is alive, on the other hand, has received the gift of moving, of forming itself from within. This kind of life pertains to a plant, and it manifests itself from the moment the seed begins to sprout.

The "process of becoming" [*Werdegang*] of the plant structure is an evolution toward a definite end, namely, the fully unfolded Gestalt with everything that belongs to it, including the ripened fruit. And this process of becoming has itself a very definite Gestalt. It has a "temporal" rather than a spatial structure, because it involves a definite kind of progression. However, in some way space also has a share in this movement, for the latter is a progressive self-forming [*Sichhineingestalten*] into space and a progressive transforming of the spatial Gestalt.

Compared with this kind of becoming, *dead things* appear as finished. Their being is characterized by inertness. We can state what they *are*, and we can speak of their essential determinateness as of the essence or nature which they *have* and which they reveal in their external appearance as well as in their doing [*Wirken, actio*] and suffering [*Leiden, passio*]. In the case of living beings, on the other hand, the essential determinateness prescribes what they are to *become* and what they are progressively to appropriate or assimilate. At the same time, however, living beings *have* in each evolutionary phase a particular essence or nature and an external appearance as well as a mode of action founded on this particular essence or nature. Here we meet once more with a phenomenon which has aroused our attention before: In living beings the essence or nature is progressively changing, and the *faculty* [*Vermögen*] (understood as *potentiality* and power) of progression has its foundation in the essential determinateness, that has evolved in any particular stage. For the actualization of this potentiality in any such phase, the corresponding material structural elements are needed.

H. Conrad-Martius has emphasized that the plant—owing to the fact that it is rooted in the ground and also reaches up into the sphere of air and light—is immersed in the elements it needs for its growth.[233] The plant is not compelled to look for its food and thus requires neither free local movement nor sensation in order to fulfill its vital task, namely, to absorb inorganic material elements and to transform them into organic ones. The plant must, on the other hand, manage with whatever it finds in its specific location, and on this natural situation depends the actual course of its evolution, i.e., on the natural habitat of the plant depends how much of that which it is capable of becoming is actualized.

Here we encounter once more the contrast between *pure form*—i.e., the *idea* of the plant or of the definite plant species, an idea which is "above" the process of evolution since it is this *essential form* that is the actuating principle in the individual plant—and the changing *actualized essence* which, to a greater or lesser degree, corresponds to the pure form. In the case of purely material structures, it is impossible to find any independent material elements—separated from the essential form—to which the defects of the entire factually existing structure might be attributed. To explain these defects, we must have recourse to external circumstances—aside from and in addition to the fundamental defect, namely, the *corruption* of all material elements after the fall, i.e., the failing away of *mass* from its union with its essential form.

In the case of living beings, on the other hand, a formative power superior to the material elements stands over against some foreign matter. Here a given matter is indeed radically transformed, i.e., changed into other material elements, vitalized, and integrated with the unified corporeal structure.[234]

The plant soul, though superior to the material elements, nevertheless remains thoroughly bound to matter [*stoffgebunden*]. Its being exhausts itself in the forming of matter. For the plant soul, therefore, the term *inner form* or *form of a body* is especially appropriate. It is *form,* i.e., formatively potent [*gestaltungskräftig*], in a larger measure than the material forms. It is nothing but the form of a body, whereas the souls of animals and the souls of human beings are in addition the essential foundation [*Wesensgrundlage*] of an inner life. The fact that a plant is an imperfect image or copy of its *idea*—the idea of the plant as well as the idea of a rose or of an oak—i.e., a somewhat stunted or crippled "specimen," may have its cause, aside from "external circumstances" (such as an unprotected location or climatic influences), in the defectiveness of the structural elements.

11. Form, Matter, and Wesen *(Essence; Nature). The Unity of the Essential Form* [Wesenform]. *Form and Act.*

After having clarified to some extent the interrelation of form and matter, we may revert once more to the problem of the interrelation of *form* and *essence* [*Wesen*]. We found in Aristotle a certain indecision in regard to the question whether the form by itself or the total composite of form and matter—whenever there is such a "composition"[235]—should be designated as "essence."

Both Aristotle and St. Thomas distinguish three kinds of *substance* (*ousia* = independent or autonomous actuality): the first existent (God); simple substances (pure spirits); and composite substances (material things and living beings: plants, animals, human beings).[236]

Concerning composite substances, St. Thomas writes:

> Form and matter are found in composite substances. Soul and body, for example, are found in human beings. It cannot be said, however, that one of these two by itself is the essence. It is evident that matter by itself is not the essence, for a thing is knowable through its essence and fixed in its species and genus. Matter, however, is neither a principle of knowledge nor does it determine anything in a genus or species. Only that by virtue of which something is actual (*quo aliquid actu est*) can thus determine a thing. Nor can the form by itself be called the essence of a composite substance, although some make an attempt to defend this proposition. It is evident, then, from what has been said that the essence is what is signified by the definition of a thing. The definition of natural substances, however, includes not only form but also matter.... Obviously, therefore, the essence embraces matter and form.[237]

If we are to understand the quoted passage correctly we must remember that what St. Thomas means by *matter* is not some determinate actuality but rather that undetermined matter which cannot actually exist by itself.[238] Formed matter has its own essential determinateness and, by virtue of it, is fixed in genus and species. Formed matter represents the lowest state of actuality. On this level matter and form must be regarded as inseparable in actual being, but as factually [*sachlich*] distinct.

To answer the question whether it is possible to speak of an essence that embraces form and matter, we must keep clearly in mind what is meant by essence. We have just heard St. Thomas define essence as that through which the thing is knowable and fixed in its genus and species. This is what can be grasped conceptually and what we previously designated as the *universal essence.* Materiality, understood as spatial fullness, belongs to the generic determinateness [*Gattungsbestimmtheit*] of the things here under discussion, and the particular mode of their space-filling belongs to their specific determinateness [*Artbestimmtheit*]. Both of these characteristics must then be regarded as belonging to the *universal essence* of these things. However, in addition, we have been discussing the *individual essence* which pertains to the individual thing and makes it what it is. Now the universal essence is not something existing aside from nor something external to the individual thing, but the universal essence is that which can be conceived as a universal in the individual.

As far as the *individual essence* is concerned, once again several interpretations seem to be possible. The essential form is that which ultimately determines the thing and thus *ultimately* makes it what it is. But because the essential forms of *composite substances* are not necessarily actualized in material fullness, their material fullness pertains to whatever they are, and their material determinateness [*Stoffbestimmtheit*] must be regarded as part of their individual essence.

In order to indicate clearly the difference between the essential form and the total essence [*Wesensganze*] which is determined by the form, we designated the latter as the "actualized essence" [*ausgewirktes Wesen*]. This difference may be noted even in purely material things, although it can be more distinctly observed in living beings, because here the essential form seizes foreign material elements which were originally separated from it. And it is from the category of living beings that St. Thomas takes his example to illustrate the interrelation of form and matter: the soul and body of human beings.

For the time being, however, we confine ourselves to the lower stage in order not to be forced to enter into an immediate discussion of those new problems which are posed by the essence or nature of human beings as such. We therefore substitute for the human soul and body the *soul* and *body* of the plant. Strictly speaking, the soul is separable from the body only if the latter is considered as a material *body* [*Körper*], i.e., in its physico-material constitution. The soul is not separable from the body if the latter is considered as *Leib,* i.e., as a be-souled or living body. A body in which there is no life and thus no soul which imparts life to it, no longer deserves to be called *Leib* (living body). Life is the being of the living being, and where there is no life, there "is" no living being.

The soul forms the *organism*, an organism whose every *part* is embodied in the living whole as a member or an *organ*. The separation of matter and form is so strongly evident in the organism because in this case a material element is present before life begins to stir and before the vital process of forming from within commences. There also remains some material element after the life that was in the organism has ceased. And for this reason we are Justified in saying that an already formed matter is being formed anew and that life "begins to stir" and again to ebb when the organism is dying. We can thus say of the "same thing" that it was alive and is now dead. In this sense St. Thomas calls it an equivocation to speak of the "eye" or the "ear" of a dead organism.[239] He means to say that the material body [*Körper*] is no longer *Leib* (a living body) once the soul has left it. The material body, however, which prior to the departure of the soul was a living body, is still there. Thus death, understood as a transition from living to dead being [*Dasein*], is no change in the sense in which we call change the metamorphoses of living beings and of dead bodies. Until the moment of death, it is the living being that undergoes all these changes and that is alive in all of them, but from the moment of death the living being is no more, and something else has taken its place. However, this happens not in the manner of one thing's being taken away to be replaced by another (a thing so similar to the first that it might be mistaken for it). What takes place is rather a genuine *transformation.* What was a living being is now a dead thing.

These processes are closely related to the problem of the unity of the essential form in a living being, that unity which St. Thomas defended with such determination against the objections of most of the thinkers of his age. The essential or substantial form (*forma substantialis*) is the form owing to which a thing has an independent or autonomous being (*esse substantiale*). St. Thomas writes:

> Two things are required for something to become the substantial form of another. First, the form must be the principle of the independent, autonomous being (*principium essendi substantialiter*) of that of which it is the form. By this I do not mean the efficacious principle of being (*principium effectivum*) but rather that formal principle by virtue of which a thing is and is called an

> existent. From this follows, second, that form and matter together have *one* being (*conveniant in uno esse*). This, however, cannot be said of the efficacious principle of being nor of that to which this efficacious principle imparts being. The composite existent as an independent, autonomous entity (*in quo subsistit substantia composita*) inheres in that one being which form and matter have in common. The latter, though one with respect to the being it has, consists of form and matter.[240]

In the context from which the above passage is taken, the attempt is made to demonstrate that the intellectual soul of human beings can truly be the form of the human body. But what is said here must apply to any matter and any form. We hold that even the lowest material structures are an inseparable[241] unity of matter and form (a form that molds matter, or of formed matter, i.e., a matter that is determined in its particularity). These material structures would be nothing unless they were thus determined in their quid [*Was*]. Their very being would be annihilated. Their being is truly *one,* because this oneness is conditioned by form and matter. The primordial "efficacious ontological principle" [*bewirkende Seinsgrund*] to which they owe their being is the divine creative act, and the being of this act differs from the being of every created thing.

The case of the plant and its essential form is somewhat more complex. A number of material elements contribute to the structural growth of the plant. The whole is a composite in a more genuine sense. The following questions then arise: Has every material element [*Stoff*] its own form? And is that life-giving form which we call the *soul* added to the other forms? Or is it the form of the soul that imparts to the entire structure whatever being it has, and is this being only *one* for the entire structure?

The material elements which contribute to the building up of the entire structure have both form and being. For the plant that grows from the seed does not come to be out of nothing. The plant comes into its being from the seed and from those structural material elements which it absorbs from the air and the soil. But the entire structure which grows from these "parts" is not the sum total of the parts, but a new structure with a new form and a new kind of being.

There is an essential difference between the seed and the newly added structural materials elements. The seed is the *beginning* of the new structure. It is the seed which "receives" or "absorbs" other material elements and converts them into a new kind of being. This new and different kind of being we call *life,* and the form which imparts this life we call a *living form* or a *soul.*

Since the entire structure is *one,* the principle which imparts unity to the whole must also be one. That which was present prior to the beginning of life is no longer the same as it was before the animation occurred. And the material elements which were present prior to the animation as well as those which remain after the animation has ceased would not be recognizable as the "same" if it were not for the sequence of mutations which occurred during the interval of life and which caused the former to become the latter. These mutations, however, have their foundation in the life principle, not in dead matter. The material body [*Körper*] which remains after the cessation of life would not be what it is unless the life principle had formed it and made it into what it is now.

This consideration seems to support the view that the soul not only imparts life—as something which accrues to an already given being of a different kind—but determines the entire being. The living being is what it is—even as a material body—by virtue of the fact that it is this specific living being. To be a living being means a structural self-building as a living body, and included therein is the self-building as a material body.

Before life began to stir, another form was present, a material form, and it was present in the foreign material structural elements. In seeds as well as in other "beginnings" of new plant life we meet with a peculiar intermediate state. They are neither dead nor are they actually alive. If the original form had remained instead of giving way to the living form, something quite different would have happened to the end product of the formative process. And when life has ceased, once again something entirely different happens to the material body that was formed by the life-soul [*Lebenseele*] than would have happened if this body were still alive.

The material body [*Körper*] is formed matter, but as such detached from union with that living form which had molded it. It is a *thing,* a structure of integral unity, and it is "actual" in the sense of exerting and receiving influences, but this actuality is not in congruity with its original essential form. Must we assume then that the being and essence of this material body are mere subsequent effects of this original actuating form? And does this "remaining" being and essence now lack a *carrying principle* [*Träger*] of its own? Or does a new, purely material form (or possibly a number of such forms) take the place of that living form which "released" the structure at the time of disintegration? I shall not attempt to answer these questions. One possible interpretation, however, would be the assumption that the forms of those material elements which contribute to the structure of the living body do not simply disappear under the dominion of the living essential form, but merely fall into disuse [*ausser Kraft treten*], and that these forms resume their proper function as soon as the essential form (which binds them) withdraws.[242]

Presupposed in this entire complex of circumstances is the "fallen" state of nature. A body that would be alive in the true and full sense of the term would not be tied to "dead" structural elements at all and would therefore not be vulnerable to death. Such a body would be formed out of the soul and commensurate with it, without absorbing any material elements. On the other hand, where "dead nature" serves as the substructure of what we call *life*—what in reality, however, is merely a faint copy of the true life—those transmutations from death to life and from life to death are found. Something is preserved in these processes, and this something permits us to speak—notwithstanding the transformation—of the "same" prior to and following the change. That which remains the same is the "this-there" [*Diesda*], the empty form of the thing, a form which is being filled with a content that is a residue of the originally formed structure.

There are certain material units which release only some individual parts of their total organic structure [*Lebensganze*]. A withered leaf on a blooming branch, the dead branch of a verdant tree—these are thingly parts [*Dingteile*] shaped by the living form, but parts which are no longer members of the living being and thus no longer permeated by its life.

St. Thomas frequently designates as act the form which imparts being to the total structure, and he equates this form to that being: "It is not unreasonable to say that the kind of being which is found in the independent, autonomous composite is identical with the form, since the composite is only by virtue of the form and since neither part of the composite has separate, independent being (*nec seorsum utrumque subsistat*)."[243]

If we are consistent in distinguishing in all finite existents between being [*Sein*] and that which is [*Seiendes*]—as seems to be required by the facts under consideration and as would also in the last analysis be in accord with the views of St. Thomas[244]—we shall find it impossible to designate the form as being.[245] And if we use the term *act* to designate *actual being*, we shall not be able to call the form an *act* but shall have to refer to it merely as to something that is *actual*, i.e., something that is actual and actuating in this particular plant and that causes the plant to be an actual thing of such and such a kind. Those material elements which contribute to the building up of the plant must then accordingly be designated as *potential*, i.e., as having the inner possibility (*passive potency*) of being "animated" by this particular form and of being integrated in the unity of the plant body as parts or members.

Here again two major stages or phases must be distinguished, namely, the capacity of *inorganic* material elements to be transformed into organic elements, and the capacity of *organic* material elements to enter into the vital unity of the plant body and thereby to receive new possibilities of actualization (*active potencies*). The life of plants is a continuous actualization of potentiatities. And if we now recall once more both the semantic differences and interrelations in the terms ἐνέργια, ἔργον, ἐντελέχεια (actuality, actuation or efficacious activity—work—perfection of being)[246]—all of them rendered by the one term *act*—we shall then designate "life" most adequately as ἐνέργια, i.e., as actual and actuating being. The actual and actuating existent [*Seiende*], on the other hand—the essential form and the living structural whole [*Lebensganze*]—is then ἐνεργίᾳ ὄν. The term ἔργον (work) may be applied to the living being in the different stages of its evolution as they devolve from the forming activity, and to every produced *effect* [*Leistung*] of the living being, to every one of its vital activities; ἐντελέχεια (perfection of being) denotes the final goal or end of the entire process of evolution. That may mean either the respective level of evolution [*Entwicklungshöhe*], i.e., the being of the fully unfolded organism, or the final structure [*Zielgestalt*] toward which the entire process of becoming moves under the directive guidance of the essential form.

In accordance with the above considerations and with the quoted passage from St. Thomas, the formal and material determinateness of animate material structures must be termed their *essence* or *nature.* For they owe what they are to the fact that specifically determined material elements are progressively transformed according to a particular formative law [*Bildungsgesetz*]. And thus also on the stage of living beings we arrive at a separation of essence and essential form τὸ τί ἦν εἶναι and μορφή.

12. Generic and Specific Determinateness of the Living Being. Generative Power

To the determinateness of the essence of living beings belong, however, other things besides the composition of form and matter, the power of the form to mold matter, and the power of self-formation inherent in the structure as a whole. As against purely material things, living beings represent a new genus of the actual. And to their generic determinateness belongs—in addition to the composition of form and matter—the supra-material plastic power of the form. The specific determinateness must be sought not only on the side of the form, as is the case with purely material structures, but the particular nature of the form also demands a corresponding specificity on the part of matter. To generic determinateness belongs, finally, not only the power for the self-formation of the individual structure, but the surpassing power of the individual structure of producing structures of the *same* species.

The term *species* thus assumes a new meaning. It no longer denotes only that which has a common determinateness of the essence, but simultaneously the totality of that which is *interrelated by a common descent.* These two meanings of *species* do not coincide. Each living being has *its* specific determinateness—which is the "same" for all the members of "its species"—and it owes its specificity to the fact that it belongs to that "whole" which as such has a common determinateness of the essence, because it stands within a relationship of common descent.

It thus pertains to the essence of life that the formative power is more than a mere power of self-formation. Life in its generic essence is "generative" or "procreative." What does this mean? As we stated previously, it means that life is capable of producing an individual structure of the same species. And if we take this statement literally, it means that a new living being, a structure composed of matter and living form, is being produced. A new living being originates and a particular material structure is formed by the generating living being and is then released to assume a separate existence of its own. The question is whether this generated being also owes to the generating being its form and its life. For example, an apple tree in its attire of ripe fruit is still a vital unity. The fruit is alive because the life stream of the tree is in it, and it owes what it is to the tree's formative power. It is still made up of members of the organic whole. But the apple which has fallen to the ground begins a separate existence of its own, and within this apple is hidden the life-bearing seed. Where then is the beginning of the new life to be found?

Aristotle sees an intimate interconnection between the self-building [*Selbstaufbau*] of living beings by means of nutrition and growth and the formation of new living beings by means of generation. He explains generation or procreation by the presence of surplus building materials in the generating living being. Out of this surplus—which must be eliminated [*ausscheiden*]—the generating being forms the seed which potentially bears within itself the new living being (cf. p.216 above). Hedwig Conrad-Martius, in her inquiry into the nature of the plant—an inquiry which she carried on within the frame of an imposing ontology and in closest contact with the most recent biological research—arrived at a similar conclusion. "Growth and reproduction ... are very intimately interrelated. Karl Ernst von Baer once designated reproduction as a 'growth beyond the measure of the individual.' But we might as well say, conversely, that growth is a kind of reproduction within one and the same individuality, for growth, too, is a continuous generation and formation of the plant or the living cell *out of its own self.*"[247]

Both growth and generation are actualizations of what Hedwig Conrad-Martius regards as *"the innermost and most genuine essence of life and of every living thing, namely self-generating potency* [*Selbsterzeugungspotenz*]."[248] Its visible expression is the *branching out* [*Verzweigung*] as the "original formal phenomenon [*Urgestaltungsmoment*] of the plant."[249] The "reproduction" [*Fortpflanzung*] in every new individual structure is, as it were, a continuation of this branching out process.

H. Conrad-Martius does not deny, on the other hand, that "growth and reproduction are to a certain extent contrasting phenomena, inasmuch as the plant in its growth reproduces itself in its *individual wholeness,* while in the process of generation it *transcends itself* to serve exclusively the preservation of the *species.*"[250] This contrast finds its "*structurally differentiated expression* in the difference between the *foliage* (which exercises the function of assimilation and nutrition and thus serves the growth and individuation of the plant) and the *blossoms* (which serve reproduction)." The same author describes the contrast "between individuation and preservation of the species ... within the vegetative organism as relatively insignificant, because the plant, according to its nature, does not yet possess a closed, inwardly centered [*geinnert, zentriert*] but rather an essentially *overt* [*offen*] individuality."

H. Conrad-Martius regards as more important for an adequate description of the plant nature the fact:

> ... that 1) both growth *and* reproduction in the plant organism proceeds *from the same essential ground* [*Wesensgrund*], namely, the existential power of self-enclosure and basic self-formation [*Selbstumfassung und Selbstbegründung*]; and that (2) consequently the principle of reproduction—i.e., generation and propagation—is the most fundamental and essential accomplishment of the plant organism, as is clearly revealed in the final formation of the blossoms and of infloresence, the "head" [*Haupt*] or crown (*corolla*) of the plant.[251]

13. Self-Formation and Reproduction. Individual Being and Species. Individual Life and the Essential Form of the Individual Being

In our context it is precisely the difference between growth and reproduction that is of decisive importance. Is it by "chance" that the apple falls to the ground? Is there a possibility that the new tree could grow on the old trunk? It may be argued that the new plant needs the nutritive elements which it assimilates from soil and air and that it must therefore—separated from the old plant—possess a sufficient "living space" for its growth. If this were the only reason for the separation, the young plant could not be regarded as a new "individual being" at all. To be sure, it would be a living material structure of a delimited spatial form, but it would then lack an *inner form* or *soul* of its own. In this case the *species* with all its "derivative specific varieties" [*Abarten*]—as a whole composed of all the material elements molded by the one form—would then represent the true vital unit [*Lebenseinheit*].

Now it is certainly important to mark out clearly that actual vital unit which, extending beyond the individual structure, comprises it. However, we must not go so far as to endanger the individual structure in its autonomous being. And it seems to me that we succumb to this danger if we do not draw vigorously enough the dividing line between growth and reproduction and therewith between the individual being and the species. If the origination of a new living being were not essentially different from the division of a cell or the branching out of a tree, its independence [*Sonderdasein*] would only be external and its individual life only apparent. The living being would then be deprived of that "self-enclosure" and "self-formation" in which H. Conrad-Martius finds the ontological foundation for both growth and reproduction. And if it is claimed that reproduction is the only or the prevalent existential meaning of the plant, the unfolding of the individual being into a structure of a particular shape is not considered in its own right.

When Aristotle speaks of a "surplus of material elements" not needed by the individual being for the purpose of its self-formation and therefore available for the formation of new individual beings, he points to the problem with which we are concerned here. We can speak of a "surplus" only if a definite measure is presupposed. And this is indeed the case. H. Conrad-Martius herself, in the chapter on "Structure and Formative Laws in the Vegetable Kingdom," demonstrated clearly and most convincingly that the formation of definite units or wholes [*Ganzheiten*] of formal structures is of fundamental importance. Certain basic types are divided into new species and subspecies, not unlike "a *central sun* or a *primordial archetype* [*Urbild*] ... that in ever new realizations is reflected in all particular individual forms. And this for no other purpose but *that of a wealth and even superabundance of forms* [*Formenreichtum und Formenüberschwang*]."[252] The *world* is a *cosmos* composed of such "wholes" which, moreover, "are found in turn to be joined together among themselves in sequences of higher form units" and which thus "from the beginning of the world—in evolutionary series and processes of wonderfully and rhythmically articulated structures—have produced an equally wonderful hierarchical gradation, reaching from the lowest to the highest formations, from the most particularized individuality to the most comprehensive universality."[253]

However, the carriers of this abundance of forms are those individual beings in which the specific particularity assumes a visible structural form [*Gestalt*]. They are bound to maintain the measure of their specific structural form, to enclose and delimit themselves in a definite manner. Whenever they grow irregularly beyond this measure, malformations ensue. The fact, however, that these individual beings are capable of absorbing a surplus of material elements becomes understandable when we consider that the meaning of their existence does not exhaust itself in self-formation but that—above and beyond self formation—they have to accomplish something else. By means of reproduction, they serve not only the propagation and preservation but also the transformation of the species as well as the formation of new varieties.

The species steps into existence, receives its formal impress, evolves, and is transformed—in individual beings. Owing to the fact that each of these individual beings efficaciously actuates beyond itself and its own existence, all of them are linked together by a causal and existential chain. But each and every link of this chain is rounded off [*gerundet*] and founded in itself, and with each and every one of them a new existence or a new life begins. Each of them is nonetheless also "overt," for each of them releases new individual beings and transmits—by transformation or variation—the particularity of the species. With the first individual being of a species there begins simultaneously the existence of the species as a comprehensive wholeness in which all those individual beings that are interrelated by common descent [*Abstammungszusammenhang*] inhere as "links" or members. The wholeness is actualized in the juxtaposition and temporal sequence of its *specimens*.

And now we ask again whether each individual being *has* its own essential form (only then does it deserve the name individual *being* [*Einzel*wezen]) and its own life. Furthermore, does each individual being receive its form and its life from the progenitor? To the first question we give the same answer as before. Yes, each individual being bears within itself its essential form. It forms itself from within in accordance with its own formative law, and this forming—from the first stirrings of life to the attainment of the fulfilled structure and beyond, as long as the transformation of material elements (i.e., the structure's "metabolism" [*Stoffwechsel*]) is maintained—is the individual's "life," which is equivalent to its *Dasein.* Included in this vital forming is the production of ripe fruit.

The individual being has its own life, a life which has a beginning and an end. But the individual has not bestowed this life upon itself. It has received it. From whom? This, it will be remembered, was our second question.

If the ripe fruit belongs to the vital unity of the generating individual being and if, on the other hand, a new life takes its start in the generated being, this seems to imply a rupture [*Bruch*] between the former and the latter. In the case of sexual generation, it is evident that what is generated by the individual being is not yet a living being. Only the "fertilized" or "fructified" ovum is fully a "fruit," but this fruit is not *ipso facto* equivalent to the independent and "living" being. Manifold are the devices which in different species of living beings serve the preparation of new life, but in every instance there seems to be an intermediate state in which the "fruit" or the seed—though *capable* of life and thereby distinguished from all dead material structures—is not yet an independent living being. In the fully developed (fertilized) seed "the new plant is contained, as it were, like a picture en miniature,"[254] i.e., there is pre-designed in the seed the structure into which the plant is to grow and the powers of organization which the plant is to actualize. Thus, only out of a grain of wheat can grow a wheat plant, and in the natural way of evolution nothing but a wheat plant could have grown out of the grain. This illustrates the essential distinction between a structure with the capacity to live and the dead *matter* of a work of art. Out of a piece of wax, for example, varied structures can be formed, and the wax that is used for the purpose of forming such structures may well be replaced by some other material.

The seed, then, bears its specific determinateness within itself as its formative law, and it owes this specific determinateness to its "descent." But the seed is that which it is to become only in *potential* potency [*der potentiellen Potenz nach*],[255] i.e., it must grow and form itself and must, moreover, conquer and subdue the matter which it needs for its growth and formation.[256] In order that this may be accomplished, however, the form must become a *living* form. And it seems to me that this "awakening of life" with which the being of the new organism as such begins is in each individual instance a new vital impulse which cannot be derived from the generative act, although this act is totally and exclusively ordained to such an awakening of life.

It is my conviction that here we find ourselves face to face with the greatest of all mysteries and miracles of life. The mere fact that things which are alive cannot come from things which are dead, but only from that which is itself alive, and that life defies all attempts to "produce" it artificially or synthetically—this fact alone is enough to arouse our awe. But what makes us see in life the mysterious revelation of the Lord of all life is the much more significant fact that all those "devices" of animate nature which aim at life do not actually produce it. They merely prepare for it and make it possible for it in each individual instance to spring, as it were, from a hidden primordial source. As far as the human soul is concerned, it is the teaching of the church that each individual soul is created directly by the hand of God. There is, on the other hand, no such doctrinal decision with respect to infra-human beings. But that reverence for the "sacredness of life" as such, which is an integral part of any truly religious attitude,[257] seems to testify to the divine origin of life in a sense which transcends the mere fact of creation.

There is no doubt, then, that we must regard each living being [*Lebewesen*] as a *genuine individual* [*Einzelwesen*]. It bears within itself its essential determinateness as a *living form* which tends to unfold itself in the life of the individual, a life which is the specific manner of its being. It has received a definite *measure* of being. That *which* it is to become is a structure ordered in accordance with a definite measure. And that life also which is to serve the forming of this structure and, beyond that, the preparation of new individual beings—the "heirs" of the specific determinateness—is "apportioned" [*zugemessen*] to the individual.

The individual being exhausts itself in these vital activities and accomplishments [*Leistungen*]. The individual is a ministering instrument of the creator in actualizing specific forms, not merely in the manner in which dead material structures are tools, but a *creative instrument* in producing itself (in the process of growth) and in generating its progeny (by means of reproduction). But the individual remains *creature* even in these creative activities. Its "creative power" (or what H. Conrad-Martius calls "creative potency") is borrowed and measured. By serving—in self-formation and reproduction—the formation, preservation, and propagation of the species and by consuming itself in these processes, the individual becomes, as it were, a "victim" of its vital task [*Lebensaufgabe*].

H. Conrad-Martius has repeatedly emphasized that the being of the plant finds its most perfect expression in efflorescence. "*The growth of flowers and blossoms is the most authentic formal expression of the innermost essence of the plant.* As a being that interminably propagates and renews itself, the plant opens, as it were, its eyes in flowers and blossoms and reveals in these lovely symbols *the nature or essence of its soul.*"[258] The same author sees in the fact that the blossom, which serves propagation, is the crown of the entire structure, a confirmation that the principal meaning of plant life is not the plant-self but rather the preservation of the species—in contrast to the animal where the life of the individual outweighs in significance the life of the species.

> The evolution of the animal proceeds along the lines of an ever richer development of sense organs, nerve centers, and of the brain structure, i.e., of those formations which support and crown the individual animal nature, a nature which is in-formed by a self-possessed inner life. This is why the animal structure gravitates toward the head, the seat of the brain, whereas the generative organs, the germ glands, which serve the preservation of the species, move to ever lower regions of the organism. In the plant, conversely the flower and *blossom* are crown and head. The plant is fully itself only where it *transcends itself* in unceasing reproduction of its own likeness. The vital activity of the plant perfects itself in the seed-bearing fruit in which it completely *surrenders its own self* for the sake of the continuous generation of the species.[259]

This description of the nature of the plant is as beautiful as it is enlightening. I, too, regard the actualization of specific forms as the most vital function of the plant organism. On the other hand, it seems necessary not to emphasize the importance of self-formation for the fulfillment of this function to such an extent that it overshadows almost completely the task of propagation or reproduction. H. Conrad-Martius herself offers cogent factual reasons for the exercise of such restraint. She points out that plants with inconspicuous blossoms (e.g., daisies) assume the appearance of one large single blossom by means of a numerical abundance of blossoms and their fitting arrangement. Such a cumulative effect cannot be explained merely by the plant's adaptation to the task of attracting insects for the purpose of pollination, for "the adaptation to a regular, individual blossom in *form, color, design, and in the formation of an apparent calyx goes far beyond that which can have any meaning for the perceptive faculties of insects.*"[260] We may say, therefore, that "*there must be an inner form urge in the more highly developed plant organisms to produce what may be called a lustrous and conspicuous flower.* ... And this tendency toward the formation of an articulate and conspicuous efflorescence reveals to us once again the innermost essence of the plant."[261]

It seems to me that this tendency of the plant toward the formation of a lustrous flower or blossom is indicative of the fact that such a blossom is first and foremost—irrespective of its significance as an organ of reproduction—the crowning perfection of the individual structure in which the all-pervasive "style" of the plant organism creates its own perfect formal expression. The plant that is adorned with blossoms has reached the highest degree of its self-formation. However, the fact that even this height is transcended, in that the blossoms serve the formation of the fruit and that out of the fruit, grow new formal structures, seems to indicate that what ultimately matters in the being of the plant is not the life of the individual. Individual life, rather, serves the plant life as such and the building up of the forms of the species. Plant life as such, however, and the abundance of forms which springs from its creative power, manifest—as does all life—that eternal being which underlies them in their ultimate ground or cause. The individual structures are variants of definite basic forms. In these structures an infinite creative power "plays" with an infinite "plenitude of ideas" [*Ideenfülle*]. The basic forms in their turn enunciate in an ever new and ever more perfect manner the particular character of the plant being as such.

> Thus the plant ... not only grows into its particular typical spatial structure, but into that *total external and internal structure* which expresses its given and continuously inherited specific character, a structure which is *at the same time* determined by ... the universal *intrinsic essence* [*Grundwesen*] of the plant in the respective degrees of its unfolding and in its specific differentiations. ... Each particular type stands thus before us as a *work of art* which is ruled and informed by a multiform total idea and which, moreover, depends on certain given conditions and on certain available material elements.
>
> This complex total idea confronts, as it were, the plant imperiously until a moment is reached where this pure form as primordial archetype is wholly filled and actualized in the plant. Then the latter evolves, forms itself, and grows out of its own inner powers.[262]

But even in the evolution of plants there are not lacking certain impediments and malformations which interfere with the total fulfillment and actualization of the *pure form* in the vegetable kingdom as it is actually constituted. Plants, too, are of the realm of fallen nature and are thus, as it were *sub ratione peccati* (stained by original sin), although the paradisiacal innocence of pure nature appears in this stage less impaired than on higher levels of being.[263] The vegetable kingdom thus reveals the universal condition as well as the unity of the entire created universe.

§5. Concluding Summary of the Inquiry into the Nature of Form, Matter, and *Ousia*

1. The Concatenation of the Different Realms of Being. Form and Matter, Act and Potency in Inanimate and Animate Nature

I find it impossible indeed to characterize to its full extent any one of the great fundamental genera of being without its relations to the others, and this includes not only the differences by which the several realms of nature are set off rigidly from each other (these differences play a major part in the discussions of H. Conrad-Martius, because she is primarily interested in pointing out the clear boundary lines), but also the demonstrable common elements. There are interrelations of causal efficacy [*Wirkungszusammenhänge*] and interrelations of meaning [*Sinnzusammenhänge*]. We find an interrelation of causal efficacy in the case of inanimate nature furnishing the material elements for the building up of the vegetable kingdom, and in the case of plants preparing—by virtue of their capacity for transforming inorganic into organic elements—the structural elements for the building up of the bodies of animals and human beings. On the other hand, we find interrelations of meaning in cases where basic forms of actuality (body, soul, spirit) are reflected in the realm of the purely material (by means of the basic modes of space filling: the solid, liquid, and gaseous phases); or where the specific differences between the being of plants and animals appear as visible symbols of feminine and masculine being; or where the individual beings as well as the totality of the species in the vegetable kingdom prefigure, in both their contrasts and their interconnections, the contrast and interconnection that exists between the individual person and the unity established by common descent (family, tribe, race).

These are mere indications of interrelations. They would have to be further elucidated by a more profound exploration of the different genera of being. This cannot be our task here. We have referred to the structural constitution of living beings only to explain the meaning of *matter* and *form* in order to arrive at an understanding of that substance which is composed of both.

Living beings are "composites" in the full sense of the term. While in purely material structures there is only uniform matter—uni-*form,* because the matter is permeated by an inherent and undetachable formative power and is divisible and compoundable [*zusammensetzbar*] only in a spatial sense—there is in living beings a manifold of material elements held together, permeated, and molded into an organic whole by a superior, living form—a whole which is proportioned in accordance with the structural law of that superior form. The superiority of the form over the matter manifests itself in the preservation and evolution of the identical structural

whole in the continuous process of "material change" (*Stoffwechsel* = metabolism). *The being of the form is life, and life is the forming of matter* in the three stages of *transformation of the structural material elements, self-formation,* and *reproduction.* The being composed of matter and

form and the progressive, never finished molding of matter by the form pertain to the *essence* of these structures.

It seems to me that Aristotle's doctrine of form and matter can be properly understood if we remember that he developed it on the basis of the observation of animate nature. The attempt to see in this doctrine a fundamental law of everything material carried with it the danger of misjudging the specific nature of purely material elements and of obliterating the boundary line between these two realms of being (form and matter). A further handicap was the lack of adequate concepts of the early stages of a natural science to which both the actual constitution of matter (such as the number and the specific qualities of the elements, their internal structure, and the laws governing their mixtures and combinations) and the composition of animate bodies were much less familiar than they are to modern and contemporary chemistry, physics, and biology with their arsenal of methodological and practical aids. Lastly, the constant tendency to regard natural organisms and works of art as analogous phenomena made it all the more difficult to determine and define strictly the nature of the *living form.*

And just as the contrast between form and matter becomes clearly evident only in the realm of life, so also the contrast between act and potency—which permeates the entire created world (the realm of becoming)—here receives its deeper significance. Hans André, who devoted much effort to the study of this problem, renders the term *act* by "determinative field of actualization" [*bestimmungsmächtiges Verwirklichungsfeld*] and the term *potency* by "determinable material field that stands in need of being determined" [*bestimmungsbedürftiges Materialfeld*].[264] Though these expressions cannot possibly comprise the entire content of the concepts of *act* and *potency* and are hardly appropriate characterizations of what these concepts basically signify (namely, actual and potential *being*), André's formulation nevertheless points to the peculiar relationships prevalent in the realm of life.

As previously stated, purely material structures—in contradistinction to living beings—are in a sense "finished" [*fertig*]. It is true that they too are subject to becoming. Being actual, they bear within themselves certain potentialities: capabilities of acting efficaciously and of submitting to efficacious action (i.e., the capability of suffering). They are thus at once "determinative" and "determinable" (i.e., they stand in need of being determined), but with respect to different objects. The actuality of purely material structures effects transformations in others and suffers its being transformed by others, but this kind of actuality does not develop and transform itself. The one exception is the process of crystallization, and this has been the reason why it proved so difficult to draw a line of demarcation between purely material structures and living beings. In crystallization we indeed still have a *becoming* that is not a mere change caused by external influences, but a "being-completed" [*Fertigwerden*] of a material structure which prior to this process was not entirely "itself." Thus we have here a *substantial becoming,* an in-forming of the matter into its commensurate formal structure.

But whereas the material structure *comes to be* finished. the living being is never finished. It is a being that is renewed again and again, a being that forms itself continuously and that is thus with respect to itself at once determinative and determinable (in need of being determined). The Aristotelian principle which states that nothing can with respect to the same object be at the same time actual and potential is not hereby impaired, since the determining element is the form, while it is the matter that is being determined. However, the whole is something that is at once generated [*gezeugt*] and produced [*erzeugt*] and that is therefore not only "efficacious" or "determinative," but quasi-creative. And while thus in one respect this whole surpasses all the efficacious capabilities and activities of purely material structures, it represents in another respect a stage of being which is inferior to fully developed capabilities (both active and passive potencies) and thus justifies our speaking of *potential potentiality.*

The undeveloped living being is not yet in possession of those powers which it is capable of attaining and destined to attain. While the developed living being possesses the faculty of sight—it is *capable* of seeing, even though at this moment it may not actually be seeing (i.e., it may not be exercising the faculty)—the undeveloped living being does not yet possess this faculty. It is not *capable* as yet of seeing, but it is capable of acquiring that faculty, so that even this capability is already a potentiality that must be regarded as a preliminary stage of actuality. And by virtue of this capability, even the undeveloped living being is distinguished from that absence of a kind of being [*Nichtvorhandensein*] which characterizes the incapability of seeing that prevails in the realm of dead things.

In the case of living beings, the acquisition of capabilities in the process of evolution is also distinct from the attainment of capabilities which we observe in purely material things. A nonmagnetic piece of iron can be made magnetic and therewith capable of attracting small pieces of iron. Here we have an illustration of the contrast between *potential potency* and *actual potency*. But the iron must "develop" this capacity. It must not first become that substantial existent in which such a potentiality has its foundation. It already possesses that particular material quality which under definite conditions and external influences makes possible the transition from the non-magnetic to the magnetic state. The living being, on the other hand, must first become that substantial existent in which there is a proper place for the faculty of seeing.

The meaning of *act* and *potency* in the case of living beings is thus even more diversified and the cleft between the two greater than in the case of material things. And it is precisely in this cleft between a mere "potential potentiality" and creative actuality that the particular kind of being is to be found that spans the opposite poles of act and potency.

2. *The Living Being as* Ousia. Ousia—*Substance*—Essentia—Wesen

It now remains for us to elucidate the particular nature of the living being as *ousia* and subsequently to answer the question which was our point of departure in this chapter: How are *ousia, essentia,* substance, and *Wesen* interrelated? We recognized that *ousia* signifies that which is or "exists in a preeminent sense" [*Seiendes in vorzüglichem Sinne*].[265] And we found that this "preeminence of being" can be of different kinds. It may denote a preeminence of that which exists over that which is merely intellectually conceived [*bloss gedacht*]. It may signify the preeminence of the actual over against the potential. And it may finally mean a preeminence of that which is independent or autonomous over against that which is dependent and therefore without a being of its own, but merely partaking of the being of some "substratum" [*Zugrundeliegendes*].

Now all these different kinds of preeminence are united in that existent which is traditionally termed a *substance*.[266] We have been using the phrase "self-dependent, autonomous actuality" [*selbständiges und selbsteigenes Wirkliches*], and this description comes very close to the conclusions arrived at by H. Conrad-Martius and presented in her treatise entitled *L'existence, la substantialité et l'âme*.[267] She too regards actual being (which she terms "existence") and substantiality as closely interconnected. The difference between "absolute being" (which we have termed "pure" or "first" being) and finite being she finds in the fact that the former is by itself (*per se* and *a se*) and that its dominion extends over *all* being, whereas finite being is said to be *self-being* [*Selbstsein*], and in its *seitas* it provides the foundation for its *in se esse* and *per se esse*. Finite being has an *essence* and it has the *power of self-being* [*Macht zu seinem eigenen Sein*]. This power is a *dynamic potentiality* in the sense that all finite actuality is constantly on the way toward its being and is therefore essentially temporal. When we designated *substance* as "autonomous [*selbsteigen*] existent," we meant to indicate that this kind of existent owns "itself" or is its own self and thus has its own essence and being. However, we understood being as the actualization [*Sichauswirken*] of the essential form, i.e., as the actualization of those potentialities which have their foundation in the essence (including temporality and the "power of being an independent self" [*Macht zum eigenen Sein*]). In the case of that particular genus of being which we term matter, this implies a self-forming [*Sich-Hineingestalten*] into space, a self-expanding, a self-offering, and self-actualizing in space.

The investigations of H. Conrad-Martius and our own concur in regarding *matter* and *mind* or *spirit* [*Geist*] as different and mutually irreducible genera of actuality. What we emphasized with respect to material elements, in contradistinction to life, namely, that in a certain sense they are "finished," H. Conrad-Martius claims equally for mind or spirit. She calls body and mind "actual existents" whose constitutional structure is completed and perfected [*vollendet*].[268] *The specific being of living beings is distinct from both body and mind (spirit) by virtue of the fact that living beings must first acquire possession of their essence or nature.* That which is alive [*das Lebendige*] is distinguished from purely material natures because it has a "center" of its own being, i.e., a *soul* or what we may call a "be-souling principle" (if we want to reserve the term *soul* for that personal soul which does not make its appearance until we arrive at the individually and *personally* formed human totality).[269] Even purely material natures or "soulless" substances do not lack—*qua* substances, *qua* independent existents—a self-like [*selbsthaft*] principle of being, an existential potency *for* their own being. This potency, however, occupies *in them* (i.e., in material natures) no "personal center," no particular "space," since these material natures are with their entire self completely "handed over to" (or, as it were, dispersed in) that self-alienation [*Selbstveräusserung*] by which they are constituted. We can and even must, on the other hand, speak of a soul or of a be-souling principle whenever "this self-like principle of being appears as a genuine "center" *within* the self. A vegetative totality is no longer merely lifted out of itself for the sake of complete self-alienation (though the substantiality of the "substrate" out of which this totality is formed remains!), but—together *with* its self-alienated (material) being—the vegetative totality is reinstated *in the self-like potency of being as in an ontological center,* and this center is then capable of embracing, forming, and organizing in a self-like manner the whole of the vegetative *totality qua* whole."

The structure of the whole is thus built up from the center of being [*Seinsmitte*]. "The soul principle, then, is situated in that potential, *pre-actual* sphere which is the constitutive element of the thing's being!" Whereas the divine *potency* wields power *over* all being and "is therefore, as it were, a *'super act'*—i.e., *more,* not *less,* than actuality—one can speak of *soul* only where it is a question of less than actual being, namely, in the case of a mere potent potency [*Kraftmöglichkeit*] *for* being."

Using our own language and terminology, we shall have to express the underlying idea somewhat differently. Divine being is for us the *pure act,* in comparison with which all finite being—in different measure and degree—is partly potential and partly actual. This also applies to the soul. As the actuating principle in the living being—the principle which forms the living being and thus makes it actual—the soul is itself actual, but its actuation [*Wirken*] is at the same time a constant actualization of its own potentialities. This supremacy of the soul over all merely potential being is implied in the term "*potent* potency" [*Kraft*-Möglichkeit]. "For the ontological potentiality of the *soul* (as is generally the case with the self-like principle of being!) is no *potency* in the sense of a purely material formative readiness [*Bereitschaft*] that stands in need of some efficacious impulse in order to become actual. The soul is rather *itself* the potent efficacious [*wirkungsmächtig*] principle. It is potency in the sense of possessing a positive *power* for being, but it is not yet this being in that fully actualized actuality that is brought about *by* the underlying ontological potency."

The soul comes out of nothingness and yet bears within itself the power for being. "This is why its nature is in a peculiar manner 'unfathomable' (in the sense of being a bottomless abyss) *and* "creative." According to its own ontological ground, the soul is placed in "nothingness," and yet, out of this same soul, the entire substance draws its being and its selfhood." The terms "self-encompassing" [*Selbstumfassung*] and "self-founding" [*Selbstbegrundung*], which H. Conrad-Martius used in her book on the plant soul, refer in all probability to this creative power of the soul with respect to its own being.

The particular nature of the soul also suggests a possibility of harmonizing the contraries of matter and mind (spirit) with the previously discussed trichotomy of body, soul, and mind (spirit). The confrontation of *matter* (in the sense of that which fills space) and *mind* (spirit) reveals an ultimate contrast with regard to *content* between two different realms of actuality. The distinction made between body, soul, and mind (spirit), on the other hand, serves to characterize three basic *forms* of actual being: that which maintains itself in a self-enclosed structure, that which tends toward formation, and that which freely gives and diffuses itself. The form toward which material elements as such tend is the form of the body. The form for which the mental (or spiritual) as such craves is the form of the mind (or spirit). The soul principle [*das Seelische*], however, being "creative" and "underground" [*unterirdisch*], does not actualize itself in a third kind of fullness of content [*inhaltliche Fülle*], but in a form that is either material or spiritual. What we customarily call *living beings* are *substances* whose being is the progressive formation of a material body out of the soul principle. That which is alive is never finished. It is forever on the way to its own self, but it bears within itself—i.e., within its soul—the power of forming itself.

We have arrived at the conclusion of our inquiry. *Ousia* in that most strict and genuine sense which Aristotle, after all, had in mind in his own investigation, is *substance,* i.e., an actuality resting upon itself and both encompassing and unfolding its own essence. *Essentia is* the *nature* belonging irrevocably to the being of this actuality as the foundation of the quidditative determinateness of such an existent. In the case of spatial material structures this nature has its roots in the matter-molding essential form. If these structures are purely material, form and matter are inseparable. The essence or nature is this definitely specified or formed materiality, and the matter is always a specifically formed matter and inconceivable without form. In the case of living beings, on the other hand, form and matter are separable or even actually separated [*treten auseinander*]. The form is then a *living form* or a soul. This soul has the power of forming and animating the whole in some specific manner. It being is life, and life is a progressive forming of matter and therewith a progressive actualization of the essence or nature which is as such constituted by this specific formation of matter.

Spatial material structures—both dead and living—do not exhaust the range and scope of what is termed *ousia.* For self-dependent, autonomous existents are also found in the realm of the spirit. And, indeed, according to what has previously been said concerning the *first existent,* it is evident that the name *ousia* applied to it in the highest and strictest sense, because the first existent possesses an infinite "preeminence" of being over and above all finite existents. But in order to be able to make some predications concerning the particular being of the infinite spirit and of infinite spirits—in contradistinction to material structures—it will be necessary to determine more clearly what is meant by *spirit* [*Geist*]. Our previous indicatory allusions to this question provide no adequate foundation for such an inquiry. However, for the time being it may suffice that we have succeeded in clarifying the nature of that basic form of being and existence which is called *ousia* or substance and which is fully realized in all the generically separate spheres of actuality.

V.

Existents As Such (The Transcendentals)

§1. Retrospect and Prospect

We have carried on an inquiry into the nature of being and have found it to be of diverse kinds. We were able to distinguish between *eternal* (infinite) and *finite* (limited) being, and in the case of every finite thing it became necessary to distinguish between *being* [*Sein*] and *existents* [*Seiendes*]. Existents reveal themselves with respect to their *content*—i.e., with respect to *what* they are—as manifold, and they could accordingly be divided into different genera. Moreover, we have seen that to the different genera of existents correspond different modes of being [*Seinsweisen*]. What we have gained so far is by no means a complete view of all genera and all modes of being.

Starting from different points of departure, we sought to gain access to an understanding of existents. We followed the *Augustinian* way, which proceeds from that which is nearest to us (because of its being inseparable from us)—the *life of the ego* [*Ichleben*]. We then followed the *Aristotelian* way, which proceeds from that which forces itself upon our attention—the world of *sensorily perceived things* [*sinnenfällige Dinge*]. In both instances we encountered existents of a particular structure that was characterized in each case by certain common structural elements. We could thus distinguish between potential and actual being and between *potential* and *actual* existents, and we discovered that both actuality and potentiality had their foundation in an *essential* being which as such is above and beyond this distinction. We have not yet determined, however, the nature of the interrelation of these two worlds—the external and the internal world—and so there remains an important, as yet unsolved problem.

Further tasks and problems of investigation are posed by the Aristotelian way. Aristotle designates the inquiry into the nature of the ὄν and the inquiry into the nature of *ousia* as signifying one and the same thing. Now we have established *ousia* to mean that which exists in a preeminent sense, and we have discovered different kinds of "preeminence of being" in different existents.[1] Should it not be possible to set forth *that meaning of being and of existents as such* which is contained in the several significations of *ousia* and which corresponds to the ὄν that determines all of these signification and yet "transcends" them all?

When Heidegger interprets *ousia* as *meaningful being* [*Seinssinn*],[2] it seems to me that this expression does not quite convey the connotations of Aristotle's use of the term. All my own efforts to understand this enigmatic word have led me to the conclusion that what is involved here is the meaning of the nature of *existents, insofar as they fulfill the meaning of being,* i.e., *the existent* qua *existing* (ὂν ᾗ ὄν). And when I understood *ousia* as "that which is or exists in a preeminent sense," I merely meant to assert that *ousia is or exists* in a *more authentic* sense than certain other things of which existence is also predicated. This implies a two-fold meaning—authentic and non-authentic—of ὄν, and ὄν in the authentic or strict sense would then have to be equated with *ousia.*[3] The task confronting us thus consists in the demonstration that the problem of the existent as such refers back to the question concerning the meaning of being.

We have so far not sought out and located all the genera of existents in which the most strictly circumscribed concept of *ousia,* i.e., *ousia* understood as the *independent autonomous existent,* is fulfilled. Following the lead of Aristotle, we have shown this kind of *ousia* to be present in sensible material things, and we have stated in a preliminary fashion only that this concept also applies to spiritual realities. This latter thesis must be implemented by positive proof. It must be shown that there are certain forms, the being of which is not constituted by the formation of space-filling matter, or the being of which does not exhaust itself in such a forming process, but which nevertheless are constituted as independent actualities. If these latter can still be called *molding* forms at all, what is it that they mold? Moreover, in this case how are the contraries form—matter and matter—spirit related to one another? How are spirit and form interrelated? And finally, are only material [*dinglich*] realties independent, autonomous existents or must independent, autonomous existence also be attributed to *ideal objects?*

Connected with these questions is one we have previously encountered in different contexts, but which we have not yet made the object of our inquiry. *Ousia* in the most strictly circumscribed sense appeared to be synonymous with the *individual nature* or the *individuum* [*Einzelwesen*]. What then is the meaning of *individuality*? And is this meaning the same in all the realms of being?

Included in the last question is still another one, and one which has a significant bearing on all the others. If we should find that the concept of the *individuum* is fully realized in different realms of being, but realized or fulfilled in different ways, and if therefore the word *individuum* has a permanent and a changing constitutive content or meaning [*Sinnesbestand*]—as is the case with ὄν and *ousia*—should we then not be compelled to understand permanent constitution as an *empty form* that is filled with different *content* in different realms of being? Or could it be that the permanent constitution is indicative of common elements of *content*, leaving a "lacuna" [*Leerstelle*] that may be filled in different ways, as we found to be the case in the relationship that exists between genus and species?[4] We encountered the contrasting elements of form and content earlier in the investigation in the course of the discussion of the formal structure of things.[5] And this contrast—without being mentioned specifically—has played a part in every phase of our inquiry because—even where we considered the differences among existents with respect to their content—we were not so much concerned with these differences as with the structure of existents as such. Thus, if we begin the present inquiry with this question concerning the meaning and the mutual relationship of form and content, new light will be cast on our previous considerations, and we shall be able to impart greater clarity to the investigations which are to follow.[6]

§2. Form and Content

We have asserted that *things* and their *properties* are *empty forms.* Thing—πρώτη *ousia*—is here understood as an independent, autonomous existent in possession of its own being and essence and both efficaciously active [*wirken*] and passively suffering [*erleiden*] the effects of external influences in accordance with its essence or nature and in a specific manner. If we now posit for *thing* "this piece of sandstone" and for *property* or quality the "red color" (of this piece of sandstone), then the empty forms are filled to the total extent of ultimate determinateness. This ultimate determinateness—i.e., the strict determination of this particular piece and this particular red color—is not verbally expressed, but is identified by the pointing finger and can be grasped only perceptually. Even that, however, which is called by a name—e.g., color, red, sandstone—is already filled with content, in contrast to the empty forms (though it has some universality and can be found in many individual things). And everything that has content can *originally* be grasped only *perceptually.*

It is true, on the other hand, that universal names can be understood in a non-perceptual manner—as occurs frequently in listening and reading, and even in speaking and writing—but in these instances we grasp the meaning of the universal names without actually seeing with our optical or mental vision the things thus signified, because we know from some previous perception what is meant by these universal names. When we hear someone speak of things or matters unknown to us, we may gain a certain understanding, but this kind of understanding remains provisional and non-authentic until it is verified in a fulfilled perception.

When we spoke of "optical or mental vision," we meant to indicate that *vision* is not synonymous with the "sensory perception" of this red color before me, but may also refer to the making present [*Vergegenwärtigung*] of a red that I have seen on some previous occasion. Immediate perception and the making present of some previous perception are both sensory intuitions, and the color of some definite individual thing is rendered accessible only by such sensory intuition [*sinnliche Anschauung*]. The meaning of "red" in general, however, and also the meaning of this particular red understood not as the color of this particular thing, but as an ultimate particularity of red which, as an *idea* or *species,* might also be found elsewhere—can neither be grasped by immediate sense perception nor be made present in sensory intuition (in memory or in imagination). Nor can, on the other hand, this meaning be understood in a purely non-perceptual manner, i.e., in that non-authentic and provisional manner which pertains to all non-perceptual understanding. This meaning can be grasped only in that most authentic *intellection* or *intelligere* which is an *intellectual vision* or intuition and as such the ground or foundation of all understanding—an intellection in which the mind assimilates its objects (both the individual elements of meaning and composite meaningful structures) and makes them its own.[7]

Is it possible then to delimit content and form with respect to each other in such a way that we say of the former that it can be perceived and of the latter that it is not perceived? Such a conclusion would be overhasty. If we take *intuition* [*Anschauung*] in the broad sense as including the most primordial kind of intellectual comprehension, i.e., authentic "understanding," then there is also an intuition or an ultimate ground of understanding with respect to forms. But the intuition of forms differs from the intuition of content. If we analyze composite contents, e.g., if we examine what imparts to the thing its "fullness," we arrive in the end at those ultimate elements of meaning [*Sinnelemente*] which we have designated as *essences*, such as redness, color, joy, sorrow, and the like. In the "intuition" of essences the intellect comes to rest. It has arrived at the deepest ground attainable, and it finds itself facing an ultimate intelligible reality [*Tatsächlichkeit*] beyond which it cannot advance. If we mark off from these contents the universal form, that "something" which still pertains to each of them, then this form too conveys an intelligible meaning, but in the understanding of this meaning one cannot rest. By its very emptiness this kind of meaning points beyond itself. It calls for fulfillment [*Ausfüllung*], because in its poverty it can give nothing to the intellect that might set the intellect at rest.[8]

With this latter observation we believe we have grasped the real distinction between *form* and *content* (or *fullness*). The two belong together. Wherever we get hold of a content, we seize it together with its form. A "content" can neither be nor be intellectually conceived without some form, even if it is a form of the most general kind. The form is, as it were, the contour of the content and thus pertains to the content in the manner in which the encompassing spatial structure pertains to a material thing. The forms can be intellectually abstracted and conceptually grasped, but they have that peculiar emptiness and poverty which characterizes them *qua* forms.

Every existent is fullness within some form. To examine and describe the forms of existents is the task of that discipline which Husserl called *formal ontology*.[9] This discipline is very closely linked with formal logic, because its forms are commensurate with those conceptual structures with which logic deals.[10]

§3. "Something," Categories, and "Existents" ["*Seiendes*"]

The most universal form is that "*something*" [*etwas*] or the "object" in the broadest sense of the term. *Every existent* is capable of filling this form. A *thing* [*Ding*], on the other hand, is a form in a more limited sense, a form which finds fulfillment only in one specific region, namely, in the realm of the *real* [*wirklich*], and not in any kind of reality, but only where this reality has an independent, autonomous being.

The "thing," as we have seen, coincides with the Aristotelian πρώτη *ousia* and with substance. We designated the Aristotelian categories as forms of existents [*Seiende*]. *Form* in this case means empty form in the sense previously described. The categories are thus the forms of things and of that which is present *in* things (their how and their what), or of that which conditions their being (their where and when), or of that which is conditioned by their being (their mutual relations, their doing [*agere*] and suffering [*pati*]).

To every form of existent corresponds a specific mode of being. To the thing-form corresponds *independent being*, and to the different forms of that which pertains or "accrues" to the thing (the *accidental categories*) correspond different modes of *dependent being* (the being *in* the thing, the being *that has its foundation in* the thingly being, etc.). The term *category* is used to designate both the forms of existents and their corresponding modes of being. But the thing and that which directly pertains or accrues to it do not exhaust the total realm of existents. *Pure forms* and the first existent have no correspondence in the structure of finite things.

If the categories are sometimes termed *genera*, it should be noted that in this case *genus* also is to be understood as designating forms of existents and not—as we have used the term in most instances—as designating some content. with lacuna to be filled in by a further determination of this content. This means that *genus*, in its formal aspect, designates the empty form of genera understood as denoting different contents.

The "something" encompasses all the Aristotelian categories and, in addition, everything that is not comprised in them, i.e., all existents [*alles Seiende*]. The one exception is the first existent, of whom it cannot be said without qualification that he is adaptable to this form. If we understand the "something," in accord with the meaning of the word, as "some or any existent," it is thereby indicated that this something is related to a *finite* existent that is placed side by side with others,[11] and this kind of relationship is in contradiction to the infinity of the all-encompassing first existent. If, on the other hand, we mean by "something" that which is "not nothing," then it finds its supreme fulfillment in the all-encompassing existent. It is thus possible to conceive the "something" as being of such vast expanse that it comprises both the existent who is everything and the existent which is not everything and yet not nothing, but this expanse comprises then also the infinite cleft (between the first existent and finite existents) which justifies us in speaking of an *analogia entis.*

Are "something" and "existents" then synonymous, and must existents themselves be understood as empty forms? Actually, we answered this question in the negative when we stated that every existent is a filling or fulfillment [*Erfüllung*] of something. The existent, in the full sense of the term, is a "filled something," and the "something" is a form of existents [*des Seienden*].

And thus we have reverted once more to the question concerning the meaning of existents as such, a meaning which must be fulfilled in every existent, whatever its form or its mode of being. We remember that St. Thomas in *De ente et essentia,* following Aristotle's definition of ὄν in Book Δ of the *Metaphysics,* distinguishes a twofold meaning of "being."[12] The first meaning is expressed in the "is" of a judgment,[13] while the second meaning denotes the being that is divided into the categories. If we are justified in speaking of *being* and *existents* in both instances, it must be possible to establish an interconnection of meaning between these two terms and their signification. This, however, can be done only after we have first attempted to determine that meaning of existents which is common to all the categories.[14]

§4. The Transcendentals (Preliminary Survey)

To determine the nature of *existents as such,* independent of their division according to different forms and different modes of being, is the function of what the *scholastics* call the *transcendentals.* They denote "what pertains to every existent."[15] In one fundamental passage at the beginning of the *Questiones disputatae de veritate,* St. Thomas mentions strictly universal determinations of existents as such the following: *ens, res, unum, aliquid, bonum, verum* (the existent, that which is determined in its content,[16] the one, something, the good, the true). In many other passages *pulchrum* (the beautiful) is added to the former and considered as a special kind of the good.[17] A further distinction refers to whether these determinations designate existents in themselves or with respect to other existents. According to St. Thomas, "*that which exists in itself* (*ens*) is *positively* designated by only one other term, namely *res* (that which is determined in its content). While *ens* denotes that which is insofar as it *is, res* denotes the *quiddity* or *essence* of the existent (*quidditatem sive essentiam entis*) or the existent with respect to *what* it is.

That which exists in itself is *negatively* determined by the term *unum* (the one), for *unum* denotes that the existent is undivided.[18] All the other transcendental determinations relate existents to other existents. Thus, if we call an existent *aliquid* (something), we contrast it with *another* existent, in a purely formal sense, *qua* "other."[19] Finally, being can be considered in its intimate *congruity* [*Übereinstimmung*] with another existent. Such a congruity can be regarded as a transcendental determination only where an existent has the capacity of being convertible with all that which is. According to Aristotle and St. Thomas, such is the case with the human *soul.* While the soul's conation *aims* at a union of the *will* with that which is, the soul's knowledge *strives* for the union of the *intellect* with that which is.

When that which is is the object of conation, it is called the *good,* and when that which is is the object of knowledge, it is called the *true.* (The *beautiful* has something in common with the good and true. It denotes that which is insofar as it is the object of *satisfaction,* a satisfaction which derives from the experience of an objective accord of existence and knowledge in their structurally graduated order.)

Thus, insofar as the existent as such is the object of knowledge, of conation, and of satisfaction, the true, the good, and the beautiful are transcendental determinations. It is necessary now to understand correctly the meaning of these transcendental determinations.

There is no doubt that they serve to characterize the existent as such, independent of the divisions which are found in those genera which differ in both form and content. The question which especially concerns us is whether the transcendental determinations are more apt to elucidate the content or the forms of existents.

§5. The Existent as Such (*ens, res*)

The basic transcendental concept is that of the *ens ut ens est* (ὄν ᾗ ὄν), i.e., the *existent as such.* According to Gredt,[20] this concept must be universal enough to comprise both *created* and *uncreated* existence, and thus also *actual* and *potential* existence, since only the uncreated existent is pure act, whereas every created existent is partially actual and partially potential. The really fundamental question, however, is precisely whether and how the forming of such a concept, comprising the created and the uncreated, is possible (i.e., objectively justified). We shall soon return to this problem.

Gredt distinguishes further[21] between two different meanings of this *ens* in the most universal sense. He states that *ens* as a *name* designates in the most universal manner *that which* is, i.e., the quid of any existent, whereas *ens* as a *participle,* designates the existent as that which is, with the emphasis on being. In the first sense every existent, according to Gredt, is called *essentially* existent, but in the second sense only God can be called essentially existent. In all other instances being is superadded to whatever existents are.

Against this separation of *ens* as "name" from *ens* as "participle" the objection may be raised that in the *ens ut ens* the aspect of being is underscored and cannot be effaced. In other words, the participial meaning is implied in the "name" *ens.* If I understand the respective passage in St. Thomas correctly, he wishes to designate by the term *res* the existent as a quid. Otherwise *res* would have no meaning of its own.[22] The statement, however, that being pertains essentially only to God presupposes that being is equated to existence and that existence is equated to actual being,[23] and this is at variance with our own standpoint.[24]

What we have designated as *essential being* cannot be said to be superadded to that which is essentially. The *whatnesses* [*Washeiten*] or *meaningful formal structures* [*Sinngebilde*] which we regarded as essentially existent are, after all, not created in the sense of being placed into temporal existence [*Dasein*], as is the case with those realities which copy [*nachbilden*] the whatnesses. If Gredt pays no heed at all to the being which pertains to the whatnesses independent of their actualization, the reason is that he regards the being of the whatnesses as purely "conceptual" [*gedanklich*]. He denies that conceptual being is being in the true sense, and he therefore excludes this kind of being from the *ens ut ens.*[25] We have previously discussed the interrelation of essential and conceptual being (cf. pp. 145ff. above) and shall soon have occasion to return once more to this problem.

We retain, then, not two different meanings of the existent as such, but only the one meaning of "that which *is*" (*ens est habens "esse" seu id quod est*).[26] With respect to this latter meaning, however, several partial significations must be distinguished. Gredt makes a distinction between *subject* and *form.* He equates the subject to *essentia.* The latter is that by virtue of which the thing is or that whereby the thing is determined in its species (*id quo res est id, quod est, seu quo constituitur in specie*). In this definition the *id quod* (that which) is conceived as one.

In this connection we previously distinguished further the "that" (*das, illud*) as the *carrier* [*Träger*] of the determinateness of the essence [*Wesensbestimmtheit*], and the "quid" [*Was*] as the determinateness of the essence itself.[27] The "that" (or this-there)—i.e., the carrier without determinateness of essence—must be regarded as an empty form, and only the filled empty form is the carrier of *being. Fullness,* however, can be attributed only to the definitely *determined* quid of the individual existent, not to the quid that is present in the general expressions "that which it is" (*das was es ist, id, quod est*). For the quid in this generalized expression is merely the empty form of the fullness. Accordingly, the question as to whether *ens* as a name of the existent designates some content is reduced to the question of whether being expresses something that relates to content or something that relates to form.

When Gredt equates form to being, this *form* must not be understood as empty form in the sense in which we have been using this term. Nor has this form the meaning of the *essential form* as we have encountered it in material things. For it is this latter form that determines the *quid* of things. My own understanding of Gredt's use of the term *form* results from the equation "essence is related to existence as potency is related to act" [*Essenz : Existenz = Potenz : Akt*].[28] The quid is here posited as "potential" in the sense of essential potentiality [*Wesensmöglichkeit*] What is added by the actualization of the quid is actual being or act.

In the case of things that are composed of matter and essential form, according to scholastic doctrine, it is the form which makes possible the transition from potentiality to actuality, and this is the reason why the form itself is designated as *act (actus formalis,* as distinct from *actus entitativus seu existentiae*).[29] Conversely, in those instances where there is no such composition of matter and form but only a composition of whatness and actual being (*essentia* and *existentia*)—as is the case, according to the teaching of St. Thomas, with pure spirits[30]—actual being (the act) may also be designated as *form.* On the other hand, the equation "form = act = being" may be understood in the sense that in God form, act, and being coincide. But because this coincidence is precisely what distinguishes God from creatures, it seems to me important to keep these concepts distinctly apart. As we cannot dispense with the several meanings of *form* (*empty form, pure form* = essence, and *essential form*), we must try to make these differentiations innocuous by some additional determinations. We can only hope that our use of the term "form" in the sense of being does not increase the danger of confusion.

We shall not resume our inquiry into the meaning of being—to which the discussion of the nature of the existent as such has carried us back—until we have analyzed the remaining transcendental concepts. For the latter permit us to grasp in the existent those elements which are hidden in it in addition to (or aside from) being, or to grasp being itself from some particular aspect. With respect to *res,* we have already stated that it is the universal name for a quid. *Res* signifies that every existent has a content or a fullness, but *res* does not determine content, because it is simply the form of fullness [*Form der Fülle*].

According to Gredt,[31] the other transcendentals are properties *(proprietates)* or predicates which either pertain to or directly derive from every existent as such. They are not completely identical in meaning with the existent, but as concepts they have a *fundamentum in re,* i.e., they have an objective foundation in the existent as such.

Gredt states that there are as many transcendental concepts apart from existents as there are modes of being (*modi essendi*) pertaining to every existent. Now we must consider carefully what is meant here by "modes of being." Up to this point we have understood this term as indicative of the distinction between actual and potential being, and those distinctions of being which correspond to the categories (independent being and the different genera of dependent being). There can be no question of either of these meanings in our present use of the term. For it is by these modes of being that existents are *distinguished* among themselves. Every existent is *either* actual *or* potential (and in case an existent is simultaneously actual and potential, it is partly actual and partly potential and not both in its total constitution), either independent or dependent. In our present inquiry, however, we are concerned with different modes of being which *all simultaneously* pertain to existents as such. We shall have to consider the question as to whether it is advisable in this case to use the expression "modes of being" at all when we analyze the transcendental concepts individually (cf. p. 289 below).

Furthermore, Gredt[32] states that the transcendentals do not *really* but only *conceptually* add anything to existents, that therefore the transcendentals are existents as such, as is indicated by the very term "transcendental." I find it impossible to reconcile the two parts of this statement if by "real" I mean not something that "exists" (as distinct from that which is merely conceptually conceived), but—in the sense of *res* being equivalent to quid—something related to *content*. The difference between the real and the conceptual is in this case (in our terminology) a formal difference (in the sense of empty form), and this formality does not then refer to something "merely conceptually conceived," but to that foundation of transcendental concepts which pertains to the existent itself. In other words, we are dealing here with the same distinction between the forms of existents and the conceptual forms (fashioned after the existential forms) as in the case of the categories. The only difference (as we have repeatedly emphasized) is that the categories divide existents according to genera, whereas the transcendentals "unfold" the totality of existents.[33] The formal structure of existents as such is unfolded [*auseinandergelegen*] in the transcendentals, each of which represents some particular "feature" [*Zug*] or aspect of this formal structure.[34]

§6. The Existent as One (*unum*)

If we call the existent *one,* and being one pertains to every existent, we thereby express that formal particularity which has its foundation in the negation of being-divided [*Geteiltheit*]. This oneness or unity is termed *transcendental* because it is a question here of the *oneness of the existent as such: That which has one being is one.*[35]

That which is one *may be,* but need not be, *simple.* It may well be a composite in the sense that not only does the quid consist of parts, but also that each part has a being of its own, and that all the parts together have entered into a unity of being. The being of a rose as such, for example, and the being of the rose's red color both belong to the *one* being of this red rose. What we mean becomes even clearer when we deal with something that is composed of independent units. A family as such has one being, although each member has his or her own being. If we dissolve the unity of being, the family *is* no more. In place of the oneness we then have a divided being, and therewith the whole is destroyed and dissolved into separate parts.

What is here designated as "oneness" or unity is an ultimate which can no longer be reduced to something else. To call this ultimate undivided being is merely an attempt to explain it by its opposite and not a reduction to something else. Gredt states quite correctly that the being-divided of existents (i.e., "transcendental multiplicity") presupposes unity.[36] Accordingly, oneness or unity must be understood as a *form* which finds a definite fulfillment In each individual existent. It is not only the form of the existent, but the form of that *being* to which this form originally pertains and by which it is distinguished from *ens, res* and *aliquid.*

§7. The Existent as Something (*aliquid*)

We started out from the form *aliquid* (something),[37] which we designated as the empty form of the existent. This definition can no longer satisfy us, since we have seen that the formal structure of the existent unfolds itself in a number of determinations. As mentioned before,[38] Gredt distinguishes three different meanings of *aliquid:* (1) *aliquid = aliqua essentia* (some or any quid), (2) *aliquid =*

non nihil (not nothing), and (3) *aliquid* = *aliud quid* (another quid). He eliminates the first meaning, because otherwise *aliquid* and *res* would be synonymous. And he eliminates the third meaning (taken from St. Thomas) because, as he points out, though the existent as one (in contrast to another) presupposes *unum,* its oneness does not derive *directly* from the existent as such. There then remains only the second meaning, i.e., *non nihil.* And in this last Gredt discerns something which, though it is not yet expressed in *ens,* nevertheless immediately derives from *ens.* The difficulty which in my opinion arises here lies in the fact that "nothing" has no meaning by itself, but can be understood only by way of contrasting it with something. If this is the case, something cannot be reduced to or derived from nothing. While this contrast may serve to clarify something, it is insufficient for any exhaustive characterization.

However, I find in the formal structure of existents one constituent part which is not expressed by any of the concepts hitherto discussed, namely, that which is. This "that which" is "something" in the sense of the *object* to which quid and being pertain as properties. And for this something I propose to reserve the term *aliquid.* In this something the *unum* also has its place (aside from having its place in being). Thus understood, the *aliquid* is not yet (in the manner of *aliud quid)* the existent in its relation to other things, but it belongs to the structure of existents as they are in themselves. The unfolding of the *ens* in *aliquid, res,* and *esse* (object, quid, and being) is the most primordial process. The object as such and as existing is *one* and is on this basis "another" in relation to other objects. The consideration of existents in relation to other things begins only with this last, derivative determination.

If we now review briefly the transcendentals which we have discussed up to this point, we find that *ens* designates the existent considered as a whole [*das Seiende als Ganzes*]: "that which *is,*" with the emphasis on being. *Res* emphasizes the quid, and *aliquid* emphasizes the that (this, [*Das*]). *Unum* is a formal property belonging as much to the this (*Das* = *object*) as to the quid [*Was*] and to being. It does not seem appropriate to speak here of "modes of being." Rather, we are dealing—if we may be permitted persistently to disregard the meaning of being—with *formal constituent parts of existents as such.* Not until we interpret *aliquid* no longer as something (i.e., as an object), but as "another something" (an interpretation which, however, already presupposes that the existent is understood as object), do we bring it into relation with other existents. And this relation is one of non-congruity with respect to both object and being. When we say "another object," this means once more an empty form. And when we say, "object, each of which has a different being," we shall only be able to decide whether such a statement can be understood in a purely formal sense on the basis of the meaning of "being."

Can the non-congruity with respect to being be designated as a mode of being? Evidently not. This non-congruity is a *relation* which has its foundation in the being of both the one and the other, and this relation, too, can be understood only on the basis of the meaning of being.

§8. An Attempt at a Formal Conception of the True, the Good, and the Beautiful

Finally, we have seen that the true and the good (including the beautiful) are called transcendental determinations which characterize existents as such in relation to, and in congruity with, other things. That existent, however, with which these transcendentals establish a relationship is not just any existent, but a very definite one, namely, the soul. And with this latter statement the bounds of a formal inquiry seem to have been overstepped.

When the congruity of existents with the *soul* or, to say it more adequately, the *spirit,* is discussed, there is always some referent to a content.[39] *Soul* and *spirit,* in the full and integral sense of these terms, are no empty forms. But when St. Thomas speaks of "something" that "is fit to be congruent with every other thing," he is using a formal expression which intentionally takes no account of the material nature of the soul. It remains undecided, however, what is meant by the word "congruence." If we interpret the sentence in a purely formal manner and designate it as "r," we may take "congruence" to mean the empty form of a relation. But, depending on whether we designate the existent as true, good, or beautiful, the meaning changes accordingly in each particular instance. It is

therefore necessary to distinguish between r_1, r_2, and r_3. This distinction is conditioned by the relation of the existent to conation, cognition, or complacency. These latter names in turn designate material essences in a definite realm of being, such as the acts of a spiritual person: a_1, a_2, a_3. Only when we succeed in finding a purely formal expression of a_1, a_2, and a_3 shall we be able to designate r_1, r_2, and r_3 legitimately as formal determinations of existents.

We find corresponding formulations in the works of St. Thomas.[40] The good and the true are not identical in meaning with the existent, but they add nothing "real" to it, nothing, at any rate, that does not belong (in the manner of an *accidens*) to the nature or essence of the existent. For since everything of a factual, objective nature is comprised in the existent, there is nothing that could be added to it. Not even certain limiting determinations, which rigidly fix the existent in a definite form and mode of being (like the determinations expressed in the categories), can be added. What is added to the existent by the good and the true can thus only be something conceptual.

> However, we call that relation purely conceptual ... by virtue of which something stands in a relationship. And this something does not depend on that to which it is related, but rather the converse is true. ... For example, this is the case with the relationship which exists between knowledge and the object of knowledge. For knowledge depends on the object of knowledge, while the converse is not true. Therefore, the relationship between knowledge and its object is a real relationship, whereas the relationship that exists between the object and knowledge is a conceptual relationship.[41]

Now what the true and the good add to the "concept" of the existent is the determination of that which imparts a perfection [*des Vollkommenheitgebenden*]. As *content,* the existent imparts a perfection to knowing, however, without entering into the intellect with its own being. And it is this perfection which constitutes the true. But insofar as an existent imparts perfection to another by virtue of its own being, this existent is called *good.*

These definitions permit a purely formal interpretation. With their aid we are capable of conceiving of the true and the good in such a manner that we do not include in the concept anything of the content of cognition and conation, and thus a_1 and a_2 must now be described as existents which are to be perfected, i.e., brought to the perfection of their being, by another existent. The existents a_1 and a_2 are distinguished from each other by the manner of their poverty or privation, and to this privation correspond the different ways in which that which imparts perfection leads these existents to the perfection of their being.

§9. The Concepts "Form—Content" [*Inhaltlich—Formal*] and "Conceptual—Factual" [*Gedanklich—Sachlich*]

It cannot be denied, however, that with *this* kind of formal determination we have not as yet gained a sufficient understanding of the meaning of the "true" and the "good." It even seems to me that this kind of determination leaves us so far removed from the world of objects that a real understanding becomes impossible. To be able to determine whether we are dealing here with something that relates to form and content, we must base our judgment on the full meaning of "true" and "good."

When we use the terms "form" and "formal" in this context, they denote—as they did in earlier passages—something which pertains to the existent (i.e., the "object" or "thing") itself, something which permits of and requires an understanding as much as does that which relates to content. Accordingly, we must distinguished carefully among: What a specific existent is with respect to its content (i.e., with respect to the fullness of its quid); the forms of existents, which pertain to this fullness (i.e., the forms of existents as such, which are called transcendentals, or the forms by which the genera of existents are distinguished—the categories, or forms of an even more limited potentiality of fulfillment); and those conceptual structures by which existents are intellectually grasped. These may, in turn, be either filled or empty with respect to content, depending on whether they are mirroring either the fullness of the existent or merely an empty form.

However, there is still another "emptiness," one that is indicative of a separation from a factual [*sachlich*] foundation. When I speak of "some or any object," these expressions admit of a factual understanding. What is meant finds its fulfillment in the empty form of the *aliquid*. The expression "non-existent object," on the other hand, admits of no fulfillment. It corresponds to empty thought. We shall have to discuss such empty thought structures in greater detail later on.[42]

§10. An Attempt at a Deeper Comprehension of Truth (Logical, Ontological, Transcendental Truth)

It is important to observe the distinctions between logical, ontological, and transcendental truth if we are to clarify what St. Thomas means by "purely conceptual relation" in the passage cited above (p. 292). He calls the relation of the object of knowledge (i.e., creaturely knowledge exclusively) a "purely conceptual relation," because the object does not depend on this knowledge. The object remains what it is regardless of whether any human being knows of it or not. Human knowledge effects no change either in the content or in the formal structure of the object. The relation of knowledge to its object, on the other hand, is called "real" because knowledge depends on its object: 1) there is no knowledge without an object, so that knowledge owes its *Dasein* to the object (though not the object alone); 2) the object imparts to knowledge its particular "content of meaning" [*Gehalt*] and therewith that which distinguishes this knowledge from any other knowledge.[43] Thus, knowledge (even with respect to its quid) can reach its completion only with a view to an object.

The "reality" of the relation thus has a twofold meaning: the relation to the object aids in construing the *quid* of knowledge and is the condition of its actuality; and the potential knowledge of reason (understood as a *faculty* or *power* of the soul) is transformed by means of the object into *act*, i.e., into vital intellectual activity.

Does this mean that the relation of knowledge to its object is something real, i.e., something that *is there* in the manner of things, thingly qualities, or events? Is this relation real in the sense in which this human being and its present knowledge are real? The answer must be in the affirmative if by "relation to the object" we mean the intrinsic tendency of knowledge toward its object, i.e., the intentionality of knowledge with respect to the object. This *intentio* is, after all, an essential constituent of the cognitive experience [*Wissenserlebnis*][44] and partakes of the latter's being.

There is nothing in the object that corresponds to this *intentio.*

However, the relation to the object is not yet that congruity (*adaequatio*) of knowledge with its object which we call truth. One can only speak of *congruity* and of *truth* when the object which is intended as real is real, if the object is actually that which our knowledge *intends* it to be, and if it *is* in precisely the manner in which our knowledge intends it to be. In such a congruity there is a coincidence of the *content* of knowledge (its *intentional content* or *logical meaning*) and the real object as it is given in a *consummate apperception* [*erfüllende Anschauung*] that includes the being, the quid, or the how of the object as well as its purely formal structure. This congruity thus presupposes two existents: an object and a knowledge which corresponds to the object. And the congruity is neither in the one nor in the other, but is itself an existent of a special kind which has its foundation in the existence of both the object and the knowledge. To say that the congruity is an "existent of a special kind" means that it belongs to that distinct genus of existence which is called a *relation* (πρός τι) in the strict and genuine sense.

Should we conclude then that truth, understood as congruity of knowledge with its object, is not a transcendental determination at all but belongs to the sphere of the categories? This would be an overhasty conclusion. The kind of truth which we have considered so far is—according to Gredt[45]—not *transcendental* but *logical truth.* It relates the existent either to a thinking which assimilates itself to that existent in a temporal process, or (and this we have not considered as yet) to a thinking by which the existent is measured and in accordance with which the existent is formed (as is the case in the relationship that exists between the thinking of the sculptor and this sculptor's works), or, finally, to a thinking with which the existent fully coincides (as is the case with the essence and knowledge of God). In any case, however, the congruity of the existent with a thinking of one kind or another has a foundation in existence as such. And this is where we have to took for *transcendental truth.*

Gredt also calls transcendental truth *ontological* truth, and he equates its meaning to *genuine purity* [*Echtheit*]. True gold is pure or genuine gold, i.e., it possesses everything that belongs to the essence or nature of gold. It seems evident, then, that therewith nothing is added to the existent. For every existent must *be* "in truth," and it must "in truth" be *that* which it is. This being "in truth" becomes meaningful only when the existent is measured by something which it itself is not, and a knowing and measuring intellect is needed to do the measuring.

When I mistake brass for gold and feel disappointed upon discovering the truth, I have found out that this thing is "in truth" not gold, but brass. I measure the thing before me by comparing it to my "idea of gold," and I discover that it does not conform to this idea, although at first it seemed to conform. But the thing must be something "in truth." On the basis of what it is, it is fit to be grasped by a knowing intellect. And what it is is in a certain manner also the basis of my initial presumptive knowledge and my subsequent disappointment. The existent as such—as it is in itself—is the precondition of the possibility of a congruity or noncongruity with the knowing intellect, i.e., of the *logical* truth or untruth. And the existent itself is—in a transcendental sense—called "true" inasmuch *as* it is the foundation of logical truth.

At this point, however, it is necessary to make some further distinctions. *My* "idea of gold" is not the ultimate measure, for this idea itself may be true or false, depending on whether or not it agrees with the *pure idea,* i.e., with the original divine archetype.[46] This latter is the ultimate measure of human *ideas* as well as of things.

A thing is what it is. This does not mean, however, that a thing is fully and wholly what it *ought* to be. It is rather more or less what it is destined to be. Here we once more encounter the contrast between the actual and essential being of thing,[47] between the essential form and the pure form.[48] Now we shall designate as *essential truth* [*Wesenswahrheit*] the congruity of some actuality with the corresponding pure form. Essential truth is yet distinct from ontological truth (in the sense of pure or genuine truth), but the latter presupposes the former because a thing can be "in truth" only to the extent that it is in congruity with a pure form. *That* peculiarity of the existent, however, which *ultimately* makes possible the existent's congruity with a knowing intellect and which merits to be called *transcendental truth* in the most authentic sense, in my opinion signifies more than is implied in the statements that the existent is in truth something and that it is in congruity with a pure form.

We have previously pointed out in a different context that every existent has a meaning [*Sinn*] or—in scholastic terminology—that every existent is *intelligible,* i.e., something which can "enter into" a knowing intellect and can be "embraced" or "comprehended" [*umgefassen*] by a knowing intellect. It seems to me that this describes the nature of transcendental truth. The terms *intelligere,* "enter into," and "comprehend" express a mutual *being-ordained* [*Zuordnung*] *of intellect and existent.* This "being-ordained" will assume a different meaning depending on the nature of the intellect that is involved. We have so far considered only that kind of knowledge which enters into an intimate contact with an existent which is independent of the knowing intellect. We have not yet discussed the knowledge of the forming artist and generally of the creative mind. We may nevertheless venture an answer to the question of whether transcendental truth is something "purely conceptual."

We have denied that logical truth is purely conceptual. We have stated that logical truth is an existent having its foundation in other existents (i.e., in the known existent and in the corresponding knowledge). Logical truth presupposes the mutual being-ordained of intellect and existent. It adds nothing to the existent as such (and by "existent" we mean here "some or any existent"). But the existent is insufficiently described if we consider it only as such or as it is in itself. It pertains to its nature to *manifest* itself [*offenbar sein*], i.e., to be at least accessible to the knowing intellect, if not—as is the case with the knowledge which the divine intellect has of existents—immediately transparent. And in relation to what "any existent" is in itself, its manifestation or revelation, or its being ordained to the spirit, are something new.

On the other hand, if we mean by "existents" "*all* that which is" in its totality, then the order which prevails in this totality is included. In other words, it pertains to that which is in its totality that it is an *ordered totality* and that each and every existent has its place therein and entertains orderly relations to all the rest. Order is thus part of the existent (thus understood). And the being-manifest or the being-ordained of the existent to the spirit (which coincides with transcendental truth) is part of this order.

Being-ordained to the spirit pertains not merely to one genus of existents, but to all that which is—to every individual existent as well as to the totality of existents. And this is why the use of the term *transcendental* is in this case fully justified. On the other hand, "spirit" signifies a genus of existence, for not all that which exists is spirit. However, the spirit is a genus in a preeminent sense because it is of the nature of the spirit to be open to all existents, to be filled with that which is, and to have its life (i.e., its actual being) in the most intimate contact with that which is.

All these determinations relate to content, and they derive from an understanding of that which pertains to the nature or essence of the spirit.[49] We therefore gain a *full* understanding of transcendental truth only if we succeed in clarifying (with respect to content) what "spirit," "overtness" of the spirit, and "being revealed to the spirit" really mean. We may then compare with these determinations those forms by means of which we previously sought to seize transcendental truth. Spirit is that genus of existents which in a definitely determined manner is ordained to all that which is. And truth is a definitely determined form of the being-ordained of all that which is to that genus of existents which in a corresponding form (not in the same form) is ordained to all that which is.

We interpreted the meaning of existents as "that which is," and we may now ask where being ordained to the spirit has its beginning. This being-ordained evidently pertains to each individual part as well as to the whole with its peculiar organic structure. I it a very special sense, however, this being-ordained pertains to being. "*To be* manifest" (or revealed), "*to be* ordained"—these verbal forms imply being, and not a special mode of being, but being as such. In short *being means* (though perhaps without thereby exhausting its full meaning) a *being manifest for* or a *being revealed to the spirit* [*Sein ist Offenbarsein für den Geist*].[50] Thus we see that our endeavor to understand the nature of transcendental truth has led us from the existent to being and from it purely formal consideration to an examination of content. But a number of further supplementary inquiries are needed before we can approach the question of the meaning of being, the central problem of our investigation.

§11. The Truth of Judgment

In the passage which served as a starting point for the *De ente et essentia* of St. Thomas and for our own discussion of existents, Aristotle distinguishes a threefold meaning of being and existents (cf. pp. 283 and 588). The Greek philosopher regards as thoroughly authentic *those* existents which are divided and classified by the categories. Transcendental investigation is used to determine what is common to the existents of all categories. As a second meaning of being Aristotle mentions the truth of judgment, and as its third meaning the "consequent" being [*mitfolgendes Sein*] which belongs to the content of certain judgments. On the basis of our previous discussion of truth, it may now be possible to gain some insight into the nature of this particular meaning of being.

If we intend to weigh the truth of judgment, we must first explain what we mean by *judgment.* This term is used with different connotations which are, however, interlinked by a common element of meaning. When I speak of "my judgment," I may have in mind the intellectual *act of the judgment* [*Urteilsakt*] which underlies the predication, "This tree is green."[51] Truth or untruth (falsehood), however, is actually not ascribed to my judgment (of which it is more often said, "I judge rightly" [*ich urteile richtig*]), but to the quid of my judgment, i.e., to the meaning of the predication. In the predication I thus assert the existence of some state-of-affairs [*Sachverhalt*]. If this state-of-affairs exists "in truth," the judgment is "true." In other words, the state-of-affairs is an existent in that sense of being that is presupposed in any truth of judgment, i.e., the state-of-affairs exists regardless of whether a judgment is passed on it or not.[52] The expression "in truth" denotes that transcendental truth which is the basis of logical truth. The *truth* of *judgment,* however, denotes nothing but *logical truth,* i.e., the congruity of the meaning of the judgment with an actual state-of-affairs.[53]

We have designated logical truth—understood as a congruity of some knowledge with an actual state-of-affairs—as an existent of a special kind, an existent which presupposes the being of the known object and the (at least potential) being of some knowing intellect. But since the possibility of such a congruity pertains to the existent as such (i.e., the congruity has its foundation in transcendental truth), the range of logical truth extends to all existents. This establishes the mutual relationship of formal ontology and logic.

Finally, let us try to arrive at an understanding of what Aristotle designates as "consequent being." When we say that this just man is an educated person, such a judgment asserts a state-of-affairs, i.e., the judgment includes everything that pertains to the actual state of this educated, just person. And the actuality of this state-of-affairs provides the measure for the truth of the judgment. However, there are several other states-of-affairs co-asserted in this judgment which—though the assertion is not specifically articulated in individual, separate judgments—provide a basis for such correlative judgments as "this one is a human being [*Mensch*]" or "this human being [*Mensch*] is just" or "this one there (this human being, this just person) is (real)."[54] We might therefore feel tempted to say that consequent being denotes the existence or reality of the co-asserted states-of-affairs and in the last analysis the being of the object (in the narrower sense of the term "object"—in our example, the being of this particular, individual human being) to which (or to whom) all the predications refer. But this is evidently not what Aristotle had in mind. Rather, "consequent" [*mitfolgend*] implies (in our example) that this just person is also an educated person, notwithstanding the fact that these predications pertain neither necessarily to the person's being human [*Menschsein*] nor to the person's justice. We are dealing here simply with a definite manner of togetherness of qualities [*Zusammensein von Beschaffenheiten*] in a thing (or in a being), i.e., with a special problem of the internal structure of a definite genus of existent, a problem which might legitimately be disregarded in the transcendental consideration of the existent as such.

§12. Artistic Truth

First of all, we attempted to gain an understanding of logical truth insofar as what was involved therein was a congruity of existents with some subsequently added knowledge. And in the course of our investigation we obtained some insight into the nature of transcendental truth. However, we stated that the being-ordained to a *spirit* [*Geist*] assumes quite a different meaning when there is no longer a question of something that is subsequently *added,* but of *creative, spiritual* [*geistig*] *activity.* The time has now come to examine this particular kind of being-ordained and its relation to transcendental truth.

The artist who creates a work of art has a knowledge which precedes the *Dasein* (being-there) of this existent, and by virtue of this knowledge the artist calls this existent into *Dasein*. The artist's *idea* provides the measure for the completed work and the basis for the artist's judgment (whether or not this work is as it ought to be). From the point of view of the medieval schoolmen, the relation between the artist and the artist's work is "real" on the part of the thing that is being created, and the relation is "conceptual" on the part of the creative intellect. The meaning of this distinction is familiar to us from our inquiry into the nature of non-creative knowledge. But whereas in this latter case knowledge owes both its *Dasein* and its content to its object, in creative knowledge the work is called into *Dasein* and comes to be *what* it is by virtue of creative activity. To say that the work was "created" means that it has a cause. It owes its existence to the real event [*Geschehen*] of creative activity, and this activity originates in the mind [*Geist*] of the artist.

On the other hand, it is not immediately evident what constitutes the nature of that relation of the artist to the work which we designated as "conceptual." The process and progress from the first inspiration of a work to its execution and completion are complex and may follow different patterns. The sculptor may first have an "idea" and then seek for suitable "material." But it may also happen that the sculptor receives the first "inspiration" at the sight of a block of marble which suggests certain possibilities of artistic formation. In the latter case we may doubt whether there can be a question of a purely intellectual relationship between the artist and this work. Though the block of marble is not yet the work, it is nevertheless an essential part of the work. The artistic "plan" or "design" owes not only its *Dasein* to the block of marble. Even the content of this plan may be co-determined by the block of marble.

If we now examine more closely what happens on the part of the artist, we find—as was emphasized earlier—that the "emergence" of the "idea" is more in the nature of receiving than of creation (cf. pp. 157f. above). The human intellect does not call *ideas* into *Dasein;* it calls works into *Dasein* which it fashions upon the model of ideas. We are then dealing here with a special kind of knowledge, a comprehension of "meaningful forms" [*Sinngebilde*] which "manifest" themselves to the intellect and stimulate its activity. But these forms do not manifest themselves immediately in full clarity and intelligibility but rather in a veiled and indistinct manner. Therefore, the first operation which the mind is required to perform is a purely intellectual one, namely, that of making the idea stand out clearly. And for a "genuine" or "true" work of art it is of the utmost importance that nothing be done aimlessly or capriciously lest the inner organic laws of the formal structure be disturbed by any arbitrary additions, omissions, or distortions.[55]

When we say that this purely intellectual operation must come "first," we do not mean to imply that this operation must be completed before the work of execution can begin. Rather, the clarification takes place step by step during and concomitantly with the execution of the work, so that the expression "practical knowledge" applies here in a true and literal sense.

The process of human "creation"[56] cannot be further pursued in this context. We merely intended to point out that this process entails a peculiar interplay of the envisaged idea, the vision of the active intellect (actuating externally through the medium of the body), and the emerging work. Only the idea itself, i.e., the *pure form* or meaningful ideal structure [*Sinngebilde*] appears here as wholly independent of both the creative intellect and the created work. Both the operation and the work (*opus*) are determined by the idea, and both are mutually conditioned by each other. And if by *idea* we do not mean pure form, but the conceptual structure which seeks to grasp the idea, then this structure too depends on these same conditions. We may thus say that the artist has "failed" in the attempt to express the idea whenever—owing to illusions and errors—the idea deviates from the pure form.

This consideration leads us to the question of the *truth* of the work of art. We call a work of art true when it *is* what it *ought* to be. However, this "ought" has a twofold meaning. It may indicate that the work of art corresponds to the intention of the artist, or that it corresponds to the pure idea. The work is not a genuine or true work of art if—though the work expresses the intention of the artist—the idea which the artist has fashioned in his or her mind deviates from the pure idea.

We must now try to determine how artistic truth is related to logical and transcendental truth. Artistic truth denotes congruity of the work with the underlying pure idea. Here we observe a kinship with *ontological* truth ("true gold," too, corresponds to the "idea of gold"). But we also observe a difference between artistic and ontological truth, a difference which corresponds to the distinction between the essence of a thing of nature and the essence of a work of art.

We mentioned earlier that human works are not *ousiai* (in the narrower sense of the term), not *substances* (cf. p. 165 above). It is true that they are "works of art" in the same sense in which things of nature may be called works of art. A "thing of nature" [*Naturding*] is. This means that in both instances we are dealing with a genus of existents. But a marble statue of Napoleon, or Napoleon as he is depicted in a work of poetry, is not Napoleon (nor a human being) in the same sense as the real Napoleon. The artistic or literary representations are *images* of the real Napoleon. They "present" him. Their characteristic attitudes (which are themselves only *images* of certain attitudes) correspond to the essence of Napoleon, but they do not own this essence because its meaning is merely conceptually "attributed" [*zugedacht*] to them.

Artistic truth denotes congruity of the work of art with a pure idea, regardless of whether or not something in the "real" world, i.e., in the world of our natural experience, corresponds to this idea. A bust of Napoleon can be "true" in this sense, even though it may bear but little resemblance to the historical Napoleon. *Historical truth,* on the other hand, is of a different kind. It denotes congruity of an *image* with that reality which it tries to depict, and the attempt at historical representation fails if the image does not resemble the primordial type [*Urbild*]. When we hear it said at times that art is "truer" than history, the frame of reference of such a statement is the relationship which exists between art and history on the one hand and their common *primordial type* on the other. The latter stands even above reality, the essence of which is determined by the primordial type.

We have learned from our inquiry into the nature of *ousia* that in created things we must distinguish between the essential form and the pure form and that real things more or less correspond to what they ought (were destined) to be. We may be sure, for example, that the life of the historical Napoleon was not a pure realization of what he ought to have been. Now it is the task of the historian to report what Napoleon actually did and how he behaved in reality. But the historian would fulfill this task in an imperfect manner if the image of Napoleon showed none of the lustre of that *pure idea* to which Napoleon ought to have corresponded. For what each human being ought to be—i.e., his or her "personal destiny"—pertains to the essence. This is why the artist, who penetrates through the purely external and factual to the primordial archetype [*Urbild*], can present more of the truth than the historian who remains within the limited circumference of external data. The work of the artist who succeeds in depicting the true *Urbild* and at the same time remaining within the bounds of tradition will be truer even in the sense of historical truth than the work of a historian who does not penetrate beyond the surface of external facts.[57]

We may call that which demands that an existent be or become what it is destined to be the existent's essentiality [*Wesentlichkeit*] or *essential truth* [*Wesenswahrheit*]. And we have distinguished this essential truth from *ontological* and *transcendental* truth (cf. pp. 295f. above). However, this distinction may be seen from yet another aspect. We have decided to call *transcendental* only that which pertains to the existent as such, not that which pertains only to one particular genus. Now essential truth—understood as a congruity of the actual essence with its primordial archetype (the pure form or idea)—is found only where we also encounter the contrast between essential and actual being, i.e., in the world of those real things which come into being and pass away in time and which in their temporal evolution copy more or less perfectly a timeless pure form. In the realm of pure forms this contrast does not exist. Their being is simply the unfolding of their quid, an unfolding which is inseparable from these forms themselves. They no longer copy or mirror anything to which they could more or less correspond. In pure forms there is therefore no place for essential truth. But since pure forms are nonetheless existents, we must also attribute to them—as we must attribute to all existents—ontological and transcendental truth. They are what they are, and to their being pertains their being manifest or that being ordained to a knowing intellect which is the presupposition of logical truth. Artistic truth (as well as historical truth) presupposes essential truth, and neither the one nor the other can be equated to transcendental truth. This means that artistic truth too is bound to a particular genus of existents, namely, to human works. But the existents of this particular genus also have—qua *existents*—transcendental truth. They are what they are—whether they be works of art or mere bungling artifices [*Machwerke*]—in truth and can be known or recognized as such.

Gredt has described and classified the congruity of the work of art with the "causative knowledge" of the artist as a special kind of logical truth. Let us try then to understand what is meant by causative knowledge.

To that which is presupposed as the cause for the coming into being of the work of art belongs above all else—as we have seen—the envisaging of the idea. The congruity of the work with the idea we have designated as *artistic truth* and have seen in it a modification of essential truth. But because the work owes its artistic truth to the *envisaged* idea of the artist and because this visualization illumines and guides the activity of the artist (by which the artist forms the idea in a proportionate matter) and is realized progressively in the growing work, there goes hand in hand with artistic truth a peculiar kind of logical truth.[58]

Transcendental truth pertains to the existent as such and preeminently to that whose nature it is to manifest or reveal its being. Existents are "divided" as to form and content into different genera and species, and concomitantly being, as well as being manifest or being ordained to some intellect, particularize themselves. The things of nature and the works of people are ordained to the human intellect in different manners, and, in turn, works are ordained in a different way to the creative, "subsequently operative," and "understanding" intellect. To these different ways of being ordained [*Zuordnungen*] correspond different modes of knowledge and of logical truth.

§13. Divine Truth

The picture changes again when by "creative intellect" we mean the divine intellect, which alone is creative in the full and true sense. As all words must be modified in their meaning when they are transferred from creatures to God, so also the word *knowledge* [*Erkenntnis*]. The German verb "*er*-kennen" conveys the meaning of a beginning, of an original temporal acquisition of knowledge. There is no knowledge of this sort in God, because God's "knowledge" is from eternity and is therefore truly a knowing which precedes all created things and is completely independent of them. In the case of human creation, on the other hand, this cannot be said without qualification.

Only divine knowledge is, as we have said, creative in the true sense, while human creation is merely a transformation of an already given matter or material in accordance (more or less) with a likewise—though in a totally different manner—given primordial type [*Urbild*]. Divine knowledge is also truly creative with respect to the work, since this work need not—in the manner of human "works"—first be transformed into an action that is externally efficacious. Divine knowledge carries within itself the creative *Fiat!* In regard to the relation of divine knowledge to created things, we may thus adopt the meaning of the *scholastic* phrase "purely intellectual—non-real," in the familiar sense that divine knowledge does not depend on created things either in its *Dasein* or in its contents. And by *relation* we means here the innate tendency [*intentio*] of knowledge toward things. That this relation is "purely intellectual" does not prevent it from being actual and efficacious in the highest degree. After all, things owe to this relation that they are and what they are. This fact we acknowledge by calling them *real* (viewed from the aspect of things).

The part which the *ideas* play in creative thinking has been discussed previously.[59] The ideas are included in the content of divine thought, together with their relationship to created things. They do not accrue to the divine intellect in any external sense. They are the divine essence itself in that self-limitation which this essence posits by determining itself as the archetype [*Urbild*] of finite things. And this in turn implies—as was pointed out before—that the *ideas* cannot be anything but "true." There is nothing else by which they could be measured in the way in which divine thinking measures things by their corresponding ideas. They are what they are, and they are manifest to the divine intellect. We can hardly speak any longer here of being *ordained,* since divine ideas are nothing but the divine intellect itself, which as such is completely manifest or intelligible to itself. In this case, then, transcendental truth and logical truth coincide. The ideas are included in divine being. And logical truth also—understood as the congruity of things (not, however, of their primordial types) with divine thought—belongs inseparably to this divine thinking itself.

Viewed from the aspect of things, however, being and truth are separate. Their *Dasein* is not simply equivalent to their being manifest or being intelligible [*Offenbarsein*] to the divine intellect. Their *Dasein* is posited as distinct from the divine intellect by the divine intellect itself, and the latter has simultaneously posited their being ordained to some knowing, created intellect, and it has also posited logical truth as a potential congruity with the created intellect. Essential truth also (as a congruity of things with their *Urbild*) has its place only in created things. From our previous discussion, we know how the possible non-congruity of things with their *Urbild* can be explained and understood.[60]

The contention that there is no longer any measure for the "truth" of divine ideas may give rise to the question which was repeatedly discussed in the medieval controversies concerning the doctrine of ideas, namely, the question of whether God is free in the formation of the ideas and thus their creator or whether ideas follow in their internal structure a necessary and unalterable law, a law with which even God could not interfere. The different answers given to this question determine essentially the opposing views of medieval *voluntarism* and *intellectualism*. Whereas for Duns Scotus—according to G. Manser[61]—the combination of simple essences to form composite ideas (which must be regarded as the archetypes of things) rests on God's free choice, for St. Thomas Aquinas the divine knowledge precedes the divine will, so that not the will (*voluntas*) but "the divine ideas and the divine nature" are "*the ultimate principle of the essence of things.*"[62]

It would be presumptuous on my part to try to decide this question. I merely venture to ask the further question whether—in view of the perfect simplicity of the divine being in whom knowledge and will coincide—a discussion of the possibility of any prior or posterior as well as of any being-conditioned of the one by the other can have any meaning. Can the divine will be conceived to be anything but free (i.e., totally independent of everything that is not the divine will itself) and simultaneously illumined through and through by that divine wisdom with which it coincides?

Ascending from finite existents, we arrive at an eternal first being, the ground or cause of all being, and we arrive at a multiplicity of ideas, which are the ground or the causes of multiplicity in the world of becoming and passing away. The knowledge of ideas (whatnesses or meaningful structures) which we actually possess reveals to us certain differences in their internal structure. There are ideas in which one characteristic feature necessarily requires others, so that these ideas cannot be conceived in any other way (e.g., pure geometrical structures, such as the circle, the triangle, etc.). And there are other ideas which leave us in the dark as to the reasons why they are constituted in this particular way and not otherwise (e.g., that people have two hands and two feet, that people need senses to acquire knowledge, that there exist certain relations of mutual dependency between body and soul, etc.). We are here face to face with a matter-of-factness the reasons or causes of which we are unable to penetrate. And such an ultimate, impenetrable fact is for us the differentiation between necessity and contingency which we find even in the realm of essential being. It seems to me that it indeed transcends the possibilities of natural reason to demonstrate that the cause of this differentiation lies in the divine essence. Even the attempt to harmonize the simplicity of the divine being with the manifold of the ideas bears the marks of a reason illumined by faith, a reason which—impelled by the words of revealed truth—seeks to grasp mysteries which defy and confound all human concepts.

§14. Transcendental Truth, Divine and Creaturely Being

We started out from the contention of Thomistic philosophy that truth pertains to the existent as such and that it adds to the individual existent merely the "intellectual" relation of that which imparts a perfection (cf. pp. 291f. above). Let us now ask what meaning truth assumes for us after we have made the above-mentioned distinctions.

We have established as the authentic meaning of transcendental truth the "being-manifest," the being-intelligible, or the being-ordained to a knowing intellect, a being-ordained which pertains to being as such and therewith also to the existent as such. When we have in mind the first existent as he is intelligible to himself, being and truth coincide, and this is why God is called *the truth.* In this case there can therefore be no question of either a being-ordained or of an imparting of a perfection. On the other hand, if we have in mind the totality of all created existents in their being-ordained to the divine intellect, this being-ordained signifies for the divine intellect neither something that is added nor something that imparts a perfection, while for finite existents this being-ordained is the foundation of all their perfection, i.e., the foundation of *that* they are and of *what* they are "in truth." And if, finally, we have in mind the being-ordained of all created existents to the created intellect, this being-ordained is the foundation of the perfection of the intellect, inasmuch as it is the existent which leads the intellect to the perfection of its being (i.e., its being active) by becoming the object of intellectual knowledge and by thereby giving to the intellect a concrete content. The being-ordained to the intellect—as has been pointed out—adds nothing to the totality of existents, because the being-ordained is always included in this totality. If by "existent" we mean *any* existent, the being-ordained to the intellect effects no change of *what* the existent is. But this being-ordained is something that is added to the quid. And for some existents the being-ordained to the intellect may also in a certain respect be the condition of the existent's perfection, because in the process of being known the existent becomes an intelligible being (an *actu intelligibile*).[63]

§15. Divine and Creaturely Goodness

Of *goodness* (as of truth) we have said that it pertains to the existent as such. The distinguishing mark of goodness we saw in the fact that *good* denotes the *congruity of the existent with the conative striving* [*Übereinstimmung des Seienden mit dem Streben*]. Moreover, the good imparts perfection not only by its content—as does the true— but also by its *being*. This distinction requires further elucidation.

Existents are good to the extent that they are perfect. And they are in congruity with the conative striving insofar as the conation is essentially a striving toward perfection. However, perfection has a twofold meaning: It means that nothing is lacking in *what* the existent is (or ought to be), and that the existent *is* in the full sense of the term (that it has attained to the highest stage of its being). Both of these conditions are fulfilled—without any limitation or restriction—only by God. He alone is both infinite plenitude and supreme actuality (pure act). He is therefore absolute perfection and absolute goodness.

Is it possible, then, to speak here of a congruity of the existent with the conative striving? If we understand striving as a tending toward an end or a goal to be attained, no such striving is possible for God. He is at the goal from all eternity. And this is precisely the ultimate aim and end of all earthly striving: a testing in the ultimate end or that fulfillment which is a "fruition" and, on the highest level, eternal bliss [*Seligkeit*]. We may therefore say that the will of God rests in his being or that the divine will is in perfect harmony with the divine being. But this is not a congruity of one existent with another, but a congruity of the one with itself.

Aside from God, no existent is perfect in this sense, because every finite existent is merely something, not everything. Every finite existent has received the measure of its quid and of its being. But a finite existent may nonetheless be called perfect if it has attained its full measure, if it is fully that which it ought to be, and if it stands on the highest stage of that level of being that can be attained by it.

If the existent is a creature in the process of evolution, the highest measure of its being is the goal of all its striving (notwithstanding the fact that there are many instances of a "false" striving—aberrations of the conative desire—which is then not "in truth" directed toward the goal). The striving finds its fulfillment in the attained highest measure, and it comes to rest in fruition when a full *congruence* of the striving and its ultimate goal has been achieved. But we may speak of congruence even prior to the attainment of the goal, because during the striving the end of the striving stands constantly before the mind's eye as that good which promises fulfillment and imparts perfection.[64]

Inasmuch as the divine will has determined every creature's measure of being, the attained fulfillment of the creature's being simultaneously signifies its congruity with the divine will and that measure of goodness that can be attained by this creature. But even prior to their perfection, all existents are—by virtue of *what* they are—in congruity with the divine will (and thus good). The divine will *is* the cause of both their being and the *quid* of their being. And the striving for perfection—being in harmony with the divine will—is also good.[65]

Included in and subordinated to that striving for the highest measure of the being of existents, which must be regarded as the fundamental striving of all created things, is a multitude of individual strivings aiming at individual *goods.* While some of these are conditions of the striving existent itself, others are modes of some other existent that may aid in the attainment of these conditions. All living beings, for example, strive for nourishment and therefore also for the food which provides proper nutrition.[66] That which—though an object of striving—is not actually suited to lead to perfection is not a true but only an apparent good, because it is not in harmony with the divine will. In the order of existents, however, every finite existent is destined to minister to the perfection of some other existent and is therefore good as a creature of God in and by itself, but also as that which imparts perfection.

Let us next ask whether it pertains to the good as such to be an actuality. According to Gredt, striving aims at something actual and not at something that is merely potential, because the actual is that which is perfect. But the same author adds that even the potential is good in a certain sense, because it is ordained to actuality.[67] This statement is certainly correct if it is a question of an existent in which are found both actuality and potentiality. Thus, the striving of a sick person aims at *actual* health and therefore also at actual medicaments, because the non-actual cannot effect a cure. But that also is good which is above and beyond the contraries of potentiality and actuality, such as, for example, health as such, or the meaning of health. The striving of the sick person, however, alms not directly at health as such, nor can health as such fulfill this striving. But—being a divine idea—health as such is in harmony with the divine will, and *actual* health is health to the extent that it is in congruity with this divine idea.

§16. The Interrelation Between Truth and Goodness

We are now facing the question of how *truth* and *goodness* are related to one another. In God these two coincide with each other as well as with being. God knows and wills his being, and both his knowing and his willing are contained in his being. However, if we understand truth as a being ordained to a finite, knowing intellect, and if we understand goodness as a being ordained to finite striving (or as a being-ordained of one existent to another existent to whose perfection the striving may contribute), truth and goodness are apart, although there persists a certain interconnection between them.

Existents are (transcendentally) true insofar as they are ordained to a knowing intellect, i.e., insofar as they are fit to become contents of intellectual knowledge. In knowing, the intellect attains to the perfection of its being. The existent, which aids the intellect in attaining this end, imparts to it perfection and is thus—insofar as it is true—also good, albeit not in an absolute sense, but only in this particular respect.[68]

Conversely, we shall have to say that the good as such (i.e., the existent insofar *as* it is good) must also be true to the extent that it can be known as good. In the case of conscious striving, the knowledge (real or supposed) of the object of the striving as good is even the very foundation of the striving. In the case of natural (non-conscious) striving, the object of the striving can be known by a rational observer as a good for the striving being. This latter relationship finds expression in the phrase "a true good." Only when the knowing of the existent as good is true, is this existent "in truth" a good. This good is then not only congruent with the striving of some creature, but also with the will of the creator and—since in God knowledge and will coincide—simultaneously in accord with this good's *archetype* [*Urbild*] in the divine intellect and this good is thus essentially true, i.e., *true* in the sense of essential truth [*Wesenswahrheit*].

The intimate interconnection and correlation of truth and goodness merely reemphasizes the fact that the existent as such is both true and good. In this formulation the meaning of *true* and of *good* remains distinct, just as *knowing* and *striving* are distinct, although they mutually condition each other. But we must still examine whether our previous contention—that the true imparts perfection as to content while the good imparts perfection by virtue of its being—remains valid (cf. pp. 291f. above).

When I recognize that this tree is green, I comprehend intellectually both the content and the reality of this state-of-affairs

[*Sachverhalt*]. Content [*Inhalt*] and reality [*Bestehen*] together are the "ingredient components" [*Gehalt*] of my knowledge. And in the consummation of this knowledge the intellect passes from *potential* to *actual* being and attains to a certain perfection of being [*Seinsvollendung*]. But the known *Sachverhalt* is not contained in this actual being and in its reality, as a part is contained in the whole. The *Sachverhalt* has not really entered into the actual being in this manner. The reality of the *Sachverhalt* and my own being remain ontically separated, notwithstanding the fact that I owe to the reality of the *Sachverhalt* that increment of being [*Seinssteigerung*] which the consummation of knowledge entails.

For this reason it is not of any decisive importance what kind of being enters into my knowledge as a content, although it is true that different contents of knowledge—arising from differences in the being of the objects known—may entail for the intellect a larger or smaller increment of its being. Thus the increment of being will differ, for example, in a sense perception and in the insight into a metaphysical problem. What matters for the intellect to attain to perfection by virtue of *some truth* is not so much that it know something actual as that it actually know. And such "actual knowledge" may have a twofold meaning. It may mean: 1) the actuality of the intellect in its knowing; and it may mean 2) that it is a question of true and not merely supposed knowledge. Even the latter type of knowledge is *actual* in the first sense, i.e., it involves an actual operation of the intellect, and to that extent it also implies a certain perfection of being, albeit not the *kind* of perfection which the intellect is destined to attain. The statement that the known object need not be an actuality applies to both supposed and true knowledge. In the latter case the non-actuality must be discerned in the knowledge.

When the physician knows that a sick person can be cured by a vacation trip, the physician recognizes in the suggested journey a *good* for the patient. The physician's intellect (and also the intellect of the patient, if the physician has succeeded in imparting to the patient the same knowledge) has been enriched by this knowledge, even though the journey may never be undertaken. However, *the* good, namely health, which is the aim of the striving of both the physician and the patient, can only be attained by the *actual* journey.

The actual vacation trip is thus the mediate or indirect aim of the striving. It includes the journey (which takes the patient to the proper destination), the atmosphere which the patient breathes at the health resort, the mineral baths, etc. We have here a chain of causally interlinked actual events which are expected to result in a decisive change in the sick person's physical condition.

If a striving is to achieve its fulfillment, the aim or end of the striving—which, unless it is a mere means to an end, is always a total complex of some actuality, an approximation to a perfection of being—must become actual in the existent, i.e., in that entity for the sake of which the end is desired.[69]

Since the striving (in the restricted and authentic sense of the term) always aims at the actualization of something not yet actual, the good which is the object of the striving as well as that for the sake of which this good is desired, are things or thingly [*dinglich*] conditions in that world of becoming in which the potential is actualized. The fulfillment of the striving is an actual resultant event [*Vorgang*] in which the end, the means to the end, and the existent which has as its end its own greater perfection, enter into a causal relationship which as such marks the unity of their being.

Now how can this explanation be reconciled with our previous contention that the true as such (or the existent as true) is also good? In intellectual striving (for knowledge), too, the greater perfection of an existent is the object of the striving, namely, the greater perfection of the intellect and therewith of the knowing human being. And this striving also finds its fulfillment in an actual resultant event, namely, in the consummation of knowledge. But the ingredient components [*Gehalt*] of knowledge, which are among the conditions of its actualization, do not enter into a causal relationship and into a unity of being with knowledge but rather into that peculiar relationship which we call intentional and which has its foundation in transcendental truth (i.e., in the being-ordained of the existent to a knowing intellect).

§17. Being, Good, and Value

We have said of truth (understood as a being-ordained of an existent to a knowing intellect) that it is distinct from the quid of any existent and comprised in being as such. Does the same statement apply to goodness? Certainly not without qualification, since owing to the difference between knowing and conative striving, being ordained has an entirely different meaning in these two instances. The being-ordained to striving—unlike the being-ordained to knowing—does not always denote a being-ordained to an intellect. For striving as tending toward the perfection of the being of the striving existent pertains to all created reality (as a becoming actuality). Aside from the conscious (intellectual) striving of rational creatures (a striving which is founded on knowledge), there is the striving of sentient (but irrational) creatures, and the natural striving of animate (but not sentient) and inanimate beings.[70] The turning of plants toward light, or the entering of soluble material elements into a crystalline form, may be named as examples of purely natural striving.

Aside from the intellect, there is no other existent which is—in the manner of the intellect—ordained to all that which is. This is the reason why *goodness* cannot denote a being-ordained of equal universality with that of truth. While all existents are good, not every existent is a good for every other existent (nor for every striving being). Only the highest good, which includes every perfection, is a good for all existents, since all owe their perfections to this highest good (including *the* perfection which they already possess, the higher perfection which they are destined to attain, and the possibility of attaining that higher perfection). Every finite good, on the other hand—and "finite" denotes not a temporal, but an objective [*sachlich*] limitation and is therefore compatible with eternity—has the meaning of that which imparts perfection only for a limited sphere of existents.[71] Thus even truth is a good only for the knowing intellect and not for non-rational creatures .[72]

On the basis of what has been said, we may now conclude that it corresponds to the meaning of the good to particularize itself in accordance with the multiple contents of existents. We call an existent that is destined to impart a perfection to some other existent(s) a *good.* That which makes it a good (i.e., its significance for others, founded upon its quid), modern philosophy calls *value.* (*Bonum* signifies both the existent as a good and the goodness of the existent.) Upon the manifold of the genera and species of existents rests the manifold of values that differ from one another.[73] The distinction between a *good* and a *value* is important in any attempt to demonstrate that goodness has its anchorage in being.

Striving as such is linked with a definite genus of existents. Only something that is in the process of becoming can strive (i.e., something that is as yet unfinished or imperfect and thus not fully actual, but simultaneously actual and potential). The actual end of the striving is the perfection of that which is as yet imperfect, and the transition from potency to act is the fulfillment of the striving. Thus we see that the entire order of goods and values is an order of the actual or real world. The immediate object of the striving of every existent is this existent's own goodness: the perfection of its quid and the highest stage of its being (i.e., its supreme actuality). All other existents which can contribute to this existent's perfection are mediately good for it. Since existents are to *actuate* [*wirken*], they must be *actual* [*wirklich*]. Actuation or efficacious activity pertains to actual being as such. The *effects* (i.e., the resultant quid of the efficacious activity), however, depend on *what the existents are.* And thus the being good of even the mediate good (i.e., of that which imparts a perfection) pertains to the being (*esse*) as well as to the quid of existents.

The entire world of becoming is permeated by that order which permits every created being (*ens*) to strive for its own perfection and to aid other created beings on their way to perfection. This order itself, however, is not subject to becoming and passing away, but is non-become and imperishable. And just as that which is signified by the term "human being" [*Mensch*] is neither born nor passes away, so also that which is signified by the word "holiness" (denoting the perfection of a person and, in a derivative sense, that which ministers to the perfection of a person or bears the stamp of a person) is not subject to any becoming, notwithstanding the fact that holiness may become actual and may therefore become the goal of striving.

Goods come to be and pass away, but that which imparts to an existent the meaning of good and which we call *value* belongs to the realm of essential being. It is pre-designed from eternity not only what an existent is, considered in itself, but also what significance, i.e., what value, attaches to it in the total context of all existents. If the existent is in truth what it ought to be, i.e., if it possesses essential truth, it is also truly good, possessing essential goodness

[*Wesengüte*], and—depending on the realm to which it belongs—truly holy, beautiful, noble, or useful.

It cannot be our task in this context to enter into a detailed discussion of the theory of good and value. We merely wanted to show that any theory of good and value must start out from the doctrine of the existent as such, and to point out the location of this starting point. Every created actuality is destined to attain to a highest measure of its being in some good that is the object of the striving. At the same time, every created actuality has for other actualities the significance of something that imparts a perfection and is therefore a good for these others. And every good thing [*jedes Gute*] as such is in accord with the eternal (divine) order of existents, an order which is the foundation of every being good and which is therefore itself good.

§18. The "Full Meaning" of the Good and the True

Have we now succeeded in presenting the good as a *formal* determination of existents, i.e., as an *empty form* which finds fulfillment in these goods and values that are differently determined according to their content? We have been able to reduce the concept of the good to that of the existent in such a manner that the good can only be comprehended from the aspect and according to the order of existence, but that there attaches to it a meaning, a "full meaning," of its own. Once we have gained insight into the interrelation of being [*Sein*] and being good [*Gutsein*], this meaning of the good is formally defined as perfection or as that which imparts perfection. Yet even natural (pre-philosophic) linguistic usage ascribes to the term "good" (and also to the term "true") a significance with respect to content, a meaning in the comprehension of which the intellect can come to rest.

We may say then that *good* is that wherein some striving finds its fulfillment. But this formulation may perhaps arouse the suspicion that we have here a *circulus vitiosus*, for *striving*, after all, is nothing but reaching out for some good. However, this difficulty resolves itself as soon as we begin to understand correctly the meaning and the implications of the terms used.

What is signified by *striving* and *goodness* (and by *knowing* and *truth*) cannot be comprehended separately, because the two concepts belong together, and the one does not "precede" the other. We can speak of truth only where a knowing intellect is in accord with some existent, and we can speak of goodness (in the realm of finite things) only where some need or want is satisfied by the attainment of its aim or end. Only when it knows can the intellect have an "authentic understanding" of what *knowledge* and *truth* really are. And only when the spirit strives or comes to rest in the possession of the object of its striving can it gain an authentic understanding of the "full meaning" of *striving* and of *good.* And upon such an authentic understanding is founded the conceptual comprehension and the orderly arrangement of what is comprehended within the frame of ultimate relations and contextual conditions [*Seinszusammenhänge*].

§19. Beauty as a Transcendental Determination

By attributing, on the one hand, a "full" meaning (with respect to content) to being true and being good, and by regarding them, on the other hand, as pertaining to being as such, we also claim a meaning with respect to content [*inhaltlicher Sinn*] for being as such. For we have seen how all the *transcendentals* refer back again and again to the problem of the meaning of being. But before we turn to this central question, we shall briefly discuss the nature of beauty, the last of the transcendental determinations.

The problem of beauty is only parenthetically discussed by Aristotle.[74] He distinguishes the beautiful from the good, inasmuch as the latter pertains to the sphere of action, whereas the former also pertains to the realm of the "unmoved," and he then defines the beautiful as such as being characterized by order, harmony, and due determinateness.[75]

The statement that the good pertains to the sphere of action may perhaps be interpreted as implying that the good is the goal of striving and, as an actuality, stands in causal relationship with the striving being. Correspondingly, the statement that the beautiful may be either in motion or unmoved would imply that for beauty actuality is not required and that the pleasure which the beautiful causes affects it as little as knowledge affects the object known. It seems that this interpretation is in accord with the view taken by St. Thomas Aquinas, for whom the beautiful, though interchangeable with the good, is nevertheless distinct from the good:

> The beautiful and the good are identical as far as the or carrier is concerned (*in subiecto*), for they rest on the same objective foundation, namely, the form. This is why the good is also praised as beautiful. Conceptually (*ratione*), however, they differ. For the good is specifically related to conative striving, since good is that which is the object of all striving. The good is thus essentially an end (*habet rationem finis*). For striving is, as it were, a movement toward its object. On the other hand, the beautiful is related to the power of knowing. For we call beautiful that which pleases when it is seen (*quae visa placent*). Beauty, therefore, is constituted by due proportion. For the senses find joy in things which are duly ordered or proportioned (*in rebus debite proportionatis*), in things which are, as it were, proportioned in a certain similitude with the senses. For the senses, like every cognitive power, are a kind of reason (*ratio quaedam*). And because knowledge comes about by assimilation and because the assimilation relates directly to the form, the beautiful in the strict and proper sense conceptually pertains to formal cause (*ad rationem causae formalis*).[76]

If everything that is good is also beautiful—since all existents as such are (metaphysically) good—it follows that the beautiful is one of the transcendental determinations of existents. Beauty—like truth and goodness—relates that which is to one distinct existent, or, more specifically, to the spirit. For beauty denotes that quality in an existent by virtue of which this existent is capable of causing satisfaction. However, satisfaction is an act of the spirit.[77] As truth leads the intellect to the perfection of its being (i.e., to knowledge) and must therefore be regarded as the proper good of the intellect, so beauty is the proper good of a special spiritual power.

What power, then, is ordained to the beautiful and finds its perfection in satisfaction? It must be that same peculiar *sense* of the spirit for *measure, due determinateness,* and *order* in which Aristotle discerned the foundation of beauty. The spirit recognizes in the known existent something which pertains to its own being. For the spirit is itself determined in its measure and species and proceeds in its activity in accordance with its own intrinsic order—that order which we call *reason.*

We stated that all created things have received a definite measure of being and that every created thing is also definitely determined in its *quid.* This is probably what Aristotle had in mind when he spoke of the "limitation" of things. Moreover, in each and every finite existent the constitutive parts are ordered according to a definite law. And this is presumably the meaning that underlies the Scriptural saying that everything was created according to measure, number, and weight.[78]

When St. Thomas (following St. Augustine) sees the foundation of the good in species, measure, and order (*species, modus, ordo*),[79] he may have been thinking of the above Scriptural passage as well as of Aristotle's definition of the beautiful. All these kindred expressions convey the same meaning, namely, that every existent as a created being is clearly determined in its *quid* and ordered according to some definite measure—both in its internal structure and in its relation to other existents.[80] The created spirit (particularly in its knowledge) as an existent is not only in accord with all other existents in that it, too, is permeated by the law and order of all that which is, but as spirit it is distinguished by the prerogative of becoming aware experientially of this accord. And this experiential awareness [*Innewerden*] we designate as "satisfaction," as "enjoyment of beauty," or "aesthetic joy."

This is not the proper place to inquire as to what extent these different expressions carry the same meaning, how the knowledge of the beautiful and the enjoyment of beauty as well as other possible attitudes with respect to beauty are related to one another, what part the senses play in this kind of joy, etc. In short, we shall not attempt to answer all those questions which are relevant to a systematic theory of the beautiful and of aesthetic experience.[81] Within our frame of reference we shall merely try to clarify the reasons for the inclusion of the beautiful among the transcendental determinations, i.e., among the properties of the existent as such. And it should be clear by now that beauty has its foundation in the structure of the existent as such and that its specific meaning refers to the possibility of an experienced relation of the spirit to existents, a relation which is itself founded on this structure. The beautiful indeed implies a relationship of a peculiar kind. It is distinct from truth (understood as an accord of knowledge and existence), and it is distinct from goodness (understood as an accord of striving and existence), and yet it has something in common with both. Like truth, beauty signifies that something is known [*ein Erkanntes*] in a large sense of *knowing*, and this something causes satisfaction when seen (visa *placent*). Thus, in contradistinction to the known truth, the something is not only known, but *pleases* (*visa* placent). And this pleasing means for the spirit a resting in the attainment of the end, as it is similarly experienced in the fulfillment of a striving. In this latter respect, then, goodness and beauty coincide.

St. Thomas describes these relationships as follows:

> When we say that the end of the striving is goodness, tranquility (that is, peace), and beauty, we are not speaking of separate ends. For it is precisely by striving for goodness that an existent simultaneously strives for tranquility (or peace). The existent strives for beauty inasmuch as the existent is inwardly determined in terms of measure and species (*modificatum et specificatum*), and this latter determination is included in the concept of the good. However, goodness adds the relationship "that which imparts perfection" to the others. Whosoever therefore strives for goodness thereby simultaneously strives for beauty. Peace or the tranquility of order, however, means the elimination of everything that causes disquietude and hinders the attainment of the end. The very fact that something is desired thus means that the desire strives for the elimination of everything that blocks the way to the attainment of the end of the desire. And this is why we say that one and the same striving simultaneously aims at goodness, beauty, and tranquility (or peace).[82]

Since goodness and truth are based on what the existent is (its *quid*) and at the same time pertain to the very being of the existent, beauty too has its foundation in the quidditive determinateness of the existent—and therefore differs according to the diverse contents of existents—and at the same time (as a *being*-ordered in due measure and as a *being*-in-accord with the order of the intellect) pertains to being as such.

If beauty is a property of the existent as such (and thus a genuinely transcendental determination) it cannot pertain exclusively to created existents, as it might appear from what has been said (since only the created, finite existent is limited according to its measure [*modus*] and *species*). just as there is divine truth and divine goodness which are the ultimate ground or cause of everything that is true and good, so there must also be divine beauty as the ultimate ground or cause of everything that is beautiful.

In this line of reasoning we receive further aid from St. Thomas. He introduces a definition of the beautiful which we have so far not considered. In the course of his discussion of the distinctions among the Divine Persons he attributes beauty in a preeminent degree to the Son, stating that "for beauty there are three requisites: 1) *integrity* or perfection (for what is deformed or defective is for this very reason ugly); 2) *due proportion* or harmony; and 3) *clarity*. This is why we call those things beautiful which have a brilliant color."[83]

An existent is perfect when it is wholly what it ought to be, when nothing is wanting to it, and when it has attained to the highest measure of its being. This perfection denotes the congruity of the existent with the divine idea which is its archetype [*Urbild*], (*Wesenswahrheit*, essential truth), and simultaneously with the divine will (*Wesensgutheit*, essential goodness). Whatever is perfect is true, good, and beautiful. And perfection also denotes implicitly that the existent has its due measure, that as a totality it is in possession of its apportioned being, and that all its parts are duly proportioned.[84] In the case of a painted image, due measure means, moreover, that the work is a faithful reproduction of the object depicted. "A painted image is called beautiful when it represents the object—no matter how ugly this object may be—perfectly."[85]

However, the "clarity" is like a splendor of brightness poured out over the existent, revealing the latter's divine origin. And it seems that this word "clarity" gives voice to the true enchantment of the beautiful. It expresses what the average human being means by "beauty" and what has such a mysterious hold on the human soul. Just as in knowing we gain an "authentic understanding" of the nature of truth and in the fulfillment of our striving an authentic understanding of the nature of goodness, so we begin to understand the nature of beauty when that "splendor" touches our soul.

We meet this splendor in the world of sense in the radiance of physical light, without which all sensuous beauty would remain hidden from us. We meet it in the radiance of color and in the loveliness of physical forms and bodies.

But this splendor is by no means confined to the world of sense. There is spiritual beauty. There is the beauty of the human soul, whose "ways and actions are duly measured and ordered in accordance with the intellectual clarity of reason."[86] The closer a created being is to the divine *Urbild*, the more perfect it is. This is why intellectual and spiritual beauty range above sensuous beauty. And because the human soul by divine grace is drawn near to the divine being in an entirely new sense, the splendor which grace pours out over a human soul surpasses all purely natural brightness and harmony.[87] However, that which imparts being and beauty to all created things and beings must be supreme beauty—beauty as such.[88] God is perfect being without any want, fault, or flaw. Even if for us he remains undefinable and immeasurable—because his infinity transcends all human measures and determinations—he is nevertheless his own measure, determined in himself in "duly proportioned" accord with himself, and wholly luminous in and for himself: that eternal light "in whom there is no shadow of darkness."[89]

VI.

The Meaning of Being

§1. The Common Constitutive Elements of Meaning [*Gemeinsamer Sinnbestand*] in All Finite Being (Essential Being, Existence, Real and Conceptual Being)

Our analysis of individual transcendental determinations has shown that there are certain distinctive differences among them. Only some of them determine existents as they are in themselves and (if we disregard for the moment the meaning of being as such) in their purely formal structure. In this manner we interpreted *ens, res, unum,* and *aliquid* (unless we wish to understand *aliquid* with St. Thomas as *aliud quid*). In the true, the good, and the beautiful, on the other hand, we recognized determinations which relate the existent as such to a sphere of being that is more limited and more definitely determined in its content—determinations to the content of which attaches a correlative meaning. *All* transcendental determinations, however, as determinations of the existent *as such,* contain or include *being,* so that the meaning of the transcendentals cannot be fully clarified unless we succeed in first clarifying the *meaning of being.* The different significations of being which we have made to stand out in the course of our investigation may serve as a starting point.[1] According to the meaning which—in the definition of the existent (ὄν, *ens*) as "something which is"—we associate with the "is," the empty something will be filled or fulfilled in different ways.

When we conceive of an *essence* [*Wesenheit*] or of a *meaningful structure* [*Sinngebilde*] as fulfillment of the something, the corresponding being is *essential being.* This latter we understood as the unmoved (non-temporal) *unfolding* of that which is contained in the unity of the meaning. In the case of simple essences, this unfolding is a simple being-spread-out [*Hingebreitetsein*] and thus a being manifest [*Offenbarsein*][2] to the understanding gaze of the spirit which comes to rest in the understanding. In the case of composite meaningful structures, we have simultaneously a confluence [*Ineinander*] and effluence [*Auseinander*] of the ordered manifold of the individual features of some structural whole [*Gefüge*]. In the case of a temporally limited spirit, there corresponds to this a knowledge that progresses and increases step by step. And of this essential being we have said that it pertains inseparably to the correlative "something." However, this kind of being is not a particular species of being, but an integral constitutive part of the meaning of all being. Just as every something has a meaning, so there is implicit in all being the particular kind of being that pertains to meaning. This holds true not only of that fullness of meaning which is equivalent to the *quid,* but also of empty something and of all empty forms. Their meaning and being pertain integrally to the structure of existents.

A special difficulty is presented by the concept of "nothingness" or of the nought [*das Nichts*], which seems to have an intelligible meaning but which is not an essence. It not only has no *full meaning,* but not even an *empty* meaning in the sense of an empty form that could be filled—as in the case of the something. In the nought we have an empty meaning that cannot be filled, and it thereby reveals its "essence-less nature" [*Wesenlosigkeit*]. This is why non-being pertains to the nought rather than being, and everything that can be predicated of it is in the nature of a negation.[3]

Essential being is thus a necessary constitutive part of all being, but in the case of every something that is not a pure, meaningful structure, something else is added to essential being. To designate this richer and fuller meaning of being, we have chosen the term *existence,* and by this we mean not only *Dasein* (being-there = *real being*), but also the being of *ideal objects* such as those with which mathematics deals. After all that has been said in our previous investigations, it need hardly be specifically demonstrated that *"Dasein"* in the sense of real being is something more than essential being (not indeed something "higher," but something *other* or *different*): something that is "placed into *Dasein,*" something whose real being has a temporal beginning. But *what* it is (its *quid,* understood as pure whatness, not as actual essence) prior to its realization has no temporal beginning. On the other hand, as far as the being of *ideal objects* (numbers, geometrical structures, pure colors, etc.) is concerned—for which we have also claimed *existence*—we have as yet not proven that their being differs from or is more than essential being.

It is easily seen that the being of ideal objects differs from real being (i.e., from the Das*ein* of things and of whatever belongs to their structure or has its foundation in them). The triangle, the circle, a series of numbers, pure colors exist without having ever had a beginning and regardless of whether or not something corresponds to them in reality. It is more difficult to show the difference between the being of ideal objects and essential being. It can be done only by inquiring into the peculiar structure of their *quid*. And this we must do in connection with the question of whether ideal objects too—like real things—can be called πρώτη *ousia*. Merely by way of intimation I should like to state that ideal objects are meaningful structures of a special kind. Their structure shows a strict lawfulness [*Gesetzmässigkeit*] not found in all meaningful structures. And to this characteristic corresponds the peculiarity of their essential being.

We have designated essential being as a being-unfolded or unfolding [*Entfaltung oder Entfaltetsein*] of pure, meaningful structures, and if it is true that their *quid* shows a specific structure, this *quid* must also unfold in a specific manner. To the strict lawfulness of these structures corresponds the strictly necessary nature of those sentences which are predicated of them as well as the specificity of those disciplines which deal with them as objects.

We may thus understand *ideal being* as a special kind of essential being, and we may say that ideal being indicates a special manner of the (non-temporal) unfolding of *ideal objects*. The sphere of essential being is not thereby transcended. On the other hand, in real being a completely novel manner of unfolding is added to the non-temporal unfolding of the *quid* of things, namely, the being-placed [*Hineingestelltwerden*] and the self-forming [*Sichhineingestalten*] of things into a temporal and special world. Underlying these processes is that being-placed and being-founded-upon-itself which we recognized as the peculiarity of thingly (i.e., substantial) being and which is the pre-condition of the "self-forming."

The relation between the essential being of the *quid* and the real being of the corresponding thing has its foundation in the essence understood as the quidditive determinateness of the thing. The thing would be unable to unfold itself if it were undetermined by its *quid*. If the essence is—as we stated—the quidditive *being* of things, this being must be distinguished from the essential being of the pure *quid*. Quidditive being is rooted in that essential form which is posited as a new beginning of being. The being of this essential form is the formation of an actual essence or nature within the context of the real world, and therewith of a structure which is determined by this essence. The being of this structure is a progressive self-disclosure of something that is self-enclosed, i.e., a transition from potentiality to actuality.

Existence denotes a kind of being that is independent of a knowing (finite) spirit, a being of objects standing in and upon themselves [*auf sich selbst gestellte Gegenstände*]. *Conceptual being* [*gedankliches Sein*], on the other hand, presupposes thinking spirits or intellects.[4] All thought is either a thinking *of* something or *about* something, or a forming of something. Once the something is filled, that which is thought or intellectually conceived acquires a *full meaning*.[5]

To think *of* something means to direct the intellectual vision to an object (in the broadest sense of the term) which is not directly seen by the eye. We do not speak of "thinking of" when we turn our intellect toward a thing which is simultaneously sensorily perceived. However, I may perceive the books on my desk and simultaneously "think of a book" which I saw yesterday. This means more than merely remembering. "Thinking of" is an actual taking hold of or apprehending and thus akin to "comprehending" [*Begreifen*]. I have either had some prior conception of the object and picture it now under the corresponding concept ("that excellent book which I read yesterday"), or the *ap*prehension [Er*greifen*] is at least an initial step toward *com*prehension [Be*greifen*]. In an indefinite distance I perceive something which I cannot yet clearly recognize, and it is precisely this indefiniteness which stimulates my intellectual curiosity and causes my intellectual preoccupation with this thing. I say to myself, "I must take a closer look at this mysterious something."

The endeavor to penetrate intellectually into the nature of this something is already a "thinking or reflection about." "Is this a tree, or is it a house?" In such instances the full meaning of the object is not yet grasped, but it is at least assumed that the object has a full meaning. And in these instances the object and the full meaning which pertains to it "in reality" subsist independently of my thinking. On the other hand, the *quid* which in my questioning I "associate mentally" [*zudenken*] with the object—"tree," "house"—depends in a certain measure on my thinking. My thinking moves this *quid* in the direction of the object, and the *quid* is thus an intellectual construct which, though deriving from some objective knowledge (in our example, from sense experience), has been abstracted from its primordial ontic foundation and now rests on a spiritual basis. And this "resting on a spiritual basis" [*vom Geist getragen sein*] or this "being in the spirit" [*im Geist sein*] is precisely what we meaning by *conceptual being* [*gedankliches Sein*]. We have called it second-hand being because it presupposes another kind of being, namely, that of existents [*Seiende*], from the knowledge of which these conceptual structures derive or according to which they are formed.

However, the being which underlies conceptual being need not be real being. Conceptual structures are *images* or *copies* of pure, meaningful structures and may derive either from the experience of real things or from the knowledge of essential potentialities [*Wesensmöglichkeiten*]. We have learned this from our analysis of artistic creation. Such creation of structures on the basis of essential potentialities we call *conceptual formation* [*gedankliches Gestalten*], and this kind of formation is of fundamental importance for accomplishments in both artistic and scientific fields.

However, the question remains whether there are not also thoughts and conceptual structures without any underlying essential being. What shall we say of the *nought,* the *nonsensical,* and the *absurd?* We have already referred to the *nought* (cf. p. 326 above). We can conceptually conceive of the nought, but it is not a "structure" [*Gebilde*]. It is without content and thus without an essence or nature. It cannot even be called an empty form, but merely the annulment, negation, or crossing out [*Durchstreichung*] of an empty form, namely, of the form of a something. The nought evinces the incapability of thought to generate by itself "something" that does not rest on an already given reality.

We speak of *nonsense* where it is a question of something that suggests a meaning but where this meaning remains unintelligible. For example, "senseless" or "meaningless syllables" (such as "ba," "ce," "dam") are of this nature. As formed sound structures they make us look for some verbal meaning, but they have none. We might say that they are in an indefinite general sense raw material for word formation. They have a kind of objective basis in the essence or nature of language. Similarly, certain series of words which do not satisfy formal grammatical laws of sentence structure, and for this reason do not yield any intelligible meaning, must be designated as "nonsensical" or "senseless" (e.g., "he and either"). Nonsense gives evidence of the fact that meaningful structures are subject to stringent formal laws.

We speak of *absurdity* [*Widersinn*] where fulfilled and objectively determined but mutually incompatible or contradictory structures of meaning are conjoined (e.g., "triangular circle"). In this case thinking joins together certain meaningful parts to form a whole without a corresponding realizable meaning. Whereas in the case of a construct of meaning that is contrary to *sense* [*Wider*-Sinn] the essence-less nature of the apparent conceptual structure is evidenced by the impossibility of a realizable visualization [*erfüllende Anschauung*]. In the case of a contra*diction* [*Wider*-Spruch], the lack of an essence has its cause in a deficiency of the form. The statement, "This leaf is green and not green," is formally and objectively unrealizable. If we substitute for this statement, "A is b and not b," the essence-less nature of this contentless, formula immediately becomes evident.

All such attempts of the thinking mind to mold meaningful structures with complete arbitrariness illustrate the difference between conceptual being and essential being. Genuine conceptual being (i.e., the being of meaningful conceptual structures) rests on the essential being of pure, meaningful structures. Genuine conceptual being differs from essential being because the being of meaningful conceptual structures is fashioned by the intellect after the model of pure, meaningful structures, and it is the intellect which sustains and maintains their being. And whenever the intellect detaches itself from the laws of pure, meaningful structures and tries to proceed "independently," it produces merely apparent structures [*Scheingebilde*], and even this can be accomplished only with the aid of partial structures which are borrowed from the realm of genuine meaning.

It pertains to the peculiar freedom of thinking, on the one hand, and to the independent lawfulness of meaningful forms [*Sinnesformen*], on the other, that the intellect is capable of playing with empty forms and of erecting large edifices of empty conceptual structures. A realizable objective meaning for such constructs may possibly be found, provided no violence is done to formal laws. But the question of whether or not there exists a corresponding objective fulfillment of meaning cannot be decided on the authority of empty thinking, but only on the basis of objective observation and insight.[6]

Keeping in mind the preceding considerations, we may now attempt to determine the common constitutive element of meaning in all (finite) being. *Finite being is the unfolding of some meaning. Essential being is a timeless (or non-temporal) unfolding above and beyond the contraries of potency and act. Real being is an unfolding that proceeds from an essential form, from potency toward act and within time and space. Conceptual being is an unfolding in more than one sense.* In their origin genuine conceptual structures are as temporal as that movement of thought [*Denkbewegung*] to which they owe their formation. However, "finished" structures possess some of the timelessness of those existents in the image of which they have been formed and in which they were "potentially" and timelessly pre-designed. On the other hand, there is in every conceptual structure a basic potentiality of a new movement of thought by means of which the conceptual structure is reproduced [*nacherzeugt*] so as to attain to a new kind of being (to become an *actu intelligible*) in some knowing intellect. Being is a mere being-thought [*Gedacht-sein*] in the case of those conceptual structures which have no correlative realizable objective meaning. This mere being-thought (*ens rationis*) is a mere apparent being [*Schein-Sein*] which simulates authentic being.

§2. Transcendental Determinations and the Full Meaning of Being

The question must now be asked whether what we have found to be the common constitutive element of meaning in all authentic being—namely, being as an *unfolding [Enfaltung*], which is only a different name, but not an explanation nor a logical reduction—exhausts the meaning of being and whether what is described therewith is a *full meaning* or merely the form of a fullness which is filled in different ways by the several modes of being. We shall be able to answer the first question when we recall what we have established with respect to the meaning of all being in our discussion of the different transcendental determinations.

Being, as the unfolding of a *quid*, denotes not only the effluence and confluence of the contents of this quid, but simultaneously the *quid's* being manifest (or becoming manifest [*Offenbarwerden*]) or its being intelligible for some knowing mind. (All being as such is *true* being.) Furthermore, being, as the unfolding of a *quid*, means that being occupies its apportioned place within the totality of all existents and thereby contributes to the perfection of this totality. (All being as such is *good* being.) Finally, it means that being is ordered according to a definite structural law and is thereby in accord with an ordering mind whose knowing is correspondingly or proportionately ordered. (All being as such is *beautiful* and *rational* [*vernünftig*] being.)

Moreover, when we speak of confluence or junction [*Ineinander*] and of the ordered parts of a whole, this implies that to being pertains oneness or *being one* [*Einssein*]. Where we have a simple *quid*, the meaning of effluence and confluence and of the order of the *parts* within the *whole* is restricted to the contraries of *form* and *fullness*, as it is intimated in the basic structure of existents: *something which is* (*etwas, was ist; aliquid, quod est*). Oneness or unity has its place in the something and in being, the two component elements of fullness.

Oneness, truth, goodness, and beauty are constitutive elements of being as such. And it also pertains to being as such to be the being of something—of a filled or fulfilled something. Since transcendental determinations unfold existents *as such*, they must needs simultaneously unfold being. However, the *full meaning* of being is more than the sum total of transcendental determinations, because the existent which *is* does not signify the empty form of the existent, but the existent in the fullness of its *quid*. The empty form, too, *is*, but only insofar as it shares in the being of that whole in the building of whose structure it aids. Being is *one*, and all that which is shares in it. Its *full meaning* corresponds to the fullness of all existents. And when we speak of *being*, we *mean* this total fullness. No finite intellect, however, is ever capable of enclosing this fullness in the unity of a fulfilled apperception. To approximate the apperception of this fullness is the infinite task and goal of human knowledge.

When we say that being is *one,* we do not have in mind the oneness of a *universal.* It is not a question of a genus that is divided into species and is particularized in individuals. The statement of St. Thomas (*De veritate,* q. 1, art. 1) that the existent is not a genus applies to the existent *as such,* but for that very reason also to being. This leaves unanswered the question of in what sense we can then still speak of different *modes of being,* of *one* existent as distinct from another existent (i.e., of numerical oneness), and of a kind of being which pertains to each and every existent as *its very own.*

§3. The Unity of Being and the Multiplicity of Existents — The Particular Being [*Eigensein*] of the Individual Existent

Let us first consider the second question. We have conducted this whole inquiry with the tacit assumption which underlies our natural experience: that there is a multiplicity of objects. Only with this assumption does it make sense to ask, for example, whether "*the* existent" means "*any* existent" or "*all* existents." If there were no multiplicity, we could speak neither of "any" nor of "all." And everything we have said concerning those things which have their own particular being (and thus everything we have said concerning *ousia*) would be meaningless.

It is well known how much Greek thought was preoccupied with the difficulty of reconciling unity and multiplicity. The Eleatic thinkers sacrificed the evident experiential factuality of multiplicity in order to demonstrate in the most stringent manner the unity of true being. On the other hand, Aristotle has received special praise for having reestablished philosophic thought on the secure foundation of experience. And the medieval schoolmen followed Aristotle in this respect.

Our own inquiry does not aim at confronting *Thomistic* and *phenomenological* theories of knowledge with each other. To do this would require a special treatise of vast scope. We are merely concerned with stressing the conviction which both theories have in common and which is significant in our context. Both see in natural experience the starting point of every kind of thinking that goes beyond natural experience. Even though not all knowledge rests exclusively on experience and even though there is, rather, a valid basis of experience which can be known by pure reason, it nonetheless remains the aim of all thinking to arrive at an understanding of the world of experience. Thinking which does not lead to the establishment of the bases of experience but to the abrogation of experience (and we do not mean the abrogation of some particular experiential fact which, after all, may always turn out to be of an illusory nature, but the abrogation of the total world of experience) is without any real foundation and inspires no confidence.

We must therefore try to understand how the multiplicity and the unity of existents, i.e., the particular being of each individual existent and *the oneness* of being, can be found side by side. And in this attempt we may be guided by what we have said concerning the meaning of the good and the beautiful. If every existent has for other existents the meaning of "that which imparts perfection," and if each existent is formed according to a structural law that is integrally adapted to a universal, then all existents together form a coherently ordered *whole:* the *oneness* of *all that which is* [*das Seiende*]. And all self-enclosed (and in their self-enclosure comprehensible) meaningful units must then be regarded as parts of all that which is. The *oneness of being* is the being of this *whole,* a being of which all the *parts* "partake."

We must carefully consider what is meant here by the *whole* and by *parts.* What comes to mind first is perhaps *nature* understood as the world of sensory experience as well as those things which in their togetherness make up the structure of nature. But this turns our thought immediately to that interlacing [*Verflechtung*] of *nature* (in the sense in which modern, rather than medieval, philosophy uses this term) and *mind.* The world which is directly accessible to sensory perception is not equivalent to the real world as such. It is not a self-enclosed whole, but is efficaciously and therefore actually linked or interwoven with the intellectual world. As an intellectually comprehensible world, moreover, it is a world for the intellect and a world which—by virtue of an *intentional* relationship—is united *with* the intellect. The worlds of nature and mind, however, do not exhaust all *that which is* if by "world of the mind" [*Geisteswelt*] we mean only a world of finite minds and of structures created by finite minds. The totality of the created world refers back, as we have seen, to those eternal and non-become archetypes [*Urbilder*] of all created things (essences or pure forms) which we have designated as divine ideas. All real being (which comes to be *and* passes away) is anchored in the essential being of these divine ideas. And all the lawfulness and order that are found in the ever-changing created world rest on the immutability of divine ideas. The manifold of divine ideas, however, is united in that *one* infinite divine being which limits and articulates itself in archetypal forms in divine ideas. The ultimate ground of divine oneness encompasses the total plenitude of being.

We have previously pointed out that the actualization of an essentially possible *quid* can neither be comprehended from the aspect of essential being (which is the being of limited meaningful structure) nor from the aspect of real being (which is the being of a finite reality), but only from the aspect of a being which is from eternity both essential and real. And thus every finite, intermediate link must ultimately refer back to this beginningless and endless, primordial ground: the first being or πρώτη *ousia.*

§4. The First Being and the *Analogia Entis*

Previously we called the first being *pure being,* and we are now in a better position to understand the meaning of this designation. We called it "pure" because—in contradistinction to that which is temporally limited, which was at one time and will be no more at some other time, and in contradistinction to that which is *objectively* limited, which is something but not everything—there is no non-being in the first being. And because there is not found in the first being any passing from potentiality to actuality (and thus no contraries of potency and act), we called the first being *pure act.* However, all this—temporal and objective boundlessness as well as immutable perfection of being (expressed in the designation *pure act*)—points to that preeminence of the eternal and infinite which is so difficult to grasp because, in the eternal and infinite, being can no longer be separated or distinguished from existence. On the other hand. in all finite things being and existence differ.

Finally, the first being is called the *first existent* (*primum ens*). But *ens*—as is the case with all transcendental terms—is predicated only in an analogical sense, i.e., in the sense of that *analogia entis* which describes the peculiar relationship that exists between finite and eternal being and which permits us to apply the term *being* to both terms of the relationship on the basis of a common constitutive element of meaning [*gemeinsamer Sinnbestand*].

1. The Meaning of Analogia Entis *in Aristotle and St. Thomas Aquinas*

When Aristotle speaks of *analogia entis,* he does not yet refer to the relationship that exists between finite and eternal being but to the fact that all existents are interrelated. "There are many senses in which we speak of existents, but all of them refer to the *one* nature (which pertains to the existent as such)."[7] And a little further on Aristotle states that every existent is said to be with reference to a first (πρὸς μίαν ἀρχήν).[8] Commenting on this passage, St. Thomas remarks that this first is neither the end nor the efficient cause. (In the example which Aristotle gives, everything is called healthy that either leads toward health as an end or causes health as an effect.) Rather, it is the *subject* (which we have called the *carrier* of being). Both he and Aristotle are thinking of *ousia,* i.e., of the independent, actual existent which exists in a more primordial or authentic sense than its variable states or properties or than that which "is said to be because it is on the way toward substance, like the processes of becoming and movement."[9]

Here we encounter once more the different *modes of being,* the meaning of which has now become questionable for us and must therefore presently be reconsidered. If thingly being is being in a more primordial and authentic sense than the dependent being of states and properties, it nevertheless refers back to an even more primordial and authentic being, namely, that first being to which all things owe their origin. What makes it possible for us to apply the term *being* to God and creatures alike is a certain *analogy of relation* or *proportion* [*Verhältnisgleichheit*] (*analogia proportionalitatis*). And St. Thomas has explicitly stated how this kind of analogy is to be understood.

> A relational or proportional accord may be of two kinds.... It is either an accord of the objects among which there exists a mutual relationship, because they are proportioned to each other

either by a definite distance or by some other relation, such as the proportional relationship that exists between the numbers one and two, since two is the double of one. Occasionally we also meet with an accord of two objects among which there exists no direct relationship but rather a mutual similarity or analogy of two proportions, as, for example, in the case of the number six, which is in a certain accord with the number four, because four is the double of two as (in an analogical manner) six is the double of three.[10]

For the first kind of accord is required—as was pointed out—a certain mutual relationship between the terms of the proportion, whereas for the second kind no such relationship is required. In the second sense "we apply, for example, the term vision (*visus*) to both optical sight and intellectual insight (*intellectus*), because the insight is in the mind as (analogically) sight or seeing is in the eye." In the case of an accord of the first kind, it is impossible:

... to make any predications that apply both to God and creatures. For no creature is related to God in such a way that the divine perfection could be determined by this relation. But when we speak of analogy in the second sense, it denotes no definite relationship between those objects which have something in common by way of analogy. And nothing therefore prevents us from applying a term analogically to God and to a creature in this manner.[11]

The infinite distance between God and the creature is thereby not diminished. This would happen only if a definite relationship or proportionality were asserted. "For the analogy of proportionality is not any greater between two and one and six and three than it is between two and one and 100 and 50. And thus the second kind of analogy does not in any way abrogate the infinite distance between God and the creature."[12]

2. *Coincidence of Quid and Being in God*

In the sense of this proportional analogy, the following statement of Gredt must be understood:

God is related to his being in a manner similar to how the creature is related to its being. Created being is the act of created

> nature or essence and is that by virtue of which created nature or essence exists. And divine being is the act of divine nature or essence and is that by virtue of which divine nature or essence exists. For divine being is grasped by us in this manner *(concipitur enim a nobis ut quo)*, although divine being is in God identical with divine essence and is self-sustaining or self-subsisting being (*esse subsistens)*.[13]

The last part of this sentence is of special significance in our context. For we may well ask whether it makes any sense to speak of an *act* of the divine essence or of a *relationship* between essence and being *(essentia*[14] and *esse)* if essence and being fully coincide. Is there still any basis for a relationship and thus for a proportional analogy?

It is necessary to keep firmly in mind that both *essence* and *being* have a different meaning in God than in creatures. And thus *relationship,* too, must needs differ in meaning. It is impossible for us to gain a full or fulfilled intuition [*Anschauung*] of self-subsisting being or of a being that has its ultimate ground in itself, that is not the being of something distinguishable from itself. If such an intuition were possible, it would mean that we could "see" God. We must conclude, therefore, that everything finite—in both its *quid* and its being—must be preformed or prefigured [*vorgebildet*] in God, because both the *quid* and the being of finite things derive from him. The ultimate cause, however, of all being and all whatness must be both being and whatness, and both in perfect unity.

St. Thomas lists three reasons for this:

> First, everything that is found in a thing in addition to its essence must derive either from the principles of the essence ... or from some external cause. ... If, then, the being of a thing differs from the thing's essence, its being must either have some external cause or it must have its cause in the principles of the thing's essence. However, it is impossible to derive the being of a thing exclusively from the principles of the thing's essence, since no thing that has a cause of its being suffices to itself to the extent that it could be the cause of its own being. Therefore, whenever we find a difference between being and essence, the existent must have its cause in another (*esse causatum ab alio*). This statement, however, does not apply to God, since God is known to be the first efficient cause. It is thus impossible that God's being differs from his essence.[15]

This argument evidently contrasts divine being with the *existence* [*Dasein*] *of real things*, i.e., with an existence that has a beginning and actualizes some potentiality. The passing from potentiality to actuality is not to be understood from the aspect of the potential but rather (and indeed exclusively) from the aspect of actuality. God, the ultimate actuality from which everything actual derives, cannot be caused by another. There is therefore in God no longer any contrast of potentiality and actuality, and his *Dasein* is without a beginning.[16]

However, might it not be necessary to differentiate conceptually between God's essence and God's existence, although in reality they are inseparable? Might not the divine essence actually be from eternity and yet differ in meaning from divine being? We find the answer to these questions in the third argument of St. Thomas:

> Just as that which is on fire (*habet ignem*) is not fire but is fiery by participation, so that which has being (*habet esse*) and is not being (*non est esse*) is being (*ens*) by participation. However, God—as has been shown (art. 3)—is his essence. For if he were not his essence, he would be an *ens* by participation and not by his essence. In this case he would not be the first existent, and to assert this is an absurdity. Therefore, God is not only his being but also his essence.[17]

St. Thomas says in effect that God is his being because he is his essence. The proof is contained in the preceding article of the *Summa Theologiae* (1, q. 3, art. 3), where St. Thomas states that God is pure form, which as such has no material carrier. In the case of things which are formed matter, something always accrues to what they are in their essence. Thus, in the case of this particular person, something which is exclusively the person's own and does not pertain to being human as such, accrues to this being human—the person's particular physical determinateness, the particular size, shape, complexion, etc.

> In the case of things which are not composed of form and matter, on the other hand—where individuation does not rest on unique individualized matter (*individuatio non est par materiam individualem*) but where the forms as such individualize themselves

> in a unique manner (*ipsae formae per se individuantur*)—the forms themselves have a self-supporting subsistence (*supposita subsistentia*). There is therefore in the forms no difference between the nature and its carrier (*suppositum*). And since God—as has been shown (art. 2)—is not composed of form and matter, he is of necessity his Godhead (*deitas*), his life, and everything else that is predicated of him in like manner.

These arguments of St. Thomas are encumbered with a number of difficult questions, and—as any student of Thomism will have gathered from our previous discussions—we cannot accept the proposed Thomistic answers. In the first place, we might mention the doctrine concerning the *principle of individuation*, the consideration of which we have so far evaded. Even at this point a thorough study of this problem would disrupt the context of our argument, and such a study must therefore be relegated to a special inquiry.[18] We shall at this time confine ourselves to what must necessarily be said if we are to clarify the mutual relationship of essence and being. The question whether in the case of human being that which pertains to a person as an individual can be causally derived from bodily material may be omitted for the time being, since this question (in our present context) relates merely to one particular example and not to the problem as such. On the other hand, the questions whether matter is to be regarded as the *carrier* of the *nature* or essence and whether, in the case of a non-material existent, carrier and nature coincide, are of immediate relevance. And of equal immediate relevance are the questions whether in the case of *pure forms*[19] being pertains of necessity to the essence and whether it is permissible to consider God as one of these pure forms.

The last two questions are clearly interrelated. In a number of passages St. Thomas has endeavored to demonstrate that only in God do essence and being (*esse,* i.e., existence) coincide and that even in created pure forms the *esse* accrues to the *essentia,* even though these pure forms are not composed of matter and form. We encountered this view in the early opusculum *De ente et essentia,*[20] and St. Thomas adheres to it in the *Summa Theologiae:*

> Though there is in the angel no composition of matter and form, there is nevertheless act and potency (actual and potential being).

This can clearly be seen from the consideration of material things in which we find a twofold composition: first, that composition of form and matter which characterizes the structure of anything in nature. But a nature thus composed is not its own being (*non est suum esse*), but its being is the act (or actualization) of the nature. Therefore, nature is related to its being as potency is related to act. If matter, their, is taken away, and if the form no longer has any matter as a foundation of its being (*subsistat non in materia*), there still remains the relationship of the form to being as such (*ipsum esse*), a relationship which corresponds to that of potency to act. And in this way must be understood the compostion which is attributed to angels. Some writers therefore state that the angel is composed of that *by virtue of which it is* (*quo est*), and of that *which it is* (*quod est*) or, according to Boethius, of *being* (*esse*) and of that *which it is* (*quod est*). For *what it is* is the form subsisting in itself (*forma subsistens*). However, *being* as such is that by virtue of which independent existence (*substantia*) is, just as running (*cursus*) is that by virtue of which the runner runs (*quo currens currit*). However, in God *being* (*esse*) does not differ from *what he is* (*quod est*), as we stated above (q. 3, art. 4). And therefore only God is pure act.[21]

If the different arguments referred to are to be reconciled without any inner contradiction, we evidently must understand the forms which "subsist in themselves" or "carry themselves" not forthwith as *actual* existents—in the sense in which God actually exists—but they are existents nevertheless. They are "self-dependent" inasmuch as they are self-enclosed units of being [*Sinneinheiten*], and what we have called essential being pertains to them irrevocably. And what they are they have not received from something else ("by participation"), but they own their *quid* by virtue of their very constitution [*als ihren eigensten Bestand*].

If by "pure forms" we mean essences, then there are other things which partake of them and which are what they are by virtue of such participation (as, for example, everything that is red partakes of redness). These pure forms themselves attain to a *share in existence* [*Anteil am Dasein*] by their actualization, and this sharing in existence does not pertain to them essentially. In the case of the angels, on the other hand, we have a different situation, because they are in no way "universals," but individuals. Nothing that is separated from them has any share in them, and they do not attain *Dasein* in another existent. Nevertheless, angels too "step into *Dasein*" and "attain to a participation in *Dasein.*" And God is distinct from pure forms precisely because being pertains to him in the same way in which the *quid* pertains to pure forms. This is the meaning of the *analogia entis* understood as *proportional analogy* [*Verhältnisgleichheit*]. There is no longer any kind of being outside or apart from God in which he could possibly gain some share.

Does this mean, however, that there is no distinction whatever between God's being (i.e., existence) and God's essence? Are his being and essence identical in meaning? St. Thomas uses such phrases as "God is his goodness, his life," etc., or "God is his being." These predications endeavor to pronounce in the form of a judgment something which actually can no longer be pronounced in the form of a judgment. For every judgment requires an analytical articulation [*Zergliederung*], but that which is perfectly and absolutely simple does not permit of any analytical articulation. At best we might perhaps legitimately say, "God is — God," and we might take such a statement as an admission of the impossibility of defining the divine essence by anything other than God himself. In other words, the name of God denotes essence and being (i.e., existence) in undivided unity.

3. The Name of God: "I Am"

I shall now attempt to approach the ultimate ontological questions from an entirely different point of view, namely by taking as my frame of reference that name by which God has designated himself: "I am who I am."[22] It seems to me highly significant that in the Scriptural text we do not read, "I am *being* [*das Sein*]," or "I am *he who exists* [*der Seiende*]," but "I am who *I am.*" One hardly dares interpret these words by using other ones. However, if the Augustinian interpretation is correct, we may conclude that he whose name is "I am" is *being in person.*

That the so-called *first existent* must be a person appears evident from much that we have previously stated. Only a person can *create,* i.e., call into being by virtue of his will. And the efficacy of the first cause can be conceived only as a *free act,* because any efficacious activity that is not a free act has a cause and is therefore not the *first efficacious activity.* Furthermore, the rational order and the purposiveness of the universe point to a person as their author. Only a rational being can posit and sustain a *rational order;* and only a knowing and willing being can posit ends and ordain certain means to these ends. Reason and freedom, however, are the essential marks of personality.

The name by which every person designates himself or herself *qua* person is the name "I" [*Ich*].[23] Only an existent who in its being is conscious of its being and simultaneously conscious of its differentiation from every other existent can call itself an "I." And of every I there is only one [*Jedes Ich ist ein Einmaliges*]. It possesses something which it shares with no other existent, i.e., something that is *incommunicable.*[24] This does not mean, however, that every I is *unique* [*einzigartig*] in the sense that it does not share its *quid* (what it is) with any other existent. For, after all, the name "I" has a universal meaning which is fulfilled wherever and whenever it is duly applied. The question of whether there pertains to every person in addition a *particularity* [*Eigenart*] which this person shares with no other person need not be considered here. At any rate, such a meaning is not implied in the name "I."

The incommunicability which pertains to every I as such is a *peculiar characteristic of being* [*Eigentümlichkeit des Seins*]. From every I emanates its own being, which we call *life.* It streams forth from moment to moment forming a *self-enclosed* [*in sich geschlossen*] existent, and every I *subsists for itself* [*ist für sich selbst da*] and subsists in no like manner for any other existent, nor does any other existent subsist for the I in any like manner.[25]

Every human being is "an I." Every human being sooner or later refers to itself as an "I." This means that, for every human being, "being I" has a beginning. It may happen that a human being pronounces the *word* "I" before it is able to realize its meaning. It is also possible that the human being understands the meaning of the word (simply as a form of "conscious life," without its being as yet able to form the *concept* "I"), before the being begins to make use of it verbally.

There are minor discrepancies between the intellectual life and its natural verbal expression, caused by the peculiarities of language as a physically conditioned means of expression as well as by the fact that speech has to be acquired by a process of learning.

Such discrepancies do not, however, void the significance of language as an essential means of expression, so that the use of the word "I" in the sense described is a sign of the awakened life of the ego. The life of the I is the ego's being, but this being does not coincide with the being of man [*Sein des Menschen*], and the beginning of the awakened ego life is not equivalent to the beginning of human existence.

The peculiar being of the ego was discussed previously.[26] We pointed out that the ego enjoys a twofold ontological prerogative with respect to those contents which fill its life: 1) The ego life is actual or actually present at every moment, whereas each of its contents has only one moment in which the height of actuality is made present; and 2) The ego life is the *carrier* of experiential contents, and the latter receive their being alive from the life of the ego and are unified by it and in it.

But despite these prerogatives, the being of the I is deficient and by itself null and void [*nichtig*]. It is empty unless it is filled with content, and it receives this content from those realms—the "external" and the "internal" world—which lie "beyond" its own sphere. Its life comes out of one darkness and moves into another darkness. There are lacunae in it which cannot be filled, and it is sustained only from moment to moment. And thus we see that while the being of the I is separated from divine being by an infinite distance, it nevertheless—owing to the fact that it is an I, i.e., a person—bears

a closer resemblance to divine being than anything else that lies within the reach of our experience. If we remove from this being of the I everything that is non-being, this will make it possible for us to conceive—albeit only analogically—of divine being.

In God there is not—as there is in the human being [*Mensch*]—a contrast between ego life and being. God's "I am" is an eternally living presence, without beginning and without end, without any voids and without any darkness. This divine ego life has all its plenitude in itself and from itself. It receives nothing from anywhere else, for it is that from which everything else receives everything. It is that unconditioned reality which conditions everything else. In this divine I there are no changing contents, there is nothing that emerges and dies away. There is no passing from potentiality to actuality or from a lower to a higher actuality. This consummate plenitude is eternally present because it is all that which is [*alles Seiende*].

The "I am" means: I live, I know, I will, I love—and all this not in the manner of a successive or coordinated series of temporal *acts,* but in the perfect unity of the eternally *one* divine *act* in which all the diverse significations of *act*—actual being, living presence, perfect being, intellectual striving, free activity—absolutely coincide. The divine I is no empty ego, but an I which harbors, encompasses, and, in sovereign self-possession, masters all plenitude.

This perfect unity may be expressed even more clearly in a language which encloses the meaning of the "I am" in one single word, as in the Latin *sum.* In the case of that I whose very being is life we can best understand that *I* and *life* (or *being*) are not two different things but inseparably one. They are the *personally formed plenitude of being.*

Form—in contradistinction to *fullness*—has the meaning of empty form, not of essential form (which is an already "formed fullness"). In this particular case, however, i.e., at the very origin of all being, there is not even any longer a contrast between form and fullness. That which is infinite and all-encompassing encompasses and encloses itself, whereas in finite things the form is an enclosure of a content which as such is distinct from the contents of other things. The *I* in this case *simultaneously* includes *form* and *fullness.* It is being in perfect self-possession and sovereign self-mastery.

The plenitude of the I also makes it understandable that in this kind of fullness *quid* and *being* coincide (and it is this problem which we found most difficult to understand). In this plenitude every *quid* is included, for this plenitude encompasses *all that which is,* and in it everything finite has its origin. Its fullness is, moreover, *the plenitude of being in every sense of the term.* The plenitude of the I is *essential being* (which as we have seen, pertains inseparably to the *quid*), and it is *actual being,* because the ego life is the height of actuality. And essential and actual being are one in this plenitude, because the divine I is an actual and living essence [*Wesen*]. But this fullness of the I is simultaneously *intellectual* being, because it encompasses itself intellectually. It is transparently intelligible [*durchsichtig*] to itself. It is fully actualized [*vollwirklich*] being, in which no potentiality remains unfulfilled. And yet there is prefigured in it also the contrast between actual and potential being, because it is God who is the author of the entire realm of becoming and passing away and who has established the order of all that which passes from potential to actual being.

At this point we find ourselves once more face to face with the great mystery of creation, i.e., with the fact that God has called forth a kind of being that differs from his own, a multiplicity of existents, in which everything that is one in God is particularized. But before we turn again to a consideration of this enigma we propose to ask once more the difficult and as yet unanswered question whether God's being is his essence or—to phrase it differently—whether in God essence and being do not only necessarily belong together but are actually identical in meaning?

As long as we understand essence (or the *quid,* if we are to maintain our previous distinction between *quid* and essence or whatness [*Wassein*]) and being in the sense in which we encounter them in everything finite, a difference in meaning will always remain. We may be convinced that *actual being* pertains to God's essence just as necessarily as essential being pertains to limited essences, but this does not mean that essence can be reduced to being or vice versa. It seems to me that such a reduction is altogether impossible, and I see the only solution of this difficulty in the assumption that in the "I am" of God both essence and being are contained without any separation [*ungeschieden*]. The separation of form and fullness as well as the separation of *quid* and being, and subsequently the division of the *quid* into separate genera and species of existents, and of being into its different modes, do not occur until we arrive at the created universe, i.e., at the totality of all existents. This means that God is not only above and beyond all the categories but even above and beyond all the transcendentals. And we remember in fact that in our discussion of each of the transcendental determinations we had to leave in abeyance the unsolved problem of being. Each transcendental determination had one meaning when we applied it to God and a different one when we applied it to finite existents. In the "I am," however, all transcendental determinations are prefigured [*vorgebildet*] without any division or separation.

4. The "Division" ["Teilung"] *of Being in the Created Universe*

The relationship between the divine "I am" and the multiplicity of finite existents is the primordial *analogia entis.* All finite being shares in a common meaning because it has its archetypal image [*Urbild*] in the divine "I am." But because being is divided in the created universe, it has not strictly the same meaning in all existents, but a different constitutive element of meaning [*Sinnesbestand*] in addition to the common one. Now it is our endeavor to understand precisely this division of being as well as the meaning of finite being and the manner in which the latter partakes of the oneness of being—as far as one may hope to understand a divine mystery.

The division should not be understood as a partitive distribution, as if the one divine being were to partition itself quantitatively—in the sense of spatial or temporal extension—in separate constitutive parts into particularized finite being. This would amount to a dissolution of the creator in creatures and to a negation of the creator—as happens in pantheism. For *analogia*, understood as a relationship between archetype [*Urbild*] and copy [*Abbild*], a contrast between eternal and finite being is an absolute requisite. And the meaning of creation, understood as a calling-into-existence, makes it mandatory that the being which begins to exist did at one time not exist. However, this requisite seems to dispense with the unity of being. For if God calls into existence something which is not he himself, something which has an "independent" or "self-dependent" being, then some kind of being, other than the divine being, must evidently exist. But if this is the case, can we then still insist that all being is *one* and that finite being partakes of this one?

It seems that this latter assertion is still correct in the sense that nothing exists that is not called forth by God, that is not prefigured in him, and that is not sustained by him in being. The independence of the created existent cannot even be compared with the independence which an image has with respect to the object represented, or with the independence which the work of art has with respect to the artist. A better comparison that might be adduced is the relationship that exists between a reflected image and the object that is reflected, or between a refracted ray of light and the unrefracted light. But even these are imperfect analogies with which we are trying to elucidate something which really allows of no comparison.

It is implicit in the very meaning of the created world that the creature can never be a perfect but only a "partial image" or a "broken ray." The eternal, uncreated, and infinite God cannot create anything that could be his equal, because there cannot be a second eternal, uncreated, and infinite being.

5. A Comparison between the Relationship of the Creator to His Creation and the Inner Relationship Which Exists among the Divine Persons

It seems to be in order to place at this point the relationship of the creator to his creation side by side with the relationship of the Father to the other Divine Persons. The *Athanasian* Creed calls the Son "generated, not created." The Son does not step into existence. He is "co-eternal with the Father." His nature is identical with that of the Father, and the same holds true of his being, since, as we have seen, being and nature (essence) coincide in God. The Son is not a partial but the total or "perfect image" of the Father. And we do well to remember that the term "image" is used here metaphorically. For even the reflected image—no matter how close it is in its being to the object which it reflects—differs as an existent from the object. Father and Son, on the other hand, are one: "*one* God and Lord."

We may best understand what is meant here by "image" if we remember that God is *spirit [Geist*]. He sees himself not in some other (different from himself)—as if he were to see himself in a painted image or in a mirror—but he sees himself in his own self. Our own self-knowledge—imperfect and far removed from divine self-knowledge as it is—offers a much better illustration. We see ourselves intellectually "as in an image" whenever we recognize our own human nature in other human beings. Friedrich Schiller's epigram, "If you want to know yourself, observe how others behave,"[27] stresses the significance of such figurative [*bildhaft*] seeing for self-knowledge. But it would not be possible for us to find the image of ourselves in others unless we knew about ourselves by virtue of a more primordial, non-figurative insight, namely, by that "self-consciousness" or immediate awareness of the self and of being which pertains to our self and our being. This kind of knowledge is not clear, distinct, and complete but rather a dark, indefinite, and unformed groping and probing [*Spüren*], but it is nevertheless the ground and the root of everything we know of ourselves and of others like ourselves in a natural manner.

God's self-knowledge, on the other hand, is perfectly clear and encompasses without any fault or impurity his entire infinite being. What our self-knowledge has in common with his is the element of *immediacy*. It is a knowledge that is not attained through any "means" or "medium"—as is the case with images—but this kind of self-knowledge pertains to intellectual or spiritual being as such. And this is why the generation of a "perfect likeness" [*Ebenbild*] of God does not mean the creation of a new being apart and aside from the divine being and of a second divine nature, but rather an internal, spiritual encompassing of the *one* divine being. The greatest difficulty which this involves for our thinking is to conceive of the being of this generated perfect likeness as of a second *Person*.[28] Does it not pertain to being a person as such, to the ego-life, to be aware of the "self"—i.e., of one's own I—and is not this essential character of being a person and simultaneously the unity of the divine being annulled if a second and third person are added?

We suggested earlier that a solution to this problem might be found if we assume that the trinity of persons pertains to the divine essence or nature as such (cf. p. 111 above). But how is this to be understood in view of all that has been said concerning divine being?

In the case of finite persons, we may understand their being persons as the form (i.e., the empty form) of their fullness. On the other hand, of God we have stated that in him form and fullness are just as unseparated [*ungeschieden*] as are *quid* and being, and as are all other things that we find separated in creatures. It is therefore evidently not possible to oppose the tri-personality [*Dreipersönlichkeit*] as form to the fullness of the one nature or essence. And what happens, if there are three persons, to the perfect unity of the "I am"? And yet it is precisely this last question which may point a way out of the difficulty.

Divine being-a-person is the archetype or paragon [*Urbild*] of all finite being-persons. The finite I, however, finds itself confronted with a Thou [*Du*], i.e., "another I" like unto itself, an existent to whom the person may turn, demanding understanding and response, an existent of whose life the I partakes in the unity of a "we" by virtue of an experienced common or communal ground of the being I.

This "we" is the form in which we experience the oneness (i.e., the being one) of a plurality of persons. And this oneness does not annul the multiplicity and diversity of persons. The diversity is not even a diversity of *being* in the sense in which we have learned to know being as pertaining to the nature of the I. The being-incorporated [*Eingegliedertsein*] into a higher unity does not annul the *monadic,* closed structure of the ego-life. But there is also a diversity of *nature* or *essence.* The community of species [*Artgemeinsamkeit*], which is the basis of the being-we [*Wirsein*], leaves room for a *personal individuality* which the we shares with no one and nothing else.

Now such a diversity of essence or nature is not found in the Divine Persons. God's "personal individuality" is all-encompassing being which, *as* all-encompassing, is unique and distinct from everything finite. Nor is there found any contrast of *universal* and *particular,* and of essential and actual being.

The Three Persons have their entire essence or nature in common, so that there remains only the diversity of the Persons as such. There is thus a perfect unity of the we, such as can never be attained by any community of finite persons. And there is yet within that unity a separateness of the I [*Ich*] and the Thou [*Du*] without which no we [*Wir*] is ever possible.

In addition to the revelation of the divine name "I am," there occurs in the Old Testament that saying of Genesis, "Let us make man according to our own image," (Gen 1:26) a phrase which our theologians traditionally interpret as a first intimation of the mystery of the Trinity. And there are furthermore the clear words of our Savior, "I and the Father are one" (John 10:30). The we, then, as a unity of I and thou, is a higher unity than that of the I. In its most authentic meaning, it is a unity of love.

Now love as a simple yea [*Jasagen*] in view of some good is possible also in the self-love of an I. But love is more than such a yea, more than a mere affirmation of value [*Wertschätzung*]. It is giving of the self to a thou, and in its perfection it is a being-one that is founded on mutual self-giving [*Selbsthingabe*]. And because God is love, divine being must be the beingone of a plurality of persons, and the divine name "I am" is thus equivalent to an "I give myself wholly to a Thou," an "I am one with a Thou," and therefore also with a "We are."

The love between God and creatures is different from that love which is the life-principle of the Divine Persons, which as such has no equal, because the love between God and creatures can never be love in its highest perfection (not even in that state of perfection which can be attained by the rational creature in the light of glory). The highest love is a mutual eternal love. While it is true that God loves his creatures from eternity, he is not loved by them from eternity. Thus, if divine love were dependent on creatures, it would be subject to change, it would lack perfect fulfillment, and God himself would be made to depend on his creatures. Thus the love between God and creatures always remains imperfect, because even though in the total self-giving of the life of glory God is capable of receiving into himself the creature, no creature—nor all creatures together—can ever comprehend or encompass God.

God's inner life is the perfectly free, immutable and eternal mutual love among the Divine Persons, independent of all created things and beings. And what the Divine Persons give to each other is one, eternal, and infinite nature and being, wholly encompassing each of them separately and all of them together. This nature and being the Father gives from eternity to the Son by generating him, and from this gift proceeds, as the fruit of mutual love, the Holy Spirit. The being of the second and third persons is thus a received being and yet—unlike created being—no newly originating being. Rather, it is the *one* divine being, simultaneously given and received, since the giving and receiving pertain to divine being as such.

Another access to the mystery of triune being may be sought in the following way. God's being is *life,* i.e., a movement from the inside out, and ultimately a generating being. The divine being is not—as is the case with finite, created things and beings—a movement into existence. Nor is it a movement transcending the individual self, as is the case in any finite generation, but it is an eternal movement within the self, an eternal self-drawing or self-creating [*Sichselbst-schöpfen*] out of the depth of God's own infinite being, an infinitely generous giving of the eternal I to an eternal Thou, and a correspondingly eternal and ever-renewed self-receiving and self-giving. And because the oneness which eternally springs from this giving and receiving brings forth once more in a *communal manner* [*gemeinsam*] that which has been given and received, the cycle of the intra-divine life completes and closes itself in the Third Person who is gift, love, and life.

6. *The Divine Word and Creation*

We have so far referred to the intra-divine life only for the sake of comparison in order to clarify the relationship between uncreated and created being. We shall have to discuss it, however, more extensively because it is, after all, essential for divine being to be tri-personal, and because as a consequence tri-personality must also be significant for the analogical image relationship [*Abbildverhältnis*] between eternal and finite being.[29] But we shall first attempt to elucidate the problem at hand—concerning the division of being—as much as is possible on the basis of what has been said.

The intra-divine processions [*Hervorgänge*] leave being undivided, but division is already prefigured in them. We previously spoke of the relationship between the divine world and the created world.[30] With regard to the divine word or *meaning* (*Logos*), i.e., divine self-knowledge personified, *Scripture* tells us that by the Logos all things were made and that in the Logos they subsist and cohere. We interpreted this coherence [*Zusammenhang*] as a meaningful interconnection [*Sinnzusammenhang*] of all existents in the Logos as a divine plan or design of the created world. And the subsistence or constitution [*Bestand*] we interpreted as a being-founded [*Begründetsein*] of created things and beings in creative archetypes [*Urbilder*] which have in the Logos a simultaneously essential and actual (and therefore efficacious) being. To resolve the difficulty as to how the unity and simplicity of the divine essence may be brought into accord with the multiplicity of *ideas,* we referred to the *Thomistic* interpretation, according to which the multiplicity of ideas has its foundation in the relationship of the one divine essence to the manifold of things and beings. Furthermore, we discovered that the being of the finite in the eternal carries a twofold meaning: 1) a being-encompassed of all finite things by the divine spirit; and 2) a causal being-founded on all finite things in the divine essence. However, we must keep in mind that "divine spirit" and "divine essence" are inseparable and that the "spiritual encompassing" of all actual and potential things by God simultaneously means their causal being-placed into an order of existents which is proportionate to them. But there nonetheless remains the contrast between the one and simple essence as causative actuality and the manifold of images or copies reflecting or mirroring this essence—both encompassed by God's all-embracing knowledge.

We have spoken of a "dual countenance" of the Logos, inasmuch as the Logos is simultaneously the known divine essence (the "image of the Father") and the archetype and cause of all created things. Since the plan of creation is—like everything else in God—eternal, the Logos and the created world belong together from eternity, notwithstanding the fact that the created world has a beginning in time and evolves in time. In generating the Son (or in "speaking out the word"), the Father hands over to the Son that created world which is providentially planned and pre-designed from eternity. And providentially pre-designed in the created world is also the multiplicity of all that which is as an organically ordered totality, as well as the being that pertains to every individual part as its very own and that yet coheres with all the rest.

7. The Distinction between Eternal and Temporal, Essential and Actual, Actual and Potential Being, and between Form and Content

To the "order" of the created world belongs *time*. It is that whereby the finite is in the strictest sense distinguished from the eternal. For though we have encountered a meaning of finitude which does not signify a beginning and ending in time, viz., the limitation of the diverse units of meaning with respect to their content, the demarcation of finitude from the unity *of divine* being must nonetheless be understood as a being-ordained toward temporal actualization. And herewith we have characterized and simultaneously tentatively outlined the contrast between *essential* and *actual being* and between *actual* and *potential* being in a dual sense: potentiality understood as a being-founded of temporal actual being upon the essential being of limited units of meaning (essential potentiality); and potentiality understood as a preliminary stage in view of some higher actuality (potentiality versus actuality) or as an inferior mode of temporal being.

Temporal actual being is not a perfectly fulfilled actuality (i.e., not pure act), but a *beginning and progressive actualization* of essential potentialities. To this kind of being there pertains the contrast between *independent* and *dependent being.* The beginning of actualization marks a transition from essential potentiality to temporal actuality or an entering into temporal existence. To progressive actualization there pertains a kind of existent that bears within itself non-actualized potentialities. Something that, though it is not yet what it is destined to be, is nonetheless already predetermined as to what it is destined to be and therefore follows a predesigned evolutionary path [*Werdegang*]. The temporal actual is standing upon or *placed upon its own self* [*auf sich selbst Gestellt*] and is *determined in its essence or nature* (*ousia* = substance). Its as yet non-actualized potencies have their foundation in the temporal actual itself. Their being shares in its being, and their actualization is its actualization and therewith its own passing over to a higher stage of being.

To *finite being*—understood as a being-objectively-limited—there pertains the distinction between *form* and *content.* The empty form marks the objective contour or limiting outline by which the finite thing or being sets itself off externally from other finite things or beings and by which it is internally integrated and ordered as a whole composed of objectively distinct and divergent structural parts. The empty form of the independent existent is that of the *object* (in the narrower sense of the term) or of the *carrier* of the *quid* and of being (*hypostasis* = *subsistens*).

VII.

The Image of the Trinity in the Created World[1]

§1. Person and Hypostasis

The search for the meaning of being has led us to that being who is the author and archetype of all finite being. This being has disclosed himself to us as being a person and even as a tri-personal being. But if the creator is the archetype of the created world, must we not of necessity find in the created world an image—be it ever so remote—of the tri-unity of the primordial being? And should it therefore not be possible to gain a deeper understanding of finite being on the basis of this image relationship?

It can be demonstrated historically that the endeavor to grasp conceptually the revealed doctrine of the Most Holy Trinity has led to the formation of the philosophic concepts of *hypostasis* and *person.* These concepts were essential not only for an understanding of the tri-personality of God but also for an understanding of the being of people and generally of thingly actuality. And this consideration may now aid us in our attempt to make the content of revelation fruitful for a deeper knowledge of finite being.

St. Augustine's 15 books *De Trinitate*[2] may well be called the foundation of all subsequent trinitarian theology. He endeavored in this work, first of all, to elaborate clearly the contents of revealed truth and then to prepare ways for human reason to arrive at an understanding of these contents. The doctrine of faith stresses the unity of *substance* (i.e., of essence or nature) in all three Persons. By virtue of this unity they are not only completely equal, but one. What distinguishes them is *relations.* The Father *generates* the Son, and both Father and son *breathe* or *spirate* the Holy Spirit. A further distinction relates to the temporal manifestation of the Second and Third Persons. Only the Son is born of a virgin, is crucified, dies and is buried, and only the Holy Spirit appears in the form of a dove or in fiery tongues.[3] These manifestations are not equivalent to the Persons themselves, and the distinctions among them should therefore not be regarded as distinctions among the Persons as such. They are rather *signs* which point toward the distinctions among the Persons.[4] The assumption of human nature into the unity of the Person of Christ in particular presupposes distinctions among the divine Persons. However, it is so very difficult for us to grasp the distinctions among the Persons as such that we may safety say that they are incomprehensible to us.

In considering the distinction in the *relations* of the Persons among themselves, we must keep in mind that in this case *relation* does not mean what it does for finite things. St. Augustine tries to explain this by demonstrating that the relations here denote neither substance nor accident.[5] They are not substantial because everything that is predicated of God substantially (i.e., as pertaining to his essence or nature)—and this includes everything except the relations—applies to all three Persons together as well as to each of them separately (irrespective of the others). And this can certainly not be said of the names of the divine Persons.[6] On the other hand, the relations cannot be accidental because—unlike all finite beings—they are not mutable, and mutability pertains to all accidents.

In the case of the divine Persons, it thus becomes necessary to distinguish between substance (which is here equivalent to *ousia* = *essentia)* and hypostasis (the carrier of substance).[7] To the unity of substance there corresponds the trinity of carriers. Calling the carriers *persons* is merely a human mode of speaking to express something ineffable.[8] Everything else that we call *person*—human beings and angels—is *rationalis naturae individua substantia* (an individual endowed with a rational nature)[9] in the sense that it contains in its *quid* something "incommunicable," something which it shares with no one and nothing else. In the case of the Trinity, however, we have three Persons who have their entire *quid* in common, three Persons none of whom is possible without the others.[10] And yet these three Persons are not more than one Person. The infinite perfection which each of them possesses separately allows of no increase.[11]

To the question of whether the name *person* is nonetheless applicable to God, St. Thomas answers:

> *Person* signifies what is the most perfect in all nature, namely, that which "stands in and upon itself" and is endowed with a rational nature (*subsistens in rationali natura*). Now, since everything

> perfect must be ascribed to God (because his essence contains in itself every perfection), it is fitting to apply to him the name *person,* not in the same sense in which this name is applied to creatures, but in a preeminent sense.[12]

We pointed out before[13] that the term is used here *analogically.* And this analogical meaning extends, according to St. Thomas, also to that original signification of the word *persona* which denotes the different character parts in a play or, more precisely, the masks through which the sound of the actors' words are heard (*personare*).

To be sure, the name *person* thus understood applies to God in view of what it expresses rather than in view of its derivation.

> For since in comedies and tragedies characters of repute are depicted, the name *person* came to be applied to designate certain dignitaries (*aliquos dignitatem habentes*). ... This is why some define "person" by saying, "The person is a hypostasis to which pertains the distinguishing quality of dignity (*proprietate distincta ad dignitatem pertinente*). And because it is a high dignity to be the bearer of a rational nature, every individual endowed with a rational nature is called a person. The dignity of the divine nature, however, surpasses every other dignity, and this why the name *person* applies to God in the most eminent sense."[14]

St. Thomas applies to God also the name *hypostasis,* without equating it to *person.* This distinction is important for our inquiry. The concept of hypostasis is determined by its relation to the concept of *substance.* The interpretation of substance = *essentia* (as it is found even in St. Thomas's own opusculum *De ente et essentia*) is thereby eliminated in favor of the version *subiectum vel suppositum quod subsistit in genere substantiae* (an object which, subsisting in itself, pertains to the genus of substance).

> Three terms are used to designate so-called substance, namely, *thing, subsistance,* and *hypostasis* (*res naturae, subsistentia, hypostasis*). They express three different points of view with respect to the object. Insofar as the object exists in itself and not in another, it is called *subsistentia,*[15] for we call subsisting what exists not in another but in itself. However, insofar as the object is the carrier (*supponitur*) of some universal nature, we call it *res naturae* (*thing*).

> Thus, for example, this particular person is a *res naturae* to which there pertains a human nature. As the carrier of accidental properties, finally, the object is called *hypostasis* or *substance.* However, what these three terms signify in common (*communiter*) within the entire genus of substances, the term "person" signifies in the genus of rational substances.[16]

Here *person* denotes the narrower concept, and rationality [*Vernunftbegabung*] denotes the *differentia specifica.*[17] If we were to adhere strictly to the fixed differences in meaning of the terms *res, subsistentia,* and *hypostasis,* we could not call the divine Persons *hypostases,* since they are not carriers of accidents.[18] However, it has become customary to understand *hypostasis* in the sense of *subsistentia,* and in this sense the term also applies to the divine Persons. But we do well to observe how *subsistere* must then be understood. St. Thomas describes *subsistens* as that which exists in itself and not in another. If we interpret this as a complete "standing in itself" [*Selbständigkeit*], it would not correspond to the way the divine Persons differ among themselves and are distinct from the divine essence. For we know that none of them can be without the others and apart from that divine essence which is common to all of them.

We have previously substituted the word *carrier* for the term *hypostasis.* But the word carrier (*suppositum*) we have already used in two significations, neither of which coincides with the meaning requisite in our present context. We call the thing (*res*) the carrier of a universal nature and the carrier of its own accidental properties. None of these meanings applies to the divine Persons, where there can be no question of accidental properties distinguishable from the essence. And the divine essence is not a *universal nature* which *individuates* itself in the three Persons, but an essence that is unique [*Einziges*] and singular [*Einmaliges*] which is common to all three Persons. That which is "carried" is the one and indivisible divine essence, and it is the Persons who carry this essence.

This concept of the carrier of the essence [*Wesensträger*], it seems to me, is highly significant for the structure of all existents. In our search for an understanding of the mystery of the Most Holy Trinity, this concept had to be brought out in clear relief. In distinguishing the divine Persons from one another, there can be no question—as in the case of corporeal things—of heterogeneous matter *carrying* a universal essential form. Nor can there be a question of distinguishing—as in the case of created pure spirits—between the contents of different forms as *carriers* of diverse properties. The spirituality, unity, and simplicity of the divine essence allows only of a carrier that is completely without matter and without content—a carrier which is nothing but the empty form of the plenitude of the essence. And this empty form we have encountered in totally different contexts. Thus, the *pure ego* appeared to us as the carrier of experiential fullness. The (finite) person appeared to us as a carrier of its individuality. The thingly form appeared to us a carrier of the fullness of its contents. And in the most universal concept of the existent as such the "object" or the "something" appeared to us as the carrier of the *quid* and of being.

It would seem that now we have at last arrived at the archetype of these different carrying forms [*Trägerformen*], so that we are in a position to understand them in relation to their archetype as well as in relation to each other. But once again we find ourselves confronted with the fact that archetype and image are separated by an infinite distance. And yet this distance and the incomprehensibility of the archetype cannot shake the certainty that the meaning of the image is determined by the archetype. Although the contrast between the one essence and the three Persons entails the separateness [*Ablösung*] of the empty form, there is no doubt that in this case form and fullness are inseparably one.

There are other instances where form and fullness depend on each other. Every existent is a filled form or a formed fullness. But the individual form is not unalterably joined with its variable fullness. There are changes indicative of partial transformations in the constitution of contents, and there are—as an outer limit—changes of the essence [*Wesenswandel*] in which the carrier remains the same while assuming a different essence. However, in God there is neither change nor transformation. In him form and fullness are inseparably one. No other fullness is conceivable that could be fitted into this form, and no other form is conceivable that could encompass this fullness.

§2. Person and Spirit [*Geist*]

Our search for the meaning of being has led us to the first being: the *Being-in-Person,* indeed, the Being-in-three-Persons. Our attempt to clarify the meaning of *person* has been undertaken in order to gain an understanding of the Being-in-Person (and the Being-in-three-Persons)—as far as we may hope to understand this mystery—and in order to gain, on the basis of the first being, new insight into finite being. However, the being-person as such, and therewith the first being as such, will remain completely veiled in darkness unless we succeed in illuminating the *nature of spirit* more than we have done so far.

We designated divine being as spiritual being. And when we called the person a carrier of a *rational* nature, we evidently also claimed for it a spiritual nature, for *spirit* and *reason* seem to be inseparably linked. However, what is the meaning of *spirit?*

We have previously made several attempts to gain access to the meaning of spirit.[19] We characterized the spiritual (or intellectual) as the nonspatial and non-material, as that which possesses an "interiority" [*Inneres*] in an entirely non-spatial sense, and which remains "within itself" while going out of itself. This going-out-of-itself pertains to the spiritual essentially. It is indicative of its being completely "selfless, "not indeed in the sense of having no self but rather in the sense of a total self-surrender without any loss of self, a self-giving in which the spiritual reveals itself completely—in contrast to the soul and its sphere, which remain in concealment.

The spirit in its purest and most perfect actualization is found in the total self-giving of the divine Persons, a self-giving in which each person totally divests itself of its nature [*Wesen*] and yet totally retains its nature, in which each person is totally within itself and totally in the others. The triune Deity *is* the authentic "realm of the spirit" and is thus the "supernatural" as such. And all the spirituality or spiritual endowment of creatures denotes an elevation or a "being-lifted-up" into this realm, albeit in varying modes and degrees.

But even all the other basic forms of being have their primordial archetype [*Urbild*] in this realm of the spirit, and it can hardly be otherwise if the realm of the spirit coincides with the first being and if *all* being has a "share" [*Anteil*] in the first being, is predesigned in it and derives from it. When we speak of "bodily" [*leiblich*] being wherever an existent owns its nature in a "born-out" [*ausgeboren*] form, we must conclude that God has a proper body [(not a material body, of course, but a spiritual body [*Geistleib*]). For he owns the total plenitude of his nature in a fully actualized, manifest, luminous form—a form which, though infinite, is enclosed with and by his own self, because he holds himself completely in the possession of his own self. There is in him nothing "pre-actual" [*vorwirklich*] that awaits formation. And yet that which pertains to the realm of the soul—the soul understood as a "creative principle" or a "source of life"—also has in God its primordial archetype, because the divine life from eternity draws creatively from the source of its own self and wells up from its own depth.[20] If the divine life were rigid and unmoved, it would not be *life,* and it is not only life but *the* life, and all earthly life is nothing but its remote image.

Might we thus not see a most intimate connection between the unity that prevails among the three basic forms of real being and the triune Deity? To the Father—the primordial creator—from whom everything derives its existence but who himself exists only by and through his own self, would then correspond the being of the soul, while to the Son—the "born-out" essential form—would correspond all bodily being. And the free and selfless streaming forth (of the Holy Spirit) would have its counterpart in the activity of the spirit, which merits the name *spirit* [*Geist*] in a special sense. We might then see a triune unfolding of being in the entire realm of reality.

But how are spirituality and personality interrelated? We have described the person as the carrier of essence or nature and, more precisely, as the carrier of a *rational* nature. By virtue of its rationality, the person is distinguished from the hypostasis which is the carrier of essence or nature in a broader sense. If there is a genuine difference between person and hypostasis—and this must be the case if it is true that an *empty form* and its *fullness* are not merely externally conjoined but belong together essentially—then in the case of the person not only the nature but also the "carrying" must be something distinctive.

We previously said of the "ego" [*Ich*] that it is carrier of its life. It is that from which inner life emanates (the *inner* life in contrast to the life of so-called *living* or *animate beings* [*Lebewesen*] which *externalizes* itself in the forming of matter). It is that which lives *in* this life and experiences [er*lebt*] this life as *its own.* It is evident that in this case carrying differs from the way in which a thing carries an essence or nature. The *ego* not only carries life, but the carrying itself is life, and to this life there pertains a being inwardly aware [*Innesein*] of itself, although this being-aware-of-itself is not necessarily *self-knowledge* (in the restricted sense of conceptual knowledge), nor necessarily a *consciousness* of the kind that generates conceptual knowledge.

There is thus an ego-life and a concomitant awareness that is not yet genuine self-understanding or self-comprehending. And we therefore cannot speak here of either *intelligere* [*Vernehmen*] or *intellectus* [*Vernunft*]. For we speak of *Vernunft* only where there is found a comprehended inner lawfulness [*Gesetzlichkeit*] of being. On the other hand, where an existent is ruled by and behaves in accordance with an intelligible lawfulness which it yet cannot understand, we speak of a hidden or latent intellect. And we call a creature *rational* or *endowed with an intellect* [*vernunftbegabt*] when it can understand the lawfulness of its own being and can act accordingly. This requires *ratio* [*Verstand*], i.e., the gift of understanding, and *liberum arbitrium* [*Freiheit*], i.e., the gift of molding one's actions out of one's own self.

If then to being-person there pertains the gift of rationality or intelligence, the person as such must possess reason and freedom. And we thus arrive at the distinction between ego and person and are justified in saying that not every ego need be a personal ego. On the other hand, every person must be an ego. It must be inwardly aware of its own being, since this is implied in the gift of intelligence.

It is highly important in our context to understand the special kind of "carrying" which being-person entails. If it pertains to the ego as such that its life emanates from its own being and that it is aware of this life as its very own, then the personal ego must in addition be capable of understanding its own life and of molding it freely out of its own self. We thus see clearly that God, who molds his life in absolute freedom and who is light through and through (from whom nothing is hidden), must be a person in the most eminent sense. And because personal life is going out of oneself and simultaneously being and abiding within oneself, and because both of these characteristics pertain to the nature of spirit, personal being must always denote spiritual being.

Finally, the question must be asked whether personal and spiritual being simply and absolutely coincide, whether "non-personal" spiritual being is conceivable,[21] and whether that which underlies the person's being-carrier must of necessity be something spiritual.[22] And this question is interlinked with another one. In what manner is the person a carrier of its *essence* or nature [*Wesen*]?

Our understanding of the person as an ego and of the ego as the carrier of its own life has made it possible for us to describe the specific manner in which the person is the carrier of its *life*. In God there is no distinction between life and essence (nature), nor between being and essence. On the other hand, where essence and life do not coincide, the meaning of "carrying" too must differ.

§3. The Human "Being-Person" [*Das menschliche Personsein*]

We are thus brought face to face with that particular being-person [*Personsein*] which characterizes created, finite persons. It may safely be assumed that pure spirits are closer to God than human beings [*die Menschen*], and because of the greater simplicity of their essence or nature, it would seem that it is easier to inquire into their being-persons. It is more natural, on the other hand, to start out from that which is nearest to us, namely, human nature. Moreover, this latter also holds a unique position from a purely objective point of view, because—owing to the fact that human nature presents a union of spirit [*Geist*] and matter—the whole of creation appears to be epitomized in it.

When we speak here of the *nature* of humans [*Menschen*] we have in mind the essence or nature of humans as such, including their being-person. And the essence—according to the results of our previous investigation—is the quidditive determinateness [*Wasbestimmtheit*], i.e., that which makes the human being a human being [*was es macht, dass der Mensch Mensch ist*]. We must then ask what pertains to the human being's being-human [*Menschsein*], and in what sense can it be said that human beings "carry" their being-human?

1. The Being of Human Beings [Das menschliche Sein] *as a Composite of Body, Soul, and Spirit* [leiblich-seelisch-geistig]. *The Peculiar Nature of the Life of the Human Spirit* [menschlichen Geisteslebens]

The being of human beings [*menschliche Sein*] is a composite of body, soul, and spirit. Insofar as human beings—according to their essence—are spirit, their "spiritual life" is an outgoing life that enters into a world which discloses itself to them, while they yet retain a firm hold on their own selves. They not only "breathe" out their essence in a spiritual manner—as does every actual formal structure—unconsciously revealing themselves, but they are, in addition, active in a personal spiritual manner. The human soul *as* spirit rises in its spiritual life beyond itself. But the human spirit is conditioned both from above and from below. It is immersed in a material structure which it be-souls and molds into a bodily form. The human person carries and encloses "its" body and "its" soul, but it is at the same time carried and enclosed by both. The spiritual life [*geistiges Leben*] of the human person rises from a dark ground. It rises like a flame that illumines, but it is a flame that is nourished by non-luminous matter. And it emits light without being light through and through. The human spirit is visible to itself without, however, being thoroughly transparent. It is capable of illuminating other things without being able to penetrate completely into their being.

We have already learned a few things about the darkness of the human spirit.[23] By virtue of its own inner light the human intellect knows about its present life and about many things which at one time were present. Its knowledge of what lies in the past, however, is fragmentary, and what lies in the future can only be anticipated with some degree of probability in some particular details. In its larger expanse, the future remains indefinite and uncertain—though conceivable in this indefiniteness and uncertainty—while the origin and ultimate end remain completely inaccessible.[24] And the immediately certain life of the present is merely the fleeting fulfillment of a passing moment, instantaneously sinking away and completely disappearing forthwith. My entire conscious life is not equivalent to "my being." Rather, it resembles the lit surface that covers an obscure depth, a depth which manifests itself in and through the medium of the surface. If, then, we want to understand the human being-person, we must penetrate this obscure depth.

2. *The Ego-Life and Body-Soul Being*

We have spoken of a twofold beyond to which the human intellect penetrates in its awake, conscious life: the external and the internal world.[25] The *external* world may in turn be understood in a dual sense: 1) It may signify everything that does not pertain to "me," i.e., to the *monadic* unity of my being, and in this case the external world would also include the inner worlds of other spirits; or 2) It may signify that which is accessible only to external perception, i.e., the corporeal world with everything that pertains to it. In this latter case the inner world of other persons would also form part of my *inner* world.

We shall confine our inquiry to the inner world of the ego. And this means in the present context not only the conscious ego-life—the present ego-life as well as the ego-life of past and future, to the extent that they are accessible by reaching backward and forward in memory and anticipation (i.e., the unity of the *stream of experiences* [*Erlebnisstrom*])—but also that which is not immediately conscious, that out of which conscious life arises.

For example, I am thinking about a difficult problem, and I have been trying in vain to find a solution. I finally give up, because today I am too dull. I cannot perceive my dullness with my external senses. (We may disregard here the externally visible characteristics which such dullness may impress upon the body.)

Nor can I be "immediately conscious" of my dullness in the way I am conscious of my thinking, the slow process of which my dullness reveals to me. But I "experience" this dullness nonetheless—it becomes evident to me in the same sense in which I experience the bluntness of a knife which refuses to cut a loaf of bread. The most original form of such an experience—upon which are based far-reaching judgments and conclusions and by which, by virtue of that which is retained in memory, that gradually accumulating sum of experiences is attained which leads to "self-knowledge"—we call with Husserl *inner perception* [*innere Wahrnehmung*]. This kind of perception differs completely from that consciousness which irrevocably accompanies ego-life (*as life of the pure I*), but it nevertheless plays an indispensable part in ego-life.

What I perceive internally and learn to know better and better in the course of my life is a thing-like something. It has enduring properties (as, for example, mental gifts—a greater or lesser facility of comprehension, keenness of judgment, the ability to discern connections and relations). It entails changing emotional states, extending to longer or shorter periods of time (such as gay and happy moods, which stimulate all sorts of activities, or depressed moods and inhibitions). It engenders varying modes of action, is subject to external influences, while it in turn exerts an efficacy that transcends its own inner world, integrating this latter with the cause-and-effect nexus of the total world of experience.

These few preliminary indications merely attempt to call attention to an existent of a highly complex structure. The example of a limited experience, from which we started out, however, may lead us further in several directions.

I have established the fact that *today* I am too *dull* to solve the problem at hand. This implies that at another time I was more keen-witted, and that I hope by tomorrow I shall have regained my former mental acuteness. If this is so, there is no question of an unchanging quality but merely of a passing condition. Moreover, I think I know what is responsible for this condition. Today my head feels as dull as if a heavy fog were weighing upon it. And this discovery points to an entirely new sphere. The fact that the head has something to do with the process of thinking opens up the entire set of problems connected with the interrelation of body and soul. What is the soul? What is the body? Is the soul that thing-like something which I inwardly perceive and experience, or is the soul the totality of body and soul? A perplexing number of questions arise, but we shall merely try to carry our inquiry forward to a point where the specific nature of the human person and therewith of being-human in general can be grasped.

My head and my entire body are physical things which I can perceive with my external senses. But in this kind of perception I am subject to peculiar limitations which I do not experience with respect to any other body. With respect to my own body, I lack full freedom of movement. I cannot view it from all sides simply because I cannot "cut myself loose from it." On the other hand, with respect to my own body I do not have to rely on my external perception. I can view it, as it were, from within. This why it is a *living body* [*Leib*] and not merely a physical body [*Körper* (*corpus*)]. And it is "my" body in a sense in which nothing external is mine, since I dwell in it as in my "native" abode. I feel what goes on in it and what happens to it, and simultaneously with this feeling I perceive it. The feeling of bodily functions and processes is as much "my life" as are my thinking and my joy, although the former are vital movements of an entirely different kind. The cold shiver which runs down my spine, the pressure on my head, the pain in my tooth—all this differs from the deliberate exercise of my thinking activity. It does not rise from an inward depth as does my joy, but I am in it nonetheless. Whatever befalls my body befalls me, and it befalls me precisely at the spot where it befalls my body. I am present in all the parts of my body wherever I feel the presence of something. This feeling may be experienced in a *nonpersonal* manner, e.g., as a mere sensation which does not actually affect the spiritual ego [*geistiges Ich*]. It does affect the spiritual ego, to be sure, to the extent that the feeling or sensation is consciously experienced. The spiritual ego can discern it and view it spiritually. But the feeling and the conscious experience are two different things. And from this consideration we may gain some insight into the possibility of a purely sentient life, a life which never assumes the form of a personal ego-life—as is the case with merely sentient beings [*Sinnenwesen*]. Bodily functions and processes *can,* however, be integrated with the life of the person. Every step and every action, if they are undertaken freely and meaningfully, are personal deeds. The body partakes of and contributes to their unity and is felt and understood in its partaking and contributing capacity. As an instrument of my acts, my body is an integral part of the unity of my personality.[26] The human ego, in short, is not only a *pure ego,* not only a spiritual ego, but also a bodily ego.

Whatever is bodily [*leiblich*] or of the body is never *merely* so. What distinguishes the body [*Leib*] from a mere physical body (*corpus*) is the fact that the body is be-souled. Where there is a body, there is also a soul. And conversely, where there is a soul, there is also a body.[27] A physical body without a soul is nothing but a *corpus* [*Körper*] and no longer a living body [*Leib*]. A spiritual nature [*Geistwesen*] without a corporeal body is a pure spirit, not a soul. Anyone who refuses to attribute a *soul* to plants should not speak of a plant body either. Rather, such a person will have to use a different name to distinguish these animate material structures from those which are inanimate or lifeless.

We have acquainted ourselves with the Thomistic doctrine of the soul which, following Aristotle, sees in the soul the essential form of all animate things and beings [*alles Lebendige*] and distinguishes different stages of such formations, depending on whether what is produced is merely a formation of animate material elements or whether the formation includes an *inner* life, and depending on whether this inner life is merely sensory or also spiritual. In accordance with these gradations in the positive functions and activities [*Leistungen*] of the soul, we distinguish among plant souls, animal souls, and human souls (i.e., vegetative, sentient, and intellectual souls) in such a way that the higher ones fulfill the functions and activities of the lower ones, adding, however, that which is their own proper function and activity.

Moreover, we have elucidated the meaning of form[28] to the effect that it imparts to the existent the determinateness of its essence or nature. In dead material structures, this includes only that which determines the specific particularity of their material being, their specific manner of forming and filling space [*Raumgestaltung, Raumerfüllung*], of movement and efficacious activity [*Wirken*], and the spiritual meaning which finds expression in the particularity of their spatial form-language. The distinguishing particularity of living (animate) forms as against lifeless (inanimate) ones consists in their supra-material [*stoffüberlegen*] power which is capable of encompassing and transforming a diversity of given material structures, of integrating them in an articulated whole, and which maintains and further develops the formed structural unity in a continuous process of metabolism. The "*being of living forms is life,* and *life is a formation of matter* in the following three stages: *the transformation of structural material elements, self-formation, and propagation or procreation.*"[29]

It is important to observe what distinguishes *life* understood in this sense, i.e., the being of animate material structures *qua* animate, from the life of pure spirits. *Matter-bound life* is the coming to be of an existent, a becoming that must gain possession of its essence or nature. It develops on the way to its full self. Spiritual life is an "unfolding" of essence or nature and as such the active manifestation of something that is already essentially perfected.[30] And here we are once more confronted with an *analogical relationship.* The term *life* is not used simply in an equivocal sense, but the two types of life show some common constitutive elements of meaning [*Sinnbestand*]. Both types are characterized by an auto-motion [*Selbstbewegung*] out of the ground of a thing's or being's own essence or nature. But in the one case the existent finds in this motion or movement the way to its own self—as something that comes to be—while in the second case the existent, as a perfected being, goes out of itself in this motion or movement, giving or surrendering its own self without, however, relinquishing or losing it. Both types of life are *images* [*Abbilder*] which in a more or less perfect manner "partake" of the fullness of the life of Divine Being.

Following the lead of H. Conrad-Martius, we have regarded it as a particular characteristic of the *soul* to be the *center of the being* [*Seinsmitte*] of the animate existent [*Lebewesen*] and the hidden source from which this existent draws its being and rises to its visible form.[31] The inanimate material structure is an autonomous [*selbsteigen*] and independent [*selbständig*] actuality with its own structural particularity and unity—a unity and particularity, however, which are not formed out of its own center and out of its own inner life. In the case of the finite pure spirit, we cannot speak of a center of being, because there is neither an *exteriority* that is naturally united with the finite pure spirit—that could be formed from within in accordance with the interiority—nor is there a self-molding out of a hidden ground.

Let us keep in mind, first of all, the meaning of *soul* as the center of being of animate material structures, i.e., of everything that "bears within itself the power of self-formation."[32] But the meaning of *soul* finds an even more authentic fulfillment where *interiority* is no longer merely a forming-of-matter but a being-in-itself [*Sein in sich selbst*], where each soul is a self-enclosed inner world, even though this "inner world" is not severed from the body and from the totality of the real world. Of this kind is the status even of the merely sentient soul [*Sinnenseele*] which lacks a spiritual life comparable with that of pure spirits. Its soul life is thoroughly body-bound [*leibgebunden*]. It does not rise above bodily life as a quasi-autonomous vital sphere of independent meaning. Whatever befalls the body is sensed and felt, and there follows a response from within, from the center of life, in the form of movements and instinctive acts which serve the preservation and heightening of bodily life. It would be wrong nevertheless to regard the animal soul as merely an "instrumental device" [*Einrichtung*] in the service of the body and as such subjected to the body. There is rather a balance between the external and the internal, whereas in the plant the external is completely predominant and in people the soul has a meaningful life even apart from the body.

The animal is a body-soul unity of formal structure [*Gestalteinheit*]. Its marked particularity expresses and reveals itself in a twofold manner, in the qualities and activities of body and soul. As this kind of a whole, the animal stands in its surrounding world, reacting to it in its own particular way. And this reaction proceeds from that innermost point of its being where the change from external impressions to responsive acts takes place. This innermost point is a *living* center where everything converges and from which everything emanates. And this interplay of stimulus [*Gereiztwerden*] and response is indicative of its *ego-life* [*Ichleben*]. However, there is no question of conscious experiences and free, authentic choices. The animal-ego is more or less at the mercy of the "drives" [*Getriebe*] of its life. It does not stand personally erect [*aufgerichtet*] behind and above them.

3. Body, Soul, Spirit, "The Castle of the Soul" ["Die Seelenburg"]

In the human soul personal erectness has become a fact. Here the *inner* life has become conscious being. The I has been awakened, and its vision moves in an outward and inward direction. The I is capable of viewing the multitude of external impressions in the light of its understanding and of responding to them in personal freedom. And *because* the human I is *capable* of doing this, people are spiritual persons, i.e., *carriers* of their own lives in a preeminent sense of a personal "having-oneself-in-hand." People do not, however, make full use of their freedom but rather abandon themselves to a large extent—much in the manner of merely sentient creatures—to the pressures and forces of external and internal "events" and "drives" [*Geschehen und Treiben*]. And they *are*, after a fashion, sentient beings and as such do not even have the power of actualizing complete freedom of action in the totality of their lives.

On the other hand, created pure spirits are limited in their freedom only by the fact that they are not the authors of their own being, but have received their being and receive it again and again as an ever-renewed gift during the entire course of their existence. And while it is true that all creaturely freedom is conditioned or relative, the being of pure spirits is nevertheless personal life in the full sense, i.e., a free and authentic engagement [*Einsatz*] of the self. Their knowledge, love, and service—and their blissful joy in knowing, loving, and serving—are a simultaneous receiving and adoptive embracing, a free self-giving of this gift of life.

The range of people's freedom does not coincide with the total amplitude of their being. And the soul is here a *central* medium or mean [*Mitte*] in a new sense. It mediates between spirituality and bodily sentient being [*Leib-Sinnenhaftigkeit*]. The traditional tripartition of body-soul-spirit must, however, not be interpreted as if the human soul were a third realm interposed between two other realms subsisting without the soul and independently of one another. Rather, it is in the medium of the soul that spirituality and bodily sentient being meet and intertwine. And this is precisely what distinguishes the particular being of the spiritual soul from the being of the sentient soul, on the one hand, and from the being of the pure spirit, on the other. People are neither brutes nor angels, because they are both in one. Their bodily sentient being differs from the sentient being of brutes, and their spirituality differs from that of angels. We have referred to these differences on several occasions. People sense or feel [*spürt*] what happens in or with their bodies, but this feeling is a *conscious* experience and is ordained to a passing over into an *understanding apperception* of the body and of bodily functions and processes as well as into an apperception of these impressions of the external world which "strike the senses."

Apperception is already a sort of knowledge and as such a spiritual activity in which knowing is confronted with the known. The body of the knower—and not merely the external world—turns into an *object,* albeit an object of a particular kind. The I disengages itself "in a certain sense" from the body and rises in personal freedom above the body's corporeality and sensuality. We say "in a certain sense" advisedly, because the I nonetheless remains attached to the sensuous organism. Spiritual life rises again and again out of sensorial life, and while the former thus never stands on its own ground, the I is capable of taking its stand in its own *higher* being and, from this vantage point, of freely mastering the *lower* being of the life of sense.

For example, the I may set for itself the goal of gaining cognitive knowledge of its own body and of its own sensory life. It learns to know the possibilities of using its body and senses as instruments of its own knowledge and action, of exercising its body and senses for certain purposes and ends, and of thereby of forming them into more and more perfect instruments. Moreover, the I has the capability of suppressing the stirrings of the senses, of withdrawing to a large extent from bodily-sensuous life, and of gaining an ever firmer foothold in the spiritual life.

The realm of spiritual life is the authentic realm of freedom. Here the I can be genuinely creative out of the depth of its own self. What we call *free acts*—a firm resolve, the voluntary inception and execution of some action, the explicit turning toward a "rising" thought, the conscious termination of a succession of ideas as well as all questioning, demanding, granting, promising, commanding, obeying—are "deeds" of the I, manifold in their meaning and inner structure, but uniform in one respect. In all of these deeds the I determines the content and direction of its own being, dedicating itself to a freely chosen experiential content and thus in a certain sense "generating" its own life. This does not mean, of course, that in these deeds the I becomes—in unconditional or absolute freedom—the creator of its own self. The I has *received* the freedom of self-determination as a gift. The "vitality" which the I displays in some freely chosen direction is a received vitality, and every deed is a response to a stimulus and a seizure of something that has been offered for acceptance. But free acts nevertheless retain that particular characteristic of self-engagement [*Selbsteinsatz*] which is the most authentic form of personal life.

All voluntary action upon the body, however, and all formative influence which the I—through the instrumentality of the body—exerts upon the external world rest upon the fact that human freedom is not restricted to the purely spiritual realm and that the realm of the spirit is not a separate, isolated sphere. The foundation upon which the spiritual life and free acts arise and to which they remain attached is the *matter* which is placed at the disposal of the human being's intellect and free will to be illumined, formed, and used.

In this way the bodily sentient life of the human being becomes a personally formed life and a constituent part of the human person. But it never ceases to be a "dark ground," and it remains the lifelong task of the free human spirit to illumine this ground more and more so as to impart to it an ever more personal form.

However, these considerations do not yet penetrate to the ultimate meaning of the realm of the soul. The soul is the "space" in the center of the body-soul-spirit totality. As sentient soul it abides in the body, in all its members and parts, receiving impulses and influences from it and working upon it formatively and with a view to its preservation. As spiritual soul it rises above itself, gaining insight into a world that lies beyond its own self—a world of things, persons, and events—communicating with this world and receiving its influences. As *soul* in the strictest sense, however, it abides in its own self, since in the soul the personal I is in its very home. In this abode there accumulates everything that enters from the world of sense and from the world of spirit. Here in this inwardness of the soul everything that enters from these worlds is weighed and judged, and here there takes place the appropriation of that which becomes the most personal property and a constituent part of the self—that which, figuratively speaking, "becomes flesh and blood."

The soul as the interior castle—as it was pictured by our holy mother Teresa[33]—is not point-like as is the *pure ego,* but "spatial." It is a space, a "castle" with many mansions in which the I is able to move freely, now going outward beyond itself, now withdrawing into its own inwardness. And this space is not "empty," even though it can and must receive and harbor a fullness in order to become capable of unfolding its own individual life.

The soul cannot live without receiving. It nourishes itself with those contents which it makes its own in an experiential spiritual manner—as the body nourishes itself with those structural material elements which it absorbs. And this comparison illustrates more clearly than the figure of "space" that it is not a question of merely filling an emptiness, but that the recipient is an existent with an essence or nature of its own (i.e., an *ousia*), an existent which has its own specific mode of receiving and which incorporates into its own being that which has been received. What discloses and reveals itself in these experiences is the very essence or nature of the soul, with all the qualities and powers that are rooted in the essence. In these experiences the soul appropriates to itself what it needs in order to become what it is destined to be. And this particular essence or nature of the soul impresses upon the body as well as upon all personal intellectual activities its definite stamp. And this same essence or nature streams forth from the body and from all personal spiritual acts in a nonconscious and non-voluntary manner.

4. *I, Soul, Spirit, Person* [Ich, Seele, Geist, Person]

I, soul, spirit, person—all these are evidently interrelated, and yet each of these words carries a special meaning which does not completely coincide with the meaning of the others. We call an existent an *I* whose being is life (not life in the sense of a forming of matter [*Stoffgestaltung*], but as an unfolding of the I in being—a being which emanates from the I itself) and who in this being is aware of itself (either in the inferior form of a dull sensorial feeling or in the higher form of an awake consciousness). The I is thus neither equivalent to the soul nor to the body. It "dwells" in body and soul. It is present at every point where something is felt or experienced as a living presence, even though it has its real "seat" at some definite "point" in the body-soul and at some definite "place" in the soul.[34] And because "its" body and "its" soul pertain to the I, the name *I* is applied to the whole human being.

Not all bodily life is ego-life. The processes of growth and nutrition, for example, take place to a large extent without our being consciously aware of them, even though we are aware of many things which pertain to these processes or are related to them. Nor is the life of the soul altogether pure ego-life. The unfolding and formation of the soul take place to a large extent without our being consciously aware of them. For example, it may happen that I believe I have "overcome" some painful experience, and I have long since forgotten it. But suddenly some new experience brings it back to my memory, and the impression which this earlier experience now makes upon me as well as the thoughts which it now evokes make me realize that it has been working within me all the time and that, moreover, without it I would not be what I am today. This earlier experience has been working "within me," i.e., within my soul, in a depth which is hidden most of the time and which only occasionally becomes overt.

The awake and conscious ego-life is the entrance portal to the soul and its hidden life, just as the life of the senses is the entrance portal to the body and its hidden life. The awake and conscious life is the entrance portal because it is a manifestation of that which takes place in the soul, and it is an actualization [*Auswirkung*] of the soul's essence.

Everything that I consciously experience issues from my soul. It is an encounter of my soul with something that "impresses" it. The starting point of the experience in the soul may lie in great depth, or it may lie closer to the surface. The location of this point, as well as the stratified order of the soul, are revealed *in* and *through* the medium of the experiences which arise out of the soul's depths. The whence as well as the stratification become overt in these experiences and attain in them to their actual, living presence. This occurs even in the original propensity of the experience, before our glance can—in *retrospection* or *reflection* (attentively, observingly, or in critical analysis)—turn toward the experience. Similarly, the primordial form of *consciousness* is a concomitant of the ego-life without detaching itself from the ego-life and without turning back toward it in a special kind of *apperception.* And this is why every human being learns to know him or herself by the mere fact of the awake life, without making the self into an object of observation and without attempting to gain self-knowledge by means of introspection and self analysis.

Primordial consciousness turns into *self-apperception* or *inner apperception*[35] only when the I rises above the original experience and turns the latter into an object. The I then envisages the soul as a thing-like substance with enduring properties, with faculties or powers which are capable and stand in need of formal development and growth, and with changing conditions and activities. However, in this way the I envisages its own self, for it recognizes itself in that which is the carrier of experiences, in that which performs acts and receives impressions. The I, from which all ego-life emanates and which in the egolife becomes conscious of its own self, is the same I to which pertain body and soul, which are both intellectually embraced and encompassed by the I. The function which in the case of the dead thing is performed by the empty form of the object is here fulfilled by the living, spiritual, personal I.

We have defined the *person* as a conscious and free I. This I is *free* because it determines its life out of its own self in the form of *free acts*. Free acts thus constitute the primary sovereign dominion of the person. But because by its actions the person exerts a formative influence on body and soul, the entire realm of "human nature" pertains to the proper dominion of the person. And because by its soul-body efficacy, the person also exerts its influence on the surrounding world, its dominion also extends to the world, which it may justly claim a "mine."

Whatever the person does freely and consciously is ego-life, but person draw their ego-life out of some greater or lesser depth. The resolve to take a walk, for example, derives from a layer that is much closer to the surface than a decision that concerns the choice of a vocation. This depth is the depth of the soul which comes "alive" and becomes luminous in the ego-life, but before its coming alive it was hidden, and it remains mysterious despite this luminosity. What human beings are "capable of doing" as free persons they learn only by doing it or, perhaps, in anticipation, when they meet with a specific *demand.*

The interconnections between I, person, and soul are gradually becoming clearer. If we understand the *pure ego* as the "point" at which all free acts originate and at which everything that is received is felt and consciously experienced, this is one possible way of looking at the matter. But this approach to the problem disregards the fact that the ego-life is firmly rooted in the ground from which it rises. The I is, as it were, the breach between the dark and deep ground and the clear luminosity of conscious life and therewith also between "potentiality" or "pre-actuality" and the full and present actuality (i.e., between potency and act). In the experience of its "capability" [*Können*], the I becomes conscious of the "powers" which are "dormant" in the soul and which sustain the ego-life. And the ego-life in turn is the actualization, the actual effectuation of these powers. It is that whereby these powers become visible.

The person—understood as the I which encompasses, cognitively illumines, and freely governs body and soul—we have described as the carrier that stands behind and above the body-soul totality, or as the comprehensive form of body-soul fullness. But what we previously stated in general terms, namely, that the empty form cannot subsist without fullness and that the fullness cannot subsist without form is here distinctly evident. The person cannot live as a *pure ego.* It sustains its life out of that fullness of the essence [*Wesensfülle*] which is resplendent in the awakeness of life, without ever being fully illumined or fully mastered. The person carries this fullness and is simultaneously carried or sustained by this dark and deep ground.

This latter consideration reveals to us the peculiar nature of the human person. We recognize now what it has in common with the being a person of God and pure spirits and wherein it differs. The human person resembles pure spirits in its free and conscious mode of life, a life which encompasses and carries its own fullness, but it lags behind them because it arises from and is carried by a dark ground and is incapable of personally forming, illumining, and sovereignly governing the totality of its "self." The human person possesses, on the other hand, a certain ontological prerogative (in comparison with created pure spirits) by virtue of its own "depth." And this means that its God-likeness differs from that of pure spirits.

This peculiar ambivalence of the being of the human person becomes even clearer when we try to determine the relationship that exists between *spirit and soul.* The human soul is often designated as a spiritual creature, and if the entire realm of reality [*alles Wirkliche*] is divided into spirit and matter, there remains no other possibility. For the human soul is certainly not space-filling and sensorial in the manner of spatial material. However, it is, and in this it differs essentially from pure spirits, naturally *bound to matter* [*stoffgebunden*]. This is clearly evident from the fact that it is the *form* of the *body.*

The human soul is the form of the body not by virtue of its lower powers, which it shares with plant and animal souls, but by virtue of its total unified essence or nature, in which are also rooted those higher powers which are the distinguishing mark of the human soul and which place it into close proximity to the pure spirits. "The spirit in the form of the soul builds up people from moment to moment, in matter and in space, as a continuously moved and self-changing nature, in such a way that the external is factually always measured and formed by the internal and innermost layers of a person's being."[36] The "internal and innermost," however, means the "most spiritual," that which is farthest removed from matter, that which moves the soul in its innermost depth. If this strikes us as strange and wonderful, we shall find it even more awesome and "miraculous" when we discover that *everything material is built by the spirit.* This means not only that the entire material world was created by the divine spirit but that *every material structure is spiritually filled* [*geisterfüllt*] and informed. Every material structure either bears, as a thing of nature, its form within itself, molding it from within, or, as a human work, has been molded from without and has, by virtue of its form, become the bearer of a meaning. The matter-molding form is not itself matter. In order to understand the manner in which this form is related to spirit, we shall have to consider the term "spirit" in a broader sense.

§4. Further Clarification of the Concept of Spirit: Spirit as Being and Life (Idea and Power)

When we designated spiritual being as free and conscious personal life, we observed that this kind of life is the "primordial form" of spiritual life. It is by no means uncommon, after all, to speak of *spirit* even when referring to impersonal structures. Thus we call a book "spirited," and it has become customary to divide the disciplines of knowledge and learning [*Wissenschaften*] into the two branches of the natural sciences [*Naturwissenschaften*] and the spiritual or human sciences [*Geisteswissenschaften*]. And the objects of the latter are not only persons and personal life but everything that has been created by the human spirit. Now we must examine the sense in which such an attribution is justified. And we must carefully consider whether the claims that are made with respect to human works are not equally valid with respect to the creative spirit [*Schöpfergeist*].

We shall do well, moreover, to keep in mind that despite the fact that in one sense we have marked off the spiritual as a definite sphere of reality from the material, we have, on the other hand, learned to know the spiritual as a basic form of being which we meet in the several spheres of reality. For example, a melody is not a mere sequence of sounds sensorially experienced. We hear in it the singing of a human soul—in jubilation or mourning, in a placid or angry mood. We understand the "language" of this melody. It touches and moves our soul; we meet in it a life that is akin to our own.

This does not necessarily mean that singers or a musicians experience inwardly what their songs or instruments express. Not even creative artists necessarily express their personal experiences. Their gift of empathy may inspire or demand this particular kind of expression, and they may then be induced to reproduce this empathetic experience in their work. And we understand this expression even without paying attention to the artist whose mediatorship has made it possible for us to gain access to it. In this way we may also understand and appreciate the meaning of a poem without paying attention to the personal characteristics of the handwriting of the poet. What the sequence of the words of a poem or the sequence of the sounds of a melody (both supported and intensified by the "corresponding" sounds of "recitation" or "recital") express is a *meaningful structure* [*Sinngebilde*] of a special kind—a structure which peremptorily demands to gain life in a human soul, and the souls of both the artist and the listener help bring about this kind of "actualization."

This brief reflection demonstrates once more what we have already emphasized in a different context. Meaningful structures are not created but merely re-created or copied [*nachbilden*] by human beings. They have an *ideal* or *essential* being of their own, and there corresponds to them a proportionate *matter* which is formed by them and by means of which they are "actualized."

Within this frame of reference, however, *matter* and *actualization* have several meanings. First, the meaning of a melody is that which molds a series of sounds or tones so that they become a unified "tone-structure." The requisite sounds or tones are a first *material element* corresponding to the melody, but not a spatial material element. Each individual soul or tone is itself a meaningful structure that has the possibility of entering into a higher unity of meaning [*Sinneinheit*].[37] The sequence of tones can in turn be actualized as sound in space and time by vibrations produced by the human voice or by musical instruments. Here we have a forming-into [*Hineinformung*] the actuality of nature and a forming-into a spatial matter. The most genuine actualization, however, takes place when the meaningful structure enters as "content" into an "experiential actuality" [*Erlebniswirklichkeit*]. And the *matter* which presents itself for such an entering is the *life* of the soul, its *spiritual* life. *Spirit* [*Geist*] *is meaning and life in full actuality.* It is a *life filled with meaning* [*Sinnerfüllt*].

Meaning and life are completely one only in God. In creatures we must distinguish between a fullness of life which is formed by meaning, and the meaning which actualizes itself in the fullness of life. Matter understood as fullness of life is not devoid of spirituality [*ungeistig*] but rather pertains to the spirit itself. Unformed fullness of life is a *power* or potency for spiritual being, a potency which must yet be brought to the perfection of its being. Meaning without fullness of life is an *idea* which becomes actual only in something that is alive. Neither meaning nor fullness of life (which pertains to the spirit) have anything to do with spatial materiality.[38] The life filled with meaning, however, is a superabundant, diffusive life. It has a form of being which we call *spiritual* [*geistig*].

In order to determine the interrelation of meaning and power (potency) in non-personal structures for which the title "spiritual" is equally claimed, we must consider these structures in their relationship to spiritual persons. The being of the former can become intelligible only when it is related and referred back to personal being (which is the more primordial of the two). Within the sphere of this primordial type of spiritual being, however, one important structural form [*Gestaltungsform*] must still be considered: that of created *pure spirits.*

§5. The Created Pure Spirits

1. Is a Philosophic Study of Angelology Possible?

The inquiry into the nature of finite being has led us to eternal being and has shown us that the latter is identical with that primordial being which conditions every other kind of being. Having learned that this primordial being is a personal being, we then reverted to the kind of being most familiar to us, namely, human being, in the hope that it might reveal to us most clearly the meaning of being a person [*Personsein*].

Now the question may be asked what possible significance our preoccupation with the so-called *pure spirits* may have in connection with our inquiry into the meaning of being. These who do not wish to relinquish the ground of experience as a foundation of all natural knowledge may perhaps be willing to admit that there is a place in philosophy for a consideration of the problem of God, on account of the fact that the conditioned nature of the contents of experience presupposes something that is unconditioned. But these same people will feel little inclination to engage in a study of angels and demons. It is quite evident, on the other hand, that such a reluctance was foreign to the medieval thinkers. In their endeavor to understand the universe of existents, good and evil spirits had a definite place, since, after all, their existence appeared substantiated by the many testimonials in the Sacred Scriptures of the Old and New Testaments and since they knew themselves surrounded at every turn by angels and demons, by the loving protection of the former and the dangerous antagonism of the latter. And because these thinkers based their discussions of angelic spirits primarily on revealed truth, we feel inclined to regard every consideration of this matter as a purely theological problem and without any philosophical relevance. Even the most recent research on the angelology of St. Thomas[39] emphasizes the prevalently theological nature of these treatises.

It must be admitted that in his *theological summa,* [i.e, the *Summa Theologiae*] the theological intention is predominant. Angels are regarded as that part of creation which represents the purest image of God.[40] However, even here St. Thomas shows himself the philosopher whose main concern it is to discover the ultimate grounds of that which is in all its structural forms. And he intimates the possibility of access to these creatures—whose existence lies outside the sphere of our immediate experience—by way of purely natural experience: "The mere fact that the intellect is higher in rank than the senses makes it rationally plausible that there must be certain incorporeal things which only the intellect can comprehend."[41] To be sure, this indicates merely that there must be, in addition to corporeal things, some spiritual things. It does not in any way conclusively prove the existence of *pure* spirits. But though St. Thomas has thus not proven this latter thesis in any strict sense, he has at least attempted to make it acceptable to natural reason.

Something would be lacking, according to St. Thomas, in the perfection of the universe and in the hierarchical order of created things if there did not exist purely spiritual beings or natures [*Wesen*] in addition to mere bodies and bodily-spiritual creatures. In his *philosophical summa* [i.e., the *Summa Contra Gentiles*] St. Thomas has listed the reasons for the existence of pure spirits[42] and has thereby expressed his conviction that this problem. concerns not only theology but also philosophy.

We need not enter into a discussion of the reason for the existence of angels, since we are not so much concerned with the question of whether or not angels do actually exist as with the question of what pure spirits are according to their essence or nature and of how their being is related to divine being.

An investigation of this sort must of necessity be carried forward by a consideration of possibilities [*Möglichkeitsbetrachtung*]. It cannot be doubted that we have some experience of spiritual creatures, namely, of our own spirit as well as of the spirits of other human beings. In the attitude of natural life as well as in the experiential disciplines of knowledge [*Erfahrungswissenschaft*]—such as the historical disciplines—we want to learn something about the factual intellectual or spiritual particularity of this or that human being or of groups of human beings. In the essentially and genuinely philosophic attitude, on the other hand, we want to know what constitutes the nature of spirit as such and what kinds of spiritual creatures can possibly exist. For such a consideration of essential possibilities and necessities, however, an experiential foundation is requisite. Once we have this kind of foundation, the investigation becomes a possibility, because every experience bears within itself some essential knowledge [*Wesenserkenntnis*] as an indispensable yet severable constituent part—an essential knowledge which is as yet hidden and opaque, but which can be brought to light and made lucid.

No experience of things spiritual would be possible if there were not implicit in human experience as such a certain understanding of what constitutes spirit and spirituality. By contemplating the nature of our own human spirit, we may therefore become aware of what pertains of necessity to spirit as such. And we are able to distinguish from the nature of spirit as such that which pertains exclusively to the particularity of human beings and might therefore be different in other spiritual beings.

The possibility of distinguishing, in the experientially given, necessary from contingent elements—contingent with respect to their generic essence—opens our eyes to other essential possibilities than the one which actually confronts us. And in our imagination [*Einbildungskraft*] we possess a spiritual power which makes it possible for us to "conceive" of such essential possibilities freely and exhaustively [*aus-denken*] This "freedom" of our imagination is no arbitrary power. It is bound to the laws of essence, and its task is the elaboration of essential *possibilities*, not essential impossibilities.

From fairy tales and legends we are familiar with spiritual beings which differ from human nature, such as elemental spirits of nature [*Elementargeister*]—dragons, water sprites, elves, goblins—and both kind and hostile fairies. We are quite capable of examining these forms and figures of our freely creative imagination and of finding out whether they represent genuine essential possibilities, in what ways they differ from the human spirit, and whether the recognition of these differences might perhaps aid in our understanding of the human spirit. But of much greater importance than these legendary creatures are for us the spirits whose reality is attested by Sacred Scripture, by Christian dogma and Christian life, and whose efficacy is so strongly felt in our own human existence. The *Church Fathers* have spared no effort in making the nature of these spiritual beings stand out in clear relief, and they were aided in this endeavor by the numerous scriptural references to angels. The most complete descriptive analysis we owe to Dionysius the Areopagite,[43] whose writings provide the foundation for the angelology of medieval scholasticism.

St. Thomas has made the most extensive use of the writings of the Areopagite. However, this is not the place to determine the relationship that exists between the works of St. Thomas and those of Dionysius. To do this, we should have to outline the total world view of the two authors and indicate the precise place occupied by their doctrine of angels. According to his own words, the main intent and concern of Dionysius (or Pseudo–Dionysius) was purely theological and exegetical. He wanted to elaborate clearly what we know about angels from the revelation contained in Sacred Scripture. However, this does not mean that the writings of Dionysius are devoid of philosophic content. All scriptural exegesis is conditioned by the mentality of the expositor. And it is quite evident that the author of these writings had mastered the concepts and contents of Greek philosophy in a sovereign manner as if they were the natural media of his own mind. But he used these philosophic concepts and contents as tools for his theological aim and thus did not proceed in a strictly philosophical manner.

As we use a travel guidebook to gain information about some foreign country or continent, so the doctrine of angels drawn from Sacred Scripture may be used as an introduction to a region of spiritual being that is not accessible to our immediate experience. And on this basic we shall now examine what knowledge concerning the essence or nature of the spirit may be derived from such a doctrinal description.[44]

2. The Angelology of the Areopagite

St. Albert the Great, in his prologue to the Areopagite's *Celestial Hierarchy,* has illuminated the basis idea of the Dionysian writings and therewith the basic design of their world view by a brief scriptural quotation: *"Ad locum, unde exeunt flumina, revertuntur, ut iterum fluant"* (Eccl 1:7).[45] God is the locus from which all that is goes forth: all natural creatures as well as all the gifts of grace and glory that are poured out over these creatures. All that is was created by the goodness of God, so that it might gain a share in divine being. This is brought about by a ray of light which issues from God and permeates the entire creation, so that every created thing and being may turn toward God and be united with him. But this illumination takes place in hierarchical gradation. The highest creatures, being nearest to God, are the first ones to be illumined by his light, to be permeated by it and turned toward God. But these highest creatures simultaneously incline toward the lower ones in order to let pour forth upon them as much of the fullness they have received as the lower creatures are capable of embracing.

These creatures nearest to God are the angels. They form a *hierarchy* of their own, i.e., a graduated order of highest, intermediate, and lower spiritual beings. The book on the *Celestial Hierarchy* is primarily concerned with an exposition of the differences that exist between the nine choirs of angels and of their relations among each other. Our own main interest, however, is to learn what characterizes celestial spirits as such, and this knowledge we shall attempt to derive from a consideration of the celestial hierarchy as a whole.

Sacred Scripture speaks of pure spirits in the same manner in which it speaks of God himself, namely, in images or metaphors borrowed from the sensory world. And these images must be interpreted according to the general and fundamental principle that everything sensible represents something spiritual. There is always present a common element which makes possible such a representation, although there is never an equality between the image and that which it represents, but always only a similitude (notwithstanding the fact that there remains an even greater dissimilitude). The intentional object [*das Gemeinte*] can be grasped only by means of these images, but this intentional object nevertheless remains wholly different from the image by means of which it becomes conceivable. And this remains true even when that earthly thing [*das Irdische*]—experientially familiar to us—by means of which we try to gain access to the supra-sensible and supra-natural, pertains to the realm of the soul or the realm of the spirit.

Anger (*Zorn, ira,* θυμός),[46] for example, in non-rational creatures is an irrational emotion, whereas in spiritual beings it signifies a virile rational power and an immutable abiding in the immovable divine dwellings. *Concupiscence* [*Begierde*] in non-rational beings is non-deliberate or non-reflected, aiming at something material and mutable, involving no conscious effort, and expressing a natural inclination or habit [*Gewohnheit*]. It indicates an irrational predominance of the physical appetite that pulls the entire creature in the direction of the desired object of sense. In pure spirits, on the other hand, this eager desire denotes that divine love with which they embrace the higher spiritual reality in an understanding and rational manner, their enduring longing for pure contemplation unfettered by any suffering, and for a union with the highest and purest love.[47]

These examples are indicative of the basic rule which must guide us in reading Sacred Scripture and in viewing the natural world. This rule is none other than the *law of analogy,* according to which everything earthly points beyond itself to something supra-earthly or supra-natural. We already encountered this law when we considered the relationship that exists between finite and eternal being, and it is this same law that opens for us the portal to the realm of finite pure spirits. The earthly hierarchy thus points toward the celestial *hierarchy.* It copies [*nachbilden*] the latter and simultaneously forms jointly with it a unity of order and efficacious activity.

But what is the meaning of *hierarchy*? Dionysius understands it as a *sacred order,* knowing and efficacious action which seeks, as far as this is possible, to imitate or copy divine knowledge and efficacious action by virtue of an infused divine illumination.[48] Its ultimate aim is the greatest possible assimilation to and union with God, who is the leader and guide in all knowing and doing. Constantly contemplating his divine beauty, the members of this sacred hierarchical order imitate this beauty as much as it is within their power to do so, and this imitation turns those who adhere to his beauty into clear and immaculate mirrors which reflect the primordial light of the sovereign deity. And those who have been filled with this light allow it—obedient to divine law and free from all envy—to flow over into the lower ranks and members of the celestial hierarchy.

Every member of this hierarchy enjoys the divine prerogative of being a *fellow worker with God* and of allowing God's efficacious action to shine forth luminously in the member's own self. It is in keeping with this sacred order that some members of the hierarchy *purify* and others are purified. Some *illumine* and other are illumined. Some *perfect* and others are being perfected. *Purification* here denotes being freed of everything that is not Godlike and that therefore impedes union with God. *Illumination* denotes being filled with divine light, and *perfection* signifies being freed of imperfection and being outfitted with that knowledge and science of the saints which impart perfection. And all these—purification, illumination, and perfection being the different effects produced by *one and the same* ray of divine life—are most intimately interconnected.[49]

The celestial hierarchy is thus that order which encompasses all celestial spirits. They all stand nearest to God because they all share most abundantly in divine being. And because they partake of sovereign divine rulership, they surpass in excellence all inanimate things, all non-rational animate beings, and all beings endowed with merely human reason. They persevere in their pure spirituality and undeviatingly reach out for the immutable love of God. They thus receive primary illuminations in a pure and immaterial manner, and they form themselves accordingly as pure spirits. The illumination which they receive through the medium of the simple divine light is for them food, refreshment, and bliss.[50] They are called *angels* (i.e., messengers) because they are first illumined by God and then act as mediators in passing on the revealed truths which we human beings receive.[51] And because all celestial spirits hold this office of messengers in common, the name *angel* is applied to all of them, although this name specifically designates the members of the lowest order of celestial spirits.[52]

It pertains to the particular nature of the highest spirits that they circle round God in purest love in a purely spiritual permanent movement, and that for them no change from the good to the less good or to evil is possible. Their knowledge of God is obtained without the use of either sensory or spiritual images and without any need of ascending to it in the manner we ascend to truth by means of the revealed word of Sacred Scripture. They are filled with the light from on high in one simple and comprehensive cognitive intuition. Included in this intuition is also their knowledge of the divine works, a knowledge and understanding which they do not have to acquire by discursive reasoning.[53] And their illumination expresses itself in *eternal canticles of praise* in honor of God.[54]

The key to the knowledge possessed by angels is found in their names. Each of these names reveals some particularity of their nature.[55] In the different appellations of the individual choirs Dionysius reads the distinguishing excellencies of their members. Dionysius says of the name *angel* as such that something of that which this name expresses pertains to all celestial spirits, though not to all in the same degree, and to only one of the nine choirs as a specific distinguishing mark of excellence.

Thus, the name *seraphim* is said to denote those spirits who inflame or generate fire, i.e., their name signifies the fire of that love which these spirits of the highest rank bear to God as well as their capability of kindling in the spirits subordinated to them a similar love. And the *cherubim* are named for their capacity to embrace the influx of the divine light and after their charismatic gift of contemplating the beauty of God and of imparting to others some of the fullness of their wisdom. And it is precisely this diffusive overflowing of gifts upon the lower orders which makes it possible for all celestial spirits to have some share in this fire of love and this plenitude of wisdom. Even the members of the lowest order of the hierarchy, however, have the power of imparting some of the bountifulness they have received. They impart a certain share of it to human beings, and—as we have pointed out—this is why they are called *angels* in a particular and specific sense.

The name *thrones* denotes elevation above all the lower ranks. The spirits so named are borne up toward the divine, and they adhere with steadfast zeal and with all their powers to the All-Highest. Thus we readily understand why this distinguishing name is reserved for some of the highest among celestial spirits. And yet, when seen in relation to all other creatures, this throning on high is a common distinguishing mark of all celestial spirits.

The name *dominions* or *dominations* designates the absolute and radical otherness of the divine as against the earthly. It denotes freedom from any earthly interest and strict rulership exercised in generous liberality and untarnished by any tyrannical perversity. These spirits are sovereignly above any contemptible servility and any abject abasement, far removed from any corruption. They are everlastingly filled with a desire for true rulership and for that source and origin of all true rulership in whose image they form themselves as well as everything that is subordinated to them.

The name *virtues* designates those celestial spirits whose excellence consists in a valiant and unshakable virility which permeates all their actions and rigidly excludes everything that might diminish the radiance of the illuminations with which God has graced them. They strive with all their might to imitate God, and in this striving they never lag in cowardly weakness behind the demands of the divine motive force. They rather contemplate unceasingly this supra-essential [*Überwesentlich*] source of power and strength and—fashioning themselves as much as possible in the image of that primordial force—they vigorously turn toward it and generate it in turn diffusely in the subordinated ranks of the hierarchy.

The name *powers* indicates a supra-natural might bestowed by the supreme and primordial power. These angelic spirits never misuse this power bestowed upon them tyrannically for evil. Rather, they employ it to turn themselves undauntedly and triumphantly toward God and to serve and aid the spirits subordinated to them with the riches of their benevolence. And they strive to approximate as much as possible the primordial archetype [*Urbild*] of all power and to reveal that power—to the extent that angels are capable of doing this—by the most resplendent display of their own mighty strength.[56]

The name *principalities* denotes the power to lead and guide in a God-like manner, the power to turn toward the eternal paradigm of all leadership and guidance and to teach others how to produce in themselves an image or copy of divine leadership and to reveal its nature, as far as this is possible.[57]

The meaning of the name *angel* we have already briefly discussed. The intermediate position occupied by *archangels*—placed between principalities and angels—may provide us with some additional information regarding the entire hierarchy of celestial spirits. As archangels represent an intermediate like between principalities and angels, so angels represent an intermediate link between created pure spirits and human beings. The highest choirs mediate between God and the lower choirs, and all created pure spirits together mediate between God and all other creatures.

There is a very special reason why all the celestial spirits are referred to as celestial *virtues* [*Kräfte*]. Since in every spiritual creature there is a distinction between *nature* or *essence* [*Wesen*], *virtue* (in the sense of strength or power [*virtus; Kraft*]), and *efficacious action* [*Wirken*], all of them may be designated as celestial natures or substances [*Wesen*] or celestial virtues [*Kräfte*].[58]

All corporeal figures and images that Sacred Scripture uses to intimate to us the nature of angels must be understood symbolically and analogically. It frequently makes use of the image of fire—streams of fire, wheels of fire, men of fire—because by virtue of its peculiar nature, fire is apt to provide an illustration of the divine nature and therefore also of the God-likeness of the celestial spirits. Sensible fire is, as it were, in all things. It passes unadulterated through all of them and is received by all, And though it is luminous throughout, it is simultaneously concealed and remains unnoticed unless it attaches itself to some matter in which it may then reveal its power. Uncontainable and invisible, it yet rules everything in which it is efficaciously active and guides it toward this thing's operation. "It is active, energetic, and invisibly present in everything ..., and regardless of how much of its luminosity it imparts, it is never diminished."[59]

If angels are customarily represented in human form, in a freely erect posture, this is to indicate their spiritual quality and their vocation of rulership. They are preferably depicted in the vigor of youth to make manifest their perpetually flourishing life. The wings signify the swiftness of their ascent to the divine heights, and the weightless quality of their wings is indicative of the unearthly lightness with which they move—unburdened by the heaviness of matter—toward the higher celestial regions.[60]

When it is said of Isaiah that he saw celestial spirits endowed with six wings and with many feet and faces, this was to intimate their multiform power of vision. And the fact that they covered their feet and their faces with their wings was to symbolize their sacred and awed fear of any forward, audacious, or impudent intrusion into the profoundest of divine mysteries. The flapping of the wings was to make the prophet understand the unceasing soaring motion with which these spirits imitate the actions and operations of God.[61]

In such manner, then, every part of the visible forms of the celestial spirits reveals something of the spiritual nature of angels. The naked feet signify unrestricted power, free from all external impediments, a power which assimilates them in the largest possible measure to the divine simplicity.[62] And, similarly, all the vestments and implements with which sacred scripture endows and equips angels must be understood symbolically.

Angels are called *winds* because of the swiftness with which they perform, complete, and perfect everything they undertake, because of the speed with which they move in every direction, and because of the ease with which they ascend and descend. And this capability makes it possible for the lower ones to rise to greater heights and for the higher ones to extend their loving care to the lower ones and to communicate with their ranks.[63] The name "wind" (*ventus;* ἄνεμος) is intimately related semantically with "breath" [*Hauch*] (*spiritus*; πνεῦμα) a term generally employed to designate spirit as such. And this reminds us of the analogical correspondence between the spiritual and gaseous.

Summarizing briefly, we may state on the basis of our inquiry into the angelology of the Areopagite that angels are *pure* spirits and that their spirituality is thus superior to that of human beings. They are *personally free, ministering* spirits who entertain a communion among themselves as well as with all other spiritual personal beings, and they abide in a *realm of giving and receiving love,* a realm the origin and end of which is the triune Godhead.

This, then, is the way Dionysius has pictured celestial spirits for us. But now the question must be asked whether this realm of pure spirits represents an essential possibility as an object of our knowledge or, in other words, whether from our human spirituality we can gain access to this realm.

3. The Possibility of Pure *Spirits*

When we say that angels are purely spiritual, this means that they are non-corporeal. They are not, like human souls, forms of a material body that is informed by them. The sensible shapes in which they at times appear to human beings are produced by them in the manner of a handiwork [*Werk; opus*], so that by means of these visible shapes they may make themselves intelligible to creatures whose knowledge is tied to sense perception. This view of the Areopagite was adopted by St. Thomas and was further elaborated in the latter's controversies with those among contemporary thinkers who held opposing opinions.[64] And in his inquiry St. Thomas shows himself not merely interested in the purely theological question of whether angels are actually of such and such a nature, but his chief interest is centered in the essential possibility of *pure forms.*

We shall begin our own inquiry not by following the line of thought suggested by St. Thomas but shall rather seek an access to the problem on the basis of personal inner experience. We know that our own human spiritual life is tied to the body in diverse ways. We derive our knowledge of the external world from sense perception which depends on bodily organs. And the entire course of our spiritual life stands in a directly experienced dependence on the condition of our bodies, on the changing states of health and sickness, of freshness and fatigue. But this relationship of dependence is not the same in different human beings, nor is it the same in a particular human being at different times. We experience in our own selves the power of the spirit of making itself to a large extent independent of these bodily influences, and we are capable of conceiving this spiritual freedom heightened to the ideal limit of a complete independence of bodily ties. And the possibility of such a conception, i.e., of an ascent which allows the spirit to "rise" in its free conjectures above the substructure of natural experience, furnishes an example or an analogy of certain modes of knowledge which transcend the boundaries of that which can be grasped by the senses. Here, then, dawns the possibility of a knowledge which no longer stands in need of sensory approaches.

4. The Possibility of Higher *(i.e., Supra-Human) Spirits*

We thus see that the mere concept of non-corporeality holds the possibility of a spirituality *higher* than our own. In our own selves we experience our being-tied-to-the-body [*Leibgebundenheit*] as a burdensome chain which impedes the flight of the spirit. Freed from such ties, the spirit will be capable of rising to greater heights than is possible for the human intellect.

However, we do well to remind ourselves that it does not essentially pertain to the nature of the body as such to impede the movement of the spirit, but only to the body in its "fallen" state. We can conceive of a bodily corporeality [*Leiblichkeit*] which does not weight down the spirit but rather serves it as an absolutely pliable instrument and medium of self-expression. In such a way we picture the state of the first human beings prior to the fall and the state of the blessed after the resurrection of the body.

Pure spirits, therefore, owe the superiority of their spiritual life not to their bodilessness [*Leiblosigkeit*] as such but rather to their freedom from bodily corporeality [*Leiblichkeit*] such as ours in our actual state. However, a purely spiritual life does not require any bodily corporeality as a means of its actualization. The fact that bodily formed beings of a spirituality higher than that of humans are possible does not therefore exclude the possibility of the existence of pure spirits.

But how are we to envisage this spiritual life superior to our own? Its features may again be revealed to us by means of a free conceptual modification and heightening of our own spiritual life, in the direction of an ideal limit and in a manner which resembles the way we "visualize" pure geometrical figures in viewing the formal structures of natural bodies. We are indeed dealing here with a kind of spiritual vision—a kind of thinking that is not *empty*, but *filled*, a comprehending seizure of essential possibilities. Such filled thinking, however, is not in the nature of ultimate fulfillment. If we are capable of "conceiving of" a spiritual life superior to our own, such a conception demands as its ultimate fulfillment the actual experiential consummation [*Vollzug*] of such a spiritual life. And to this we do not attain in our earthly existence.

(a) *Higher Knowledge*

Our human *knowledge* is acquired in a step-by-step process. From that which is immediately accessible to us we work our way gradually—by means of conceptual thinking, judgments, and conclusions—toward other things which we do not grasp immediately. In this manner we gather in a continuously progressive movement—and notwithstanding the circuitous ways on which we may embark due to error and self-deception—a growing treasure of knowledge. However, this entire movement is directed toward an end or goal and a resting at the goal. This end or goal is the *contemplation of that which is* [*des Seienden*]. In the realm of sense knowledge, the goal is sensory apperception, not simply sense "impression," but an intellectually filled [*geisterfüllt*], understanding apperception. In the realm of discursive or syllogistic reasoning, the goal is insight into states-of-affairs [*Sachverhalte*].

As far as such a manifold of cognitive efforts—corresponding to the different genera of existents—in their entirety is concerned, it is possible to demonstrate in detail at which kind of fulfilled apperception they aim. And once the aim or end has been reached, we somehow experience a blessed moment of rest. However, this rest must needs be of short duration, because we always reach only a partial aim or end, one that points beyond itself and posits new tasks. It can nevertheless be said that the fulfilled apperception in which we are allowed to rest is cognition or knowledge in the true and genuine sense, and all thinking efforts are merely ways and means to that end. And from our actual experience or resting at the goal we may arrive at the idea of a spirit that is absolved of the labor of the way, because this spirit rests from the very beginning at the goal of our laborious striving—the contemplation of the plenitude of that which is.

This restful abiding in the contemplation and possession of all that which is can be from the first beginning and truly all-embracing only in the case of that spirit who is himself the plenitude of being and who imparts to all existents their being. And that spirit is God. However, it is possible to conceive of finite spirits who own, from the very beginning of their existence, the full measure of that knowledge of which they are capable by virtue of their nature, a knowledge free from deception and error and a knowledge which they possess in the integral unity of a completely fulfilled life without any diminution and relaxation. An increase in their knowledge would be conceivable only if God were to elevate them above their own nature by imparting to them some measure of the infinite and inexhaustible plenitude of his being. Such a bestowal we call *grace,* and Dionysius describes it as an *illumination.*

For the time being we confine ourselves to a consideration of the natural knowledge of angels. This knowledge exceeds human knowledge in that it is a resting at the goal, a spiritual contemplation or vision of that which is in its plenitude. And this prerogative of angelic knowledge is closely linked with still another essential particularity [*Wesenseigentümlichkeit*] of pure spirits (to which we shall refer presently): They do not "evolve" or "develop," but enter into existence "completed" or "perfected" [*fertig*]. But before we turn to a discussion of this peculiar characteristic, we shall have to give some additional attention to their spiritual life.

(b) *The Unity of Life*

Our knowledge is the foundation upon which we base our position and attitude with respect to existents and with respect to our activities in the world. To the knowing of things there pertains an understanding of their significance for us and of what they mean to each other. We experience this significance inwardly in the form of a vital awareness of values, an awareness which, as a response of our inner life, commands certain attitudes of mind and will and stimulates corresponding active impulses and operations. Our knowing, feeling, willing, and acting are neither completely separated from and independent of each other, nor are they inseparably one. They are rather mutually conditioned by correlative dependencies. They can be individually articulated as independent movements, and the adequate interconnections are by no means always clearly realized. A blindness to values sometimes goes hand in hand with a keen sense for the pure matter-of-factness of things. And we often find a *dead* recognition of values, i.e., a recognition which rationally acknowledges the value-significance of things while no corresponding inward movement ensues. Again, there may be a vital awareness of values, but willing and doing may fall to respond owing to weakness, indolence, irresoluteness, or infidelity. These things are variable in different human beings, and they vary in the same human being at different times. There are moments at which our entire spiritual power awakens to the fullness of its life and at which this life appears collected in perfect unity. Knowledge, love, and action are then inseparably one. And these summits of human existence open to us once again the prospect of a spiritual life which holds itself on this summit immutably and without relaxation. The life of angels must be conceived in such a way.

(c) *The Unity of Power* [Kraft]

In the writings of Dionysius, we found the remark that in angels we must distinguish between essence or nature [*Wesen*], power [*Kraft*], and efficacious action [*Wirken*]. In the creatures we know from natural experience efficacious activity or operation is the "actualization" of a power which was previously a mere potency (δύναμις). To the manifold of active operations—differing as to end and content—of any independent substantial actuality (i.e., *ousia*) there correspond diverse powers or potencies into which the *one* natural power, i.e., the power pertaining to the nature or essence of the actual thing, is divided,

We have been using the term *Wesen* (nature; essence; substance) in a dual sense, namely (1) to designate the specific determinateness conceivable as a universal, and (2) to designate that which makes the individual what it is. It is the conviction of St. Thomas that in the case of angels this distinction does not apply, because every pure spirit embodies an individual species.[65] We need not enter into a discussion of this question at this time, since even where the specific determinateness—with respect to its content—is supplemented by an individual determinateness, the *actual essence* (or nature) contains in itself both determinations in the unity of the individual whole. It is the precise object of our present inquiry to learn how essence, power, and powers (i.e., potencies) are related to each other.

It pertains to the essence or nature of human beings that they possess certain powers (or faculties), e.g., reason and free will. And it pertains to the essence or nature of this particular human being [*Mensch*] that his reason is lucid and his will is resolute. Every active operation of reason and will is a "feat of power" [*Kraftleistung*], and in every such active operation a vital spiritual power is formed in a definite manner. We have made it plain that *spirit* [*Geist*] in the full sense of the word is meaningfulness [*Sinn*] and life and that these two are related to each other like form and matter, inasmuch as meaningfulness imparts to the indefinite fullness of life a determinateness with respect to content. In connection with the term *matter,* however, we have pointed out that in this particular case there can be no question of *space-filling* matter. We also have to remind ourselves again that what we call *form* in material spatial structures is at once meaningfulness and power and that the power is the "feat" or "accomplishment" of the process of formation, whereas the meaningfulness determines the manner of the formation. Meaning and power (or fullness of life) must be distinguished in the individual spiritual *accomplishment* [*Leistung*] as well as in the *power* (potency) on which this performance or accomplishment is based.

The one spiritual power which is the property of human beings is formed by the manifold of the determinateness of meaning [*Sinnesbestimmtheit*], so that it becomes a manifold of powers (potencies). The unity of this diversified forming process is evidenced, on the one hand, by the fact that in a human being who possesses great spiritual power all accomplishments are powerful and, on the other hand, by the fact that strong engagement of this power in one definite direction hampers its actualization in another direction.

To the essence or nature of this particular human being [*Mensch*] there pertains a definite measure of power [*Kraftmass*] that characterizes her individuality, and in addition there pertains to her one prevalent direction of her active operation, a direction which is her very own by virtue of her particular nature. This measure of power must, however, not be conceived as a statically fixed quantity. Human spiritual power is subject—as is the entire essence or nature of the human being—to the law of evolution, and only gradually and under appropriate conditions does it reach the height of actualization attainable to it. The possible courses of this evolution, however, are pre-designed in the essential form [*Wesensform*], and they differ in individual human beings.

Now let us ask which of these conditions and relations apply equally to pure spirits and which of them must be conceived differently. If it is true that meaningfulness and fullness of life pertain to spiritual actuality as such, then both of these must also be found in angels. Compared with human spirituality, theirs is superior and therefore comprises a far greater spiritual fullness [*Geistesfülle*]. And this is indicated by the name *powers* or *virtues* [*Kräfte*].

But is this spiritual fullness of the angels likewise something undetermined and determinable, something that undergoes different kinds of actualization because their being is manifold? Is this fullness perhaps a sort of spiritual *matter* (which would not contravene their incorporeality [*Körperlosigkeit*])?

At any rate, the formative actualization of angels cannot be conceived in the manner of a temporal evolutionary process. They are what they are destined to be according to their nature from the very beginning of their existence, and they are also immediately at the summit of their power. Nor is this power, as is the case with human beings, subject to fluctuations owing to the influence of changing external conditions. Their power is not consumed in operative accomplishments. It undergoes no change. However, it may be heightened supernaturally by the influence of grace.

Is the power of angels to be conceived as formally actualized [*ausgeformt*] in a manifold of different powers? The names of the angels seem to suggest such formal actualization. The fact that the seraphim owe their name to the fire of their love and the cherubim to the luminosity of their knowledge seems to indicate that in each of these choirs a different power or virtue is characteristically prevalent. But such a prevalence has a different meaning in angels than in human beings. The *power* of angels is no *mere potency* which is now operative and then again passes over into a state of mere possibility, which may unfold but, under adverse conditions, may remain forever non-unfolded. The power of angels is forever and ever vitally efficacious in the precise manner and direction prescribed by the range of their nature and in the highest measure attainable to them. It therefore seems more appropriate to speak in the case of angels not of *powers* but rather of *one* power that is formed and is efficacious in diverse ways. Angels are distinguished among themselves by the measure of power which they own according to their nature and by the diverse manner in which their power is formed. And to this unity of power corresponds that integrated and collected unity of their lives of which we spoke earlier: the inseparable unity of knowledge, love, and service.

5. *Actuality and Potentiality.* Potentia Oboedientialis. *Nature, Freedom, and Grace. Evil*

St. Thomas asks the question whether in pure spirits the distinction between actuality and potentiality is valid, and he answers in the affirmative. In the first place, he says, pure spirits are created, and in the act of creation their "potential" essence or nature becomes actual. Moreover, the contraries of actuality and potentiality are found in angels in yet another sense. True enough, these spirits are placed into existence with a "completed" or "perfected" [*fertig*] nature and not, like people, with a nature capable and in need of further development. They need not "become" what they are destined to be, and they have no undeveloped natural capabilities. But, as has already been pointed out, they are nevertheless capable of an increment in their being [*Seinssteigerung*] by the influence of *grace* and *glory*. Like human beings, they are endowed with *potentia oboedientialis,* i.e., a ready capacity [*Aufnahmebereitschaft*] for the reception of divine being. St. Thomas says of this capacity that by virtue of it "anything which the creator wishes to take effect in a creature may actually come to pass."[66]

Grace is the means to unite God and creatures and to make them one. According to what it is in God, grace is the divine love or the divine being, as *bonum effusivum sui,* i.e., a goodness which effusively diffuses or imparts itself while maintaining itself undiminished. According to what it is in creatures, grace is what creatures receive into themselves as imparted divine being, an imparted similitude of the divine nature,[67] and as such limited and created, but replenished by the inexhaustible source of infinite divine being, and capable of unlimited growth.

Some of the statements we have made may sound as if grace were a "second nature" or even not at all distinct from nature. However, the distinctions between grace and nature are far-reaching indeed. Nature, though created and bestowed by God, separates the creature from the creator (yet not in the sense in which evil separates the creature from God, and therefore not in the sense in which a fallen nature is separated from God). A "thing of nature" is placed outside God—though, in another sense, it remains "in him," since there is nothing that "is outside him"—and stands on its own [*auf sich gestellt*]. It is substance or πρώτη *ousia,* bearing within itself its own being and nature [*Wesen*]. On the other hand, grace unites the creature with God. It is infused into the creature, making the latter a "grape on the vine," while grace at the same time remains deeply and firmly implanted in God.

Such an influx of grace is possible in the full sense only in the case of creatures who are *free.* Dead things may serve as instruments of divine efficacious action, and in this sense they may then be said to "contain" grace or to be means of grace (e.g., the sacraments),[68] but they can never be "full of grace" or, as in the case of a person, become *bearers* [*Träger*] of grace. Human beings and angels who are filled with grace are personal bearers of grace, although God, as the living dispenser of grace, never ceases to be the one and only authentic bearer of grace.

Grace calls for a "personal" receptive response. It is a call or a knocking of God, and the person who is thus called is to listen and to open: to open the door of his or her own self so that God may enter. The ready capacity to receive or the *potentia oboedientialis* in the more restricted and authentic sense, therefore, is a capacity to *obey,* to listen to God and to freely surrender one's self to him. The person-to-person relationship makes possible that being-one [*Einssein*] which can come to pass only among persons. And in the relationship between God and the free creature, being one results from the communication and communion of grace.

Grace thus presupposes freedom as well as *nature,* since there must be free creatures if the efficacy of grace is to find fertile ground. On the other hand, nature does not presuppose freedom and is not "personally" received. Rather, creatures find themselves in existence, already endowed with a specific nature which, unlike grace, they are not free either to "accept" or "reject."[69] And angels, too, are placed into existence already endowed with their natures. They have no free choice in this matter. The possibilities of a free and decisive stand with respect to their natures are even fewer in the case of angels because they possess no natural powers of evolution which might be influenced by their free decisions.

All nature thus means limitation, confinement, restraint. No creature is absolutely or unconditionally free. Only the Creator is bsolutely and unconditionally free, because his self is his freedom. And yet there exists in free creatures—in angels and in human beings—a possibility of saying "yes" or "no" to their own natures, which is equivalent to a possibility of saying "yes" or "no" to the Creator. The *non serviam* of Lucifer and the free assent of the first human beings (Adam and Eve) to the serpent's tempting promise, *eritis sicut Deus,* were acts of rebellion against these creatures' own creaturely natures and therewith also against the Creator.

What is the meaning and the effect of such a rebellious attitude? For a creature to aim at equality with the Creator is an absurd and impossible goal, a goal that is not only unattainable in view of the weakness of the creature but also impossible of being granted fulfillment by the Creator, *since* such an aim is intrinsically nonsensical or absurd.

The other side of the question concerns the refusal of the creature to acknowledge the limitations imposed upon it by its creaturely nature and to admit that the creature is subject to God. Is there any way for the creature to free itself from these bounds and bonds—if not by self-exaltation, then perhaps by self-annihilation?

The angel, as a non-corporeal being, lacks the power of a human being to destroy its own body and thus to put an arbitrary end to its bodily life. The angel's purely spiritual life consists—as we have pointed out—in knowing, loving, and serving. All this requires freedom and therefore in some manner and measure the possibility of rejecting and frustrating this kind of life. *Cognition* (in the broadest sense of the term) is the acquisition or possession of knowledge. This entails in creatures a *receiving* (which as such is not in the power of the creature, since it presupposes something that is "donated," and ultimately a donor) and free *acceptance* or *assent.*

In this connection several things come to mind which pertain to the freedom of action of the knowing being. In human sense perception, the things and events of the external world are given in order to be accepted. It is in people's power to move closer and closer toward these things and events and also to use other means which may aid them in acquiring more exact knowledge. But when we use the term "acceptance" we think not so much of the efforts connected with gaining exact sense knowledge, but rather of what is implied in the word *assent* or *belief* [*Zustimmung oder Glauben*] (in the broadest, non-religious sense of the term, such as the English word *belief* has): I am to believe or give credence to what I see or hear. And in view of the inescapable obtrusiveness with which the things and objects of our immediate environment urge themselves upon us, it appears hardly possible to refuse assent to what is "given" in this manner. There are instances, however, when we do not trust our own eyes and ears. Though we may have distinctly understood some words that were spoken to us, we believe we may have heard wrongly. Or we may see something quite tangibly and may yet feel inclined to believe that what we see is an optical illusion. In such instances there are usually some more or less rational "reasons" for refusing assent. However, these reasons are *motivating* causes. They move the will, but they do not force it. And there are other instances where no reasonable ground for doubt exists and where nonetheless credence is refused to something that is highly credible, while, on the other hand, credence is freely given to something wholly incredible.

The more knowledge becomes allied with reason, judgment, and discursive thinking, the greater is the share that freedom has in it. A correspondingly greater effort is then required for the acquisition of knowledge. The number of reasons for and against assent grows larger, a comprehensive perspective becomes more difficult, and there is consequently more leeway for free decision. Whether we like it or not, it is an inescapable and important fact that in the spiritual life frequently *stat pro ratione voluntatis* (will usurps the place of reason). And in many instances this does not necessarily denote "irrationality." It simply means that in certain situations there is no possibility for us to resolve the problem at hand in any other way.

Though angels have an original store of knowledge, not acquired in the course of their existence but pertaining to their very being, they have nevertheless received this knowledge simultaneously with their being. A refusal to "accept" amounts in this case to a rebellious opposition to their own true being. And such an attitude is found wherever and whenever the creature demands equality with God. Lucifer knows full well the distance which separates his being from divine being, but he "refuses to admit" what he yet knows to be true. He thus becomes the "father of lies." For a lie is not, like an error, a failure to recognize the truth or putative knowledge but rather an attempt to destroy the truth, an abortive attempt since truth shatters every lie.

The meaning of the above statement can perhaps be further clarified. Let us imagine a created spirit whose entire being consists in knowing. In this case the attempt to deny truth within the total circumference of this spirit's knowledge would necessarily lead to its own complete annihilation if its knowledge depended exclusively on its freedom. But this is not so. The created spirit has not given itself its being and its knowledge, and it therefore cannot take them away. What it negates nevertheless remains constantly in its sight. It is maintained in being as an unwilling witness to the power which it defiantly opposes and denies, the power which alone—since it is the power which alone was capable of creating the spirit—could annihilate it. But the being of such a spirit exhausts itself in negation and rebellion. It opposes itself to the entire divine order of being and therewith also militates against this spirit's own true being. It is a being which constantly consumes and devours itself and is in this sense an empty and futile being.

The idea of a spirit whose entire being consists in knowing is, however, an untenable assumption. Since knowledge implies and entails freedom, a knowing spirit is of necessity also one which wills.

But because such a spirit possesses its knowledge as an original gift, no acquisitive effort is required with respect to this kind of knowledge. The perfection of knowledge consists in this case in an inward affirmation, in a yea-saying [*Jasagen*] to God, to all created things and beings, and therewith also to this spirit's own being. This harmonious accord and concord is love, joy, and willingness to serve. Rebellion against being, on the other hand, turns all this into the very opposite. Negation of being must simultaneously be hatred of being—hatred of self, hatred of God, and hatred of all existents—and a constant impotent and destructive warfare against all that which is. This does not mean, however, that Satan does not want to be himself. It means that he does not want to be what and how he is in reality and truth. He wants to be like God, and he therewith, even in warring against God, affirms divine being.

In their doctrine of evil, both the Areopagite and St. Thomas spared no effort to elucidate with all possible precision that all being and all existents as such are good. Evil, they argue, can therefore be nothing but a privation of being, and even "evil" spirits are good insofar as they are and have preserved their nature [*Wesen*].[70] They are still, after all, pure spirits, and they are still in possession of a keenness of intellect, a power of will, and a fullness of strength which make them superior in rank to human beings. And while these natural gifts are good in themselves, the perverse use which they are making of them is evil. Added to this, as an evil resulting from punitive judgment, is the loss of the supernatural gifts, especially the cessation of their union of grace with God.

This doctrine of evil was elaborated in the course of the fight against two erroneous teachings: against *Manichaean dualism,* which assumes two independent primordial grounds or causes of all that which is, a primordial principle of good and a primordial principle of evil; and against the view which indeed acknowledges God as the one and only primordial ground or cause of all that which is, but which for that very reason makes God responsible for evil.

On the other hand, if evil is not positive being (but rather a privation of being), both pitfalls are avoided. This is why Christian theologians have used all their ingenuity of mind to demonstrate that evil is neither an independent, positive existent, nor anything in an existent, nor anything possessing a mode of positive existence.

However, it seems to me that in all these endeavors the distinction between a purely natural want or privation—as, for example, an innate debility of reason—and that which is evil in a genuine sense—such as the misuse of a "good" or sound reason for evil purposes—has not been sufficiently stressed. True enough, the theological distinction between sin and evil (as a result of divine punishment [*Strafübel*]) takes this difficulty into consideration, but in the metaphysical discussion of the problem the contrast between these two kinds of evil is neutralized by the grouping together of both kinds under the heading "not-being" or "privation of being."

The German language expresses the different concepts of being which are here involved by the semantic distinction between *schlecht* (bad) and *böse* (evil), both having their equivalent in the Latin *malum.* We speak (in German) of *böse Geister* (evil spirits), not of *schlechte Geister* (bad spirits), and we speak, on the other hand of *schlechte* (bad, poor) mental faculties or endowments, not of *böse* (evil) faculties.

Now "evil" in the strict and authentic sense of the term always and exclusively has its source in free will. The devil does not have a deficient nature, but he has perverted his good nature into evil by using it in a manner contrary to nature. Natural reason hesitates to accept a doctrine which sees evil a mere want or debility, because we definitely experience evil as an efficient hostile force. This force is nothing but the power of the free, spiritual person, and it does not have its origin in the created spirit. Free will—even the free will of the highest among the angels—is therefore not an autonomous ground or source of being, on a level, as it were, with the being of God. Free will is incapable of generating any existent out of its own being, and it thus shares in that nullity [*Nichtigkeit*] which characterizes all created things in relation to and in comparison with the creator. On the other hand, free will is capable of giving a certain direction to action, even if the thus directed action is strictly opposed to the divine will. And an "evil" act is precisely an act of the creaturely will that is in opposition to the divine will. Such an act of the will is certainly something that positively is. It even ranks among the highest existential actualities in the being of creatures. But the direction of such free decision against God is "negative" and strictly contrary to that which is.

We might well call the creaturely will which rebels against the divine will "primordial evil" [*das Urböse*], if only we keep in mind that primordial evil is not a *primordial existent* [*Urseiendes*]. The freedom of the creature is the condition which makes evil possible, and if we regard all natural defects, including everything that is known as "physical evil," as evils resulting from divine punishment [*Strafübel*], we may conclude that everything that is *schlecht* (bad) may likewise in the last analysis be traced back to freedom of will. Both the possibility of evil and the possibility of created grace are rooted in the freedom of created spirits.

Grace is an elevation of creaturely being by means of union with God and effusion of divine being. Evil, as a perversion of the creaturely will, is a barrier that cuts off the influx of grace and therewith annuls the elevation of being effected by grace. Moreover, evil is a kind of being that opposes itself to the existent's own original nature and is thus "perverted" being in the literal sense. The existent's nature or essence is thereby not annihilated, but "perverted," i.e., changed into a negative counterpart [*Gegenbild*] of its positive substance. Theologians call this change a "hardening in evil" or "impenitence" [*Verstockung*].

In human beings we find—in accord with their temporal growth or development—a gradual "formation of habits" in good as well as in evil. And to the lability of the human situation between good and evil corresponds the possibility of a conversion, i.e., a restoration of the original direction of human nature after the "fall." But there also remains the possibility of repeated lapse. On the other hand, it is in accord with the "perfected" nature of pure spirits that their fall is a radical perversion consummated in a single moment of decision and therefore leaving no possibility of conversion.

The passing of angels from essential possibility to actual existence by means of a divine creative act, as well as the perversion of their being by a rebellion of the will, and the elevation of their being by grace, indicate that the contraries of actuality and potentiality have a place in angelic beings in more than one sense. On the other hand, the rising from a preliminary stage of actual being to full actuality—as it occurs in human beings and lower animate creatures in the "progressive development" of their innate powers or potencies—is not found in angels. And one additional difference should be noted. People, after they have learned to walk, to speak, to play musical instruments, have developed their corresponding *potencies* into *definite skills* which they are able to use freely. They are able to use them, *can* use them, but do not have to use them. There is neither any need nor any possibility for them to make constant use of all their acquired skills (and this is a mark of their limited freedom), since certain activities mutually exclude each other and since their limited power is incapable of exercising all acquired skills simultaneously. Similarly, people never have an immediately present or an enduring grasp of the total treasury of knowledge which they have acquired in the course of their lives.

Is there also found in angels such an intermediate stage between capability (potency) and an activity (act) which is equivalent to an acquired skill or habit [*habitus*] that can be freely used? If we assume a corresponding condition in angels, it could at any rate not be an intermediate stage, since there are in angels no undeveloped faculties and therefore no contraries of *potentia* and *habitus*. The only question that requires an answer is the following: Can the always available powers [*potentiae*] of angels be regarded as being intermittently at rest? Against such an assumption there speaks the unity of their undivided power, a power which is not subject to natural fluctuations and which admits—strictly speaking—of no separate capabilities. The nature [*Wesen*] of angels is constantly efficaciously actual by virtue of its fullness of power [*Kraftfülle*] and in a kind of knowledge

that is fully alive [*voll-lebendig*] in love and service.

But the life of angels is nevertheless not wholly immutable. The elevation of which their being is capable owing to the influx of grace means a heightening and enrichment of their entire lives. And both an increment of knowledge and a change of activity appear possible even within the sphere of their natural being. For, on the one hand, they are, according to their nature, not omniscient, omnipotent, and omnipresent (like God) and, on the other hand, they are not self-enclosed [*abgeschlossen*] and fixed [*festgelegt*] to such an extent that it would be impossible for them to receive novel and unfamiliar contents or to move freely in the direction of things that lie outside of their original spheres of action.

To "receive" and to "move" must here, of course, be understood in a spiritual sense. St. Augustine and St. Thomas speak of an intercommunication of angels which they call "speech." But this kind of speech needs no external means of communication. It consists in turning toward one another and in a mutual overtness.[71] In this manner they share in each other's personal life, and such a sharing implies a reciprocal movement and entails an enrichment on the part of the lower members of the celestial hierarchy.

In a similar manner we may perhaps conceive of the communion between guardian angels and the human beings entrusted to their care. If they do not already know by virtue of their own nature the secrets of the human heart, their attentive listening to a call for help may disclose to them something new and unfamiliar. Their aid to human beings, however, must be thought of as having a beginning and being transitory rather than as having been foreseen and preordained from the very inception of their being. In this respect their action differs radically from the working of Divine Providence.

However, the picture changes when in addition to the natural knowledge of angels, we consider their supernatural knowledge or, more precisely, that knowledge which permits them to see all created things in God. St. Thomas, following St. Augustine, speaks in this connection of the matutinal knowledge of angels.[72] In this kind of knowledge many things which they do not know by virtue of their own nature become accessible to them, so that they need not rely on natural communication for the side of creatures. At this juncture, however, our main intent has been to elucidate the natural possibilities that are within the reach of angels. We have pointed out before that every supernatural elevation of being serves to heighten and enrich existence.

In some such manner, then, mutability and change in the life of angels must be conceived, on both natural and supernatural levels. And their being is always life. There is nothing in them that is not alive, and there is no part of their being that is not spiritual life. This is the prerogative by which pure spirits excel those other spirits who are the forms of a body that is bound to space and to matter.

To the pure spirituality of angels there corresponds a less inhibited freedom and a more unlimited being-person [*Personsein*] than are found in human beings. Pure spirits are not absolutely and unconditionally free, since they have received their being and their delimited nature as gifts. And they are unable by their own power to break through the boundaries imposed thereby. But they are masters of their own being in the sense that their being is at their free disposal and that they can completely and unreservedly engage in the kind of life for which they were created. In this realm there are no natural events that follow rigid laws which leave no room for free action, such as are found in the corporeal world. Life in its totality is here equivalent to freedom of action and the responsibility of personal decision. Angels know of only one alternative, for or against God, and there is no room for sliding into estrangement and separation from God unless these are actually willed. And from this consideration additional light falls on that unique and irrevocable decision of angels which determined their eternal destiny.

6. *Form and Matter, Essence* [Wesen] *and the Carrier of the Essence* [Wesensträger] *in Pure Spirits*

The fact that St. Thomas designates angels as *subsisting forms* is closely connected with the particular manner of their being-persons [*Personsein*].[73] He means to indicate that they have no space-filling matter as a foundation of their being, that they are not "in another" but "in themselves," or that "they carry themselves." However, we may remind the reader that we have placed the empty form of the object between the *foundation* and *carrier*, even in those instances where space-filling matter is an essential constituent part of a thing. In turn, we regarded the *person* as a carrier in a preeminent sense because a person not only has and embraces, but "possesses" its essence or nature, which means that a person is master of its own self in several ways. And the being-persons of pure spirits is a purer fulfillment of the idea of personality because there is nothing in their being that eludes this power of free self-mastery.

But if we distinguish between essence and carrier of essence, is it still possible to speak of a "self-carrying" or "self-subsisting" form? Before answering this question, we might do well to clarify another problem. According to Aristotle and St. Thomas, *form* and *essence* (or nature) coincide where no space-filling matter is involved. But now we have discovered that there exists something even in the sphere of pure spirituality which in a certain sense may be called *matter*—not in the sense of that which fills space, but in the sense of a determinable indeterminateness.

Those familiar with the ontological view of Duns Scotus will remember that the *Doctor Subtilis* claims for angels, as for all finite existents, a composition of form and matter, a view which Scotus maintained and defended with all the admirable keenness of his mind.[74] He has no intention denying the incorporeality of pure spirits. The *materia primo prima,* which they share with all finite existents, is not space-filling matter, but something which particularizes itself in both the corporeal and spiritual worlds in accordance with different forms. The matter of the world of spirits thus differs generically from the matter of the corporeal world.

The *materia primo prima* is, according to Duns Scotus, the lowest stage of that which is [*des Seienden*]. It was created by God as an existent with a being of its own, and it is differentiated but not separated from, and it is integrated with the composite of form and matter. The *materia primo prima* is equivalent to the *potentia passiva.* On the one hand, it contains that possibility of non-being (and thus of possible annihilation) which pertains to the nature of all created things as such, and, on the other hand, it contains a ready receptive capacity [*Aufnahmebereitschaft*] and a capability of being formed [*Formungsfähigkeit*].

It is not possible for us to expound the Scotist theory of matter in every detail. All we are attempting to do is to relate what we have described as the *power* [*Kraft*] or *fullness* of life of angels to that matter which Duns Scotus ascribes to pure spirits. What, we have in mind pertains, we believe, to spirit as such and therefore also to the divine spirit. For this reason it cannot be equated with passive potency or with the possibility of non-being.

We must remember in this connection what provided the starting point of our entire inquiry into the nature of being, namely the plenitude of divine power—*potentia Dei*—in which there is no unfulfilled potentiality, which rather is fully actual and fully efficacious being: an infinite plenitude of power that is simultaneously an infinite plenitude of being, two plenitudes which are yet inseparably one.

In all finite actuality there is power mingled with debility, being mingled with non-being, and being and power are never inseparably one. And in every finite actuality there is found *active* and *passive potency*, the possibility of acting efficaciously and the possibility of being acted upon or of suffering (*pati*). The possibility of acting efficaciously we call *power* or *force*, and this we ascribe to the form, for it is the form which effects formation. The possibility of being acted upon is what makes possible the reception of a structural form [*Gestalt*]. The reception of a structural form presupposes in turn something which is either not yet structurally formed at all or not completely formed or separable from its structural form.

Now the *materia primo prima* is conceived as that which is completely formless. This can certainly not be said of the power of angels, for this power bears the imprint of the spirit who owns it. This power is full of meaning [*sinnvoll*], and it is efficaciously actual and active in the life in which it manifests itself. And the individual essence or nature of angels, in which meaningfulness and power interpenetrate, is indissoluble. Meaningfulness and power are not "constituent parts" separable from one another, and a "transformation" of the power of angels, in the manner in which a piece of wax is transformed, is therefore inconceivable.

We have found, however, that finite spirits are not completely and thoroughly determined in their nature [*durchbestimmt*]. They are capable of receiving the influence of a new fullness of power and of being [*Kraft- und Seinsfülle*]. And it pertains to the nature or essence of the personal spirit to be capable of receiving an extraneous fullness of power and being, unless this spirit—in the manner of the divine spirit—already comprises all plenitude primordially.

Now this capacity to receive [*Aufnahmefähigkeit*] we call *passive potency*. It is a potency that depends on extraneous efficacious action. But *active* and *passive* potency must have something in common. This is indicated not only by the common name *potency*, but it can also be factually demonstrated. For that which receives and that which is received interpenetrate in the act of reception. They become one, and this is possible only if there exists a common essence or nature [*Wesensgemeinsamkeit*]. That which one angel imparts to another angel by virtue of his efficacious power is akin to that wherein it is received. Moreover, the formed and efficacious power in the receiving angel is inseparable from the power of forming and receiving. For it is precisely the formed and efficacious power as such which in the act of receiving is raised to a higher and richer efficacy. What we call the *power* of angels is thus simultaneously *active* and *passive* potency.

We follow Duns Scotus in ascribing active potency to form. If we also follow his lead in designating passive potency as matter, it would appear that form and matter constitute an inseparable whole. And this, if I understand him correctly, seems indeed to be the opinion of the *Doctor Subtilis,* for he states that form and matter are united or one in the highest degree in angels. "The *more actual* the form is, the *more it penetrates into the interior* of matter, uniting matter with itself. Now the forms of angels and of the rational soul are the *most actual* forms. They therefore unite matter completely with themselves, and by virtue of their unifying power they are free from *extension* and have no corporeal form."[75]

Accordingly, we may designate angels (with St. Thomas) as pure (i.e., non-corporeal) spirits, but not as pure forms, because there pertains something to their structure that undergoes formation.

In line with what we have previously stated,[76] we are making a distinction between that which is the ultimate foundation of formation and the carrier of the essence or nature. The essence or nature as a composite whole of form and matter rests or stands on itself. And in this self-dependent essence or nature-the Aristotelian πρώτη *ousia* (which in contemporary German philosophy is sometimes referred to as *Selbstandwesen*)—we are able to discern something which "carries" the entire fullness of the essence or nature as well as form and matter. Spiritual beings, insofar as they carry their essence or nature, we call persons. On this level form and matter, efficacious action and receptivity, show the characteristic formation of personal being.

7. *The Realm of Celestial Spirits and Their Mediatorship*

From pure spirits' capability to receive the influence of other spirits there follows something else, something that plays an important part in the angelology of Dionysius. None of the angels is a self-enclosed world apart from the others. They all stand together in the "realm" of spirits, and all are, each in his apportioned place, integrated in a communal life of a firmly ordered "statelike structure" [*Staatsgebilde*]. This "city of God," as we may well call it since all the life that flows through it and all the rulership that pervades it issue from God, is the ideal archetype of all human community and social order, insofar as these latter rest on a purely spiritual foundation. In reading the description which Dionysius gives of the relationships prevailing in the superordinated and subordinated ranks of the celestial hierarchy, we get the impression that he must have had before his mind's eye the human de-ordinations and perversions of the ideal community he envisaged in its purity in the realm of angels. This is why he states with such emphasis that the *dominion* and *rulership* of the celestial spirits are not tarnished by either tyranny or servitude.

When we attempt to gain access to the realm of celestial spirits on the basis of what we know of human communal life and social order, we must, of course, confine ourselves to a consideration of the purely spiritual foundations of human society and exclude everything that derives from the corporeal-bodily nature [*Leib-Körper-Natur*] of people. And since it is impossible to present in this limited space a descriptive analysis of all those social structures in which human beings are conjoined as constituent members, we had best center our attention on that structure which among all earthly orders stands in closest proximity to the realm of celestial spirits, namely, the *church*. In this we follow Dionysius, who likewise sees an intimate relationship between the ecclesiastical and celestial hierarchies.

On the one hand, we regard the earthly church, like the state, as a structure that rests on a juridical foundation and represents a sovereign order. As such it is based on the freedom of the persons who are its members. Such a juridical constitution implies the need for a lawgiver (one or several persons) who lays down its law, who, by virtue of his free will, establishes the rule and regimen of its life.[77] Furthermore, such a structure requires certain representative administrators [*Träger*] of this legal order to whose care is entrusted the observation and execution of the law. Finally, it requires *subjects* who are directly affected by this order of law and who submit to it by virtue of their freedom.[78]

All these requisites are fulfilled in the earthly church. Its sovereign lord and lawgiver is God (visibly represented by his supreme vicar on earth and by the bishops,to the extent that the latter share in the legislative power of the church within the circumference of their own juridical sphere). Its executive organs[79] are the members of the different ranks of the priesthood. Its subjects are the members of the *laity*.

This juridical structure, however, by no means expresses fully and exhaustively the nature of the church. It is not the church's real and innermost essence. True enough, for many years the church was primarily seen from this aspect, and those outside its fold often take such a superficial view even today. But many of our contemporary theologians, as well as the faithful generally, have regained that larger and deeper perspective which St. Paul expressed in the words, "head and body—one Christ." This means to say that the church is not an arbitrarily and artificially constructed institutional "mechanism," but a living or organic whole. In an analogical manner, the primary element in a state or a nation is as a rule the organically evolving folk community [*Volksgemeinschaft*], while the external formal order is subsequently added as a definitive external arrangement and a free confirmation of something that has grown naturally.

The life which pulsates in this organic whole of the church is not the natural life of the individuals and groups that constitute its membership. What animates and vitally informs the church is rather the new life of *grace*, a life which the church imparts to its members. Without the life of grace there would be no church. However, grace is imparted or participated *divine* life, and this life the church receives from its divine head. It is one and the same Christ who imparts life to the church and who lays down the law which this imparted life is to obey. All the "laws" and the entire "institutional organization" of the church serve only one purpose: the communication, preservation, and restoration of divine life.

Since the "living building stones" of the church are human beings, the structure and the institutional organization of the church pay regard to human nature. For this reason, Christ, the head of the church, is both God and human. He communicates his divine life to the church through the medium of his human nature. He addresses people in human language, and he has so ordered the institutional organization which serves the communication of his life that his voice can become audible to the soul by way of the body.

If we now imagine a church composed of pure spirits, then everything that is conditioned by a bodily nature must be excluded, but everything that is of the essence of the church as such must be retained: the divine head as the source from which flows the life of grace and as the lawgiver, and finite persons as free recipients, guardians, and mediators of the life of grace. This is precisely the nature of the "celestial hierarchy." The celestial spirits are open to the divine influence, and they are therefore capable of receiving into themselves the life which flows from the divine source. They are also open to each other, so that the higher ones are capable of communicating their spiritual life to the lower ones, and the lower ones are capable of receiving the gifts of the higher ones.

Now let us ask whether it is possible for us to gain an insight into the nature of such a communion and communication of life on the basis of what we know of human social and communal life. All mutual relations and all intercourse among human beings are founded upon bodily-physical expressions and manifestations of the inner life.[80] But bodily-physical expression is a gateway to inner life, making intimate contact possible and (within certain limits) even a union of minds. In a genuine pupil-teacher relationship, for example, pupils receive and appropriate not only what is contained and expressed in the words of the teacher—detached, as it were, from the teacher's personal life. The spoken word as such, the inflection of the voice, the face—in short, everything that is conveyed by the term *expression*—permit pupils to gain access to the teacher's personal life and to a hitherto unknown spiritual world. Pupils begin to share in a foreign life, a life that fills them and forms them and that comes to be, within the limits of their receptive capacity and their willingness to learn, an integral part of their own spiritual being.

Such spiritual formation may come about in diverse ways and may have correspondingly diverse effects. Independent, resolute, and studious persons will face other human beings in a conquering mood, eager to gain hold of their spiritual world and to appropriate whatever appears commensurate with their own personal growth. And such persons will reject whatever appears noncongenial. Weak, non-energetic persons may unwittingly be overwhelmed and carried away by the force of a stronger life. They may be carried away without being able to appropriate and actualize this life force independently. Or they may be crushed by it, so that their own personal life will be unable to unfold properly. 

The manner and measure of receptive appropriation depend, of course, not only on the recipients but also on the givers. The latter may give themselves wholly or with more or less reserve. They may withhold some of their knowledge, their personal convictions, their individuality. Their self-communication may be in the nature of an imperious conquest or of humble service. There is thus on the side of both teachers and pupils a possibility of either overtness or concealment of the self, and it depends on the freedom of the individual whether the one or the other prevails. We are not defenseless prey to that which, by means of phenomena of expression, tries to force itself upon us from the outside. Nor are we compelled to surrender or communicate unreservedly all that which is alive within us. Both the communication and the appropriation of spiritual possessions and personal life are to a large extent left to our free choice. And what results from this free giving and receiving is in the nature of a spiritual transaction that involves and entails the communal life of spiritual persons, the spiritual growth and spiritual formation of individuals, and the creation of an intimate spiritual association.

On the basis of such a conception of the communal life of spiritual persons, it is quite possible to envisage a spiritual communion that is not dependent on the media of bodily-physical expression. We can readily understand that in the case of pure spirits, a freely willed overtness suffices for both communication and appropriation. And we are also able to conceive of a spiritual communal life that is free of all those perversions and corruptions which darken the picture of human relations and associations. Such corruptions may merely be faults deriving from the imperfection of the human capacity of self-expression: an inability of adequate self-communication by means of bodily-physical manifestations and a corresponding inability to understand bodily-physical expressions. But we have also already referred to those de-ordinations which have a purely spiritual root and are caused by a perversion of the will.

Now in angels there is neither false self-assertion nor a withholding, for the sake of *self-aggrandizement,* of the received fullness of grace, nor a presumptuous self-sufficiency that closes itself to the influx of the abundance of grace. The higher angels communicate their riches generously and ungrudgingly, and if they withhold anything, they do so out of tender regard for those weaker spirits who are not quite equal to the bountifulness of these spiritual gifts. The realm of celestial spirits is thus perfect in itself. Each member spirit stands in its proper place and desires no other. Each is sheltered and shielded in its entire essence. Each is unfolded without restraint and reserve, and each—nourished by the primordial source of love—bears fruit and dispenses love within the domain allotted to it.

There is, however, one basic aspect of the celestial "hierarchy" which may yet present some difficulties, namely, the mediatorship of angels. Is it actually necessary for the lower spirits to receive all their life of grace from the higher ones and for human beings to receive their life of grace from angels? Is there no immediate access to God?

There can be no doubt that God needs no such mediation. He holds every creature in his hand and can exert his influence on each and every one of them immediately. And he does not withdraw or exclude himself when he makes his "first-born sons" his coworkers. He is present in all the actions and operations of his creatures. And he is efficaciously active in a particular manner in all the working of grace, which is an effusive communication of divine life. Therefore, even though millions of angels were to mediate between God and ourselves, this would not mean any separation or unbridgeable distance between him and us, because in every single "mediator" he himself would still be vitally and intimately near and present to us.

It cannot be our task here to determine whether such mediatorship is a fact. All we are trying to ascertain is whether this mediatorship is an essential possibility. And it can hardly be denied that it is. The innermost essence of love is self-giving [*Hingabe*]. God who is love generously gives himself to those creatures whom he has created for love. And why should not those spirits who are nearest to him be privileged to share in all his gifts and dispensations and aid him in passing them on? For it is precisely in this manner that the realm of love is built, a realm in which all are one, in which God enters into union with all creatures to whom he gives himself and who in turn surrender themselves to him. And all creatures together are united with each other and with God by partaking of his succoring love and by mutually sharing their aspiring and ascending love of God.[81]

§6. Meaning and Fullness, Form and Matter. The Contrast between the Creator and His Creation and the Image Relationship

The inquiry into the nature of those finite pure spirits who stand nearest to God has served to bring into proper perspective the specifically creaturely qualities in creatures. God is infinite plenitude and perfect or *pure* form because there is nothing in him that stands in need of formation, nor is there in him any possibility or potentiality of receiving extraneous influences. All finite existents, on the other hand, have limited fullness. Though they are formed, they are not thoroughly formed, i.e., not formed to the extent of their ultimate perfection. And this fullness of finite existents, which is capable and stands in need of further formation, is the *matter* which pertains to all finite actuality. This creaturely fullness is—in addition to creaturely limitation—that which places the creature over against the creator as the "totally other." And this fullness is also that which keeps the creature—subsequent to its creation and its therewith established (relative) autonomy—subject to the divine formative power. By virtue of this fullness, the creature can plastically mold itself by means of its own formative power, i.e., by means of the formative power of its own form, and the creature remains always open to the extraneous influences exerted by other creatures. Form and matter are closely interconnected, and they share in the fullness in common. Form is shaped or determined and efficacious fullness. Matter is an undetermined fullness that is subject to formation and efficacious action. In the process of formation, matter is received into form. The undetermined fullness is turned into a determined, formed fullness that is efficaciously activated by the form.

That element in the form which determines the fullness we have designated as meaning [*Sinn*] or idea. In thinking of God, we can only think of meaning and fullness, and we think of both as being in perfect unity. The division of being in creatures causes a partition into several realms of being that differ with respect to form and matter. Physical-corporeal matter is a non-determined spatial fullness [*Raumfülle*], while spiritual matter is a non-determined fullness of life [*Lebensfülle*]. Physical-corporeal forms mold themselves (or their matter) into space and into a world of corporeal things. Spiritual forms mold their fullness of life into a spiritual realm of persons and creative deeds which are all spiritually and causally interlinked. But the spiritual and corporeal worlds are not unrelated to each other. That which is not pure spirit is a structure that is formed by spirit, either immediately by the divine spirit or mediately by created forms out of proportionate matter. In the structures of nature [*Naturgebilde*] matter and form are joined in an essential union [*Wesenseinheit*]. And all human works presuppose such structures of nature. These latter are then given a new meaning through the instrumentality of an efficacy that works upon them from without.

In their unity of meaning and life all created structures are images [*Abbilder*] of the divine essence [*Wesen*] from which they are distinguished by their materiality [*Stofflichkeit*]. And we shall now make an attempt to describe finite being in terms of its image relationship to divine being. However, we can only do this by turning our eyes first on divine being.

We have ascended to divine being by starting out from creaturely being and by proceeding from the finite and conditioned to the infinite and unconditioned author and archetype [*Urbild*] of everything finite and conditioned. We have also already crossed that borderline which is indicative of what can be learned about the creator from creatures and of what God has himself revealed concerning his own nature. Without crossing this borderline, it would be impossible to learn anything about creaturely being as viewed from the perspective of divine being. We thus look in the Triune Deity for the archetype of what in the realm of creaturely being we have designated as meaning and fullness of fife.

As far as *meaning* [*Sinn;* idea] is concerned, we may refer to our earlier discussions.[82] We regarded the *Eternal Word* (the Logos) as that *unity of meaning* which, as the archetype of all finite units of meaning, encompasses the total plenitude of meaning [*alle Sinnesfülle*]. The church designates in her creed the Holy Spirit as the author of life, as the "vivifier" or "life-giver" (*vivificans*). Ultimately, however, only the one who does not receive life but is "life in person" can vivify or give life. In the *Holy Spirit* we thus see the divine fullness of life.

It need hardly be emphasized that this statement does not imply a partition or division of the divine essence. The one essence owned in common by all the Divine Persons is life and love, wisdom and power. Aside from the relations of the three Persons to one another, nothing can be predicated of one of them that does not pertain to all of them. And if, within the indivisible unity of God, we distinguish certain *attributes* and ascribe some of them to this person and others to that person, we are thereby merely attempting to make the incomprehensible intelligible. And yet what the creaturely image reveals to us of the divine archetype serves to make us see creaturely being in a new light.

But to make us understand (as far as one can speak of "understanding" in these matters) the Holy Spirit as the dispenser of life and as the archetype or paradigm of all creaturely life, something must first be said concerning the position of the third person in the Deity.

As was emphasized in our earlier discussion, the only distinctions among the Divine Persons concern their relations to one another, relations which are explained by the different manner of their procession. Thus, the Father is called *Father* because everything proceeds from him, while he proceeds from no one and nothing else. The Son is called *Son* because he proceeds from the Father. And "he is called the *Word of the Father* because he proceeds from the Father as an effect or act of the intellect, as a conception of the spirit, and this latter name is also applied to the word that is inwardly produced by the intellect in us."[83] The third Person is called the *Holy Spirit* "because this person proceeds from the Father through the Son in a single spiration in the manner or mode of love, and it is this first and highest love which moves and guides hearts to a sanctity which is essentially love for God."[84]

We have been trying to understand the plurality of the Divine Persons from the fact that God is *love* and that love is a free self-giving of an I to a Thou, and a union of both in a We.[85] Because God is spirit, he is fully transparent to himself and generates from eternity the "image" that pertains to his own being, an image in which he sees himself as he is in himself—his co-essential Son, Eternal Wisdom, or the Word. And because God is love, the "image" which he generates of himself is love also, and the mutual relationship of Father and Son is a loving self-giving and a union of love. But because love is the highest kind of freedom,[86] a giving of self as the act of one who fully possesses himself (i.e., a *person*)—in the case of God, however, the act of a person who is and loves not in the human manner, but who is love or whose very being is love—the divine love must itself be a Person: the Person of Love. And when Son and Father love each other, their mutual self-giving is simultaneously the free act of the Person of *Love*.

However, love is *life* in its highest perfection. Love is being which eternally gives itself without suffering any diminution, and it is thus infinite fecundity. The Holy Spirit is therefore the *gift* as such: not merely the mutual self-giving of the Divine Persons to one another, but the self-giving of the deity *ad extra* [*nach aussen*]. The Holy Spirit thus comprises in itself all the gifts of God to his creatures.[87] Because God's wisdom foresaw from eternity all created things and being, the Logos as Wisdom in Person is the universal archetype of the determinateness of all creaturely essences or natures, the eternal paradigm of everything they are destined to be. And because God's creative will, his existence-creating and life-imparting love have from eternity apportioned to creatures their *power of being* [*Seinsmacht*] or the *power* of unfolding their essence or nature, the Holy Spirit—as the person of life and love—is the archetype of all creaturely life and efficacious action as well as of that spiritual radiance of their essence or nature which is a property even of material structures. And if, finally, in the standing-upon-itself [*Aufsichselbstgestelltsein*] of every independent actuality πρώτη *ousia*) we may see an image of the Father as the primary unconditioned principle, then the entire structure of created existents ("that which is") turns into an image of the Triune Deity. But because all that which is is *one* and because there is never an *empty form* without fullness, and the fullness of the essence is simultaneously a meaningfulness and powerfulness which form themselves into existence, all that which is analogically mirrors the unity of the divine essence.[88]

§7. The Image of the Trinity in Inanimate Corporeal Things

From this vantage point we may now gain an understanding of the essential form [*Wesensform*] as the potent formative principle that imparts meaning and perfects being. The essential form exercises this function even in the lowest realm of actuality, i.e., in the realm of purely corporeal things. Their power of being is a potent force for filling space and for being efficaciously operative in space. Corporeal structures are molded by the formative force that is operative within them and with the cooperation of external causes. There is on this lowest stage no matter that temporally precedes formation, but there is nonetheless a union of form and matter. The fullness is here *spatial fullness* [*Raumfülle*]. It is formed, albeit not thoroughly or completely formed and therefore capable of further formation. And this fullness is therefore *matter* in the dual sense of that which fills space and of that which, though undetermined, is determinable.

The creation of the corporeal world signals the origination of form and matter and the separation of space-filling matter and spirit. The spirit creates for itself in space and in the filling of space an extraneous *means* or *medium* for its self-representation. In this the spirit is taking one further step beyond the stage represented by the setting apart of the world of ideas from the Divine Spirit. Material formation is a kind of self-mirroring of the spirit in the medium of spatial structures.

The forms of corporeal things are the mean [*ein Mittleres*] between the personal spirit and space-filling matter, and they point the way from the former to the latter. In their meaningfulness and self-unfolding power they are akin to the spirit, but they lack the conscious freedom and auto-motive vitality that are requisites of spirituality in the full sense. The spirit uses these forms as bridges to a world of spatial structures, a world which is to serve the spirit as a means of self-expression. As the language of the spirit, these forms are pronouncements of the spirit and as such intelligible to the spirit, although they are not intelligible to themselves. As forces they are in motion and cause motion, although they do not cause their own motion.

The spirit as a principle of understanding (*intellectus*) enunciates the word or the meaning, and this word remains intelligible, i.e., accessible to the spirit. The spirit in its motion (*voluntas*) imparts to the meaning motion, mobility, and motivating force (*motum, mobile et motivum*). The primary movement is formation, i.e., the forming of matter into space. This first movement is a presupposition for the second movement, namely, the efficacious operation of the formed material structures—the material bodies—in space, of their movements and changes as well as of the movements and changes which they cause. These movements and changes and their causal relations permeate the entire texture of the spatial-material world or nature. But just as the "word spoken" by the Creative Intellect remains intelligible for the created intellect, so that which is efficaciously operated and endowed with an efficaciously operating power by the Creative Will remains accessible to the created will.

At this point we do well to remind ourselves of what we have previously said concerning the different possible states or conditions of the created world. That material nature which we know from experience is neither a pure expression of the divine plan of creation nor a pure actualization of the divine will—neither a pure formation from the inside *ad extra* nor a frictionless, mutually promotive cooperation of forces. But owing to the fact that the actual "fallen" state of material nature points beyond itself to an original state of "integrity," the possibility of such an original state can be envisioned.

For the purpose of throwing further light on the composition of material-corporeal structures, we recall that in the preceding discussions the terms body, soul, and spirit were used with different connotations. In the sense suggested by experience, body, soul, and spirit are bound to specific realms of actuality. In this sense, the soul is the supra-material [*stoffüberlegen*] form which animates a body, molding it from within, in accordance with the specific essence, in a temporal process of evolution and with the aid of extraneous structural material elements. The living body [*Leib*] in this sense is this particular physical body [*Körper*] which is animated and formed by the soul. And spirit [*Geist*] in this sense denotes an incorporeal, rational, and freely active essence or nature (either the human soul or a pure spirit). In a somewhat broader sense, the term "spirit" is also applied to non-personal structures, namely, to meaningful structures [*Sinngebilde*] which are intelligible to personal intellects and are significant for their lives.

If we understand the terms body, soul, and spirit in this sense, then a corporeal structure that has not been molded by a supramaterial form in a vital evolutionary process is not a living body [*Leib*], the corresponding form is not a soul, and there can, of course, be no question at all of a freely active spirit [*Geist*]. But this *dead physical body* [*Körper*] nevertheless has, like every creaturely being, a *meaning* [*Sinn*], and it is therefore in the broader sense of the term a spirit-filled [*geisterfüllt*] structure and thus a structure through which the Creator Spirit speaks to the created spirit. By enunciating its meaning with the aid of its sensible appearance, this structure steps outside itself [*geht aus sich heraus*] and has some amount of *spiritual being.*

This brings us to the second meaning of body, soul, and spirit, according to which they signify the basic forms of actual being. In this sense, the being of the soul denotes the fluid mobility that tends toward formation. The being of the body denotes the possession of a thoroughly formed essence or nature. And the being of the spirit denotes a free self-transcending [*Herausgehen aus sich selbst*], a free self-enunciation or ex-spiration of the essence. And this triune manner of unfolding also holds true in the case of *dead things,* inasmuch as they too attain to the form that corresponds to the determinateness of their essence only in the course of their temporal existence, inasmuch as they actually possess their thoroughly formed essential structure, and inasmuch as they enunciate or ex-spirate their essence.

We thus encounter in the realm of material being a twofold triunity: first, in the structure of existents, inasmuch as they stand upon themselves as thingly carriers of their essence or nature and inasmuch as, by virtue of their essence or nature, they are meaningful and unfold their being with the aid of that potent force which pertains to the essential form. And, second, this unfolding of being proceeds again in a triune manner: It is a self-forming into a structure that pertains to a particular essence or nature [*wesenseigentümliche Gestalt*]. It implies possession of a thoroughly formed essence or nature. And it is a self-transcending in efficacious action *ad extra,* in active involvement in the causal texture of corporeal nature and in a radiation of the individual essence or nature that extends into the spiritual world. Lastly, the triple unfolding of being in the material realm has an analogue in the three basic modes of space-filling: the liquid, solid, and gaseous formation of matter.

§8. The Image of the Trinity in Non-Personal Animate Beings

That which is efficaciously operative in the formation of animate beings and exercises its efficacy as the "center" or "core" of a structural unity we have designated as a supra-material form, living form, or soul. This form or soul, though delimiting and enclosing itself from within, receives into itself, embodies in its structure, and transforms extraneously existing material elements, and it produces or generates new independent structures of the same species. We are dealing here with a kind of formation in which life is *auto*-motive [Eigen*bewegung*]—a self-enclosed cyclic movement that yet procreatively reaches out beyond itself. This kind of life is an image of divine self-sufficiency and self-sustenance as well as of divine self-giving and creative productivity.

That which is alive or animate is more self-sustaining than the material-corporeal thing because it has a genuine primordial source in its own self, and it is therefore a more strongly marked image of the Father. As a self-enclosed and self-delimited structure, the animate being is a complete unity of meaning [*Sinneinheit*] and as such a more strongly marked image of the Logos. It bears within itself the power of unfolding its own essence or nature and of generating new structures, and in this vitality and fecundity it is a more strongly marked image of the Holy Spirit.

The *power of being* or the *life-force* of the animate creature is, on the other hand, proportioned to the structural unity into which it is to unfold as well as to the new "births" which it is to produce. And just as its essence or nature is not already completely actualized from the outset but is evolving and becoming more and more actual in a temporal process, so it also does not bear within itself from the outset the measure of power [*Kraftmass*] that is proportionate to its essence or nature, but must progressively gain possession of it. To attain this goal as well as to complete itself in its structural unity, the animate creature has to rely on the material elements of the corporeal world. Just as it is capable of receiving into itself and of formally appropriating foreign material elements, so it is also capable of making use of these elements' internal forces and of transforming these forces into vital energy. For this reason the more or less perfect unfolding of the animate creature's essence or nature depends on its *environment*.

In plants, formation is no more than a mere forming of matter [*Stoffgestaltung*]. Plants have not yet attained to the state of "being their own selves" and thus of forming themselves from within. The *animal soul* has reached that stage. It continues, like the lower forms, in the spatial forming of matter, but beyond this its *life is an internal movement* and the *forming of a soul structure* [*seelische Gestalt*]. The intake of food is "felt." The taste of the received material elements is experienced as a sensory impression "from without," and satiation is felt as resulting from bodily functions and as a physical state. Both the taste of food and satiation with food are intimately associated with an "internal impress," with satisfaction or repugnance, and with the more durable inner states of contentment or discontentment. And even the actual measure of power as well as its increase and decrease are felt in specific *vital emotional states* [*Lebensgefühle*].

All of this has its *raison d'etre* in the nature of the soul, which on this level has a tendency to unfold in a threefold manner: in the direction of material corporeality, in the direction of its own self, and in the direction of self-transcendence. For every external sense impression is an encounter with the surrounding world, and the contrast between the *self* and the external world is *felt*, so that the life of the soul compels a constant reckoning and coming to terms [*Auseinandersetzung*] with the external world. And body and soul are being formed in these encounters.

This forming of the individual being, however, is preceded by that original formation which results from the specific determinateness of the essence or nature. The *life force* is here a *body-soul* power. And this means not only the power of forming matter into a living body [*Leib*], but the capability of moving and activating in space the already formed body in diverse ways—always. however, in accordance with the specific essence or nature. And in this process the body receives its complete "actual formation" [*Ausgestaltung*]. Moreover, it means that the animal soul is capable of moving itself and of being active in diverse ways, and in these movements and activities the original "design" of the soul-structure expresses itself in a concrete manner.

What the animal "encounters" in its surrounding world sets it in motion internally and causes it to assume specific attitudes with respect to the things and beings encountered. Reactions of fear, rage, etc., are responses to received impressions. Although they originate internally, they tend to manifest themselves externally, and they produce several effects. These "responses" impress a definite stamp upon the body—a bodily *expression* of the soul, which may be a temporary formation or a set of "features" of enduring character. And these responses cause certain externally manifest bodily activities, such as movements of flight or grasp, and they leave definite "traces" in the soul, such as an inclination and readiness for the resumption of identical positions and attitudes as well as enduring inner modes of behavior [*habitus*].

In these attitudes and responses the *single* power of the soul is being articulated and formally developed into a manifold of *powers* (faculties, skills, inclinations) without yet losing its unity. And the *life* in which this power of the soul unfolds itself is being formed into vital movements of varying content.

All these manifestations of the animal soul reveal a supramaterial quality which far surpasses that of the plant soul. The animal soul possesses an inner individual life that is detached, as it were, from space-filling matter, that is mirrored in the already formed material structure (the body) by constantly occurring transformations (in the phenomena of expression), and that turns the body into an instrument of the individual's activities in the external world. This is made possible by the dual nature of the body, which is a body in the corporeal world and simultaneously an animate structure formed by the soul, and by the dual nature of the soul, whose life is an internal movement and simultaneously an external formation of matter. The result is the transformation of soul movement into body movement and of body movement into purely material corporeal movement.

On the other hand, however, the life of the animal soul remains tied to and conditioned by the body. Everything that befalls the animal soul is occasioned by the body, and it affects the body in one way or another. And the power of the soul which exerts and consumes itself in its inner life (as well as in its external forming of matter) is nourished by the influx it receives from the corporeal world through the medium of the body. But this same power is also diminished and consumed by the resistance it meets in its encounters with the external world.

With the awakening of an inner life, an entirely new kind of image relationship to the Deity appears: a relationship which is an analogical counterpart of the duality of an inner personal life and a self-transcending forming of an external world. And this inner life bears within itself the seal of the Trinity. As a life that *stands upon itself* [*eigenständig*] it is an image of the Father. As a *meaningful* [*sinnerfüllt*] life—full of meaning by virtue of its contents, even though these contents are not yet rationally understood by an ego—it is an image of the Son. And as *life,* as manifestation of *power,* as radiation of the essence or nature, it is an image of the Holy Spirit. But the entire inner life, the forming of the body, and the active operation upon the external world are at this stage still things that merely "happen" [*Geschehen*]. They happen without being either understood or freely willed and are therefore not personal acts of a free spirit.

§9. The Image of God in Human Beings [*im Menschen*]

1. The Human Soul as Compared with Lower Forms and with Pure Spirits

All the forms of corporeal structures are in a stage of "transition" from personal spirit to space-filling matter. They are ways or means by which the spirit forms itself into space. These forms pertain to the spirit as its products and—in their ascending scale from the lower to the higher ones—they bear within themselves more and more of the nature of the spirit. Where there is found an internal individual life—such as in the animal soul—a preliminary stage of spiritual life has been attained. And where the individual life of the soul has received a personal formation, the spirit nature is fully marked and expressed. Therefore, the *human soul* is not a mean between spirit and matter, but a *spiritual creature*—not only a formed structure of the spirit, but a *forming spirit*. But the human soul differs generically from pure spirits on account of the fact that it does not cease to be a medium and a transition. As the form of the body, it forms itself into space like the lower forms. Its spirituality shows distinct traces of its being tied to matter, and its spiritual life rises from a hidden ground.

We shall attempt, then to show how the human soul, as a matter-molding form, differs from the lower forms, and how, as spirit, it differs from the higher spirits. The forming of bodies and souls of both animals and human beings takes place initially, i.e., before birth and during the earliest stages of life, in an involuntary manner. And while this involuntary forming does not cease, even in human beings, during the entire course of life, a second manner of forming is added, intervening in the first and gaining more and more ground as soon as the process of *education* begins. The *habituation* of the child, which may be compared to the training of animals,[89] represents an intermediate stage between completely involuntary formation (as we observe it in physical growth and in the forming of limbs and bodily organs and generally in what is known as *physiological processes*) and voluntary or willed formation (as, for example, the free control of physical deportment and facial expression). The child is *habituated* or *conditioned* to sleep and to eat at definite hours, and with proper guidance it "learns" to walk and" speak" (at this early stage speaking merely means imitating certain words) until the time arrives when reason awakens and the child becomes able to use its will and to understand what it is asked to do.

At this early stage of the child's development, the formative will of the adult person makes use of certain plastic urges and impulses of the infant and, while the resulting behavior may resemble very closely that of free, rational persons, there is as yet no question of *personal* formation in the true sense. This latter becomes possible only with the inception of a genuine intellectual life, i.e., at the moment when the I [*das Ich*] "awakens" and acquires full consciousness of itself—a consciousness which may pass over into a genuine *understanding* of the person's own life as well as of all the meaning encountered in the external world—and when the I learns to determine itself, i.e., to give direction to and become personally engaged in its own actions.

Education presupposes freedom and understanding because it addresses itself to the will and points out the direction which the will is to follow in its acts. Whether the will actually follows this direction rests with the will's own free decision. *Physical education* thus means much more than merely bodily hygiene, physical exercise, or physical habituation. It means directing the will to a planful, conscientious, and free forming of the body. And such a free forming is possible because of the fact that the soul is the form of the body, so that the soul's attitude expresses itself naturally in the body. However, in the soul there dwells the I, and the soul's modes of action are the life of this ego, so that the I—within certain limits—may itself either evoke or (to an even larger extent) suppress or stifle these modes of action. And the same holds true with respect to the ways in which the soul affects the life of the body. The I is capable of either initiating and increasing or arbitrarily thwarting and canceling this influence of the soul on the body. Expressions of joy, for example, can be suppressed as well as artificially produced.

We thus see that the body can be formed at will. But because what is taking place here is an exerting of some influence on something that is in a process of evolution, a keen observer will be able to distinguish what is "genuine" from what is "faked" or "feigned." Only where not only the bodily expression but even the affections and emotions are restrained and controlled, does external self-restraint assume the features of natural expression. And where the equanimity of the soul is the result of an internal collectedness, the external "composure" appears as the final consummation of a thoroughgoing forming from the vital center of interiority.

Our considerations have made it clear that free formation or self-formation extends not only to the forming of the body but also, and even prevalently, to the forming of a person's soul. Human beings are spiritual persons because they are free not only with respect to their bodies but also with respect to their souls, and they exercise power over their bodies only to the extent that they exercise power over their souls. The soul's capability of self-formation is related to what it has in common with the pure spirit and simultaneously to that wherein it differs from the pure spirit. Both the human soul and the pure spirit are conscious or—in the case of the human soul—become conscious of their ego-life and are capable of freely influencing its course. But the human soul differs from the pure spirit in that its free modes of action are not co-extensive with the soul's total being but are rather an exertion of influence on something that is engaged in a process of evolution, and these free modes of action leave certain traces in the soul by virtue of which the soul attains to its final structural formation and firm contour. The pure spirit, on the other hand, receives its nature as a readmade formal structure, a structure which, while it unfolds in its life, does not undergo any change.[90] The human soul must gradually gain possession of its essence or nature, and its life is the way that leads to that goal. This is why in the case of the human soul *formation* is possible and necessary. But so that this formation may be *free*—and not an involuntary occurrence in the manner of the animal soul's being formed by the natural process of its evolution—the human soul must have self-knowledge and be capable of taking a stand with respect to its own self. It must find itself in a dual sense: It must *learn to know* itself, and it must *come to be* what it is destined to be. And freedom has a share in the attainment of both of these ends. But the cognitive finding itself of the human soul, too, has more than one meaning because, as we have indicated on several occasions, *knowledge* and the *self* are both equivocal terms.

2. *Stages of Self-Knowledge*[91]

It cannot be our task here to unfold the meaning of the word *knowledge* in its every aspect. We shall confine ourselves to pointing out different possibilities and stages of self-knowledge, since they will reveal to us something about the essence or nature of the spiritual soul.

The most primordial form of self-knowledge is that consciousness which is associated with the life of the ego. The ego [*Ich*] is in this case conscious of "itself" and of its life. The *self* owes its most primordial meaning to the fact that to its being, i.e., its life, there pertains a being-there-for-itself [*Für-sich-selbst-dasein*] (= being conscious [*Bewußtsein*]), a reflection that is immanent in all spiritual life. This consciousness is not an individual *act,* not an independent experiential unit. Nor is the self-conscious ego an *object.* This means that at this stage there are as yet no opposites of knowledge and an object known, as there are in external and internal apperception.

We mentioned before that the primordial, undivided ego-life already implies a cognitive transcending of the sphere of the *pure ego.* I experience my vital impulses and activities as rising from a more or less profound depth. The dark ground from which all human spiritual life arises—the soul—attains in the ego-life to the bright daylight of consciousness (without, however, becoming transparent). The ego-life thereby reveals itself as a soul-life, and the soul-life—by its going forth from itself and by its ascending to the brightness of light—simultaneously reveals itself as spiritual life. The *self* expands from a point-like *pure ego* by adding to itself that "space" of the soul which is circumscribed by the ego, but the self is not able to raise up this space as a whole into the brightness of light. It is a space which the ego is able to traverse. but unable to fill.[92] Ego and soul are not merely juxtaposed, but inseparably linked. To the human soul there belongs a personal ego that dwells in the soul, that embraces the soul, and in whose life the being of the soul becomes a living and conscious presence. And the human ego is so constituted that its life rises out of the dark depth of the soul. 

The illuminable darkness of the soul makes it understandable why self-knowledge (in the sense of knowing one's own soul) must be regarded as a gradually increasing possession. If such a gradual acquisition is to be a real *task*, it must be presupposed that the eventual possession is achieved freely. The primordial kind of consciousness, which is integrally associated with all ego-life, is simply given without being initiated by an act of will. But this primordial consciousness may pass over into cognitive *activity* which as such is free. And because it is free, the passing over into it must also have been freely attainable from the outset.

For example, when I turn toward a joyous emotion in a spiritual movement or impulse, this turning toward is no longer—like the accompanying consciousness—a co-constitutive part of joy but a *novum*, i.e., an independent experiential unit. The joyous emotion and the comprehending grasp which attentively turns toward this emotion are opposed to each other as object and objectively oriented cognition.[93] Attentive turning toward the object is the first step in the acquisition of knowledge in the more restricted and genuine sense of the term. It is the first step on the way to an intellectual appropriation which establishes with certainty *what* the known object is, an appropriation that grasps and classifies the object conceptually and that inquires into its contextual relations, its whence, whither, and why, its conditions and effectual consequences.

The being and life of the soul are as manifold as the modes of knowledge by means of which it can be comprehended. Our attention may turn toward the content of an experience—such as joy—in order to establish therein and thereby what joy as such is. We may well disregard here such general knowledge of the essence

[*Wesenserkenntnis*] since it does not lead us any further (at any rate not immediately) in our inquiry into self-knowledge. However, it may happen that our attention turns toward that previously hidden depth which has been illumined in our experience. For example, I may have accomplished something of which hitherto I had not thought myself capable, and in this accomplishment I begin to realize for the first time "what sort of human being I am." And this, too, may come about in different ways. There is a way of looking at ourselves in the manner we look at other human beings: observing, as it were, from without, verifying, examining.[94] This is what we call *inner apperception*. Self-experience and self-observation are based on this kind of apperception, and they in turn lead further on in the same direction. And self-education, too, may take its start from inner apperception.

To use an example, I have lately been trying to do some painting, and I have made the discovery that I am not doing too badly. I have therefore decided to further develop my newly discovered talent. Or, as another example, I may have "caught" myself in passing hasty judgments on others, and I know this to be a bad habit which I must try to overcome. Such factual verifications, in which I see myself as an object, reveal—as we stated before—the soul as a thing-like whole endowed with qualities which manifest themselves in the soul's attitudes and acts and which, on the other hand, can be influenced by these attitudes and acts. And because these attitudes and acts are "mine," i.e., manifestations of my freedom, I have the power of cooperating personally in the formation of my soul.

However, this manner of looking at the molding one's self does not penetrate to the essence of the soul and therefore does not permit a genuine forming of the essence. This essence of the soul is revealed in the primordial experience, not in the subsequent verification. For the soul's essence not only "manifests" itself in this primordial experience, but is *alive* and clearly evident in it. And a genuine forming of the essence is possible only as a primordial life-process.

By "essence of the soul" we do not mean the *universal* essence (i.e., what a soul is as such), but the specific nature of the individual human soul or its *personal particularity*. If, for example, on the basis of some instruction or indoctrination, I have gained the conviction that it is wrong to pass hasty judgments, and if in the previously described manner I have come to notice this fault in myself and have resolved to make every effort to overcome it, it is quite possible that I may succeed and that I subsequently change in a manner distinctly noticeable to myself and to others. And yet this does not necessarily imply that something is happening in the depth of the soul. I am still "fundamentally the same human being that I was before."

It is an entirely different matter if, for example, by my hasty judgment I have seriously hurt another human being and have suddenly become aware of "what I have done." In this case I *experience* in a primordial and genuine manner what is involved in passing judgment. I am seized with horror in view of the grave consequences of my behavior, and I detest myself on account of my thoughtless and inconsiderate attitude. This is that true contrition, that sorrowful remorse, which makes the soul capable of genuine inward renovation. Here the very root of the evil is exposed and eradicated.

The question which naturally suggests itself, as to what elements in such a process are natural and which are supernatural, need not be discussed at this time, since we shall first have to gain a clear insight into the natural structure of the soul before it will be possible for us to understand where in the soul may be found the precise place that disposes it for the reception of supernatural influences.

We have repeatedly described the soul as a sort of "space," and we have spoken of its "depth" and its "surface." The same idea is expressed in the metaphor of the *castle of the soul,* a castle that has outer and inner chambers as well as an innermost abode. The "I" inhabits this castle, and it may choose to reside in one of the outer chambers, or it may retire into that nearer and innermost abode. And the examples we have cited may now aid us in gaining an understanding of the meaning of these metaphors which, after all, are nothing but a necessary expedient in any attempt to describe in a tangible manner situations and conditions of the soul which are of a completely non-spatial nature.

That ego which apprehends, observes, and works upon its own self as if this self were a purely external thing evidently does not have its seat in the interior of the castle. It almost seems as if this ego had left the castle in order to be able to look at it from the outside. To be sure, it cannot really do this. For the observation of one's self is *ego-life,* and the ego possesses no life that is not soul life.

Without its relation to the soul, the ego-life would be nothing at all. And thus, if the ego intellectually adopts the point of view of a spectator in order to look upon its own self, it nonetheless remains inseparably tied to itself, notwithstanding its transposed standpoint. We may safely assert, however, that in this case the ego has abandoned the natural locus of its being, its actual center of gravity, that it has deviated from the primordial direction of "its life" and is thus not in possession of its full, unbroken, and undivided vital power. However, once the ego has reached a point where it is no longer wholly and indivisibly itself, it is unable to encompass itself wholly with its personal transforming power.

3. The Essence (Nature), the Powers, and the Life of the Soul

We have called the soul as a whole the essential form [*Wesensform*] of the body. But, as we have already seen in the case of the animal soul, the soul itself is something that has been formed, and it bears its form within *itself*. That which forms the *powers* (faculties) and the *life* of the soul is its essence,[95] and this formation rests on the fact that, as was stated above, we must distinguish in the essence between *meaning* and *power*. Meaning is revealed in the final structure [*Zielgestalt*] to which the soul is ordained by the determinateness of the essence, while power or potency of being [*Seinsmacht*] has been given to the soul so that it may come to be what it is destined to be. This power unfolds in the *life* of the soul in the threefold sense of the forming of the body, the inward, non-conscious activity of the soul, and its conscious ego-life.

Ego-life, in turn, is something that has been formed and that is filled with meaning. It receives the determinateness of its meaning, though not exclusively, from the essence of the soul. Ego-life is—not exclusively, but prevalently—a reckoning and coming to terms [*Auseinandersetzung*] of the soul with something that is not the soul's own self, namely, the created world, and ultimately God. The life of the ego receives impressions, works upon them creatively, and responds to them. In this way the manifold of its meaningful contents and its articulation in coordinated and consecutive self-enclosed experiential units acquires determinateness, while the unity of the *stream of experiences* rests upon that flux of life which continuously permeates all experiential units.

In accordance with the basic trends or directions of the ego-life (receiving, working creatively upon that which has been received, and responding) the *single* power of the soul forms itself simultaneously into a plurality of differentiated *powers* (potencies) with diverse directions: cognitive powers that are ordained to receiving (*inferior* and *superior*, or *sensory* and *spiritual* powers, proportionate to the structure and articulateness of the objective world), internally retaining and creatively working powers (of which more will be said presently), and responsive powers. The latter are known in scholastic terminology as *vires appetitivae* (powers of appetitive striving) and are traditionally divided into inferior and superior powers, the powers of sense appetite and of will.[96] The development of a diversity of *powers* does not do away with the unity of the soul and its single innate power. This is experimentally demonstrated by the fact that strong engagement and consumption of power in a specific kind of activity means a curtailment of the power available for activities of a different kind and direction.

We must further remind ourselves that in the human soul—and likewise in the essential forms of lower animate beings—the measure of power that pertains to them according to the determinateness of their essence is not present from the beginning of their existence, but must be acquired in the course of their evolution and growth. While their soul life as such constantly consumes power, it also aids in opening up to the soul new sources of power. This comes about, first of all, in the process of the building up of the body, since the power of the soul is replenished again and again by the growing body (even though both the life of the body and the inner life of the soul constantly consume power). Secondly, the soul receives the influences of that trans-subjective [*ich-jenseitig*] world which becomes accessible through the medium of ego-life. The bright sunshine and the radiance of the azure sky, a serene landscape, the gay laughter of a child, or some consoling word of encouragement—all of these may serve to awaken new life in the soul. What strikes the senses in all these experiences is a spiritual reality which asks to  be admitted into the soul, so that this reality may gain life in it. But in being received into the soul, this same spiritual reality displays new life-giving power. And in this process of receiving and giving a new relationship between *meaning* and *power* is revealed. The meaning—divorced from the life context of spiritual persons—that we encounter in those interpersonal structures which owe their being to the creative work of the spirit is, as it were, charged with power (i.e.. with *potential energy*) and is discharged as soon as it re-enters into the life context of a spiritual person. This discharge takes place in the interiority of the soul, which works creatively upon the received contents of meaning.

4. *The Interiority of the Soul*

If we are to gain clear insight into the peculiar nature of the human soul, it is of the greatest importance that we first acquire an adequate understanding of the interiority of the soul. Cognitive powers exercise, as it were, external functions and services in the castle of the soul. They admit or even draw in the things of the external world. The senses are the portals through which "sensible" things enter. And reason penetrates as a conqueror into that spatial distance which lies beyond the sensory realm, and into that "interiority" of things which, though it does not strike the senses, nonetheless becomes accessible by means of sensible exteriority. Both sense perception and intellectual knowledge are experiential units which endure for a shorter or longer period of time. They pass and make room for new vital impulses and movements. But the passing of these experiential units does not mean that their content is lost. The meaningful content, once received, is inwardly retained—for a shorter or longer period of time, and possibly forever.

The primary mode of inner reception and retention is related to the *retentive power of the memory*.[97] What disappears from consciousness is not lost to the soul. It is retained and brought back from time to time "to the light of day"—sometimes in the form of a memory in which the entire former experiential unit "comes to life again." At other times it is brought back as a constitutive part of the soul's gradually increasing treasury of knowledge and experience, and quite apart from the circumstances associated with the original reception. For example, in this manner we make use of a doctrinal proposition for the purpose of a demonstration, or we use a general moral precept to aid us in a present decision. How long something is retained in memory depends—not exclusively, but to a large degree—on how deeply it has originally penetrated. And the depth of the original penetration depends in turn on the depth of the original reception.

The activity of the intellect is regarded in some quarters as something relatively superficial. Such a devaluation of the intellect is usually a reaction against an age of *enlightenment* and its one-sided overestimation of reason.[98] What lends such a view some persuasive force is the fact that a certain kind of intellectual activity leaves the depths of the soul untouched. But this superficiality does not have its cause in the nature of the intellect. It is more correct to say that in such superficial intellectual activity the true power of the intellect is not fully unfolded. It may happen that two human beings listen jointly to the same news and that both have an intellectually clear grasp of its contents, such as, for example, the news of the Serbian regicide in the summer of 1914. However, the one "thinks no more about it," goes calmly on his way and a few minutes later is again busy with his plans for a summer vacation. The other is shaken in his innermost being. With his mind's eye he envisages the approaching general European war, and he sees himself uprooted in his professional life and involved in the great world historic events. His thoughts cannot detach themselves from what has happened, and he lives henceforth in feverish anticipation of the things that are to come. In his case the news has struck deeply at his inner life, and he understands the external events from the point of view of his own interiority. And because his full intellectual power is alive in his understanding, his mind penetrates into the context and into the "consequences" of the external event.[99]

In this latter kind of thinking "the entire human being" is engaged, and this engagement expresses itself even in the external appearance. It affects the bodily organs, the heartbeat, and the rhythm of breathing, the individual's sleep and digestion. He "thinks with his heart," and his *heart* is the actual *living center* of his being. And even though the heart signifies the bodily organ to whose activity bodily life is tied, we have no difficulty in picturing the heart as the inner being of the soul, because it is evidently the heart that has the greatest share in the inner processes of the soul, and because it is in the heart that the interconnection between body and soul is most strikingly felt and experienced.

In its innermost being the essence of the soul is completely overt to itself. When the ego lives in this interiority, i.e., in the ground of its being where it is truly at home and in its own, it experiences in some measure the meaning of its being and feels the collected power that precedes the division into individual powers or faculties. And when the ego's life issues from this interiority, it lives a *full* life and attains to the height of its being. Any contents received from without that penetrate to this interiority remain not merely a possession of the memory but may "become flesh and blood."[100] Such contents may then become a vitalizing source of strength in the soul. It is equally possible, on the other hand, that elements enter that are foreign to the essence of the soul, elements that devour the soul's life and that may become a deadly peril unless the soul eliminates them by using all its collected strength.

The inner transformation of that which penetrates into the depth of the soul does not take place instantaneously but requires a shorter or longer period of time. Linked with the inner transformation is usually some particular attitude or possibly some active tendency *ad extra.* The message which penetrates into the interiority of the soul (from without) finds this interiority already in a certain disposition which the soul experiences as a definite *mood* [*Stimmung*]. That which enters may bring about a change in this disposition. For example, the soul may feel itself threatened in its very being, and it may respond to this threat with horror and fear—indications of the changed inner disposition. While prior to this threat the soul was in peace and at rest "in and with itself," it is now dominated by tumultuous unrest and engaged in a defensive warding off of the danger that threatens from without.

Up to this point we have been dealing with an occurrence that takes place within the soul and the soul's "response" has been involuntary. But such an occurrence may well create the predisposition for free action, an action that finally extends to the external world.

Everything that penetrates into the interiority of the soul is an appeal or a call to the *person,* an appeal to the person's *intellect,* i.e., to that power which "understands" what is happening; an appeal also to *reflection* [*Besinnung*], i.e., to that power which searches for the *meaning* of that which approaches the soul; and an appeal to *freedom,* since even the intellectual search for meaning is already free activity. However, beyond this the soul is required to behave and act in accordance with the meaning for which it searches. A scholar who is deeply absorbed in his work and who suddenly discovers that the house is on fire must interrupt his work and try to extinguish the fire. It would be as unreasonable for him to continue in his work as it would be—"frightened stiff"—to do nothing at all.

The personal spiritual life of the soul is organically integrated into a large context of meaning which is simultaneously a context of causes and effects. Every understood meaning demands a corresponding attitude and behavior and has at the same time the motivating power of impelling the soul to comply with the demand. This "being moved" of the soul *by* something meaningful and powerful and *toward* a meaningful and powerful attitude and behavior we traditionally call "motivation."[101]

Here we again see how in all spiritual life meaning and power are intimately interrelated. And it becomes evident at the same time that what takes place in the being-moved of the soul has to do not with a natural process but with a *call* and *response*. And the person is not "forced" by that which approaches. Although the person may initially be moved to an involuntary attitude of response, it need not and must not allow itself simply to "drift," but the person is expected to "take a stand" with respect to its own position—either negating it or freely affirming it. The person is to use its reasoning power to clarify its position, to discover by way of understanding in what manner it ought to behave, and finally to engage its personal power freely in pursuing the required course.

The personal I is most truly at home in the innermost being of the soul. *When* the I lives its life in this interiority, it is then capable of freely disposing of and of freely engaging the soul's collected power. In this interiority the I is also closest to the meaning of every event, most open to the demands with which it is confronted, and in the best possible position to evaluate the significance and the import of these demands.

Few humans beings, however, live such "collected" lives. The ego of most of them takes its stand on the surface. Although the ego is on some occasions shaken and drawn toward the depth of the soul by "great events" and then attempts to correlate its behavior with the significance of these events, it returns to the surface sooner or later. And that which approaches the soul from without is indeed often of such a nature that it can without too much difficulty be effectively "dealt with" and disposed of from a superficial or, at any rate, from a not very deeply anchored standpoint. The ultimate depth of the soul is not required to understand in some measure such external events, nor is it necessary that the soul respond by an engagement of its fully collected power.

But it is nevertheless true that only those who live collectedly in the depth of their personalities are able to see even the "little things" in their larger context, and—measured by ultimate criteria—these persons are the only ones capable of evaluating these little things correctly and of ordering and regulating their attitudes and actions correspondingly. Their souls are on the way to the ultimate formation and perfection of their being. On the other hand, in those who only occasionally enter into the depth of the soul and who habitually abide on the surface the depth remains inarticulate and cannot mold the outer layers with its forming power.

Moreover, it is probably that some human beings never attain to this ultimate depth. Not only do they never attain to the perfection of their being and to the thorough formation of their souls in the sense of a determinateness of the essence [*Wesensbestimmtheit*], but they do not even gain that "initial" or "preliminary" possession of themselves which is a presupposition for any self-possession in the full sense. This preliminary stage is attained even in the case of an only transient abiding in the depth, and the attainment of this stage entails an—at least darkly anticipatory—knowledge of the meaning of personal being, of the personal power that is required for any working and striving toward the ultimate goal as well as of the obligation to strive toward that goal.

Such knowledge often comes in the wake of those "illuminations" of the depth as may accompany crucial events in one's own personal life, but it may also be mediated by rational argument and doctrinal instruction and, above all, by a doctrine of religious faith which pictures human life in this perspective. Reason and faith are both appeals of the soul, calling it "to enter into its own self" and to mold human life from the innermost center.

The innermost center of the soul is the "most spiritual" part of the soul. Although impressions which are mediated by the senses penetrate to this depth and although what happens in this interiority is actually effective even in the formation of the body, the being of the spiritual soul is detachable from all sensuality and corporeality. We are able to conceive of an "inner life" of the soul that persists even in separation from the body and after the cessation of all sense impressions. In this manner we envisage the life of the soul after death and prior to the resurrection of the body. And in this manner the soul lives—according to the testimony of the mystics—in those ecstatic states in which the soul is enraptured [*entrückt*], in which the senses are non-receptive to any external impressions and the body in death-like rigidity, while the spirit acquires in contemplation its greatest vitality and attains to the plenitude of being.

From the innermost center of the soul there issue also issues that *radiation* of the personal essence or nature which is an involuntary spiritual emanation of the personal self. This radiation, which issues from the person and captivates others, is the stronger the more collectedly a human being lives in the innermost center of the soul. And the more this is the case, the more strongly marked are all the free spiritual manifestations of a person's individuality, since this individuality is ultimately domiciled in the soul's interiority. And, lastly, the more a human being is at home in the interiority of its soul, the stronger is the body impregnated with this inner life and "spiritualized" by it. Here, then, is the true center of the being of body, soul, and spirit.

But wherein can the life of the soul consist when the soul no longer receives external impressions and when it is also no longer preoccupied with what it has retained in memory? We have stated that in its interiority the soul is completely open to itself. This means that it feels or experiences what it is and in what state or condition it is, but it does not mean that the soul is able in this life to know itself naturally "as it is known" (1 Cor 13:12), i.e., as God knows it. We are using the word *spüren* (to feel) advisedly, because this inner experience of the soul is evidently a spiritual experience, but it is not clear intellectual knowledge that can be grasped conceptually and expressed verbally. And something analogous takes place when the soul does not abide in itself but becomes externally active in its dealings with the world. Then it is the *voice of conscience* that guides it to right action and restrains it from doing wrong, that pronounces judgment on its deeds and on the condition in which the soul finds itself after it has performed them. Conscience reveals the roots of these deeds in the depth of the soul, and conscience relates the I—notwithstanding the ego's free mobility—to this depth. This voice from the deep recalls the I again and again to its proper place and condition and demands that the I answer for its actions and gain an understanding of their effects and consequences. For all actions leave a trace in the soul, which is differently disposed before and after the act.

The soul is something in and by itself. Its whatness has been placed into the world by God. And the specific quality of this whatness impresses its stamp upon the entire life in which this individual whatness unfolds. This is the reason why it is justly said that "if two do the same thing, it is still not the same." The soul in its interiority feels *what* it is and *how* it is. This is a dark feeling that cannot be expressed in words, but it indicates to the soul the mystery of its being (*as* mystery), without clearly revealing this mystery.

Moreover, the soul bears in its whatness the determination of what it is to *become*—by virtue of what it receives and by virtue of what it does. The soul feels whether or not what it receives into itself is compatible with and beneficial for its own being, and whether or not what it does is in accord with the meaning of its being. And this compatibility or incompatibility is manifested in the condition in which the soul "finds" itself after each contact and encounter with the world.

A conscious life of the soul in the depth of its interiority is, of course, possible only after the awakening of reason. At the time of this awakening the soul already bears the stamp of what has previously happened in it and to it. The soul is thus not capable of comprehending itself from the very beginning of its existence and of understanding the precise condition in which it was at the beginning. Its natural life is moreover directed from the outset toward dealing with the world and toward its active insertion in the world. This is why the natural direction of the soul life is a going-out-of-itself rather than a turning-into-itself and an abiding "in and with itself." The life of the soul must be *drawn* into itself, and this is brought about by the *demands* with which the soul meets and by the *voice of conscience.* But quite naturally the urge and pull toward the outside will always be stronger, so that abiding within is usually of short duration.

It must also be taken into account that the ego, when it turns into itself and severs all links with the external world, does not normally find a great deal. And by "turning into itself" we mean not only a closing of the portals of the senses, but a disregarding of what the memory retains of the impressions of the world and of what the ego *perceives* in itself when it regards itself as a "human being in this world"—in short, a disregarding of the part which the ego plays in the world as well as a disregarding of all the talents and capabilities which the ego possesses.

As objects of inner apperception, experience, and observation, human beings—their souls at least as much as their bodies—offer ample material for consideration, reflection, and discussion. And it is therefore hardly surprising that to many people their "own ego" (understood in this sense) is more important than all the rest of the world. But what is taken hold of in such inner perception and observation is, first, forces and faculties which serve human activities in the world and, second, the results of such activities. What is involved here is not the true interiority of the soul, but merely the residue of the original life of the soul, or those crusts which, steadily growing, cover and hide the inner life of the soul.

When human beings actually withdraw from all these surface activities into the interiority of their souls, they find most assuredly not nothing, but there is nonetheless an unaccustomed emptiness and quiet. Listening to "one's own heartbeat," i.e., to the inward being of the soul, cannot satisfy the vital actual impulses and urges of the ego. The ego will therefore not tarry long in this region unless it is held fast by something else, unless the interiority of the soul is filled with and moved by something other than the external world. And this is precisely what the masters of the *inner life* of every age: They were drawn into the innermost center of their being by some force stronger than the entire external world, and they thus experienced the breaking through of a new, mighty, superior life—a life supernatural and divine. "If thou seekest an exalted place, a sacred place," writes St. Augustine, "then offer God this inner life as a temple. 'For the temple of God is holy, and thou art this temple.' Wilt thou pray in the temple? Then pray within thine own self. But before thou doest, thou shouldst be a temple of God, for in his temple he listens to the one who prays."[102] And again: "Call me back from my errant ways. Be thou my guide, and I shall return into myself and into thee."[103]

Mystical infused graces impart to the soul an experience of what faith teaches on the indwelling of God in the soul. Those who seek God guided by faith are by their own free effort setting out on the same road and are headed for the same goal to which the mystic is drawn by the grace of infused contemplation. They withdraw from the senses, from the "images" of memory, and even from the natural activities of intellect and will, into the empty loneliness of their inner life to abide there in the darkness of faith—in a simple, loving lifting up of the eyes to the hidden God, who is present under a veil.[104] Here they will rest in deep peace because they have reached the place of their tranquillity—until it may please the Lord to transform faith into vision. This, in very sketchy outline, is the *Ascent of Mount Carmel* as taught by our holy father St. John of the Cross.[105]

5. *Capability* [Können], *Obligation* [Sollen, *the "Ought"*], *and the Inner Life*

Another access to the indwelling of God in the soul and to the place where the soul's being appears anchored in divine being is gained—likewise on the basis of inner awareness—by starting out from the experience of what a person *can do* and what a person *ought to do,* or from the relationship of the freedom of the I to the power which commands. The power which is at a human being's disposal as an already present possession—and even the maximum measure intended for a human being according to the determinateness of its essence—has a *measure.* It is a "measured," finite quantity. Every free act is a *performance* that consumes power, so that in the end a natural exhaustion may ensue unless there is a sufficient influx of power from those sources to which we have previously referred. It may therefore happen that the ego no longer feels adequate to a demand that is made upon it. For example, a physician who, after a strenuous day's work, receives a night call from a sick person, may feel that it is beyond his power to comply with such a demand. However, this fact does not silence the *demand.* A human life is at stake, and the physician may tell himself, "You can because you ought." This saying perhaps struck us as strange when we read it in Kant's *Critique of Practical Reason,* but in our example it suggests itself as an adequate expression of the experienced demand. However, it may well be that in some particular instance the feeling of inability was due to a self-deception and that our natural powers, if strained to the limit, were really capable of performing this particular work. But it is also possible that the *ought* may at times be obligatory even beyond our natural power.[106] In the demand of duty is revealed the freedom of the I even with respect to its own nature, and this is the real meaning of Kant's saying. It does not mean, however, that the I by its own power is capable of feats that are beyond the capability of its nature. For such a view would attribute to the I a creative power with which no creature is endowed. If, then, there is an obligation that is beyond the natural power of the I, the source of the additional strength must lie outside the person's nature. And it is faith that provides the answer as to where this source of strength must be sought.

God demands nothing of human beings without at the same time giving them the power to comply with the demand. This is what faith teaches us, and this teaching is confirmed in the experiences of the life of faith. The innermost being of the soul is like a vessel into which flows the spirit of God (i.e., the life of grace) if the soul by virtue of its freedom opens itself to this vital influx. And the spirit of God is meaning and power. God imparts to the soul a new life that makes it capable of doing things to which by its own nature it would be totally inadequate, and he simultaneously gives a definite direction to the soul's activity. In the last analysis, therefore, every *meaningful* demand which is made upon the soul with obligatory force is a *word of God.* For there is no *meaning* that does not have its eternal home and abode in the *Logos.* And anyone who willingly receives such a word of God simultaneously receives the divine power to comply with the demand.

Every increase in grace, however, leads in addition to a strengthening of the human being's spiritual being and opens up to the soul a richer and more penetrating insight into the *divine word,* into the supernatural meaning that underlies every event and that becomes

articulate in the interiority of the soul as an "inspiration" [*Einsprechung*]. This is why a soul which, by virtue of its freedom, leans upon the spirit of God or upon the life of grace is capable of total renovation and transformation. Its free activity, borne and sustained by the life of grace, wields power over all the involuntary acts of the soul.

Since it is not possible in this context fully to demonstrate the cooperation of nature, freedom, and grace in the forming of the soul, we shall attempt to illuminate this cooperation by just one example. Perhaps our previous contention that "there is nothing freer than love" or that "love is the height of freedom" has met with amazed protest because, from the natural point of view, love and hate appear as irresistible elemental forces engulfing the soul. People are wont to say even of their inclinations and aversions that they "can do nothing about them." And the soul really does "respond" to the "impression" it receives from a human being—sometimes at the first meeting, at other times after prolonged acquaintance—in an involuntary manner: with affection, with aversion, or possibly with indifference. The soul feels itself attracted or repelled. And these attitudes may be thoroughly meaningful expressions of the soul's encounter with a being foreign to its own. The soul feels attracted to a person by whom it expects to be aided and benefited, and it shrinks back from a person who seems to endanger its own being. And yet in such involuntary reactions there is ample room for grave self-delusions and misjudgments. Outward appearances may hide the true being of a person and thus veil the significance which one person has for the other. Such natural inclinations and aversions are therefore neither to be passed over lightly, nor is it "reasonable" simply to give in to them. They can and must be examined and tested with the aid of reason, and the judgments must be influenced by the will. The free play of inclinations and aversions is subject to the divine commandment, "You shall love your neighbor as yourself." This commandment is valid unconditionally and without qualification. The "neighbor" is not the one whom I "like," but any and every human being with whom I come into contact, without exception.

And again it is said, "You can, for you shall." God demands it, and he does not demand the impossible. He rather *makes* possible what would be naturally impossible.[107] Those saints who, trusting in this divine promise, resolved to practice heroic love of their enemies experienced the freedom of love. It may well be that a certain antipathy persists for some time, but it has no power to influence that basic attitude and those acts which are inspired and guided by supernatural love. In most instances the initial aversion will soon give way to the superior force of that divine life which fills the soul more and more. For love, as we know, is in the last analysis and in its ultimate meaning a surrender of one's being and union with the beloved. Therefore, the one who does God's will learns to know the divine spirit, the divine life, and the divine love, i.e., that person learns to know God himself. For by doing what God demands of us with total surrender of our innermost being, we cause the divine life to become *our* own inner life. Entering into ourselves, we find God in our own selves.

When the soul has been filled with divine life, it has become an image of the triune God in a new sense, in a higher sense than other creatures are, and in a sense that makes it superior even to its own natural structure. But before we discuss this new kind of soul image, we must first further elucidate the natural image relationship.

6. The Image of God in the Soul and in the Total Human Being (Preliminary Outline)

God created human beings in his image. The Creator-God is a triune or tri-personal God. We have attempted to penetrate into the mystery of the Most Holy Trinity, and we have tried to draw the picture of the human being. Will we now succeed in bringing to light the image relationship that exists between human beings and their creator?

In the case of lower creatures we have seen the similitude with the divine archetype primarily on the side of the form, because matter—in the dual sense of that which fills space and of the determinable indeterminate—is with respect to God the totally other. Only as formed matter does matter partake of the Godlikeness of created things and beings. And yet matter cannot be dispensed with for two reasons: 1) *as* formed matter it is a symbol; and 2) the *whole* (i.e., the composite of form and matter) is that which stands upon itself (i.e., *ousia* or substance). As *ousia* this whole is an image of the primordial existent [*des Urseienden*] or of the Father, and, as a whole filled with meaning and power it is an image of the triune Deity.

Ascending from lower to higher forms, we finally arrived at the human soul. If we regard the soul as the form of the body, we shall have to seek the divine image in the total human being. For once again it is the unified whole that has been placed into existence as an autonomous being. And it is the soul which makes this totality meaningful and alive.

But because the soul has neither its only nor its true being in the informing [*Hineingestaltung*] of the body (since the soul is capable of living independently in separation from the body), the soul in and by itself may be regarded as an image of the triune God. As a personal spiritual nature [*Wesen*] it stands upon itself, is filled with meaning and power, and forms itself in accordance with its meaning. We shall later on make an attempt to delineate the divine image in the being of the soul as well as in the total human being (body, soul, and spirit) more clearly and comprehensively.

7. *The Image of God in the Natural Spiritual Life* [natürlichen Geistesleben] *of Human Beings*

It should be pointed out, first of all, that the spiritual life of human beings, too, must be regarded as threefold [*dreifaltig*] and triune [*dreieinig*]. We are indebted to St. Augustine for his pioneering work in exploring these dimensions of the human intellect. He designates as both *three* and *one*[108]: (1) love as such[109]; (2) *mind, love,* and *knowledge;* and (3) *memory, intellect,* and *will.*[110]

St. Augustine starts out from the premise that God is love. This in itself already circumscribes the Trinity, for love implies a lover, a beloved, and love as such. When the mind [*Geist*] loves itself, lover and beloved are one, and love (as pertaining to both mind and will) is one with the lover. The created mind which loves itself thus becomes an image of God. But to love itself, the mind must know itself. *Mind, love,* and *knowledge* are thus *three* and *one.* They are held in proper relationship when the mind is loved neither more nor less than is its proportionate due, i.e., not less than the body and not more than God. These three (mind, love, and knowledge) are one because both knowledge and love reside in the mind, and they are three because love and knowledge are distinct in themselves and related to one another. They resemble two corporeal material elements in a chemical combination or mixture. Each of them is in every part of the whole and yet distinct from the other. Mind, love, and knowledge are each wholly in and by themselves and yet wholly in the others. The mind knows and loves itself wholly. Knowledge illumines itself as well as love, and therewith also the knowing and loving mind. And love embraces itself as well as knowledge, and therewith also the loving and knowing mind.[111]

Self-knowledge is born of the mind as the Son is born of the Father. The Son can be known before he knows himself, and he acquires his knowledge by inquiring and learning. That which is found (*repertum*) was born (*partum*). The desire to find it pertains to the will, is of the nature of love, and becomes love at the moment of the finding. Thus knowledge is generated by love, but love as such is not generated. The word that is generated by the spirit of love is loved knowledge. When the mind knows and loves itself, it receives the *word* as a *gift from love.* Love is in the word, the word is in love, and both are in the one who loves and speaks. The mind with its self-knowledge is thus an image of the Trinity.[112]

The second symbol—that of *memory, intellect,* and *will*—St. Augustine believes to be even more illuminating. It derives from a more exhaustive analysis of the interrelation of love and knowledge. No one, says St. Augustine, can love something of which that person has no knowledge at all. The eagerness to know the unknown results from our cognitive awareness of the significance of the knowledge of the unknown. When the intellect loves itself, it must also have some knowledge of itself. And when it seeks to gain knowledge of itself, some knowledge must precede this seeking. The intellect must know itself as not knowing. With the help of what it knows, it inquires into that which it does not know.[113]

Why is it, then, that the intellect, which after all is in its own self, yet seeks itself? The reason is that the intellect adheres to bodies, lives with bodies, as it were, and must therefore return to itself. As soon as the intellect understands the command, "Know thyself!" it actually knows itself. It realizes that it is in its own self and thus need not seek itself as one seeks something that is absent. It needs merely address itself to its own self as to something that is present. It knows that it *is, lives,* and *knows,* and that knowing is its specific being and life. In this kind of knowledge the functions of memory, intellect, and will are united. They are simultaneously three and one and thus an image of the Trinity.[114]

More recently Theodor Haecker has again emphasized the need for a deeper exploration and affirmation of the truth "that the knowledge of human beings is most genuine, most replete with beauty, and most blissful when it rests on the *analogia Trinitatis*" and "that with human beings and through human beings this applies to the entire created universe, which is *similitudo,* i.e., a similitude of God through and through."[115] Haecker, too, points to the endeavors of St. Augustine in this direction, but he refers only to the trinity of memory, intellect, and will. And he regards this tri-partition as not quite satisfactory, because it seems to him that without memory no intellectual activity is possible. Although he thus agrees with the *Thomists*—who insist on the bi-partition of intellect and will—he contends that Thomism has thereby lost track of the idea of analogy.[116]

For Haecker the true tri-partition of intellectual life is that of *thinking, feeling,* and *willing.* He calls this a discovery of modern psychology and states that the discoverers were unaware of the fact that they actually had laid the foundation for a new and more adequate understanding of the *analogia Trinitatis.* The establishment of feeling as a province of equal rights with thinking and willing is of such importance to Haecker because for him *love* has its true abode in feeling. He finds one of the weakest points of Thomistic psychology in its contention that love has its habitat in the will. Though Haecker is aware that love is intimately linked with thinking and willing, he insists that it truly abides in the boundlessness of feeling.

I have the impression that Haecker's justified criticism does not "invalidate" St. Augustine's main thesis. No other thinker has made it so clear that love is the motive force of thinking. The fervor of his own love urges the saint on to an ever more rigorous exertion of his intellect. He does not rest satisfied with a solution he has found, but tries to penetrate deeper and deeper. And because in his inquiry he starts out from the inner life, he assigns to love an important part in the work of knowledge. In his thinking he delves deeply into love because of his conviction that love is for us the way that leads to a knowledge of the Trinity.[117] For it is said that "the one who abides in love, abides in God." Therefore, those who gain a correct knowledge of love will advance to a knowledge of God. That is the saint's guiding principle.

Does this mean that St. Augustine simply wants to equate love and will? He places longing desire in the will and says that this desire is something in the nature of love, and that desire turns into love when the desired thing, i.e., knowledge, has been attained. And there no doubt exists a close relationship between love and will. The one who loves feels the urge to fulfill the commandments of God: he desires to conform his own will to the will of God. The will grows out of love, and from willing springs action. In fulfilling the divine commandments, however, we gain a deeper knowledge of God, and thereby in turn our love increases. And while love for its part seeks to gain ever deepening knowledge, it is from the very outset not possible to have love without having knowledge. Love comprises in itself knowledge and presupposes a certain kind of knowledge. The spiritual life is an ascending life, and every basic form of spiritual life conditions by its own ascent the ascent of the other forms and is in turn stimulated and further advanced by these other forms. It is precisely the inextricable junction and simultaneous difference of these basic forms of spiritual life that makes them an image of the triune God.

What, however, are these basic forms? Is it necessary for us to decide in favor of one of the proposed tripartite divisions and to reject the others? St. Augustine's way of proceeding seems to indicate that this is not a question of an either/or. The three and one may well be regarded as a basic law of spiritual life (as well as of all created things and being)—a basic law that recurs again and again in all the ramifications of spiritual life, similar to the manner in which the structural law of an animate being is found in every part of that being.

St. Augustine's view that three and one is already found in love as such appears quite plausible. And equally plausible is the contention that love is not possible without knowledge and that the mind unfolds itself in love as much as in knowledge. Knowledge results from the operation of the mind, and it is not possible without memory. For St. Augustine *memoria* evidently has several connotations, but in our present context we may disregard the fact that *memoria* may mean both a distinct spiritual power or *potency* and the efficacious operation of this power. Since we are primarily concerned here with the spiritual [*geistig*] *life,* we may confine ourselves to a consideration of the efficacious *operation* [*Leistung*] of the memory.[118] But even in this restricted sense, *memoria* has several meanings. It means: 1) the "inner awareness" [*Innesein*] which pertains to all spiritual life and by virtue of which it has "consciousness" prior to the knowledge which derives from a special intentional act[119]; 2) the "retention" of that which has once become known; and 3) the "remembrance," i.e., the re-emergence of that which has been retained.

The first kind of *memoria* is the original form of knowledge. The other two are stages in the process and progress of knowledge and make this progress possible. But without memory no willing would be possible either, for willing—if it is to arrive at actualization and execution—requires inner awareness, retention, and remembrance or re-emergence. Without memory there would be no "stream" of spiritual [*geistig*] life and thus no spiritual being at all. It is therefore understandable that St. Augustine assigns to memory an independent position, alongside of intellect and will, and a fundamental position at that, for *memoria* is inserted in the precise place where in the preceding tri-partition (mind [*Geist*] — love — knowledge) the mind was located.

If we take seriously the contention that we are dealing here with a created image of the uncreated Trinity, we may conclude that the "enunciation" of the eternal Word presupposes a primordial self-knowledge on the part of God (in a non-temporal sense), so that the original form of *memoria* would have to be attributed to the Father. The eternal Word, "outborn" [*ausgeboren*] knowledge, has always been equated to the Son, and the Holy Spirit is called the Person of Love. St. Thomas followed in the main the Augustinian tri-partition (mind — love — knowledge), because he saw the *true* image of God in the procession of the Word from knowledge and in the procession of love from both intellect and knowledge (cf. *S.Th.* I, q. 93, a 6), but he did not reject the other tri-partition (memory — intellect — will). In both divisions no rigid distinction is made between love and will.

Real clarity in this matter can be obtained only by a more thorough analysis of each of these tripartite divisions. St. Augustine designated the desire for knowledge as something that pertains to the will and as something in the nature of love. But the desire for knowledge is neither the one nor the other in the full sense. Those who "desire" knowledge long for its possession. Without knowledge they feel imperfect. But this desire may express itself in an attitude in which the individual expects to receive the desired thing without any effort of self-activity. Those who "will" knowledge—in the full sense of the term "will"—engage themselves fully in the endeavor to attain it. They are resolved to do whatever may lead to the possession of knowledge. And once they envisage ways and means to that end, their willing passes over into action. Willing is thus distinguished from mere desire by the firm resolve, by the free self-engagement of the person who wills.

Once the desire is fulfilled it ceases. The possession of the desired thing terminates the desire, but possession does not put an end to willing and much less to loving. I want to possess not only the knowledge which I lack, but also the knowledge which I have already gained. In this latter case volition is an assent to that which has been obtained and a readiness to do whatever can make the possession secure. This willing (as volition) cannot be said to be more perfect than the volition that aims at an as yet unattained goal. On the other hand, love fully unfolds itself only in the possession of its object.

Desire, volition, and love have in common that they affirm a good. Desire is directed toward the reception of the desired good. Volition is directed toward this good's actualization through personal active engagement, should such personal engagement be necessary. Love is a self-surrender to the loved good. And such self-giving in the true sense is possible only where a person is the object of love, so that love in the full and authentic sense proceeds from person to person, notwithstanding the fact that there are certain desires "in the nature or manner of love" which tend toward impersonal things. Self-surrender aims at union [*Einswerden*], and it attains to its perfection only when the gift of oneself is accepted by the beloved person. To be perfect, love thus demands a mutual self-giving of persons. And only in this kind of self-giving can love be affirmation [*Jasagen*] in the full sense, since it is only in self-giving that one person discloses or reveals himself to the other.

A genuine knowledge of persons is possible only in the oneness of the union of persons. Love in this highest kind of fulfillment, therefore, includes knowledge. It is simultaneously a receiving and a free act. It thus also includes the will and it is the fulfillment of desire. But love in its highest perfection is fully actual only in God: in the mutual love of the Divine Persons, in the mutual self-giving of Divine Being. Love is the being of God, the life of God, the essence of God. It is fully adequate and proportionate to each of the Divine Persons as well as to their unity.

In the finite image that which is one in the divine archetype appears divided. Here love, knowledge, and will do not coincide, despite the fact that love contains something of the nature of knowledge and something of the nature of the will. For love cannot be completely "blind," and love is free. As was previously stated (in following Duns Scotus), there is nothing that is freer than love, for love commands not only some individual personal urge or impulse, but the personal self in its totality.

Love as such assumes different modes and forms in the realm of the finite. As the love with which the lower loves the higher it is more in the nature of desire and primarily disposed to receiving. As the love with which the higher loves the lower, it is more in the nature of a free giving out of personal superabundance. But to be love in the true sense, it must always be a self-giving [*Hingabe*]. Therefore, a desire which looks only for personal gain without a willingness to self-giving does not merit the name of love.

It may justly be said that the finite spirit attains in love to its supreme fullness of life. If St. Augustine in his tripartite division (memory — intellect — will) no longer refers specifically to love, this omission can be justified in view of the fact that love must be regarded as the origin and end of this threefold spiritual activity. We pointed out before that knowledge and volition (or willed action) are conditioned by love and lead in turn to a higher degree of love.

But how is love related to memory? The positive functions of memory—the inner awareness that pertains to the life of the spirit as such, retention, and remembrance—have their place in the "interiority" of the spirit. In knowledge and volition, on the other hand, the spirit steps forth from itself, even where its knowledge and volition are directed toward itself. In the operation of the memory, the spirit abides in itself. It collects an inward possession which occasionally bears fruit in remembrance. Without a memory, the spiritual person could not possess itself and could thus not give itself, i.e., the person could not love. On the other hand, the spiritual life and spiritual possessions are inwardly appropriated and retained the more firmly and securely, the more deeply a received experience was anchored in the spirit's interiority. And since love is deeper than anything else, memory has its most unshakable ground in love.

We may thus say that intellect, will, and memory have their origin and end in love. However, they signify different directions of the spiritual life. Through the media of reason and will the spirit steps forth from itself—in knowledge, in order to receive into itself that which is and as it is; in volition, in order to form that which is at will and thus to confirm it as it were in its being and thusness [*Sosein*]. In memory the spirit preserves, orders, and adjusts itself internally with the aid of what it receives into itself.

But memory by no means exhausts the breadth and depth of "inner being." The life of which I become aware in the most primordial activity of *memoria* is an unfolding of the individuality of the human person. It is in their interiority that human beings *feel* how they are "disposed," what the place, condition, and prevalent mood of their existence is. And in this interiority there is also the seat of *emotional life,* although this latter is not confined to inner emotional states and moods. Not only in knowing and willing but also in feeling, the spirit steps forth from itself or transcends itself. Its reception of that which is proceeds from an interiority of definite contour and of such and such a mood and is therefore not merely a rational knowing, but also a *feeling* or *emotional reception* [*fühlendes Aufnehmen*]. And in this process of receiving, that which is is seized and understood in its value and in its significance for the person's own being. Feeling and willing, the person takes a stand with respect to that which is. Feeling thus stands—conditioned as well as conditioning—between rational knowledge and volition.

We therefore distinguish a triple unfolding of spiritual life *ad extra*—in rational knowledge, feeling, and volition—and these three are yet *one, as* an unfolding of the spirit and by virtue of the fact that they mutually condition each other. On the other hand, we also distinguish a threefold inner life: 1) a cognitive inner awareness of the person's own being in the original form of the memory (which is simultaneously the original form of knowledge); 2) an emotional self-awareness [*Sichfühlen*]; and 3) a volitional affirmation of the person's own being.

The *inner being* of the spirit, the spirit's *self-transcending ad extra* [*das Nach-aussen-gehen*], and the *dialectic encounters* [*Auseinandersetzung*] *between the within and the without* are the *basic directions or dimensions of the spiritual* [*geistig*] *life.* The memory in its threefold activity is itself a tri-unity which makes possible the structure of inner being as well as transcending *ad extra.* And feeling, as emotional self-awareness, as emotive awareness of values, and as a definite emotional attitude [*Stellungnahme*] is again a tri-unity. A more penetrating analysis would show that the same holds true *mutatis mutandis* with respect to knowledge and volition. But the greatest tri-unity of all is love. It is all-encompassing, and it unites and unifies the internal and the external.

But what kind of love is capable of accomplishing this? Can it be that self-love of the intellect which was the starting point of St. Augustine's discussion? The saint himself went beyond this initial stage. When he considered the spirit [*Geist*] in relation to external things, he discovered in it a threefold life, albeit not a true image of the Deity, because in this relationship the spirit is dependent on something inferior to itself.[120] To be an image of the eternal, the spirit must be directed toward the eternal. It must *embrace* the eternal in *faith,* retain it in *memory,* and lovingly seize it with the *will.* In this threefold activity of the spirit St. Augustine discerns the tri-unity or trinity of the inner person.[121] But even this does not yet yield a true image of God, since faith is temporal and transitory and will eventually give way to vision.[122] That which truly mirrors the Trinity in the human soul must be something that endures. It must be retained by the immortal soul and can therefore be found only in the immortal part of the soul.[123] However, this is true only of that spirit which in the process of thinking recognizes itself after having previously known itself by the most primordial activity of the memory, and which lovingly strives for the fruition of itself.[124] It seems that St. Augustine sees in the spirit (understood in this sense) a true—albeit not the highest—image of God. And it may appear strange that the saint values self-love so highly. But we must keep in mind that in an earlier passage he cautioned that it must be the *right* kind of self-love, that we are to love our neighbor as we love ourselves for the sake of God, and that we are to love only God for his own sake.[125] The *right kind* of self-love can thus be understood only on the basis of the love of God.

We arrive at the same conclusion when we recall what we said earlier with respect to the nature or essence of love. If love in its highest fulfillment is mutual self-giving and a union of persons, then a plurality of persons is required. That "adhering" to one's own person, that self-assertion, which are character marks of a perverted self-love, are diametrically opposed to the divine nature which, as we know, is purest self-giving. As was previously pointed out, the one and only perfect actualization of love is the divine life itself, the mutual self-giving of the Divine Persons. Here each Person finds himself in the other, and since both their life and their nature are one, this mutual love is simultaneously self-love and a self-affirmation of the Persons' nature or essence. In the realm of creatures, the closest approximation to this pure love, which is God, is the self-surrender of finite persons to God.

No finite spirit [*Geist*], to be sure, is capable of wholly embracing the Divine Spirit, but God—and he alone—embraces and encompasses wholly every created spirit. Those who surrender their selves to him attain in loving union with him to the highest perfection of their being and to that love which is at once knowledge, surrender of the heart, and free act. That love is wholly turned upon God, but in union with divine love the created spirit also embraces its own self—in knowledge, in joyful bliss, and in free self-affirmation. The surrender of oneself to God is simultaneously a surrender of one's own self—a self which God loves—to the entire created world, and in particular to all spiritual beings united with God.[126]

8. The Supernatural Image of God: The Indwelling of God in the Soul

Of this self-surrender of love, however, human beings are incapable by their own nature. If it is true that they can attain even to the knowledge and truly fulfilled love of other human beings only if the others lovingly reveal themselves—everything else that is called knowledge of human nature and love of human beings is only a preliminary stage and a way that leads to such knowledge and love—how can human beings attain to the love of God, whom they do not see, unless God loves them first? For no natural knowledge of God, ascending from creatures, discloses his hidden nature or essence. All such natural knowledge—despite the analogy by which creature and Creator are linked—can comprehend him only as the totally other. In uncorrupted created nature this might be sufficient for the creature to recognize that a greater love is due to the Creator than to any creature. But in order to give ourselves to him in love we must first learn to know him as the divine lover. And only he himself can reveal himself to us in this capacity. In a certain manner this is accomplished by the word of revelation. And the acceptance of divine revelation by faith already presupposes that God has turned to the soul in love. But this gift of love is perfect only when God gives himself to the soul in the life of grace and glory, when he imparts to the soul his divine life, when he draws the soul into his divine life.

The divine life which unfolds in the God-loving soul can be no other than the triune life of the Deity, for it is the triune God to whom the soul gives its own self. It surrenders its self to the will of the Father, who generates in the soul anew, as it were, the Son. The soul unites itself with the Son. It desires to disappear in him, so that the Father may see in the soul nothing but the Son. And the life of the soul unites itself with the Holy Spirit and thus becomes an outpouring of divine love.

It is quite evident that the image of God that is found in the created spirit by virtue of the union of love, the gift of grace and glory, incomparably excels any mere natural image. The term "image" is hardly appropriate here unless we understand it in the sense in which the Son is called the image of the Father. We are dealing here with a genuine father-child relationship—the sonship of divine adoption [*Gotteskindschaft*].

Since the soul receives into itself the spirit of God, it may be called a "spiritual vessel."[127] But the word "vessel" very inadequately expresses the kind of reception that takes place in the soul. For a spatially extended vessel or receptacle and that which is poured into it or received remain apart. They do not unite to form *one* being, and when the two are again "separated," the vessel and its content are what they were prior to their being united (unless we are dealing with material elements which "impair" or "corrode" each other, but in this case the vessel is "deficient" and, to the extent that it can be impaired by the received content, it is or becomes unfit as a vessel).

Much more intimate is the union of matter with the form that abides in it—such as the union of body and soul. Here we have an inner junction which can no longer be understood in any spatial sense. And when the two are separated, they are both no longer what they were in their union nor what they were prior to their union. For both are one single being. The body owes its being to the soul, and, on the other hand, it pertains to the being of the soul to form itself into the body or to inform the body. In the case of the union of the soul with the divine spirit, however, God and the soul do not become one in *this* manner, i.e., not as parts of *one* being. Divine being is neither augmented nor diminished nor changed in any other way by its union with human beings. The soul, to be sure (and therefore the entire human being), undergoes a radical transformation in this union, and it yet persists in its own being and does not become part of the divine being. But this union may nonetheless be designated as even more intimate and as an inner junction in a more genuine sense than the union of soul and body. For the soul forms itself into the body as into a foreign medium, as into a generically different material element. God and the soul, on the other hand, are both *spirit* and interpenetrate or permeate each other as only spirit and spirit can interpenetrate, i.e., by virtue of a free and personal self-giving which, though it presupposes a difference of being, is nonetheless—despite the infinite distance between uncreated and created being—an essential communion [*Wesensgemeinsamkeit*] that makes possible an *entering* into one another in the true and full sense.

9. Spirit [Geist] *and Soul*

The spiritual nature [*Geistnatur*] of the soul is presupposed for its union with God (i.e., for its life of grace and glory). In this union the soul ascends to a height of being that places it side by side with pure spirits. But the soul is distinguished from pure spirits in that this union (the life of grace and glory) is in the case of the soul an "ascent" or an "elevation." For the being of pure spirits consists in the most real sense in their free self-surrender to God and his service—the only alternative possibility being the refusal of self-surrender on the part of evil spirits. The soul, on the other hand, has to fulfill a double (or triple) task. It has to form itself by unfolding its own essence or nature; it has to form or inform the body; and it is to ascend above itself to union with God.

The previously mentioned distinction between body, soul, and spirit now becomes more intelligible. As the form of the body, the soul occupies that intermediate position between spirit and matter which is peculiar to the forms of corporeal things. As spirit the soul has its being "in itself," and it may in personal freedom rise above itself and receive into itself a higher life. The soul not only radiates its essence or nature in an unconscious and involuntary manner—which is true of every type of spiritual being and even of the being of lower creatures—but it steps forth from itself (i.e., transcends itself) in personal freedom. As was emphasized before, this does not mean that spirit and soul are juxtaposed in human beings, but rather that the one spiritual soul unfolds its being in several ways. Nor is the division to be understood in the sense in which we distinguish spirit [*Geist*] (= *mens*) and sensuality as superior and inferior "parts" of the soul, or in the even narrower sense in which, in the higher part of the soul, *Geist* (= *Verstand, intellectus*) as a cognitive faculty may be set off from the will. The soul is spirit [*spiritus*] in its innermost essence or nature, and this spirit nature underlies the actual deployment of all its *powers* (faculties).

There are some passages in the epistles of St. Paul which, it seems to me, hint at the distinction between soul and spirit with which we are here concerned. Speaking of the resurrection of the dead,[128] St. Paul writes, "What is sown as a natural besouled body *(corpus animale;* σῶμα ψυχικόν) rises a spiritual body *(corpus spirituale;* σῶμα πνευματικόν). If there is a natural besouled body, there is also a spiritual body, as it is written: 'The first Adam was made a living soul *(anima vivens;* ψυχὴ ζῶσα*)*, and the last Adam was made a life-giving spirit *(spiritus vivificans;* πνεῦμα ζῳοποιοῦν).' It was not the spiritual life that came first, but the besouled physical life, and then came the spiritual."[129]

In our context we are not so much interested in the distinction between the besouled body and the spiritual body as in that which underlies this distinction, namely, the "living soul" and the "life-giving spirit." We call that soul "living" which bears its own (natural) life within itself and which imparts life to the body. But this soul is not a gushing spring that generates life in the manner in which the "life-giving spirit" of the new Adam generates life. The true life-giving or life-awakening spring is the soul of Christ, because this soul bears within itself the plenitude of the divine spirit and because this soul in the boundless freedom of the divine Person of Christ has full command over its own plenitude of life. The soul of Christ is not only implanted in the body in a natural manner,[130] but it was "given the power" to begin, to end, and to resume its life in the body. There issue from it not only "streams of living water"[131] (as is the case with other souls which have received the gifts of grace), but it has full *command* over its plenitude of life, even in making this plenitude efficaciously actual in other souls. The soul of Christ has command over all created spirits. It has the power of calling departed souls back into the soulless body and of expelling evil spirits from the dominion they have conquered.

Thus in the soul of Christ there combine and interpenetrate that natural linkage of the soul with the body which makes the soul a *soul* and the sovereign rulership of the Divine Person which is far superior to the personal freedom of all created spirits. However, all this would not be possible if the human soul were "alive" only in the manner of the animal soul, if it were not by its very nature a personally formed spirit capable of receiving into itself divine life. And this is why every human soul can be elevated to a height that makes it capable of dominating its body and its own nature.[132] Either as a *charismatic* gift of grace or as an eternal reward in the life of glory the soul may obtain a share in the sovereign ruling power of Christ. The division between the *soul* being (i.e., the body-bound being) and the *spiritual* being (i.e., the God-centered being) of the human soul is found in the soul's very essence or nature. This is why the *Word of God* may rightfully be called more penetrating than a "double-edged sword," for it "extends even to the division of the soul and the spirit."[133] This saying refers to the word of divine judgment, which will uncover the most secret thoughts and intentions of the heart and which will be passed in accordance with the soul's inner direction and disposition, which will then lie revealed. On the basis of this divine judgment the soul may then be elevated from its natural bondage [*Gebundenheit*][134] to the body and to itself, to a position in which it freely rules over the body, over itself, and over the divine life with which it is filled.

Of this filling or fulfillment it is said: "... for without measure is the gift God makes of his spirit."[135] The created spirit, however, the soul as a spiritual essence, the soul as it is according to its nature, has a measure, and in this sense the spirit is given to the soul "according to its measure." But the spirit of God is beyond all measure, and when he gives himself, he does not bind himself to the measure of the being to whom he gives. Although it is true that the comprehensive capacity of the finite spirit is limited and thus incapable of receiving into itself the infinite, its comprehensive capacity is strengthened by that which is imparted to it, so that the limits of its being filled and being elevated are not restricted to any finite measure.

To describe in full extent the transformation of the soul—the transformation of its power and of all its activities—under the influence of the received divine life is too formidable a task to be undertaken in this summary outline.[136]

10. The Threefold Formative Power of the Soul. Body, Soul, and Spirit

At this time we must again remind ourselves that the being of the human soul is not exhausted in its spiritual life. If we go back to the root of human being, we find a threefold direction in its unfolding: the forming of the body, the forming of the soul, and the unfolding in spiritual life. All this is done by the formative power of the soul, although this power (in its threefold formative efficiency) is *one*. It effects the forming of the body in the manner in which a plant soul is formed, and yet that which results is a human soul. What is formed by this power is a human body, a means and field of expression for a free spirit—not a plant structure. This formative power is alive in the body and forms itself in the manner in which an animal soul is formed, and yet quite differently, since the life of the senses in its entirety is united with and formed by the

spirit. And this formative power of the soul rises to a spiritual life of equal rank with the life of the pure spirits, but this spiritual life, nevertheless, has its own particular form, because it is rooted in bodily-sensory life. In this manner the separate realms of the created world are joined in human beings in the unity of an essence or nature, while outside of human beings they are linked only by a causal nexus and by an interconnection of meaning.

The threefold formative power of the soul must be regarded as a tri-unity, and the same is true of the end product of its forming activity: body—soul—spirit. If we attempt to relate this tri-unity to the divine trinity, we shall discover in the soul—the wellspring that draws from its own sources and molds itself in body and spirit—the image of the Father; in the body—the firmly designed and circumscribed expression of the essence or nature—the image of the eternal Word; and in the spiritual life the image of the divine Spirit. If we further keep in mind that *body* [*Leib*] is not to be understood as merely an animate physical entity [*Körper*] but as the "outborn" structure of the essence or nature; that, correspondingly, *soul* signifies not merely the essential form of a corporeal animate being, but every kind of primal life source; and that, lastly, *spirit* [*Geist*] denotes free self-transcending, we shall be able to discern this tri-unity even in the soul as such. The soul draws from its own source. It forms itself into a firmly designed and circumscribed structure. And it steps forth from itself (transcends itself) in its spiritual life. Its self-forming into foreign matter in the process of the formation of the body may then be compared to the becoming incarnate of the Word, and its stepping forth from itself into an external world—upon which the soul impresses its own stamp—may be compared to the sending of the divine Spirit into the created world.

The soul in its threefold formative power and the threefold deployment of its being—even on its natural level—can be regarded as an image of the Triune Deity. And when it then opens itself in its innermost being to the influx of divine life, the soul (and through it the body) is formed into an image of the Son of God. Then "streams of living water" emanate from it—streams which effect a renewal of the face of the earth out of the Spirit. The human spirit, when it is permeated and guided by the Divine Spirit, recognizes in the divine light—underneath all the disfiguring veils—the original form of the created world and becomes capable of cooperating in the task of its restoration.

§10. The Difference Between the Image of God in Rational Creatures (Angels and Human Beings) and in the Rest of Creation

The union of the soul with the triune life of the deity presupposes the spiritual nature of the soul, i.e., its personal spiritual essence. The human spirit—even on the purely natural level—is an image of God in a much more genuine sense than are other created things and beings, because the human being is a person and as such capable not only of involuntary and unconscious spiritual stepping forth from itself [*Ausgehen von sich selbst*], but of living a free and conscious spiritual life. We thus understand why St. Thomas recognizes only in the human spirit and in the angels an *image* of God. We found ourselves unable to follow him in his contention that the rest of creation shows merely a *vestige (vestigium)* of the triune God.[137] It is our conviction that a certain image character can be found and demonstrated in the entire created universe.

On the other hand, we must distinguish between a proximate and a more remote image-character—a distinction which St. Thomas expresses by the terms *imago* and *similitudo*.[138] He proposes to speak of *similitudo* where there exists a correspondence in the genus or in some quality or property, and of *imago* where there is a common species. In relation to God all these expressions cannot be understood in a literal sense. Since God is not included in any species nor in any genus and since he has no qualities or properties, nothing can really correspond to him or be congruous with him. However, everything has its primordial paradigm [*Urbild*] in the simple divine essence, and the image may be more proximate or more remote. And because rational creatures resemble the Creator in that quality by which they excel all other creatures—their personal spirituality—we may speak here of a *God-likeness* [*Ebenbildlichkeit*] which they alone possess.

All creatures have a triune structure as substances that stand upon themselves and that are filled with meaning and power. And all self-dependent structures pertain to a triune (body—soul—spirit) unfolding of their being.

In corporeal nature the threefold deployment of being expresses itself in the solid, liquid, and gaseous phases. In the realm of animate being the specific expression of the ternary unfolding is found in plant life, animal life, and human life. On the human level, all the lower stages are, as it were, once more recapitulated or epitomized. Only spiritual persons, however, partake of the personal essentiality of God. They alone have a personal spiritual life and with it a spiritual fecundity that remotely resembles the processions in the trinitary life of the Deity. When knowledge perfects itself in word and speech, it is as if something had detached itself from the creative spirit like a ripe fruit. And when the spirit contemplates this self-created formation, there ensues that joyful affirmation which bears some resemblance to the "nature of love."

At this point an objection may be raised which puts into question the entire notion of a divine image in the created world. It might be argued as follows: It is undoubtedly possible to discover a three-and-one everywhere and to discover a personal, spiritual fruit-bearing life in created spirits, but a tri-personality cannot be found in any creature. What we designate in the creature as an image of the Divine Persons are not persons. All we discover are different traits in one person (or in some impersonal structure), and these different traits may then be said to be related to one or the other Divine Person.

To escape this difficulty, it might be suggested to regard as tri-personality a plurality of spiritual persons (e.g., man, woman, and child), but both St. Augustine and St. Thomas have refuted this proposition.[139] It is, after all, the individual human being in whom the image of God is said to be found regardless of whether this individual generates other human beings or not. Besides, physical generation is something which human beings have in common with brutes, and something which sets them apart from pure spirits, from God and angels. On the other hand, this latter argument is valid only if we understand generation or procreation in its animalic form and forget that in human beings it can and should be something else, namely, a free, personal act, so that the physical bodily union becomes an expression of the mutual self-giving of the souls of free persons who become one in love and who, in their common procreative will, become fruit-bearing not merely in a physical bodily sense.[140] Becoming one in love entails a spiritual receiving-into-oneself of the beloved being and makes the one who loves an *image* of the beloved. And the fruit of such a union bears the stamp of a community of essence or nature [*Wesensgemeinsamkeit*].

Such generation is possible only for spiritual persons (not for lower animate beings), and it is possible also as a "purely" spiritual generation—in the loving union of these pure spirits who reveal themselves completely to each other and are fruit-bearing in this union of essences or natures. They bear fruit by virtue of the atmosphere which radiates from them on their environment and perhaps also by means of the works which they produce in common and through which they "propagate" their spirit.

We may say that every communion and community of finite persons has its primordial paradigm [*Urbild*] in the Divine Trinity, although the image—in this case as in any other finite image of the eternal—is infinitely far removed from the *Urbild* and very imperfect. This imperfection is revealed in the fact that the community of essence or nature is always only a partial one and that it is not a primordial community, but is founded on the primordial particular nature or essence [*Eigenwesen*] of individual persons. This imperfection is further revealed by the fact that in such a finite community of essence or nature we have an open plurality of persons in place of the Third Person of the Trinity. And just as the archetypal Divine Being appears in the image of the created world refracted or dispersed in the multiplicity of that which is, in the manifold of things and beings, so also is the image of the Trinity a refracted one. Individuals and communities reflect the divine archetype in diverse ways, and they supplement each other in their image-character. Furthermore, no finite communion or community is a strictly defined and circumscribed [*geschlossen*] triunity.

More perfect than the image of the divine tri-personality in the created community is the one previously referred to, namely, the image that is found—by virtue of the indwelling of the Divine Persons—in the individual soul in the life of grace and glory, since this kind of life is an actual living-with and conforming-to the tripersonal divine life.

Both a genuine natural communal life and the life of grace and glory presuppose personal self-giving and are therefore special character marks by which created spirits—angels and human beings—excel all other things and beings in the created universe.

§11. The Difference Between the Image of God in Angels and in Human Beings

According to what was previously said regarding pure spirits, it should now be possible to show in what way the image of God in pure spirits differs from the image of God in human beings. The basic structure which pertains to every *ousia is* also found in pure spirits. Every one of them stands upon itself and has its own essence or nature which it unfolds in its life by virtue of its own power. But these spirits attain to their firmly defined and circumscribed essential form not in any temporal mode of unfolding. They *own* or *possess* a firmly circumscribed essential form (their "spirit body" [*Geist-Leib*]) without first having to mold it. Their *life* is a free, spiritual self-transcendence [*Herausgehen aus sich selbst*] .Are we therefore justified in attributing to them bodily and spiritual being but no soul being? They evidently have no soul in the sense of a dark ground which tends toward being formed. But inasmuch as they possess their essence or nature not only as something that is firmly circumscribed and that radiates *ad extra,* but are inwardly in motion and capable of hiding or disclosing their "inner" lives, we may speak of a ternary unfolding of being even in pure spirits.

To their *spiritual being,* i.e., to their self-transcendence, we previously gave a threefold appellation: knowledge — love — service. We did so without having in view the image of the Trinity. According to the Augustinian tripartition (mind — love — knowledge), love and service would have to be grouped together. If we keep in mind the three principal directions or dimensions of the life of the human soul—receiving, inner assimilation of the received content, and responsive activity *ad extra*—knowledge would correspond to receiving and service would correspond to responsive activity. And what about love? Love mediates between the two terms and shares in both. It is a receiving into the innermost core of being and simultaneously a response issuing from the center of interiority.

We must take into consideration, however, that in the case of angels these processes denote no temporal succession. Their spiritual life is unified (and therein closer to the divine life), and only an objective order prevails in this unity. Their spirit nature is empowered to receive into itself foreign spirituality, to unite it with their own inner lives, and to disclose their own interiority to others.

This latter characteristic describes the essential nature of their service. In all this, however, love (as self-giving) is of basic importance. It opens the created spirit to the divine life, it allows the spirit's own nature to be permeated by the divine spirit, and it radiates this same spirit, so that the divine spirit may seize and embrace the spirits of the lower ranks of the celestial hierarchy.

Because of the purity of their self-giving, the communal life of angels is also a purer image of the tri-personal divine life. Every celestial spirit is united to a higher one (if not immediately to God himself) by love, and this union bears fruit by awakening the divine life in the lower spirit.

Lastly, the pure spirits' life of glory partakes of the life of the triune God in a manner unattainable for any human being in the course of this being's earthly life (excepting, of course, Christ who combined in his life the state of the "earthly pilgrim" with the state of the inhabitants of heaven).

Pure spirits resemble rays by which the eternal light is imparted to the created world. This light has to traverse a greater distance and a longer way to illumine those spiritual beings who are enveloped by a material shell and who rise like a spring from a hidden depth. But this very concealment and spring-like nature imparts to these spiritual beings some of the unfathomableness of the Divine Being. And in their (relative) autonomy they appear to be more self-dependent [*auf sich selbst gestellt*] than pure spirits who are wholly borne up by God. Finally, by their being tied to matter these spiritual beings are in a peculiar manner intimately related to him who descended into the depths of earthly existence—the incarnate Word. Our final effort, therefore, shall be devoted to an attempt to disclose something of this mysterious relationship.

VIII.

The Meaning and Foundation of Individual Being

In the course of our discussion of the human being's personal being we frequently had to touch upon another question, a question which we also encountered in some other contexts and which must be clearly answered if the nature of human beings, their position in the order of the created world, and their relationship to divine being is to become intelligible. This question concerns the *individual being* (i.e., individuality) of human beings, and it can be discussed only in connection with an analysis of *individual being* in general.

§1. The Individual Thing [*Einzelding*], Individuation [*Einzelheit*], and Unity [*Einheit*] (Individual Being [*Einzelsein*] and Oneness [*Einssein*])

It is necessary, first of all, to establish with all possible clarity what is meant by individual being [*Einzelsein*], a term which is by no means unequivocal. As *individuum* (i.e., an individual thing [*Einzelding*]) we usually designate what Aristotle called τόδε τί (this thing there), i.e., a thing that can no longer be named (since all names have a general meaning), a thing that can only be identified by the pointing finger. Avicenna uses the term *signare* or *designare* for this pointing out, and St. Thomas adopts this terminology.[1] We have previously tried to show that Aristotle saw in the τόδε τί the πρώτη *ousia*.[2] Though it has a universally comprehensible nature or essence that can be expressed conceptually—*this* human being is a "human being," and the being human is universally comprehensible—this does not exhaust the quid of its being. And what the individual thing is above and beyond its universally conceivable nature is its exclusive and immediate property. This is why individuality as such has been designated as *noncommunicability* (*Unmitteilbarkeit* = that which cannot be communicated).[3]

The *universal essence or nature* is that which a thing shares with others. But what is that which the individual thing shares with no other thing, that which makes it an *individual thing?* The individual thing is defined by St. Thomas as "that which is undivided in itself, but set apart from everything else."[4] This inner non-dividedness [*Ungeschiedensein*] is equivalent to unity or oneness [*Eines-sein*].[5] Transcendental unity, however, pertains to that which is [*das Seiende*] as such, not only to the individual thing but also to the *universal.* The signification of the term "human being" [*Mensch*]—the *meaning* or the *essence*—is *one:* undivided in itself and set apart from every other meaningful structure [*sinngebilde*]. But this essence is not absolute, i.e., in every respect, indivisible and therefore not absolutely incommunicable.[6] It is that in which all human beings share by virtue of their being human. And this is why the transcendental unity does not suffice to define and determine the nature of individual being.

And what about *numerical unity* [*zahlenmässige Einheit*]? Does it suffice? What is numerically one is opposed to multiplicity and is simultaneously a presupposition of multiplicity. It is that of which a structural quantity ("multiplicity") is composed. To "multiplicity" there pertains a common element which makes it possible to combine one plus one plus one ... " to a quantitative unity. If we take an extreme case, this common element may be nothing but the common empty form of "something." In this manner we may group together "number," "color," and "poem" as "three objects" (*object* in the broadest sense of the term). We may also speak of "three meaningful structures, "since each of them is determined in its content, although as far as their contents are concerned, the three have nothing in common. Each of them is numerically one, but it is nonetheless not an individual thing. This means that numerical unity is equally insufficient to define and determine the nature of individual being.

We have the extreme opposite of the example in which the empty form is the only common element in the case where several things are not distinguished at all by their content. Let us think, for instance, of "three copies" of a book or reproduced picture. Here we actually say that "the same" is present so and so many times, and it would seem indeed that in this case individual being can be comprehended only by means of numerical unity. But even here the two terms (individual being and numerical unity) are not simply equivalent. According to Gredt, individuation [*Einzelheit*] "is that whereby in the corporeal order of beings of the same species differ among themselves in a purely numerical manner."[7] This statement implies that individual being *underlies* any numerical determinateness and that therefore the former does not coincide with the latter. And Gredt adds in the same passage: "We do not recognize the specific difference of individual being because we do not grasp individual being as such in its essence." This evidently means that though two individual things of the same species differ in their essence, we are incapable of grasping this difference. Obviously, Gredt distinguishes here between *individual being* and *universal being* (generic and specific determinateness), as we have done in our earlier discussion of this problem.[8] This sounds as if we had to assume a difference among individual beings with respect to *content* and simultaneously a determinateness of the individual being's content that would transcend the universal determinateness of the individual essence—a determinateness which, however, cannot be grasped in its content, but only in its empty formality as that which underlies numerical unity and numerical computation. But things must make themselves known to us as differentiated if we are to be able to recognize their differences and their numerical multiplicity. "We distinguish ... individual corporeal things among themselves, "says Gredt, "by accidental, externally and sensorially noticeable characteristics, especially by their external form and their position in space and time."[9]

§2. A Critical Appraisal of the Thomistic Doctrine on the Ground or Foundation of Individual Being

The Thomistic presentation of the problem gives rise to some questions: 1) Is the difference between individual and individual really one of content? *Can* or *must* this difference relate to content? 2) Why do we have to confine these differences to the *corporeal* world?

These two questions cannot be discussed separately, for they are both occasioned by the Thomistic idea concerning the ground or foundation of individual being (the *principle of individuation*), and they must therefore be answered jointly on this common basis.[10]

1. The Individual Being of Corporeal Things

We shall attempt, first of all, to gain a clear understanding of the Thomistic answer to the problem. The undividedness of the individual thing—in contrast to the undividedness of the universal—is an *absolute* undividedness. The universal is *one* and undivided only with respect to its *meaning*. In its actualization it divides itself by communicating itself:

> The universal generic essence or nature appears divided in things by specific differences and is in this manner communicated to those species subordinated to it. Similarly, the universal specific essence or nature appears divided by individual differences and is in this manner communicated to the individual things subordinated to it.[11]

The unity of the individual thing, however, denotes "a state of existence that bars out any division and any communication to subordinates." Whenever a thing differs numerically from other things of the same species, this difference must add "something positive to the universal essence or nature of the species [*Artwesen*]," and this addition "cannot be due to the specific essence or nature as such. ... If the specific essence or nature owes this perfection—by virtue of which it is indivisible and incommunicable to subordinates (which, in the Thomistic view, is true in the case of angels)—to its own self, then it differs from every other specific essence or nature by virtue of its own self, and there cannot exist a community of several beings according to species."[12]

On the other hand, whenever the species is divisible and communicable the indivisibility and incommunicability must have their cause in something else. And since that which determines the species is the form, the essential nature of individual being—the inner principle whereby individual things exist (*principium individuationis formale*)—must be sought on the side of *matter*. Only in the corporeal world, therefore, can there exist individual things of the same species.

"According to the Thomists, the principle of individuation (the root principle: *principium individuationis radicale*) is quantitatively determined matter *(materia signata quantitate)*, i.e., matter differentiated or set apart by quantitative extension."[13]

What is meant by this *designation* [*Bezeichnung*] is not the actual quantitative determinateness of the *finished* [*fertig*] matter. If this were the case, individuation would be reduced to an accidental property, which is impossible 1) because properties owe their individual being exclusively to the thing to which they pertain; and 2) because the properties of a thing—including its quantitative determinateness, its actual structure or quantitative extension—change, while the thing remains the same. It is rather a question of the relationship of matter to an as yet not determined quantity (*quantitas indeterminata*). The coming to be [*Enstehung*] of a corporeal thing is preceded by a "preparatory predisposition of matter" [*Stoffzubereitung*] by which matter is ordained to *this* particular quantitative extension.

"A particular matter is thus differentiated and set apart (i.e., designated as separable) from the rest of matter, even before the quantitative extension actually comes to be, because this particular matter—by virtue of the preceding preparatory predisposition—is related to and requires *this* particular quantitative extension."[14] In this manner "the quantitative extension exerts an influence on the determinateness of individual being ... not in relation to the definite size and form of the individual, but exclusively as a quantitative extension that is posited as distinct and set apart from every other quantitative extension."

2. *The Formal Structure of Things* (*Matter, Form, Self-Dependence or Subsistence* [Selbstand], *Existence* [Dasein])

In his attempt to prove the validity of the Thomistic thesis, Gredt makes the following statement: "The cause of the individual being of corporeal substances must be something within these substances that makes them individual things by multiplying them simultaneously within the same species."[15] We have already pointed out why this result cannot be achieved by adding accidental properties. As constitutive structural parts of the thing as it is in itself (i.e., the *substance*) Gredt mentions "matter, form, self-dependence [*Selbstand*],

and existence [*Dasein*] (*materia et forma et subsistentia et existentia*)."[16] If we group together matter and form as the quid [*Was*] of the thing, we discover in this quid the basic structure of existents as such—"something which is." For an understanding of this basic structure and therefore also for the theory of individuation, the following sentences, it seems to me, are of decisive importance: "Self-dependence [*Selbstand,* subsistence] and existence [*Dasein*], however, must be eliminated as principles of individuation from the outset, since they already presuppose the essence or nature as individual being. For only an individual being (not a universal) can be self-dependent [*selbständig,* subsistent] and can exist in and for itself." These two sentences, which in the passage referred to appear without any further proof, must be examined very carefully.

3. Subsistence [Selbstand] *and Absolute Self-Dependence* [Vollselbständigkeit] (Subsistentia *plus* Suppositum = Hypostasis)

We shall first try to gain further information on the meaning of subsistence [*Selbstand*]. Gredt tells us that it means "a double independence of the essence [*Wesen*] in existence [*Dasein*]: (a) independence of a carrier [*Träger*] to which the essence would be attached; (b) independence of any other substantial essence with which the self-depending essence would share its essence, so that its existence would depend on the substantial essence in such a manner that it would exist only jointly with this essence and not by and for itself."[17]

Carrier [*Träger*] in this context differs in meaning from what we previously designated by that name—the empty form of *something* or the *object* which encompasses the essence. The term is used here in the sense in which a thing is called the carrier of its properties. *Being a carrier* in our sense coincides, rather, with the kind of independence listed under (a). It means "to carry itself, i.e., to exist in and for itself."[18] *Carrier* thus understood is not an object in the broadest sense of *something* ("something," understood as an encompassing empty form with a fullness of content, lacks independence, as is the case with properties), but an object in the restricted sense of that which stands upon itself [*des auf sich Gestellten*].

However, we must remember that our own concept of carrier, too, has a double meaning. Strictly speaking, the *object* is the carrying principle, while the fullness of the essence is that which is carried. Neither of the two is possible without the other, and only the composite of both can be said to "exist in and for itself." Similarly, only the composite can be said to "carry itself." And this latter predication can be made of the composite only because there is something in the structure which is the genuine carrying principle. Both the matter and the form of corporeal things—excepting the human soul—lack (according to Gredt) the first kind of independence, because the one without the other is "neither capable of carrying accidents nor capable of carrying itself."[19] The human soul, on the other hand, possesses this kind of independence, "because it carries (*substat*) the spiritual accidents as well as itself when it is separated from the body, i.e., the soul is in and by itself (*subsistit*)." And because of the soul's separability from the body, the second kind of independence or self-dependence—the one mentioned under (b) above—may also be attributed to it. The soul is nevertheless only "imperfectly self-dependent" because "notwithstanding the fact that it has its being exclusively for itself, it is by its very nature ordained to sharing its being with some other." The soul is "complete as a substance" but "incomplete as a species," because by its nature it is a form that can be communicated to a proportionate matter and when thus communicated, it shares its being with matter. To the substance (which is also complete as a species) it pertains to be fully "self-dependent" [*ein Vollselbständiges*] (suppositum; ὑπόστασις).

That which is fully self-dependent is absolutely non-communicable, and it is that which is most complete in the order of subsistence [*Fürsichsein*]. It is so much in and for itself and owns its being so exclusively that it could not possibly be communicated to some other, to share its being with it. That which is fully self-dependent is therefore defined as the perfect individual substance, i.e., the substance which incommunicably exists in and for itself. When the fully self-dependent has a rational nature, it is called a *person. Subsistence* (*Selbstand* = standing upon itself) *as the determinateness whereby the fully self-dependent is being formed must be defined as that whereby the individual substance in its determinateness becomes subsisting and incommunicable.*

The fully self-dependent is to the essence or to the nature as the whole is to the determinateness of its parts. The fully self-dependent is therefore that *which* is, while the nature is that *whereby* the fully self-dependent is this specific determinateness. And the fully self-dependent is that which possesses the nature, while the nature is that whereby the fully self-dependent is determined in its species. Moreover, the fully self-dependent as that *which* is, is also that *which* is active, while the nature is that whereby the fully self-dependent is active.[20]

In the preceding passages Gredt's formulations again differ from our own. We should have to say that the fully self-dependent is "something that is." The *quid* in this composite expression we reserved for the fullness of the essence [*Wesensfülle*]. We are speaking of full "self-dependence" or completeness in itself, nonetheless, because the quid is in the form of the *object* (in the restricted sense of the term: the object as that which stands upon itself, and on the highest stage the *person* which, like the more generalized *carrier,* we understood in the double sense of the carrier of the essence and the composite of carrier and that which is carried—form and fullness). And the quid derives its *self-dependence* from the fact that it is in the form of the object. We are thus in factual agreement with Gredt when he calls *subsistence* [*Selbstand*] a "positive perfection," because subsistence imparts independence, and independence is a perfection.[21]

Moreover, Gredt explains *Selbstand* as a perfection which definitely confines [*abschliessen*] the individual substance:

> ...inasmuch as the substance is essence and nature. For *Selbstand* is that whereby the nature is completely self-dependent and thus definitely confined [*abgeschlossen*]. This definitive confinement, however, is not to be understood in a negative sense only—in the sense that nothing further accrues to the nature—but as a positive perfection, since the nature is thereby individually confined in such a way that it becomes capable of acting as a carrier by receiving into itself accidental properties as well as existence [*Dasein*], although these accidents and this *Dasein* do not fuse with the nature.[22]

We may add that the thus completed and confined whole—the *nature* made to stand upon itself or placed into itself—is capable of carrying the properties accruing to the essence because in this composite whole the *carrier* of the nature or essence can and must be distinguished from the essence or nature. It is therefore quite in conformity with our own interpretation when Gredt declares that the *Selbstand* differs *factually* from "the nature which possesses *Selbstand*" and that the *Selbstand* is "the confining boundary line with the nature [*die der Natur innerliche Abschlussgrenze*]."[23]

Just as we sustained the separability of the nature from the carrier of the nature [*Naturträger*] by the doctrine of faith (on the *one* nature and the *three* Persons in the Deity), so we sustain in this case the same kind of separability by referring to the assuming of a human nature by the Divine Person of Christ. And when we speak of a *modally* objective distinction in contrast to an absolutely objective distinction, this evidently corresponds to the distinction we established between the *content* and the *empty form* of existents, both of which we regarded as pertaining to the "object" [*Sache*], i.e., to the existent [*das Seiende*] as such.

4. *Subsistence* [Selbstand], *Substance* [Selbständiges], *and Individual Being* [Einzelwesen]

But now we must examine the question of how the *Selbstand* is related to the individual thing and to the differences among individual things [*Einzelheitsunterschied*]. For it is this question which has caused us to interpose this entire discussion concerning subsistence. According to Gredt, "*Selbstand* is a perfection accruing to the individual substance."[24] The further explanation makes it clear that *substance* is here equated to *essence* or *nature* [*Wesen*]:

> The self-dependent, subsistent essence is the carrier of the accidents, for the essence is in and for itself. It carries itself and everything pertaining to itself. However, we cannot conceive the essence as such as the carrier of the accidents. For the essence as such as well as the individual essence (e.g., humankind) comports itself as a part—a part that accounts for the species—that is not self-subsistent [*selbständig für sich*]. This part is within the self-subsisting whole. Being human is in the human being. The essence as such is thus not self-dependent. It is not the carrier of its own self and therefore incapable of acting as a carrier in receiving the accidents. If the essence as such were to receive the accidents, it would receive them as pertaining to its own self. The accidents

> would then merge with the substantial essence. Thus, the received color would make people white. But this cannot be, since the accidents remain extraneous and are objectively distinct from the essence. The self-dependent, self-subsistent essence, therefore, adds a perfection to the individual substance by virtue of its self-subsistence [*Selbstand; Fürsichsein*], and this added perfection makes the self-subsistent essence capable of acting as a carrier in receiving the accidents.

In our previous discussions we attempted to establish as the true meaning of substance (= πρώτη *ousia)* the standing upon itself, the being founded upon itself [*das in sich Gegründete*] or self-dependence [*das Eigenständige*]. This πρώτη ousia, however, is the individual thing, i.e., the thing which is already confined in its *Selbstand,* the essence which is carried by its carrier. It is therefore not possible to designate the *Selbstand* as something that accrues to the individual substance. The *Selbstand* must rather be understood as something that inwardly pertains to the individual substance, as something that can merely be abstracted from the fullness of the essence of the individual substance, as the empty form that encompasses the substance.

It is important, moreover, to note what is meant here by *individual essence* [*Einzelwesen*]: the "part that accounts for the species" of the individual thing (e.g., the humanity of this individual person). Accordingly, each individual thing has *its* essence, but this essence is the *same* as that of all the other members of the same species. I pointed out before that I find it impossible to accept this point of view. It seems to me that the essence of Socrates is found in his being Socrates (which includes his being human), and I hold that this essence differs not only numerically but by virtue of a special particularity from the essence of any other human being.

I shall revert to this problem in the course of the following discussion. For the time being, I am chiefly interested in discovering the root principle of individual being in all those instances where there exist many individual things that are alike and that all belong to the same species. For I do not deny, of course, the possibility that there exists a multiplicity of individual things which are alike. I therefore prefer to choose my example from the field of purely corporeal things. It is not difficult to conceive of ten completely alike pebbles. Each of them is an independent individual thing. We can distinguish them from each other only by their different position or situation in space, a difference which is due to their material nature. For whatever is material [*stofflich*],[25] is spread out and fills space, so that one particular position in space cannot be occupied by several things, and one particular part or particle of matter cannot fill several parts of space (of proportionate size or quantity) simultaneously.

5. *Matter Considered as the Ground* [Grund] *of Individual Being. Arguments against This Theory*

In the Thomistic view, matter is not only the means by which individual things are distinguished from each other, i.e., the epistemological cause of their individual being, but the ontological cause of individuation. Gredt states:

> In matter we find the conditions for the individuation of the substance. Matter does not (like the form) determine the species, since matter is a common, wholly indefinite, substrate [*Untergrund*]. Nor does matter presuppose (as do *Selbstand* and *Dasein*) the already individualized substance, since matter belongs to the essential constitution [*Wesensbestand*] of the substance as such. But matter multiplies the form and the substance as a whole in a purely numerical manner without causing a change in the species, because matter does not cause differences in the species-determining forms as such, but only in the substrate. The form is thus or thus solely because it is in this or that matter. *Every form is transcendentally related to a matter that is definitely marked by its quantitative extension, and this transcendental relation is an internal property of the form* and is maintained even when the form (as in the case of the human soul) is separated from matter. Being the ultimate, incommunicable substrate, matter simultaneously prevents any further multiplication. It causes the substance to become incommunicable, i.e., it makes it an individual thing. For an individual thing is that which cannot be communicated to subordinates. The substance which has come to be from the combination of matter and form cannot in turn be communicated to a further substrate (and thus multiplied) in the manner in which the form is communicated and multiplied.

> However, the matter which differentiates and individualizes the corporeal substance is not matter as such [*an und für sich* (in and by itself)]. For matter as such is undetermined and is a common element in all corporeal things. Nor can matter as such be the *ground or principle of individuation or the causal principle of numerical difference.* This causal principle *is* rather that matter *which is determined and divided by its being ordained to a definite quantitative extension.* Among all other accidents only quantitative extension is numerically distinguished by its essence from any quantitative extension of the same species. It is distinguished by position, order, and contiguity. By its essence, quantitative extension denotes parts which by their very position are numerically distinct from each other. Constancy of extension denotes coherent parts which by their very position are numerically distinct from each other. ... Quantitative extension is thus in and through itself a mode of individuation.[26] It is therefore the condition of the individuation of the substance as a transcendentally required extension (*ut connotata*) which designates the parts of the matter and—as divided extension—sets these parts off from each other. If this premise is correct, matter provides the causal principle or the ground of individuation. For by virtue of its essence (as ultimate substrate), matter cannot be communicated to any other material element from which it is set apart. Therefore, matter is also individualized in and by itself and thus apt to individualize the form and the substance.[27]

The following questions arise in connection with Gredt's presentation of the problem of individuation and his proposed solution:

1. Can matter by itself actually accomplish what is here ascribed to it?
2. Is the determination of the species [*Artbestimmung*] the one and only function of the form?[28]
3. Is individual being "presupposed" for self-subsistence [*Selbstand*] and existence [*Dasein*], as Gredt tries to prove?[29]

To answer the first question, there is no need to discuss once again the problem of original or prime matter, since according to Gredt it is not unformed prime matter that is the root principle of individuation (prime matter functions in his discussion only as the "ultimate substrate"), but that matter which is characterized by "undetermined quantitative extension" or that matter "which is determined and divided by its being ordained to extension." But what else is this signification or ordination than a primary "formation"? Spatial extension and "divisibility" characterize the form of matter as such. They are that which distinguishes material (space-filling) things generically from spirits (when we try to characterize the former by what they *are* rather than by what they *are not* [e.g., lifeless, non-conscious, etc.]). To every material thing there pertains *its* matter, and the matter pertaining to it is pre-designed in the form. This is why in my rendition of Gredt's argument I have underscored the words: Every form "is transcendentally related to a matter that is definitely marked by its quantitative extension, and this transcendental relation is an internal property of the form" (cf. p. 479 above). However, I do not subscribe to the conclusion, "The form is thus and thus solely because it is in this or in that matter." I should rather say, "The matter is thus and thus, because it belongs to this or to that form."

To be sure, we must not fail to take into consideration the relationship that exists between *material elements* as specifically determined constitutive parts of the spatial-corporeal world or *nature* (*nature* in the sense in which it is contrasted to *spirit*)—constitutive parts which are, however, not self-contained structural units—and material things as the structural units into which these things are divided and in which they "occur." *Every matter* or *material element*—such as gold, iron, etc.—*is a whole, but* not indivisible and therefore *not an individual thing,* not an *individuum.* It pertains to the individual thing to be specifically determined and definitely confined or circumscribed as a structural unit. Both of these characteristics are pre-designed in the form of the individual thing.

We pointed out before[30] that the external spatial limits of corporeal things are to a large extent determined by external influences. A "piece of matter" can be smashed or sliced or "divided" in some other manner. From such division result several individual things of the same material determinateness and either the same or a different size and shape. However, the spatial limits do not depend exclusively on external factors or influences. There is innate in every material thing a directive and formative power, a power which is proportionate to the thing's specific material determinateness [*Stoffbestimmtheit*]. If the view to which we previously referred were correct, that every material element is "really and truly" [*eigentlich*] destined to crystalline formation, then every material element would—without disturbing influences from the outside—"mold itself" and (correspondingly) divide itself into its particular crystalline form.

A crystal is an individual thing (an *individuum*) in the full sense of the term: a structure that consists of a number of cohering crystals, a whole that is composed of many individual things. A crystal that is smashed to pieces does not remain the same thing, but gives way to a number of new things which come to be "out of it." The individual, undivided crystal is "thoroughly formed" [*durchgeformt*] from within. The pieces which result from the smashing—and likewise the spatially separate parts of non-crystallized material elements—owe their spatial limits as well as their individual being partly to an external influence. I say partly, for (as was also pointed out before) their specific constitution is not a matter of indifference. In these pieces and parts there lies the general possibility of being cut up, and, furthermore, the mode and manner of the cutting up is predesigned in the specific material nature of the pieces and parts.

According to what we have stated so far, the question whether unformed matter suffices as a causal principle of individual being must be answered in the negative (cf. p. 480 above). Only formed matter can be this root principle, because (spatial) material being as such already denotes a being-formed, a being-placed into a genus of existence that is determined with respect to its content—the genus of quantitative extension, or of that which fills space and is divisible. By virtue of this generic nature, material substances bear in themselves the conditions of their being divided into individual things. But this generic nature is not a sufficient reason for the actual division.

The determinateness of the species [*Artbestimmtheit*] by which material substances are distinguished from one another takes us one step further on the road to individual being. The determinateness of the genus [*Gattungsbestimmtheit*] is as yet not a form. That which would be determined by it exclusively would be lacking that degree of determinateness which is required for actual being. The specifically determined material substance (e.g., gold) is (by virtue of its specific determinateness) not only capable of being divided in some manner, but is ordained to or destined for definite modes of division and for a limited choice among possible delimiting spatial structures.

But even the determinateness of the species does not yet coincide with the essential form. The two could be equated only if we were to assume that the whole of some specifically determined matter (e.g., "all the gold that there is") was originally placed into the world as a self-contained thing, i.e., if we could conceive of an order of creation in which the *elements* would originally come into existence as self-contained and separate material wholes [*Stoffganze*], to subsequently enter—by virtue of the "primary motive impulse"—into that great nexus of cause and effect [*Wirkungszusammenhang*] by which they are divided, to enter moreover into mixtures and combinations and thus to effect the building up of the manifold of self-contained individual corporeal things. If this were the case, it would not be necessary to attribute to individual things (as they actually exist) a form of their own. The original unified whole of matter would then be the large *individuum* that bears within itself the form which determines the species. But this form would then not only be the root principle of the determinateness of the species (as marking the distinction from other material substances), but it would simultaneously be the principle or cause of the *thorough forming* [*Ausformung*] of the whole into parts and pieces of definitely shaped spatial limits, and the form would accomplish this by its own efficacy and its efficacious interplay with other material substances.

However, this interpretation gives rise to serious doubts and objections. First of all, each self-contained and spatially separate part or piece of a material substance has a *being of its own.* It unfolds its specific essence or nature in effects which are actively and passively related to the immediate corporeal environment. This unfolding may possibly also be due to the formative influence of spiritually directed operations. In all this the part or piece of matter is independent of "others of its kind" [*seinesgleichen*], and in this sense it has its own destiny [*Schicksal*]. However, that which with its being and efficacious activity stands upon itself is a true *substance* or πρώτη *ousia* whose activity, passivity, and unfolding proceed from its own essential form. Furthermore, individual things come to be not only as parts or pieces of existing material substances, but as material quantities which are new as far as the determinateness of the species is concerned. After all, we know from everyday experience that—by combination and dissolution, by mixture and separation—composite material substances come into being from simple material elements, and vice versa. And there is no reason to assume an *original state* in which all the possible simple and composite material substances (or even the mere elements) were already extant and set apart from each other. What we read in Genesis (Gen 1:2) about the original *Tohuwabohu* (chaos) rather suggests that the separation of material elements and substances and the naturally ordered and regulated sequence of becoming and passing away was preceded by a state of confusion which permitted no thorough forming of material substances. Much of what Thomism attributes to the *materia prima* might be predicated of this primordial confusion. In this mixture there was the "possibility (or potentiality) of the becoming of all things," i.e., of the self-forming manifold of the entire corporeal world. Although this mixture was not yet full actuality, it was not nothing, but rather a preliminary phase of the actual world. And it might be said that in every actual thing there is part of this mixture as a "foundation" [*Unterlage*] of further formation.

On the other hand, this primordial mixture could not be called wholly undetermined. It would contain the specifically determined material elements, but restrained by their mutually exercised influences in such a way that their free unfolding would be impeded. Besides, this description pictures only one possibility of such an original state. It is not certain that it corresponds to actual fact, and other possibilities are conceivable. For example, it is just as plausible (as an essential possibility) that the created universe proceeded from the hands of God as a well-ordered and articulated world of fully formed things, albeit capable of undergoing transformations, not a world of finished and immutable things, because otherwise becoming and passing away, movement and change, would be incomprehensible. And it is these movements and changes which determine the face of the earth and the "natural course of events" [*das Naturgeschehen*]. Therefore, regardless of whether we envisage the genesis of things as a progressive evolution from chaos to cosmos or as a continuous transformation of a primordial cosmos, we are dealing with a sequence of formations and it must remain undecided whether these formations are to be conceived as temporally separated works of creation or as merged in *one* creative *Fiat!*

On the lowest stage of existents there are the specifically determined material elements and substances. They are specifically distinguished from each other by their forms, but they are simultaneously endowed with directive and formative powers which ordain them to their being divided into individual structures of a combined and specific particular [*arteigentümlich*] spatial form. The division and confining enclosure [*Umgrenzung*] take effect as was pointed out before—not exclusively as an unfolding from within but with the cooperation of external influences. It is a transformation in the sense that the part-structures take the place of the whole. The whole "passes away" so that "out of it" may arise the part-structures. And every new structure that thus comes to be has *its* form, a form which contains in itself the particularity of the species. It is the meaning of the being of material substances to serve the building up of spatial structures in which the spirit creates for itself a means of expression. The thoroughly formed structures are thus the language of the spirit, and the end and aim of the forming are "expressive, meaningful structures." External influences may either work in the direction of this end or they may act as impediments. The end structures toward which the forming tends may require for the attainment of the quantitative extension that is proportionate to their essence either a division or a combination of originally present quantities of matter.[31] In some instances the constitutive parts are preserved in the whole (that grows out of them) as independent units with a form of their own (as is the case, for example, with a group of boulders). In other instances the constitutive parts become dependent parts of the whole (as is the case with the quantities of water which a river absorbs from its tributaries).

I believe we are now in a position to answer the question of whether the one and only function of the form is the determination of the species (cf. p. 480 above). The essential forms of material things give to things not merely the determinateness of the species, but they are efficacious matter-forming forces, and as such each of them is an individual actuality. Such a form is already efficaciously active in every spatially enclosed partial quantity of a material substance. But the partial quantity which is not yet thoroughly formed in the sense of the determinateness of its species is only a stage that marks the transition to individual things or to structures composed of individual things, in which the end-structures find a more or less perfect actualization. The generic nature of matter as such makes possible the co-existence [*Nebeneinander*] of things that are alike.[32] However, this generic nature is not the ground or the root principle of individual being, but that which is required by the form.

Not the essential form but only the pure form or the essence (cf. chap. III, §§2, 3, and 10) of which things "partake" by their essential form is what is "communicable" to a multitude of individual things. Therefore it is not possible to speak of a "communication" of the essential form to its corresponding matter. According to my view of the relationship existing between form and matter in purely material things, the term "communication" [*Mitteilung*] is not appropriate at all, since form and matter cannot do without one another. The being of the form is the forming of matter, and the genesis of matter coincides with the self-molding of the form into space. Matter as such, to be sure, is not communicable at all. In itself and by itself it has neither meaning nor efficacy—neither *something* which could be communicated nor the power to communicate. It is simply that which receives, partakes, and is divisible.

We thus attribute to the form the individual being of the thing.[33] The question is whether individual being is something that accrues to the form or something which pertains to the form internally as a constitutive structural part. By saying that the essential form is incommunicable, we have already established this form as an individual "in itself." But the mere being-individual of one thing—as far as the content is concerned—differs not at all from the being individual of another thing. The being individual pertains to the *empty form* of the thing. If two individual things are to be distinguished as this or that, they must have something distinctive above and beyond their being individual. In the case of material things that are alike, this element of distinction is their share in matter [*Stoffanteil*] by which they differ spatially from each other. We shall have to ponder the question whether in the case of individual things of a different genus this share in matter is replaced by something else. But before we turn to a consideration of this question, we must first inquire into the relationship that exists between individual being, on the one hand, and *Selbstand* (subsistence) and *Dasein* (existence) on the other.

6. *Subsistence* [Selbstand], *Individual Being* [Einzelsein], *and Existence* [Dasein] *in Material Corporeal Things and in Ideal Objects*

According to Gredt[34] individual being is a presupposition of any *Selbstand* (subsistence). This is easily understandable from my own point of view, as far as material-corporeal things are concerned, since I attribute individual being even to the form, and since the form cannot be without matter. The very meaning of the form *is* the forming of matter [*Stoffgestaltung*]. The same observation holds true with respect to the relationship that exists between individual being and *Dasein* (existence), since the essential forms of material things have *Dasein* only in matter. But the question must be asked whether the same relationship exists where the independent objects are not material things. In other words, are there any independent things which are not individual things? And must we distinguish individual being from *Selbstand* in those individual things which admit of no disjunction of form and matter?

Relative to the first question, I have in mind so-called *ideal objects.* "The triangle" is contained in every individual triangle—it is thus communicable and is not an individual thing—and even the fully determined triangle with a definite size of angles and a definite length of sides seems to admit of further individuation. After all we speak of *congruent* triangles, and we are able to conceive of any number of triangles which are distinguished from each other only by their position in space. Is "the triangle," then, an independent object? It is a meaningful structure [*Sinngebilde*] which is one in itself and distinct from any other meaningful structure, and it follows in its structure a strict norm, a norm by virtue of which it becomes an object of true (and necessarily valid) judgments. And yet it lacks the full determinateness which is required for independence. It pertains to the meaning of the triangle that it contributes to the structural formation of independent objects. It is therefore not an independent existent and not an *object* in the more restricted sense of the term.

Let me ask then whether the triangle A B C with a length of sides a, b, c and a size of angles α, β, γ is independent? This triangle appears to be fully determined—nothing seems to be lacking in its internal structure—and yet something definitely conclusive [*ein Abschluss*] is missing, something what would make it "stand." According to its meaning, it is something extended, and to being-extended there pertains a definite position or location in space. The triangle that is determined in its position or location is an individual triangle. It is fully determined and non-communicable, which means that numerically differing structures cannot partake of it in the sense in which they can partake of the triangular structure A B C, which is thus "individuated."[35]

Is the individual triangle something independent? Or is it once again something which, according to its meaning, is merely destined to contribute to the structural formation of something that is independent? These questions lead me to a consideration of the relationship of geometrical structures to the world of things. There is no doubt that it pertains to the meaning of the being [*Seinssinn*] of geometrical structures to be of vital importance for the structural formation of the corporeal world, of material things. But geometrical structures do not enter into things as structural parts. They are not properties or qualities of things, i.e., they do not coincide with the spatial structure of things, but they are related to them as the archetype is related to the image. I tried to explain this previously by pointing out that purely geometrical structures do not occur in nature at all, but are merely "ideal limits" which the material bodies with their bounding lines and surfaces more or less approximate. Purely geometrical structures are the *measure* according to which the corporeal world has been fashioned.[36] This means that these structures are independent with respect to things. They contain no thingly carriers [*dingliche Träger*].

Do purely geometrical structures then carry themselves or is their carrier perhaps something else than a material thing? They are usually regarded as something *mental.* They are said to be "in the mind" [*im Geist*]. This view is correct if the mental is conceived not as being produced by the human mind or intellect, but as an *intelligible* or as that which the intellect can embrace and which in this sense can enter into the intellect.

Pure geometrical structures, therefore, do not have the human intellect as a personal carrier as is the case with thinking and actual thought content (in the sense of a product of thinking). Is their personal carrier then perhaps the Spirit [*Geist*] of God? This is true in the sense in which it is said that all being proceeds from God and is sustained and maintained by God, and in the sense in which in particular every *meaning* has its home and abode in the Logos. But just as things in their actuality are created and sustained by God and are yet *by* the act of creation placed outside the divine being and into and upon their own being, so the meaningful structures [*Sinngebilde*], the archetypes of actual things, are in a way placed outside of the Divine Spirit—yet nonetheless encompassed or enclosed by the Divine Spirit—as self-contained units and as a "creation anteceding creation." The human intellect discovers these meaningful structures and has to adapt its thinking to their norm. The world of things is fashioned in their image and according to their measure. This is why Hering designates them as *primary existents* [*das erste Seiende*].[37]

These meaningful structures are arranged among themselves in an order which permits "those which are communicable" to contribute to the structural formation of the others and thus to fulfill their meaning. Those individual structures, on the other hand, which are fully determined as to their content are "without need or want" [*unbedürftig*], no longer dependent on any other structure of their species, independent with respect to their actualization and indifferent in their independence as to whether or not they are intellectually thought or conceived as human beings. And yet it cannot be said that they are altogether independent of any personal intellect, not only on account of the relationship that exists between all finite beings and the infinite Creative Spirit, but also because individual geometrical structures are in a special manner dependent on the spirit [*Geist*]. They are not *actual,* and they are not in space in the manner actual things are in space. They "are not there or present" as something that strikes the senses or that makes itself felt by its effects. They are not efficaciously active nor do they fill space, although they have a spatial extension and occupy a position in space. They delimit or circumscribe a piece of space

[*Raumstück*], but they do not occupy it in such a way that it becomes non-accessible to other structures. We may even venture to say that they are merely intellectually "conceived" [*gedacht*] in space. No definite place can be ascribed to them, but merely "some" piece of space proportionate to the determinateness of their extension. We can therefore place them in different positions, and we can conceive of them as being in motion, although they never move themselves (i.e., have their own motion), nor can they be "actually" moved (i.e., within the context of the natural course of things and events).

However, these liberties with regard to pure geometrical structures are given to us by virtue of their very essences and we thus could not "take" these liberties unless the structures in question were of this particular nature. The non-actuality of ideal objects also accounts for the peculiar nature of their independence. They do not "stand upon themselves" in the manner of *substances.* They do not possess themselves and they have no power of being [*Seinsmacht*] that would allow them to unfold their essence in a temporal measured *Dasein.* Their being is no self-unfolding at all but rather an accomplished unfolding [*Entfaltetsein*]. And those possibilities which have their *raison d' être* in them—such as the possibility of being placed in different space positions or the possibility of being divided and joined together (as happens in geometrical "constructions")—are not possibilities of individual action, but possibilities for the intellect to deal with them in a specific manner without thereby "impairing" their structures as such. And these possibilities have significance not only for the intellect but also for the structures with which the intellect deals. The triangle A B C is an individual triangle. It has a definite extension, and by virtue of this extension it has a claim to a place in space. But this triangle is not in a place in space "by virtue of its nature" [*von Natur aus*], nor can it "appropriate" or "maintain" its place. It has to be "placed" into the position in space, and this placement can be brought about only by a thinking intellect. The position in space which causes this triangle to be fully determined and distinct from other triangles must be "intellectually intended" [*zugedacht*] for it. It can be moved or transposed from one position to another and even the difference of its position from that of other triangles is not irrevocable. If we prove the congruence of two triangles, we demonstrate their equality by means of their coincidence, i.e., we place them into an identical position. Though they thereby become non-distinguishable from one another, one cannot say that the two triangles have become one.

We shall now attempt to determine the relationship that exists between individual being, *Selbstand* (subsistence), and *Dasein* (existence). A certain class of individual objects is independent in the sense of being fully determined as to its content. These objects do not adhere to a *carrier* (as the properties of things adhere to things), but they are themselves carriers of an essence or nature and carriers of properties or qualities. However, their independence is not unlimited, since the particular nature of their being makes them quasi-dependent on some thinking intellect. Their being is no actual *Dasein.* We cannot say that "there are" triangles in the sense in which we say that there are (i.e., exist) rocks and human beings. Individual being and *Dasein,* therefore, do not necessarily go together. With the particular nature of the being of such structures as triangles, however, is conjoined a particular characteristic of their individuality. Each of them is itself, this one triangle and no other, and it can be grouped together with others of its kind to form a multiplicity. But the multiplicity of all these structures of the same kind cannot be a finite number. An infinite number of them is possible—not only in infinite space, but even in a finite piece of space, as they do not "contend with each other" for space. And since for them the difference between potentiality and actuality does not exist, there are as many of them as are (ideally) possible, i.e., any number in the sense of an open infinity.

How, then, are *Selbstand* (subsistence) and individual being related to one another in these structures? We call them "independent" or "self-dependent" because they are self-contained and fully determined, because they embrace or "carry" their own quid. And we call them "individual" because each of them is this one [*dieses eine*] and no other. Each of them is this one not on account of the fact that it occupies a position proportionate to its extension, but, conversely, on account of the fact that the structure is this one, it has *its* extension and is therewith allotted a proportionate position. Individuality and independence are both anchored in the structure itself, owing to the fact that the structure is *something* or an *object* (in the restricted sense of the term), i.e., the carrier of a quid and an essence. And while independence pertains to the whole—i.e., to the carrier plus that which is carried—individual being already attaches to the carrier as such and to everything which the carrier carries and encloses in itself: the essence and all its parts, and its accruing properties and qualities.

Selbstand (subsistence) and individual being thus have a common ground or foundation in the formal structure of existents. They mutually need and require each other, so that the one cannot be said to be "prior" to the other. Whatever is independent must also be an individual. But an individual must not necessarily be independent. However, if it is not independent, it must be a structural part of something that is independent.

As far as the relationship to *Dasein is* concerned, we have seen that there are individual and independent structures (albeit in a somewhat modified sense) of which no *Dasein* can be predicated. But whatever is actual is either individual and independent or a structural part of something that is individual and independent or a whole that is made up of independent individual things. Individuality and independence may be said to be factually prior to *Dasein* (actual being, existence).

Moreover, we have learned that we must distinguish between the being-different [*Unterschiedensein*] and the being-distinguishable-in-its-difference [*Unterscheidbarkeit*] of individual objects. Being different rests on its carrier. The knowability of differences rests, in the case of material things, on their participation in matter, and in the case of pure geometrical structures it rests on their position or location in space. In both instances this knowability has its foundation in the spatial nature of objects.

7. *The Individual Being of Created Pure Spirits*

By establishing being a carrier [*das Trägersein*] as the ground or foundation of individual being, we are referring individual being back to the formal structure of existents. It is thereby set apart from the spatial nature of definite genera of existents. A nonspatial structure, too, can be an individual. This fact is familiar to us and is also well-known to *Thomists* who regard pure spirits as *substances,* i.e., as being individual, self-dependent, and actual. But Thomists must of necessity try to find another foundation of these spirits' individual being than the one assumed in the case of spatial-corporeal material things, since in these latter they regard matter as the root principle of differentiation. This is why Thomists designate angels as *pure forms*[38] which are "individualized by themselves and which cannot be multiplied within the same species. In the order of these pure spiritual forms, there are therefore as many species as there are individuals."[39]

According to my own point of view—which distinguishes even in pure spirits between the determinateness of the species and its carrier (in this case the carrier is the person)—the personal carrier is the ground or root principle of individual being. And since we do not find the root principle of individual being in the "communication" or, more precisely, in the self-molding of the form into space-filling matter, but see in this a kind of communication [*Mitteilung*], rather than the unfolding of the essence of a definite genus of forms, the "non-communicability" [*Unmitteilbarkeit*] of spiritual forms to space-filling matter constitutes in my opinion no proof of the non-communicability of the determinateness of the species to a multiplicity of individuals. On the other hand, nor can *spiritual matter* which I attribute to pure spirits be regarded as the root principle of the individuation of the species, since form *and* matter are individuated and are in this case inseparably one.

If it is true that there do not exist several alike [*gleich*] angels of the same species and that one angel is distinguished from the other not only numerically but by his or her unrepeatable individual *particularity* [*Eigenart*], the reason must be a different one. Gredt attributes to pure spirits "a certain kind of infinity. They are not absolutely but relatively infinite, i.e., they are infinite in their species, so that *one* individual fills, as it were, the entire circumference of the species...."[40] In this kind of "infinity" we might find an explanation of the fact that there do not exist several alike angels of the same species. They are not "needed" for a thoroughgoing formation of the species. St. Thomas also refers in this context to the idea of the *preservation of the species*. Since pure spirits are immortal, only one individual is needed to make secure the preservation of the species, whereas in the case of material structures, a multiplicity of individuals is needed because they are transitory.[41] But this does not prove that a multiplicity of spirits of the same species is impossible. As we shall have to revert to the relationship that exists between species and individuality [*Art und Eigenart*],[42] we confine ourselves for the time being to a further exploration of the problem of individual being with respect to the knowability of differentiation [*Unterscheidbarkeit*].

Two pure spirits differ from one another because they are persons and are as such both individual and independent. But what is it that makes them distinguishable from one another? Space cannot in this case be the medium that accounts for their being different. Can it be *time?* There are temporal structures which are distinguishable from each other only by their position in time, just as spatial structures which are alike are distinguishable from each other only by their position in space. If "the same" tune is played twice (assuming that it is played at the identical place and in a completely identical manner), we have two time structures which are separated by their temporal sequence. If they are played simultaneously (which can be done only in an imperfect, approximate manner), they would be indistinguishable from one another. In a similar manner, two alike spirits (assuming such a possibility) would be distinguishable from one another only if they were to come into existence at different times.

However, it seems that in this case still another possibility would have to be considered (a possibility which is nonexistent in the case of original temporal structures), namely, the return of the same spirit after an interruption of its *Dasein.* When "the same tune" is played again, that which is designated as the same, i.e., the tune as a "time structure," is not something individual [*ein Einzelnes*] but something that can be "communicated" [*ein Mitteilbares*]. The processes in which the same is actualized are numerically separate, and it would therefore be meaningless to say that "the same" tonal process [*Tonvorgang*] returns.

To the tune or melody in our example there corresponds, when we are dealing with a spiritual person, the "course of life" as a time structure. We regard the course of life of a human being as something unique [*ein Einmaliges*] that cannot be repeated. But that world view which sees in world history an ever repeated cycle and which assumes a return or rebirth of souls points to a possibility which seems to be rooted in the essence or nature of the person as such—

and this despite the fact that many objections can be advanced against such a view by both faith and natural reason. The person is a *carrier* in a different sense than any impersonal something. The life of the person "springs" from personal being as from a source, and it is conceivable that this life might end without the person itself being annihilated, and the person might then begin a new life.[43] The possibility of distinguishing whether in the case of temporally separate identical courses of life it was a question of the same person or of different persons could be located in the person itself.[44] The person might be able to identify itself in the "new life" as the same ego that was alive once before in the manner in which we "rediscover" ourselves after certain interruptions of our conscious life.

Now the same situation prevails quite generally with respect to the possibility of distinguishing persons from each other. The fact that every person is able to distinguish itself from all other persons—irrespective of whether they live at the same time or at some other time, and irrespective of whether they are alike or different—has its reason or cause in the particular nature of that self-consciousness that pertains to the personal being of the ego. However, to recognize other persons as numerically distinct, another medium or means for establishing this distinction [*Unterscheidungsmittel*] is needed. This other medium or means is—with respect to persons as well as other beings and things—the difference in content which, aside from the difference of the temporal determinateness, is by far the most important means for the recognition of these *distinctions.*

Things which are, as the saying goes, "so much alike as to be mistaken for one another" and which we are able to recognize as numerically different only by their position in space and time are, according to common experience, much rarer in occurrence than those things which are sufficiently distinguishable from all others by their *individual peculiarity* [*Eigenart*].

Of course, no one denies the actual differences among things. These differences are even at times so exaggerated as to lead us to the conclusion that no things whatsoever exist "in reality" that are completely alike. They are merely so similar as to be non-distinguishable from each other. This is the reason why an *individuum* is usually regarded not only as something that is numerically one and distinct from everything else, but also and even primarily as something that differs from everything else with respect to content. However, these two characteristics must be kept strictly separate. Even if complete alikeness were not found in reality, it is at any rate intellectually conceivable, and such complete alikeness in no way impedes numerical differentiation. And since differentiation in number and differences in content carry not only a different meaning but must be considered as actually separate, it is highly probable that they also differ in the ground or root principle of their being [*Seinsgrund*].

St. Thomas too distinguishes strictly between numerical differentiation and non-alikeness [*Ungleichheit*] (= differences in content). The latter he designates as difference according to form (*formalis*) and the former as difference according to matter (*materialis*). By *form* he means, of course, the essential form, and formal difference is therefore for him equivalent to specific difference [*Artverschiedenheit*]. "For since matter is for the sake of form, the material difference exists exclusively for the sake of the formal difference."[45] This is then given by St. Thomas as the reason why a multiplicity of alike structures (for the sake of the preservation of the species) is found only in transitory material things. The actual occurrence of a multiplicity of things belonging to the same species is thus explained by their purpose, but it is not shown that the numerical differentiation as such is anchored in the very structure of beings. I have attempted to show that the latter is actually the case, and I am convinced that the root principle of individual being is found in the formal structure of objects as such, and especially in the fact that the carrier which confines or sets apart the essence or nature of objects as their empty form is not communicable. This holds true irrespective of the differences in the content of the genera of existents and is therefore valid for every genus. The differences in the content of individual things, on the other hand, are not caused by their formal structure, and this is why these differences may have different causes in different genera.

8. The Cause of the Differences of Content in Spatial-Material Things

We are tracing back causally the manifold in the natural constitution of material individual things of identical determinateness of species to the differences of those external influences which—in cooperation with the determinateness of the species—are responsible for the "fate" of individual things and their particular actual *formal structure* [*Gestalt*]. When St. Thomas says: *Individuum est de ratione materiae,* he expresses his conviction that not only the individual being of things rests on their participation in matter, but also the nature of their contents, to the extent that the latter does not rest on the determinateness of the species, a determinateness which is shared by all the other individual things of the same species.

There is no need to discuss once more the nature of individual being. As far as the natural constitution of individual things is concerned, we do well to remind ourselves that we must not expect to meet with matter that is not determined in its species. We may say of the individual material thing that it owes the determinateness of its species to its form, but we may say just as well that the individual material thing has *this* determinateness of species because it is "a piece of *this* matter." What distinguishes the individual pieces of this matter with respect to their content—differences of size, shape, color—is accounted for by the fact that matter as such (according to the determinateness of its genus) lends itself to being cut up into pieces [*zerstückbar*], that it is capable of receiving influences, varying according to the determinateness of the species, from other material substances (but also from spirits), and that the spatially separated pieces are subject to various influences.

We must keep in mind, furthermore, that to each material substance belong certain formative powers which are proportionate to the determinateness of its species, powers which ordain the material substance to a particular individual formation and make it capable of expressing a *meaning* that addresses the comprehending intellect through the medium of the sensible shapes of material structures. The external influences may deliver or set free these internal formative powers, or (in "fallen" nature) they may impede and counteract these powers. As far as the *language* is concerned by which material structures express and convey their meaning, the manifold of content in structures of the same species may be meaningful and may be pre-designed as a possibility in the determinateness of the species. Thus, not every non-alikeness within a species can be regarded as an *accidental* change caused by external influences.

The possibilities of varying formation are pre-designed in the formal determinateness of individual material elements and substances as well as in the total order of the material world.

9. The Relationship Between the Specific and Individual Essence or Nature in Sub-Human Animate Beings

Only where we are dealing with *supra-material* [*stoffüberlegen*] forms, i.e., forms which come into *Dasein* in some previously existing and determined matter and which mold an individual structure (i.e., an *animate being* [*Lebewesen*]) out of this matter and other added elements, do we find a possibility of distinguishing *within* the individual thing between form and matter as root principles of the specific and individual natural constitution of the individual thing. In this case the particularity of the species is differently marked and expressed according to the structural material elements which the individual form encounters. This does not mean, however, that the varying formation of the specific particularity is caused exclusively by the diversity of the structural material elements.

I previously pointed out that the particular nature of the genera of animate beings, in contradistinction to lifeless things, accounts for the difference in the manner of their origin and formation. There is in animate beings neither "disintegration" [*Zerfallen*] nor "accidental junction" [*Zusammengeraten*] of material quantities but rather a forming process that issues from a vital center (i.e., a self-formation) and a generation of individuals by individuals. The whole of the species is in this case not a material whole (either spatially coherent or in pieces), but a cohesion by virtue of generation or common descent. As compared with lifeless material structures, the individual here has a greatly heightened significance with respect to the whole of the species. Each individual structure is an articulate unity with a meaning and expressive worth of its own, and not merely a transitional stage with respect to the actual end structures [*Zielgestalten*], as we have seen it to be the case with material quantities in their relationship to thoroughly formed structures.

The being of animate creatures is *self*-formation in the sense of a forming of the individual structure from its vital center and not merely an unfolding of the particularity of the species under the influence of forces effective from the outside. And proportionate to this is a collected power and, springing from it, a stronger activity and efficacy of the self. But each individual being also has on this level a heightened significance *for* the whole of the species. The individuals *embody* the species and *preserve* it by means of propagation, and in the individuals the species also experiences a progressive *transformation.* It is divided into *varieties* [*Spielarten*], and in these varieties it becomes more clearly evident that material structures, from the point of view of the particularity of the species, are no mere *accidental formations*—more or less perfect actualizations, depending on favorable or unfavorable external circumstances—but they express the particularity of the species in several ways and directions and may therefore be regarded as *end structures* that are intentionally pre-designed in and with the particular species.

In addition, there exists the dual possibility that the species either "makes its original appearance" already divided into several different mutually irreducible *branches* or that one single core relationship of descent [*Abstammungszusammenhang*] with progressive particularizations and ramifications must be assumed. Neither pure reason nor experience provide any criteria that would enable us to decide whether the one or the other is the case. But there can be no question of an absolute either/or. Even if it were necessary originally to assume separate varieties, a progressive particularization and transformation could not be denied. It takes place in and through individual beings: in and *through* the "fate" which befalls them and which is significant for their formation, and by the combination of different inherited characteristics in those individuals which are generated by sexual procreation.

Although every individual being is an independent actuality (a πρώτη *ousia* or substance), the totality of all individuals interrelated by *common descent* must be regarded as an actual whole with vital laws of its own (albeit not an independent whole, since it is actual only *in* individuals and is thus no actual *substance*).

The individual being is thus a carrier of the particularity of the species and of its evolution. The being-individual and the particular form of the individual are as links in a chain. And this is why I cannot accept without qualification St. Thomas's *de ratione materiae,* i.e., the contention that the diversity of content within a species has its reason or cause in matter. The essential forms of animate beings are living forms and as such capable of unfolding and transformation. In this they follow their own formative laws. The material structural elements cooperate in the achievement of the final result, but they do so in a servile manner. I do not go so far as to assume at this stage for every individual being a form differing in content from all other forms. The particularity of the species demands here that it find expression in different specific *varieties*, the carriers of which are individuals, and there is not only no need for *unique* individuals, but the preservation of the once definitely marked varieties is even a necessary task and a requirement. Because the individual being comes to be and passes away, it must generate others "of its kind and like unto it" [*seinesgleichen*], so that the *form* [*Gestalt*] is not lost. Preservation and evolution must go side by side in the unfolding of the particularity of the species if the meaning of their being [*Seinssinn*] is to be fulfilled. The question of whether the co-conditioning external circumstances lead to the result that in their actual constitution no two individuals are ever completely alike need not be answered in this context. The abundance of life can make itself manifest not only in the manifold of different formal structures but also in the growing fullness of structures which are alike.

10. The Specific Particularity [Arteigentümlichkeit], *the Individual Particularity* [Eigenart], *and the Individual Being* [Einzelsein] *of Human Beings*

Thomism regards human beings as a species of the genus *animate being*, and in its attempt to establish the cause or the root principle of individual being, it makes no distinction among plants, animals, and human beings. And, as a matter of fact, much of what has been stated above in this respect applies *eo ipso* to human beings [*Menschen*]: The being-human [*Menschsein*] as such is the common essence or nature of all individual human beings, an essence or nature that is always and everywhere the same. However, in addition, every human being possesses something in his content by which he is distinguished from other human beings. And here again we find a branching out of humankind into *particular species* (races, peoples, tribes, generations, families), i.e., groups of individuals who are distinct from others by their interrelationship of common descent and by the common elements of their individual particularity [*Eigenart*]. The individuals are carriers of the particularity of the species and of the specific formation which is achieved with the aid of external circumstances. The material constitution of the individual being and of the *environment* into which the individual is integrated are co-determining factors. The question is whether in this case, too, individual being and particular species are merely like links in a chain. If we consider the dual meaning of human *life*—that on the one hand, it is matter-forming life (like that of animals and plants) and, on the other hand, a spiritual, personal, internal life, self-contained and yet self-transcending; a world-embracing life that discloses itself to fellow humans and that is ever renewed from these sources; and, lastly, a life that is freely determined by the I [*Ich*]—then we must ask whether this radical dichotomy of human life is not also of major significance for the individual being and the individual particularity of human beings.

It has already become clear that the individual being of human beings—like the individual being of every spiritual person—differs from the individual being of all non-personal things. This implies that life (on the level of personality) emanates from the I and that the personal I holds command over it in a dual sense: so as to become conscious of it as of a life that is set apart from everything else; and so as to mold this life freely. But we have seen, moreover, that the I is not to be conceived as a mere *pure ego* [*ein blosses reines Ich*]; that the pure ego is, as it were, only the portal through which the life of the human person passes on its way from the depth of the soul to the lucidity of consciousness. And the innermost center of the soul, its most authentic and most spiritual part, is not colorless and shapeless, but has a particular form of its own. The soul feels it when it is "in its own self," when it is "self-collected." This innermost center of the soul cannot be grasped in such a manner that it could be given a universal name, nor can it be compared with anything else. It cannot be divided into properties, character traits and the like, because it is located in greater depth than any of these. The innermost center of the soul is the *how* (ποῖον) of the essence itself and as such impresses its stamp on every trait of character and every attitude and action of human beings, and it is the key that unlocks the mystery of the structural formation of the character of a human being. By means of these "expressions," the innermost essence of the soul also becomes manifest externally. We "feel" the ineffable in the soul's essence also in our communication with others. It is that which ultimately accounts for the fact that we are either "attracted to" or "repelled by" a human being. This ineffable in the soul's essence may cause a feeling of kinship with others, and yet my own intrinsic *nature* [*meine Art*] and that of the other cannot be neatly taken apart so as to make manifest what we have in common and in what we differ. In this sense, then, we must admit that the essential difference [*Wesensunterschied*] in individuals cannot be grasped.

Is there such a thing as a perfect alikeness or equality among human beings? The phenomenon of the "double" [*Doppelgänger*] is familiar to us from literature, but it is presented there as something preternatural—either as a product of a pathological imagination or as a phantom of hell. This proves nothing, of course, but it indicates at least that people experience their own selves as unrepeatable. And certain reasons why this is the case—reasons which are, to be sure, not absolutely conclusive—may be adduced. It is, of course, possible that human beings resemble each other so closely that they are constantly mistaken for each other (e.g., in the case of identical twins). People who know such persons intimately are nevertheless capable of noticing the differences. And these persons themselves feel their being different so distinctly—even if they are as close to one another as they are to no one else in the world—that they are unable to understand how it is possible to mistake them for each other. And what matters is not so much that actually the one person's nose may be a slightly different shape or that the color of the eyes may show a slight variation—the stranger may notice such differences and may remember them for the purpose of future identification—nor does it matter that a certain talent is more conspicuous in the one than in the other. What really matters is, rather, that each of these persons feels himself in his innermost essence as an "authentic individual" and is so regarded by those who have truly "grasped" or "apprehended" the nature of his personality.

Is it possible to explain such a radical difference of individual essences by the fact that human souls abide in bodies which consist of spatially separated material elements? Certainly not. But then what justifies us in assuming as real such a difference of the essence? What convincing reason can be adduced for safely trusting our "feeling"? I answer, first of all, that this *feeling* is not to be understood as a mere state of the soul to which no further significance attaches. The *feeling* of which we are speaking here has of cognitive value and significance. It reveals to us something which becomes accessible by this very feeling. This feeling is in fact a spiritual *act,* a spiritual *apperception.* We call it a "feeling" because it is a "dim" apprehension, an apprehension that lacks the clarity and distinctness of a conceptually expressible, rational insight, and because it is an "apperception in which the heart is engaged" [*Wahrnehmen mit dem Herzen*]. Whatever is felt in this manner speaks to the inwardness of the soul and tends to being received in this inwardness. And we speak of *apperception* because this kind of apprehension has in common with sense perception that something unique and actual is apprehended. But that which is apprehended is something spiritual and as such not accessible to the senses, even though it manifests itself by means of sensible signs or symbols (i.e., by the bodily *expression* of that which pertains to the soul). And this kind of apperception, like sense perception, is open to deception. But to dispense with it altogether on this account would be just as unreasonable as to renounce completely the use of the senses as a means of knowledge on account of the fact that the senses are "delusive."[46]

If we then feel our own essence or nature as well as the essences or natures of others to be thus constituted, and if we feel this "thus" [*So*] to be something "unique," then this feeling, as a special mode of primordial experience, bears within itself its own justification. It would appear that, with the contention of the uniqueness of this "thus," we have transcended the frame of an individual experience and have ventured to pronounce a sentence that lays claim to universal validity. It is indeed the meaning of such a dictum that no other thus resembles this one. The reason for this lies in the formal structure of the person: in the uniqueness of the I as such that is conscious of its own self, that embraces the particularity of its own essence as its "very own," and that ascribes to every other I the same uniqueness and individual *particularity* [*Eigenheit*]. However, the content of the "thus" cannot be apprehended and expressed universally.

§3. Some Reflections on the Meaning of Human Individual Being on the Basis of its Relationship to Divine Being

I believe I am justified in assuming, on the basis of innermost self-consciousness and our understanding of the general form of the being-person deriving therefrom, the uniqueness of the innermost center of each human soul and therewith the entire human person, insofar as the person receives its form from this deepest interiority. We shall now attempt to gain an insight into the meaning of this fact. Such an understanding becomes possible on the basis of the relationship of the soul to God.

1. The Vocation of the Soul to Eternal Life

We have learned to know the innermost being of the soul as the "abode of God." By virtue of its pure spirituality, this innermost being is capable of receiving into itself the Spirit of God. And by virtue of its free personal nature, this innermost being is capable of surrendering itself in such a way that this reception can become efficacious.

The vocation to union with God is a vocation to eternal life. As a purely spiritual form, the human soul is immortal *by virtue of its very nature* [*natürlicherweise*].[47] As a spiritual personal substance, moreover, the soul is capable of a supernatural augmentation and elevation of its life, and faith tells us that God *wills* to give the soul eternal life, i.e., an eternal participation in his life.

The individual soul with its "unique" individuality is thus not something transitory, destined merely to impress upon itself for a limited span of time the stamp of its specific particularity, and during this span of time to hand on this specific particularity to its "progeny" so as to preserve it beyond the duration of the life of the individual. Rather, the soul is destined for eternal being, and this destination explains why the soul is called upon to be an image of God in a "wholly personal manner."

Sacred Scripture offers much support for such an interpretation. Thus, we may understand the words of the Psalmist: *Qui finxit sigillatim corda eorum* ("he has formed the heart of each of them individually"),[48] in the sense that every individual human soul has proceeded from the hands of God and bears a special seal. And when we read in the Apocalypse of St. John, "I shall give the victor ... a white stone, and on the stone will be inscribed a new name, known only to the one who receives it,"[49] are we not to assume that this name signifies a *proper* name [*Eigenname*] in the strict and full sense of the term, i.e., a name which enunciates the innermost essence or nature of the recipient and reveals to this recipient the mystery of his or her being that is hidden in God? For God this name is not new, but a "new" name is given to the victorious human being. While on earth, this person bore a different name. For human language, after all, knows of no genuine proper names. It names things as well as persons after some universally apprehensible traits of character. Human beings "characterize" things and persons by compiling the greatest possible number of such traits. The innermost and most authentic nature of human beings remains hidden most of the time. It is veiled by that stamp or style of character which individual human nature has assumed in the course of the individual human life under the influence of the environment and especially under the influence of *social intercourse.* Whatever we know or divine of this deeply hidden nature in ourselves and in others remains dark, mysterious, and "ineffable." But when our earthly life ends and everything transitory falls away, then every soul will know itself "as it is known,"[50] i.e., as it is before God: in the what, the why, and the whither which God had in mind when he created this personal soul, and this is essential in the status which it has attained in the orders of nature and grace by virtue of its free choices.

We also have to consider what it means for the soul to receive God into its innermost being. The omnipresent God is, of course, present always and everywhere—in inanimate and irrational creatures which are unable to receive him in the manner the soul receives him, in the "outer mansions" of the soul where the soul is unaware of his presence, and in the innermost being of the soul, even though the soul may not abide in its own interiority. It is therefore not possible to assume that God enters into a place where he was not present before. To say that the soul receives God means rather that it opens itself and gives itself freely to him to bring about a union that is possible only between spiritual persons. It is a union of *love:* God is love, and the participation in divine being which is granted in this union must be a participation in divine love [*ein Mitlieben*].

God is the plenitude of love. Created spirits, however, are incapable of receiving into themselves and of sharing to the fullest extent the total plenitude of divine love. Their share in divine love is rather determined by the measure of their being, and this implies not only a "so much" [*Soviel*], but also a "thus" [*So*]. In other words, love always bears the stamp of personal individuality. And this explains in turn why God may have chosen to create for himself a special abode in each human soul, so that the plenitude of divine love might find in the manifold of differently constituted souls a wider range for its self-communication.

2. *A Comparison Between the Individual Particularity* [Eigenart] *of Human Beings and of Angels*

If we attribute to every human soul an unrepeatable individual particularity, does this mean that we place people on a footing of equality with angels? Does it mean that every human being is a "species by itself" and, if it does, what would be the relationship of this species to the human race?

To the essence of the human being as such there pertains a dual nature: The human being is a spiritual person and he is shaped [*gestaltet*] as a body. As a spirit, the human being belongs to the same genus of existents as other created spirits. As a structural composite of a corporeal body and a soul the human being belongs to the genus of animate beings. But because the spiritual and the body-soul being of the human being are not externally juxtaposed, but *one*, it seems to me that we are justified in speaking here of a particular genus. The intellectual-spiritual life of the human being differs from that of angels in that the former rises from a hidden depth and in that the formation of the corporeal body also proceeds from this hidden depth. Angels have no soul in the sense of a center of being [*Seinsmitte*] which unfolds in a temporal process of evolution by forming itself into a corporeal body and into a spiritual life. The meaning of their being is no other than the unfolding of what they are (they do not have to become what they are) in a life of pure self-giving to God: in knowledge, love, and service. And angels all share in common in this generic nature. What distinguishes them from each other is the *how* or the *mode and manner* of their knowledge, love, and service. In this how their individual *particularity* unfolds itself. Their knowledge and love are not separated, since in the vision of God, which is nothing but a union of love, the essence or nature of God (which is love) is known by participation [*Mitlieben*]. Their service, however, is an actualization of their love. And because love differs according to the nature of personality, their entire spiritual life is different from that of the human being.

I pointed out before that the "communication" of such an individual particularity to a plurality of personal carriers is, properly speaking, not wholly inconceivable[51] just as "doubles" are conceivable among human beings. But if even where human beings are concerned strong reasons seem to speak against the possibility of such *individual specification* [*Vereinzelung*], one further reason can be adduced in the case of angels. As indicated before, one single individual angel suffices for the unfolding of the entire riches of the species. The meaning of this statement may be illustrated by the contrast between the realm of angels and the realm of humankind.

Even the individual human being is incapable of unfolding in its life all the possibilities which have their ground or foundation in its essence or nature (in the sense of the individual essence or nature). The individual human being's power is so limited that he or she has to pay for the highest accomplishments in one field by shortcomings or deficiencies in other fields. We may therefore assume that the perfection of the individual human being in the state of glory will not only free each human being from the impurities of its corrupt nature but also unfold its as yet unfulfilled possibilities. However, even then the individual human being will not be a perfect expression of the "essence of the human being" [*Wesen des Menschen*].

It pertains to the essence of the human being that the individual is a *member* of the human race and that this individual realizes himself as a whole (with all the possibilities implied therein) in a *humankind* [*Menschheit*] in which the individuals inhere as "members of one another" [*Glied zu Glied*]. To be a member of this totality, every individual must be an embodiment of universal human nature. But this latter is only a frame which is to be filled with the manifold of the individual member beings [*Gliedwesen*]. We may perhaps draw a comparison between this relationship and the one that exists between color and specific color gradations [*Farbarten*], since it pertains to the essence of specific color gradations to be *color,* and it pertains to the essence of color to be *a* color. And yet the latter relationship is quite different, since the individual human being is in his content not merely a particularization of something more universal, but a member of a whole that realizes itself as a *vital unity* [*Lebenseinheit*] and that can achieve its unfolding only in the vital context of the whole, in its particular place and in cooperation with the other members.

An important part in all this is played not only by the vital laws of propagation, the care and the division of labor required for providing the necessities of life—functions and activities which human beings have in common with the lower animate beings—but also by those laws of spiritual life by virtue of which all the products and creations of the human mind become the common property of humankind, "food" for the souls of contemporary and succeeding generations, or orders of life endowed with directive force and formative power. By virtue of its spirit nature [*Geistnatur*], humankind is called to a communal life which—after having grown from a temporally, spatially, and materially determined soil—eventually annuls the limitations of time and space.

However, since the individual soul comes to bloom in a place prepared for it—prepared by the historical evolution of the people of its earthly homeland and by the generations of its earthly family—and since, after its pure and full unfolding at its predesigned

place, the soul is to be inserted as a flower in an eternally imperishable wreath, it does not seem fitting to see in its essence or nature a *species* that can be *individualized* in a multiplicity of alike structures. Now in a wreath a rare and exquisite flower may well be surrounded by many insignificant small blossoms almost completely alike to each other and therefore mutually replaceable. Similarly, in the history of the human race as well as in the narrow circle of our own experience we are able to distinguish the "great," "strong," "outstanding" personalities from those "average human beings" among whom we can hardly discover any significant differences. But we already know that only a superficial observer sees things in this way. When the troops who have been marching in rank and file disband, every soldier who was trotting along and was strictly keeping pace with the others, having perhaps almost forgotten that he is an individual, becomes once again a small, self-contained universe in his own right. And where the curious spectators along the way saw merely a homogeneous mass, the mother or bride was able to discern in the crowd him whom they were expecting, the individual, him whom none of the others resembled. The mystery of his being which their love divined is fully known only to the all-seeing eye of God before whom all human standards of "great" and "small," "significant" and "insignificant" come to naught.

There is no denying, of course, that in the kingdom of heaven, too, there are the "great ones" and the "little ones"—differences which may be traced back to preparation in earthly life: to the endowments of the individual person and to the use this person has made of his or her God-given "talents." Human beings may "find their own selves"[52] to a greater or lesser degree, but there is also the possibility of losing oneself. For those who do not find themselves do not find God either, and do not attain to eternal life. Or, more precisely, those who do not find God do not attain to their own selves—no matter how much they may be preoccupied with themselves—nor to that source of eternal life which lies in wait for them in their own innermost being.

To the dual meaning of the word "humanity" [*Menschheit*]—which is now used to designate universal human nature, and then again to designate the living whole of humankind—corresponds a dual relationship of the individual human being to "humanity." The individual human being is an embodiment of the *universal,* and this human being is a member of the whole. The individual angel, too, is the embodiment of a universal "angelic nature," but the angel is not a member of a whole in the same sense as a human being. We are justified in speaking of an "angelic world" in which every individual angel represents a specific phase or stage of spiritual personal being and forms with others, as it were, a harmony of many voices. And, as was mentioned earlier, it is the opinion of the Doctors of the Church that angels communicate with each other and meaningfully to each other, inasmuch as they mutually illumine each other. But no angel owes its nature to another member of the angelic hierarchy,[53] and no angel needs any of the others for the unfolding of its nature. They form a unity as the "heavenly court" which surrounds the throne of the All-Highest.

We experience a human being's being a member [*Gliedsein*] of humanity or humankind as a fact. To be sure, individuals must be far advanced in their development to embrace humanity as a whole and to know of their obligations to this whole. At the time of the awakening of their reason, human beings discover themselves only as members of a more limited community (viz., the family and other cultural and educational communal associations), and they never gain a total and uninhibited perspective of the larger communities (not even of their township and much less of their tribe, nation, race, and humankind as a whole), although there are certain ways in which they experience the reality of these communal organisms. To become acutely aware of the integral unity of those more limited units of which we are members and to become conscious of our membership in them, it is of special importance that we experience their difference from other similar communities which yet strike us as *foreign*. On the other hand, to gain an acute awareness of humanity or humankind as of the totality which encompasses and sustains us, it is of signal importance for us to realize experientially that common bond which links us—notwithstanding all the differences—with peoples and individuals of every age and clime, and to be conscious of the fact that by our contacts with foreign members of the human race our own being is enriched and perfected.

3. The Unity of the Human Race. Head and Body One *Christ*

This ever fragmentary, often misinterpreted, and sometimes completely misunderstood experience[54] receives firm support and a clear meaning from the doctrine of creation and redemption, which derives the origin of all people from one ancestor and which envisages as the goal of the entire evolution of the human race its union under *one* divine-human head, in the *one* "Mystical Body" of Christ. The fact of *original sin*—that all the children of Adam come into this world separated from one another and with a heart and mind "whose thinking and striving ... are inclined toward evil"[55] from the days of their youth—would be completely incomprehensible without the premise that in "this *one* man (Adam) all have sinned."

In this connection several things need to be clarified. According to the doctrine concerning humankind's original state

[*Urstand*], sanctifying grace was bestowed by God upon the first human beings as a free gift, beyond anything that was due to human nature as such, and this gift was intended also for all their descendants. Now the withdrawal of the gift of grace as a punishment for the disobedience of Adam and Eve appears quite plausible. The fact that this punishment was also to be inflicted on the descendants of our first parents may evoke some speculation concerning the justice and goodness of God, and yet this divine judgment is even understandable from a point of view which regards individual human beings as wholly independent or as standing upon themselves [*auf sich selbst gestellt*]. If grace is a free gift which God bestowed on Adam and which for Adam's sake he intended to bestow also on all the children of Adam, we may well imagine that the loss of the highest good must have struck Adam all the harder because, owing to his guilt, all his descendants too would be deprived of this good.

A different problem is posed by the fact of bodily death which "has come into the world through sin" and which "has passed into all human beings."[56] For this seems to imply a decisive change in human nature. It is true that the gift of immortality and the complete absence of bodily suffering are not regarded as being part of the human being's constitution in the original state, but as something which was to be earned and gained together with the state of glory by the human being's persevering cooperation with grace.

According to St. Thomas, the "immortality of Adam" should not be understood "as if he had been protected from within his nature against any deadly influence from without, such as against wounds inflicted by the sword and the like, but rather in the sense that he was preserved from death by divine providence."[57] But even though Adam was not protected from any injury by his natural endowment, he did not bear within himself the seed of corruption. He would not have died a "natural death" and, if he had not fallen, his descendants would not have been afflicted with "hereditary diseases" and "miscarriages." Accordingly, not only the withdrawal of certain gifts and the decree of death—both, as it were, to be carried into effect and to be suffered as something approaching people from without—must be regarded as a punishment of sin, but also the mutation of human nature and the transmission of this changed nature by propagation. This presupposes in turn that unimpaired human nature, too, was originally destined to be transmitted by way of propagation. And here we encounter again the same mystery that has puzzled us before: that by way of procreation new individual beings proceed from the generating agents and that nevertheless each of these generated beings stands upon itself and is as it were, a first beginning. If this appears mysterious even on the level of lower animate beings, it is all the more mysterious in the case of human beings, to whose nature it pertains to possess a spirit soul [Geist-Seele], and who receive this soul not from their ancestors, but directly from God.

From actual experience we know that there exist similarities between the progenitors and the progeny that indicate an inherited disposition. And it is equally obvious that these similarities extend not only to particularities of the body but also to those of the soul. The very nature of the soul, as form of the body, implies that the body owes its formation [*Gepräge*] to the soul (as far as the specificity of the essence [*Wesensart*] is concerned, and not the accidental deviations from it). St. Thomas traces even the corruptibility of the body back to that changed relationship of body and soul which was caused by the fall of humanity. "The precise reason," he writes, "why our body is corruptible lies in the fact that it is not completely subjected to the soul. For if it were completely subjected to the soul, the immortality of the soul would be transmitted to the body, as will be the case after the resurrection of the body."[58]

It seems then that from the point of view of theology and the doctrine of faith (if we remember the previously quoted passage in St. Paul's Epistle to the Romans, which has been embodied in the Catechism as an authoritative explanatory statement on the nature of original sin) our first ancestors have transmitted to us a body-spirit nature, a nature in which "the flesh" wars against the spirit, in which our reason (as compared with the state of our unstained nature) is darkened, our will weakened, and our heart inclined to evil. But despite the fact that the consequences of sin manifest themselves in the souls of the descendants, the root of the evil seems in this case to lie on the side of the body. The change of nature took place in the first human beings. It was then that the human will divorced itself from the divine will in a free, personal act, and the consequence was a profound disturbance in the order of human nature. But "in us corruption comes about in a reversed sequence: For whereas in Adam the soul corrupted the body and the person corrupted human nature, in us the order is reversed."[59]

Can this significant passage in *De veritate* aid us in solving our difficulty? That human nature which was to be the common property of the entire human race had, as it were, been given into Adam's safe-keeping. In his capacity as a "living soul" he bore within himself the power to animate and dominate not only his own body[60] but also to form the seed out of which new individuals of his own species were to proceed. A prelude and in a sense a prototype of this kind of procreation we find in the account of Genesis with respect to the creation of woman. God took the *matter* for the creation of Eve from the body of Adam, but he breathed into this matter the soul. Does this not indicate that these two were to be *one*[61] and yet *two,* each of them self-dependent and self-contained by virtue of their individual souls? And is not the same law also valid with respect to procreation? The latter forms and nourishes the "fleshly" structure that is destined to receive the spiritual soul and to become *one* with it. In this manner the new human being is linked with its progenitors and yet separated from them.

However, in the case of both relationships—that of man to woman and that of progeny to progenitors—we must carefully consider to what extent the soul is involved, and in the second instance special consideration must be given to the question of how this share of the soul is portioned out to the soul of the newly generated creature and to the souls of the progenitors. Aside from the fact that according to my conviction of the thoroughgoing union of soul and body, all bodily processes (if they are really *bodily* [*leiblich*] and not merely corporeal [*körperlich*] are simultaneously soul processes, the relationship of woman to man is according to the will of the creator certainly not to be conceived as a purely or prevalently bodily relationship. Sacred Scripture tells us that Adam has to be given a "helpmate" (Gen 2:18), so "that he be not alone"—two expressions which suggest above all a soul relationship. "God created man in his image ..., man and woman he created them" (Gen 1:27), and he gave them the blessings of fruitfulness (Gen 1:28).

God created Adam and Even in his image as spiritual personal beings. And this is why it was "not good" that such a creature be alone, since the most sublime meaning of all spiritual-personal being is mutual love and the union of a plurality of persons in love. The Lord gave Adam "a helpmate like unto himself" (*adiutorium simile sibi*, in the translation of the Vulgate; the Hebrew *eser kenegdo* places stronger emphasis on the equality)—a companion who was to Adam as one hand is to the other, almost completely his likeness and yet a trifle different, and who was thus capable in body and soul of a complementary activity of her own.

Now when we understand "being-in-one-flesh" not merely as an essential communion of the bodily nature of two persons but simultaneously as an interpenetration of vital processes and functions resulting in a unity of being, then an even more intimate union is possible among souls, since the being-one that is found in spiritual life—the creaturely image of the mutual love between the eternal Father and the divine Son—has no equal in the realm of corporeal being. Every creature has its own nature and not, like the Divine Persons, one common nature. But human souls are capable, by virtue of their free spirituality, of opening themselves in loving self-giving to one another and of receiving one another into their own selves—never, to be sure, as completely as is the case with a soul that abides in God, but in some greater or smaller measure. And this receiving is not merely a knowing comprehension which leaves the *object* [*Gegenstand*] standing by itself at a distance and is thus of small significance for the soul, but an inward reception of the object, a reception which aids in nourishing and forming the soul.

We may therefore interpret the text of Genesis in the sense that woman was placed by the side of man so that they might mutually aid one another in perfecting their being. The power of self-giving, however, determines not only the measure of the mutual help but also the measure of what can be received into the individual soul and therefore the degree to which the being of the individual soul can be elevated. And if it is true that to the nature of woman there pertains a greater power of self-giving, we must conclude that in the union of love she will not only give more but also receive more.

The fruitfulness or fecundity of animate beings, i.e., the power of generating out of their own selves other beings like unto themselves, must be regarded as part of their God-likeness, an image of the *bonum effusivum sui*, i.e., of the self-diffusive goodness of God.

If humans rank above the lower creatures because as spirit they imitate God, their generative power too must be rooted in the spirit. We may regard it as being in conformity with the meaning of the original order of creation that bodily union was meant to be an expression and actualization of the union of souls and the consummation of a communal generative will in union with the divine creative will. An independent life of the instincts and urges, on the other hand, a life that has divorced and emancipated itself from this original context of meaning, appears as a consequence of the fall and of the necessarily ensuing abrogation of the original order.[62]

The child is the fruit of mutual self-giving and, more than that: it is the very embodiment of the "gift." Each of the two spouses receives in the child an "image" of his or her own being as well as well as the gift of the other spouse's being. The gift (i.e., the child) is a third person, an independent creature and, as a "creature" in the full sense of the word, a gift of God. Is there a further possibility of knowing what this creature receives, at the moment of conception, immediately from God, and what it receives mediately from its parents? Does the new structure, which owes its corporeal existence to the common generative will of the parents, receive from them also the form of its soul, a form that corresponds to the particular individuality that is alive in the generative act and to the particular nature of the parents' oneness [*Einssein*]? Or with the soul of the child, does God *give* to the parents a gift proportionate to their nature, in the manner he gave to the first male a proportionate female companion? We may leave this question undecided, although it would seem that the second possibility is more in harmony with the teaching of the church that every soul is directly or immediately created by God. However, either possibility makes it understandable that the new creature has a particular individuality of body and soul from the first moment of its existence in the maternal womb, a particular individuality which, though akin to that of the parents, is nonetheless something quite different.

It must be considered, furthermore, that the new human being is from the first moment of its existence the carrier—albeit not a free, conscious carrier—of its own being and initiates its own evolution. It takes in nourishment, it grows, and it forms itself. Must we not assume, then, that the soul too, even in this earliest stage, receives impressions and initiates its own formation [*Ausgestaltung*]? Biologists are in disagreement on this point, but the practical wisdom of the people accepts it as a fact that the mental and emotional disposition of the mother in the period between conception and birth is of decisive importance for the future life of the child.

Neither one nor the other possibility can be termed an essential necessity [*Wesensnotwendigkeit*]. Although dogmatic theology takes no explicit stand on this question, there are some pronouncements which seem to suggest certain conclusions. If it was possible that the Most Blessed Virgin at the moment of her conception was preserved from the stain of original sin, it would seem that the unification of the soul with the body and the beginning of human existence must be relegated to this particular moment. If the being of the soul is actualized in a twofold manner, in the forming of the body and in the *inner* life, we may also assume that the inner life and the receptivity for external impressions have their beginning at the moment of conception. This view is confirmed by the teaching regarding the consecration of St. John the Baptist in his mother's womb on the occasion of the meeting between Elizabeth and the Blessed Virgin (known as the Visitation) and by the scriptural report that the child in the womb "leaped with joy" (Lk 1:41 and 44). And if there is such receptivity of the soul,—even though this receptivity is dim rather than clear and fully conscious—it is safe to conclude that the strongest natural influences issue from the soul of the mother and through her mediating instrumentality.

Just as the mutual self-giving of the parents and their common generative will prepare the existence of the child and the endowments of its future life, so the growth of the child and the forming of its body and soul demand the loving self-giving of the mother and her dedication to the task of motherhood. The paradigm of this is the *Fiat!* ("Be it done unto me") of the Mother of God (Lk 1:38). This *Fiat!* enunciates her loving self-surrender to God and to the divine will and simultaneously her own generative will and her readiness to dedicate her body and her soul to the service of motherhood. Is it even possible to conceive of the relationship of the Mother of God to her child otherwise than as a loving embrace with the whole power of the soul? This motherly love, to be sure was different from ordinary motherly love because this child's soul was illumined by the light of reason from the very beginning of its existence and was therefore for its part capable of free personal self-giving and of free receiving. And must we not further assume that the Son of Man, who wanted to be human in everything (sin excepted), accepted from his mother's love not only the flesh and blood needed for the forming of this body, but also nourishment for his soul? And is not this the deepest meaning of the Immaculate Conception that the mother whom the Son, the purest in body and soul, wanted to resemble had herself to be immaculately pure?

The motherhood of Mary is the paradigm of all motherhood. Like Mary, every human mother is called to be mother with her whole soul, so as to pour the abundant riches of her soul into the soul of her child. And the more of the nature of the spouse she has in loving self-surrender received into her own self, the more the individuality of the child, through her mediatorship, will be co-determined by the individuality of the father. Moreover, in most instances the mother exercises in her later life a role of mediatorship between father and child. The preeminent significance of motherhood in relation to human fatherhood seems indicated by the very fact that Jesus was to be born of a human mother, but not generated by a human father. Since the entire life of Jesus was lived for our sake, everything in his earthly life has exemplary significance. In order to be human in body and soul, he had to be born like a human being. And since it was to be his nourishment to do the will of his heavenly Father (Jn 4:34), the mother whose nature was to be his first nourishment had to give herself over to the will of the heavenly Father with the whole power of her soul.

We believe we have now gained a better understanding of the fact that humanity's descent [*Abstammung des Menschen*] from human progenitors makes them like unto others in body and soul and that they may nonetheless glory in being children of God and bearing in their souls the special and indelible seal of God. And it thus also becomes understandable to a certain degree why the break in human nature that was caused by the guilt of our first parents reappeared in their descendants. But how are we to interpret the saying that "in the *one* (Adam) all have sinned"? For this evidently means more than merely that all of us who are descended from Adam and Eve bring with us into the world the consequences of their fall as an innate inherited evil. We cannot assume, on the other hand without infringing upon the freedom and responsibility of the individual human being or upon the justice of divine judgment that the action of Adam was imputed to the entire human race without a personal share on our part in Adam's guilt, simply for the reason that Adam is the "head" of the human race.

It seems to me that the solution to this difficulty is found in the fact that God foresaw in the first sin all future sins and that he saw in our first parents all of us who "are all convicted of sin" (Rm 3:9). To the person who would indict our first parents for having brought down upon us the burden of original sin, our Lord might give the same reply that he gave to those who accused the adulteress: "Let whoever of you is without sin throw the first stone at her" (Jn 8:7). We cannot excuse ourselves by saying that for us who are burdened with original sin it is more difficult than it was for people in the original state to preserve our purity from the stain of personal sin. Though it is more difficult, it is not impossible, and even after the fall there is no necessity that forces us to sin. And, moreover, who would dare to assert that he or she would have remained steadfast where our first parents fell?

It seems then that we are forced to the conclusion that we were all judged in Adam and Eve because we deserved to be judged. They stood under the divine judgment for all of us, because every personal sin means a yielding to the whisperings of the serpent, and because their fall is repeated by all succeeding generations.

But the glance of the Divine Judge saw by the side of the first human pair, and by the side of all those whom our first parents "represented," a second pair that were not included in his judgment: the *new Adam* and the *new Eve*—Christ and Mary. He heard their *Fiat voluntas tua!* and *Fiat nihi secundum verbum tuum!* ("Thy will be done!" and "Be it done unto me according to they word!") They are the true parents and the true paradigms of a humankind that is united with God and in God. Christ—not Adam—is the *first-born* of God and the head of the human race. He is the first-born not only as the eternal Son of God but also—as I see it—as the Father of the elect, as the Word made flesh, whose earthly pilgrimage and heavenly glory were from eternity in God's plan. The resurrected Christ, the King of Glory, is the paradigm and the head of the human race—the end form [*Zielgestalt*] to which every human being is ordained and from which it receives its meaning.

If it is true that the entire creation was prefigured and predesigned in the Logos, this is true in a very special sense of the human race. For it is, after all, the meaning of being human to embrace and unite heaven and earth, God and creation. The human body is composed of the material elements of the earth. It is unified and structurally formed by the soul which—as a spiritual-personal substance—is nearer to God than all nonpersonal structures and capable of being united with him. No closer and stronger union of separated natures is possible than that union in one Person as it was consummated by the incarnation of the Word.

By virtue of the incarnation, human nature—first of all, in Christ himself—is filled with divine life to a degree proportionate with the divine will. By virtue of the personal freedom with which the God-Man has sovereign command over his two natures, he may allow the divine life to overflow into human life or he may restrain this influx. But by virtue of this influx, Christ is a *life-giving spirit* from the very first moment of his human existence.

The *living soul* of natural man has the power to form those material elements which are at its disposal for the building up of its body into a unity, and to maintain and animate this unity in its own structure for a certain length of time. Beyond this, the soul has its *inner* being and the capacity to receive into itself new life from extraneous sources and thereby to experience an increase, a strengthening, and a heightening of its own life. The soul does *not* have the power to form out of its own self—without the aid of existing material elements—a body (a *spirit-body* [*Geistleib*]) *in the* manner in which the Holy Spirit formed those visible structures in which it appeared to human beings (the dove and the fiery tongues), or in the manner in which the angels formed those human bodies in which they showed themselves on earth. Nor has the soul the power to impart to the earthly body the invulnerability and immortality which are promised for the life of glory, or to generate out of its own self new life and impart it to others. All this requires a divine creative power. And the soul of Christ has this power. It flows into his soul from the Godhead with whom his soul is united. From the soul of Christ, therefore, issue forth streams of living water. They flow into his own body—a body which did *not* ordinarily manifest the qualities of a transfigured body, for the one reason that the will of the

Lord, in order to make possible the suffering and death of Christ, restrained in a miraculous way the natural effects of the union of the two natures[63]—and they flowed into the bodies and souls of those who were privileged to experience in their own selves the miraculous power of the Deity.

The union of the two natures in Christ is the basis of the union of other human beings with God. By virtue of this union of the two natures, Christ is the mediator between God and humanity [*Mensch*], the one and only "way" that leads to the Father (Jn 14:6). Is this saying true only in view of the justification which was wrought by the Redeemer and which leads fallen humanity back to God, or does it apply to humanity even prior to the fall and independently of it? The main body of theological tradition regards the fall as the direct cause of the Incarnation. But it would seem that the words of the Credo—*...qui propter nos homines et propter nostram salutem descendit de coelis*—admit of a broader interpretation.

The *church's doctrine of justification,* formulated by the Council of Trent as a result of the controversies concerning the heretical teachings of the sixteenth century,[64] bases the *need for justification* on the fact that "by the transgression of Adam all people *lost their innocence* (Rm 5:12 and 18) ... and to that extent became *slaves of sin* (Rm 6:20)..., that not only the pagans were ... no longer capable of freeing themselves from or rising above sin by the power of their own nature, but not even the Jews by the letter of the law of Moses. For though the power of *free decision* was *by no means extinct* in them ... it was greatly weakened and inclined toward evil."[65] Therefore, "they would never be justified" unless they they were reborn in *Christ,* since this rebirth is effected "by the *merit* of his *suffering,* by virtue of the grace by which they are made just."[66] Accordingly, justification consists *not only* in the *remission of sins,* but justification "is a sanctification and *renovation* of the inner person [*Mensch*] by a free acceptance of grace and of those gifts by which unjust persons become just and are turned from enemies into friends, so that they are made, *in hope, heirs of eternal life*" (Tit 3:7).[67]

> The *one formal cause* of justification is the Justice of God, not the justice by which he *himself* is just, but the justice by which *he makes us just.* ... For if we are clothed by him with this justice, we shall be renewed in the spirit of our heart (*spiritu mentis nostrae*), and

> we shall *not only be deemed just, but* shall be called just in truth, and shall *be* just indeed, since we shall receive justice into ourselves, each one according to the measure which *the Holy Spirit apportions to everyone as he will* (1 Cor 12:11) and in accordance with the receptive disposition and cooperation of each individual.[68]

> For though no one can be a just person except by sharing in the merits of the suffering of our Lord Jesus Christ, the imparting of justice in the justification of the godless person is brought about in such a way that—by the merit of Christ's hallowed suffering—*God's love is poured forth by the Holy Spirit into the hearts of those* (Rm 5:6) who are to be justified, and his love firmly *adheres* in them (*inhaeret*). ... *In* their justification, people thus receive the infused gifts of *faith, hope, and love,* together with the remission of their sins by Christ Jesus, into whom they are engrafted.[69]

From the above quotations several conclusions may be derived which are significant in our context. By his suffering and death, Jesus Christ atones for the sins of all people and thus satisfies divine justice. Human nature lends itself to this atonement as a fitting instrument, because it contains the possibilities of suffering and of death. That the atonement is of sufficient, indeed of superabundant value, is evident from the fact that it is the work of a divine person. It is thus as infinite in its nature as was the offense against God, and there is no human accomplishment, not even all the good works performed by the entire human race, that could serve as a substitute.

But how are we to understand that Christ's atonement is to be credited to us and that we are thereby freed from guilt? Is this liberation from guilt a free gift of divine mercy? This is, of course, precisely what it is. There existed no obligation on the part of God to forgive sin for the sake of the merits of Christ. And yet this remission of sin is not *merely* a gift. It is necessary that those human beings who had turned from God through sin and who are called to conversion and justification by the *prevenient,* awakening, and sustaining grace of Christ "prepare themselves by their *free* assent and their cooperation with grace. When God touches the hearts of human beings with the illumination of the Holy Spirit, human beings, in accepting this divine inspiration (which they might well be able to reject), do not remain entirely passive. *Without the grace* of God, on the other hand, human beings would not be able, by the mere power of their free will, to ... move themselves toward justice...."[70]

The "preparation" consists in the following steps: When sinners "are awakened and supported by divine grace," they must:

> ... *receive into themselves faith* from hearing (Rm 10:17), must *freely* move toward God, with faith in the truth of what God has revealed and promised ... believing above all that God justifies the godless person by his grace, by the redemption that is in Christ Jesus (Rm 3:24). Realizing that they are sinners, they turn from the fear of divine justice, which has shaken them wholesomely, to the *contemplation* of God's mercy, *rising* to new *hope,* trusting that God will be merciful for Christ's sake, and *beginning to love* him as the source of all justice. They therefore, in hatred and abhorrence, *take a stand against sin* ... with that contrition which is a prerequisite for the reception of baptism. ... Finally, *they resolve* to receive baptism, to begin a new life, and to obey the divine commandments.[71]

When sinners thus accede to the counsels of God and make (speaking in a human manner) the divine inclinations their own, then God is prone to see in Christ any repentant sinner and to accept Christ's atonement for all sins. We must not forget, however, that our relationship to Christ differs from our relationship to Adam. We would be able to sin, even without the guilt of Adam, and every one of us might have fallen in his place. But without Christ we would be unable to find our way back to God, and none of us could make atonement in Christ's place. It is an incitement of grace, i.e., a divine act of which no human being is capable (the human being can only serve as an instrument of grace), that calls us back to God: to repentance, penance, expiation, and faithful adherence to the Redeemer. This grace, which prepares us to return to God, we owe to the merits of Christ. And because these merits are superabundant, the mercy of God upon sinners is equally so. Christ not only awakens us by the call of grace and lifts from us the burden of sin, but he makes us *just,* i.e., *holy,* filling us with divine life and leading us as children to the heavenly Father. By justification we have once again become children of God, as Adam and Eve were before the fall.

And now we ask further: To whom did the first human beings owe their adoption as children of God? This adoption was a gift of God and—as is every gift of God—a gift of the divine Trinity, and thus also of the Son. But was this gift given to human beings independently of the human nature of Christ? This would appear irreconcilable with the idea of "head and body, one Christ" which plays such a prominent part in the theology of St. Paul and which has acquired special significance for our own time. If Christ is the "head" of the redeemed human race and if the life of grace overflows from him into all those who are redeemed, then our first parents, too, are members of his Mystical Body. And if they were "redeemed," i.e., ransomed from sin *through* the suffering of Christ, but *prior* to the temporal actualization of this suffering, then they were also—as members of the Mystical Body of Christ prior to the incarnation—already in possession of that grace which pertained to humankind's original state [*Urstandsgnade*]. For according to the teaching of the church, they died in the state of grace, even though they did not attain to eternal bliss until after Christ had died on the cross. Perhaps we may even venture to say that in a certain sense the creation of the first human being may be regarded as a beginning of the incarnation of Christ. It is certain, at any rate, that in the God-Man abides not only the entire plenitude of divinity, but also the entire plenitude of humanity. And it seems to me that it pertains to the meaning of the Mystical Body of Christ that there is nothing human—sin excepted—that does not pertain to the vital unity of this body. Indeed, even sin is committed by the members of this body, although sin proceeds, of course, not from the head and brings death upon these members.

The life of grace flows into the members because *by their very nature* they are related to the head and—as spiritual beings and by virtue of their free openness—capable of receiving into themselves his divine life. The linkage between head and members has a threefold foundation. It rests upon *nature, freedom,* and *grace.*

The entire human race is the race of Christ, although humanity as a whole is related to the person of the divine Word in a different way than that individual human nature which the Word assumed when it was born of the Virgin, and this humanity [*Menschheit*] begins its existence in the first human being.

I shall now make an attempt to gain some understanding of the relationship that exists between Adam and Christ. The first man (Adam) has, like every creature, his paradigm [*Urbild*] in the divine Word. As a spiritual person, Adam was, like every human being, a more perfect image of God than all nonpersonal creatures, and he was capable of being personally united with God. Moreover, he was, again like every human being, related in a special manner to the *humanity* of Christ. But Adam's *special* relationship to Christ distinguished him, nonetheless, from all other human beings. He was destined to be the *representative of Christ* as the head of the human race. We must assume, therefore, that no other human being was in his nature as Christlike as was Adam.[72]

The humanity of Christ was distinguished from that of all other human beings not only by his being free from all sin but by the fact that there was in him the "total plenitude of humanity." In him the entire specific essence [*Artwesen*] of the human race was not only partially, as is the case with all other human beings, but fully actualized. And of his plenitude we all have received our share, not only "grace for grace" (Jn 1:16), but even in our nature, so that each of us in our own particular individuality might imitate the original prototype in the manner in which every member of a living structural unit embodies in its own particular way the essence of the whole, and in which all members together build up the total structure.

This is what makes the figure of the savior, as it is depicted in truthful simplicity in the Gospels, so mysterious and unfathomable. He is "wholly human" [*ganz Mensch*] and precisely for this reason unlike any other human being. He cannot be apprehended and comprehended as a "character" like Peter or Paul. Any attempt, therefore, to bring us into intimate contact with our Lord by depicting his life and character in the manner of a biographical portrait means really an impoverishment and a narrowing down of his life to some particular aspects, and in some instances it even means a distortion and falsification.

We see then that the fullness of humanity is actualized in a dual manner: in the person of Christ and in the entire human race. In the person of Christ it appears veiled during the course of his earthly life, but radiantly unveiled in the glory of the resurrected Savior, sitting at the right hand of the Father. And the road of the human race is a way that has its first beginning in Christ and that leads back to Christ in the end. He created man in his image, an image which he had designed from the beginning, to realize it eventually in his own person.

In his inviolate nature Adam was the purest image of this original prototype, and he possessed, moreover, the generative power to produce an even more comprehensive image in the totality of his descendants. Divinity and humanity were not united in him, as they are in Christ, in one person. But Adam was united with Christ by grace (in the manner in which one person may enter into union with another person), and he had been elevated to a participation in divine life. In this union the free descending of God and the freely ascending self-surrender of humanity meet. Because Adam possessed a more perfect knowledge of God and of creatures than did people after the fall, and because his will was still unimpaired, we may well imagine that Adam received the first infusion of grace with a lucid consciousness and a free resolve (i.e., not in the manner in which sanctifying grace is received in the baptism of infants, but rather in the manner grace is received by the created pure spirits). We may also assume that Adam had a knowledge of Christ as the future divine-human head of the human race and as the Son of Man in his flesh, and that he therefore freely responded to the call of grace as a token of his union with the God-Man and as a free assent to his own vocation as the chosen ancestor of the human race, which was to be generated for Christ and for the sake of Christ.

The recognition of the *Redeemer* cannot, on the other hand, have preceded that "knowledge of good and evil" which is linked with the fall. This latter knowledge is, rather, due to the revelation which followed upon the judgment that was pronounced after the fall (Gn 3:15).

Although we may justly ascribe to Adam a richer endowment with the gifts of nature and grace than was given to all his descendants (excepting the "Son of Man" and his mother), he cannot have been in possession of that plenitude of all gifts which we attribute to Christ. For only the God-Man was to bring to perfect fulfillment what had been initiated in Adam. Moreover, the fact that Adam needed as a *complement* a female companion and that Adam and Eve were destined to generate a *race* [*Geschlecht*] of human beings, seems to indicate that Adam did not in and by himself embody the fullness of humanity, but that this fullness was to be realized in and through the entire human family.

Christ does not generate according to the body, since he is the Creator prior to all time, the one who is perfect and who leads to perfection in the temporal order. Although he was born in time, like a human being, and as a descendant of Adam, his being-human is not a received being like that of all the other children of human beings: he was not "thrown into existence" as are all other human beings—but he came into the world because he so willed it just as he died because he willed it, and at the time he willed it. And all human being [*menschliches Sein*] that precedes and follows his earthly life is oriented toward his being and is called forth by his being as by its final cause [*Zielursache*]. But because God "created us without our cooperation, but did not want to save us without our cooperation," he made dependent on our free assent and willing collaboration not only the reception of sanctifying grace in every human being, but even the incarnation of the Redeemer, from whom grace emanates and flows into us.

In the covenant of the Old Testament this cooperation consisted in the trusting expectation of the promised Messiah, in being mindful of the task of propagation for the sake of this promise, and in the obligation to prepare the ways of the Lord by faithful obedience to his commandments and zeal in his service. All of this finds its crowning fulfillment and its most perfect expression in the *Fiat!* of the Virgin, and it finds its continuation in every efficacious action that serves the spreading of the kingdom of God by working for our own salvation and for the salvation of others.

In this manner, by the cooperation of nature, freedom, and grace, the body of Christ is built up. Every individual human being is created to be a member of this body. And this is the reason why even on the purely natural level no human being is like the other—we recall that these reflections on the Mystical Body were to aid our understanding of the meaning of human individuality—but every human individual is a variation of the common human essence or nature, an individual structural unit, and simultaneously a constructive part of a structural totality [*Gesamtgestalt*].

However, it is of the very essence of humankind that every individual as well as the entire human family are to become what, according to their nature, they are destined to be in a process of temporal unfolding, and that this unfolding depends on the cooperation of each individual as well as on the common effort of all. The corruption of human nature after the fall is the reason why a pure unfolding and a corresponding pure activity of the will is made possible only by redemptive grace. This grace also initiates the future fulfillment of the original ordination of the natural being of people: their participation in divine life by means of free, personal self-giving. A humanity united in Christ and through Christ is the temple in which the Triune God has his abode.

So far we have spoken of the Mystical Body of Christ only in a narrower sense. However, it is possible to conceive of the Mystical Body in a broader sense. St. Thomas calls Christ—not only with respect to his divinity but also with respect to his humanity—the "head of the angels," because both angels and human beings are ordained to the same end, the fruition of divine glory, and they therefore form one body. According to St. Thomas, Christ is the head of this body, set by God the Father (Eph 1:20) not only above all people, but also above all dominations, principalities, virtues, and powers.[73]

We may go even one step further and may comprise in the Mystical Body the entire creation: in its natural order, because everything was created in the image of the Son of God and because the Son, by his incarnation, entered into the total context of the created universe; and in the order of grace, because grace flows from the head into all the members: not only into human beings, but into all creatures. As the entire subhuman nature was implicated in the fall of man, it is also to share in the restoration of man wrought by redemption. And though in the case of angels we cannot speak of *redemption,* since for them there is no possibility of a return or a conversion after their fall, it may nevertheless be assumed that those angels who persevered in their allegiance to God were able, by virtue of the grace merited by Christ, to give resplendent proof of their loyalty, and that they owe their glory to Christ.

Notwithstanding this possibility of a broader interpretation of the doctrine of the Mystical Body, we may and must continue to see in humankind the Mystical Body of Christ in the narrower sense. For humankind is the portal through which the Word of God entered into the created world. Human nature has received the Word, and the Word is linked in a special way with human beings, by virtue of a unity of common descent—not with subhuman nature and not with angels. As the head of humankind, which combines in itself the higher and the lower reaches of being, Christ is the head of creation in its totality.

Editors' Appendix

To the First German Edition[1]

1. Historical-Archival Responsibility

Finite and Eternal Being was written in the years 1935/36. Begun shortly after the end of the novice year in the spring of 1935, the work bears the completion date of September 1, 1936.

This is authenticated by the following:

1) The relevant references in Stein's preface to *Finite and Eternal Being* (cf. pp.xvii ff. of this volume). E. Stein writes (p. xxviii) "After the author had been received into the order of the Discalced Carmelites and had completed the year of her novitiate, she was ordered..." (She took religious vows on April 21, 1935.) E. Stein adds to the signature of the preface: "Cologne-Lindenthal, September 1, 1936."
2) A handwritten letter by E. Stein to Mrs. Malvine Husserl (wife of E. Husserl), which is in the possession of the Husserl Archives. In writing on February 29, 1940 from the Carmel in Echt, she says: "As you know, in the years 1935/36 I wrote a two-volume work on the basic ontological questions, comparing and contrasting Thomism and phenomenology."

   We are reserving a comparative critique of disagreements, i.e., inexact or false citations, for another place. This will appear at the completion of the publication of the collected works.

Two drafts are to be distinguished in the naming of the work, even though there certainly is no doubt about the final intentions of the author. The original draft of the title from the years 1935/36 reads:

Edith Stein (Sister Teresia Benedicta a Cruce, O.C.D.)
Finite and Eternal Being
(Variant: On Eternal and on Finite Being)
A Survey of the *Philosophia perennis*

In the definitive draft of the title from the years 1938/40 Edith Stein writes:

Sister Teresa Benedicta a Cruce, O.C.D.
Finite and Eternal Being
An Attempt to Ascend to the Meaning of Being

We present the following as authentication of this:

1) For the original draft of the title
   a) The wording of the manuscript (the crossed out title in the table of contents of volume 2, p. 1);
   b) The wording of one of E. Stein's handwritten loose notes which is in the possession of the Husserl Archives. This note was found among other papers during the reconstruction of Stein's manuscript. It reads:

   "Title and first sentence for a new, improved edition of *Potency and Act:*
   On Eternal and Finite Being
   A Survey of the *philosophia perennis*
   I do not understand the *philosophia perennis* as a scholastic system, but as the ceaseless search of the human spirit for true being."

2) For a final draft of the title:
   a) The wording of the manuscript (title page of Volume II with erasures which unambiguously indicate a later revision of the main title). Since E. Stein left the manuscript back in Cologne when she fled to Holland on New Year's Eve 1938, (cf. below), the revision of the main title and the change of the subtitle were undertaken before this date.
   b) An inscription in E. Stein's handwriting on the galley proofs of Volume II, p. 1 (in the possession of the Husserl Archives[2]);
   c) An inscription on the cover of the content and name indices (from the years in Echt of 1939/42 in the possession of the Husserl Archives);
   d) An inscription in a typewritten table of contents (volumes I and II) whose pagination agrees with the Borgmeyer galley proofs. E. Stein sent this table of contents to Rev. Prof. Van Breda at the beginning of the year 1940. Moreover, this table of contents cannot have been composed in the year 1939 for the following reason: The table of contents bears the pagination of the galley proofs of Volume II. However, the Borgmeyer galley proofs of the second volume were first delivered during the year 1939, i.e., after E. Stein's flight to Echt.

e) The previously mentioned letter to Mrs. Malvine Husserl of February 29, 1940 in which E. Stein refers to the title of the work: "Finite and Eternal being" (a reference to the revision of the main title with no mention of the subtitle);

f) A document which, in contrast with the previous documentation, permits the inference that the revision of the main title had already been done in July of 1938 (there is no information about the subtitle): A strikeout in the Borgmeyer publishing contract which E. Stein sent as an enclosure to the letter of February 29, 1940. In §2 of this contract of July 22, 1938 the text reads, "...the exclusive right of the publisher to the work of 'Sr. Teresa Benedicta a Cruce, *Finite and Eternal Being*."[3]

Finite and Eternal Being was to be published by Borgmeyer in Breslau (Frankes Verlag und Druckerei), the same house which had already published Stein's translation of St. Thomas Aquinas's *De Veritate*. The printing began in the fall of 1936, but, after a number of month-long pauses, finally had to be suspended in 1939. According to Nazi repressive measures, no works from the pens of non-Aryan authors were to appear in print. Up to this time the first volume of the work had been completely made up into pages; the galley proofs of the second volume, including the two appendices and notes, had been set.

The above statements are based on the following source (in possession of the Husserl Archives):

1) Stein's letter of February 29, 1940 [to Malvine Husserl], already mentioned several times;

2) The Borgmeyer proof sheets (page and galley); see below.

A comprehensive account of all the details, together with a critique of variant readings, is planned within the framework of our archival-biographical study.

We now want to turn to the question of the archival status that is the basis for the present edition of the work. An exact description of this status appears necessary to us for two reasons:

First of all, hereby the fact and the necessity of a revision in content and form becomes evident. For the present edition is in no way a reprinting of the Borgmeyer corrected proofs, but a revision of the text which is based on a comparative study of the various drafts of the text, the corrections, etc.

Secondly, this description forms the factual basis for the elucidation of the revision.

The following are in the possession of the Cologne Carmel:

1) The manuscript of the work which E. Stein left at her mother house as a remembrance when she fled to Holland at the end of December 1938. Thanks to the judicious measures of the Reverend Prioress, Teresa Renata de Spiritu Sancto, the manuscript remained undisturbed when the convent itself went up in flames in 1944.

   Description:
   1368 single pages, 21 x 16.5 cm. (including the main text of 1099 pages, the preface and table of contents of 36 pages, Appendix I of 78 pages, and Appendix II of 155 pages).
   Script: Ink with later editing in ink and pencil; supplements typewritten.

2) The galley proofs of the first and second volumes with occasional entries of Stein's corrections.

In the Husserl Archives there are the following:

1) Galley proofs, page proofs of the first made-up proofs and page proofs of the second made-up proofs (improvements of the first made-up proofs) of the first volume. Galley proofs and page proofs are filled with corrections in E. Stein's hand.

   Clarification of the reconstruction of the first volume from these particulars:

   On the one hand, there are missing page proofs of respective galleys in the made-up proofs as well as in the first composition. On the other hand, there are duplicate pages of a large number of page proofs and galleys.

   The restored first volume was therefore put together: from the page proofs of the second made-up proofs supplemented by page proofs from the first made-up proofs. At the same time, corrections were taken into consideration which were entered into the galleys or into the first made-up proofs by E. Stein, whose improvements were in fact overlooked in the next printing.

2) The galleys of the second volume, including Appendices I and II, which also contain corrections in E. Stein's hand.

Since the second volume could no longer be made up (cf. above), there are no page proofs for it.

However, in contrast with the first volume, there are no duplicate pages of the galleys.

3) A complete typewritten copy with strikeouts of the second appendix; we were able to be put it together from damaged loose sheets.

4) The manuscript of the subject matter and name index of *Finite and Eternal Being*.

Description:

A notebook with an alphabetical index, 21 x 15 cm., 113 pages with writing, with approximately 30 inserts (loose pages or notes).

Handwriting: ink and pencil

Title on the inside cover: Subject matter and name index for *Finite and Eternal Being*. An examination of the contents, however, resulted in the conclusion that the index referred exclusively to the made-up first volume.

No date. From the back side of the inserted pages, it clearly follows that the index was completed in Echt. Since, further, the page numbers depend on the made-up proofs of the first volume and E. Stein was already in Echt when the first page proofs were delivered (letter of February 29, 1940), it may be concluded that the index is from the time in Echt.

5) A typewritten table of contents of the galleys of the first volume and a typewritten table of contents in duplicate of the galleys of the second volume.

This duplicate execution was written before the delivery of the last 40 galleys of text with the corresponding four galleys of notes (Appendix II, Section B). One of these two copies contains the expansion of the incomplete table of contents of Appendix II entered later on the typewriter.

2. Relationship of the Present Work to *Potency and Act*

As E. Stein herself says in her preface, *Finite and Eternal Being* resulted from a reworking of a comprehensive study which bears the title *Potency and Act* and was conceived before E. Stein's entrance into the Cologne Carmel. Nothing further about this has been established to date.

Since *Potency and Act* is in the possession of the Husserl Archives,[4] the attempt will be made here to verify the relationship between the two works archivally and to illuminate them in terms of content. This means that all doubts about the contents and value of this study, which are based on the false premise that *Potency and Act* is an obscure "first-draft," will thus be laid to rest.

First of all, two archival pieces of proof:

1) The note in E. Stein's hand cited above on p. 530 in connection with the original concept of the title;
2) The relevant reference by E. Stein in her preface to *Finite and Eternal Being* (see the first page of the Author's Preface).

So now we have the point of departure for the illumination of the contents: the title page, the main divisions of the Table of Contents, and an abridged rendering of the preface to *Potency and Act*.

Since *Potency and Act* will not be published in the collected works (E. Stein herself designates it as a prelude to *Finite and Eternal Being*), the opportunity of becoming informed about the construction of this work is now offered to the specialist:

a) Reproduction of the title page:

Potency and Act
Studies on a Philosophy of Being
by
Edith Stein

b) Main divisions according to the table of contents with the addition of paragraph numbers and pages:

Table of Contents

c) An Abridged reproduction of the preface:

Preface

The following investigations are undertaken as an attempt at gaining access to understanding the method of St. Thomas. When I began to study the writing of Aquinas, the following question continuously disturbed me: What method is actually being used here? Being accustomed to the phenomenological way of working, which makes use of no traditional doctrines but investigates everything that is necessary for the resolution of a question itself *ab ovo,* I ran into a procedure in which sometimes Scriptural texts, sometimes citations of the Fathers, sometimes statements in ancient philosophy were brought into play in order to draw conclusions from them. One very soon has the impression that this procedure is not "unmethodical".... Reliability is vouched for by the profusion of conclusions which one reaches by this path.... One also quickly understands that the "authorities" are not brought in without selection and examination.... But even when the examination appears to be positive, it is mostly not presented to our eyes. Propositions are handled as if they have long been recognized as general knowledge with which one can work without doing anything more. What are the criteria concealing their truth? One gets a clue to this from the way opposing views are handled. When these are said to be contradicted, as soon as their inconsistency with certain propositions has been proved, there must, on the other hand, be an agreement with these propositions that is

> presented as valid. So, beginning with the negative, one is led to a basic stance on truths which serve as criteria for everything else. Yet the comparative consideration of positive arguments also helps to trace the method.... The arguments of the theological *summa* often appear on closer examination to have holes in them. The outcome is indeed plausible but the evidence is not really "conclusive." But it reaches finality as soon as one brings in what the saint said in another place (e.g., perhaps when he dealt extensively with the same question in the *Quaestiones disputatae*.... If one were to work through all of the works of the saint in this way and bring together from everywhere that which must be referred to in certain places in order for the final structure to bear its load, then one would have to get to all of the basic Thomistic concepts and propositions. One would then have insight into the method and at the same time into the systematic structure of this whole work. A prodigious interpretative task would be concluded.... But this by no means achieves what the philosopher owes to St. Thomas. In fact, one may say that the result would be just the mental preparation for the real philosophical work. The mental investigator [*Geisteswissenschaftler*] will be satisfied when she has discovered the inner structure of a mental world that is complete in itself and can follow its movements from the foundation to the summit.... The philosopher must not only be able to see and point out *that* another proceeded in such and such a way. She must not only have insight into the structure of propositions and conclusions; but she must *grasp why* these results occurred. The philosopher must descend to the reasons themselves and grasp *them*, i.e., must be gripped by them and forced to a decision in favor of them to an *internal* agreement leading to the conclusions based on them and eventually go even further than her predecessor has gone. Or she must master *them*, i.e., penetrate to freedom from them and make a decision for another direction. To be compelled by the "theses" of St. Thomas in this way meant to conquer them philosophically for ourselves. To master his theses meant to be "finished with them" philosophically...."

A look at these quotations reveals that the study of this work is incessant in its attempts to gain insight into the development of the trains of thought that would be carried forward in *Finite and Eternal Being*. Between the formulation of these two works, there are five decisive years (1931–1936) in E. Stein's philosophical and human development which are reflected in the original and in the later handling of the question of being.

Thirdly, as a supplement to the above account, we present an abbreviated archival description of the work.

> The Husserl Archive possesses a hand-corrected typewritten manuscript which we were able to put together from the heavily damaged pages of two manuscripts (carbon copies).[5]
>
> The manuscript contains VII and 437 pages in quarto. Pages 5, 8, 12, and two supplementary pages referred to on p. 76 are missing from this. They could no longer be found in spite of many attempts.
>
> The preface is dated in E. Stein's hand: Breslau, in September 1931.

Now we want to turn to the question of the kind of development that becomes evident to us in comparing the two works *Potency and Act* and *Finite and Eternal Being.*

The position of E. Stein on the question of being as such, as well as to the ideas of the philosophers who set the standards for her lines of thought, already seem to have been determined in 1931. As a result, they undergo no basic changes in the revision. Nevertheless, the significance of this revision is not entirely in terms of form, but also as to content. The comparison of the three titles (cf. p. 529f.) already indicates a shift in the emphasis of the contents, i.e., it indicates a shift and amplification of the point of view from which the question as to being will be taken up. The beginning studies on the philosophy of being lead E. Stein to the idea of the *philosophia perennis* as a ceaseless search by the human spirit for true being. However, since the knowledge of a subject, in correspondence to the deepest characteristic of Stein's personality, means taking a position on this subject, E. Stein follows the inner call to a ceaseless search.[6] Yet now this means searching for the *meaning* of being. And as an encompassing "recognition," the results of this search are posited in an ascent to the meaning of being. E. Stein herself describes this process in the following simple words: "The point of departure from the Thomistic act-potency doctrine has been retained—but only as a starting point. At the center is the *question concerning being.* The comparison and contrast between Thomistic and phenomenological thought results in the actual handling of this question."

This citation from Stein's preface to *Finite and Eternal Being* (cf. p. xxvii) is supplemented by four comparable indications:

a) In *Potency and Act* E. Stein takes a position against the Thomistic doctrine that matter (*materia*) is to be designated as the basis for individual being (*principium individuationis*), and is here already searching for an answer to this question by making a distinction between the concept of matter as filling up space and as determinable indeterminability.

In *Finite and Eternal Being* she retains the basic idea that the principle of form is a unity and must be determined exclusively by the mind and is thereby led to the conclusion that, on the one hand, where space-filling matter is an essential part of a thing, one must distinguish between the basis and the bearer and to consider the empty form of the object as the bearer in the real sense. On the other hand, in place of the subsisting form of pure spirits which St. Thomas accepts, she is led to posit the *materia primo prima* of Duns Scotus. *Materia primo prima* is equivalent to *potentia passiva*, since the possibility of not being and thus the destruction of everything created is at the same time equivalent to the possibility of being conceived and of having form.

b) At the same time, in connection with the form-matter problem and the separation of potency and act within the psychological itself, E. Stein is led to address the *life force* as the *psychological* [*seelische*] *material:*

> The diversity of all species of psychological acts is somewhat analogous to the diversity of sensory qualities, the qualities of material things. Just as the latter indicate the matter which shapes them by substantial forms, so that which is constantly real to the psyche is formed somewhat analogically to matter. Just as the matter of physical bodies and their accidents only changes from potential to actual being by uniting with a substantial form, so too in regard to the psychological accidents of this *psychological matter*. The contents of psychic acts could only come into existence in a living completion of acts by the psychic subject. Every act denoted by a species is a *piece of psychic life*. Have we not here the sought after *psychic matter*, the analogue of physical matter? Just as there belong to every substantial form in the physical realm a certain number of material traits, so every psyche has a certain amount of *life force*. (*Potency and Act*, p. 355)
>
> In a certain sense all being is *from above*, insofar as nothing is which has not received its being and that which it is from the highest being.

This is even true of that which stands in the uttermost contrast to the highest being, the lowest in the realm of being, that which—considered in itself—*is* not yet and is not yet *something*, but is pure receptivity for being and for being something [*Was*], which it gets through the substantial form. This pure potentiality has confronted us with double force: as *matter* that takes up space and as *life* that pushes forward into time and throughout time. Substantial forms, which are immersed in this mere potential and give it being and content, can be designated relative to this potential as *from above* and everything that is in relation to form as *from beneath*. The substantial forms that correspond to twofold *matter* are different from each other: *material forms* and *living forms*. In a certain sense, organic form lies between material and animal forms in that it, on the one hand, is apprehended as of a material kind and on the other hand as of this kind, i.e., as organic. (*Potency and Act*, p. 360f.)

In working through these thoughts, E. Stein in *Finite and Eternal Being* also advances on the designated trail in order to see herself linked once again to the thoughts of Scotus. In further following the position already taken, in a) above, regarding the Aristotelian-Thomistic concept of *form that carries itself*, she believes she recognizes her concept of psychic matter (life force) in the *potentia passiva* of Duns Scotus. And this leads her into considering pure spirits and to the conclusion of designating angels with St. Thomas as pure, i.e., bodiless, spirits, but not as pure forms, because there belongs to their structure something that underlies their formation.[7]

c) *Potency and Act* seems at first glace to be a large- scale execution of the "dialogue" between Edmund Husserl and St. Thomas Aquinas begun in the year 1929,[8] where E. Stein in a didactic manner offers a series of strict phenomenological analyses and defines her respective standpoint in relation to her results. On closer examination of this work, this means that it does actually concern a comparison and contrast by E. Stein of E. Husserl and the phenomenological school (especially that of H. Conrad-Martius) on the one hand and Thomistic doctrine on the other. Accordingly, the presentations have the character of a personal study and are neither supported nor proved by citations from the literature, etc.

In contrast, *Finite and Eternal Being* presents a thoroughgoing comparison and contrast not only with Thomas of Aquinas, but also with Greek philosophy (Plato, Aristotle), with the Church Fathers (especially Augustine), and with the scholastics in general. By a detailed consideration of Thomism and supported by a thorough study of the relevant literature and Christian dogma, the presentations of this work are evidently solidly founded on citations and references.

When E. Stein in her characteristic modesty points out in her preface to *Finite and Eternal Being* that it is customary for *some* thinkers to gain access to the "things" ["Sachen"] by concepts which another mind has already given to them, that other thinkers, by contrast, are called to a method of immediate investigation of things and only arrive at an understanding of the works of other minds by the help of what they are able to work out for themselves, then the above comparison of these two works gives us points of objective reference for E. Stein's phenomenological stance and phenomenological way of working. She begins *ab ovo* in order to test the results of her own thought afterwards and to measure it against the presentations of the authoritative philosophers. This is also how she works with the relevant technical literature. The commentary is not made up of snippets cut out of the analyses of philosophical researchers. Rather, she bases her personal interpretation on primary sources by thoroughly considering the technical literature, i.e., the original lines of thought are sifted through citations of the literature.

d) However, at the same time, *Finite and Eternal Being* also delivers a thoroughgoing expansion and deepening of her own lines of thought. Certain characteristic remarks from *Potency and Act* can show that this process of inner growth had already begun during the working out of the first draft of her ontology:

> All of these are only titles for more extensive analyses in which the *similitudo* and *maior dissimilitudo* of God and created subjects would be pursued in all directions. (*Potency and Act*, p. 133)
>
> Naturally, the individual factors and their interrelationships working in a generation must be investigated more precisely in order to

grasp more closely the possible achievements of the entelechy, its extent and its limits. (*Potency and Act,* p. 347)
It should especially be shown that and how things are perceived occasions increases in power. (*Potency and Act,* p. 405)

Finite and Eternal Being is an explicit witness that these are not all empty phrases, but about a self-conscious growth of the self beyond itself. For instance, how does E. Stein pay attention in her revision to the above-mentioned requirement for a more extensive analysis of *similitudo* and *maior dissimilitudo?* A whole section of the book is dedicated to the *analogia entis.*[9] At the same time, by means of this comprehensive survey, the idea of the absolute is enhanced: Over against the Thomistic impetus of the triunity of everything in the world, E. Stein seeks—reminiscent of similar contemporary currents—to prove the image of God in the whole of creation. Setting aside the Thomistic limitation of the concept of *imago* to human existence [*Sein*], E. Stein follows the vestige (*vestigium*) and image (*imago*) of divine being in all created existence (*Finite and Eternal Being,* p. 355). A glance at the table of contents of *Finite and Eternal Being* will show that the same process can also be discerned regarding other questions.

3. Editorial Comments

Revision of the Organization of the Work

The manuscript, the Borgmeyer corrected proofs, and the table of contents show the work divided into two parts: Preface and Chapters I-V included in the first volume, Chapters VI-VII along with Appendices I and II in the second volume.

The reasons for this bifurcation are clearly of a technical nature: Volumes I and II contain no special subtitles; the chapters are continuously numbered (Volume II begins with chapter VI). The small size of Borgmeyer's typing area did not permit a printing of the work in one volume.

Considering this, the present edition unites the work into one volume without thereby, as implied by the above statements, injuring its construction. References to places in the work are adjusted to correspond.

E. Stein left two appendices to follow the last chapter: Appendix I: The Interior Castle; Appendix II; Martin Heidegger's Existential Philosophy.

Appendix I gives a presentation, largely in citations, of the essential thoughts and guiding principles that Holy Mother Teresa [of Avila] enunciates in *The Interior Castle.*

Appendix II, also largely in the form of citations, contains Heidegger's lines of thought, on which E. Stein takes a position in the second part of this appendix. Since this appendix had already been completed with the work in the year 1936, only the relevant publications of Heidegger are considered which had appeared before this time*: Being and Time; Kant and the Problem of Metaphysics; On the Essence of Ground; What is Metaphysics?*

These two appendices consisting of a total of four and a half signatures were not taken up in the present edition of the work. Instead of this, Stein's own personal reflections developed in the appendices have been introduced in footnotes at those places in the work where she herself refers to the appendices.

The change in the original conception seemed to be necessary for the following reasons:

The construction of the work achieves a unity and completeness. Since E. Stein limits herself in presenting the thoughts of others to citations of the original texts, by leaving out these sections and merely printing Stein's comments, the length of the book could be shortened. The appendix on Heidegger originates, as noted, from the year 1936. Its publication would require a thorough revision on the part of the author herself.

Further, [Stein's] name and content index was foregone within the frame of the present edition, since the rough draft in E. Stein's hand was not completely worked out. Also it is related exclusively to the first five chapters of the work (the first volume according to the original division of the work) and is based on references to the page numbers of Borgmeyer's proofs. The publication of [Stein's original] index would require a thoroughgoing revision and expansion of the key words as well as page citations for the present edition. Moreover, the printing of the index would cause an appreciable increase in cost. The possibility was therefore considered of permitting the index to appear at a later date as a separate appendix to the work.

Revision of the Text

On the one hand, in comparing the manuscript and Borgmeyer's corrected proof sheets, there appeared variations in the wording, partly stylistic and partly as to content. On the other hand, when comparing Borgmeyer's galley proofs and page proofs, it became evident that there are corrections in E. Stein's hand in the galleys which were not considered in the page proofs.

The basic principles of the revision were: 1) an attempt to retain the final line of thought or the temporally last draft of her thoughts; 2) consideration of E. Stein's stylistic wishes.

The examination of the differences in content led to the conclusion that in no cases did the differences involve basic questions which, for example, would indicate a change of standpoint or a change in the conception of the line of thought. Therefore, we permitted ourselves to omit a critical commentary on the text.

In isolated places where clarification of sentence construction seemed indispensable, we have indicated this by brackets (<>). The same goes for places where we wanted to indicate the singularity of the expression.

Revision of the Notes

The revisions of the notes, first of all, concerned references to the literature. This was unavoidable for two reasons: On the one hand, there are in Borgmeyer's corrected proofs, as well as in the manuscript, a considerable number of incomplete or missing references. On the other hand, they lack any consistent formulation.

Further, it was advisable to substantiate them in terms of content, to expand on insufficient references, and, as already indicated, to correct corresponding references in certain places in the work. We omitted indicating the page numbers, etc., that we augmented, since we were able to come up with authentic references by our research.

Finally, the improvements that resulted from a comparison of the manuscript with Borgmeyer's corrected proofs could be carried into the notes (see above, *Revision of the Text*).

Technical Printing Revisions

Without relevant references on the part of the author, Borgmeyer's edition of the work lacks clarity and the professional precision of the form of the text, both conditions for the readability of a text that is difficult in its contents and style.

A comprehensive technical editing revision thus appeared unavoidable. Due to untoward circumstances, this could no longer be done entirely as the editor and the publisher themselves would have liked. Nevertheless, at this time we owe the publisher, Herder, and in particular his readers thanks for their ready cooperation and their professional support of our efforts.

Fr. Romaeus Leuven, O.C.D.
Dr. L. Gelber

Notes

Foreword to the ICS Publications Edition

1. Stein's own account of her early life and student years can be found in Edith Stein, *Life in a Jewish Family,* trans. Josephine Koeppel (Washington, D.C.: ICS Publications, 1986). For her doctoral dissertation, see Edith Stein, *On the Problem of Empathy,* trans. Waltraut Stein, 3d rev. ed. (Washington, D.C.: ICS Publications, 1989).

2. Edith Stein, *Self-Portrait in Letters, 1916–1942,* trans. Josephine Koeppel (Washington, D.C.: ICS Publications, 1993), Letter #135 (24 February 1933), 134.

3. The recently rediscovered letters of Edith Stein in the archives of the State University of New York at Buffalo are contained in the Marvin Farber collection, which includes over 80 boxes of material divided into two overlapping categories. The boxes listed under "22/5F/768" contain correspondence and papers on phenomenology and philosophy in general. Archivist Christopher Densmore helped to locate the materials cited here, which we brought to the attention of the German editors of Edith Stein's works. Some of these letters have subsequently appeared in the third volume of the new "Edith Stein Gesamtausgabe," in Edith Stein, *Selbstbildnis in Briefen II (1933–1942),* ed. Maria Amata Neyer (Freiburg: Herder, 2000). See also the "Foreword to the ICS Edition" in Edith Stein, *Knowledge and Faith,* trans. Walter Redmond (Washington, D.C.: ICS Publications, 2000).

4. Letter 664 in Stein, *Selbstbildnis in Briefen II,* 445–446. The translation of the Stein letters in the Buffalo archives is by Sr. Josephine Koeppel, O.C.D.

5. Kaufmann to Farber, 7 May 1940, Farber series 22/5F/768, box 11-2.

6. Letter 672 in Stein, *Selbstbildnis in Briefen II,* 672.

7. Letter 676 in Stein, *Selbstbildnis in Briefen II,* 462–463.

8. Farber to Stein, 9 May 1941, Farber series 22/5F/768, box 22-20.

9. Letter 704 in Stein, *Selbstbildnis in Briefen II,* 506.

10. Farber to Stein, 25 October 1941, Farber series 22/5F/768, box 22-20. The essay on Pseudo-Dionysius appears in Edith Stein, *Knowledge and Faith,* 83–134.

11. Private letter of Sr. Fleurette Sweeney to ICS Publications.

Preface of the Author

1. *Festschrift* in honor of Edmund Husserl's seventieth birthday (Halle: Verlag Niemeyer, 1929), pp. 315ff. [See Edith Stein, *Knowledge and Faith,* trans. Walter Redmond (Washington, D.C: ICS Publications, 1999), pp. 1–63.]

2. *Des hl. Thomas von Aquino Untersuchungen über die Wahrheit* (Breslau: Verlag Borgmeyer, 1931–1934); the first volume was published in 1931, the second in 1932, and the index in 1934. [See Edith Stein's *Werke,* Vol. III.—ICS Ed.]

3. E. Przywara, S.J., *Analogia entis* (Munich: Kösel-Pustet, 1932).

4. These forms of consciousness constitute the field of research which Edmund Husserl has demonstrated as the object of *transcendental phenomenology.*

5. Cf. *Analogia entis,* p. 25.

6. Ibid., p. 24

7. Cf. chap. I, §4.

8. Cf. the appendix, pp. 541ff.

Chapter I

1. G. Manser, O.P. In *Das Wesen des Thomismus: Divus Thomas,* 1924, p. 10 he calls the doctrine of act and potency the "innermost essence of Thomism." Manser's most important work of the same title (2d ed., Freiburg, 1935) is entirely based on this idea.

2. *Quaestiones disputatae de potentia,* q. 1, a 1.

3. Aristotle, *Met.* Z 1028 b 1. Cf. the passage in Plato's *Sophist* (244a) which Martin Heidegger placed at the beginning of *Sein und Zeit* (p. 1): "For manifestly you have long been aware of what you mean when you use the expression *'being'* [*Seiende*]. We, however, who used to think we understood it, have now become perplexed." [See Martin Heidegger, *Being and Time,* trans. John Macquarrie and Edward Robinson (New York: Harper & Row, 1962), p. 1.—ICS Ed.] Concerning the difficulty of finding an adequate translation for the Greek *ousia,* we shall soon have more to say.

4. Albert the Great, who himself felt so heavily the burden of the ἀπορούμενα says at the end of his treatise *De causis et processu*

universitatis that he did not write this study on his own initiative but that it had been "wrested from him" by the constant urging of his "companions" to give them an explanation of Aristotle. The socii to whom he refers were probably the young Dominican scholastics who were attending his lectures. Cf. Roland-Gosselin, *Le "De ente et essentia"* (Le Saulchoir: Kain-Belgique, 1926), p. 179.

5. Cf. Roland-Gosselin, ibid., pp. XVf.

6. Although not all the manuscripts bear this title, it may be assumed that it was so named by the saint himself.

7. This name is today hotly contested among Catholics themselves. In recent years the controversy has been especially lively in France. An excelled summary of the question is presented in *La Philosophie Chrétienne* (Kain-Belgique, 1933), a report on the second "Journée d'Etudes de la Société Thomiste," which convention was held at Juvisy on September 11, 1933.

8. Published in Leipzig by Verlag Alfred Kröner in 1934.

9. *Die deutsche Thomasausgabe* published by Anton Pustet, Salzburg, since 1933 [and continued after World War II by Kerle Verlag, Heidelberg—TRANS.]. To date, volumes I, II, III, IV, V, VI, VII, IX, XI, XX, XXV, XXVII, XXIX, and XXX have appeared. [The editing and translation are a joint undertaking of German and Austrian Dominican and Benedictine scholars presenting the *Summa Theologiae* in both Latin and German.—TRANS.]

10. Hense Edition (Teubner Verlag, 1914), Letter 18 (quoted by Roland-Gosselin in ibid., pp. 8ff).

11. *Ens* follows ὄν in strict analogy of word formation; it is derived from *esse* [to be] but is infrequently used.

12. The equation *esse* — *essentia* = *Sein* — *Wesen* could be expressed more easily in middle high German where *wesen* is used as a verb alongside of *sîn* [*sein*].

12a. [I thought it advisable to include this particular passage of Edith Stein's work, notwithstanding the fact that it deals with certain specific difficulties encountered in a translation from Latin into German. The reason for this inclusion is an obvious one: the difficulties of a translation from Latin into English—as indeed of any translation—are *mutatis mutandis* the same.—TRANS.]

13. Examples which illustrate the flexibility required in the rendition of particular terms may be found in the Latin-German

glossary appended to the author's translation of Aquinas's *Quaestiones disputatae de veritate,* i.e., *Des hl. Thomas von Aquino Untersuchungen über die Wahrheit* (Breslau: Borgmeyer, 1934). For example, see the terms *ratio* or *intellectus.*

14. In all such instances I have added the Latin text in parentheses.

15. Cf. the essay "Um den deutschen Thomas" by A. Dempf and W. Moock in *Hochland* (November 1934): 175ff.

16. This does not mean, of course that it is impossible to gain access to the spirit of the Middle Ages without studying the sources in the original. We have in mind those who, intent upon making an access for others possible, find it necessary to discover it first for themselves.

17. Cf. Aristotle, ibid., 1047–50, and this volume, pp. 223–225ff. below.

18. In the discussion at Juvisy (September 12, 1933) a threefold meaning of the term "Christian philosophy" was proposed (cf. *La Philosophie Chrétienne,* pp. 115ff.):

1) The Church fathers designated Christianity as their philosophy because they saw in it the fulfillment of the aspirations of the Greek philosophers and because Christian doctrine made use of philosophic concepts. Understood in this sense, there is no difference between *Christian philosophy* and theology. (The fathers differ in their views on pagan philosophy: Some regard it as a stepping stone to "Christian philosophy," while others condemn it *in toto*).

2) In ancient and modern times attempts have been made to construct a philosophy which uses both natural reason and supernatural faith as sources of knowledge. Those who see in philosophy a purely natural science—and this is the Thomistic point of view—deny that either this *Christian philosophy* or the philosophy of the church fathers have any claim to the title "philosophy." They argue that the philosopher "ceases to be a philosopher and becomes a theologian at the very moment he begins to make use of revealed truth as such" (cf. P. Daniel Feuling, O.S.B. ibid., p. 129).

3) The term "Christian Philosophy" is customarily used to designate that medieval thinking which undeniably developed under the influence of Christianity. In this latter sense the term is used in the encyclical *Aeterni Patris* and by both Etienne Gilson (in *The Spirit*

of Medieval Philosophy [New York: Charles Scribner's Sons, 1936]) and Jacques Maritain, whom we follow in our own discussion. According to this interpretation, Thomistic philosophy is indeed a *Christian philosophy,* notwithstanding the fact that it wants to be a natural discipline and therefore sets itself off from theology. And it is precisely the strictest Thomists who affirm the essential incompatibility of the terms "Christian" and "philosophy." See, for example, P. Mandonnet, O.P., in *La Philosophie Chrétienne,* pp. 62ff. and Feuling, ibid., p. 125).

19. *Summa contra gentiles* 1, 2.

20. Ibid., 1, 3.

21. *Von der Christlichen Philosophie,* translated from the French and introduced by Balduin Schwarz (Salzburg, 1935).

22. Ibid., p. 56.

23. Ibid., pp. 58f.

24. It is unavoidable that we anticipate here certain ideas which will be discussed in greater detail in later sections of this work.

25. What is said here of written documents applies equally to all those devices which tangibly embody the results of scientific research, such as graphs and every kind of pictorial documentation and illustration, including all "contrivances" [*Apparate*] which, though used as material aids in the exploration of truth, are nonetheless already the results of scientific reflection.

26. Edmund Husserl, *Logische Untersuchungen* I (Halle, 1913), p. 12.

27. Ibid., p. 60.

28. *Summa Theologiae* [hereafter *S.Th.*—Trans.] I, q. 1, a 1, *corpus articuli.*

29. One is bound to receive a profound shock when one looks at what remains of the former realm of the soul. The attempt of psychology to divorce itself totally from all religious and theological considerations has yielded a psychology without a soul. Both the nature and the faculties of the soul were designated as mythological concepts and therefore eliminated until, in the end, the impulses and activities of the soul were explained as composites of simple sensations. Even all the powers of the intellect, of sentiment, and of life itself were drained out of the soul. Today this scientific psychology of the nineteenth century has been abandoned in principle

[at least on the European continent.—Trans.]. The rediscovery of the intellect and the efforts on behalf of a genuine science of ideas [*Geisteswissenschaft*] are foremost among the decisive changes which have taken place in the realms of knowledge and science.

30. This does not mean that philosophy exists for the sake of these other disciplines but rather that, to the extent that they are genuine sciences, they are rooted in philosophy.

31. *S.Th.* II-II, q. 45, a 2; Maritain, ibid., p. 60.

32. In the course of discussions at Juvisy, P. Daniel Feuling proposed the following definition of philosophy: "Philosophy is the purely natural, rational knowledge of beings [*des êtres, des Seienden*] and of being [*de l'être, des Seins*] in the light of the highest causes and ultimate reasons—insofar as the given phenomenon (φαινόμενον) allows natural reason to seize upon and comprehend the being (νούμενον) of existents, whether it be in the manner of evidence or of probability or of opinion, according to the particular conditions of the specific case" (ibid., p. 126). "Knowledge of beings and of being in the light of the highest causes and ultimate reasons"—this definition is in accord with our own description. If philosophic knowledge is confined to the sphere of natural reason (considered as definitive and irrevocable)—and this meaning is implied in Feuling's definition—then something decisive has already been said concerning the relationship existing between philosophy on the one hand and faith and theology on the other: Revealed truths cannot actually enter into the structure of philosophy. This amounts to a rejection of the second meaning often associated with the term "Christian philosophy" (cf. n. 18, above). A discussion concerning the necessary validity of the phenomenal data would require a more detailed inquiry into the meaning of the given phenomena than is warranted at this time.

33. Heidegger has never abrogated the ancient meaning of the term *metaphysica generalis* as denoting the science of *existents as such* [*vom Seienden als solchem*] but merely emphasized that first of all the meaning of being [*Sein*] should be made clear. In this demand we agree with him. He then advanced one step farther, asserting that in order to understand the meaning of being, we must first inquire into the ways in which people understand being. And because he found the reason for the possibility of an understanding of being

[*Seinsverständnis*] in human finitude [*Endlichkeit des Menschen*], he proposed as the proper way of arriving at a foundation of metaphysics the discussion of human finitude. This proposition must be challenged on two counts: First, *metaphysics is concerned with beings as such and not with human being alone.* If philosophers disregard the meaning of being which is implied in the understanding of being and simply "project" [*entwirft*] the human *Seinsverständnis,* they run the risk of cutting themselves loose from the true meaning of being. If my interpretation is right, Heidegger has succumbed to this danger. Second, since there are finite existents which lack *Seinsverstandis,* the understanding of being cannot be called a property of finitude as such. *Seinsverstandis is* rather the distinguishing mark which sets off personal-spiritual beings from other (inferior) kinds of being. Within the circumference of *Seinsverstandis,* the *human* understanding of being must be distinguished from that of other finite intelligences and, moreover, every *finite* understanding of being must be distinguished from the *infinite* (divine) *Seinsverstandis.* In short, the true meaning of *Seinsverstandis* cannot be determined without a prior clarification of the *meaning of being.* And thus *the question as to the meaning of being is and remains* the *basic one in any attempt at laying the groundwork of metaphysics.*

34. 1 Corinthians 13.

35. Grace does not exempt Christian scholars from the need for a solid scientific and philosophic erudition—to the extent that such a training is within their reach—just as it does not in other respects absolve them from their natural vocational duties. Those who in a fallacious trust in the aid of grace would disregard these obligations could, of course, fall far behind the achievements of thorough and conscientious non-Christian scholars.

36. Maritain, ibid., p. 73.

37. Ibid., p. 74.

38. Ibid., pp. 72f.

39. Cf. *La Philosophie Chretienne,* p. 100.

40. Cf. note 18, above.

41. *Analogia entis,* 1, 45.

42. Ibid., p. 45. According to Przywara (p. 3), "metaphysics" means a "going behind" to reach the "background" of "physis" (the latter understood as the "mode of being" [*Seinsweise*] in which existents

are founded and in which they act). This describes adequately the Aristotelian *first philosophy* which concerns itself with that which is as such—not with its multiple individual, concrete species. As we indicated above (cf. §2) and as we shall demonstrate later on in greater detail, the central problem of metaphysics is the inquiry into the actual meaning of that which is *(ousia)*, and it seems that Przywara has the same problem in mind in his explanation of "physis." This *first philosophy* is equivalent to a *philosophical metaphysics* if natural reason is engaged in tracing the ultimate reasons of actual being [*Sein*], to the extent that it is within its power to do so. If, however, the aid of theology is invoked, then the philosopher arrives at what Przywara calls a *theological metaphysics*. In a significant letter, Fr Roland-Gosselin, O.P., has pointed out how difficult it is to draw the correct dividing line between philosophy and theology (cf. *La Philosophie Chrétienne*, pp. 153ff.): "Both philosophy and theology establish their foundations by permitting faith to influence reason. Christian theology and Christian philosophy as historic structures originated simultaneously, and both considered first and foremost the needs of theology. They were not greatly concerned with the question as to what extent the distinctions and conceptual formulations demanded by theology could be accepted and justified by a strictly philosophical method. Perhaps there are still many points at which the precise boundaries have to be drawn."

43. *Analogia entis*, 1, 58.

44. The *theological "Summae"* make the findings of philosophy subservient to theology, while the *philosophical "Summae"* extend the striving for an understanding of that which is [*des Seienden*] to the facts of revelation.

45. This term *visio* is very descriptive, because for us seeing (vision) is the most penetrating and most convincing kind of knowledge. We must, however, remain conscious of the fact that this *visio* differs essentially from any optical vision. It denotes not an understanding from without, from a distance, as it were; it is rather a knowing that is completely one with the reality known. It resembles perhaps most closely the manner in which we know ourselves, i.e., our own existence.

46. *Catechismus Catholicus*, 13th ed. (Rome, 1933), Pro adultis, q. 515, p. 242.

47. Cf. Aquinas, *De veritate,* q. 14, a 7, ad 7 (*Untersuchungen über die Wahrheit,* II, 28).

48. Ibid., q. 14, a 2, *corpus articuli,* p. 9.

49. "Urquell," in *Gedichte des heligen Johannes vom Kreuz* (Munich, 19240, pp. 17f. [Stein quotes from a German translation of St. John of the Cross's poetry. For the original Spanish, with an English translation, see "Song of the soul that rejoices in knowing God through faith," in *The Collected Works of St. John of the Cross,* trans. Kieran Kavanaugh and Otilio Rodriguez, rev. ed. (Washington, DC: ICS Publications, 1991), pp. 58–60.—ICS Ed.]

50. John of the Cross, *The Living Flame of Love,* quoted from the German edition of John's *Werke* (Munich, 1924), 3: 170. [In the ICS Publications translation this passage is rendered: "In this matter of striving for perfection, not to go back is to go forward; and the intellect goes forward by establishing itself more in faith. Thus it advances by darkening itself, for faith is darkness to the intellect" (*Living Flame,* 3.48). See *Collected Works of St. John of the Cross,* rev. ed. (1991), p. 693.—ICS Ed.]

Chapter II

1. Martin Grabmann, *Die Werke des hl. Thomas von Aquino. Eine literarhistorische Untersuchung und Einführung* (Munich, 1921), pp. 275ff.

2. Page numbers refer to the critical edition of M. D. Roland-Gosselin, O.P (Bibliotheque Thomiste, VIII) [Kain, Belgium: Le Saulchoir, 1926—Trans.].

3. Ibid., p. 35.

4. Ibid., p. 36.

5. St. Augustine, *De Trinitate,* X, 3.

6. St. Augustine, ibid., XV, 12.

7. Cf. Edmund Husserl, *Ideen su einer reinen Phänomenologie und phänomenologischen Philosophie* (Halle: Max Niemeyer, 1913), pp. 48ff. [available in English translation as *Ideas: General Introduction to Pure Phenomenology* (London: Allen and Unwin, 1931).—ICS Ed.]. See also, *Méditations Cartésiennes* (Paris: A. Colin, 1931), pp. 66ff. This latter work is based on a series of lectures which Husserl delivered in Paris in 1929.

8. In an essay entitled "Die Zeit" [Time], published in *Philosophischer Anzeiger II,* 2 and 4 (1927/28), pp. 143–182, 345–390, Hedwig Conrad-Martius presents a profound analysis of the frailty of temporal being and of the way temporal being is related to eternal being.

9. Husserl uses the term "act" to designate that in which I am. Since we have started out, however, from the scholastic concept of act and are trying to find its objective bases and since, on the other hand, we do not know as yet how the phenomenological and the scholastic concepts of act are related to one another, it seems advisable to avoid this term for the time being and speak instead of an "intellectual movement."

10. The question of whether this is the only possible point of departure need not be answered at this time.

11. "*...inter creatorem et creaturam non potest tanta similitudo norari, quin inter eos maior sit dissimilitudo notanda*" (Fourth Lateran Council, 1215, Dz., 432).

12. Cf. pp. 56ff.

13. Cf. "Die Zeit," 2:170ff., 4:387. H. Conrad-Martius confines the meaning of the term *actuality* to the non-dimensional [*punktuell*] *"Existenzberührung"* and therefore does not apply this term to eternal being.

14. Ibid., pp. 172f.

15. Ibid., pp. 154f.

16. Ibid., p. 157.

17. Ibid., p. 166.

18. Ibid., p. 167.

19. Ibid., p. 346.

20. Ibid., p. 348.

21. Ibid., p. 349.

22. Let us emphasize once more that we are using the term *actuality* in a sense differing from the meaning attributed to it by H. Conrad-Martius. We designate as actuality the height of being [*Seinshöhe*] as such. This why we speak of actuality *also* and even *preferably* with respect to God, while for H. Conrad-Martius the concept of actuality denotes merely a "passage" from one state of being to another.

23. St. Augustine, *De Trinitate,* I, 1.

24. Here we do well to remember that only the *pure* act is being in *absolute perfection,* while there are various degrees of perfection in the realm of *actual* being.

25. This term is quite common in phenomenology. *Experience* [*Erlebnis*] in this context does not signify—as it does sometimes in ordinary linguistic usage—something especially meaningful or soul stirring, but simply an enduring unified structure, arising and abiding in the individual self.

26. I am assuming here that the joy is related to the message conveyed to me, and not—which would also be possible—to the fact that it is conveyed to me.

27. In this Husserl differs from the way this term is traditionally used. He does not call *transcendent* what goes beyond our experience, but designates as transcendent the objects of experience, with the exception of those *immanent* objects which are constitutive elements of human consciousness.

28. The phenomenologists call this the *sphere of immanence.*

29. Cf. Husserl, *Ideen,* p. 160.

30. The term *eternal* is used here in the popular sense of a temporal endlessness rather than in the genuine sense of supratemporal pure being.

31. We shall soon have more to say concerning this problem.

32. Husserl terms that which in this manner reaches out of the past and future into the present the *retentional* and the *protential,* respectively. (Cf. "Vorlesungen zur Phänomenologie des inneren Zeitbewusstseins" in *Jahrbuch für Philosophie und phänomenologische Forschung* IX, 1928, prepared for publication by the author of this present volume in 1917/18.) These terms are indicative of the fact that the contents of past and future are "held" by the present now. One must be careful not to misinterpret the metaphor "stream of experience" lest we make it appear as if past and future were "standing" behind and in front of me as something into which in retrogression or progression I might be able to enter.

33. This span of time, however, cannot be said to be "filled" in the strict sense, because that which has passed no longer "stands" exactly at the place where it once stood.

34. Cf. Martin Heidegger, *Sein und Zeit* (Halle, 1927), p. 179. [See Heidegger, *Being and Time,* pp. 223–224.—ICS Ed.] This manner of speaking indicates that human beings find themselves in existence [*in Dasein*] without knowing how they have come into it; they do not exist by themselves and through themselves and they cannot expect from their own being an answer regarding their whence. This question whence, however, is not thereby silenced. No matter how hard one may try to circumvent it or to prohibit it altogether as a meaningless question, it imperiously rises again and again out of the very nature of the human being: Apparently groundless in itself, this being calls for a firm ontological ground; and since it is "thrown" being, the question concerning the thrower cannot be suspended or suppressed.

35. In a similar manner St. Thomas finds the distinction between the higher and lower pure intelligences in the fact that the former possess more actuality and less potentiality than the latter.

36. Heidegger, *Sein und Zeit,* pp. 184ff. [Cf. Heidegger, *Being and Time,* pp. 228ff.—ICS Ed.] The central theme of Heidegger's inaugural lectural at the University of Freiburg (entitled "What is Metaphysics?") is the concept of nothingness [*Nichts*]. [Cf. also *Existence and Being* (Chicago: Henry Regnery Company, 1949), pp. 25–131 and 255–392.—ICS Ed.] The mood in which people are brought face to face with *nothingness* is *anxiety* [*Angst*]. In the anxiety or dread which accompanies the experience of the *gliding away of all existents, including our own selves,* nothingness is revealed. "In the luminous night of the nothingness of dread the *primordial* overtness [*Offenbarkeit*] of that which is *as such* becomes manifest: It is, it exists and is thus *not nothing.* The immersion of existence in nothingness [*die Hineingehaltenheit des Daseins in das Nichts*] on the basis of hidden dread is a going beyond existents in their totality; transcendence.... *The inquiry into nothingness spans the totality of metaphysics,* for being and nothingness belong together..., because *being* itself is *finite* in its essence and is only revealed in the transcendence of an existence projected into *nothingness*" (p. 26).

When *ancient metaphysics* [according to Heidegger] advanced the proposition *ex nihilo nihil fit* [nothing can come from nothing], it understood *nothing* as unformed matter and admitted as being only that which is formed [*das Gebilde*]. *Christian dogmatics,* on the other hand, denies the truth of the proposition *ex nihilo nihil fit,* and asserts instead *ex nihilo fit — ens creatum* [the created being is made out of nothing]. Christian dogmatics thus understands *nothing* as denoting the absence of any existents apart from the divine existence. In both instances the question concerning being and nothingness as such remains unasked (p. 25).

It is evident that Heidegger's inaugural lecture was intended for a non-professional audience and was meant to be provocative rather than instructive; it therefore lacks the stringency of a scientific treatise. The terms and phrases used sound at times more mythological than philosophical. Heidegger speaks of the nothing [*Nichts*] almost as if he were referring to a person whose long suppressed rights must be vindicated. One is reminded of that "nothing that once upon a time was everything."

Is it really true that ancient metaphysics understood the nothing as unformed matter? If this *were* the case, it could not have formulated the proposition *ex nihilo nihil fit,* for according to the point of view of ancient metaphysics every "formed thing" is "formed" from unformed matter. Ancient [and medieval] metaphysics makes a distinction between the absolutely nonexistent and a nonexistent which yet is (in the mode of potency). And this latter kind of nonexistent is the matter out of which everything is formed that is in the "strict" sense.

And how are we to understand the phrase *ex nihilo fit — ens creatum?* It must unquestionably be understood in the sense that the creator in his creative act is not determined by any other existent and there is no other existent aside from the creator and his creation.

Is it then correct when Heidegger asserts that in Christian dogmatics the questions concerning the nature of both being and nothingness remain unasked? This assertion is correct inasmuch as it is not at all the function of Christian dogmatics as such to *ask* questions but rather to *teach* Christian doctrine. (True enough, Christian dogmatics may ask whether or not some proposition is an article of faith, but once a proposition has been established as Christian dogma, there is no occasion for any further questioning.)

This, however, does not mean that Christian dogmatics is indifferent with respect to the problem of being and nothingness. In speaking of God, it speaks of being. And it speaks of nothingness in many contexts as, for example, when it speaks of creation and describes a created being as an existent whose being includes some not-being [*Nichtsein*]. Precisely because we are "so *finite*...that we...find it impossible to bring ourselves face to face with nothingness by our own will and resolution," the revelation of the nothingness in our own being marks at the same time our breaking through this finite, empty being of ours to the infinite, pure, and eternal being.

37. Heidegger, *Sein und Zeit,* p. 266. [See Heidegger, *Being and Time,* pp. 310–311.—ICS Ed.]

38. Cf. the third way of St. Thomas, in the *S.Th.* 1, q. 2, a 3.

39. Ibid., 1, q. 3, a 4.

40. Ibid., 1, q. 11, a 3.

41. H. Conrad-Martius has formulated a demonstration of the existence of God in this way: "*If* temporal existence...*then* also of necessity eternal existence," but she never personally "followed up the implications of this rational conclusion" ("Die Zeit," pp. 371f.).

42. St. Augustine, *De consensu Evang.* IV, 10, 20 (cf. Przywara, ibid., pp. 207f.).

43. St. Augustine, *In Ps.* 99, 5f. (cf. Przywara, pp. 201).

44. St. Augustine, *In Ps.* 134, 6 (Cf. Przywara, ibid., pp. 203f.).

Chapter III

1. It will be shown later that there is a real distinction between *eidos* and μορφή (cf. Chapt. IV, §8 and §19,2).

2. Two careful and illuminating phenomenological studies deal with these problems: J. Hering, "Bemerkungen über das Wesen, die Wesenheit und die Idee" (in Husserl's *Jahrbuch für Philosophie und phänomenologische Forschung,* IV, [1921], pp. 495ff.), and R. Ingarden, "Essentiale Fragen" (in Husserl's *Jahrbuch,* VII [1925], pp. 125ff.). The latter is also available in a special edition. Hering's study is the more fundamental of the two. Ingarden follows Hering in this discussion of *Wesen* and *Wesenheit,* but in his elaboration of the doctrine of ideas (which is only sketchily treated by Hering) he proceeds independently.

3. Hering, *Bemerkungen,* p. 510.

4. Hering himself regards the expression "to be realized" as inadequate (p. 510, n. 2), but the Platonic expression "to partake" or "to participate" is hardly more adequate.

5. It should be understood that the Aristotelian term πρώτη *ousia* is used by Hering in a sense differing from the way Aristotle uses it. It is applied by him to the very thing to which Aristotle emphatically refused to have it applied. Hering's entire treatise may therefore not be regarded as an attempt to interpret Aristotle notwithstanding his heavy leaning on the language of Aristotle's *Metaphysics.* His is rather a thoroughly independent and objective approach to the problems with which both Plato and Aristotle were concerned, and in some respects he offers a progressive clarification of these problems.

6. See §11 of this chapter.

7. We refer here to only one of the many meanings of this semantically complex word. It is possible to distinguish *ratio* from *intellectus* by defining *ratio* as reason *engaged* in a discursive movement of causal relations, and *intellectus* as reason *resting in the understanding* of the ultimate meaning.

8. Hering, *Bemerkungen,* p. 522. We question Hering's statement that essences can become wholly [*restlos*] intelligible. It would rather seem that in this ground of all understanding we are facing an ultimate that forces us to acknowledge an impenetrable mystery (cf. chap. III, §10 and chap. IV, §19,7).

9. Joseph Gredt, O.S.B. in his *Elementa philosophiae Aristotelico-Thomisticae,* 5th ed. (Freiburg im Breisgau, 1929, I:12) lists among the several terms for *conceptus* also *idea ab* εἰδω and thus seems to equate concept [*Begriff*] and *eidos* [*Wesenheit*] (essence). The reason for this lies in the fact that in traditional logic the term *concept* is used in a broader sense than we are using it in the following pages. In traditional logic *several concepts* of the *concept* are marked off from one another, especially the *subjective* (that *whereby* we conceive something) from the *objective* (*what* we conceive). Moreover, what in traditional logic is termed *idea* cannot simply be equated with *essence.*

10. Among these new questions is, for example, the problem of *universals,* so heatedly disputed in the Middle Ages. But a discussion of this problem presupposes a much more far-reaching clarification of basic principles than we have achieved at this time.

11. Cf. *De veritate,* q. 26, a 4–5 (*Untersuchungen über die Wahrheit,* II: 379ff.).

12. "Passion" is here understood as a state or condition of the soul [*seelischer Zustand*]. On the concept of *passion* compare the Latin-German vocabulary list in *Untersuchung über die Wahrheit* (p. 39) and the places cited there.

13. *De veritate,* q. 26, a 4 (*Untersuchungen über die Wahrheit,* II: 380).

14. *Untersuchung über die Wahrheit,* II: 383.

15. Hering, *Bemerkungen,* p. 497.

16. Ibid., p. 496.

17. Cf. Husserl, *Ideas,* §2, p. 9.

18. From this must be distinguished the ποῖον (quality [*Beschaffenheit*]): the being-brown of this particular horse is something different from its brown color.

19. In modern philosophy, *object* denotes what stands opposite [*Gegen-stand*] the knowing *subject.* Medieval philosophy, too, often uses the word in this sense. But primarily it sees in the object a *subiectum,* i.e., a *substrate,* a foundation, or a *carrier* in one sense or another. (Cf. the pages which follow, and Gredt, ibid., II: 135).

20. This is termed *substantia subsistens* or *hypostasis.* An object in this sense entails no relationship to a knowing subject; such a relationship to a knowing subject is implied, however, when the object is understood as an *ob-iectum* or a *Gegen-stand.*

21. Hering, *Bemerkungen,* p. 498.

22. Ibid., p. 499.

23. These determinations correspond to the different modes of *predication* which Aristotle summarily designated as *categories.*

24. The *fortuitous* may be defined as "that which has no foundation in the nature."

25. We might venture to say that it follows from the nature of humanity that no action can be derived with necessity from the nature of a *particular* person.

26. The term *intentio* is therefore frequently used to designate the concept.

27. We assume here that nothing of the present experience has been lost and that I am able to revive in my memory every detail of my past experience. This means, of course, that we assume an ideal situation.

28. See pp. 151f.

29. The problem of the *bearer* will have to be discussed at length later on (cf. pp. 211ff.).

30. It seems reasonably safe to use the term *nature* in the dual sense implied here. "Animate natures" [*Lebewesen*], "soul natures" [*seelische Wesen*], are not *natures* in the sense in which the term is used here. They are objects to whose nature it pertains to have life or a soul.

31. This is the ever repeated objection of Aristotle to the Platonic doctrine of ideas.

32. Faith teach us that man [*Mensch*], who in the state of innocence recognized the nature of things, was also able to call them by their proper names: "As Adam named each of the living beings, so are their names" (Gn 2:19). The language of paradise was lost together with the innocence and the knowledge of paradise.

33. It is impossible to discuss here the *Platonic doctrine of ideas* in its historical structure, but all the problems which are discussed in this section are directly related to it. The great difficulty with which both Plato and Aristotle had to contend lay in the fact that they found themselves face to face with the entire realm of *ideal being* and naturally had a difficult time groping their way through the complexities of this vast territory. In their attempt to get hold of the *ideas,* they seized alternately upon *natures* [*Wesen*] and *essences* [*Wesenheiten*] or *ideal objects*. It proved impossible to subsume all these rich contents under *one single* concept. It seems to me that the beginnings of a phenomenological theory of essences, as it is incorporated in the works of Husserl and his school, for the first time points the way to an understanding, a just appraisal, and a fruitful elaboration of the life work of Plato and the metaphysics of Aristotle.

34. Cf. Aquinas, *S.Th.*, III, q. 7, a 2; *De potentia,* q. 9, a 1. [In the *Summa Theologiae,* St. Thomas says: *Est enim de ratione individui quod non possit in pluribus esse...; est in se indivisum et divisum ab omnibus aliis.* (*loc. cit.*)—TRANS.]

35. Cf. pp. 80f. above, where it was shown that the being of the quid may also be understood in a different sense.

36. This makes it quite clear that there is a difference between the full quid and the nature quid.

37. One might suspect that only the quid but not the nature (understood as the to be [*esse*] of the quid [*Was*-Sein]) admits of

an actualization. The *Wassein,* however, also becomes actual only with and in the object.

38. Cf. pp. 277ff. below.

39. Anticipating the results of our future inquiry, we might adduce for the purpose of comparison the interrelation of body and soul: The soul attains to being in the body, but the body attains to being *by virtue of* the soul, not vice versa.

40. Cf. pp. 177ff. and pp. 254f., below.

41. This world of essential being may be regarded as the one which Plato had in mind when he spoke of the *realm of ideas.* Only a further investigation could show how this realm of ideas is related to the scholastic *intelligibile,* i.e., to that which is *intelligible* or accessible to the knowing mind (cf. pp. 99ff. below).

42. The same is of course true of the term *Wesenheit* (essence). Cf. pp. 93f. below for the way St. Thomas makes use of the term *quidditas* (*Washeit*).

43. In his *Ideas* (pp. 8ff.) Husserl speaks of the possibility of knowing the quid of an individual object of experience by means of *ideation* or by an *intuition of the essence* [*Wesensanschauung*]. This peculiar kind of intuition, which is distinct from all experience, uncovers the contents of factual experience without engaging in the actual *positing* of the experience (i.e., without conceiving of the thing in its *reality*), and it posits these contents as something which could just as well have been realized elsewhere, i.e, apart from the content in which it was experienced. For Husserl *universality* thus pertains to the *nature as such* regardless of the degrees of universality within the essential sphere [*Wesensgebiet*]. This kind of interpretation is evidently possible only on the basis of the aforementioned dual nature of the nature [*Doppel-"Wesen" des Wesens*]. It takes into consideration only one aspect, namely *essential being,* and it cuts that connection with reality which attaches to the nature not merely externally but which pertains to it intrinsically. On the basis of this initial cut which separates fact from nature, it becomes understandable why Husserl had to arrive at an idealistic interpretation of reality, whereas his associates and disciples (Max Scheler, Alexander Pfänder, Adolf Reinach, Hedwig Conrad-Martius, Jean Hering, and others), guided by the full meaning of the term *nature,* became ever more confirmed in their realistic ways of thinking.

44. We shall encounter this kind of nature again under the name of *Wesensform* (cf. chap. IV, §3, parts 7, 8, and 19 below.)

45. Hering, *Bemerkungen*, p. 503.

46. Ibid.

47. Husserl has such a *Wesenslehre* in mind when he speaks of a *material ontology* (cf. *Ideas*, pp. 4ff.). Some references to such a theory will be found in the following section.

48. Hering, *Bemerkungen*, pp. 505ff.

49. Ibid., p. 509. The term μορφή (form) is here used in a broader sense than in Aristotle, who means by μορφή merely the inner form of an *object*, i.e., of an independent and real existent. See also the discussion in the following section.

50. Ibid., p. 515.

51. Not to be mistaken for the identically named essences.

52. Hering, *Bemerkungen*, pp. 516f.

53. Ibid., pp. 517f.

54. Ibid., p. 518.

55. Ibid., p. 522.

56. Ibid., p. 522.

57. Ibid., pp. 523f.

58. From such sounds must be distinguished *pure* sounds (*ideal objects*), which are neither the sounds of a violin nor the sounds of a flute.

59. Aristotle, to be sure, coined this phrase with a view to the actual *nature* rather than with a view to *essential being*. For a further discussion of the meaning of τὸ τί ἦν εἶναι, cf. pp. 138ff. below.

60. *Essence* [*Wesenheit*] does here not denote that marked contrast to *nature* [*Wesen*] that we have previously elaborated. *Essentia* may have both meanings.

61. *De potentia*, q. 3. a 5, ad 2.

62. *De veritate*, q. 3, a I *corp. art.* (*Untersuchungen über die Wahrheit*, I: 93).

63. Here we touch on the problem of *individuation*. But our present investigation does not propose to pursue this line of thought any further.

64. Cf. Gredt, ibid., I: 96.

65. Ibid., I: 97.

66. *Concept* (here as well as in our earlier discussion and in our quotations from Gredt) is understood in the sense of *formal concept* [*Formalbegriff*], i.e., as a mental structure.

67. The distinctive character [*Eigentümlichkeit*] of *thoughts* as the actual sphere of the objects of logic, and of *concepts* as *elements of thought,* is clearly and convincingly discussed especially in the introduction (pp. 139ff.) and section II (pp. 271 ff.) of Alexander Pfänder's "Logik," *Jahrbuch für Philosophie und phänomenologische Forschung,* IV (1921).

68. Pfänder, ibid., p. 275.

69. Let us observe at this point that the terms *matter* and *form* are used here in a sense differing from the way they are used in cosmology [*Naturphilosophie*], where they designate the *matter* and *essential form* [*Wesensform*] of natural objects.

70. The Thomists distinguish between *universale* and *commune:* They call *commune* any one in which several things share in some manner; and they call *universale* that which several things have in common insofar as it can be identified with them and has *become multiplied in them* (*multiplicatum in illis*). Thus the *commune* does not determine whether what is possessed in common by a number of things (*communicatur in pluribus*) is numerically the same or not. The *universale,* on the other hand, compels such a determination, for it is never numerically the same in several things. Thus the divine nature is *common* (*communis*) to the three Divine Persons, but it is not related to them in the manner in which the *universale* is related to the objects that are its subordinates (*inferiora*). A room, for example, is a place that is *common* to several human beings [who are in it], but it is not a *universale* (cf. Gredt, ibid., I: 96).

71. Aquinas, *In Met.* I.7, lect. 13.

72. We shall make no attempt to translate the term *species intelligibilis* until we have had an opportunity to clarify its meaning to such an extent that an unequivocal translation is possible. We might perhaps speak of the *form of cognition* [*Erkenntnisform*] and thereby suggest its meaning in a preliminary way.

73. Aquinas, *In Met.*, 1.1, lect. 10.

74. What is "actualized" in this process is not the object, but knowledge.

75. We lay stress on the word "additional" because, as we shall presently demonstrate, this same has its *own specific* mode of being, aside from those possible modes of being that may be added.

76. It will be shown later (chap. IV, §4) that something of all that which is intellectually grasped can enter into the knowing mind and can form it.

77. Because we regard the nature quid as the *same,* we cannot accept without qualification Pfänder's assertion that the content of the concept [*Begriffsinhalt*] does not coincide with any element in the object; nor can we follow him in his rejection of the doctrine of abstraction.

78. I confess that so far no one has been able to convince me that what Aristotle (in the *Metaphysics*) objected to in the doctrine of ideas was actually held by Plato.

79. Husserl followed the first two ways in his *Ideas,* and the third way in his *Logical Investigations.*

80. We shall have to ask later whether and to what extent such fanciful thinking is possible (cf. chap. VI, §1).

81. The meanings of "mediacy" and "immediacy" of course need further clarification.

82. We must remember here the twofold meaning of possibility: (1) the possibility of the nature [*Wesensmöglichkeit*], which accounts for actual being with its preliminary stages, and (2) these preliminary stages themselves.

83. Conrad-Martius, "Die Zeit," p. 373.

84. Ibid., p. 372.

85. Cf. Aquinas, *De veritate,* q. 4, a 1, ad 5-6 (*Untersuchungen über die Wahrheit,* I, 115ff.).

86. This is my attempt to translate the Greek συνέστηχεν (Lat., *constant*).

87. According to St. Anselm of Canterbury, *Fides quaerens intellectum* and *Credo ut intelligam.* Cf. also Alexander Koyré's introduction to this Latin-French edition of St. Anselm's *Proslogion,* published under the title *Fides quaerens intellectum* (Paris, 1930).

88. "All things" means all that is created.

89. The same interpretation, substantiated by quotations from St. Augustine and Origen, may be found in J. Dillersberger, *Das Wort vom Logos* (Salzburg, 1935), p. 35.

90. The divine nature is a *commune,* not a *universale* (cf. pp. 99f. above).

91. St. Anselm, *Proslogion* (chap. II, p. 12 in Koyré's edition).

92. Aquinas, *S.Th.* I, q. 2, a 1, ad 2.

93. Aquinas, *S.Th.* I, q. 2, a 1, *corp.art.*

94. For this reason the usual refutation of the ontological argument—pointing out that this argument "illegitimately passes from the logical to the ontological order"—is not convincing. It is really a question of passing from the nature to being [*vom Wesen zum Sein*], and, while it is true that such a passage is inadmissible in the case of all finite natures, the conclusion that it is equally inadmissible in the case of the infinite nature is unwarranted: It is precisely the difference in the interrelation of nature and being which most decisively distinguishes the infinite nature from everything finite.

95. Augustine, *De Trinitate,* V, 1, 2 (Pryzywara, *Augustinus,* p. 231).

96. The way in which intention [*Meinung*] is related to fulfillment [*Erfüllung*] is discussed by Husserl in his *Logische Untersuchungen,* VI (third volume of the second edition).

97. Cf. A. Koyré, ibid., p. V.

98. In the language of Holy Scripture, the godless person is called an *insipiens* (a fool). Cf. St. Anselm, *Proslogion,* chs. III-IV.

99. Since in God *quid* [*Was*] and *nature* [*Wesen*] are non-distinguishable, we may speak of his *Wesen,* whereas in the case of finite existents we had to speak of their *nature quid* [*Wesenswas*].

100. This decision was pronounced on the occasion of the condemnation of the *ontologism* of A. Günther (cf. Denzinger-Bannwart, *Enchiridion Symbolorum,* 11th ed. [Freiburg i. Br., 1910], 1659-1665.)

101. According to St. Thomas, the essential differences among things are unknown to us; the only way to characterize them would be with the aid of those *accidental* differences which derive from the essential ones (cf. *De ente et essentia,* chap. V and our own statements concerning the nature and the knowledge of natures [*Wesenserkenntis*], pp. 102ff. above).

102. Cf. Aquinas, *De veritate,* q. 2, a 5, *corp. art.*

103. Ibid., q. 3, a 2, *corp. art.* (*Untersuchungen über die Wahrheit,* I, 99).

104. St. Thomas encloses everything that acquires actuality at any time in this phrase.

105. Cf. chap. VI, §5.

106. Moreover, to every individual existent there pertains a definite position or situation in space by which it is distinguished from others—those completely like it otherwise. But the situation does not pertain to them in the same strict sense as does their size or extension. Something that is "the same" can be conceived in many different positions or situations.

107. Finite existent in this sense means not that which *has a beginning* but that which *has limits.*

108. Cf. the following passage in H. Conrad-Martius, where she speaks of the Creator and his creation: "It might be…the meaning or *one* meaning of creation to present in a finite unfolding [*Enfaltung*] what God himself is. The deity manifests itself in creation in the totality of its personal form [*Gesamtgestalt*]. God can neither create nor sustain his creation out of a vacuum or into a vacuum. He creates and sustains his creation necessarily, out of the eternal plentitude of his eternally formed nature" ("Die Zeit," p. 377).

109. Cf. P. E. Longpré, O.F.M., "Duns Scotus, der Theologe des fleischgewordenen Wortes," in *Wissenschaft und Weisheit,* vol. I (1934), pp. 243ff.

110. The Nicaean Creed says *per quem omnia facta sunt* (by whom all things were made).

Chapter IV

1. Cf. Aristotle, *Met.* Δ 7, 1017a; E 1, 1025b, 1027b.

2. I hesitate to translate "*in re*" by "in reality" [*in Wirklichkeit*] because what is meant is more comprehensive than the *reality of nature* [*Naturwirklichkeit*].

3. Aquinas, *De ente et essentia,* chap. I (Roland-Gosselin, pp. 2f.).

4. We have no intention of discussing here the question of whether these two propositions express two different ways. But we should like to call attention to what Pfänder in his *Logik* (ibid., p. 1791) says concerning the *copula,* viz., that it expresses two things: 1) the relationship existing between the predicative determination [*Prädikatsbestimmtheit*] and the objective determination of the subject [*Subjektsgegenstand*]; and 2) the affirmation of this relationship.

5. For a further discussion of the concept of *Sachverhalt,* cf. A. Reinach, "Zur Theorie des negativen Urteils" in *Gesammelte Schriften* (Halle, 1921) and A. Pfänder, ibid., pp. 147ff. and 184ff.

6. This is why Pfänder's assertion that the judgment projects [*entwirft*] the *Sachverhalt* is open to misinterpretation.

7. Aquinas, *De ente et essentia,* chap. I (ibid., p. 3).

8. Ibid.

9. Καθ' αὑτὰ δὲ εἶναι λέγεται ὅσαπερ σημαίνει τὰ σχήματα τῆσ χατηγορίας ὁσαχῶς γὰρ λέγεται, τοσαυταχῶς τὸ εἶναι σημαίνει (Aristotle, *Met.* Δ 7: 1017a, 22ff.)

10. *Substance* and *ousia* are linguistically unrelated to each other. The linguistic meaning of *substance* is close to the Greek ὑπόστασις. Cf. Gredt, ibid., vol. II, p 126f. and chap. VII, §1 for the scholastic usage of these terms and for the factual connection between substance and subsistence. For the use of the term *substance* in particular cf. pp. 191ff. below.

11. Cf. the third chapter of Aristotle's *Categories.*

12. For the meaning of this statement, cf. pp. 139ff. below.

13. Aristotle, *Met.* Ζ 1, 1028b, 2ff.

14. δαιμόνια: This word may refer either to the gods of the popular religion or to the celestial bodies.

15. Aristotle, *Met.* Δ 8, 1017b, 10-26.

16. In another passage the *objects of mathematics* and the *ideas* are discussed separately. Plato, too, could not make up his mind whether to put the two together or whether to interpret them as different kinds of being (cf. Aristotle, *Met.* Ζ 7, 1028b, 20ff.).

17. It should be noted that Aristotle, in developing the conception of the idea in the sense of *ousia,* does not mean to imply that this is his own interpretation. The reason for the obscurity of this passage is the ambiguity of the Aristotelian μορφή (form). It is on the one hand—like Plato's *eidos*—the actual object of knowledge and as such universal, eternal and immutable. But since Aristotle, unlike Plato, refuses to grant to the μορφή an independent being separate from things, he attributes to each and every thing its *own* μορφή and thereby marks each μορφή as an individual. Cf. Clemens Bäumker, *Das Problem der Materie in der griechischen Philosophie* (Münster, 1890), pp. 281ff. It is clear therefore that a distinction must be made between μορφή and *eidos,* between the inner form

and the essence, and also between the individual and universal nature, as we have done in the preceding chapter and as we shall continue to do in our future considerations.

18. The term χωριστή *ousia is* rendered in Latin by *substantia separata.* While the medieval thinkers associate this expression primarily with pure spirits, Aristotle has in mind the Platonic ideas.

19. *Met.* Z 2, 1028b, 8–32.

20. *Met.* Z 3, 1028b, 33ff; 1029a, 1–7.

21. This means that neither affirmative nor negative predications can be made of pure matter. It is completely undetermined in itself, and all determinations "follow" from the determination of the whole into the structure of which matter enters.

22. *Met.* Z 3, 1029a, 10–34.

23. Cf. pp. 134ff. and pp. 184ff. below.

24. According to the way the problem is presented in the doctrine of the categories, we may be in doubt whether our statement holds true also in the case of δευτέρα *ousia* (the *quid* or *whatness* of the thing). The whatness, to be sure, is predicated of the thing (e.g., *This* is a *human being*). But, without being *what* it is, the thing would be *nothing.* Therefore, it seems that the *what* is not that which "accrues to" or "falls to" the thing [*nichts "Zukommendes"*]. Aristotle himself maintains that the *what* is already a "substratum" [*ein "Zugrundeliegendes"*]. The possibility, on the other hand, of making some predication points to the potential separability of the *what* from whatever is "determined" by this *what* (cf. pp. 216f. below).

25. *Eidos* and ιδέα both belong to the linguistic stem that is found in the Latin word *videre* [to see]. The ideas are for Plato something that can be seen or visualized. The Latin term which is formed linguistically by analogy to *eidos* is *species* (from *spicere* = to behold).

26. *Met.* Z 3, 1029b, 3ff.

27. *Met.* Z 4, 1029b, 13ff.

28. Hering actually designates the nature or essence [*Wesen*] as τὸ τί ἦν εἶναι (ibid., p. 496.)

29. Definition in this sense must then be understood as the conceptual formula of the nature or essence and not as some "univocal determination" that merely serves to mark off one thing from another.

30. This is no doubt the way that Aristotle understood the τὸ τί ἦν εἶναι.

31. The term "*universal* essence" is a somewhat loose expression: All human beings possess *their* human being [*Menschsein*], but *qua* human beings they are "among others like unto them" [*seinesgleichen*], and that which is "alike" can be abstracted [*ist abhebbar*] as a *universal.*

32. Cf. Ueberweg-Heinze, *Geschichte der Philosophie,* vol. 1, §49, p. 251.

33. Understood in the sense in which we have determined this concept in chap. III, secs. 2 and 3.

34. Here, it seems, we recognize the difference between τὸ τί ἦν εἶναι and μορφή, which is an exclusive property of the individual thing. Speaking in Aristotelian terms, we should, however, have to admit that in the case of *pure forms* τὸ τί ἦν εἶναι and μορφή actually coincide. Nevertheless, the one term designates the essence insofar as it is comprehensible universally, while the other term designates something which is a property of the individual thing. And in the individual thing—if it be a compound of matter and form—the *what* and the form do not coincide (cf. pp. 321ff. below).

35. Heidegger, in *Kant und das Problem der Metaphysik* (Bonn, 1929, p. 231) interprets τὸ τί ἦν εἶναι as that which always was and still is [*was immer schon war*] and finds in it *the moment of enduring presence* [*das Moment der standigen Anwesenheit*]. Similarly, he interprets *ousia* as presence or as a being present (cf. *Sein und Zeit,* p. 25). He conceives of both terms as expressions of a "spontaneous and self-evident understanding of being on the basis of temporality." We ourselves, on the contrary, regard the understanding of being as the basis for the understanding of time (cf. chap. II, §3 and chap. III, §1). Nor are we able to find in the Aristotelian texts any support for the opposite view.

It is evident that Heidegger's entire analysis of the problem is determined by a definite preconceived idea of being. This preconceived idea is not simply that *pre-ontological understanding of being* [*Seinsverständnis*] which is part of the being of man [*menschlichen Sein*] and without which no inquiry into being is possible. Nor is it a question of that genuine ontology at which Heidegger himself ultimately aims, i.e., an inquiry which views being in its purity and as a whole in order to make it itself "speak" [*es selbst zum "Sprechen" zu bringen*]. Rather, everything is designed from the outset to demonstrate the temporality of being. This is why the horizon of the eternal is everywhere rigidly barred out. This is why no allowance is made for an *essence* [*Wesen*] distinct from *Dasein* [human existence], an essence which could be actualized in *Dasein.* There cannot and must not be a *meaning* [*Sinn*] distinct from the understanding, a meaning which could be grasped by the understanding. Nor must there be *eternal truths* independent of human knowledge. For if any of these were admitted, the closed circle of the temporality of being would be broken, and this must not happen no matter how much *Dasein,* understanding, and the process of "un-covering" ["*Entdecken*"] demand in the interest of their own elucidation that there be something that is timeless, independent, something which through them and with them enters into temporality.

If all such necessary frames of reference are arbitrarily excluded, the philosophic language assumes a peculiarly grim and contemptuous tone. For example, *eternal truths* are then described as pertaining to the "those residues of Christian theology within philosophical problematics which have not as yet been radically extruded" (cf. *Sein und Zeit,* pp. 229f.). What is conspicuous here is an anti-Christian resentment which, though generally restrained in its expression, is perhaps indicative of a continued struggle of the author with his own inherited Christian substance [*keineswegs erstorbene christliche Sein*].

The same bias is shown in Heidegger's treatment of medieval philosophy: It figures chiefly in brief marginal notes which suggest that there is hardly any need to make it the object of a serious philosophic analysis. Medieval thinking appears in Heidegger's view as a devious way of reasoning; it is said to have neglected or forgotten the genuine inquiry into the meaning of being.

Might it not have been worth the effort to ask whether perhaps in the speculation on the *analogia entis* the proper inquiry into the meaning of being remained alive? A careful consideration of the problem would also have shown that the Thomistic tradition understands *being* by no means in the sense of the "enduring constitution" (i.e., in the sense of "*Vorhandensein*" or *dingliches Beharren*) of the things of nature (cf. M. Beck, ed. *Philosophische Hefte,* vol. 1 [Berlin, 1928], p. 20).

Moreover, it is very peculiar when in the discussion of the concept of truth Heidegger badly presents the truth of judgment as practically the only meaning of truth that was elaborated by the Thomistic tradition, notwithstanding the fact that St. Thomas in the first of his *Quaestiones de veritate,* in his answer to the question, "What is truth?", distinguishes a fourfold meaning of truth and by no means regards the truth of judgment as primary (even though it is the "first" truth in the human perspective). When, following Hilary, St. Thomas designates the true as the *self-revelation and self-explication of being* (*De veritate,* q. 1, a 1, *corp. art.; Untersuchung über die Wahrheit,* I, 5), we are even reminded of Heidegger's own description of "truth as re-velation" or "truth as an un-covering" [*Wahrheit als Entdecktheit*]. And how could truth ever be legitimately termed an "existential" if not in the case of the first truth? For only God is "in truth," without any restriction or limitation, while the human mind, as Heidegger himself emphasizes, is simultaneously "in truth and untruth."

Most of the critics of *Sein und Zeit* have regarded it as their main task to demonstrate that Heidegger's philosophy has its roots in the thinking of the leading philosophers of the last four centuries (Kierkegaard, Nietzsche, Marx, Bergson, Dilthey, Simmel, Husserl, Scheler, etc.). (Cf. M. Beck, ed., *Philosophische Hefte* [July 1928] and A. Delp, *Tragische Existenz* [Freiburg i. Br., 1935].) It seems to have escaped their attention how strongly Heidegger's thinking was determined by his wrestling with Kant's philosophy. These ties are revealed in Heidegger's treatise on Kant. Hardly less significant, however, is the philosopher's constant preoccupation with the original problems of Greek philosophy and with the varied treatment these problems have received in the later history of philosophy. It would be rewarding to reexamine in a special investigation the relationship of Heidegger to Aristotle and the scholastics on the basis of his citations and interpretations. But this cannot be our task here.

36. Aristotle, *Met.*, Δ 26, 1023b, 26-32.

37. *Met.* Δ 28, 1024a, 29ff.

38. *Met.* Δ 28, 1024b, 1ff.

39. Ibid.

40. *Form* is used her in the sense of *empty form* [*Leerform*] (cf. pp. 205ff. below).

41. *Met.* Δ 28, 1024b, 10ff.

42. In this connection, Bäumker speaks of *conceptual matter* [*begriffliche Materie*] (op. cit., p. 293).

43. Aristotle, *Met.*, Δ 25, 1023b, 18f.

44. *Met.*, Δ 25, 1023b, 24.

45. The *contrary* was previously defined as that which is the most different of the things within a genus or that which differs in such a way that it cannot belong at the same time to the same subject (*Met.* Δ 10, 1018a, 28ff.).

46. *Met.* Δ 10, 1018b, 1ff.

47. *Met.* Z 4, 1030a, 10–14.

48. *Met.* Z 4, 1030a, 17ff.

49. Thus, for instance, we call "healthy" the human being who is in the state of health, the means which produce this state, and the symptoms by which this state is recognized. This presents an example of a common semantic basis in different meanings of the same word. (Many such instances occur in the writings of Aristotle and St. Thomas.)

50. These considerations refer to certain *ontological relations* between the *universal* and the *particular* corresponding to the *logical* relations which exist between the concept and that which is encompassed by its *ambit* [*Umfang*] and which constitutes the synthetic *content* [*Inhalt*]of the concept.

51. Heidegger, *Sein und Zeit,* 6th ed. (Tubingen, 1949) p. 7. Hedwig Conrad-Martius comments as follows on Heidegger's discussion of *Dasein:* "It is as if a door which had remained locked for ages and of which people had come to believe that it could never be opened, was—after long, careful and tenacious preparation—suddenly blown open with tremendous force and then immediately slammed shut, bolted, and so strongly barricaded that there seems no possibility of ever opening it again" ("Heidegger's *Sein und Zeit,*" in *Kunstwart,* 1933). "Heidegger," the same author continues, had "elaborated his conception of the human self with an inimitable philosophic energy and keen insight and therewith had in his hands the clue to an ontology which—by banishing all the specters of subjectivism. relativism, and idealism of the presently ending era

of philosophic thought—might have brought about a return to a genuine cosmology and the idea of a divinely informed universe." Heidegger is the thinker who, first and foremost, "reinstated being fully into its authentic rights," even if he did so only within the limited sphere of the self [*Ich*]. The *being of the self,* according to Heidegger, is determined by the fact that the self is *capable of understanding the nature of being* [*es versteht sich auf das Sein*]. With this approach, the way is cleared for arriving—unperturbed by the critical question of how the knowing ego can reach out beyond itself—at an exhaustive analysis of this understanding of being (which forms an integral part of human existence) and thus for a comprehension not only of the human being's own being but also of the being of the world and ultimately of that divine being in which all creaturely being has its ground. But what happens? The *Ich* is thrown back upon itself. To justify his starting out from an analysis of human *Dasein,* Heidegger states that only an existent [*ein Seiendes*] to whose nature belongs an understanding of being [*Seinsverstandnis*] can ask and answer the question concerning the meaning of being. And the inquiry must begin, he says, with the analysis of human *Dasein* because *Dasein is* capable of understanding not only its own being, but also other modes of being. But does not the very opposite follow from Heidegger's argument? The very fact that human beings are capable of understanding not only their own being but other modes of being as well suggests that human beings in their endeavor to explore the meaning of being do not have to rely on their own being exclusively. Doubtless, it is essential to pose the question relating to the understanding of one's own self [*das eigene Seinsverständnis*] and it is quite legitimate to start out with an analysis of one's own being. If this method is adopted, the roots of the understanding of being are revealed, and critical objections can be warded off from the outset. But this procedure by no means obviates the possibility of starting out from thingly existents or from the first existent. It is true that if this latter way is adopted, we will not obtain conclusive evidence concerning the nature of human existence, but merely certain indicative evidence, which must then be followed up. However, the converse is also true: The analysis of human existence likewise provides us only with a certain indicative evidence concerning other modes of being, and these other modes must then in turn be subjected to a "questioning" analysis if we are to arrive at an understanding. These other modes of being, to be sure, will not "answer" our questions in the way a human being would answer them. A thing has no *Seinsverständnis* and cannot engage in a discussion of the nature of its being. But the thing nevertheless *is* and has a *meaning* which "speaks" to us in and through its external appearance. And this kind of self revelation pertains to the meaning of all thingly being.

52. Cf. Hedwig Conrad-Martius, "Dasein, Substantialität, Seele." This treatise is available only in a French translation (cf. *Recherches Philosophiques,* Paris: 1932-1933). However, I had access to the German manuscript and was able to quote from it (cf. pp. 272ff. and n. 267 below).

53. In regard to what follows, see our discussion of universals in chap. II, §9.

54. When I say "*belongs* to that person's essence" rather than "*is* that person's essence," I thereby indicate in a preliminary fashion that I do not regard the being-human [*Menschsein*] as the complete essence of the individual human being, but only as a part of an individual's essence.

55. Cf. chap. III, secs. 6 and 8.

56. Cf. in chap. III, §10 the discussion of the relationship that exists between the *ideas* and the *Logos.*

57. When Aristotle states that the δευτέρα *ousia* (understood as genus or species) is not in the individual thing, this holds true of the *concepts* of genus and species as well as of genus and species as comprehensive wholes, but not of the *determinateness* of genus and species.

58. The distinction between τί and τί εἶναι—the what and the essence—is a significant one. There corresponds to it, on the one hand the effectuated distinction between genus and species, understood as universal *being,* and, on the other, the distinction between the *determinateness* of genus and species (cf. pp. 150f.).

59. Cf. Hering, op. cit., pp. 496f. and 504ff.

60. Cf. chap. III, §4.

61. In Aristotelian terms, not only the τί εἶναι (the being of the quid = whatness [*Was*-Sein]) but also—and perhaps even principally—the sheer *quid* [*Was*] (τί) is to be regarded as δευτέρα *ousia.*

62. Hering, op. cit., p. 496.

63. It is not necessary to discuss here the question of whether such an ultimate determinateness—i.e., one which goes beyond the specific determinateness—is also found on the level of infra-human structures (cf. chap. VIII, §2).

64. This does not necessarily mean that it can also be conceptually expressed.

65. This "everything" must, however, be understood *cum grano salis.* It remains for an investigation of human nature or essence to examine to what extent that which actually belongs to the being of human beings is truly *essential.* At this point we are interested only in the clarification of the concept of *form,* and we are using the form of the human being merely as an example which may aid us in this procedure. It seems legitimate in this context, therefore, to underscore somewhat heavily the element of unity in the concept of essentiality [*das Wesenhqfte*].

66. Cf. Homer's *Iliad,* can. 16, 19, 21.

67. "Unfolding" [*Sichauseinanderlegen*] and "fully disclosing itself" [*Sichvollaufschliessen*] are expressions which denote two different meanings of *Entfaltung* (cf. pp. 159ff.) A third meaning is conveyed by the term *Entfaltetsein,* i.e., the fully actualized unfolding (cf. pp. 160f.).

68. We are referring here only to pure spatial structures and tone sequences, not to the *symbolic values* which may be associated with them.

69. These two elements may, however, appear in separation from one another: An essential trait of character may be visible at a time when it is not disclosed in vital action (e.g., the trait of cruelty in a firmly set facial expression).

70. Here we come close to the meaning which modern philosophy and psychology associate with the term *act.*

71. According to what has been said before, it is clear that this constancy must not be understood as a "standing in time" but rather as a special kind of "being conserved" (cf. chap. II, §3).

72. Cf. Otto von Bismarck, *Gedanken und Erinnerungen* (Stuttgart: Volksausgabe, 1913), vol. II, pp. 62ff. [English edition, translated by A. J. Butler Smith (London: Elder, 1889).—Trans.]

73. Ibid., p. 67.

74. The essence reaches the height of being in being active [*im Tatigsein*] if (and to the extent that) it actualizes itself in time.

75. Homer, *Iliad,* can. 1.

76. Ibid., can. 8.

77. Ibid., can. 17.

78. Aristotle, *Met.* Z 7, 1032a, 12–25.

79. *Met.* Z 7, 1032a, 31; 1032b, 1–2. We recall that Aristotle designated as *ousia* in a preeminent sense not only the thing in its entirety but also its μορφή and ὕλη (cf. p. 132 above.)

80. If we define art (τέχνη; ars) in that broadest sense in which this term may be applied to every purposively planned "making," we are justified in calling artisans and physicians "artists."

81. Aristotle, *Met.* Z 7, 1032b, 11–14.

82. Ibid., 1032b, 31ff; 1033a, 1–5.

83. Ibid., 1033a, 21ff.

84. Here *eidos* does not mean *archetypal form* [*Urbild*], nor does μορφή denote *essential form* [*Wesensform*]. Rather, both terms refer to the visible spatial structure [*Raumgestalt*] and are therefore distinguished from τὸ τί ἦν εἶναι. It will become clear later on that in all material things *Wesensform* and *Raumgestalt* are closely related to one another.

85. Aristotle, *Met.* Z 8, 1033b, 5–13.

86. Ibid., 1033b, 16–20.

87. Ibid., 1033b, 31f.

88. Ibid., 1034a, 2–8.

89. What is meant here is the δευτέρα *ousia,* i.e., what the thing is.

90. *Ousia* ἐντελεχείᾳ *ousia* = πρώτη *ousia* = a thing of the same species.

91. Aristotle, *Met.* Z 8, 1034b, 14–19.

92. These are the questions which more than any others challenged the critical thinking of the medieval commentators on Aristotle—Arabs, Jews, and Christians alike.

93. Aristotle, *Met.* Z 1, 1042a, 27f.

94. Ibid., 1042b, 1–3.

95. The earlier Pre-Socratics saw in this prime matter, πρώτη ὕλη, the primordial ground [*Urgrund*] (ἀρχή; *principium* [*Prinzip*]) of all being. However, for most of them the *Urstoff* was a definite element and not—as for Aristotle—something wholly indefinite.

96. Bäumker, op. cit., p. 284.

97. Cf. Roland-Gosselin, op. cit., pp. 59ff. and 104ff.

98. Aquinas, *De ente et essentia,* p. 10. Cf. *In Boëthium de Trinitate,* q. 4, a 2.

99. Aristotle, *Met.* Z 4, 1044a, 28.

100. Ibid., 1044a, 31f.

101. *Met.* Z 2, 1043a, 4ff.; 1043b, 21ff.

102. This function is exercised by the demiurge in Plato's *Timaeus.*

103. Aristotle, "Dialog über Philosophie," *Hauptwerke,* ed. and trans. by Wilhelm Nestle (Leipzig, 1934), p. 27.

104. Ibid., p. 30.

105. Ibid.

106. Also significant in this respect is Aristotle's version of Plato's parable of the cave (cf. ibid., p. 32).

107. *Met.* Λ 7, 1072a, 21 ff.

108. The discussion of matter and form in Book H of Aristotle's *Metaphysics* is immediately followed by the discussion of potency and act in Book Θ.

109. *Met.,* Δ 12, 1019b, 22ff. and H 1, 1046a, 4ff.

110. *Ontological* ground is here opposed to *logical* ground: The "being" contained in it is distinguished from being merely intellectually conceived [*blosses Gedachtsein*]. It embraces *Dasein* as well as *what comes to be* [*Werden*] and *what comes to pass or happens* [*Geschehen*].

111. *Met.* Δ 11, 1019a, 19f.

112. *Met.* H 1, 1046a, 10f. Cf. also our discussion of act and potency in chap. 1, §1; chap. II, §1; chap. III, §8: and pp. 220f. below.

113. *Met.* H 1, 1046a, 23f.

114. G. Manser, O.P., *Das Wesen des Thomismus,* 2d ed. (Freiburg [Switzerland]: Paulus Verlag, 1935), pp. 601f.

115. When we speak of an "indefinite something" in everyday language, we do not refer to something which is in itself indefinite, but to something which *we* cannot define.

116 For our own attempt solution of this problem cf. pp, 193ff. and 264ff. below.

117. Manser, *Das Wesen des Thomismus,* 2d ed., p. 28.

118. How these two pairs of contraries are related to each other will have to be further examined.

119. As an aid to readers who are as yet unfamiliar with the *Metaphysics* of Aristotle, it may be well to mention that most of the references to these questions are found in Book Δ, which is largely devoted to the clarification of basic principles.

120. The spontaneous movement [*Eigenbewegung*] in a living being, for example, is distinguished from the falling motion or any other purely physical motion to which this being is subject.

121. Unfortunately, the manuscripts differ precisely in this particular wording. In the Paris manuscript (E) the μή (not) is omitted, and this omission completely changes the meaning of the entire passage. This version thus refers again exclusively to the products of art as exemplifications, so that "nature" would actually denote the "prime matter" out of which the things of nature come to be. A second version, on the other hand, designates as "natures" the natural materials which are given and which the creative work utilizes.

122. Here as well as in other passages Aristotle applies the term ὕλη (matter) and even the term πρώτη ὕλη (prime matter) not to what is indefinite, but to definite materials (e.g., bronze or water).

123. Both Aristotle and Plato explain the solubility of metals by saying that their primordial principle is water.

124. *Met.* Δ 4, 1014b, 16 to 1015a, 19.

125. The Greek term ἀρρύθμιστον means "that which lacks due order or proportion."

126. Aristotle, *De anima* B 4, 415a, 14ff. (quoted from Aristotle's *Hauptwerke,* ed. Nestle, pp. 156f.).

127. Ibid., p. 157.

128. Does *ousia* (substance) here signify the individual thing, τόδε τί, or—as it did in the previous passages—its form? As the immediately following discussion of the significance of nutrition shows, substance and form are in intimate touch with each other in living beings.

129. Ibid., pp. 157f.

130. The combination and separation of material elements follow the same laws that are observed in the chemical processes of external nature and can be expressed in the same formulas. The process of nutrition is nevertheless not a purely chemical process but rather a vital operation [*Lebensvorgang*]: What use the living

being makes of the received nourishment depends on this being's total constitution and disposition.

131. A work of art can be called "besouled" only in an analogical sense. The "idea" which is "alive in it" is not really alive. It is merely "loaned" to it.

132. We may disregard here the unique case of the first being in whom being and existence coincide, because in him the contraries of act and potency are likewise suspended.

133. Cf. Bäumker, op. cit., pp. 212f. and Aristotle, *Physics* I 8, 191a, 23 to 191b, 34.

134. Cf. Bäumker's critique of the Aristotelian concept of matter (op. cit., pp. 247ff.)

135. Ibid., p. 252.

136. Ibid., pp. 184ff.

137. Where *intellect* [*Geist* (mind, spirit)] and *matter* [*Stoff*] are contrasted with each other, matter is to be understood as what fills space [*raumfüllend*]. Later on we shall have to discuss the question of whether it is possible to speak of matter also in the realm of the spiritual (cf. chap. VII, secs. 5 and 6).

138. The following discussion is based on the investigation of *Materialitat* in H. Conrad-Martius's "Realontologie" (*Jahrbuch fur Philosophie und phänomenologische Forschung,* VI [Halle, 1923]), pp. 159–333. Page numbers refer to the special reprint of this treatise.

139. Ibid., p. 33.

140. "Material" *[stofflich]* is here to be understood in the sense in which we have been using this term, i.e., as a translation of the Aristotelian ὕλη = *materia.* But since H. Conrad-Martius in addition distinguishes between *matter* [*Materie*] and *material element* [*Stoff*], we shall, in presenting her line of argument, speak likewise of matter [*Materie*].

141. Ibid., p. 37.

142. Ibid., p. 42.

143. Ibid., p. 43. "Body" is not to be understood here in the narrow sense of a human or animal body. It. denotes—in the most general sense—the whatness [*Washeit*] which is effectually embodied in a real carrier [*Träger*]. In this sense we may speak also of a "spiritual body." A corporeal body denotes substantial plenitude in spatial form (cf. pp. 31ff.).

144. Ibid., p. 48.
145. Ibid., p. 51.
146. Ibid., p. 52.
147. Ibid., p. 56.
148. It should be pointed out that the terms *immanence* and *transcendence* are here not used in the sense in which Husserl uses them. Any relation to consciousness is lacking. *Immanence* here simply means self-possession, and *transcendence* denotes that which is "outside itself" [*ausser sich*].
149. Ibid., p. 60.
150. Ibid., p. 61.
151. Ibid., p. 63.
152. Ibid., p. 64.
153. Ibid., p. 67.
154. Ibid., p. 69.
155. Ibid., p. 71.
156. Ibid., p. 72.
157. Ibid., p. 73.
158. Ibid., p. 76.
159. Ibid., p. 80.
160. Ibid., p. 81.
161. Ibid., p. 82.
162. Ibid., p. 83.
163. Ibid., p. 84. While we accept as valid the unity of *Kraft* and *Stoff* as formulated by H. Conrad-Martius, we cannot admit that *Stoff* is an "effectual realization" [*Auswirkung*] of force.
164. Ibid., p. 87.
165. Ibid., p. 88.
166. This is not yet the place to enter upon a discussion of the difference between *mixtures* [*Mischungen*] and *combinations* [*Verbindungen*].
167. We shall have occasion to point out that a specific spatial limitation also pertains to the particular nature of the purely material (cf. pp. 217ff. below).
168. Cf. Aristotle, *Met.* Z 7, 1032a–b; and p. 173 above.
169. H. Conrad-Martius, "Realontologie," p. 90.
170. Ibid., p. 97.
171. Ibid., p. 98.
172. Ibid., p. 106.

173. We shall have to discuss later the way in which in these three modes, the basic forms and domains of actual being (i.e., corporeal being, the being of the soul, and spiritual being), are symbolically and analogically represented.

174. Ibid., p. 112.

175. Cf. Manser, *Das Wesen des Thomismus,* pp. 602, 610, 614.

176. Aquinas, *De anima,* a 9, ad 10.

177. Cf. chap. III, §3 above.

178. It should be pointed out that in logic mental structures are themselves made the "objects" of thought. There is formed a concept of the concept, a concept of the judgment, and a concept of the conclusion. Judgments are passed on concepts, on judgments, and on conclusions. Conclusions are drawn with respect to all of these mental structures. Logic thus "creates," in a certain sense, its own objects, but it does so on the basis of more primordial objects which as such logic cannot create.

179. A "mental structure" is itself a "form of being," because the mental as such has a being of its own—a "second-hand being." Thus we see that logic and formal ontology are interrelated in more than one way.

180. For a further discussion of the concept of *Sachverhalt,* cf. A. Reinach, *Zur Theorie des negativen Urteils* in *Gesammelte Schriften* (Halle, 1921), pp. 56ff., first published in the Lipps-Festschrift (Leipzig, 1911).

181. Cf. Aristotle, *Met.* Z 3, 1028b, 36ff. and pp. 142ff. above.

182. *Stoff* can be regarded as an *object* only when it is *formed matter,* i.e., a thing. Totally unformed prime matter [*Urstoff*] would not only be no object in the narrower sense but not even an object in the broader sense of a definite something.

183. But aside from this "so-called" colorlessness there is also a *genuine colorlessness* (e.g., the colorlessness of water, glass, etc.). It seems then that there exist colorless things and that color does not pertain irrevocably to the structure of the thing as such. This question, however, need not be further discussed here.

184. Cf. our discussion of Aristotle's definition of the genus (chap. IV, §§2 and 7).

185. Our investigation of the essential form will yield a further meaning of *carrier* (cf. chap. IV, §§4 and 5).

186. This theory of the origin of organic beings differs from that held by Aristotle. According to the Greek thinker, the seed already bears within itself the plastic form of the new organism (cf. *De generatione animalium,* II, 4.) This difference will be discussed in a later passage (cf. pp. 254ff. below).

187. This is also the view of St. Thomas concerning the unity of the essential form, as he expressed it so frequently and with such emphasis (e.g., in *De anima* a 9, *corp. art.).* The teaching of St. Thomas on matter and form will be discussed after we have brought our analysis of the Aristotelian doctrine to a satisfactory conclusion.

188. The possibility of such a transformation of the essence [*Wesenswandel*] was previously mentioned (cf. Chapt. III, §4).

189. In a particular case our knowledge may find it impossible to determine whether a change of essence occurs or whether one object is "annihilated" [*"zu nichts wird"*] and *another* object comes into being. The saying, that neither can something which is become nothing nor can something come from nothing, is valid only if we bar out divine omnipotence which can both "create" and "annihilate." Whether God actually uses his power to annihilate is a theological question which need not be discussed here.

190. The older atomistic doctrines attributed to atoms a definite spatial structure. From this point of view, the assumption that the form of the "smallest parts" determines the formation "of the whole" is conceivable.

191. Cf. chap. IV, §3, subsecs. 2, 3, 5, 18, and 20.

192. Cf. chap. IV, §3, subsec. 3.

193. Cf. Aristotle, *De generatione animalium,* II, 4.

194. Cf. Aristotle, *Met.* Z 8, 1033b.

195. Ibid., H 4, 1044a 36f. However, Aristotle used the term *eidos* rather than μορφή.

196. Ibid., H 8, 1049b 5.

197. Ibid., H 8, 1049b 6–12.

198. Ibid., H 8, 1050a, 7–10.

199. Aristotle here uses the expression *being-in-the-form,* which we previously understood as indicative of the meaning of nature or essence (cf. pp. 155f. above).

200. Aristotle, *Met.* Z 8, 1050a, 15f.

201. Ibid., 1050a, 21–23.

202. Ibid., 1050a, 24–28. The sentence, ὅμως οὐθὲν ἧττον ἔνθα μὲν τέλος ἔνθα δὲ μᾶλλον, τέλος τῆς δυνάμεώς ἐστιν, has been translated and interpreted in different ways.... [W.D. Ross translates: "...yet nonetheless the act is in the former case the end and in the latter more of an end than the potency is," in *The Basic Works of Aristotle,* ed. by Richard McKeon (New York: Random House, 1941), p. 830.—TRANS.]

203. *Met.* Z 8, 1050a, 28–38. It should be noted that in all these passages no distinction is made between *being* and *that which is* [*Sein und Seiendes*] nor between *operation* and *that which operates* [*Wirken und Wirkendes*] (cf. p. 257 below).

204. Cf. pp. 10f. above.

205. Aristotle, *Met.* H 8, 1034a, 2ff.

206. Ibid., A, 3ff.; Δ 2 (*Physics* II,3).

207. Cf. pp. 223ff. above.

208. Cf. chap. III, §4 (pp. 75–76 above).

209. Cf. chap. III, §12.

210. Cf. Aquinas, *De veritate,* q. 4, a 6 (*Untersuchungen über die Wahrheit,* I, 124f.).

211. Aquinas calls the being of these eternal archetypes "potential being" and yet "higher...than the actual being which things have in themselves, because the active potency is more perfect than the act which is its effect." See Aquinas, *De Veritate,* q. 4, a 9, ad 3 (*Untersuchungen über die Wahrheit,* I, 125).

212. Aristotle *Met.* Λ 7, 1072a, 21ff.

213. *Met.* Λ 10, 1075b, 35.

214. Ibid.

215. Ibid., 1072b, 2–3.

216. A. Lasson, *Aristoteles' Metaphysik,* p. 172.

217. In the case of structures on a higher level, the already formed matter is temporally prior to any further formation.

218. We need not think here of the verbal sounds themselves but rather of those meaningful structures which are expressed and conveyed by verbal sounds.

219. Cf. chap. VII, §5, subsec. 6, below.

220. Cf. chap. IV §3, subsec. 14, above.

221. In a theological perspective, this fall might be linked with the fallen state that is a consequence of original sin. The "fallen"

state of external nature is then a grandiose symbol of the fallen state of human beings. It should be added, however, that such an interpretation is not supported by any specific dogmatic declaration, although many Scriptural passages seem to point in that direction.

222. This law of measure differs in plants, animals, and humans.

223. Aristotle and many others assumed a "spontaneous generation" [*"Urzeugung"*], an essential impossibility.

224. H. Conrad-Martius, *Die "Seele" der Pflanze* (Breslau, 1934), p. 58. The above data concerning the life-like phenomena observed in the formation of crystals are taken from this book.

225. Aquinas, *Summa contra Gentiles,* II, 68: "We always find that the lowest stage of the higher genus touches on the highest stage of the lower genus...and this is why, according to blessed Dionysius (*De divinis nominibus,* chap. 7), *Divine wisdom links the lowest stage in the higher sphere of being with the highest stage in the lower order.*"

226. Cf. chap. III, §12.

227. Lamentations 4:1.

228. *Matter* in a second specific sense denotes that which as such is capable of being formed [*das Gestaltungsfähige*]. Spatial matter, too, is matter in this second sense of the term, but that which as such is capable of being formed need not necessarily be spatial.

229. H. Conrad-Martius, in her "Realontologie" and in her essay on "Colors" (cf. *Husserl Festschrift,* Halle, 1919) has attempted to disclose some such relationships. And the philosophic endeavors of Gertrud Kuznitzky are prompted by a similar intent. (Cf. "Naturerlebnis und Wirklichkeitsbewusstsein," [Breslau, 1919]; "Natur als reine Erscheinung," *Archiv fur die gesamte Psychologie,* 50 [1925] 3, 4; "Die Seinssymbolik des Schönen und die Kunst," [Berlin, 1932].)

230. H. Conrad-Martius, "Realontologie," p. 93.

231. Ibid., p. 94. In the sphere of purely material being, these three realms are symbolically represented by the three phases of the solid, the liquid, and the gaseous (p. 97).

232. The forming plant soul is contrasted with the sentient soul of the animal (cf. especially chap. II of *Die "Seele" der Pflanze*).

233. Ibid., p. 44.

234. The "plastic arts" imitate in their own particular ways this formative operation of the *living form* or *soul.*

235. In view of the union of form and matter as we found it constituted the term "composition" seems hardly appropriate.

236. Cf. Aquinas, *De ente et essentia,* ed. Roland-Gosselin, p. 5.

237. Ibid., p. 7.

238. St. Thomas's concept of prime matter is distinguished from that of Aristotle by the fact that the angelic doctor regards prime matter as created. He agrees with Aristotle, however, in conceiving of prime matter as being contained *in* corporeal things as a constitutive element that bears within itself the potentiality for all forms and that can therefore receive into itself different forms.

239. Aquinas, *De anima,* a 1.

240. Aquinas, *Summa contra Gentiles,* 2, 68.

241. The unity is "inseparable," inasmuch as matter cannot be without form, and form cannot be without some matter. "Inseparable" does not mean, however, that the possibility of a transformation is rigidly excluded.

242. We may refer here to what St. Thomas describes as the virtual preservation of the forms of elements, in combinations or in mixtures (cf. p. 203 above).

243. Aquinas, *Summa contra Gentiles,* 2, 68.

244. Even in the case of *pure forms,* St. Thomas distinguishes what these forms are from their being (cf. p. 32 above).

245. We are already familiar with the view of Aristotle which prompted him to equate form, act, and being (cf. pp. 222ff. above).

246. Cf. pp. 10f. above and pp. 277–278 below.

247. H. Conrad-Martius, *Die "Seele" der Pflanze,* p. 59.

248. Ibid., p. 115.

249. Ibid., p. 113.

250. Ibid.

251. Ibid.

252. Ibid., p. 73.

253. Ibid., p. 82.

254. Ibid., p. 70.

255. Ibid., p. 112.

256. This distinguishes the seed essentially from the dead material structures of crystals, which likewise attain to their specific form in a gradual process of formation. In the formation of crystals

a given matter is simply arranged in a specific order, but no *novum* is generated.

257. This attitude finds its expression in the Mosaic law in the prohibition placed on the consumption of blood, because blood is the carrier of life (Leviticus 17:10ff.).

258. H. Conrad-Martius, *Die "Seele" der Pflanze,* p. 70.

259. Ibid., p. 71. The life of the plant, as it is described here, appears to me as a perfect symbol of the idea of the timeless woman (i.e., the mother) as depicted by Gertrud von Le Fort in *Die Ewige Frau* (Munich, 1934), pp. 97ff.

260. Conrad-Martius, *Die "Seele" der Pflanze,* p. 78.

261. Ibid., p. 79.

262. Ibid., p. 80.

263. Regarding the "innocence" of flowers and blossoms, cf. ibid., p. 84.

264. H. André uses these terms in his own writings as well as in his introduction to *Die "Seele" der Pflanze* by H. Conrad-Martius (ibid., pp. 13f.).

265. Cf. chap. IV, secs. 4 and 5.

266. In the more recent German translations of the works of St. Thomas Aquinas the term *Selbstandwesen* [a nature or essence standing firmly in itself] has been adopted.

267. H. Conrad-Martius, "L'existence, la substantialité et l'âme," *Recherches Philosophiques* (Paris: Boivin & Cie, 1932–1933). This treatise is the introduction to H. Conrad-Martius's imposing ontology, the outlines of which are indicated in her study on the plant soul. "Existence" is there understood as "actual being" and is thus conceived in a narrower sense than in our investigation. And her distinction between "existence" and "essential being" correspondingly differs from the distinction we have made between "actual" and "essential" being. It seems to me that the essential being of H. Conrad-Martius comprises several elements which were clearly distinguished in the investigations of both this and the preceding chapter (cf. especially chap. IV, §5.)

268. We shall not at this time discuss the justification of such a claim with respect to mind or spirit, because we have not yet undertaken those investigations which may eventually provide a foundation for such a discussion (cf. chap. VII).

269. In the preceding discussions we have not made this qualification, but have used the term *soul* in the general sense of *living form.*

Chapter V

1. Cf. the tabular classification on pp. 152–153 above.

2. Cf. O. Becker, "Mathematische Existenz," *Jahrbuch für Philosophie und phänomenologische Forschung* (1927), p. 471, n. 2. Although in the preface to *Sein und Zeit* Heidegger states that his book aims at an elaboration of the "meaning of being" [*"Sinn des Seins"*], he does not say that this expression is to be understood as a translation of the Aristotelian term *ousia.*

3. Cf. p. 285 below, where this problem is further discussed.

4. Cf. chap. IV, §3, subsec. 15.

5. Cf. chap. IV, §3, subsec. 17.

6. For this reason it seems advisable to leave unanswered for the time being the question concerning higher essential forms and related questions concerning the nature of spirit.

7. This intellectual intuition is lodged in sense intuition as the species red is lodged in the distinct color of the individual thing. This observation seems necessary lest what has been said be misconstrued as favoring a doctrine of illumination or as an attack on the theory of abstraction.

8. This *intuitive understanding of empty forms* must be clearly set apart from the e*mpty (i.e., non-perceptual) understanding of words.* Such words may "mean" empty or filled forms. Husserl designates empty forms as *formal categories* (cf. *Ideen,* p. 21), and the corresponding intuition he calls categorial intuition (cf. *Logische Untersuchungen,* II, pp. 128f.).

9. Husserl demarcated the special field of format ontology in the first volume of *Logische Untersuchungen* (Leipzig, 1900; 2nd. ed., Halle, 1913); in the first section of *Ideen;* and in *Formalen und transzendentalen Logik* (Halle: Max Niemeyer, 1929).

10. Husserl even made formal ontology a part of logic. On the other hand, those who with Pfänder regard "thoughts" as the proper objects of logic will have to insist that ontology and logic are separate disciplines.

11. Thus, St. Thomas Aquinas understands *aliquid* (something) as *aliud quid* (another *quid*) that is contrasted with other *quids* (cf. *De veritate,* q. 1, a 1, *corp. art.;* and p. 277 above.) Gredt (op. cit., II, 12) distinguishes a threefold meaning of *aliquid:* (1) *aliquid* = *aliqua essentia* = any *quid;* (2) *aliquid* = *non nihil* (not nothing); (3) *aliquid* = *aliud quid.* Cf. pp. 289ff. below.

12. Cf. chap. IV, §1; *Met.* Δ 7, 1017a, 7.

13. Here again a twofold distinction is possible: First, we may have in mind that being which is affirmed in every judgment—the state-of-affairs [*Sachverhalt*] to which the truth of the judgment corresponds. Second, in the passage referred to, Aristotle speaks of still another special kind of being, which is contained in the content of certain judgments. He calls it "consequent" [*"mitfolgend"*] being, and by this he means the being that is attributed to an object in a predication which adds something to the concept of the subject, as is the case, for example, in the sentence, "The just man is liberally educated," or "This living creature is a human being." The being of the *Sachverhalt* and the corresponding truth of the judgment, which can be gathered from the "is," pertain to every judgment as such and are formally alike in all instances. On the other hand, the being that belongs to the content of the judgment and that is likewise expressed in the "is," is multiform. This being depends on and is related to the inner structure of the object of which something is predicated, the context of determinations of the object's how and what, and to the object's relation to other objects. And this kind of being is distinguished from the being of the categories (understood as the universal forms of existents) in that it is connected with the relations of the predications to their object and not with the corresponding forms as they are in themselves (cf. Aquinas, *In Met.,* I, 1, 9.)

14. Cf. pp. 285ff. below and chap. VII.

15. Cf. Aquinas, *De veritate,* q. 1, a 1, *corp. art.;* and Gredt, *Elementa,* II, 11ff.

16. I prefer not to render *res* as *thing* [*Ding*], because we have used this latter term to designate a definite form of existent, whereas what is meant here is something which applies to every existent.

17. Cf. Aquinas, *S.Th.* I, q. 5, a 4, ad 1; and Gredt, op. cit., pp. 28f.

18. From this *transcendental unity,* St. Thomas distinguishes *numerical unity* or unity as *number,* which as such belongs to the category of quantity.

19. Cf. pp. 290ff. below.

20. Cf. Gredt, op. cit., II, 1ff., n. 614.

21. Ibid., p. 4, n. 615.

22. Gredt, too, expresses himself to this effect (cf. ibid., p. 12, n. 623).

23. *Esse* = *existentia* = *id quo res existit seu quo est extra causas et extra nihilum* (cf. Gredt, ibid., p. 5, n. 616.)

24. Cf. the table on pp. 152–153 above.

25. Gredt calls *transcendentale* only the *ens* that signifies everything *actual.* On the other hand, that *ens* which relates to both the actual and the conceptual he calls *supertranscendentale* (op. cit., p. 7, n. 618).

26. Ibid., p. 4, n. 616.

27. Cf. chap. IV, secs. 3, 17, and 18 and the discussion of *aliquid* on pp. 289ff. below.

28. Gredt, op. cit., p. 5, n. 616.

29. Ibid., I, p. 222, n. 258.

30. Cf. the previously cited passage (pp. 32–33ff.) from *De ente et essentia.*

31. Gredt, op. cit., II, p. 11, nn. 621 ff.

32. Ibid., p. 14.

33. Ibid., nn. 626ff.

34. Strictly speaking, the meaning of *transcendentals* is threefold: *names (ens, unum,* etc.), corresponding *concepts,* and *objective reality* which is intellectually grasped by means of concepts, i.e., the formal structure of that which is. We shall see, however, that not all transcendentals allow of a purely formal interpretation (cf. pp. 291, 297f., and 317f. below).

35. To this oneness, Gredt (op. cit., n. 630) opposes *non-transcendental* oneness, i.e., oneness of the *quid* (in several respects).

36. Ibid., p. 18, n. 632.

37. Cf. pp. 282ff., above.

38. Cf. chap. V, n. 11, above.

39. What is meant here is, of course, not the soul as a basic form distinct from the spirit, but the *spiritual soul* as a knowing soul.

40. Cf. Aquinas, *De veritate,* q. 21, *corp. art.* (*Untersuchungen über die Wahrheit,* II, 175f.).

41. Ibid. (*Untersuchungen über die Wahrheit,* II, 170–171).

42. Cf. chap. VI.

43. We are speaking of "*Gehalt*" rather than "*Inhalt,*" because we are not dealing here with content in the sense in which we have been using this term. It is not a question of that *quid* of knowledge which distinguishes it from feeling and willing, or which distinguishes *this* knowledge from another knowledge regarding the same object, but it is a question of the intention or objective meaning of knowledge [*was es "meint," seinen "gegenständlichen Sinn"*]. It pertains to knowledge as such to have an *intention* (in the phenomenological sense), i.e., to tend toward an object. And all knowledge is determined in accordance with its respective object. Husserl distinguishes between "intentional content" and "real content" (cf. *Logische Untersuchungen,* II, pp. 397ff.).

44. The *intentio* belongs to the "real content" of knowledge.

45. Cf. Gredt, op. cit., p. 19, n. 634.

46. This kind of agreement will be discussed later on (cf. pp. 304f. below).

47. Cf. chap. III, §9.

48. Cf. chap. IV. §4, subsec. 2.

49. We mean that which pertains to the spirit in the strictest and most authentic sense of the term, i.e., to the *content* of the *personal* spirit [*Geist*].

50. However, this definition does not exhaust the full meaning of being.

51. If someone is said to have "sound judgment," what is meant is not some individual act, but the *faculty of judgment.* However, this meaning need not concern us here.

52. It is quite a different question to determine whether the *Sachverhalt* fits into the Aristotelian doctrine of categories and how the *Sachverhalt* is related to the πρώτη *ousia.* This problem must be discussed separately.

53. It is possible to conceive of logical truth more broadly than of the truth of judgment, so that the latter appears included in the former. This applies insofar as the act of judgment and the judgment itself as definitely formed intellectual structures presuppose

a certain kind of "knowledge" and as such a certain congruity with some existent—in our example, the sense perception of a green tree and the "meaning" of this perception.

54. This is the case where it is a question of a judgment based on actual experience [*Erfahrungsurteil*] and not a question of a judgment based, for example, on a sentence that is found in a story. In this latter case a different kind of being (in place of the real being) would be asserted.

55. Cf. chap. IV, §3, subsec. 2 (pp. 157f., above).

56. What we have stated regarding the work of art also applies to the activity of the craftsman and to scientific research.

57. Deviating from historical truth, the artist may invent occurrences which, though they have never taken place, are essentially possible and fitting to make intelligible the nature of Napoleon. The artist deviates much further from historical truth, however, when he or she depicts a Napoleon who does not correspond at all to the real person (and consequently not to Napoleon's *Urbild* either). The work may nonetheless show some measure of artistic truth if the character depicted by the artist has "authenticity," i.e., if the image corresponds to some essential possibility of the original character. However, it might be questioned whether in this case the artist has the right to call such an image "Napoleon," for if the artist uses this name, the artist thereby advances a certain claim and assumes an obligation to historical truth.

58. Distinct from this kind of logical truth is *the* logical truth which attaches to the knowledge of the connoisseur who later critically evaluates the work of art.

59. Cf. chap. III, §12 and chap. IV, §4, subsec. 3.

60. Cf. chap. IV, §4, subsec. 2.

61. Cf. G. Manser, *Das Wesen des Thomismus,* p. 168.

62. Ibid., p. 176.

63. A corresponding relationship exists between sensible things [*Sinnendinge*] and sense knowledge.

64. In the case of conscious striving, the end stands before the mind's eye of the striving agent, while in unconscious—instinctive or natural—striving the end may be envisaged by some knowing and understanding spectator.

65. As a *conscious* striving, it is *morally* good.

66. That which is not desired for its own sake is traditionally called a *bonum utile.*

67. Gredt, op. cit., II, 25.

68. In other respects the existent maybe bad or evil. We thus speak of an evil deed. And the existent may even be bad for the knowing human person if that person's good knowledge concerning an evil act becomes a temptation to sin.

69. This need not always be the striving being itself. In our example the striving of the physician is directed toward the health of the patient.

70. Cf. Aquinas, *De veritate,* q. 22, a 1, 3, and 4.

71. An insight into these matters may aid in the elaboration of the true meaning of a "relativity of values" (which has nothing to do with "subjectivity").

72. However, indirectly the known truth may also be a good for nonrational creatures. Insight into the nature of matter and of material elements may induce a people to give them a form which corresponds to their nature.

73. This consideration forms the basis of Max Scheler's material doctrine of value (cf. *Der Formalismus in der Ethik und die materiale Wertethik* [Halle, 1913]). The formal laws which permeate this sphere have been elaborated by Husserl in his lectures on *formale Axiologie und Praktik* in a strict parallelism to formal logic. Unfortunately, this significant piece of research has never been published.

74. Cf. Aristotle, *Met.* M 3, 1078a, 30ff. In this passage Aristotle refers to "another place" where he intends to treat more extensively of this problem. However, it is not clear what other place in his writings he may have had in mind.

75. Aristotle uses the terms "order," "harmony," and "due determinateness" or "limitation" (τάξις, συμμετρία, ὡπρισμένον) τοῦ δὲ χαλοῦ μέγιστα εἴδη. Rolfes (cf. op. cit., II, p. 112) translates: "The principal forms of the beautiful" [*die Hauptformen des Schönen*]. However, evidently this does not mean that there are different *species* [*Arten*] of the beautiful but rather that order, harmony, and due determinateness are to be understood as those basic traits of the existent which account for its being beautiful.

76. Aquinas, *S.Th.* I, q. 5, a 4, ad 1.

77. Even sensuous beauty can (*as beauty*) be only intellectually conceived. St. Thomas endorses this view when he emphasizes that

it is especially the higher ("spiritual" [*"geistig"*]) senses which are instrumental in making possible our access to the beautiful (ibid., I/II, q. 27, a 1, ad 3) and that only a human being but not an irrational animal, finds joy in beauty (ibid., I, q. 9 1, a 3, ad 3).

78. Wisdom 12:21. In this passage we read that the Egyptians were punished strictly in accordance with the measure of their sins. This order of divine justice, however, is traced back to the universal order of the created world.

79. Cf. Aquinas, *De veritate,* q. 21, a 6.

80. In the passage referred to in the previous note, St. Thomas means by "order" those mutual relations among creatures by which one creature becomes for the others that which imparts perfection and thus a good.

81. It is equally impossible to discuss here the related problems of Kant's aesthetics as expounded in the *Critique of Judgment,* or those of the modern aesthetics of empathy [*Einfühlungsästhetik*] as it was developed by Th. Lipps.

82. Cf. Aquinas, *De veritate,* q. 22, a 1, ad 12.

83. Aquinas, *S.Th.* I, q. 39, a 8, *corp. art.*

84. When we add that the existent is duly ordered, this means that it occupies its apportioned place in the total context of existents.

85. Aquinas, *S.Th.* I, q. 39, a 8, *corp. art.* Inasmuch as every created thing is an image of a divine *Urbild,* due measure coincides with essential truth [*Wesenswahrheit*].

86. Ibid., II/II, q. 145, a 2, *corp. art.*

87. Cf. Aquinas, *In Psalmum,* 23.

88. Cf. Aquinas, *In Dionysium de divinis nominibus,* chap. 4, lect. 5. Regarding the views of St. Thomas on the nature of the beautiful, cf. Martin Grabmann, *Die Kulturphilosophie des hl. Thomas von Aquin* (Augsburg, 1925), chap. V, pp. 148ff.

89. I John 1:5.

Chapter VI

1. Cf. the table on pp. 152–153 above.

2. In this being manifest or being intelligible we recognized the authentic meaning of transcendental truth.

3. Cf. the supplementary discussion of *conceptual structures* on pp. 329f. below.

4. The question of whether a plurality of finite intellects is required need not concern us in this context, nor need we consider the infinite spirit at this time.

5. However, we shall have to examine what occurs when we think of something "nonsensical" [*"unsinnig"*] or "absurd" [*"widersinnig"*].

6. Cf. the critical appraisal of Hilbert's formalism in O. Becker's essay on "Mathematische Existenz," *Jahrbuch für Philosophie und phänomenologische Forschung* 8 (1927): 441ff. and 472ff).

7. Aristotle, *Met.* Γ 2, 1003a, 33f.

8. Ibid., 1003b, 5f.

9. Aquinas, *In Met.* I, 1, lect. 4.

10. Aquinas, *De veritate,* q. 2, a 11, *corp. art.* (*Untersuchungen über die Wahrheit,* I, 74f.)

11. Ibid.

12. Ibid., q. 2, a 11, ad 4 (I, 76).

13. Gredt, op. cit., II, 7 (n. 618, 2).

14. The distinction between essence as whatness [*Was*-sein] and essence as pure quid [*Was*] (to which we referred in chap. III, §3, subsec. 4) is not found in St. Thomas. His *essentia* comprises both. To be sure, aside from *essentia,* St. Thomas uses the term *quidditas* (whatness [*Washeit*]), but without distinguishing clearly between these two terms.

15. Aquinas, *S.Th.* I, q. 3, a 4, *corp. art.*

16. This is stated in the second argument of St. Thomas, in the same place.

17. Ibid.

18. Cf. chap. VIII, §2.

19. Following St. Thomas, by pure forms we mean here pure spirits (e.g., the angels) and not, as we did in previous passages, essences as archetypes [*Urbilder*] of things.

20. Cf. chap. II, §1 above.

21. Aquinas, *S.Th.* I, q. 50, a 2, ad 3.

22. Exodus 3:14. The Hebrew words, *Ah'jäh, aschér äh'jäh,* have been translated and interpreted in a number of ways: I am who I am; I shall be who shall be; I shall be who I am. We follow the above-mentioned Augustinian version, according to which God enunciates in the "I am" his own name in the strictest and truest sense [*eigentlichst*] (cf. pp. 59–60 above).

23. Concerning the being of the I [*Ich*], cf. chap. II, §§6 and 7.

24. This is the way Thomism understands *individuality.*

25. It seems to me that Leibniz's "monad" shows some of this peculiar characteristic.

26. Cf. chap. II, secs. 6 and 7.

27. "Willst du dich selber erkennen, so sieh, wie die andern es trieben."

28. We have previously alluded to the difficulty involved in the attempt to reconcile the unity of the divine being with the trinity of the divine Persons (cf. n. 105 in chap. III, above).

29. Cf. chap. VII, §6ff.

30. Cf. chap. III, §10, especially the cited scriptural passages from John 1:1ff. and Colossians 1:17.

Chapter VII

1. St. Thomas Aquinas makes a distinction between *vestige* [*Spur*] and *image* [*Abbild*]. He speaks of *vestigium* [*Spur*] where merely the *causality* of the cause can be inferred from the effect (as fire may be inferred from the phenomenon of smoke), and he speaks of *imago* [*Abbild*] only where we find in the effect a *representation* of the cause by an analogous form (as the statue of Mercury represents Mercury). Like St. Augustine, St. Thomas sees a *vestigium* of the Trinity in the entire created world, but an *imago* only in rational creatures, i.e., in creatures endowed with reason and [free] will (*S.Th.* I, q. 45, a 7). It seems to us, however, that there is also a certain image quality where St. Thomas sees merely a *vestigium* of the Trinity, and we are therefore using the term "image" exclusively (cf. §6ff. below).

2. Cf. Minge, *Pat. Lat.* 42.

3. Ibid., I, 4.

4. Ibid., II, 9.

5. Ibid., V, 2ff.

6. Generally speaking, it is quite possible to call each of the divine Persons "Father" in relation to all the "children of God." And one might also call each of the divine Persons "Holy Spirit," because each of them is both spirit and holy. But only the second person can be called "Son," and only the third person can be called "Gift" (cf. ibid., V, 11).

7. Ibid. IV, 8.

8. Ibid., V, 9.

9. Cf. Aquinas, *S.Th.* I, q 29, a 1, 1.
10. Cf. Augustine, *De Trinitate,* VI, 7.
11. Ibid., VI, 8.
12. Aquinas, *S.Th.,* I, q. 29, a 3, *corp. art.*
13. Cf. chap. VI, §4, subsec. 4.
14. Aquinas, *S.Th.,* q. 29, a 3, ad 2.
15. In accordance with our strict distinction between existent [*Seiendes*] and being [*Sein*], we should prefer the term "subsistent" (*subsistens*).
16. Aquinas, *S.Th.,* I, q. 29, a 2, *corp. art.*
17. St. Thomas points out, however, that the Greek thinkers customarily also used *hypostasis* in this narrower sense (ibid., a 2, ad 1).
18. St. Thomas mentions this objection in ibid., q. 29, a 3, 3.
19. Cf. chap. IV, §3, subsec. 20 and §4, subsec. 8.
20. Cf. H. Conrad-Martius, "Realontologie," pp. 94ff.
21. Cf. chap. VII, §4, below.
22. Cf. this chapter, §3.
23. We have discussed these darknesses insofar as they relate to the immediate comprehension of the ego life. The lacunae and defects in the knowledge of objects which lie beyond the sphere of the ego [*ich-fremde Gegenstände*] need not concern us here.
24. Origin and end remain inaccessible as long as we rely on that consciousness which pertains to life itself and do not accept the aid of experiences not our own, of intellectual judgments and inferences, or of the truths of faith-aids which the pure intellect does not require for self-knowledge.
25. Beyond both lies the way into the "higher" beyond of divine being.
26. My body is part of my personality not *only* in this capacity, but for the time being we confine our analysis to this particular aspect.
27. The separation of body and soul in death is the scission [*Durchschneidung*] of a natural unity and does not destroy the intimate interconnection between the two, although both suffer a certain diminution of their nature.
28. *Form* understood in the Aristotelian-scholastic sense, not in the sense of *empty form.* Cf. chap. IV above, especially the summary in §5.

29. Cf. chap. IV, §5, subsec. 1, above.
30. Cf. chap. IV, §5, subsec. 2, above.
31. Cf. chap. IV, §4, subsec. 2 and §5, subsecs. 2 above.
32. Cf. chap. IV, §5, subsec. 2 above.
33. Cf. "The Interior Castle," in *The Collected Works of St. Teresa of Avila,* trans. Kieran Kavanaugh and Otilio Rodriguez, vol. 2 (Washington, D.C.: ICS Publications, 1980). In depicting the "castle of the soul" as the "house of God," our holy mother Teresa is merely attempting to elucidate her own spiritual experiences. Calling the soul back from its forlornness in the external world, our Lord draws it ever closer to himself, until he can at last unite it to himself in the soul's very own center. St. Teresa was not interested in the question of whether the structure of the soul, aside from being the abode of God, has an independent meaning of its own and whether there is perhaps another entrance "portal" to the soul's inwardness besides contemplative prayer. However, both of these questions must be answered affirmatively.
34. Cf. A. Pfänder, *Die Seele des Menschen* (Halle: Max Niemeyer, 1933): "The soul subject has a *definite location* within its *consciously* experienced environment. On the one hand it is in a certain sense the center of its own soul and of its own soul life. On the other hand, it is located behind the eyes, roughly in the center of the head.... The subject comes closer and closer to itself by moving from the other parts of its own body back to this center of the head. From this central point the soul subject orients itself in its own body and in the consciously experienced body environment. Instinctively, therefore, other human beings (and also some animals) turn their gaze toward this place in the head behind the eyes whenever they want to turn their attention to this soul subject" (p. 20).
35. The two do not coincide, since the apperception of the body is included in self-apperception and since access to the body may also be gained by means of external apperception—by means of expressive bodily phenomena—and since, by way of the body, external access may also be gained to the soul.
36. This fortunate description is from D. Feuling, O.S.B. "Das Kartenlesen," in *Benediktinische Monatsschrift* XVII (1935, 9/10): 393.
37. Cf. our previous discussion of the dual meaning of *matter* as that which fills space and as that which permits of further formation.

38. We shall have occasion to speak more at length about this non-spatial materiality (cf. §§5 and 6).

39. Cf. the German *Thomas-Ausgabe,* vol. IV: *Schöpfung und Engelwelt* (Anton Pustet: Salzburg, 1936), pp. 499 and 559.

40. Cf. Aquinas, *S.Th.* I, q. 50, a 1.

41. Ibid., q. 50, a 1. *corp. art.*

42. Cf. Aquinas, *Summa contra Gentiles,* II, 91 (in the German edition, *Summe wider die Heiden* [Leipzig, 1935], II, 398ff.)

43. The writings which are traditionally linked with the name of Dionysius the Areopagite are found in Minge, *Pat. Graec.* vols. III/IV. They include "On the Celestial Hierarchy," "On the Ecclesiastical Hierarchy, "On the Divine Names," "On Mystical Theology," and ten epistles. These writings, forming a unified whole, exerted a decisive influence on medieval theology and mysticism, an influence which is effective even today. The author mentions in addition several works which are no longer extant, especially the "Theological Instructions," which contained his doctrine of the Holy Trinity. He calls himself Dionysius and mentions as his teachers and masters Hierotheus. a disciple of St. Paul, as well as St. Paul himself. For this reason his medieval commentators (St. Albert the Great, St. Thomas Aquinas, and others) identified Dionysius with the so-called Areopagite. Prominent scholars of the sixteenth and seventeenth centuries (Baronius, Bellarmine, Baltasar Corderius, S.J., editor and translator of the Dionysian writings) concurred in this opinion and defended their stand against the critical objections of the humanists. The most recent research has arrived at the conclusion that the Dionysian writings did not originate before about 500 A.D. (Cf. especially the contributions of J. Stiglmayer, S.J. and H. Koch, listed in the article on "Dionysius the Areopagite" in *Lexikon für Theologie und Kirche,* edited by Buchberger, vol. III [Freiburg im Breisgau, 1931], pp. 334f.) Although it is not possible for me to present any conclusive argument concerning this question, I may be permitted to say this much. The writings of the Areopagite are an overwhelming hymnic praise of the greatness and love of God, and they are permeated and impregnated even in the minute details of verbal expression with the spirit of devout and pious reverence. I therefore find it impossible to attribute to the author of these writings any willful imposture. If any imposture actually occurred, we may

perhaps surmise that other authors, in using the works of Dionysius—the *Monophysites,* according to Stiglmayer, used the authority of the Areopagite to defend their own position—may have found it opportune to interpolate certain passages which specifically refer to the authorship of Dionysius the Areopagite. In Dionysius, then, we venerate an unknown saint as well as one of the most influential—if not *the* most influential—among the Greek fathers. Stiglmayer suggests that the name "Dionysius" may be a pseudonym of Patriarch Severus of Antioch, who was a Monophysite. It is impossible for me at this time to consider the arguments which may be advanced for and against such an opinion.

44. It need hardly be stated explicitly that we do not place revelation on the same level with that natural experience which—in our example of the travel guidebook—is gained by others and is then substituted for personal experience. Since in our present inquiry we are not interested in experimental or experiential scientific verifications, it does not greatly matter from what source we draw our descriptive outline, as long as our description represents a genuine essential possibility.

45. "The rivers return to the place from which they emanate, so that they may stream forth again" (cf. Albert the Great, *Opera omnia,* vol. XIV, Borgnet edition [Paris, 1982], p. 1).

46. "Anger"—*ira,* θυμός—is here to be understood in that broad sense in which this term is used in scholastic psychology, denoting a passionate opposition to something that curbs desire (cf. Aquinas, *De veritate,* q. 25, a 2ff.; q. 26, a 4–5; *Untersuchungen über die Wahrheit,* II: 343ff., 379ff.).

47. Cf. Dionysius, *On the Celestial Hierarchy,* II, §4 (Minge, PG 3, 141C–144A).

48. Ibid., III, §1 (Minge, PG 3, 165D). Today the concept of hierarchy, as it is commonly understood, has been narrowed down, so that it designates merely the graduated order of ecclesiastical ranks and functions. The concept has become static, while Dionysius uses it in a prevalently *dynamic* sense. It encompasses that divine *life* which permeates all ranks and "estates" [*Stande*] of a sacred order which embraces and links heaven and earth.

49. Ibid., III, §2 (PG 3, 166A–C).

50. Ibid., VII, §4 (PG 3, 212A–D).

51. Ibid., IV, §2 (PG. 3, 180A–B).
52. Ibid., V (PG 3, 196B).
53. Ibid., VII, §2, 3 (PG 3, 208B–210A).
54. Ibid., VII, §4 (PG 3, 210D–212A).
55. Ibid., VII, §1 (PG 3, 206B–D).
56. Ibid., VIII, §1 (PG 3, 237B–240B).
57. Ibid., IX, §1 (PG 3, 258B).
58. Ibid., XI, §1 (PG 3, 284B-C).
59. Ibid., XV, §2 (PG 3, 328C–329C). In reading and interpreting this passage, we must keep in mind that the ancients regarded fire as an element. This view need not be refuted here because in our context we are not so much concerned with a scientifically correct definition of fire as with the symbolic value and signification of the *phenomenon* of fire.
60. Ibid., XV, §3 (PG 3, 329C–332C).
61. Ibid., XIII, §4 (PG 3, 304D–305A).
62. Ibid., XV, §3 (PG 3, 329C–332C).
63. Ibid., XV, §6 (PG 3, 333C–336A).
64. Cf. Aquinas, *S.Th.* I, q. 50ff.
65. Aquinas, *S.Th.* I, q. 50, a 4.
66. Cf. Aquinas, *De veritate,* q. 8, a 12, ad 4 (*Untersuchungen über die Wahrheit,* I: 228). Among the endowments which God bestows upon angels—over and above their nature—St. Thomas mentions the vision of the divine essence, a vision of which no creature is capable by its own nature (cf. Ibid., q. 8, a 3, *corp. art.; Untersuchungen über die Wahrheit,* I: 201f.).
67. Cf. Aquinas, *S.Th.* III, q. 62, a 1, *corp. art.* The life of grace and the life of glory are both an imparting of divine being to creatures. According to theological doctrine, they differ in that grace is given as a preparation for glory. Glory is the reward for the creature's free cooperation with grace, and it is given to the creature as a definitive possession. The beatific vision of God which the citizens of heaven enjoy is reserved to glory, whereas grace leaves "earthly pilgrims" in the darkness of faith.
68. The Holy Eucharist differs in this respect from the other sacraments, since in the case of the Holy Eucharist *dead* matter is transformed into the living body of Christ, which forms part of the unity of the person.

69. The new [spiritual] birth of new-born children does not contradict this statement. The call of God's grace is addressed to all souls, and in the rite of baptism the church accepts the profession of faith from a person who acts as a proxy for those souls who cannot yet answer for themselves. But while God unites to himself the immature soul on the basis of a profession of faith by proxy, whether or not union with God endures depends on this soul's future personal decision.

70. Cf. Dionysius, *De divinis nominibus,* chap. 4, §23 (PG 3, 724B–725C) and Aquinas, *S.Th.* I, q. 64, a 1, *corp. art.*

71. Cf. Aquinas, *De veritate,* q. 9, a 4, *corp. art.* (*Untersuchungen über die Wahrheit,* I: 253f.).

72. *De Veritate,* q. 8, a 16f. (*Untersuchungen über die Wahrheit,* I: 237ff.).

73. Cf. Aquinas, *De spiritualibus creaturis,* especially a 5, ad 8.

74. The following exposition is based on the *Quaestiones disputatae de rerum principio,* edited by Marianus Fernandes Garcia, O.F.M. (Quaracchi, 1910), q. 708. The authenticity of this work is regarded as certain by Ephrem Longpré. (Cf. the article "Stand der Skotusforschung 1933" in the Franciscan review *Wissenschaft und Weisheit* I, 1 [1934]: 67.)

75. *Quanto forma* actualior, *tanto* magis se intimat *materiae, et unit eam sibi: sed forma Angeli et animae rationalis sunt* actualissimae; *ergo omnino se uniunt materiam, ac per hoc nec in* quantitatem *prorumpunt, quia virtutis* unitivae *sunt; nec habent aliquam formam corporalem...* (Dun Scotus, *De rerum principio,* q. 7, a 2, n. 215 [Quaracchi, 1910], p. 137.)

76. Cf. chap. IV, §3, subsec. 18.

77. Even the *eternal* law, i.e., a law which is and remains law independent of any positive (or arbitrary) legal enactment, must be "posited" in order to become an obligatory rule and order of life in any actually existing state or statelike structure.

78. Cf. Edith Stein, "Eine Untersuchung über den Staat" in *Jahrbuch für Philosophie und phänomenologische Forschung,* 7 (1925), translation forthcoming from ICS Publications.

79. The fact that the same persons simultaneously have *legislative power* (in the name of God) and *executive power* presents no difficulty. In the government of states, too, such a combination of powers in one and the same person is not uncommon.

80. The term "expression" is here used in that very broad sense which includes linguistic expression as well as any other kind of either voluntary or involuntary external manifestations.

81. From the point of view of theology, it may perhaps be doubted whether the part played by angels in mediating between God and human beings can be reconciled with the position of Christ as king of all creation and with the position of Mary as queen of the angels and mediatrix of all graces. It cannot be denied that Dionysius has but little to say about the humanity of Christ. The most significant passages (which might also be adduced as arguments against any Monophysite interpretation) are found in the *Ecclesiastical Hierarchy.* And he refers to the Mother of God only once and in a context of minor relevance. It seems to me, however, that the Dionysian angelology does not actually jeopardize the royal dignity of the God-Man and his mother. It is quite conceivable that the savior in his own human life was strengthened by grace by the mediating ministration of angels (cf., e.g., Mt 4:11 and Lk 22:43), although in his ascension he rose, above and beyond all the angels, to the throne of God. Is it not the deepest meaning of this "ascending" (of Christ and Mary) that they were filled with an abundance of divine life which surpassed by far the measure of grace allotted to all other creatures? And when we see Christian art portraying Christ and Mary carried aloft by angels, does not this ministration signify that the celestial spirits impart to them the bountifulness of the divine life which the angels themselves have received, up to the time when Christ and Mary, risen above all the angels, could now in their turn give from their plenitude to the entire church, to angels, and to human beings?

82. Cf. chap. III, secs. 2 and 12; chap. VI, §4, subsec. 6, above.

83. *Secunda Persona Sanctissimae Trinitatis appellatur* Verbum Patris, *quia a Patre procedit secundum actum intellectus, ut conceptus mentis, sicut etiam in nobis interior mentis conceptus* verbum *dicitur* (*Catechismus Catholicus,* 11th ed. pro adultis [Rome, 1933], chap. III, 86, p. 112).

84. *In sacris Litteris appellatio* Spiritus Sancti *tertiae Sanctissimae Trinitatis Personae reservari solet, quia ipsa a Patre per Filium unica spiratione procedit per modum amoris, et est primus summusque Amor, qui animos movet agitque ad sanctitatem, quae demum amore in Deum continetur* (ibid., chap. III, q. 119, pp. 12–13).

85. Cf. chap. VI, §5 above.

86. Cf. Duns Scotus, *Quaestiones disputatae de rerum principio,* q. 4, §6.

87. Cf. Augustine, *De Trinitate* XV, 17ff.

88. We speak here of an "image" and not, like St. Thomas, of a mere "vestige," because we find in creaturely autonomy of being [*Seinsselbständigkeit*] and in creaturely fullness of meaning and life a genuine likeness [*Abbildlichkeit*] of divine autonomy and plenitude of meaning and life, not a mere sign or trace of the authorship of the triune God (cf. chap. VII, n. 1, above).

89. The habituation of the child is not identical with animal training because the soul life of the child is a preliminary stage of a personally formed intellectual and spiritual life, and the initial stage contains the possibility of passing over into the higher stage.

90. The one exception is that perversion of the essence or nature that followed upon the singular decision of the fallen angels.

91. Our holy mother Teresa remarks that it is truly a strange and even a pathological state of mind which prevents people from knowing or recognizing their own houses. And yet it is a fact that many souls are "so sick and so used to busying themselves with external things...that they find it impossible to enter into their own inner being." As a consequence, they have forgotten how to pray. The *first mansion,* therefore, into which one enters through the portal of prayer is *self-knowledge.* The knowledge of God and the knowledge of self mutually support one another. Through self-knowledge we come nearer to God, and this is why self-knowledge remains indispensable, even after we have arrived at the innermost mansions of the soul. On the other hand, "We shall...never attain to perfect self-knowledge unless we strive at the same time for a deeper knowledge of God."

92. We pointed out before that by virtue of the interconnection existing between ego, soul, and body, the body is also included in the self.

93. The question of whether such an *objectification* is possible as long as the joyous emotion is alive or only after it has subsided need not be discussed in this context.

94. There is, on the other hand, a way of "co-experiencing" the life of others [*"mitzuleben"*], and this mode of knowing is more closely

related to primordial, personal life than a mere observing from without. Knowing of one's self and knowing others intertwine in a peculiar manner and mutually condition each other. There is no need, however, of discussing this problem any further in our present context.

95. "Essence" is here again understood as individual essence, as that which pertains to this particular person, making that person what he or she is.

96. A more detailed discussion of these powers is one of the tasks of *systematic psychology* [*Seelenlehre*]. The importance of this task was realized by older *metaphysical psychology,* while *empirical psychology* of the nineteenth century neglected this aspect in favor of a one-sided consideration of the conscious life of the soul. In A. Pfänder's *Die Seele des Menschen: Versuch einer verstehenden Psychologie* (Halle, 1933) we find a vigorous attempt to elucidate the structure and life of the soul by relating them to the soul essence.

97. In the Thomistic view, the memory is not regarded as an independent basic power or faculty in addition to reason and will, but is (as sensory and intellectual memory) proportioned to the lower and higher cognitive faculty. As a matter of fact, without the work of the memory, no knowledge would be possible. On the other hand, we find in the writings of our holy mother Teresa and of our father, St. John of the Cross, the Augustinian (*De Trinitate* X) trichotomy of reason, memory, and will.

98. This happened, for example, in the *sentimentalism* of the eighteenth and in the romanticism of the early nineteenth centuries. The anti-intellectualism of the present age is primarily a reaction against neo-Kantian rationalism.

99. St. Thomas regards it as a special endowment of higher spirits that—as compared with lower ones—they embrace more with one single glance and thus have greater power of *synthetic vision* (cf. *De veritate,* q 8, a 10; *S.Th.* I, q 55, a 3. He explains this by pointing out that their *forms of cognition* are more universal. However, it appears certain that for such a synthetic vision there is also required greater power of the intellect, a power which enables these spirits to actually penetrate into everything that is within their intellectual reach.

100. The German novelist, Marie von Ebner-Eschenbach. once stated that true education [*Bildung*] is what remains after we have

forgotten everything we have learned. By this she evidently means that which has become flesh and blood.

101. Cf. A. Pfänder, *Motive und Motivation* (Münchener Philosophische Abhandlungen, Lipps-Festschrift [Leipzig, 1911], pp. 163ff.) and Edith Stein, *Philosophy of Psychology and the Humanities,* trans. Mary Catharine Baseheart and Marianne Sawicki (Washington, D.C.: ICS Publications, 2000), pp. 39ff.

102. Augustine, *In Io.* 15, 25.

103. Augustine, *Soliloquia,* II, 6, 9.

104. Such a detachment from the world and the self, however, will be meaningful and fruitful only under the guidance of grace and within the limits prescribed by grace.

105. Cf. *The Collected Works of St. John of the Cross,* trans. Kieran Kavanaugh and Otilio Rodriguez, rev. ed. (Washington, D.C.: ICS Publications, 1991).

106. This does not mean that each and every demand made upon us—even if it is right and just in itself—is obligatory in this manner. All *ultra posse nemo obligatur* [nobody is obliged to do things that are beyond the person's power] is certainly valid with respect to human demands, whereby the *posse* is determined according to the measure of a person's natural power.

107. St. Jerome says concerning the command to love one's enemies: *Multi praecepta Dei imbecillitate sua, non Sanctorum viribus aestimantes, putant esse impossibilia quae praecepta sunt.... Sciendum est ergo, Christum non impossibilia praecipere, sed perfecta* (Many measure the commandments of God by their own weakness rather than by the strength of the saints, and they therefore believe that it is impossible to fulfill that which has been commanded.... But we must remember that Christ does not demand the impossible, but that which is perfect.) Cf. *Commentary on Matthew 5 and 6,* bk 1; *Roman Breviary,* Feria VI *post Cineres.*

108. Cf. Augustine, *De Trinitate,* VII, 10; IX, 2.

109. Ibid., IX, 1–5, 10, 12.

110. Ibid., X; XII, 4; XIII; XIV.

111. Ibid., IX, 1–5.

112. Ibid., IX, 10–12.

113. Ibid., I, 1–4.

114. Ibid., X, 8–12.

115. Theodor Haecker, *Schöpfer und Schöpfung* (Leipzig, 1934), p. 145.

116. Could it have escaped Haecker that St. Thomas discusses extensively the image of God in people (cf. *S.Th.* I, q. 93)?

117. Augustine, *De Trinitate*, VIII, 7.

118. St. Thomas emphasizes that the image of God is to be sought primarily in the *activity* of the spirit, because only in regard to this activity is it possible to speak of *progressions* [*Hervorgänge*]. Cf. *S.Th.* I, q. 93, a 7.

119. Cf. the discussion of the stages of self-knowledge in chap. VII, §9, subsec. 2, above.

120. Cf. Augustine *De Trinitate*, XI, 5.

121. Ibid., XIII, 20.

122. Ibid.,XIV, 2.

123. Ibid., XIV, 3–4.

124. Ibid., XIV, 6.

125. Ibid., VIII, 8.

126. H. Scholz, in a study entitled *Eros und Caritas: Die platonische Liebe im Sinne des Christentums* (Halle, 1929), a work that shows a keen and profound understanding of the phenomena of philosophy and religion, finds an *aporia* in the Scriptural saying, "God is love" (p. 54). The author asserts that besides love we must assume in God at least *one* additional spiritual quality, namely, wrath. Scholz thus presents his own version of St. John's saying that the kind of love that is predicated of God cannot be predicated of any other being. His main difficulty arises from the fact that he had initially defined love as a state or condition of the heart [*Gemütsverfassung*]. He must therefore look for a subject of such a state or condition. In strict opposition to the classical philosophy and theology of the Catholic church, Scholz sees in the *actus purus*—in God who is love, wisdom, and goodness as such and who is all this in one—the "epitome of subjectless qualities." It seems to me that Scholz arrives at this conclusion because he pays no attention to the *law of analogy* which in my opinion is the basic law of all theological thinking. This law makes it impossible to transfer to God the categories of the finite completely unchanged. In God there are neither states of heart nor qualities. Everything that is attributed to him must be understood analogically. (Cf. also our previous discussion of the analogy between

the natural and the supernatural on pp. 454ff. above.) And that which is separated in creatures is one in God. Equally radical is the difference between Scholz's philosophic approach and our own. Although he defines clearly the nature of a Platonic idea, his way of procedure seems to imply that no ideas (in the sense of essences) exist. If this were so, there would be no possibility of measuring the different *concepts* of love—which Scholz elaborates in a historically accurate manner—by the objectively basic standard of the "*idea* of love" and of finding out how much or how little of this fundamental reality of the idea these concepts contain and express.

127. The Litany of Loreto calls the mother of God a *vas spirituale* [spiritual vessel]. But what is said here of the soul of Mary is applicable to every human soul, because every human soul is destined to become a spiritual vessel. The only difference is that Mary realized this destiny of the human soul in the most perfect manner.

128. 1 Cor 15:35.

129. 1 Cor 15:44–46.

130. This may mean two things: 1) The *weight* imposed on the soul by that material body which was assumed by Christ for the duration of his *earthly* life together with a human nature, a weight of which the resurrected Christ was freed; 2) The self-forming of the soul into a proportionate body, a characteristic which was retained even by the transfigured Christ.

131. John 7:38.

132. The words of the gospel of St. John, stating that we have been given "power" (ἐξουσία, potestas) of being children of God (John 1:12), make it evident that to those who accept the divine Word "new life" is given as something over which they have free command.

133. Hebrews 4:12.

134. Understood according to the first of the two meanings mentioned in n. 130 above.

135. John 3:34.

136. A vivid picture of the inner life of the soul is presented in *Das Ideal des geistlichen Lebens,* edited by Odilo von Zurkinden, O.S.B. (Munich, 1936). The unnamed author is the same Carthusian to whom we also owe a book entitled *Im Banne des Dreieinigen.* Further ample illustration is offered in the mystical writings of all centuries.

Excellent contributions to a description of the transformation of the powers of the soul under the influence of the Holy Spirit are contained in Sister Isidora's *Die sieben Gaben des Heiligen Geistes* (Freiburg i. Br., 1926.). See also Sister Teresia Renata de Spiritu Sancto, O.C.D., *Die siebenfache Gabe* (Freiburg i. Br., 1936).

137. See the first note to chap. VII, above.

138. Cf. Aquinas, *S.Th.* I, q. 93, a 2 and 9.

139. Cf. Augustine, *De Trinitate* XI, 5–6; Aquinas, *Sum theol.* I, q. 93, a 6, ad 2.

140. Cf. chap. VIII, §3, subsec. 3, below.

Chapter VIII

1. Cf. the scholarly treatise on the problem of individuality by Roland-Gosselin in *Le "De ente et essentia"* (Le Saulchoir: Kain-Belique, 1926), p. 51.

2. Cf. chap. IV above.

3. Cf. Aquinas, *S.Th.* I, q. 29, a 3, ad 4.

4. Ibid., a 4, *corp. art.* Cf. also J. Gredt, *Die aristotelisch-thomistische Philosophie,* vol. I (Freiburg i. Br., 1935), pp. 80f. This is the freely translated German version of the same author's Latin compendium to which we referred frequently in our previous discussion.

5. Cf. chap. IV, §6 above.

6. Cf. pp. 165f. above.

7. Gredt, *Die aristotelisch-thomistische Philosophie,* I, p. 81.

8. Cf. chap. III, §5.

9. Gredt, *Die aristotelisch-thomistische Philosophie,* I, p. 81.

10. Cf. Gredt's lucid presentation (ibid., I, pp. 241ff.). It may be asked, however, whether the Thomistic answer is altogether acceptable. If not, a separate discussion of the two questions seems necessary.

11. Ibid., I, p. 241.

12. Ibid., I, p. 242.

13. Ibid.

14. Ibid., I, p. 243.

15. Ibid., I, p. 244.

16. Ibid., I, p. 303.

17. Ibid., II, p. 114.

18. Ibid., II, p. 113.

19. Ibid.
20. Ibid., II, pp. 114f.
21. Ibid., II, pp. 115f.
22. Ibid., II, p. 117.
23. Ibid., II, p. 118.
24. Ibid., II, p. 116.
25. *Matter* is here to be understood in the restricted sense of that which fills space.
26. In the footnote (*Die aristotelisch-thomistische Philosophie,* I, p. 246), Gredt distinguishes *this* individuation of the "*required* extension" from that of the "*adherent* [*anhaften*] extension," which is said to be founded on the individuality of the substance.
27. Ibid., I, pp. 244–246.
28. My answer is found on pp. 485f. below.
29. My answer is found on pp. 487ff. below.
30. Cf. chap. IV, §4, subsec. 6.
31. The quantitative dimension or size is not irrelevant for the meaning of a structure, but is pre-designed in accordance with this meaning perhaps not unequivocally, but at any rate by certain limits which signify a minimum or maximum.
32. This likeness may be a mere likeness of species [*Artgleichheit*] leaving room for differences in the individual structure, or it may be a full likeness of structure [*Gestaltgleichheit*], so that the spatially separate quantity of matter remains as the only mark that distinguishes the content of one thing from the contents of the others. *Structure* [*Gestalt*] signifies here more than more spatial structure [*Raumgestalt*]. What is meant is the entire individual "particularity" [*Eigenart*] of the structure insofar as it has found an "expression."
33. Duns Scotus does likewise, if I understand him correctly. He sees the *principium individuationis* as something that has the marks of a positive existent, as something that sets the individual form of the essence apart from the universal form of the essence (cf. R. Messner, O.F.M., "Das Individualprinzip in skotistischer Schau," in the periodical *Wissenschaft und Weisheit* I (1934): 8ff.).
34. Gredt, *Die aristotelisch-thomistische Philosophie,* II, p. 116.
35. However, it is possible for several individual triangles to be in the same position and to become thus indistinguishable for us (cf. pp. 485f. above).

36. "Thou hast ordered everything according to measure, number, and weight" (Wisdom 11:21).

37. Cf. chap. III, §2 above.

38. I agree with this view as long as *matter* is understood exclusively as that which fills space. But we have been able to discover in angels something which is to be considered as *matter* in the sense of a determinable indeterminateness. For this reason I have designated them not as pure forms, but as pure spirits (Cf. chap. VII, §5, subsec. 6 above).

39. Gredt, *Die aristotelisch-thomistische Philosophie,* I, p. 250.

40. Ibid.

41. Cf. Aquinas, *S.Th.* I, q. 47, a 2 *corp. art.*

42. Cf. chap. IV, §3, subsec. 2, above.

43. Some sort of being, of course, would have to be attributed to the person during the time his or her personal life is interrupted.

44. We leave out of consideration here divine omniscience which can, of course, always distinguish among those things which are for us indistinguishable.

45. Aquinas, *S.Th.* 1, q. 47, a 2 *corp. art.*

46. Cf. Husserl's "principle of principles": "that every primordial intuition is a valid source of knowledge" [daß *jede originär gebende Anschauung eine Rechtsquelle der Erkenntnis* sei...], *Ideen,* p. 43.

47. Like all created things, the soul could be annihilated by God, but this would not be a "natural end."

48. Psalms 32:15.

49. Revelation 2:17.

50. 1 Corinthians 13:12.

51. Cf. p. 489 above.

52. Since the soul is a personal-spiritual structure, its innermost and truly authentic being—its essence from which flow its powers and the complex fluctuations of its life—is not merely an unknown X that serves to explain the knowable facts about the soul, but something that may, despite its mysterious character, become to some extent lucid and tangible for us. The entire spiritual life of the soul is a *conscious* life, and this makes it possible for the soul to view and reflect upon its own self, even without entering into itself through the portal of prayer (cf. chap. VII, n. 33). What kind of a self the soul finds in such self-reflection depends, however, on the nature

of the portal through which it enters into itself. It is possible, for example, to gain access to our souls by means of existential communication with other human beings. Another impulse to self-reflection and introspection derives from the strengthening of personal life during the period of growth from childhood to adolescence. Lastly, we may think of the scientific exploration of the *inner world,* a region of being which has become one of the main objects of scientific research. Ultimately, however, the question urges itself upon us as to whether, after, all, the one and only way to the interiority of the soul is not through the portal of prayer. It would be a formidable but eminently worthwhile task to recapitulate once more the history of psychology with a view to discovering how basic religious beliefs and basic concepts of the soul—in individual scholars as well as in different epochs—are related to one another.

53. It was laid down by dogmatic definition that angels do not proceed from one another (Denzinger 533). In everything else dogmatic theology leaves a great deal of freedom regarding the different views on angels. The church teaches in its dogmatic declarations merely that angels are pure spirits created by God (Denzinger 428, 1783).

54. These misinterpretations account for the one-sided exaggerations of nationalist and internationalist ideologies.

55. Genesis 8:21.

56. Romans 5:12.

57. Cf. Aquinas, *De veritate,* q. 24, a 9, *corp. art.* (*Untersuchungen über die Wahrheit,* II: 308).

58. Ibid., q. 13, a 3, ad 2 (*Untersuchungen über die Wahrheit,* I: 381).

59. Ibid., q. 2, a 6, ad 5 (*Untersuchungen über die Wahrheit,* II: 358).

60. Only in a limited sense are we permitted to speak here of a "forming" of the body by the soul, since the first human beings must be conceived from the outset as fully developed and not in need of any further evolution.

61. "Two in one flesh" (Gen 2:24).

62. Cf. the passages dealing with marriage in the book of Tobit (6:17–22 and 8:4ff).

63. Cf. Aquinas, *S.Th.* III, q. 45, a 2, *corp. art.*

64. Cf. Denzinger 793ff.

65. Ibid.

66. Ibid., 795.
67. Ibid., 799.
68. Ibid.
69. Ibid., 800.
70. Ibid., 797.
71. Ibid., 798.
72. The Mother of God occupies an incomparable position, since her close intimacy with her son was of a different kind.
73. Cf. Aquinas, *S.Th.* III, q. 8, a 4, *corp. art.*

Editors' Appendix to the First German Edition

1.[To clarify how the German work translated in the foregoing pages was edited from various manuscript versions by the Archivum Carmelitanum Edith Stein, we have included here the editors' "appendix" from the first German edition of *Finite and Eternal Being*. It should be noted, however, that some of the information in this section has now been superseded. The German text of *Potency and Act*, for example, was published in 1998, and the original appendices to *Finite and Eternal Being* have appeared in volume 6 of *Edith Steins Werke*. A new critical edition of *Endliches und Ewiges Sein* is currently in preparation.—ICS Ed.]

2. When E. Stein was deported in 1942, she left behind an extensive collection of her own writing and manuscripts at the Carmel in Echt, which her fellow sisters hid at a neighboring monastery in Herkenbosch. After the destruction of this monastery at the end of 1944, Fr. Avertanus, the provincial of the Discalced Carmelites at that time, was able to recover most of Stein's papers from the ruins of the monastery. Rev. Prof. Van Breda, O.F.M. Director of the Husserl Archives, is to be thanked for taking the initiative for this personal intervention. By these actions the many thousands of pages of this extensive intellectual legacy of E. Stein could be turned over by the archivist of the Husserl Archives to Dr. L. Gelber who would be responsible for the reconstruction and scholarly evaluation.

When we speak, at this point or later, of E. Stein's manuscripts in the possession of the Husserl Archives, we are referring to these manuscripts of the above-mentioned legacy. The author's rights to these works belong exclusively to the Dutch provincial of the Discalced Carmelites. [This has subsequently changed.—ICS Ed.]

3. In the way in which the title was written, a switch in the capitalization of certain words is evident. We have presented the style of the actual supportive material in its original form.

4. We were able to reconstruct the work by sifting through Stein's literary remains.

5. Also, a typewritten copy of the work with corrections in E. Stein's hand belonged to Mrs. Hedwig Conrad-Martius.

6. In this respect, see in the abbreviated rendering of the preface to *Potency and Act* on the previous page and the definition of the philosophical task vis-à-vis the cultural sciences.

7. See *Finite and Eternal Being*, pp. 409ff. and also in the author's preface the general mention of this position regarding the doctrine of Duns Scotus (p. xxxi).

8. See "Husserl and Aquinas: A Comparison," in Edith Stein, *Knowledge and Faith*, trans. Walter Redmond (Washington, D.C.: ICS Publications, 2000), pp. xix–xx, 1–63.

9. Chapters VI-VIII were originally foreseen as the second volume of the revised work. See in the following the remarks on the revision of the organization.

Index

Other Volumes in the *Collected Works of Edith Stein* Series Available from ICS Publications

Vol. 1: *Life in a Jewish Family.* Edited by L. Gelber and Romaeus Leuven. Translated by Josephine Koeppel (1986).

Vol. 2: *Essays on Woman.* Edited by L. Gelber and Romaeus Leuven. Translated by Freda Mary Oben. 2d edition, revised (1996).

Vol. 3: *On the Problem of Empathy.* Translated by Waltraut Stein. 3d revised edition (1989).

Vol. 4: *The Hidden Life.* Edited by L. Gelber and Michael Linssen. Translated by Waltraut Stein (1992).

Vol. 5: *Self-Portrait in Letters.* Edited by L. Gelber and Romaeus Leuven. Translated by Josephine Koeppel (1993).

Vol. 6: *The Science of the Cross.* Edited by L. Gelber and R. Leuven. Translated by Josephine Koeppel (2002).

Vol. 7: *Philosophy of Psychology and the Humanities.* Translated by Mary Catharine Baseheart and Marianne Sawicki (2000).

Vol. 8: *Knowledge and Faith.* Edited by L. Gelber and M. Linssen. Translated by Walter Redmond (2000).

Other Works About Edith Stein Available from ICS Publications

Herbstrith, Waltraud, ed. *Never Forget: Christian and Jewish Perspectives on Edith Stein.* Translated by Susanne Batzdorff. Carmelite Studies 7 (1998).

Neyer, Amata. *Edith Stein: Her Life in Photos and Documents.* Translated by Waltraut Stein (1999).

Sullivan, John, ed. *Holiness Befits Your House: Canonization of Edith Stein—A Documentation* (2000).

WWW. ICSPUBLICATIONS.ORG

The Institute of Carmelite Studies promotes research and publication in the field of Carmelite spirituality. Its members are Discalced Carmelites, part of a Roman Catholic community—friars, nuns, and laity—who are heirs to the teaching and way of life of Teresa of Jesus and John of the Cross, men and women dedicated to contemplation and to ministry in the church and the world. Information concerning their way of life is available through local diocesan Vocation Offices, or from the Vocation Directors' Offices:

2131 Lincoln Road, NE, Washington, DC 20002–1199

P.O. Box 3420, San Jose, CA 95156–3420

5151 Marylake Drive, Little Rock, AR 72206–9436